D1315995

MCTS 70-680 Cert Guide: Microsoft® Windows 7, Configuring

Don Poulton

Pearson
800 East 96th Street
Indianapolis, Indiana 46240 USA

MCTS 70-680 Cert Guide: Microsoft® Windows 7, Configuring

Copyright © 2011 by Pearson Education, Inc.

All rights reserved. No part of this book shall be reproduced, stored in a retrieval system, or transmitted by any means, electronic, mechanical, photocopying, recording, or otherwise, without written permission from the publisher. No patent liability is assumed with respect to the use of the information contained herein. Although every precaution has been taken in the preparation of this book, the publisher and author assume no responsibility for errors or omissions. Nor is any liability assumed for damages resulting from the use of the information contained herein.
ISBN-13: 978-0-7897-4707-5
ISBN-10: 0-7897-4707-3
Library of Congress Cataloging-in-Publication Data is on file.
Printed in the United States of America
Eighth Printing: April 2014

Trademarks

All terms mentioned in this book that are known to be trademarks or service marks have been appropriately capitalized. Pearson IT Certification cannot attest to the accuracy of this information. Use of a term in this book should not be regarded as affecting the validity of any trademark or service mark.

Warning and Disclaimer

Every effort has been made to make this book as complete and as accurate as possible, but no warranty or fitness is implied. The information provided is on an "as is" basis. The authors and the publisher shall have neither liability nor responsibility to any person or entity with respect to any loss or damages arising from the information contained in this book or from the use of the CD or programs accompanying it.

Bulk Sales

Pearson IT Certification offers excellent discounts on this book when ordered in quantity for bulk purchases or special sales. For more information, please contact

> **U.S. Corporate and Government Sales**
> **1-800-382-3419**
> **corpsales@pearsontechgroup.com**

For sales outside of the U.S., please contact

> **International Sales**
> **international@pearson.com**

Associate Publisher
Dave Dusthimer

Acquisitions Editor
Betsy Brown

Development Editor
Box Twelve
Communications, Inc.

Managing Editor
Sandra Schroeder

Project Editor
Mandie Frank

Copy Editor
Mike Henry

Indexer
Tim Wright

Proofreader
Megan Wade

Technical Editor
Chris Crayton

Publishing Coordinator
Vanessa Evans

Multimedia Developer
Dan Scherf

Interior Designer
Louisa Adair

Cover Designer
Gary Adair

Composition
Mark Shirar

Contents at a Glance

Table of Contents

About the Author

Don Poulton (A+, Network+, Security+, MCSA, MCSE) is an independent consultant who has been involved with computers since the days of 80-column punch cards. After a career of more than 20 years in environmental science, Don switched careers and trained as a Windows NT 4.0 MCSE. He has been involved in consulting with a couple of small training providers as a technical writer, during which time he wrote training and exam prep materials for Windows NT 4.0, Windows 2000, and Windows XP. Don has written or contributed to several titles, including *Security+ Lab Manual* (Que, 2004); *MCSA/MCSE 70-299 Exam Cram 2: Implementing and Administering Security in a Windows 2003 Network (Exam Cram 2)* (Que, 2004); *MCSE 70-294 Exam Prep: Planning, Implementing, and Maintaining a Microsoft Windows Server 2003 Active Directory Infrastructure* (Que, 2006); and *MCTS 70-620 Exam Prep: Microsoft Windows Vista, Configuring* (Que, 2008).

In addition, he has worked on programming projects, both in his days as an environmental scientist and more recently with Visual Basic to update an older statistical package used for multivariate analysis of sediment contaminants.

When not working on computers, Don is an avid amateur photographer who has had his photos displayed in international competitions and published in magazines such as *Michigan Natural Resources Magazine* and *National Geographic Traveler*. Don also enjoys traveling and keeping fit.

Don lives in Burlington, Ontario, with his wife, Terry.

Dedication

I would like to dedicate this book to my wife Terry, who has stood by my side and encouraged me throughout the days spent writing this book. This project would not have been possible without her love and support.

Acknowledgments

I would like to thank all the staff at Pearson IT Certification and in particular Betsy Brown for making this project possible. My sincere thanks goes out to Chris Crayton for his helpful technical suggestions, as well as Jeff Riley, development editor, and Chris Cleveland, development editor liason, for their improvements to the manuscript.

—Don Poulton

About the Technical Reviewer

Christopher A. Crayton is an author, a technical editor, a technical consultant, a security consultant, a trainer, and a SkillsUSA state-level technology competition judge. Formerly, he worked as a computer and networking instructor at Keiser College (2001 Teacher of the Year); as network administrator for Protocol, a global electronic customer relationship management (eCRM) company; and at Eastman Kodak Headquarters as a computer and network specialist. Chris has authored several print and online books, including *The A+ Exams Guide, Second Edition* (Cengage Learning, 2008); *Microsoft Windows Vista 70-620 Exam Guide Short Cut* (O'Reilly, 2007); *CompTIA A+ Essentials 220-601 Exam Guide Short Cut* (O'Reilly, 2007); *The A+ Exams Guide, The A+ Certification and PC Repair Handbook* (Charles River Media, 2005); *The Security+ Exam Guide* (Charles River Media, 2003); and *A+ Adaptive Exams* (Charles River Media, 2002). He is also co-author of *How to Cheat at Securing Your Network* (Syngress, 2007). As an experienced technical editor, Chris has provided many technical edits/reviews for several major publishing companies, including Pearson Education, McGraw-Hill, Cengage Learning, Wiley, O'Reilly, Syngress, and Apress. He holds MCSE, A+, and Network+ certifications.

We Want to Hear from You!

As the reader of this book, *you* are our most important critic and commentator. We value your opinion and want to know what we're doing right, what we could do better, what areas you'd like to see us publish in, and any other words of wisdom you're willing to pass our way.

As an associate publisher for Pearson IT Certification, I welcome your comments. You can email or write me directly to let me know what you did or didn't like about this book—as well as what we can do to make our books better.

Please note that I cannot help you with technical problems related to the topic of this book. We do have a User Services group, however, where I will forward specific technical questions related to the book.

When you write, please be sure to include this book's title and author as well as your name, email address, and phone number. I will carefully review your comments and share them with the author and editors who worked on the book.

Email: feedback@pearsonITcertification.com

Mail: Dave Dusthimer
      Associate Publisher
      Pearson IT Certification
      800 East 96th Street
      Indianapolis, IN 46240 USA

Reader Services

Visit our website and register this book at www.pearson ITcertification.com/register for convenient access to any updates, downloads, or errata that might be available for this book.

Introduction

MCTS Windows 7 Configuring Cert Guide (Exam 70-680) is designed for network administrators, network engineers, and consultants who are pursuing the Microsoft Certified Technology Specialist (MCTS) or Microsoft Certified IT Professional (MCITP) certifications for Windows 7. This book covers the "TS: Microsoft Windows 7, Configuring" exam (70-680), which earns you the Microsoft Certified Technology Specialist: Windows 7, Configuration certification. The exam is designed to measure your skill and ability to implement, administer, and troubleshoot computers running all editions of Windows 7. Microsoft not only tests you on your knowledge of the desktop operating system, but also has purposefully developed questions on the exam to force you to problem-solve in the same way that you would when presented with a real-life errors. Passing this exam demonstrates your competency in administration.

This book covers all the objectives that Microsoft has established for exam 70-680. It doesn't offer end-to-end coverage of the Windows 7 operating system; rather, it helps you develop the specific core competencies that you need to master as a desktop support specialist. You should be able to pass the exam by learning the material in this book, without taking a class.

Goals and Methods

The number-one goal of this book is a simple one: to help you pass the Microsoft MCTS Windows 7, Certification Exam (exam number 70-680) and thereby earn this certification. It is also the first step in obtaining the MCITP certification in either Enterprise Desktop Support Technician 7, which validates technical skills and the ability to operate effectively in a support center, or Enterprise Desktop Administrator 7, which validates skills for deploying operating systems and desktop applications and for managing the client life cycle.

Because Microsoft certification exams stress problem-solving abilities and reasoning more than memorization of terms and facts, our goal is to help you master and understand the required objectives for the 70-680 exam.

To aid you in mastering and understanding the MCTS certification objectives, this book uses the following methods:

- **Opening Topics List:** This defines the topics to be covered in the chapter; it also lists the corresponding 70-680 exam objectives.

- **Do I Know This Already? Quizzes:** At the beginning of each chapter is a quiz. The quizzes, and answers/explanations (found in Appendix A), are meant to gauge your knowledge of the subjects. If the answers to the questions don't come readily to you, be sure to read the entire chapter.

- **Foundation Topics:** The heart of the chapter. Explains the topics from a hands-on and a theory-based standpoint. This includes in-depth descriptions, tables, and figures geared to build your knowledge so that you can pass the exam. The chapters are broken down into several topics each.

- **Key Topics:** The key topics indicate important figures, tables, and lists of information that you should know for the exam. They are interspersed throughout the chapter and are listed in table form at the end of the chapter.

- **Memory Tables:** These can be found on the CD-ROM within Appendix B, "Memory Tables." Use them to help memorize important information.

- **Key Terms:** Key terms without definitions are listed at the end of each chapter. Write down the definition of each term and check your work against the complete key terms in the glossary.

Study and Exam Preparation Tips

It's a rush of adrenaline during the final day before an exam. If you've scheduled the exam on a workday, or following a workday, you will find yourself cursing the tasks you normally cheerfully perform because the back of your mind is telling you to read just a bit more, study another scenario, practice another skill so that you will be able to get this exam out of the way successfully.

The way that Microsoft has designed its tests lately does not help. I remember taking Microsoft exams many years ago and thoroughly understanding the term "paper certified." Nowadays, you can't get through a Microsoft exam without knowing the material so well that when confronted with a problem, whether a scenario or real-life situation, you can handle the challenge. Instead of trying to show the world how many MCSEs are out there, Microsoft is trying to prove how difficult it is to achieve a certification, including the newly created MCTS and MCITP as well as the MCSE and MCSA, thereby making those who are certified more valuable to their organizations.

Learning Styles

To best understand the nature of preparation for the test, it is important to understand learning as a process. You are probably aware of how you best learn new material. You might find that outlining works best for you, or, as a visual learner, you might need to "see" things. Or, as a person who studies kinesthetically, the hands-on approach serves you best. Whether you might need models or examples, or maybe you just like exploring the interface, or whatever your learning style, solid test preparation works best when it takes place over time. Obviously, you shouldn't start studying for a certification exam the night before you take it; it is very important to understand that learning is a developmental process. Understanding learning as a process helps you focus on what you know and what you have yet to learn.

People study in a combination of different ways: by doing, by seeing, and by hearing and writing. This book's design fulfills all three of these study methods. For the kinesthetic, there are key topics scattered throughout each chapter. You will also discover step-by-step procedural instructions that walk you through the skills you need to master in Windows 7. The visual learner can find plenty of screen shots explaining the concepts described in the text. The auditory learner can reinforce skills by reading out loud and copying down key concepts and exam tips scattered throughout the book. You can also practice writing down the meaning of the key terms defined in each chapter, and in completing the memory tables for most chapters found on the accompanying CD-ROM. While reading this book, you will realize that it stands the test of time. You will be able to turn to it over and over again.

Thinking about how you learn should help you recognize that learning takes place when you are able to match new information to old. You have some previous experience with computers and networking. Now you are preparing for this certification exam. Using this book, software, and supplementary materials will not just add incrementally to what you know; as you study, the organization of your knowledge actually restructures as you integrate new information into your existing knowledge base. This leads you to a more comprehensive understanding of the tasks and concepts outlined in the objectives and of computing in general. Again, this happens as a result of a repetitive process rather than a singular event. If you keep this model of learning in mind as you prepare for the exam, you will make better decisions concerning what to study and how much more studying you need to do.

Study Tips

There are many ways to approach studying, just as there are many different types of material to study. However, the tips that follow should work well for the type of material covered on Microsoft certification exams.

Study Strategies

Although individuals vary in the ways they learn information, some basic principles of learning apply to everyone. You should adopt some study strategies that take advantage of these principles. One of these principles is that learning can be broken into various depths. Recognition (of terms, for example) exemplifies a rather surface level of learning in which you rely on a prompt of some sort to elicit recall. Comprehension or understanding (of the concepts behind the terms, for example) represents a deeper level of learning than recognition. The ability to analyze a concept and apply your understanding of it in a new way represents further depth of learning.

Your learning strategy should enable you to know the material at a level or two deeper than mere recognition. This will help you perform well on the exams. You will know the material so thoroughly that you can go beyond the recognition-level types of questions commonly used in fact-based multiple-choice testing. You will be able to apply your knowledge to solve new problems.

Macro and Micro Study Strategies

One strategy that can lead to deep learning includes preparing an outline that covers all the objectives and subobjectives for the particular exam you are planning to take. You should delve a bit further into the material and include a level or two of detail beyond the stated objectives and subobjectives for the exam. Then you should expand the outline by coming up with a statement of definition or a summary for each point in the outline.

An outline provides two approaches to studying. First, you can study the outline by focusing on the organization of the material. You can work your way through the points and subpoints of your outline, with the goal of learning how they relate to one another. For example, you should be sure you understand how each of the main objective areas for Exam 70-680 is similar to and different from another. Then you should do the same thing with the subobjectives; you should be sure you know which subobjectives pertain to each objective area and how they relate to one another.

Next, you can work through the outline, focusing on learning the details. You should memorize and understand terms and their definitions, facts, rules and tactics, advantages and disadvantages, and so on. In this pass through the outline, you should attempt to learn detail rather than the big picture (that is, the organizational information that you worked on in the first pass through the outline).

Research has shown that attempting to assimilate both types of information at the same time interferes with the overall learning process. If you separate your studying into these two approaches, you will perform better on the exam.

Active Study Strategies

The process of writing down and defining objectives, subobjectives, terms, facts, and definitions promotes a more active learning strategy than merely reading the material does. In human information-processing terms, writing forces you to engage in more active encoding of the information. Simply reading over the information leads to more passive processing. Using this study strategy, you should focus on writing down the items highlighted in the book: bulleted or numbered lists, key topics, notes, cautions, and review sections, for example.

You need to determine whether you can apply the information you have learned by attempting to create examples and scenarios on your own. You should think about how or where you could apply the concepts you are learning. Again, you should write down this information to process the facts and concepts in an active fashion.

Common-Sense Strategies

You should follow common-sense practices when studying: You should study when you are alert, reduce or eliminate distractions, and take breaks when you become fatigued.

Pretesting Yourself

Pretesting enables you to assess how well you are learning. One of the most important aspects of learning is what has been called *meta-learning*. Meta-learning has to do with realizing when you know something well or when you need to study some more. In other words, you recognize how well or how poorly you have learned the material you are studying.

For most people, this can be difficult to assess. Memory tables, practice questions, and practice tests are useful in that they reveal objectively what you have learned and what you have not learned. You should use this information to guide review and further studying. Developmental learning takes place as you cycle through studying, assessing how well you have learned, reviewing, and assessing again until you feel you are ready to take the exam.

You might have noticed the practice exam included in this book. You should use it as part of the learning process. The ExamGear test-simulation software included on this book's CD-ROM also provides you with an excellent opportunity to assess your knowledge.

You should set a goal for your pretesting. A reasonable goal would be to score consistently in the 90% range.

Exam Prep Tips

After you have mastered the subject matter, the final preparatory step is to understand how the exam will be presented. Make no mistake: A Microsoft Certified Technology Specialist (MCTS) exam challenges both your knowledge and your test-taking skills. Preparing for the 70-680 exam is a bit different from preparing for those old Microsoft exams. The following is a list of things that you should consider doing:

- **Combine Your Skill Sets into Solutions:** In the past, exams would test whether you knew to select the right letter of a multiple-choice answer. Today, you need to know how to resolve a problem that might involve different aspects of the material covered. For example, on exam 70-680, you could be presented with a problem that requires you to understand how to incorporate drivers in an unattended installation, as well as what errors you might see if you installed a computer that used a device driver incompatible with Windows 7. The skills themselves are simple. Being able to zero in on what caused the problem and then to resolve it for a specific situation is what you need to demonstrate. In fact, you should not only be able to select one answer, but also multiple parts of a total solution.

- **Delve into Excruciating Details:** The exam questions incorporate a great deal of information in the scenarios. Some of the information is ancillary: It will help you rule out possible issues, but not necessarily resolve the answer. Some of the information simply provides you with a greater picture, as you would have in real life. Some information is key to your solution. For example, you might be presented with a question that lists a computer's hard disk size, memory size, and detailed hardware configuration. When you delve further into the question, you realize that the hardware configuration is the problem. Other times, you will find that the hardware configuration simply eliminates one or more of the answers that you could select. For example, a portable laptop does not support dynamic disks, so if the hardware configuration is a portable laptop and one of the answers is a dynamic disk configuration, you can eliminate it. If you don't pay attention to what you can eliminate, the answer can elude you completely. Other times, the hardware configuration simply lets you know that the hardware is adequate.

- **TCP/IP Troubleshooting Is Built Right In:** Because TCP/IP is a core technology to the Windows 7 operating system, you are expected to know how to configure the operating system, how to recognize IP conflicts, and how to use the TCP/IP tools to troubleshoot the problem. Furthermore, Microsoft expects you to know how to work with the new version 6 of TCP/IP along with the traditional version 4 that has been used for many years. You should also be able to discern between an IP problem and something wrong with the OS or hardware, or even some combination that involves IP along with some other element.

- **It's a GUI Test:** Microsoft has expanded its testing criteria into interface recognition. You should be able to recognize each dialog box, properties sheet, options, and defaults. You will be tested on how to navigate the new interface: for example, the Aero and Aero Glass desktop themes used by Windows 7, as well as the Category View shown in Control Panel. If you have reverted your Windows 7 desktop to the Windows Classic theme and you have not yet learned the new interface, you might end up selecting answers that are deliberately placed to confuse a person used to the old Windows desktop. Of course, if you know the difference between the two, you'll be able to spot the old ones and avoid them.

- **Practice with a Time Limit:** The tests have always been time restricted, but it takes more time to read and understand the scenarios now and time is a whole lot tighter. To get used to the time limits, test yourself with a timer. Know how long it takes you to read scenarios and select answers.

Microsoft 70-680 Exam Topics

Table I-1 lists the exam topics for the Microsoft 70-680 exam. This table also lists the book parts in which each exam topic is covered.

Table I.1   Microsoft 70-680 Exam Topics

Chapter	Topics	70-680 Exam Objectives Covered
1	Leading Up to Windows 7	(n/a)
	Windows 7 Editions	
	Features of Windows 7	
	A Quick Tour of Windows 7	
	Patches, Hotfixes, and Service Packs	
2	Identifying Hardware Requirements	Installing, Upgrading, and Migrating to Windows 7
	Performing a Clean Installation of Windows 7 as the Sole Operating System	■ Perform a clean installation
	Dual-Booting Windows 7	
	Other Windows 7 Installation Methods	
	Troubleshooting Windows 7 Installation Issues	

Table I.1   Microsoft 70-680 Exam Topics

Chapter	Topics	70-680 Exam Objectives Covered
3	Upgrading to Windows 7 from a Previous Version of Windows	Installing, Upgrading, and Migrating to Windows 7
	Migrating from Windows XP	■ Upgrade to Windows 7 from previous versions of Windows
	Upgrading from One Edition of Windows 7 to Another	
4	Migrating Users from One Computer to Another	Installing, Upgrading, and Migrating to Windows 7
	Migrating Users from Previous Windows Versions	■ Migrate user profiles
	Side by Side versus Wipe and Load	
5	Planning a Windows 7 Deployment	Deploying Windows 7
	Capturing a System Image	■ Capture a system image
	Preparing System Images for Deployment	■ Prepare a system image for deployment
	Deploying Windows System Images	
	Troubleshooting an Unattended Installation	■ Deploy a system image
6	Understanding VHDs	Deploying Windows 7
	Creating and Deploying VHDs	■ Configure a VHD
	Offline Servicing and Updating VHDs	
7	Installing and Configuring Device Drivers	Configuring Hardware and Applications
	Maintaining Device Drivers	■ Configure devices
	Troubleshooting Device Drivers	Monitoring and Maintaining Systems That Run Windows 7
	Configuring Updates to Windows 7	■ Configure updates to Windows 7
8	Configuring Application Compatibility	Configuring Hardware and Applications
	Configuring Application Restrictions	■ Configure application compatibility
	Configuring Internet Explorer	■ Configure application restrictions
		■ Configure Internet Explorer

Table I.1   Microsoft 70-680 Exam Topics

Chapter	Topics	70-680 Exam Objectives Covered
9	Understanding the TCP/IP Protocol Configuring TCP/IP Version 4 Configuring TCP/IP Version 6 Resolving IPv4 and IPv6 Network Connectivity Issues	Configuring Network Connectivity ■ Configure IPv4 network settings ■ Configure IPv6 network settings
10	Configuring Networking Settings Configuring Windows Firewall	Configuring Network Connectivity ■ Configure networking settings ■ Configure Windows Firewall
11	Configuring Shared Resources Configuring Security Permissions Configuring Data Encryption	Configuring Access to Resources ■ Configure shared resources ■ Configure file and folder access
12	Configuring User Account Control Configuring Authentication and Authorization Configuring BranchCache	Configuring Access to Resources ■ Configure User Account Control (UAC) ■ Configure authentication and authorization ■ Configure BranchCache
13	Configuring BitLocker and BitLocker To Go Configuring DirectAccess Configuring Mobility Options Configuring Power Options	Configuring Mobile Computing ■ Configure BitLocker and BitLocker To Go ■ Configure DirectAccess ■ Configure mobility options
14	Configuring Remote Management Configuring Remote Connections	Configuring Network Connectivity ■ Configure remote management ■ Configuring Mobile Computing ■ Configure remote connections

Table I.1   Microsoft 70-680 Exam Topics

Chapter	Topics	70-680 Exam Objectives Covered
15	Managing Disks and Volumes Managing File System Fragmentation RAID volumes Configuring Removable Drive Policies	Monitoring and Maintaining Systems That Run Windows 7 ■ Manage disks
16	Windows System Monitoring Tools Configuring and Working With Event Logs Managing Computer Performance Configuring Additional Performance Settings	Monitoring and Maintaining Systems That Run Windows 7 ■ Monitor systems ■ Configure performance settings
17	Using Windows Backup to Protect Your Data Creating a System Recovery Disk	Configuring Backup and Recovery Options ■ Configure backup
18	Restoring Files and Folders System Restore Recovering Your Operating System from Backup Advanced System Startup Options	Configuring Backup and Recovery Options ■ Configure system recovery options ■ Configure file recovery options

How This Book Is Organized

Although this book could be read cover-to-cover, it is designed to be flexible and enable you to easily move between chapters and sections of chapters to cover just the material that you need more work with. If you do intend to read all the chapters, the order in the book is an excellent sequence to use.

Chapter 1, "Introducing Windows 7," is an introductory chapter that is designed to ease readers that are new to Windows 7 into this book. It provides a broad description of the components of the Windows 7 operating system, including the major items that are new or recently updated, the Windows interface, and the Control Panel components.

The core chapters, Chapters 2 through 18, cover the following topics:

- **Chapter 2, "Installing Windows 7":** This chapter identifies hardware requirements for Windows 7 and covers installing Windows 7 on a new computer without an operating system.

- **Chapter 3, "Upgrading to Windows 7":** This chapter covers upgrading a computer running an older version of Windows to Windows 7. It discusses which upgrade paths are supported by Microsoft and which situations require a clean install of the operating system.

- **Chapter 4, "Migrating Users and Applications to Windows 7":** This chapter discusses the procedures available for getting users of older computers working on new Windows 7 computers with a minimum of delay.

- **Chapter 5, "Deploying Windows 7":** A large organization typically has hundreds to thousands of computers that must be installed with or upgraded to Windows 7. This chapter discusses methods you can use to perform such deployments in a rapid, timely fashion.

- **Chapter 6, "Configuring Virtual Hard Disks":** Virtualization is becoming increasingly prevalent in the corporate world these days, and this chapter discusses methods available for creating and using virtual hard disks.

- **Chapter 7, "Configuring Devices and Updates":** This chapter covers procedures you might use to set up and configure a variety of hardware devices, including use of the drivers that interface these devices with the Windows operating system. It also covers methods you might use to ensure that computers are kept up-to-date with the latest Microsoft patches, hotfixes, and service packs.

- **Chapter 8, "Configuring Applications and Internet Explorer":** Applications are the heart of any work done by users with Windows 7 computers. This chapter discusses methods you might use to set up applications and configure or troubleshoot options with these applications and Internet Explorer.

- **Chapter 9, "Configuring TCP/IP":** This chapter discusses versions 4 and 6 of the TCP/IP protocol together with setting up network connections and name resolution. It also discusses network connectivity problems.

- **Chapter 10, "Configuring Network and Firewall Settings":** This chapter focuses on the use of wired and wireless devices for network connections, configuring and troubleshooting firewalls, and methods for remote management of users and computers.

- **Chapter 11, "Configuring Access to Local and Shared Resources":** This chapter covers sharing of files, folders, and printers and restricting access to these resources by users and groups. It also covers the use of the Encrypting File System (EFS) to provide an extra layer of security to sensitive documents.

- **Chapter 12, "Configuring Access Controls":** This chapter covers all aspects of authenticating users to resources, including the BranchCache feature for authenticating users in remote locations. It also discusses the use of User Account Control (UAC) for enhancing the security of computers and the data they contain.

- **Chapter 13, "Configuring Mobile Computing":** This chapter covers topics of special interest to users with portable computers, including data protection, network access, file and folder access, and power options.

- **Chapter 14, "Configuring Remote Management and Remote Connections":** More and more users need to connect to corporate networks from diverse locations such as home, hotels, and client locations. This chapter covers all methods used for creating, authenticating, and troubleshooting these remote connections.

- **Chapter 15, "Disk Management":** This chapter discusses methods you would use for installing and managing disks and disk volumes and troubleshooting problems you might encounter with disks.

- **Chapter 16, "Managing and Monitoring System Performance":** This chapter focuses on computer performance and looks at factors that might cause degraded performance and steps you might take to restore performance to an acceptable level.

- **Chapter 17, "Configuring Backups":** Data on a disk volume can easily be lost if a backup is not available, and days or weeks of work could be wiped out. This chapter discusses how you can back up data so that the risk of loss is minimized.

- **Chapter 18, "Configuring System and File Recovery":** This chapter covers methods you can use to recover computers that have encountered startup and other problems. It also covers options for recovering files when corruption or other damage has occurred.

In addition to the 18 main chapters, this book includes tools to help you verify that you are prepared to take the exam. The DVD includes the glossary, practice test, and memory tables that you can work through to verify your knowledge of the subject matter.

This chapter covers the following subjects:

- **Leading Up to Windows 7:** Windows 7 is the latest in a long hierarchy of Microsoft operating systems. This section traces the history of Windows as it has unfolded in the past 20-plus years.

- **Windows 7 Editions:** Microsoft makes several editions of Windows 7 available for different purposes. This section compares and contrasts the available Windows 7 editions.

- **Features of Windows 7:** Windows 7 presents many new and improved features designed to help users work smartly and securely. This section provides a brief overview of new and improved features in Windows 7.

- **A Quick Tour of Windows 7:** This section introduces the Windows 7 desktop, with its Start menu and taskbar. It also provides a brief introduction to the new concept of Libraries and the features of the Control Panel.

- **Patches, Hotfixes, and Service Packs:** This section describes and compares the methods used by Microsoft to keep its operating systems current and secure.

CHAPTER 1

Introducing Windows 7

In the years since it was first released, Windows XP has become nearly ubiquitous throughout the homes and offices of PC users worldwide. Although it's a very stable, easily used operating system, it has become plagued with security problems in recent years. Service Pack 3 (SP3) certainly helped overcome these problems, but a new upgrade to the operating system was sorely needed to overcome security problems and provide an enhanced productivity environment for home and business users alike. Windows Vista appeared in January 2007 and offered many improvements to security; however, this operating system required considerably greater hardware resources than Windows XP and would not run on most of the computers in use at that time. Companies were slow to migrate to Vista, and in many cases, downgraded new Vista computers to the more manageable Windows XP. Windows 7 represents Microsoft's effort to provide a stable, reliable, and secure operating environment for the millions of users who have come to depend on Microsoft's operating systems, both at work and at home.

Leading Up to Windows 7

The PC has transformed over the past quarter century from a standalone computer that performed little more than word processing and spreadsheet functions to a portable multimedia machine supporting a diverse set of applications. Microsoft has been at the forefront of this development, providing the most ubiquitous operating system to power PC applications—Windows.

From its humble beginnings in the 1980s, Microsoft built Windows up to a popular consumer-oriented offering that most people first saw as Windows 3.0 (quickly supplanted with Windows 3.1 and Windows for Workgroups 3.11) in the early 1990s. As this decade progressed, Microsoft released Windows 95, which sported the first graphical user interface (GUI) that is the oldest original ancestor to the currently used GUI. This was followed by Windows 98 and then Windows Millennium Edition (Windows Me). However, these versions of Windows were partially based on DOS, which was the base operating system that worked underneath Windows. This posed severe limitations in their usefulness, especially in corporate environments.

Parallel to this development of a consumer-oriented 16-bit operating system, Microsoft was working with IBM to build a new industrial-strength networking system, based on IBM's popular OS/2 operating system. This partnership soon fell apart, but Microsoft continued to develop a new, 32-bit networking in the form of Windows NT 3.1. NT stands for "New Technology," and 3.1 referred to the fact that the interface resembled Windows 3.0. This was followed by Windows NT Workstation 3.5 (released in 1994); Windows NT Workstation 3.51 (released in 1995); Windows NT Workstation 4.0 (released in 1996), which had the new interface matching Windows 95; and Windows 2000 Professional. Microsoft also introduced server versions of each of these operating systems.

At this point, Microsoft brought the home and corporate user versions together under the Windows NT kernel. The home user version became Windows XP Home Edition, whereas the corporate version was Windows XP Professional. These differed in that Windows XP Professional contained additional components (many of which had been present in Windows 2000) designed for integration into corporate, server-based networks. Microsoft also added a complete entertainment software package including support for watching and recording TV shows and working with digital music and videos to Windows XP Professional to create the Windows XP Media Center Edition.

Almost as soon as Microsoft introduced Windows XP, it publicly announced initial plans for the next release of Windows, which it code-named "Longhorn" and originally planned to release in 2003. But as security problems mounted, Microsoft was forced to repeatedly delay the introduction of this release and work on enhancing the security behind Windows XP, a task that included the introduction of many security patches and three service packs. Microsoft targeted Longhorn's release for 2006 and revealed that Longhorn would incorporate major security enhancements beyond that of XP SP2, including technologies that would improve the resistance to such attack vectors as viruses, spyware, and other forms of malicious software. But yet again, in 2006, Microsoft pushed the final release of Longhorn (now known in its client versions as Vista) back into 2007, announcing that corporate versions would be available in November 2006, and the final public release was set for January 30, 2007.

Although Windows Vista brought many improvements and enhancements to the computing world, this operating system was negatively viewed by large segments of the population for a considerable number of reasons including the following:

- Windows Vista required more powerful hardware to utilize all new features including the new Windows Aero interface while maintaining decent performance. In addition, power requirements often resulted in poor battery life on laptops running Vista.

- The new User Account Control security feature generated too many prompts for users to proceed with common actions. Consequently, many users simply turned UAC off, thereby negating its security benefits.

- The new interface required a steep learning curve that made it more difficult for corporations to transition to the new version of Windows and resulted in an increase in support calls.

- Companies were required to purchase new, expensive licenses compared to Windows XP, representing additional cost for corporations who already have an investment in Windows XP.

- Many applications used in business would not run properly under Windows Vista, and even use of application compatibility settings often did not improve this situation.

- Many hardware devices did not have appropriate drivers for Windows Vista, especially in the 64-bit versions that required only signed drivers installed in kernel mode. These devices often ran poorly or did not run at all under Windows Vista.

Other common reasons included poor game quality, poor game performance, overall slower performance, and software bloat. Even though Microsoft tried to address some of the complaints with Service Pack 1, Windows Vista was not widely accepted. Many purchased Windows Vista only to use the downgrade license to run Windows XP, particular within corporations.

So, Microsoft placed high priority in readying a new version of its flagship operating system with the strong hope of alleviating these concerns and developing a secure, well-planned version of Windows that would be much more well accepted by individuals and corporations around the world. The result was Windows 7, which Microsoft released to manufacturers on July 22, 2009, and to the general public on October 22, 2009.

Why name this version Windows 7, you might ask? Although Microsoft has used various names for its NT-based operating system in the past decade, these were equipped with version numbers, and you can define a hierarchy of operating systems, as follows:

- Originally, Windows NT 3.x was known as such because it used the same GUI as Windows 3.0, 3.1, and 3.11. So, it was logical that Microsoft named its next version as Windows NT 4.

- While in beta, Windows 2000 was actually known as Windows NT 5. You can still see this if you look at the My Computer Properties dialog box in this version of Windows.

- Windows XP was actually version 5.1, which you can also see in the My Computer Properties dialog box.

- Windows Vista consequently became version 6 of the now venerable Windows NT kernel.

- So, consequently, it was logical that the next version of Windows would be known as Windows 7 (although some tech websites suggest that this version is actually 6.1). Many observers in the computing world expect that Microsoft's next version of Windows, sometime in the decade to come, will be Windows 8.

Windows 7 Editions

Microsoft designed six major editions of Windows 7, each suited for a different segment of the general population: Windows 7 Starter, Windows 7 Home Basic, Windows 7 Home Premium, Windows 7 Professional, Windows 7 Enterprise, and Windows 7 Ultimate. Table 1-1 compares the editions of Windows 7 and compares the basic features available with each.

Table 1-1   Windows 7 Editions

Edition	Designed for	Notable Features
Starter	Small notebook computers (netbooks)	A fundamental, entry-level version available in all markets for small form-factor computers. Limited to running three programs at a time.
Home Basic	Designed to run on lower-powered systems frequently found in emerging markets	Provides basic computing needs such as email, Internet browsing, and photo viewing.
Home Premium	Most home users, including music, photo, and video usage	A standard, consumer-level version that provides a full, rich computing environment including features such as Aero Glass, Mobility Center, and Windows Media Center.
Professional	Business users who need enhanced business-style networking capabilities	Domain membership, advanced backup capabilities including shadow copy, Encrypting File System, and Remote Desktop.
Enterprise	Business users who need advanced computing and security functions	Advanced business capabilities, including seamless corporate network connectivity and AppLocker software restriction capabilities. Available only through software agreement contracts.
Ultimate	Home and business users who desire the complete experience	A total computing package including all features available in other editions, plus ability to use multiple languages.

Each Windows 7 version includes all features of lower versions, with no trade-off on features when upgrading to a higher version. This is in contrast to Windows Vista, where the Business version (which compares to Windows 7 Professional) lacked numerous features that were available in the Home Premium version, such as Windows Media Center.

NOTE   Microsoft makes the Enterprise version of Windows 7 available only to Enterprise Agreement (EA) or Software Assurance (SA) customers, who must purchase a minimum of 250 Windows 7 licenses. You can only install Windows 7 Enterprise as a clean installation. Smaller businesses should deploy Windows 7 Ultimate if they need the enhanced features available to Windows 7 Enterprise.

Table 1-2 provides additional detail on the components included in the various editions of Windows 7. We introduce many of these features in the following sections.

Table 1-2   Components Included in Windows 7 Editions

Component	Starter	Home Basic	Home Premium	Professional	Enterprise and Ultimate
Internet Explorer 8	x	x	x	x	x
Windows Search	x	x	x	x	x
HomeGroup membership	x	x	x	x	x
Action Center	x	x	x	x	x
Parental Controls	x	x	x	x	x
Windows Media Player	x	x	x	x	x
Taskbar Thumbnail Previews		x	x	x	x
Create ad-hoc wireless networks		x	x	x	x

Table 1-2   Components Included in Windows 7 Editions

Component	Starter	Home Basic	Home Premium	Professional	Enterprise and Ultimate
Internet Connection Sharing		x	x	x	x
Support for multiple monitors		x	x	x	x
Aero Glass and advanced window navigation			x	x	x
Scheduled backups			x	x	x
Ability to create a homegroup			x	x	x
Complete PC Backup and Restore			x	x	x
Windows Media Center			x	x	x
DVD video playback and authoring			x	x	x
Ability to join a domain				x	x
BitLocker drive encryption				x	x
Support for multiple processors				x	x
Remote Desktop				x	x
Advanced network backup				x	x

Table 1-2   Components Included in Windows 7 Editions

Component	Starter	Home Basic	Home Premium	Professional	Enterprise and Ultimate
File encryption using Encrypting File System (EFS)				x	x
Windows XP Mode				x	x
Advanced security capabilities, including BitLocker, AppLocker, DirectAccess, and BranchCache					x
Multilanguage User Interface (MUI)					x

NOTE   The Starter and Home Basic editions of Windows 7 are not generally used on computers found in most developed areas of the world, such as the U.S., Canada, and western Europe. They are not important from the viewpoint of Microsoft exams and will not be discussed further in this book.

Features of Windows 7

Windows 7 builds upon the vast array of new features first introduced with Windows Vista. Every edition of Windows 7 includes all features supported by the next lower edition of Windows 7. Because many people are coming directly from Windows XP and have not had much (if any) experience with Windows Vista, the following lists include some of the features first introduced with Vista. These lists are not designed to be exhaustive; they merely introduce the most important new features included with Windows 7. As you study this book, you will learn most of these features in detail.

Productivity Improvements

Windows 7 includes a number of new features and enhancements that are designed to improve the way users interact with their computers. The basic productivity enhancements included with most editions of Windows 7 include the following:

■ **Improved User Interface and Start Menu:** The new look to the user interface is similar to that introduced with Windows Vista and includes translucent window borders. Although similar to the Windows XP Start menu, the Windows 7 Start menu includes a new instant search assistant that directs you to any program or file on your computer. Further, many items on the Start menu include jump lists, which enable you to access tasks associated with programs on the Start menu or documents recently accessed with these items. You can also pin items to the jump lists.

■ **Improved Taskbar:** Windows 7 minimizes the buttons to running programs into small icons, thereby reducing taskbar clutter and allowing more icons to be visible at all times. You can see a thumbnail view of each running document by hovering your mouse over the taskbar icon, and you can bring it to the front by clicking the taskbar icon. Icons to common Windows programs are always displayed on the taskbar. You can also pin frequently used programs to the taskbar so that you can open them with a single click. Simply drag the desired icon to the taskbar. Figure 1-1 shows the Windows 7 desktop with the improved Start menu and taskbar.

Figure 1-1   The Windows 7 desktop, Start menu, and taskbar.

■ **Homegroup Networking:** Microsoft has facilitated networking of Windows 7 computers located in a non-domain environment by introducing the concept of *homegroups*. This is simply a group of Windows 7 computers connected by a high-speed local area network (LAN) and sharing resources such as files, folders, and printers with each other. You can create a homegroup or join an existing one during Windows setup, or later by running the wizard accessed from the Windows 7 Control Panel, as shown in Figure 1-2. When creating a homegroup, you are presented with a password that protects access to the homegroup; to join additional computers to the homegroup, you must enter this password. Note that computers running older Windows versions cannot join a homegroup.

Figure 1-2   Homegroups facilitate networking of Windows 7 computers in a nondomain environment.

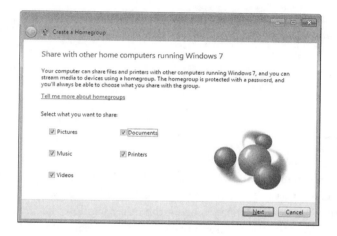

- **Libraries:** One of the most significant new features from a user viewpoint is the concept of *libraries*, which are collections of Windows folders, such as Documents, Pictures, Videos, and Music. These replace the special shell folders such as My Documents that were found in previous Windows versions. Links to these libraries appear on the Start menu, and you can also access them by clicking the icon pinned to the taskbar (it looks like a set of folders in a plastic bracket). See Figure 1-3. Libraries serve to aggregate items located in one or more folders each, and you can add or remove folders from each library as desired. They can even include folders stored on other computers within your homegroup. You can also create additional libraries if you choose. Furthermore, when you set up homegroup networking, these libraries are automatically shared with other computers in the homegroup.

- **Aero Glass:** Available on all Windows 7 editions except Starter and Home Basic, this is the desktop appearance first introduced with Vista featuring translucent title bars that reveal objects hidden beneath them. You can also hover your mouse pointer over taskbar buttons to reveal live thumbnails of the document or program to which the button relates. A feature known as Flip 3D enables you to display live windows of each open document in sequence by pressing the Windows+Tab key combination, facilitating your selection of the correct one. You can configure all these features from the Display applet in Control Panel. Aero Glass in Windows 7 includes the following additional new features:

Figure 1-3 Libraries collect folders that contain commonly used items.

— Aero Shake: To focus on a single window on a crowded display, simply shake your mouse back and forth on the title bar of the desired window. This minimizes all other windows. Repeat to bring the other windows back.
— Aero Peek: Enables you to make the windows transparent to reveal hidden icons and gadgets. You can also show the desktop from a tiny button at the right corner of the taskbar.
— Aero Snap: Enables you to resize open windows by dragging them to the edges of the display. You can expand windows vertically, display them side-by-side with other windows, or maximize them to the entire screen.

■ **Windows Live Essentials:** Microsoft has simplified the Windows 7 footprint by removing some programs such as Windows Mail from Windows 7. These have been replaced with a series of free programs available for download at http://download.live.com/. This includes Windows Mail, Messenger, Writer, Photo Gallery, Movie Maker, Family Safety, and Toolbar. By downloading these programs, you can customize your Windows experience according to your needs and desires.

■ **Improved Power Options:** Microsoft has tweaked the three power plans introduced with Windows Vista (Balanced, High Performance, and Power Saver) with the idea of optimizing energy use even further. For example, when using either the Balanced or Power Saver power plan, your processor will run at as low as 5% of its maximum performance, or as high as 100%, according to demands of currently running software. Further, your notebook display will dim slightly after even a minute or two or nonuse.

- **Sleep Mode:** Combining features of Windows XP's Standby and Hibernation modes and first introduced in Windows Vista, sleep mode enables you to preserve open documents and programs on shutdown, enabling you to resume work rapidly from where you left off.

- **Windows Experience Index:** Introduced with Windows Vista, this is a performance scoring metric that assesses the capability of several hardware and software components on your computer. It includes such components as the processor, memory, graphics card, and hard disk and displays a base score that relates to the weakest performing component on your computer. Thus, it suggests which component you should upgrade to improve your computer's overall performance.

- **Windows XP Mode:** You can install a virtual copy of Windows XP on a computer running Windows 7 Professional or higher and run older Windows XP business software that might not run properly on Windows 7 on this virtual computer. The Windows 7 Start menu integrates programs installed on Windows XP Mode with those directly installed on Windows 7 for further user convenience.

- **Support for Document Metadata:** As in Windows Vista, Windows 7 can search for documents, pictures, and so on with the aid of metadata included with many file types—that is, data about data. The Windows Search service indexes many types of metadata and enables you to filter search results to view data that contains specific property values. For example, you can filter images to display only those taken with a specific camera within a specified block of time.

Security Improvements

As you know, Windows Vista and previous Windows versions have been subjected to a never-ending flow of new vulnerabilities. Microsoft has introduced several new features designed to improve the security of computing in Windows 7:

- **Secure Startup:** This feature prevents unauthorized users from accessing sensitive data during startup by encrypting the system drive. It utilizes a hardware module called the Trusted Platform Module (TPM), which is found on many recently manufactured computers. New to Windows 7 is a TPM Management Microsoft Management Console (MMC) snap-in that can be used to reset TPM security settings.

- **User Account Control (UAC):** First introduced with Windows Vista, UAC causes all users, even administrators, to operate in a limited mode that prevents actions that might be detrimental to system security. When users need to perform potentially risky tasks, Windows presents a dialog box requesting permission or administrative credentials to perform the task. In Windows 7, you can choose from several levels of protection by UAC. This follows complaints by Vista users that UAC produced too many prompts (even for actions such as moving, renaming, or deleting image files under certain conditions) that hindered their productivity and caused many users to disable UAC completely.

- **Credential Manager:** Windows 7 stores credentials used to log on to servers, websites, or programs in a secure location called the *Windows Vault* that protects these credentials while facilitating the ease of logon to the required locations. This includes NTLM or Kerberos credentials used to log on to Active Directory domains as well as certificate-based credentials.

- **AppLocker:** A new, easily administered tool that enables administrators to specify what programs are allowed to run on the desktop in a domain-based environment. You can specify applications that are allowed or denied execution, and you can create exceptions to these rules as desired. AppLocker replaces the older Software Restriction Policies used in previous Windows versions.

- **BitLocker and BitLocker To Go:** First introduced in Vista and enhanced in Windows 7, BitLocker enables you to encrypt any hard drive partition to prevent unauthorized individuals from accessing data contained therein. The new BitLocker To Go extends this protection to removable devices such as USB flash drives and portable disks. Even if a thief removes a protected drive from its computer and installs it in another computer, he cannot access the data contained on the drive. Included is a data recovery agent that enables administrators to secure drives and store access credentials so that authorized access is never lost.

- **Enhanced Auditing:** Auditing capabilities have been enhanced in Windows 7 so that corporations can meet the increasingly stringent data security regulations. Additional Group Policy settings enable you to find out why certain users have access to specific information or have been denied access, and you can also discover which changes specific users or groups have made.

- **Enhanced Storage Access:** Provides new Group Policy settings that enable you to manage portable data storage devices such as USB flash drives, which can be easily lost or stolen. You can configure certificate usage, specify the types of devices allowed on the network, and perform other actions that secure data on such devices.

- **Windows Biometric Service:** Provides improved support for the use of fingerprint readers for authenticating users and elevating their privileges through UAC. New Group Policy settings enable you to administer the use of biometric devices.

- **Action Center:** Replaces the Vista Security Center and brings a large set of security features together in one location. Action Center enables you to track items such as Windows Firewall, Windows Update, antivirus, antispyware,

Internet security settings, UAC, and Network Access Protection from one location. Action Center also enables you to manage backup and problem troubleshooting.

- **New Internet Explorer 8 Security Features:** Microsoft has improved and secured web browsing with new capabilities including the Internet Explorer Enhanced Security Configuration, which adjusts security levels for the existing Internet security zones. This configuration automatically adds the Microsoft Update website to the Trusted Sites security zone, so that problems in obtaining updates for Windows are reduced. Protected Mode, which was first introduced in Internet Explorer 7, can now be applied to sites in the Local Intranet zone. Internet Explorer 8 also adds InPrivate browsing mode, which hides your browsing history when using public computers and turns off the ability to store items such as cookies, usernames, and passwords.

- **Improvements to Windows Firewall:** Although not much changed from the Vista version, Windows Firewall now includes an enhanced interface and automatic configuration of settings according to the type of network (home, work, or public) that you have selected when you first configure networking on your computer.

- **Windows Defender:** First introduced in Windows Vista, Windows Defender monitors your computer for signs of spyware infection and block actions of malicious programs such as their installation.

- **Parental Controls:** Introduced with Windows Vista, these controls enable parents to set limits on their children's activities by setting time limits, restricting games, allowing or blocking specific programs, and so on. In Windows 7, website blocking and Internet activity reporting have been moved to the new Windows Live Family Safety program, which is a free download from the Windows Live website.

Chapter 8, "Configuring Applications and Internet Explorer"; Chapter 10, "Configuring Network and Firewall Settings"; and Chapter 12, "Configuring Access Controls," provides details of most of these features.

A Quick Tour of Windows 7

Windows 7 builds on the enhanced visual experiences in Windows Vista to improve your overall computing experience. This section introduces many of the new and enhanced features you will become familiar with as you begin to work with Microsoft's latest operating system.

Start Menu and Taskbar

Figure 1-4 shows the new Windows 7 Start Menu, which follows the same basic design first seen in Windows Vista but includes several enhancements, as indicated from top to bottom on the figure:

- **Jump Lists:** Many of the items on the left side of the Start menu link to jump lists, which are lists of program features associated with the primary item, or of documents that you have recently opened from the indicated program. Hover your mouse pointer over an item with an associated jump list and the list replaces the right side of the Start menu. For example, the Getting Started jump list contains links to items you might want to configure when you first log on to Windows 7. You can then click any item in the jump list to open it.

- **All Programs:** When you select this feature, the list on the left side of the Start menu changes to display a menu of all available programs, many of which are categorized into folders. You can simply click through the folders on this menu to locate any program on your computer. This behavior is similar to that of Vista and different from that of Windows XP.

- **Windows Search:** This feature works in a similar manner to that of Windows Vista, enabling you to perform instant searches for programs, files, email, and other items on your computer, as well as search the Internet for anything you can imagine. Simply type the name of the item you want to locate and Windows 7 will display matches for your search in the left pane of the Start

Figure 1-4   The Windows 7 Start menu offers several enhancements from the Start menu included with Windows Vista.

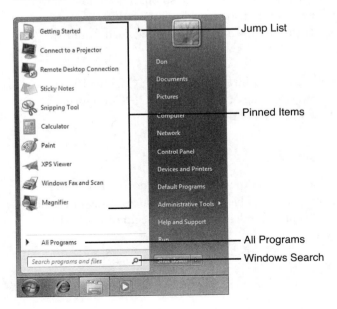

menu within a few seconds. If you type the name of a program on your computer and press Enter, Search will locate and open that program. You can also perform instant searches from any folder window. Note that you can perform a similar search from any Windows Explorer window.

- **Pinned Items:** Windows 7 no longer pins items such as Windows Mail and Internet Explorer to the top of the Start menu. Instead, these items have taskbar buttons that enable you to quickly access them from that location. You can still pin programs to the Start menu as you did in Vista; simply right-click the desired program in the All Programs list and choose **Pin to Start Menu**.

The new Windows 7 taskbar, shown in Figure 1-5, combines features of the taskbar and Quick Launch area formerly present in Windows XP and Vista. By default when you first install Windows 7, the taskbar contains three buttons to the right of the Start button, which represent Internet Explorer, Windows Explorer, and Windows Media Player. Each time you open an application, a button representing this application is added to the taskbar. You can add applications to the taskbar; simply find the desired application from the All Programs list in the Start menu, right-click it, and choose **Pin to Taskbar**. You can also pin items to the taskbar by dragging and dropping them to the taskbar. These remain on the taskbar whether the program is running or not; if you want to remove a button from the taskbar later, simply right-click it and choose **Unpin this program from Taskbar**.

Figure 1-5   The Windows 7 taskbar offers buttons for running applications as well as buttons from which you can launch applications.

Taskbar buttons can take on any of the three following appearances:

- For a pinned program that is not running, a simple icon for the program appears. Click the button to open the program.

- If a single instance of the program (or a single Windows Explorer window or Internet Explorer tab or page) is running, the button is enclosed by a single rectangular frame. Mouse over the button to view a thumbnail of the application; click it to bring it to the front. If the application is already in the front on your desktop, clicking its taskbar button minimizes the application.

- If multiple instances of the program (or of Explorer windows or Internet Explorer tabs or pages) are running, the button takes on a pseudo-3D appearance that looks like stacked frames. If you mouse over the button, a series of icons representing each instance or tab appears; click the desired one to bring it to the front.

Configuring Windows 7 Start Menu and Taskbar

Windows 7 provides several options for configuring the properties of the Start menu and the taskbar. Right-click **Start** and choose **Properties** to bring up the Taskbar and Start Menu Properties dialog box, which enables you to configure properties related to the taskbar, Start menu, notification area, and toolbars.

Start Menu Properties

As shown in Figure 1-6, you can configure the following properties of the Start menu tab:

Figure 1-6   The Start Menu tab of the Taskbar and Start Menu Properties dialog box enables you to configure several options for the Start menu.

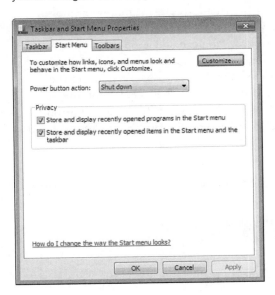

- **Customize Button:** Select this button to bring up the Customize Start Menu dialog box (see Figure 1-7). You can choose which options appear on the Start menu. In particular, selecting the Display As a Menu option enables a jump list for items displayed on the right side of the Start menu.

- **Power Button Action Button:** Select this option to display different possible actions that can occur when you press the computer's power button. By default, this is Shut Down, but you can also choose from Switch User, Log Off, Lock, Restart, or Sleep.

- **Privacy Options:** If additional users are accessing your computer and you do not want them to know which files and programs you have recently accessed, clear either or both of the check boxes in this section.

Figure 1-7   You can configure which items appear on the Start menu from the Customize Start Menu dialog box.

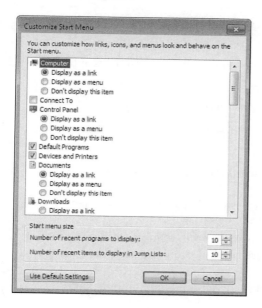

Taskbar Properties

Selecting the Taskbar tab of the Taskbar and Start Menu Properties enables you to configure the items shown in Figure 1-8.

Figure 1-8   The Taskbar tab enables you to configure several taskbar properties.

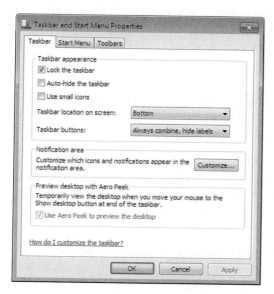

Except for the Show window previews option, these properties function as they did in Windows XP:

- **Lock the taskbar:** Determines whether the taskbar is always visible at the bottom of the display.

- **Auto-hide the taskbar:** Determines whether the taskbar disappears automatically after a program is started.

- **Use small icons:** Shrinks the size of icons on the taskbar buttons.

- **Taskbar location on screen:** Enables you to choose between top, bottom, left, or right.

- **Taskbar buttons:** Provides the following three options for display of taskbar buttons.
  — **Always combine, hide labels:** Provides the default Windows 7 view already described.
  — **Combine when taskbar is full:** Displays icons in a similar fashion to that of Vista with descriptive labels that are combined only when a large number of applications are open.
  — **Never combine:** Offers a similar display but does not combine icons for open programs.

- **Notification area:** Click **Customize** to display the Notification Area Icons applet of Control Panel, which enables you to choose what items are displayed in the notification area (formerly known as the system tray). Some third-party programs add options to this applet when installed.

- **Preview desktop with Aero Peek:** Enables viewing of the desktop by hovering the mouse over a small area to the right of the clock at the end of the taskbar.

Toolbars

Click the Toolbars tab to configure the taskbar to display toolbars for Address, Links, Tablet PC Input Panel, iTunes, and the Desktop (see Figure 1-9). These toolbars appear on the right side of the taskbar, next to the Notification area.

Libraries

As already discussed, Microsoft has created the new Libraries location, which is simply a shell folder that provides access to files and folders with a common theme (refer to Figure 1-3). Each library is simply a pointer that opens a window containing all subfolders and files within the library. By default, the following four libraries are provided:

- **Documents:** Includes the My Documents and Public Documents folders

- **Music:** Includes the My Music and Public Music folders

Figure 1-9 The Toolbars tab enables you to display several toolbars on the desktop.

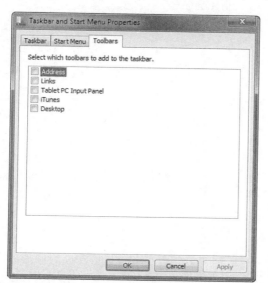

- **Pictures:** Includes the My Pictures and Public Pictures folders

- **Videos:** Includes the My Videos and Public Videos folders

You can add additional folders to a library at any time. Right-click the desired library and choose **Properties** to display the dialog box shown in Figure 1-10. To add a folder, click **Include a folder** and browse to the desired folder. To remove a folder, select it and click **Remove**.

You can also create new libraries at any time. Right-click a blank area in the Libraries window and choose **New > Library**. Provide a name for the library and then follow the procedure in the preceding paragraph to add folders to your library.

By default, all libraries are shared when the computer is in a homegroup or workgroup. You can modify this behavior as desired. We discuss sharing of libraries and folders in more detail in Chapter 11, "Configuring Access to Local and Shared Resources."

Control Panel

Microsoft has continued the idea of categories that first appeared in Windows XP and was enhanced in Windows Vista and has included links that assist you in performing many common tasks (see Figure 1-11).

This section provides a quick introduction to the Control Panel features. You learn about many of these features in detail in subsequent chapters of this book.

Figure 1-10 Each library has a Properties dialog box that enables you to perform actions such as adding and removing folders accessed from the library.

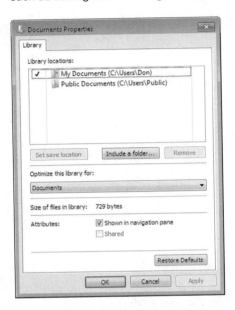

Figure 1-11 The Windows 7 Control Panel offers links to frequently used applets.

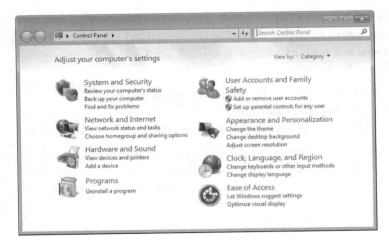

System and Security

Shown in Figure 1-12, the System and Security category includes several tasks that enable you to configure performance options and obtain information about your computer. Note that the left side of the window includes links to other Control Panel categories. This feature assists you in navigating among categories and is displayed for all Control Panel categories.

Figure 1-12   The System and Security category includes basic system- and security-related configuration tasks.

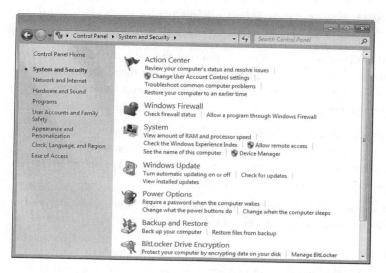

The task options available through the System and Security category include the following:

- **Action Center:** This new applet provides a one-stop connection to many security- and maintenance-related tasks.

- **Windows Firewall:** Builds on the firewall first introduced in Windows XP SP2 that protects your computer against both incoming and outgoing threats. You can configure which programs are permitted to send or receive data across the firewall.

- **System:** Provides a summary of information related to your computer, including the hardware configuration, computer name, workgroup or domain information, and activation status. You can also access this information by clicking Start, right-clicking Computer, and choosing Properties from the context menu.

- **Windows Update:** Enables your computer to download various updates, including patches and hotfixes, from the Microsoft Windows Update website. You can view and download available updates and Windows Ultimate Extras from this location, and you can also configure settings that control the downloading and installation of updates.

- **Power Options:** Enables you to select a power plan to conserve energy by turning off items such as your display or hard disks after a period of inactivity or maximize performance of your computer. You can also customize a power plan to suit your needs.

- **Backup and Restore:** Enables you to perform automatic backup copies of files and folders on your computer, thereby protecting them against system or disk failure. We discuss backup and restore in detail in Chapter 17, "Configuring Backups."

- **BitLocker Drive Encryption:** Enables you to encrypt the contents of your hard drive so that intruders or thieves are unable to access your data. You can also enable BitLocker To Go, which protects the contents of removable drives from unauthorized access.

- **Windows Anytime Upgrade:** Available on all editions except Ultimate, this option enables you to upgrade your computer to a higher edition of Windows 7. You can go online, choose the desired edition, and purchase it, or enter an upgrade key if you have already purchased your upgrade.

- **Administrative Tools:** Links to a large number of administrative tools, many of which we discuss in subsequent chapters of this book.

Network and Internet

As shown in Figure 1-13, the Network and Internet category includes several tasks that enable you to configure connections to your LAN or the Internet, as well as several other network-related tasks.

Figure 1-13   The Network and Internet category enables you to perform network-related tasks.

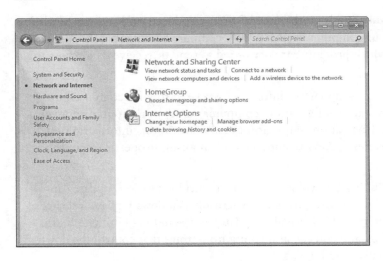

The task options provided by the Network and Internet category include the following:

- **Network and Sharing Center:** Enables you to establish and configure options related to networks accessible to your computer. It provides a local view of the network to which your computer is attached, and enables you to perform several tasks related to sharing of items such as files, folders, printers, and media. You can view the current status of your network connections, enable or disable network connections, and diagnose connectivity problems.

- **HomeGroup:** Enables you to modify sharing options for libraries and printers. You can also stream pictures, music, and videos to other networked devices, and modify homegroup security options.

- **Internet Options:** Enables you to configure the properties of Internet Explorer 8. You can specify your home page, delete your browsing history, modify tabbed browsing, configure security and privacy options, and many more actions. We look at these options in Chapter 8.

Hardware and Sound

Shown in Figure 1-14, the Hardware and Sound category includes applets that enable you to configure all your computer's hardware components.

Figure 1-14 The Hardware and Sound category enables you to manage a diverse range of hardware components.

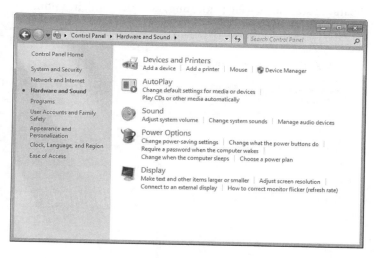

The Hardware and Sound category includes the following applets:

- **Devices and Printers:** Enables you to add printers and fax devices and configure properties of these devices. You can view and manage print queues, configure printer permissions, modify settings related to a specific printer type, and troubleshoot problems related to printers and faxes. You can configure mouse properties such as button settings, pointer appearance, scroll wheel actions, and so on. You can also access the Device Manager, which enables you to view information on hardware devices on your computer. Device Manager enables you to enable or disable devices; identify resources used by each device; identify, update, and roll back device drivers; and so on.

- **AutoPlay:** Enables you to configure default actions that take place when you insert media of a given type such as audio CDs, DVDs, blank discs, and so on.

- **Sound:** Enables you to configure the settings associated with audio recording and playback devices. You can create and modify sound schemes that include the sounds associated with Windows and program events.

- **Power Options:** Enables you to choose and configure a power plan. These are the same options as those accessed through the System and Security category.

- **Display:** Enables you to specify the size of text and other items on the screen. Links from this applet enables you to adjust screen resolution and the use of Clear Type text, and access the Magnifier tool, which can temporarily enlarge a portion of your screen.

Programs

Shown in Figure 1-15, the Programs category includes applets that enable you to configure features related to applications installed on your computer, including programs that run by default at startup as well as locating, downloading, installing, and removing of applications.

Figure 1-15   The Programs category lets you manage applications on your computer.

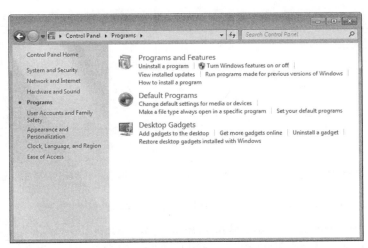

Applets provided by the Programs category include the following:

- **Programs and Features:** This is a complete reworking of the Add or Remove Programs applet in Windows versions prior to Vista, and enables you to uninstall, change, or repair applications installed on your computer.

- **Default Programs:** Enables you to configure which applications Windows uses by default for opening files of a specific type. You can also control access to various types of applications and configure AutoPlay settings.

- **Desktop Gadgets:** Enables you to add desktop gadgets (which were displayed in the Sidebar in Windows Vista but now can be placed anywhere on the desktop). You can also configure properties of individual gadgets. Note that, unlike Vista, no gadgets appear on the desktop by default; you need to enable them. You can also access the Desktop Gadgets applet by right-clicking the desktop and choosing Gadgets.

User Accounts and Family Safety

As shown in Figure 1-16, the User Accounts and Family Safety applet enables you to configure several options related to user accounts and logon credentials.

Figure 1-16   The User Accounts and Family Safety category enables you to configure user account properties.

Applets provided by the User Accounts and Family Safety category include the following:

- **User Accounts:** Enables you to create or remove user accounts and modify use account properties.

- **Parental Controls:** Enables you to configure which applications Windows uses by default for opening files of specific type. You can also control access to various types of applications and configure AutoPlay settings.

- **Windows CardSpace:** Enables you to configure information used when logging on to online network services. You can keep track of memberships at online services and websites and modify personal information sent to these sites.

■ **Credential Manager:** Enables you to configure the Windows Vault, which stores credentials used for logging on to other computers or websites.

Appearance and Personalization

As shown in Figure 1-17, the Appearance and Personalization category enables you to configure properties of your computer related to how items appear on the display.

Figure 1-17   The Appearance and Personalization category enables you to configure appearance-related options.

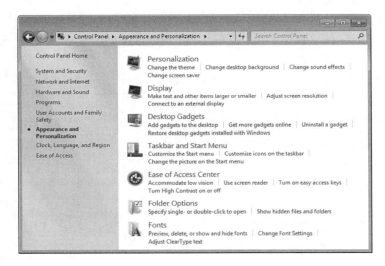

The Appearance and Personalization category includes the following:

■ **Personalization:** Enables you to configure a large range of mostly display-related options such as color and appearance of windows, desktop background, screen saver, Windows themes, display resolution and refresh, and so on. You can go online to get additional themes.

■ **Display:** Enables you to configure display properties. These are the same options as those provided in the Hardware and Sound category.

■ **Taskbar and Start Menu:** Same as accessed by right-clicking Start and choosing Properties, as already discussed.

■ **Ease of Access Center:** Contains several accessibility options that enable vision- and mobility-challenged users to use the computer. You can access a wizard that helps you select the appropriate options for individuals with different requirements.

- **Folder Options:** Enables you to modify how folder windows display their contents. You can configure whether files open with a single- or double-click, show hidden files and folders, and so on.

- **Fonts:** Enables you to manage fonts stored on your computer. You can add or remove fonts and display samples of fonts installed on your computer.

Displaying File Extensions

As in previous Windows versions, Windows 7 does not display extensions for common types by default. To display file extensions, access the Folder Options applet, click the **View** tab, and clear the check box labeled **Hide extensions for known file types**. This helps you distinguish between files with otherwise similar names. It also helps guard against undesirable files with double extensions; for example, `data.txt.exe` would appear as `data.txt` and could hide a malicious executable if you have not cleared this check box.

Clock, Language, and Region

The Clock, Language, and Region category contains two applets that enable you to configure the time and date displayed on your computers; configure your time zone; and select how your computer displays items such as dates, times, numbers, and currency according to the country in which you live. You can also add or remove display languages, set which language is displayed by default, and adapt your keyboard for specific languages.

Ease of Access

The Ease of Access category provides access to the Ease of Access Center, which is also included in the Appearance and Personalization category. It also includes the Speech Recognition applet, which enables you to configure microphones and train your computer to understand your voice. You can take a tutorial that shows you how to use speech on your computer and view or print a list of speech-related commands.

Patches, Hotfixes, and Service Packs

With millions of lines of code in any application, you can imagine that there will be some errors that were not caught in testing, especially considering how many different uses that millions of people will find. This was something that users have expressed concerns about since the early days of computing and no program has ever worked perfectly under every circumstance. The frustration of not being able to get work done because of some bug in the software generated complaints. Microsoft's solution to bugs was to create bug fixes, also called *hotfixes*. More recently, Microsoft created security fixes known as *patches* and began to release these on the second Tuesday of every month, which has become known in Microsoft circles as "Patch Tuesday."

After a certain amount of time, people had to install so many patches and hotfixes that Microsoft packaged them into a single installation called a *service pack*, or SP for short. Of course, hotfixes created after the first service pack required Microsoft to incorporate all those fixes into another service pack.

Service packs gave the developers an opportunity to release additional features. For example, SP2 for Windows XP added Windows Firewall, Windows Security Center, and a pop-up blocker for Internet Explorer. Each service pack is cumulative, so when you install a service pack, you need to install only the latest one released to gain all the fixes and features in previous SPs.

Service Packs Are Not Necessarily the Best Thing Since Sliced Bread

Each service pack usually causes a few unexpected errors with a variety of applications and/or hardware devices. As an administrator, you should install service packs with the same amount of caution that you would use to deploy the operating system itself, by first testing it in your own environment with your own applications and hardware, and then running a pilot test of the update on a group of (forgiving, you hope) users. After you are sure that the service pack will cause fewer errors than the ones that it fixes, you should roll it out to your users.

Summary

This chapter has provided you with an overview of the basic features of the Windows 7 desktop operating system. The information here will guide you as you explore the configuration tasks associated with Windows 7 computers and networks in the chapters to come.

This chapter covers the following subjects:

- **Identifying Hardware Requirements:** This describes the hardware requirements your computer must meet in order to run Windows 7 properly.

- **Performing a Clean Installation of Windows 7 as the Sole Operating System:** This section describes the procedure for performing a basic installation of Windows 7 from the DVD-ROM media.

- **Dual-Booting Windows 7:** You can install Windows 7 alongside another operating system so that you can choose which operating system to start when you turn your computer on. This section describes how to perform these actions.

- **Other Windows 7 Installation Methods:** You can install Windows 7 by using installation files copied to other locations, such as removable USB hard drives or network shares, or Windows Deployment Services installed on a server.

- **Troubleshooting Windows 7 Installation Issues:** Problems can and do occur when installing Windows 7. This section describes some of the problems you might encounter and suggests ways to troubleshoot them.

CHAPTER 2

Installing Windows 7

The Microsoft 70-680 exam assesses your ability to install, configure, and administer Windows 7 and focuses on how to do so in a business environment. Basic to any installation type is the manual, clean installation of Windows 7 on a new computer.

As an adjunct to Murphy's Law, what can go wrong during an operating system installation does go wrong, and then the situation needs troubleshooting. Windows 7 is no exception. Knowing how to handle the unexpected error makes all the difference to a network administrator or engineer.

"Do I Know This Already?" Quiz

The "Do I Know This Already?" quiz enables you to assess whether you should read this entire chapter or simply jump to the "Exam Preparation Tasks" section for review. If you are in doubt, read the entire chapter. Table 2-1 outlines the major headings in this chapter and the corresponding "Do I Know This Already?" quiz questions. You can find the answers in Appendix A, "Answers to the 'Do I Know This Already?' Quizzes."

Table 2-1 "Do I Know This Already?" Foundation Topics Section-to-Question Mapping

Foundations Topics Section	Questions Covered in This Section
Identifying Hardware Requirements	1–4
Performing a Clean Installation of Windows 7 as the Sole Operating System	5–6
Dual-Booting Windows 7	7–8
Other Windows 7 Installation Methods	9–10
Troubleshooting Windows 7 Installation Issues	11–14

1. What is the minimum amount of RAM required for a basic Windows 7 installation?
   a. 256 MB
   b. 512 MB
   c. 1 GB
   d. 4 GB

2. What is the minimum processor speed required for a Windows 7 computer?
   a. 1 GHz
   b. 2 GHz
   c. 3 GHz
   d. 4 GHz

3. What is the minimum amount of hard drive space required for a 32-bit Windows 7 installation?
   a. 10 GB
   b. 15 GB
   c. 16 GB
   d. 20 GB
   e. 40 GB

4. Which of the following is the standard networking protocol used by Windows 7?
   a. NWLink
   b. NetBEUI
   c. IPX/SPX
   d. TCP/IP

5. Which of the following are items you should have on hand before beginning a Windows 7 installation? (Choose all that apply.)
   a. Windows 7 drivers from the manufacturer for any hardware not appearing in the Windows Logo Program
   b. BIOS that meets the minimum requirements for Windows 7 compatibility
   c. Windows 7 product code
   d. Internet connection
   e. A CD-ROM drive
   f. Backup of all your existing data and the drivers for your backup device

6. Which of the following settings can you configure during an installation of Windows 7 from a DVD-ROM? (Choose all that apply.)

   a. Username and password

   b. Domain membership

   c. Date, time, and time zone

   d. Network settings type

   e. Desktop gadgets

7. You need to edit settings while configuring your computer to dual-boot Windows 7 with Windows XP. What utility should you use?

   a. `boot.ini`

   b. `bootcfg.exe`

   c. `bcdedit.exe`

   d. `winload.exe`

8. You want to set your computer up to triple-boot Windows 98, Windows XP, and Windows 7. What should you do first?

   a. Install Windows 7

   b. Install Windows 98

   c. Install Windows XP

   d. Install MS-DOS

9. If you want to use a USB hard drive to install Windows 7, which of the following should you do before beginning the installation?

   a. Configure the BIOS to boot from the USB device

   b. Insert a floppy disk with MS-DOS boot files

   c. Insert a CD-ROM with MS-DOS boot files

   d. Press the F10 key

10. What is the first thing you should do after turning the computer on, to start installing Windows 7 by means of WDS?

    a. Press the Esc key.

    b. Press the Del key.

    c. Press the F10 key.

    d. Press the F12 key.

    e. Nothing; just wait until Windows 7 completes installation, and then log on with your username and password.

11. Which of the following are possible problems that could cause a Windows 7 installation to fail? (Choose all that apply.)

   a. Incompatible BIOS

   b. Incompatible hardware

   c. Insufficient hard disk space

   d. Incompatible hard disk, network adapter, or other device drivers

   e. Inability to access the network because of name or IP address conflicts

12. Which command would you choose to display a computer's TCP/IP connections and protocol statistics?

   a. `ipconfig`

   b. `ping`

   c. `nbtstat`

   d. `netstat`

13. What key would you press during startup to access the Advanced Boot Options menu?

   a. Esc

   b. Delete

   c. F8

   d. F10

14. Which Setup log records modifications are performed on the system during Setup?

   a. `netsetup.log`

   b. `setuperr.log`

   c. `setupapi.log`

   d. `setupact.log`

Foundation Topics

Identifying Hardware Requirements

Microsoft has defined the minimum level of hardware requirements for computers running Windows 7. These represent the bare minimum required to run the core features of Windows 7 and provide a basic user experience. Computers meeting these requirements are considered "Windows 7–Capable" computers. Unlike Windows Vista, Microsoft has not defined any premium-ready hardware requirements level.

Table 2-2 lists the base hardware requirements for Windows 7. Although these are the minimum hardware requirements for supporting the operating system, they are not necessarily adequate to support additional applications or for reasonable performance. When designing the hardware requirements for installation, you should allow for extra RAM and hard disk space and probably a faster processor for applications.

Table 2-2   Hardware Requirements for Windows 7

Device	Minimum Supported Hardware
Processor	32-bit (x86) or 64-bit (x64) running at 1 GHz or higher
RAM	1 GB (32-bit) or 2 GB (64-bit)
Graphics processor	DirectX 9-capable with WDDM 1.0 or higher driver
Hard disk	At least 16 GB (32-bit) or 20 GB (64-bit)
Disk drives	DVD-ROM drive
Other	Standard keyboard and mouse or other pointing device

If you want to access a network, you should have a network adapter installed that is compatible with the network infrastructure. For Internet access, at a minimum you need a 14.4 Kbps modem or higher to dial up to an Internet service provider (ISP). Video conferencing, voice, fax, and other multimedia applications generally require 56 Kbps modems, microphone, sound card, and speakers or headset. Video conferencing itself requires a video conferencing camera. Other required hardware depends on purposes you might use Windows 7 for, such as the following:

- Complete Media Center functionality requires a TV tuner.

- BitLocker requires the Trusted Platform Module (TPM) 1.2.

- Windows XP Mode requires an additional 1 GB RAM, an additional 15 GB of available hard disk space, and a processor such as Intel VT or AMD-V that is capable of hardware virtualization.

Hardware Compatibility

Microsoft makes it easy to check your hardware's compatibility by providing a list of supported hardware. Microsoft designed the *Windows 7 Logo Program for Hardware* with the aim of assisting users to identify hardware components that are compatible with Windows 7 and the Windows Server 2008 Release 2 (R2). Microsoft states that the "Windows 7 Logo Program is designed to help your company deliver compatible and reliable systems, software, and hardware products." This program is similar to that initiated with Windows Vista and replaces the Hardware Compatibility List and Windows Catalog that were previously used with older Windows versions. Companies that produce computers with hardware carrying the Compatible with Windows 7 Logo can assure their customers that they are purchasing machines that are designed and tested for compatibility with Windows 7 and that devices in these machines will continue to be supported by means of Windows Update.

> **NOTE** For more information on the Windows 7 Logo program, refer to "Windows 7 Logo Program for Hardware Overview" at http://www.microsoft.com/whdc/winlogo/about_Win7.mspx.
>
> The Windows 7 Logo program is not comprehensive. You can check hardware compatibility by contacting the manufacturer of the device if you cannot find it on the Microsoft website.

An issue that can interrupt the installation process is the use of incompatible critical device drivers. If a compatible driver is not available, Setup stops until updated drivers are found. Operating system upgrades will not migrate incompatible Windows XP drivers. The only way to ensure a smooth installation is to make certain you have all the drivers available at the start of the installation process. Do not be concerned about unattended installations because there is a folder in which you can place any additional or updated drivers for hardware that is not included in the base Windows 7 files.

Before you deploy Windows 7 on any system, you should ensure that the hardware and Basic Input/Output System (BIOS) are compatible with the operating system. Older hardware may not have a compatible BIOS even though the devices within the PC itself are all listed in the Windows 7 Logo program. The original equipment manufacturer (OEM) should have an updated BIOS available that can be downloaded from the OEM's website.

If you have an Internet connection, you can use the Windows Update feature to connect to the Windows Update website during setup. Windows 7 automatically downloads and installs updated drivers during the setup process from the Windows Update website.

NOTE   More information on Windows Update is provided in Chapter 7, "Configuring Devices and Updates."

Software Compatibility

One of the more difficult parts of the development and testing phase of an operating system deployment project is to handle software compatibility, or rather, software *incompatibility*. The operating system that you deploy is important because it provides the basic functionality for the computer, but productivity usually depends on business applications that are installed, which makes applications more important to the organization. If an application is not compatible with the operating system, you have the following options:

- Upgrade the application to a compatible version

- Replace the application with a similar type of application that is compatible with Windows 7

- Retire the application

Before you are faced with these decisions, your first task in determining software compatibility is to identify all the applications that are used *and* that will be installed in your deployment project. You should develop a matrix of applications that is organized according to priority of business productivity and by number of users that use the application. For example, if you determine that 100% of all your users use APP A, but that it does not directly contribute to business productivity (such as an antivirus application), you would place it in the high use, low productivity quadrant. If you determine that 10% of your users use APP B, and it contributes highly to business productivity, you would place it in the low use, high productivity quadrant. If 5% of users use APP C and it has no impact on business productivity, you would place that in the low use, low productivity quadrant. The applications in that low use, low productivity quadrant are the ones that you should analyze for potentially retiring. If you find that 90% of all users use APP D and it is considered business-critical, you would put APP D in the high use, high productivity quadrant. All applications in this quadrant should receive priority during the project. Figure 2-1 attempts to place these applications into this perspective.

You might decide to include additional criteria to your matrix to better pinpoint the applications that will require more of your time during the project. For example, you could identify which applications are developed for Windows 7 and which are developed specifically for older Windows operating systems, as well as which

Figure 2-1   You should prioritize all applications used in your company according to their usage and productivity.

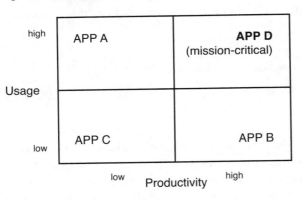

have been developed in-house. Applications that have been developed for Windows 2000, Windows XP, or Windows Vista might not run properly on Windows 7. Those applications developed for older versions of Windows, such as Windows 9x/NT, are more likely to be incompatible with Windows 7. Antivirus applications are typically incompatible if they were developed for older Windows versions. In nearly all cases, applications that worked properly on Windows Vista should work with Windows 7. If problems do occur, you should be able to run these applications in compatibility mode. Compatibility mode is discussed in Chapter 8, "Configuring Applications and Internet Explorer."

NOTE   If you have applications that work properly with Windows XP but are incompatible with Windows 7, you might want to consider installing Windows XP Mode. This installs a virtual copy of Windows XP on your Windows 7 desktop, on which you can install these applications. After you have installed the applications in this manner, they are available directly from the Windows 7 Start menu and can even be pinned to the Windows 7 taskbar.

After you have an inventory of your current software, you should then build a test lab and test the applications with Windows 7. With each application that has compatibility problems, you should decide whether the application is important enough to fix. If it is important, you should then determine the fixes you need to undertake to make it compatible. You can then package the fixes using the Microsoft Application Compatibility Toolkit. This toolkit assists software developers and corporate IT professionals in determining whether their applications are compatible with Windows 7; it also enables these individuals to determine how applications are affected by the update to Windows 7. Finally, you should test the deployment and perform a quality assurance check on the test PCs to see whether the applications install and run properly.

NOTE   For more information on the Microsoft Application Compatibility Toolkit, refer to "Microsoft Application Compatibility Toolkit (ACT) Version 5.6" at http://technet.microsoft.com/en-us/library/cc722055(WS.10).aspx.

Network Requirements

In a Windows 7 deployment, you must be able to identify which network protocols and network hardware are used on your network. Network protocols affect how you configure the computer, especially if there is some problem with addressing. When you install Windows 7, it will not connect to the network properly if it does not use a compatible protocol or does not have a correct address.

The network hardware you use affects the options you have available for deployment. For example, if you have no servers on your network and/or no peers with enough hard disk space to hold the installation files, you will be unable to install Windows 7 over the network—attended or unattended. If you have servers but they do not run Windows 2003 or Windows 2008, you will not be able to use Windows Deployment Services (WDS). If you do not have sufficient bandwidth, you will not be able to run the installation across the network either.

NOTE   WDS is an automated deployment function that provides a means of performing on-demand, image-based installation of operating systems across a network connection from a server to the computer on which the operating system is to be installed. WDS is discussed in Chapter 5, "Deploying Windows 7."

To assess your network, collect the following information:

- Network protocols

- Addressing format and address resolution

- Naming conventions and name resolution

- Network servers, including server operating system, names, IP addresses, domain membership, file and print services, directory services, and authentication

- Network sites and available bandwidth between the sites

- Routers, hubs, switches, printers, bridges, other peripherals, firewalls, and proxy servers

A thorough network assessment includes physical and logical diagrams of all sites, documenting each physical link, its speed, IP address, and available bandwidth, and the location of each piece of equipment. The logical portion should show server roles, Domain Name System (DNS) servers, Windows Internet Naming Service (WINS) servers, Dynamic Host Configuration Protocol (DHCP) servers, trust relationships, and your domain architecture.

When the Windows 7 computer is a network client, you need to determine how to connect that client to the network. Keep in mind that large networks tend to be hybrids, having a mixture of network media. If one client is intended to connect to a token ring network, whereas another is intended to connect to a wireless network, you need to plan for the appropriate network adapter, drivers, and installation method.

The standard network protocol for Windows 7 is *Transmission Control Protocol/ Internet Protocol (TCP/IP)*. If you intend to connect to a network that has NetWare servers that do not use TCP/IP, you also need to configure the NWLink protocol, which is Microsoft's equivalent to the Internetwork Packet eXchange/Sequenced Packet eXchange (IPX/SPX) protocol. On the other hand, you should not install any additional protocols if they are unnecessary because they will generate additional network traffic.

DHCP servers automatically provide IP addresses to each DHCP client on the network from a pool of addresses. When a network device releases its IP address, the address can be reused for another DHCP client. This averts IP address conflicts and helps distribute IP addresses efficiently, along with extended information such as DNS server data. Even if your network uses DHCP services, you should be aware of IP addresses used on each network link. This helps if you have to troubleshoot a problem with connectivity. If your network uses static IP addresses, you need to have an IP address for each network client you install.

The file-sharing capabilities in Windows 7 are simplified such that all users have identical rights to files based on how you originally share the resource. This means that either all users can read the files or all users can change the files. You can control which users are permitted to do by configuring the access control list (ACL) for the appropriate files and folders, provided you are using the New Technology File System (NTFS). Right-click the file or folder, choose **Properties**, and then select the **Security** tab of the dialog box that appears. Users and permissions are discussed further in Chapter11, "Configuring Access to Local and Shared Resources."

File System Considerations

Windows 7 supports three file systems:

- File Allocation Table 16 (FAT16)
- File Allocation Table 32 (FAT32)
- NT File System (NTFS)

FAT16 (often simply called FAT) is a 16-bit file system, whereas FAT32 is a 32-bit file system, both of which have grown out of the Windows 95/98/Me family. NTFS is the 32-bit file system that has come from Windows NT. For more information on Windows 7 file systems, search for "File systems" in Windows 7 Help and Support Center.

In a corporate environment or in any peer-to-peer network, you should consider NTFS to be the optimum file system to use. It has the basic functionality that FAT16 and FAT32 provide, plus it supports improved security, file encryption, file compression, and larger partitions and files. For scalability, NTFS can ensure your file system will support the larger hard disks and will not degrade in performance.

Fault-tolerant features are incorporated in NTFS. The file system automatically repairs disk errors without displaying error messages. When Windows 7 writes files to the NTFS partition, it saves a copy of the file in memory. It then compares the file on the disk to see whether it is the same as the copy in memory. If the two copies aren't equivalent, Windows 7 marks that section of the disk as bad and rewrites the file to another disk location.

NTFS also enables you to perform several operations related to file and folder security. The security within NTFS enables you to set permissions on folders and individual files. FAT16 and FAT32 do not. Furthermore, to use the Encrypting File System (EFS), you must have NTFS as your file system. EFS enables you to protect your files and folders from unauthorized access on the local hard drive through the use of public key security. In addition, you can set disk quotas. When multiple people use the same computer, you can control the amount of disk space each person can use on that computer. When you have configured disk quotas, a user looking at the available disk space will see only the amount of space available for that user's disk quota. If users attempt to exceed their allotment, they are given the message that the disk is full.

Native NTFS file compression enables users to select individual files or folders to compress. Because the file system takes care of the compression algorithm, any Windows application can read or write a compressed file without having to manually decompress the file beforehand. File compression is supported only when NTFS has a cluster size of 4 KB or smaller.

NOTE   Windows 7 does not allow you to format a partition greater than 32 GB with the FAT32 file system; you must use NTFS. If you have a larger partition that was formatted under a different operating system, you can still use it with Windows 7.

Product Activation

The highly controversial Windows Product Activation (WPA) was first introduced by Microsoft in Windows XP and Office XP to deter piracy. The premise is that each computer installed should have a unique identifier associated with the software with which it was installed. The WPA feature, however, does cause some planning issues for a large deployment. In a simple installation of a single Windows 7 system, WPA is just a matter of contacting Microsoft via the Internet (the easiest method) or phone and obtaining the unique identifier. In a large deployment, Microsoft has introduced an update to WPA called Volume Activation, which enables straightforward activation of multiple computers.

How WPA works is straightforward: It generates a unique identifier for your computer by combining your hardware ID with the product key. This ID is sent to Microsoft, which then checks to see whether that product key has been used for more than the number of systems that the End User License Agreement (EULA) allows, which is simply one system. If this check passes, your computer receives a confirmation code that activates Windows 7 and the issue of WPA goes away. If the check fails, your system is not activated and some features on your computer will not operate after the 30-day activation period is over; for example, the desktop background will be set to plain black.

If you have a computer that is not connected to the Internet and does not have a modem available for connection purposes, you are required to manually activate it. To do so, you run through the WPA process when prompted to activate the computer, and you will obtain an installation ID number. Then you call the Microsoft Activation Call Center to obtain a confirmation ID. Finally, you input the confirmation ID number in WPA.

When you use WPA, regardless of the method, the information in the ID submitted to Microsoft indicates the following:

- System volume serial number
- Network adapter Media Access Control (MAC) address
- CD-ROM or DVD-ROM ID
- Display adapter ID
- CPU ID and the CPU serial number
- Hard drive ID
- IDE controller ID

Performing a Clean Installation of Windows 7 as the Sole Operating System

In an attended installation, someone is required to interact with the computer while it executes the installation process. This is a process that IT professionals should be familiar with but one the average user will rarely, if ever, need to perform. With OEMs releasing new computers with the operating system preinstalled, and with organizations ensuring that only IT staff installs and configures computers, it's likely that the only non-IT professionals who will run fully attended installations are those who purchase Windows 7 off the shelf and install it on their existing home computers.

As an IT professional, you should run through at least one or two attended installations even if you are planning to deploy only unattended installations of Windows 7 throughout your organization. By going through the process, you can see each stage of installation and relate it to sections within the answer files and with the unattended process later. If you need to troubleshoot an unattended installation, you will be better able to identify the point at which the installation failed if you have already become familiar with the attended installation process.

Performing an Attended Installation

You can run an attended installation process for either an upgrade or a clean installation of Windows 7. Upgrading to Windows 7 is covered in Chapter 3, "Upgrading to Windows 7," so we will be walking through a *clean* installation process in this section.

Before you begin, check to make certain that you have gathered all the information you need and are prepared to install. You should have the following:

- A computer that meets the minimum hardware requirements (refer to Table 2-2).

- Windows 7 drivers from the manufacturer for any hardware that does not appear in the Windows 7 Logo Program. It's imperative that you have the hard disk drivers, especially if they are RAID or SCSI devices.

- Windows 7 DVD or installation files available across a network.

- BIOS that meets the minimum requirements for Windows 7 compatibility.

CAUTION   Ensure that you have the latest BIOS available before beginning Windows 7 installation. Windows 7 requires Advanced Configuration and Power Interface (ACPI) capability in the BIOS; you cannot use older power management systems such as Advanced Power Management (APM).

- Product code, which should be listed on the DVD package or provided to you from the network administrator.

- If across a network, a boot disk that can access network shares and appropriate network adapters.

- Internet connection for Automatic Updates and access to updated drivers and WPA.

- A backup of all your existing data and the drivers for the backup device so that you can restore the data.

When you have all the preceding items in hand, you're ready to install Windows 7. Your first step in the installation is to boot up the computer into the setup process. This process involves running Setup.exe, which is the application that installs Windows 7 on a new computer or updates an older Windows computer to Windows 7. Use the following procedure to install Windows 7 using a bootable DVD-ROM rather than a network installation:

Step 1.   Insert the Windows 7 installation DVD and boot the computer. If you receive a message that the DVD has been auto-detected and a prompt to Press any key to boot from CD or DVD, press the spacebar or any other key within five seconds or the computer will attempt to boot from the hard disk.

Step 2.   A message stating that Windows is loading files appears. After a minute or so, the Install Windows dialog box shown in Figure 2-2 appears. If you need to change the language, time and currency format, or keyboard or input method settings, do so. Otherwise, click **Next** to proceed.

Figure 2-2   The Install Windows dialog box offers options for language, time and currency, and keyboard or input method.

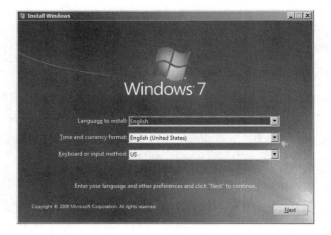

Step 3.   You are informed that Setup is starting, and then another Install
Windows dialog box (see Figure 2-3) asks you to read the license terms.
You must select the I accept the license terms check box to accept the
licensing agreement as indicated at the bottom of the screen. Then click
Next.

Figure 2-3   You must accept the license terms to install Windows 7.

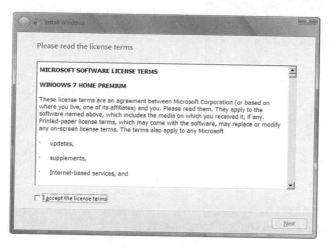

Step 4.   The next screen offers you a choice of upgrade or clean installation.
The Upgrade option will be disabled (grayed out) unless you are running the installation on a computer running a compatible copy of
Windows Vista with sufficient free disk space to accommodate the upgrade. Select the **Custom (advanced)** option to continue.

Step 5.   The next screen shows the available partitions and unpartitioned disk
space where you can install Windows 7. Make certain you select a partition that has enough available disk space, preferably 40 GB but at least
16 GB for an x86 installation or 20 GB for an x64 installation. If unpartitioned space is available, you can select the unpartitioned space and
create a new partition for the operating system at this point. Click **Next**.

Step 6.   The next window tracks the progress of installing Windows 7 and informs you that your computer will restart several times, as shown in
Figure 2-4. Take a coffee break.

Step 7.   After the final reboot, Setup displays the window shown in Figure 2-5.
Type a username in the text box provided. Also accept the computer
name provided or type one of your choosing. Then click **Next**.

Step 8.   Setup asks you to type and confirm a password and to specify a password hint. The password you provide is for a local user account on the

computer running Windows 7. If you want, you can leave the password blank. If you do type a password, you must type a password hint in the space provided. If you forget your password later, Windows will display this password hint.

Figure 2-4   Tracking the progress of Windows 7 installation.

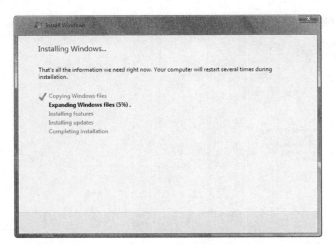

Figure 2-5   Setup asks you to provide a username and computer name.

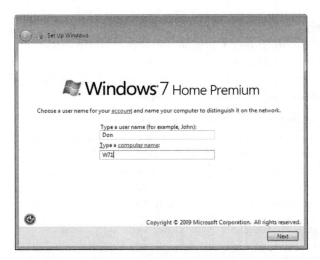

Step 9.   Setup displays the dialog box shown in Figure 2-6, asking you to type your Windows product key (found on the case for your installation DVD). Type the product key and then click **Next**.

TIP   In Windows 7, unlike versions of Windows prior to Vista, you can leave the product key blank. If you do so, you will receive a warning message and will be prompted to select the edition of Windows 7 you want to install. You will have 30 days to activate Windows, at which time you must supply a valid product key. You can use this feature to preview any edition of Windows 7 and select the most appropriate edition for your requirements.

Figure 2-6 Type your product key when prompted by this dialog box.

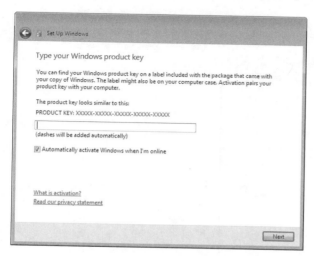

Step 10. On the next screen (see Figure 2-7), select the **Use recommended settings** option to provide the highest security level.

Figure 2-7 The Help protect Windows automatically screen enables you to choose the appropriate security level. You should always select the Use recommended settings option.

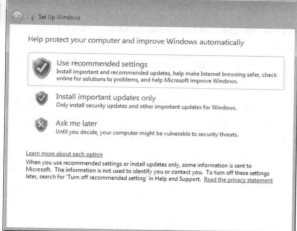

Step 11.   On the next screen, set the current date, time, and time zone. If this computer connects to the Internet, you can simply select the correct time zone and later make certain that Windows 7 automatically synchronizes with an Internet time provider.

Step 12.   On the next screen (see Figure 2-8), select the location that best describes your computer's current location.

Figure 2-8   Windows 7 provides three options that govern how network settings are applied.

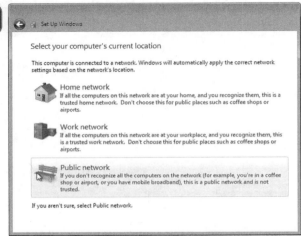

Step 13.   Windows applies networking settings according to the location you selected and then displays a window informing you that settings are being finalized. After a minute or two, Windows 7 displays a Welcome screen and a message that it is preparing your desktop.

Step 14.   After another minute or two, the Windows 7 desktop appears. The computer attempts to access the Internet to download and install updates from the Microsoft website, and a message at the bottom of the desktop informs you of the update progress. You are now ready to work with Windows 7.

You have just completed a full, manual installation of Windows 7 from scratch. In a typical installation, you would next join a workgroup or domain, install additional applications, restore data from backup, and customize the desktop to meet your needs.

Dual-Booting Windows 7

As in previous versions of Windows, you can install Windows 7 alongside a different version of Windows in a dual-boot configuration. *Dual-boot* refers to installing two operating systems (for example, Windows XP and Windows 7) side-by-side on the same computer so that you can choose between booting the computer to one operating system or the other. By specifying a partition that does not have an operating system installed in step 5 of the procedure outlined in the previous section, you can select a different partition on which to install Windows 7. This retains all applications and settings you have configured in the previous version of Windows and creates a clean installation of Windows 7 on the partition you have specified. You can even create multi-boot systems with more than two different operating systems, including different editions of Windows 7, on the same computer. Dual-booting or multi-booting has the following advantages:

- You can test various editions of Windows 7 without destroying your current operating system.

- If you are running applications that are not compatible with Windows 7, you can boot into an older operating system to run them.

- Developers can test their work on different Windows versions without needing more than one computer.

Boot Management Programs Used by Windows 7

Windows 7 includes several new boot management programs, which were first introduced in Windows Vista and Windows Server 2008, and replace the older programs used with Windows NT/2000/XP/Server 2003. These include the following:

- **Bootcfg.exe**: Enables you to edit, modify, or delete boot entry settings in the boot.ini file used in Windows XP and older Windows operating systems.

- **Bcdedit.exe**: An editing application that enables you to edit boot configuration data on Windows Vista/7. This is the only program that offers boot management editing capabilities for Windows 7.

- **Winload.exe**: The operating system loader, included with each instance of Windows Vista, Windows 7, or Windows Server 2008 installed on any one computer. Winload.exe loads the operating system, its kernel, hardware abstraction layer (HAL), and drivers on startup.

- **Winresume.exe**: Included with each instance of Windows Vista, Windows 7, or Windows Server 2008 installed on any one computer, this program resumes the operating system from hibernation.

Setting Up a Dual-Boot System

The procedure for setting up a dual-boot operating system can vary, but you should generally proceed along the lines of the following:

Step 1.   If you haven't already installed the oldest operating system, install and configure it first. For example, you would install Windows 2000, then Windows XP, and then Windows 7 in that order if you wanted a triple-boot configuration with these three operating systems.

Step 2.   While running the older operating system, insert the Windows 7 DVD-ROM.

Step 3.   When you receive the option with a choice of upgrade or clean installation (step 4 of the previous procedure), select the **Custom (advanced)** option to continue.

Step 4.   The next screen displays the list of available partitions, which will include the partition or partitions on which you have installed the older operating system(s). Select a different partition or create a new partition from unpartitioned space, and then click **Next**.

Step 5.   Follow the remaining steps in the previous procedure to complete the installation of Windows 7.

CAUTION   Dual- or multi-boot systems also require you to think through the file system choice. If you need to dual-boot Windows 7 with operating systems earlier than Windows 2000, remember that these older operating systems support only certain file systems. Windows 98/Me support FAT and FAT32 file systems, and Windows NT 4.0 supports FAT and NTFS file systems. If you need Windows 7 plus one of these operating systems to read the same data, ensure that your data is located on a partition formatted with one of these file systems. Also ensure that Windows NT 4.0 has at least Service Pack 5 (SP5) installed. However, remember that the partition on which you install Windows 7 must be formatted with the NTFS file system.

Other Windows 7 Installation Methods

The installation we have already described is the straightforward installation of Windows 7 from the DVD media you would receive if you went to a computer store to purchase a new or upgrade copy of Windows 7. You can also use other sources for the Windows 7 installation files, including USB portable drive, network shares, and Windows Deployment Service (WDS).

USB

You can copy the installation files from a Windows 7 DVD-ROM to the root of a partition on a USB portable hard drive and use this to install Windows 7 on another computer. When you insert the DVD, select the **Open folder to view files** option, select all the files, and copy them to the root of a partition on the portable hard drive.

> **NOTE**   You can also download a Windows 7 ISO image from http://store.microsoft.com/Help/ISO-Tool and copy this image to a USB flash drive. Follow the instructions provided on that web page to save the file to your USB drive or burn it to a DVD.

At the computer on which you want to install Windows 7, insert the USB hard drive and then turn the computer on. Access the BIOS setup screen and select the **Boot** option. Specify the USB drive as the primary boot device, and then save your changes. Reboot the computer; it should boot from the USB drive and you should receive the `Windows is loading files` message. Then proceed to install Windows 7 as already described.

CD

Similar to Windows Vista, the Windows 7 setup files are too large to be contained on a CD-ROM disc. If you have a computer with a CD drive but not a DVD drive, or if the DVD drive is not bootable, you might be able to create a startup CD that will enable you to boot your computer and connect to Windows 7 installation files located on a USB portable hard drive or network share. This option might also be useful if the BIOS in your computer does not support booting from a USB portable hard drive or network share.

Network Share

If the Windows 7 installation files are available from a shared folder on a server or another network device, you can use this location to install Windows 7. Ensure that the computer is connected to the network on which the shared folder can be accessed and turn it on. Access the BIOS setup screen and select the **Boot** option. Select the option to boot from a network share and then select the correct share.

Save the changes and reboot the computer; similar to the option for booting from USB, you should receive the `Windows is loading files` message. Then proceed to install Windows 7 as already described.

WDS

First introduced with Windows Vista, WDS provides a means of performing on-demand, image-based installation of operating systems across a network connection from a server running WDS to the computer on which the operating system is to be installed. You can install WDS on a server running Windows Server 2003, Server 2008, or Server 2008 R2 and use it to install Windows 7 or Windows Server 2008/2008 R2 on destination computers.

Understanding WDS

WDS provides several advantages to the administrator who needs to install Windows 7/Vista/2008/2008 R2 on a large number of computers, including the following:

- WDS enables you to install Windows 7 on computers at a remote location across a wide area network (WAN).

- WDS provides native support for Windows Preinstallation Environment (PE) and the Windows Image Format (WIM) file format. We discuss the WIM file format in Chapter 5, "Deploying Windows 7."

- WDS reduces the complexity associated with large deployments, thereby reducing total cost of ownership (TCO).

- WDS simplifies the duties associated with management of an installation server.

- WDS simplifies the procedures required to recover an installation from system failures that occur during installation.

You can create installation images of Windows 7, Windows Vista, Windows Server 2008, or Windows Server 2008 R2 that include complete computer configurations, including such items as applications and desktop settings, and use WDS to push these images out to client computers on the network. The capabilities of WDS include the following:

- Enable users to install an operating system on demand. On starting a client computer that is equipped with the Preboot eXecution Environment (PXE), the computer connects to a WDS server, which then installs the operating system across the network without the need for a DVD.

- Provide images of the operating system that are complete with specific settings and applications such as those required by a corporate workstation policy. You can designate the group of users provided with a certain image or series of images.

- Create images that enable the automated installation of Windows 7, Windows Vista, Windows Server 2008, or Windows Server 2008 R2.

NOTE   We discuss the use of WDS for deployment of multiple Windows 7 installations in detail in Chapter 5.

Requirements to Use WDS

You can install WDS on a server running Windows Server 2003 or Windows Server 2008 from the Windows Automated Installation Kit (AIK) by using the `Windows_deployment_services_update.exe` program included in the AIK. In addition, the following server components must be available on the WDS server or on another server available to the WDS server:

- **Dynamic Host Configuration Protocol (DHCP):** Provides TCP/IP configuration parameters that enable the client computer to create its own network connection.

- **Domain Name System (DNS):** Provides name resolution services so that the client computer can locate the WDS server by name.

- **Active Directory Domain Services (AD DS):** WDS operates only in an AD DS–enabled domain environment. You cannot use WDS in a homegroup or workgroup environment.

In addition, you must have the Windows AIK media available either on the WDS server or at an accessible location, as well as a separate partition on the WDS server that is formatted with the NTFS file system. You must be using a domain account with membership in the local Administrators group on the WDS server.

Client computers must meet the proper design specification to be installed with WDS. This includes the capability for remote booting, which is usually accomplished by adding a network interface card (NIC) that is equipped with a PXE ROM–enabled chip, along with support in the BIOS for booting the computer from this NIC. In addition, the client computer can have only a single disk partition. (Any additional partitions are destroyed when the operating system is installed, and the entire disk is formatted as a single NTFS partition.)

To install Windows 7 on the remote computer, simply connect it to the network and turn it on. When prompted, press **F12** to use PXE for booting from the network share and accessing the DHCP server. If more than one boot image is available, you will need to select the appropriate image. Then follow the instructions provided by the WDS user interface to complete the Windows 7 installation.

NOTE Details of installing and configuring WDS on the server are beyond the scope of the 70-680 exam and this book. For more information on this topic, consult "Windows Deployment Services Getting Started Guide" at http://technet.microsoft.com/en-us/library/cc771670(WS.10).aspx.

Troubleshooting Windows 7 Installation Issues

At some point, before a computer can be used, an operating system must be installed. Problems often occur during an operating system installation, which requires troubleshooting. Windows 7 is no exception. Whatever method you have used for installation—one of the installation methods described in this chapter or a deployment that is described in Chapter 5—problems can occur. Network administrators and engineers need to know how to handle unexpected errors.

In this section you review the common problems that can occur during installations. You also discover how to troubleshoot problems with the various types of installations and the troubleshooting methods to follow when faced with a failed installation of Windows 7.

Troubleshooting Process

When you troubleshoot any problem, whether it is during installation or otherwise, there is a simple cyclical methodology that can help you achieve a solution. This is shown in Figure 2-9. As you can see, it consists of five phases:

Figure 2-9 The troubleshooting methodology is circular until a solution is found.

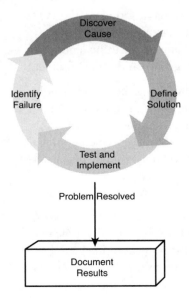

Step 1.   Identify the point of failure.

Step 2.   Discover the cause of the failure.

Step 3.   Define a solution.

Step 4.   Test and implement the solution.

Step 5.   Document the results.

This is not a straightforward linear process because all troubleshooting is based on theory. Your job is to come up with a theory about why the computer is failing and then test your theory. If your test proves the theory to be wrong, you need to return to the original phase—identifying the point of failure.

Identifying the Point of Failure

The first phase of troubleshooting is determining what the problem is. Given that some symptoms can be caused by a variety of different failures, you need to remain open to any possibility.

Let's say, for example, that Windows 7 Setup does not boot from the DVD-ROM. The point of failure is limited to

- DVD-ROM drive

- DVD-ROM device drivers

- BIOS

- Installation media

- Lack of power (computer is not plugged in)

Given that any one of these items could be the failure, you should look closely at the clues that your computer has given you. If, for example, you can see that the BIOS has started, the light on your keyboard is on, and the monitor is displaying data, you can discard the last item as a point of failure. You should select one of the most likely points of failure and then move on to the next phase.

Discovering the Cause of the Failure

The difference between the point of failure and the cause of failure is the same as the *what* and *why*. A point of failure can be the DVD-ROM. The *cause* of the failure could be that the DVD-ROM drive is not plugged into the power cable, the DVD-ROM drive is not a bootable drive, or the DVD-ROM drive electronics failed.

During this second phase, you should select the most probable cause of failure. Ask yourself, "If the problem is the *what*, *why* did it fail?" and consider your answer to be the next part of your theory that you need to test.

Defining a Solution

The third troubleshooting phase is to define a solution. This is the answer to the question "*How* do you fix it?"

For example, if you have decided that the DVD-ROM drive is the problem and that it failed because it is not a bootable drive, your solution might be to install the operating system over the network from another computer's shared DVD-ROM drive.

Testing and Implementing the Solution

Testing and implementation are often the same phase when it comes to troubleshooting because your test is usually to carry out the solution you just defined. If the solution worked, it was implemented. Otherwise, you simply tested a possible solution with negative results.

If your test produces a negative result, you should return to the first phase—identifying the point of failure. For example, if you test the solution by trying to install Windows 7 from another computer's shared DVD-ROM drive and you are unable to gain access to the media, you can theorize that the installation media is the point of failure. From there, you can theorize that the DVD is damaged. Your solution might be to replace the DVD. You can then test again and move through the cycle as needed until you succeed.

Documenting the Results

Always document your results when you are troubleshooting. Not only is documentation generally considered a good practice, but it is a key to making sure you don't make the same mistakes twice.

Troubleshooting an Attended Installation

When you are sitting in front of a computer, watching it go through the various installation phases, it's easier to troubleshoot a problem as it occurs than to resolve a failed installation after the event. The Windows 7 Setup process is so streamlined that you usually do not encounter problems during installation. However, when a problem does occur, it's frequently related to lack of preparation. This basic problem manifests itself in the following symptoms:

- The BIOS is not compatible with Windows 7.

- The hardware is not compatible with Windows 7.

- There is not enough space on the hard drive to install the operating system.

- The drivers for the hard disk, network adapter, or other devices are incorrect or incompatible.

- The computer cannot connect to the network because the name or IP address conflicts with another computer on the network.

Typically, fixing a problem or running the installation again takes much longer than gathering the tools and information you need before you start the installation. As it happens, an ounce of preparation is equal to a pound of troubleshooting.

This section reviews specific problems that you might encounter during installation. These consist of media errors, insufficient hard disk space, unrecognized DVD-ROM drive, a network that can't be accessed, and problems that require an advanced startup.

Media Problems

Windows 7 can be installed directly from a bootable DVD-ROM drive. If the disk does not boot, check to see whether the drive can be configured as a boot drive and whether this is set in the computer's BIOS. If you are installing from a bootable DVD-ROM and your computer has difficulty reading from the disc, the quickest way to resolve the problem may be to simply use a different Windows 7 Setup DVD-ROM. Even though a DVD-ROM has worked in the past for other installations, it might have become scratched or otherwise damaged. If you inspect the data side of the disc and discover fingerprints, a simple cleaning might fix the problem. To determine whether the problem is with the DVD-ROM or with the DVD-ROM drive, test the disc on another computer. If you have the same or similar errors reading the disc, you should contact Microsoft for a replacement.

If you boot from a DVD-ROM and the Setup process begins but is unable to copy files to the computer, you might have an unsupported DVD-ROM drive. In addition, make sure you have a DVD-ROM drive and not a CD-ROM drive; the latter cannot read the Windows 7 DVD-ROM disc. Try to install Windows 7 from another location—either from another DVD-ROM drive or across the network. Another option is to copy the Setup files to a local hard drive before beginning Setup.

For network installations, you can boot to the network from either the computer's existing operating system or a Setup floppy boot disk. If you have problems with the boot disk, test it on an alternative computer to see whether the disk needs to be re-created.

Insufficient Hard Drive Space

The minimum hardware requirements for installing Windows 7 state that you should have 16 GB of available drive space for a 32-bit installation or 20 GB for a 64-bit installation. If your hard drive is smaller than these amounts, you should add a new hard drive or replace the drive.

CAUTION   These are minimum amounts required for installing Windows 7. In reality, you will want as much hard drive space as you can obtain; when you install all the applications you will be using and add data, the gigabytes will mount up rapidly. This is especially true if you will be storing a large number of photos or videos. Even if you store your data on a separate partition or drive, updates installed via Windows Update take up additional space and add their own uninstallation files. These can reduce the amount of available space on your Windows partition to a small amount in no time flat.

Unrecognizable DVD-ROM Drive

If the Setup program doesn't recognize the DVD-ROM drive, check whether the DVD-ROM drive is compatible with Windows 7. If it is, you might be able to load updated drivers from the manufacturer. A much easier solution is to install across a network or to copy the files to a local drive before running Setup.

Unavailable Network

Network connectivity can be a problem caused by simple errors, such as the following:

- The password is incorrectly typed. Check to make sure that the Caps Lock key isn't on.
- The wrong domain name is used. Check to make sure that the domain name has been entered correctly.
- The network cable is not connected.
- The IP address is incorrect.
- A name conflict exists, the name is too long, or the name contains illegal characters.
- The computer was unable to obtain an IP address from the DHCP server.
- The network adapter drivers are incorrect or malfunctioning.
- The DNS server or domain controller is not online.
- There is no computer account created in the domain.
- The IP address of the default gateway is incorrect.

For each of these problems, there is generally an easy solution. To determine which of the errors specifically applies to you or if there is another error preventing network connectivity, you can use the IP utilities listed in Table 2-3.

Table 2-3   IP Utilities

Utility	Command	Usage
Packet InterNet Groper (Ping)	ping	Uses an echo command to establish whether packets can be routed at the Network layer on a network.

Table 2-3 IP Utilities

Utility	Command	Usage
File Transfer Protocol	ftp	Uploads/downloads files on a network. The ftp command helps you determine whether Application layer functions can work on the network.
Telnet	telnet	Establishes a character-based session with a Telnet server across a network. The telnet command helps you determine whether Session layer functions can work on a network.
Line printer daemon	lpr	Executes a print job on a network printer. Helps you print setup logs and other files that list errors and problems that might have occurred.
Ipconfig	ipconfig	Shows the IP configuration of network adapters installed in a computer. From the results of this command, you can determine whether you have incorrectly addressed the adapter or the default gateway or whether the adapter was unable to obtain an address from the DHCP server.
Name Server Lookup	nslookup	Checks DNS entries.
Netstat	netstat	Displays Transmission Control Protocol/Internet Protocol (TCP/IP) connections and protocol statistics. To find all the applicable switches, type **netstat /?** at the command prompt, as shown in Figure 2-10.
Nbtstat	nbtstat	Similar to netstat, except that it resolves NetBIOS names to IP addresses. To find all applicable command switches, type **nbtstat /?** at a command prompt.
Trace Route	tracert	Shows all the routing hops that a packet takes to reach a destination on a network.

If everything physically checks out with your computer and you are able to install and boot the computer but cannot connect to the network, you should determine whether the adapter is working and then review your network adapter configuration settings. Use the following procedure to determine whether the adapter is functioning.

Step 1. Click **Start**, right-click **Computer**, and select **Properties**.

Step 2. In the System applet shown in Figure 2-11, see the Computer name, domain, and workgroup settings section. Make certain that the name is unique for the network and that the workgroup or domain name is spelled correctly.

Figure 2-10 The **netstat** command with switches is used for troubleshooting network connectivity.

Figure 2-11 The System applet enables you to verify computer name, domain, and workgroup settings.

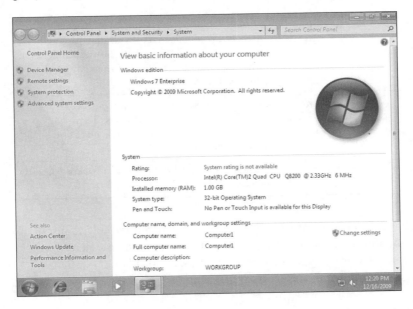

Step 3. On the left side of the applet, under Control Panel Home, click **Device Manager**.

Step 4. If you receive a User Account Control (UAC) prompt, click **Yes**.

Step 5. Expand the Network adapters section, as shown in Figure 2-12.

Figure 2-12   Device Manager displays the network adapter.

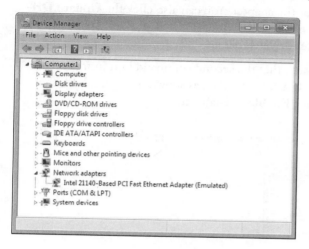

Step 6.   Right-click the network adapter and select **Properties**. The Properties dialog box displays (see Figure 2-13).

Figure 2-13   The network adapter's Properties dialog box provides device information.

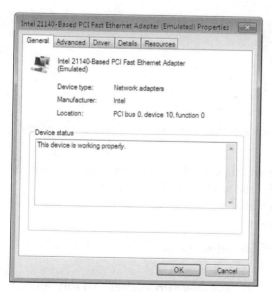

Step 7.   Ensure that the General tab states that This device is working properly.

Step 8.   Click the **Advanced** tab to check the adapter's configuration.

Step 9.   Click the **Driver** tab to determine whether you are using the current/latest driver for the adapter. You can also click the **Update Driver** button to install a newer driver or click the **Roll Back Driver** button to revert to an older driver version.

Step 10.   On the Driver tab, ensure that the second command button from the bottom reads Disable. If it reads Enable, as shown in Figure 2-14, the adapter is disabled; click **Enable** to enable it.

Figure 2-14   The Driver tab informs you whether the adapter is disabled.

Step 11.   Click the **Resources** tab to see whether there are any hardware conflicts to resolve.

Step 12.   Click the **Power Management** tab, if available, to see whether Power Management has been configured to turn the device off. This tab is present only for device drivers that support power management standards, such as network adapters.

Step 13.   Click OK to close the Properties dialog box and then click the red X to close Device Manager.

Step 14.   Click **Start**, right-click **Network**, and select **Properties** to display the Network and Sharing Center. If the network adapter is not functioning, the diagram at the top of this page displays a disconnected symbol in the form of a red X, as shown in Figure 2-15.

Figure 2-15   If the network adapter is not functioning, you see a red X at the top of the network diagram.

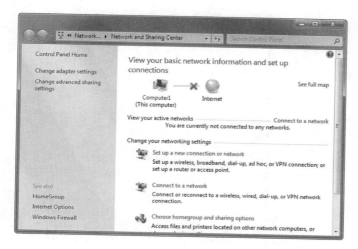

Step 15.   On the left side of the Network and Sharing Center, click **Change adapter settings**. This brings up the Network Connections dialog box showing your local area connection.

Step 16.   Right-click the connection and select **Properties**. If you receive a UAC prompt, click **Yes**. You should see an adapter in the Connect Using text box. (If you don't, that means it's disabled or not working.) You should also see the following protocols listed in the This Connection Uses the Following Items list:

- Client for Microsoft Networks or alternative client if connecting to a different type of network

- Quality of Service (QoS) Packet Scheduler

- File and Printer Sharing for Microsoft Networks

- Internet Protocol Version 4 (TCP/IP)

- Internet Protocol Version 6 (TCP/IP)

- Other network protocols

Step 17.   If you have determined that there is a TCP/IP problem from the results of running an `ipconfig` command, select the **Internet Protocol Version 4 (TCP/IP)** option and then click the **Properties** button. The Internet Protocol Version 4 (TCP/IPv4) Properties dialog box opens, as shown in Figure 2-16. Click **Use the following IP address** to configure the IP address, subnet mask, and default gateway.

Figure 2-16   The Internet Protocol (TCP/IP) Properties dialog box shows how the network adapter's IP address is configured.

Advanced Startup

Sometimes you can install the Windows 7 operating system but cannot get the computer to boot normally. You can use options in the Advanced Boot Options Menu by pressing **F8** during the initial boot sequence. Use the Safe Mode option to load the minimum necessary operating system drivers and then continue to troubleshoot the problem by making configuration changes as appropriate. You can also select **Safe Mode with Networking** to access network or Internet resources.

Another useful option is Enable Boot Logging. Boot logging stores information about drivers that initialize upon startup in the %system root% directory in a file named Ntbtlog.txt. You can identify incorrect, missing, or possibly corrupted drivers and replace them as necessary.

NOTE   Chapter 18, "Configuring System and File Recovery," discusses advanced startup and recovery options in more detail.

Refer to Compatibility

The previous sections referred several times to checking the compatibility of your hardware, BIOS, and drivers. This is probably the main issue that affects a new installation of Windows 7. Compatibility with Windows 7 means that Microsoft supports the driver or the device. If you have hardware that is not listed in the Windows 7 Logo Program for Hardware, even if Windows 7 installs and appears to work correctly, Microsoft will not provide any technical support in the event of an error.

TIP Check your hardware first. When you have an installation failure, check hardware compatibility first.

Application compatibility is another significant concern. Because many unattended installations of Windows 7 automatically incorporate applications, you can encounter *application compatibility* errors that are caused by the applications rather than the operating system. To reduce application errors significantly, you should prepare in advance as follows:

- Inventory the applications on the network.

- Investigate the compatibility of the applications with Microsoft and the manufacturers.

- Test the applications.

- Resolve application compatibility issues and incorporate the resolutions in the installation process.

- Test hotfixes, service packs, and application updates.

- Incorporate hotfixes, service packs, and application updates into the installation process.

- Create standard software images so that all users have identical application installations.

Strip the PC

Back when we first became involved with computers, having a hard drive larger than 10 MB was a big deal. The hardware for a standard PC was limited to a VGA monitor, simple CPU, hard drive, 5-1/4″ floppy disk drive, keyboard, and mouse. Installing the operating system software on one of those babies was a matter of knowing each device's resources and manually setting pins on adapters that you added before you started feeding installation floppy disks into the computer for a two-hour stretch, while manually selecting or inputting the device drivers for your computer into the Setup program. If you encountered an error, you checked your resources and pin settings and then started over again because there was no such thing as advanced startup or repair options.

How times have changed! With today's hardware automatically detected by Plug and Play, there is much less hardware tweaking needed. You'd think that would make installation easier, but, unfortunately, that's not always the case.

continues

There are currently hundreds of different types of devices that can be attached to various brands of computers. Thousands of different configurations and millions of lines of operating system code are supposed to recognize every possible hardware combination and make it all work together seamlessly with whichever version of device driver it happens to have available to it.

The fact is that errors abound, and the methods of resolving or working around them to have a functioning PC are convoluted at best. So, the best way to resolve a problem with the operating system installation is to strip the PC. Remove every unnecessary hardware component, including detaching the printer, and take out any extra network adapters. This can greatly help you successfully install Windows 7 on a PC. After you have Windows 7 installed and running, you can then add each component back to the computer, one at a time, rebooting and testing the computer between each device installation. If the first hardware component checks out okay, add a second, retest, and then go on to the third. Continue this for all devices. At some point, you will either discover the errant component or be able to attribute the error to a conflict that no longer exists.

Troubleshooting Failed Installations

A network administrator's best friend in a crisis is an error log file. This is also true for Windows 7 installation failures. While installing, Windows 7 Setup generates log files that point you in the right direction when you need to troubleshoot.

The Action log (`Setupact.log`) reports which actions Setup performed in chronological order. This log indicates which files were copied and which were deleted. It records whether any external programs are run and shows where errors have occurred.

Setup creates an Error log (`Setuperr.log`) to record only the errors. Given that the Action log is extremely large, this log makes it easier to review errors and their severity levels. Although you might see some errors in the Action log, you probably won't see them in the Error log unless they are severe. For example, the Action log reports an error if Setup cannot delete a file because the file was already moved or deleted, but that error does not appear in the Error log. Table 2-4 describes some of the more important logs created during installation.

Table 2-4   Windows 7 Setup Logs

Log File Name	Description
`%systemroot%\panther\miglog.xml`	Records information about the user directory structure, including security identifiers (SIDs).
`%systemroot%\panther\setupact.log`	Records modifications performed on the system during Setup.

Table 2-4 Windows 7 Setup Logs

Log File Name	Description
`%systemroot%\inf\setupapi.dev.log`	Records data about Plug and Play devices and drivers. Check this file for device driver installation information.
`%systemroot%\inf\setupapi.app.log`	Records data about application installation.
`%systemroot%\setuperr.log`	Records errors generated by hardware or driver issues during Windows installation.
`%systemroot%\debug\netsetup.log`	Reports the results of a computer attempting to join a workgroup or domain. Check this file if you have trouble joining a domain.
`%systemroot%\security\logs\scesetup.log`	Logs the security settings for the computer.

NOTE Additional logs are created at different steps of the setup phase. For additional information, refer to "Windows 7, Windows Server 2008 R2, and Windows Vista setup log file locations" at http://support.microsoft.com/kb/927521.

Stop Errors or Blue Screen of Death

If you receive a *Stop error* that appears on the Microsoft blue screen (commonly known as the blue screen of death), you have encountered a serious error with the installation. Stop errors have some instructions to follow on the screen. Not only should you follow the instructions, but also you should check the compatibility of the hardware before attempting to install again. Use the following steps to resolve a Stop error:

Step 1. Shut down the computer.

Step 2. Remove all new hardware devices.

Step 3. Start up the computer and remove the associated drivers. Shut down.

Step 4. Install one of the removed hardware devices. Boot the computer and install the appropriate driver. Reboot. If no BSOD occurs, continue adding devices, one at a time.

Step 5. Open **Device Manager** and look for devices with a yellow exclamation point or red X. Run hardware diagnostic software.

Step 6. Check for hardware compatibility and BIOS compatibility. Check to see whether you have the latest available version of the BIOS.

Step 7. Check the System log in Event Viewer for error messages. These might lead to a driver that is causing the Stop error.

Step 8.   Visit http://search.microsoft.com and perform a search on the Microsoft Knowledge Base for the Stop error number (for example, Stop: 0x0000000A). Follow the instructions given in the Knowledge Base article(s) for diagnosing and repairing the error.

Step 9.   Disable BIOS options such as caching or shadowing memory.

Step 10.   If the Stop error specifies a particular driver, disable the driver and then download and update the driver to the latest version available from the manufacturer.

Step 11.   Video drivers are commonly the cause of a BSOD. Therefore, switch to the Windows 7 low-resolution video (640×480) driver (available from the advanced startup options menu) and then contact the manufacturer for updated video drivers.

Step 12.   If using a Small Computer System Interface (SCSI) adapter and device, ensure that the SCSI chain is properly terminated and that there are no conflicts with the SCSI IDs.

> **TIP**   The code and text associated with a Stop error are a great help in troubleshooting. For example, an error could be STOP 0X00000D1 (DRIVER IRQL NOT LESS OR EQUAL). You can search for this code number and text on Microsoft's website for an explanation of the cause and possible ways to fix the problem.

Stopped Installation

Windows 7 might stop in the middle of an installation. This can happen because of a hardware conflict, incompatibility, or unsuitable configuration. To resolve the conflict, you should follow the usual procedure of removing all unnecessary devices from the computer and attempting installation again. After Windows 7 is installed, you can add one device at a time back to the computer, load the latest manufacturer's drivers, and boot to see whether the computer functions properly. It is important that you add only one device at a time so that you can discover which device (or devices) might have been the cause of the problem.

Exam Preparation Tasks

Review All the Key Topics

Review the most important topics in the chapter, noted with the key topics icon in the outer margin of the page. Table 2-5 lists a reference of these key topics and the page numbers on which each is found.

Table 2-5   Key Topics for Chapter 2

Key Topic Element	Description	Page Number
Table 2-2	Hardware requirements for Windows 7	51
List	Items you should have on hand before starting a Windows 7 installation	59
List	Procedure for installing Windows 7 from an installation DVD	
Figure 2-7	Use recommended settings to ensure your computer is adequately protected	63
Figure 2-8	Network options determine how security settings are applied	64
List	Reasons you might want to set up a dual-boot system	65
List	Requirements for using WDS for installing Windows 7	69
List	Major reasons Windows 7 might fail to install properly	72
Table 2-4	Important Windows 7 setup log files	82

Complete the Tables and Lists from Memory

Print a copy of Appendix C, "Memory Tables" (found on the CD), or at least the section for this chapter, and complete the tables and lists from memory. Appendix D, "Memory Tables Answer Key," also on the CD, includes completed tables and lists to check your work.

Definitions of Key Terms

Define the following key terms from this chapter, and check your answers in the glossary.

application compatibility, Windows 7 Logo Program, file systems, File Allocation Table (FAT), NT File System (NTFS), Setup.exe, Windows Deployment Services (WDS), Basic Input/Output System (BIOS), stop error, Transmission Control Protocol/Internet Protocol (TCP/IP)

This chapter covers the following subjects:

■ **Upgrading to Windows 7 from a Previous Version of Windows:** This section shows you how you can upgrade from Windows Vista to Windows 7.

■ **Migrating from Windows XP:** A direct upgrade from Windows XP to Windows 7 is not possible; however, Microsoft has specified ways in which you can get from Windows XP to Windows 7. This section shows you what you must do to accomplish this task.

■ **Upgrading from One Edition of Windows 7 to Another:** Certain upgrade paths are available among the various editions of Windows 7. This section identifies these upgrade paths and shows you how to perform these upgrades.

CHAPTER 3

Upgrading to Windows 7

A lot of individuals have purchased computers running Windows Vista since its rollout in early 2007, and most have been disappointed to a certain extent because of the problems encountered with this operating system, which we have already discussed in Chapter 1, "Introducing Windows 7." Microsoft has provided paths for upgrading these computers to Windows 7. Further, some users of Windows XP computers would like to take advantage of the latest and greatest of Microsoft operating systems. In this chapter, we look at which computers can be upgraded directly to Windows 7 and which computers require a complete reinstall of the operating system.

Many users are attracted by the features available in higher editions of Windows 7, such as Ultimate, but might have purchased a computer on which a lower edition of Windows 7, such as Home Premium, has been preinstalled. For those users, Microsoft has made upgrade paths available that enable them to move to a higher version of Windows 7. As with the upgrade of an earlier version of Windows, these paths enable users to retain Registry settings and account information from the lower version of Windows 7.

"Do I Know This Already?" Quiz

The "Do I Know This Already?" quiz enables you to assess whether you should read this entire chapter or simply jump to the "Exam Preparation Tasks" section for review. If you are in doubt, read the entire chapter. Table 3-1 outlines the major headings in this chapter and the corresponding "Do I Know This Already?" quiz questions. You can find the answers in Appendix A, "Answers to the 'Do I Know This Already?' Quizzes."

Table 3-1 "Do I Know This Already?" Foundation Topics Section-to-Question Mapping

Foundations Topics Section	Questions Covered in This Section
Upgrading to Windows 7 from a Previous Version of Windows	1–4
Migrating from Windows XP	5–7
Upgrading from One Edition of Windows 7 to Another	8–10

1. Your computer is running Windows Vista Home Premium. Which of the following can you upgrade directly to in one step, without performing a clean installation? (Choose all that apply.)

   a. Windows 7 Home Premium.

   b. Windows 7 Professional.

   c. Windows 7 Enterprise.

   d. Windows 7 Ultimate.

   e. You cannot upgrade directly to any of these operating systems; you must perform a clean install of Windows 7.

2. Your computer is running Windows XP Professional. Which of the following can you upgrade directly to in one step, without performing a clean installation? (Choose all that apply.)

   a. Windows 7 Home Premium.

   b. Windows 7 Professional.

   c. Windows 7 Enterprise.

   d. Windows 7 Ultimate.

   e. You cannot upgrade directly to any of these operating systems; you must perform a clean install of Windows 7.

3. You are preparing to upgrade your Windows Vista computer to Windows 7. Which of the following tasks should you perform before beginning the upgrade? (Choose all that apply.)

   a. Run the Windows 7 Upgrade Advisor.

   b. Run Windows 7 Anytime Upgrade.

   c. Check for any available upgrades for your computer's BIOS.

   d. Scan your computer for viruses.

   e. Remove or disable your antivirus program.

   f. Install the latest service pack for Windows Vista.

4. You insert the Windows 7 DVD-ROM in the drive of your Windows Vista computer and select the option to install Windows and to get the latest updates. You receive the Which Type of Installation Do You Want page, but the option to upgrade is disabled (grayed out). Which of the following is the most likely reason that this option is not available?

   a. You have not accepted the license agreement.

   b. Your computer is running a 32-bit version of Windows Vista, but you have inserted the 64-bit Windows 7 DVD.

   c. Your computer is running Windows Vista Home Premium, and you are attempting to upgrade to Windows 7 Professional.

    d. Your computer is running Windows Vista Home Premium, and you are attempting to upgrade to Windows 7 Ultimate.

5. Your computer is running Windows XP Professional. You want to upgrade to Windows 7 Ultimate. Which of the following is the cheapest and simplest way to perform the upgrade?

    a. Insert the Windows 7 DVD and upgrade directly to Windows 7 Ultimate.

    b. Insert the Windows 7 DVD and upgrade to Windows 7 Professional. Then use Windows Anytime Upgrade to upgrade to Windows 7 Ultimate.

    c. Insert the Windows Vista DVD and upgrade to Windows Vista Ultimate. Then insert the Windows 7 DVD and upgrade to Windows 7 Ultimate.

    d. Insert the Windows 7 DVD and install a clean copy of Windows 7 Ultimate.

6. Your computer is running Windows XP Professional. You insert the Windows 7 DVD and choose the option to perform a clean installation of Windows 7. You then select the same partition on which the Windows XP system files are located and proceed with the upgrade. Which of the following best describes what happens to your Windows XP system files?

    a. The Windows XP system files are overwritten with the Windows 7 system files.

    b. The Windows XP system files are placed in a new folder named `Windows.old`.

    c. The Windows XP system files remain in the same location in an unaltered state, and you create a dual-boot system.

    d. The Windows XP system files are moved to a new partition, and you create a dual-boot system.

7. Fred has saved a large number of Word documents on your computer running Windows XP Home Edition. He installs Windows 7 Home Premium on your computer, using the same partition on which Windows XP was installed. He does not reformat this partition. What happens to these documents?

    a. They are placed in the `Windows.old\Documents and Settings\Fred\My Documents` folder.

    b. They remain in the `Documents and Settings\Fred\My Documents` folder.

    c. They are placed in the `Users\Fred\My Documents` folder.

    d. They are lost; Fred must restore them from backup.

8. Your computer runs Windows 7 Home Premium and you want to upgrade to a higher edition of Windows 7. Besides Windows 7 Ultimate, what edition can you upgrade to?

   a. Starter

   b. Home Basic

   c. Professional

   d. Enterprise

9. Your computer runs Windows 7 Home Premium and you want to upgrade to Windows 7 Ultimate. You have gone online and purchased a Windows 7 Ultimate upgrade license. What should you do?

   a. Run Windows Anytime Upgrade, enter the key code for the Ultimate upgrade, and let the upgrade proceed.

   b. Insert the Windows 7 DVD, select the option to install Windows, enter the key code for the Ultimate edition, and run the upgrade.

   c. Insert the Windows 7 DVD, select the option to repair Windows, enter the key code for the Ultimate edition, and run the upgrade.

   d. Insert the Windows 7 DVD, select the option to perform a clean install of Windows, enter the key code for the Ultimate upgrade, and let the upgrade proceed.

10. You have upgraded your computer from Windows Vista Home Premium to Windows 7 Home Premium. However, you are dissatisfied with the performance of your computer and want to revert to Windows Vista. You verify that a `Windows.old` folder exists. What should you do?

   a. Access the System and Security applet in Control Panel and select Uninstall Windows 7.

   b. Access the Programs applet in Control Panel and select Uninstall Windows 7.

   c. Use the Windows Recovery Environment and the `Windows.old` folder to recover Windows Vista.

   d. You cannot revert to Windows Vista; you must reformat the partition containing Windows 7 and perform a clean installation of Vista.

Foundation Topics

Upgrading to Windows 7 from a Previous Version of Windows

Upgrade paths from previous Windows versions depend on the operating system version currently installed. Table 3-2 lists the available upgrade paths for older operating systems.

Table 3-2   Upgrading Older Operating Systems to Windows 7

Operating System	Upgrade Path
Windows Vista Home Basic	Can be upgraded directly to Windows 7 Home Basic, Home Premium or Ultimate.
Windows Vista Home Premium	Can be upgraded directly to Windows 7 Home Premium or Ultimate.
Windows Vista Business	Can be upgraded directly to Windows 7 Professional, Enterprise, or Ultimate.
Windows Vista Enterprise	Can be upgraded directly to Windows 7 Enterprise.
Windows Vista Ultimate	Can be upgraded directly to Windows 7 Ultimate.
Windows 9x/Me Windows NT 4.0 Workstation Windows 2000/XP Professional	Cannot be upgraded. You need to perform a clean installation of Windows 7.
Non-Windows operating systems (UNIX, Linux, OS/2)	Cannot be upgraded. You need to perform a clean installation of Windows 7.

NOTE   Theoretically, you can upgrade Windows XP computers to Windows Vista and then upgrade to Windows 7. However, the licensing costs for such an upgrade would be higher than that of purchasing a clean copy of Windows 7; besides, such older computers might not meet Windows 7's hardware requirements.

CAUTION   In addition to the limitations presented in Table 3-2, you cannot directly upgrade a 32-bit Windows Vista operating system to a 64-bit Windows 7 operating system. You also cannot directly upgrade a 64-bit Windows Vista operating system to a 32-bit Windows 7 operating system. Both of these scenarios require a clean installation of Windows 7, regardless of the edition being upgraded.

Preparing a Computer to Meet Upgrade Requirements

In addition to running one of the supported versions of Windows mentioned here, a computer to be upgraded to Windows 7 must meet the hardware requirements previously described in Chapter 2, "Installing Windows 7." Furthermore, all hardware components should be found in the Windows 7 Logo Program for Hardware. Older software applications also might not be compatible with Windows 7. Such applications might need to be upgraded or replaced to work properly after you have upgraded your operating system.

Windows 7 Upgrade Advisor

Microsoft provides an Upgrade Advisor that generates reports describing hardware and software components that might not be compatible with Windows 7. You can download and install this program free from http://www.microsoft.com/windows/windows-7/get/upgrade-advisor.aspx. This report identifies any hardware or software problems associated with the computer to be upgraded.

NOTE   In general, nearly all computers that can run Windows Vista can also run Windows 7. However, it is still worthwhile to run the Windows 7 Upgrade Advisor to reduce the likelihood of encountering problems during or after upgrading to Windows 7. In particular, many antivirus programs that are compatible with Vista will not work with Windows 7.

Use the following procedure to obtain a system compatibility report from the computer to be upgraded:

Step 1.   Download the Windows 7 Upgrade Advisor from the website already mentioned. Read the information provided and then click the **Download** button.

Step 2.   On the **File Download–Security Warning** dialog box, click **Run** to run the advisor now or **Save** to save it to your hard disk and run the advisor later.

Step 3.   If you receive a User Account Control (UAC) prompt, click **Continue**.

Step 4.   The Windows 7 Upgrade Advisor Setup Wizard starts with a **Welcome** page as shown in Figure 3-1. Select the radio button labeled **I accept the license terms** and then click **Install**.

Step 5.   The installation takes a minute or two to complete. When the wizard displays the **Installation Complete** message, click **Close**.

Step 6.   The Upgrade Advisor adds an icon to your desktop. Double-click this icon to run the advisor, and then click **Continue** to accept the UAC prompt.

Figure 3-1   You must accept the license terms to run the Windows 7 Upgrade Advisor.

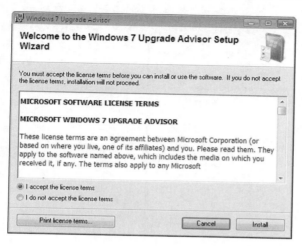

Step 7.   The Windows 7 Upgrade Advisor displays the page shown in Figure 3-2. Ensure that you have connected and turned on all peripheral devices (such as printers) so that they can be checked. Then click **Start check**.

Figure 3-2   The Windows 7 Upgrade Advisor displays this introductory page.

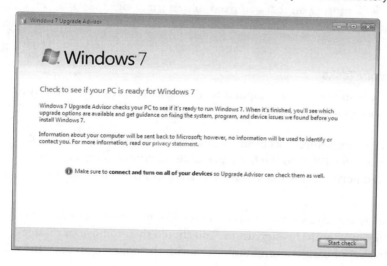

Step 8.   The Upgrade Advisor checks the hardware and software on your computer and then displays a report window similar that shown in Figure 3-3, which indicates any issues it might have found with your computer. Click the links provided if you need additional information.

Figure 3-3   The Windows 7 Upgrade Advisor informs you of any issues related to system, devices, and programs.

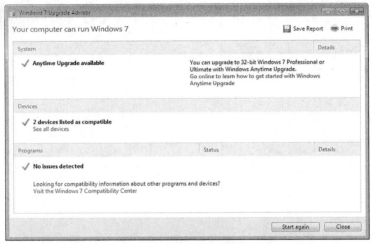

NOTE   You can also run the Windows 7 Upgrade Advisor on a computer running Windows XP. The only prerequisite to run this program on a Windows XP computer is to install .NET 2.0 Framework or higher. The steps are similar to those described here, and you will receive a report similar to the one shown in Figure 3-3. Among other items, it will inform you that you need to perform a clean installation of Windows 7.

Additional Preparatory Tasks

Before you upgrade a Windows Vista computer to Windows 7, you should perform several additional tasks, as follows:

- Check the BIOS manufacturer's website for any available BIOS upgrades, and upgrade the computer's BIOS to the latest available functional version if necessary. You should perform this step before a clean install or an upgrade to Windows 7.

- Scan and eliminate any viruses from the computer, using an antivirus program updated with the latest antivirus signatures. You should then remove or disable the antivirus program because it might interfere with the upgrade process. In addition, you should use a third-party program to scan for and remove malicious software (malware).

- Install any upgrade packs that might be required to render older software applications compatible with Windows 7. Consult software manufacturers for details.

■ Install the latest service pack for Windows Vista (SP2 at the time of writing), plus any other updates that Microsoft has published. At the very minimum, you must have Vista SP1 installed.

Upgrading the Computer to Windows 7

After you have checked system compatibility and performed all tasks required to prepare your computer for upgrading, you are ready to proceed. The upgrade takes place in a similar fashion to a new installation, except that answers to some questions asked by the Setup Wizard are taken from the current installation. Perform the following procedure to upgrade a Windows Vista computer to Windows 7.

Step 1.   Insert the Windows 7 DVD-ROM.

Step 2.   If you receive a UAC prompt, click **Continue**.

Step 3.   When the Windows 7 screen appears, select **Install now**.

Step 4.   Setup copies temporary files, and then the Get Important Updates for Installation page appears. If you are connected to the Internet, select the **Go online to get the latest updates for installations** option. Otherwise, select the **Do not get the latest updates for installation** option.

Step 5.   Accept the license agreement and then click **Next**.

Step 6.   On the Which type of installation do you want? page, shown in Figure 3-4, select **Upgrade**.

Figure 3-4   The Which type of installation do you want? page offers you a choice between upgrading or performing a clean installation.

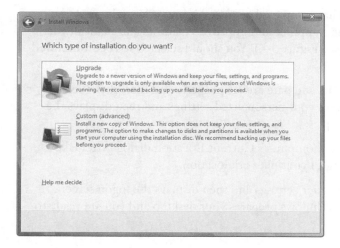

Step 7.   Setup checks for compatibility issues and displays the Compatibility Report page with information about any applications or drivers that are

not supported in Windows 7 (see Figure 3-5). Note the information provided and then click **Next**. If the compatibility check does not find any issues, this page might not appear.

Figure 3-5   The Compatibility Report screen describes items that might be incompatible with the upgrade to Windows 7.

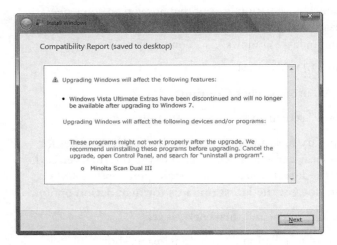

Step 8.   The Windows 7 upgrade proceeds in a fashion similar to that of a clean installation. It asks for only any information it cannot retrieve from the previous Windows installation.

Step 9.   After installation has completed and the computer has rebooted, the Help protect your computer and improve Windows automatically dialog box appears (see Figure 3-6). You should select **Use recommended settings**.

Step 10.   Ensure that the time and date are set properly and then click **Next**. Windows configures your personalized settings and then displays the Windows 7 desktop.

Step 11.   On the Select Your Computer's Current Location dialog box, make a selection according to your network location.

Step 12.   Windows finalizes your settings and then displays the logon screen. After you log on, Windows prepares your desktop and you are ready to use Windows 7.

Figure 3-6   Select **Use recommended settings** to ensure optimum protection for your computer.

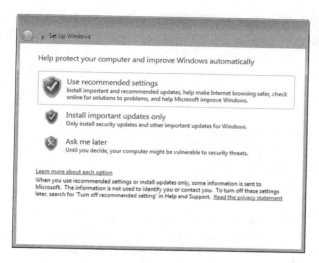

Migrating from Windows XP

As you have seen, Microsoft does not provide a direct upgrade route from Windows XP to Windows 7. If your computer running Windows XP meets the hardware requirements for running Windows 7, you have two choices for upgrading to Windows 7:

- Upgrade your computer to Windows Vista and then upgrade from Windows Vista to Windows 7. This procedure is time-consuming, is expensive (you will need to purchase upgrade editions of both Windows Vista and Windows 7), and is consequently not recommended.

- Back up all your files and then do a clean install of Windows 7. You will need to reinstall all applications on your computer after you have installed Windows 7.

Use the following procedure to upgrade a Windows XP computer:

Step 1.   Back up all files before starting, especially those on the partition to be used for the Windows 7 operating system files.

Step 2.   Use one of the procedures detailed in Chapter 2 to install Windows 7 on your computer. When you are offered a choice of upgrade or clean installation, the upgrade option will be unavailable and you must choose the clean installation option.

Step 3.   If you want to retain the Windows XP operating system files, select a different partition when offered a list of available partitions. Doing so will create a dual-boot system, as discussed in Chapter 2.

Step 4.   If you choose the Windows XP partition, the old operating system files will be retained in a `Windows.old` folder as discussed in the next section. Do not format this partition.

Step 5.   After you have finished the installation of Windows 7, you can migrate your settings to the new installation by following procedures covered in Chapter 4, "Migrating Users and Applications to Windows 7." You will need to reinstall all your applications on Windows 7.

NOTE   For more information on upgrading from Windows XP to Windows 7, refer to "Installing Windows 7 on an Existing Windows XP Computer" at http://technet.microsoft.com/en-us/library/dd939987(WS.10).aspx.

TIP   Windows 7 requires the NTFS file system. If you are performing a clean installation of Windows 7 on a computer that was running Windows XP, remember that the partition on which you install Windows 7 must be formatted with the NTFS file system. If the Windows XP computer was using a FAT or FAT32 partition, you must execute the `convert c: /fs:ntfs` command from XP before installing Windows 7.

The `Windows.old` Folder

When you upgrade a previous version of Windows to Windows 7, Setup.exe stores copies of the previous operating system subfolders and files in the `Windows.old` folder so that they are available in case you need them. This also happens if you perform an in-place upgrade or reinstallation of a Windows 7 system. This folder assists you in migrating some of your settings to Windows 7 after upgrading from Windows XP. You will find the following subfolders present:

- `Windows.old\Windows`: Contains files from the old Windows operating system.

- `Windows.old\Documents and Settings`: Contains the following subfolders:
  — `Windows.old\Documents and Settings\Administrator`: Contains personal files stored by users of the default Windows XP Administrator account. If you did not use this account, this subfolder might not contain any personal files.
  — `Windows.old\Documents and Settings\All Users`: Contains any documents you might have stored in My Shared Documents (as accessed from the default Windows XP Start menu).
  — `Windows.old\Documents and Settings\`*`Username`*: Contains personal files for the user *username*, such as documents, pictures, and Internet Explorer favorites. If you had multiple users on the Windows XP computer, you will find a separate folder labeled with the username for each user.

- **`Windows.old\Program Files`**: Contains folders for applications that were installed on Windows XP. You might be able to migrate program settings from this folder.

We look at migrating these folders and settings to your Windows 7 computer in Chapter 4. You can also use cut and paste to move their contents to the Windows 7 locations, such as the Documents folder accessed from the Windows 7 Start menu.

NOTE   For more information on moving files and settings, refer to "How to restore your personal files after you perform a custom installation of Windows Vista or of Windows 7" at http://support.microsoft.com/kb/932912.

Removing the **`Windows.old`** Folder

After you have restored files and settings from the `Windows.old` folder and are confident that you do not need anything left behind in this folder, you can use Disk Cleanup to remove this folder and reclaim its disk space. Perform the following procedure:

Step 1.   Click **Start > All Programs >Accessories > System Tools > Disk Cleanup**. You can also type **disk** into the Search box in the Start menu, and then click **Disk Cleanup** from the results list.

Step 2.   If you have more than one disk partition, the Disk Cleanup: Drive Selection dialog box appears. Select the partition on which you installed Windows 7.

Step 3.   Disk Cleanup calculates the amount of space you can free up and then displays the dialog box shown in Figure 3-7, showing you what items can be freed up. Click **Clean up system files**.

Step 4.   If you receive a UAC prompt, click **Yes**, and if you are again asked for a partition, select the Windows 7 partition again.

Step 5.   The Disk Cleanup dialog box reappears. Select **Previous Windows Installation**. Also select check boxes for any other files you want to delete, click **OK**, and then click **Delete Files** to confirm your action.

Figure 3-7 The Disk Cleanup dialog box enables you to remove unnecessary files and folders.

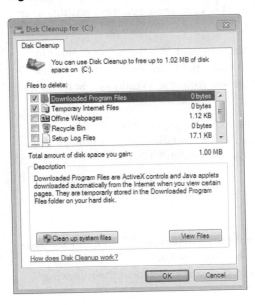

Upgrading from One Edition of Windows 7 to Another

Chapter 1 introduced you to the editions Microsoft has produced for Windows 7. Just as you can upgrade Windows Vista to Windows 7, you can also upgrade a lower edition of Windows 7 to a higher one. Table 3-3 summarizes the available upgrade paths.

Table 3-3 Upgrading One Edition of Windows 7 to a Higher One

Windows Edition You Are Upgrading	You Can Upgrade to This Edition
Windows 7 Home Basic or Windows 7 Starter	Windows 7 Home Premium
	Windows 7 Professional
	Windows 7 Ultimate
Windows 7 Home Premium	Windows 7 Professional
	Windows 7 Ultimate
Windows 7 Professional	Windows 7 Ultimate
Windows 7 Ultimate	Cannot be upgraded further

Windows Anytime Upgrade

The Windows 7 DVD-ROM contains the code for all editions of Windows 7. When you enter the license key, this tells Setup which edition of Windows 7 you are installing. As mentioned in Chapter 2, you can also install Windows 7 without entering a license key and then select the desired edition. Doing so enables you to preview the capabilities of a given edition before making a purchase decision.

Upgrading Windows 7

Use the following procedure to upgrade one edition of Windows 7 to a higher one:

Step 1.   Click **Start > Control Panel > System and Security > Windows Anytime Upgrade**.

Step 2.   As shown in Figure 3-8, Windows Anytime Upgrade enables you to compare the available editions of Windows 7 or enter an upgrade key that you have already purchased.

Figure 3-8   Windows Anytime Upgrade enables you to upgrade your edition of Windows 7.

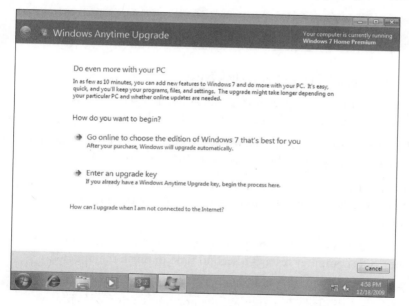

Step 3.   If you want to review a summary of available features in different editions, click the **Go online to choose the edition of Windows 7 that's best for you** link. While online, you can purchase the license for the edition you want to upgrade to. When finished, close Internet Explorer to return to Windows Anytime Upgrade.

Step 4.   To upgrade to a higher edition of Windows 7, click the **Enter an upgrade key** link. This takes you to the window shown in Figure 3-9.

Figure 3-9   Windows Anytime Upgrade instructs you to enter the upgrade key you purchased to begin the upgrade.

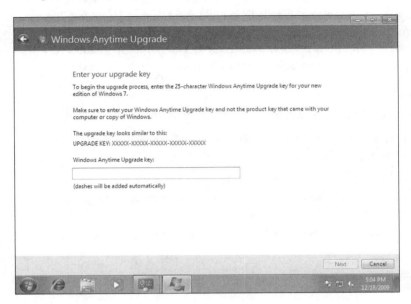

Step 5.   Type your upgrade key and then click **Next**.

Step 6.   Windows verifies your upgrade key and, after a few seconds, displays a message to Please accept the license terms. Click **I Accept**.

Step 7.   Follow the instructions provided to save work and close open programs, and then click **Upgrade**. If you receive a UAC prompt, click **Yes**.

Step 8.   Windows Anytime Upgrade displays the screen shown in Figure 3-10 as the upgrade takes place. The process might include the downloading of updates.

Step 9.   After 10 minutes or so, the computer restarts and the upgrade process finishes. The computer restarts a second time to finish the upgrade.

Step 10.   After this reboot, the Windows 7 logon screen appears with the username(s) you specified while running the previous edition of Windows 7. Select an appropriate username and type the password, if configured.

Step 11.   You are informed that the upgrade was successful. If desired, click the link provided to find out what's new. Otherwise, click **Close**.

Uninstalling Windows 7

In some cases, you might be able to uninstall Windows 7 and revert your computer to a previous version of Windows. Microsoft supports the following scenarios for uninstalling Windows 7:

Figure 3-10   The Windows Anytime Upgrade process includes the downloading and installation of available updates.

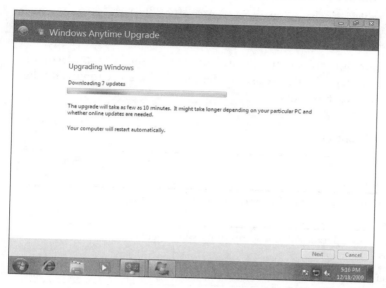

- **After Installing Windows 7 over an Earlier Windows Installation:** If the Windows.old folder already mentioned in this chapter still exists, you might be able to recover the older Windows installation by using the Windows Recovery Environment. Refer to http://support.microsoft.com/kb/971760/ for more details. We discuss the Windows Recovery Environment in Chapter 18, "Configuring System and File Recovery."

- **After Installing Windows 7 on a Computer That Did Not Have a Previous Operating System Installed:** Use the Windows XP or Vista installation media to install the desired version of Windows over the Windows 7 installation. You will lose all data from the Windows 7 installation, so be sure to back up any data of value before starting.

- **After Upgrading from Windows Vista:** Microsoft does not provide a direct uninstall path (unlike the uninstall path provided in Windows 2000). You need to use the same procedure as mentioned for installing Windows 7 on a computer without a previous operating system.

- **After Creating a Dual-Boot or Multi-Boot System:** Back up your programs, files, and settings from the Windows 7 partition. From the other operating system, delete or format the Windows 7 partition. This frees up all the disk space from this partition, allowing its use by the other operating system.

NOTE   For more information on these methods of uninstalling Windows 7, refer to "How to Uninstall Windows 7" at http://support.microsoft.com/kb/971762.

Exam Preparation Tasks

Review All the Key Topics

Review the most important topics in the chapter, noted with the key topics icon in the outer margin of the page. Table 3-4 lists a reference of these key topics and the page numbers on which each is found.

Table 3-4   Key Topics for Chapter 3

Key Topic Element	Description	Page Number
Table 3-2	Lists operating systems that can or cannot be upgraded to Windows 7	91
Figure 3-3	The Windows Upgrade Advisor warns of possible upgrade problems	94
List	Tasks you should perform before upgrading to Windows 7	94
List	Identifies methods you can use to upgrade Windows XP to Windows 7	97
Table 3-3	Lists supported upgrades from one edition of Windows 7 to a higher one	100

Complete the Tables and Lists from Memory

Print a copy of Appendix C, "Memory Tables" (found on the CD), or at least the section for this chapter, and complete the tables and lists from memory. Appendix D, "Memory Tables Answer Key," also on the CD, includes completed tables and lists to check your work.

Definitions of Key Terms

Define the following key terms from this chapter, and check your answers in the glossary.

Windows Anytime Upgrade, Windows Upgrade Advisor, Disk Cleanup,
`Windows.old`

This chapter covers the following subjects:

- **Migrating Users from One Computer to Another:** This section discusses methods you can use for migrating user files plus desktop and application settings from one computer to another and contrasts methods according to the volume of users being migrated.

- **Migrating Users from Previous Windows Versions:** This section discusses procedures you can use for migrating users running Windows XP and other older Windows operating systems to new Windows 7 computers.

- **Side by Side Versus Wipe and Load:** This section compares and contrasts these two methods that you can use for preserving documents and settings when upgrading a large number of users to Windows 7.

CHAPTER 4

Migrating Users and Applications to Windows 7

Many companies will be purchasing new computers with Windows 7 already loaded or upgrading computers from Windows XP or Vista. Users who will be working with these computers might have been using Windows XP computers for several years, and these computers will have applications with user- or company-specific settings as well as important data on them. Microsoft provides tools to assist you in migrating users and applications to new Windows 7 computers, and they expect you to know how to perform these migrations in an efficient manner as part of the 70-680 exam.

"Do I Know This Already?" Quiz

The "Do I Know This Already?" quiz enables you to assess whether you should read this entire chapter or simply jump to the "Exam Preparation Tasks" section for review. If you are in doubt, read the entire chapter. Table 4-1 outlines the major headings in this chapter and the corresponding "Do I Know This Already?" quiz questions. You can find the answers in Appendix A, "Answers to the 'Do I Know This Already?' Quizzes."

Table 4-1 "Do I Know This Already?" Foundation Topics Section-to-Question Mapping

Foundations Topics Section	Questions Covered in This Section
Migrating Users from One Computer to Another	1–5
Migrating Users from Previous Windows Versions	6–8
Side by Side Versus Wipe and Load	9–10

1. You have been called to help a home user who has bought a Windows 7 computer move her documents and settings from her old computer running Windows XP Home Edition to the new computer. What tool should you use?

   a. Files and Settings Transfer Wizard

   b. User State Migration Tool (USMT)

   c. Windows Easy Transfer

   d. Windows Automated Installation Kit (AIK)

2. Your company is migrating 50 users in one department from old computers running Windows XP Professional to new computers running Windows 7 Professional. What tool should you use?

   a. Files and Settings Transfer Wizard

   b. User State Migration Tool (USMT)

   c. Windows Easy Transfer

   d. Windows Automated Installation Kit (AIK)

3. Which of the following items are components included with USMT 4.0? (Choose three.)

   a. ScanState.exe

   b. LoadState.exe

   c. Migwiz.exe

   d. MigApp.xml

   e. Migapp.exe

4. You are charged with the responsibility of migrating 100 users in the same department to new Windows 7 Ultimate computers. What program should you use to collect user settings and data from their old computers?

   a. ScanState.exe

   b. LoadState.exe

   c. Migwiz.exe

   d. Fastwiz.exe

5. You have stored user settings and data from all the employees in your company's marketing department on a file server. You have also set up new Windows 7 computers for these employees and installed all required applications. What program should you use now to transfer the user settings and data to these new computers?

   a. ScanState.exe

   b. LoadState.exe

   c. Migwiz.exe

   d. Xcopy.exe

6. You have used the Custom (Advanced) option to upgrade your Windows Vista Home Premium computer to Windows 7 Home Premium. You have taken care not to format the system drive. What should you do to restore your documents and application settings to the Windows 7 installation with the least amount of effort?

   a. Copy these items from the backup disk you created before you performed the upgrade.

   b. Use the Files and Settings Transfer Wizard to migrate these items from the `Windows.old` folder.

   c. Copy these items from the `Windows.old` folder to their locations in the new Windows 7 installation.

   d. Use Windows Easy Transfer to migrate these items from the `Windows.old` folder.

7. You have upgraded your Windows Vista Ultimate computer to Windows 7 Ultimate by using the Upgrade option provided by the Setup Wizard. What should you do to restore your documents and application settings to the Windows 7 installation with the least amount of effort?

   a. Use the Files and Settings Transfer Wizard to migrate these items from the `Windows.old` folder.

   b. Copy these items from the `Windows.old` folder to their locations in the new Windows 7 installation.

   c. Use Windows Easy Transfer to migrate these items from the `Windows.old` folder.

   d. You don't need to do any of these actions. The Upgrade option preserves all your documents and settings in their proper locations for use with Windows 7.

8. You are planning to perform a scripted migration of all users in your company from Windows XP to Windows 7. You have a server running Windows Server 2008 R2 available with plenty of disk space to hold everyone's documents and settings. You have even downloaded a script from Microsoft and modified it to suit the needs of your migration. But you are unable to find the migration tools. What should you do?

   a. Insert the Windows 7 DVD-ROM and browse to the `Support\Tools\USMT` folder.

   b. Download the Windows Preinstallation Kit (Windows PE) from Microsoft.

   c. Download the Windows Automated Installation Kit (AIK) from Microsoft.

   d. You don't need to use any fancy tools. The old-fashioned DOS `xcopy` command will work just as well.

9. Which of the following best describes the wipe and load method of migrating a series of users to Windows 7?

   a. Windows Easy Transfer is used to collect user settings and data from old computers and store them to a network location. Windows Easy Transfer is then used to restore these settings to new Windows 7 computers.

   b. ScanState.exe is used to collect user settings and data from old computers and store them to a server. LoadState.exe is used to restore these items to new Windows 7 computers.

   c. Windows Easy Transfer is used to collect user settings and data from old computers and store them to a network location. Windows 7 is installed on the same computers by formatting the hard disk and performing a clean install. Then Windows Easy Transfer is used to restore these settings and data to the same computers.

   d. ScanState.exe is used to collect user settings and data from old computers and store them to a server. Windows 7 is installed on the same computers by formatting the hard disk and performing a clean install. Then LoadState.exe is used to restore the settings and data to the same computers.

10. Which of the following best describes the side by side method of migrating a series of users to Windows 7?

   a. Windows Easy Transfer is used to collect user settings and data from old computers and store them to a network location. Windows Easy Transfer is then used to restore these settings to new Windows 7 computers.

   b. ScanState.exe is used to collect user settings and data from old computers and store them to a server. LoadState.exe is used to restore these items to new Windows 7 computers.

   c. Windows Easy Transfer is used to collect user settings and data from old computers and store them to a network location. Windows 7 is installed on the same computers by formatting the hard disk and performing a clean install. Then Windows Easy Transfer is used to restore these settings and data to the same computers.

   d. ScanState.exe is used to collect user settings and data from old computers and store them to a server. Windows 7 is installed on the same computers by formatting the hard disk and performing a clean install. Then LoadState.exe is used to restore the settings and data to the same computers.

Foundation Topics

Migrating Users from One Computer to Another

Windows 7 provides two tools that assist you in migrating users from old computers to new ones. Windows Easy Transfer is a wizard-based tool that replaces the Files and Settings Transfer Wizard used in Windows XP and is designed to facilitate the migration of one user or a small number of users, including their data and profiles. If you have a large number of users to migrate in a corporate environment, the User State Migration Tool (USMT) 4.0 is designed for this purpose. Running from the command line, you can customize USMT to suit the needs of your migration requirements.

User State Migration Tool

Intuitively, you might first think that migrating a large number of users to new Windows 7 computers could be a simple as using the xcopy command or a tool such as Robocopy to move files from their old computers to a network share, and then moving them back to the new computers later. However, users like to store data on various locations on their local hard drives; they have customized application settings and specific files (such as Microsoft Outlook PST files) that might be hard to locate after such a move is finished. Users also like to set up individual desktop preferences, such as wallpapers and screen savers. Using USMT enables you to move all these items and more in a seamless manner to their appropriate locations on the new computer so that the user can resume working on this computer with minimal delay.

You can use the USMT 4.0 to quickly and easily transfer any number of user files and settings as a part of operating system deployment or computer replacement. It includes migration of the following items:

- Local user accounts.

- Personalized settings from these accounts, such as desktop backgrounds, sounds, screen savers, mouse pointer settings, Internet Explorer settings, and email settings including signature files and contact lists.

- Personal files belonging to these accounts including user profiles, the Desktop folder, the My Documents folder, and any other folder locations users might have utilized. New to USMT 4.0 is the capability to capture files even when they are in use, by means of Volume Shadow Copy technology. We discuss Volume Shadow Copy in Chapter 18, "Configuring System and File Recovery."

- Operating system and application settings, including the Applications folder within Program Files, user profile folders, or storage folders on the local disk defined within specific application settings.

This tool reduces the costs of operating system deployment by addressing the following items:

- Technician time associated with migration
- Employee learning and familiarization time on the new operating system
- Employee downtime and help desk calls related to repersonalizing the desktop
- Employee downtime locating missing files
- Employee satisfaction with the migration experience

USMT consists of two executable files, ScanState.exe and LoadState.exe, and three migration rule files, MigApp.xml, MigUser.xml, and MigDocs.xml. You can modify these migration rules files as necessary. They contain the following settings:

- **MigApp.xml**: Rules for migrating application settings
- **MigDocs.xml**: Rules that locate user documents automatically without the need to create custom migration files
- **MigUser.xml**: Rules for migrating user profiles and user data

NOTE You should not use MigDocs.xml and MigUser.xml together in the same migration. Otherwise, some migrated files might be duplicated if these files include conflicting instructions regarding target locations.

You can also create customized .xml files according to your migration requirements, as well as a Config.xml file that specifies files and settings to be excluded from migration (such as a user's large folder full of images and music). ScanState.exe collects user information from the old (source) computer based on settings contained in the various .xml files, and LoadState.exe places this information on a newly installed Windows 7 (destination) computer. The source computer can be running Windows XP, Vista, or 7.

New to USMT 4.0 is the capability to migrate from previous Windows installations contained in Windows.old folders. You can also use ScanState.exe in the Windows Preinstallation Environment (PE) to collect data from offline Windows operating systems.

CAUTION USMT is designed specifically for large-scale, automated transfers. If your migrations require end-user interaction or customization on a computer-by-computer basis, USMT is not recommended. In these cases, use Windows Easy Transfer instead.

Using the USMT involves running `ScanState.exe` at the source computer to collect the user state data to be migrated and transferring it to a shared folder on a server and then running `LoadState.exe` on the destination computer to load the user state data there, as shown in Figure 4-1. When migrating multiple users, you can create a script to automate this process.

Figure 4-1   To use USMT, run **ScanState.exe** at the source computer to transfer the files to a shared folder on a server and then run **LoadState.exe** at the destination computer to load the data there.

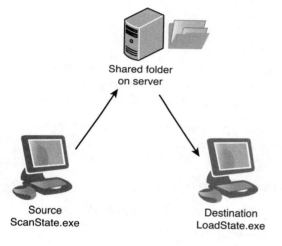

Shared folder
on server

Source
ScanState.exe

Destination
LoadState.exe

NOTE   You can use a server running Windows Server 2003 or 2008 for these procedures. You can also use a computer running Windows Vista or Windows 7.

Preparing the Server to Run USMT

You need to create and share the appropriate folders on the server before running USMT. This procedure requires the Windows Automated Installation Kit (AIK), which you can download as an `.iso` file from http://www.microsoft.com/downloads/details.aspx?FamilyID=696dd665-9f76-4177-a811-39c26d3b3b34&displaylang=en and burn to a blank DVD disc. Use the following procedure:

Step 1.   Create and share a folder named USMT on the server. The migrating user should have Read permission to this folder, and the local administrator on the destination computer should have at least Modify permission to this folder. Ensure that this folder has enough storage space available to meet the needs of all computers to be migrated.

Step 2.   Create and share a folder named MyStore on the server. Both the migrating user and the local administrator on the destination computer should have at least Modify permission to this folder.

Step 3.   Create two subfolders in the USMT folder named Scan and Load, respectively.

Step 4.   Insert the Windows AIK disc and follow the instructions in the Setup program that automatically starts to install Windows AIK.

Step 5.   Copy all files from the C:\Program Files\Windows AIK\Tools\USMT\x86 (or amd64) folder created during the Windows AIK installation to the USMT shared folder.

Step 6.   Make any required modifications to the .xml files included in this folder, or create any additional .xml files as needed.

Collecting Files from the Source Computer

After you have created and shared the appropriate files on the server, including the USMT folder and its contents, you are ready to scan the source computer and collect information to be exported to the new computer. Use the following procedure:

Step 1.   Log on to the source computer as the migrating user. This user should have permissions to the shares on the server as described in the previous procedure.

Step 2.   Map a drive to the USMT share on the server.

Step 3.   Open a command prompt and set its path to the mapped USMT share.

Step 4.   To run ScanState, type the following command:

```
scanstate \\servername\migration\mystore /config:config.xml
/i:miguser.xml /i:migapp.xml /v:13 /l:scan.log
```

In this command:

/i: is the include parameter, which specifies an XML file that defines the user, application, or system state that is being migrated.

/config: specifies the config.xml file used by scanstate.exe to create the store.

servername is the name of the server on which you installed the Windows AIK tools.

l: is a parameter that specifies the location of Scan.log, which is the name of a log file that will be created in the USMT share and will hold any error information from problems that might arise during the migration. If any problems occur, check the contents of this file.

The v:13 parameter specifies verbose, status, and debugger output to the log file.

NOTE   Both ScanState and LoadState support a large range of command-line options. Refer to the USMT.chm help file in the Windows AIK for a complete list and description of the available options. Also refer to "ScanState Syntax" at http://technet.microsoft.com/en-us/library/dd560781(WS.10).aspx.

Loading Collected Files on the Destination Computer

Before loading files to the destination computer, you should install Windows 7 and all required applications on this computer. However, do not create a local user account for the migrating user (this account is created automatically when you run LoadState). Join the computer to the domain if in a domain environment. Then perform the following procedure:

Step 1.   Log on to the destination computer as the local administrator (not the migrating account).

Step 2.   Map a drive to the USMT share on the server.

Step 3.   Open a command prompt and set its path to the mapped USMT share.

Step 4.   To run LoadState, type the following command: (The set of .xml files should be the same as used when running ScanState.)

```
loadstate \\servername\migration\mystore /config:config.xml
/i:miguser.xml /i:migapp.xml /lac /lae /v:13 /l:load.log
```

Step 5.   Log off and log on as the migrating user and verify that all required files and settings have been transferred.

In this command, /lac and /lae specify that local accounts from the source computer will be created and enabled on the destination computer. The other parameters are the same as defined previously for the ScanState tool. Note that passwords are not migrated (they are blank by default). For more information on LoadState, refer to "LoadState Syntax" at http://technet.microsoft.com/en-us/library/dd560804(WS.10).aspx.

NOTE   For more details on all three USMT procedures, refer to "Step-by-Step: Basic Windows Migration Using USMT for IT Professionals" at http://technet.microsoft.com/en-us/library/dd883247(WS.10).aspx.

Windows Easy Transfer

Windows Easy Transfer enables you to transfer files and settings from an old computer to a new one across a network or by means of an external hard drive, a USB flash drive, or the Easy Transfer cable. You can purchase the Easy Transfer cable from a computer store or on the Web. This cable uses USB to link to cables and transfers data at about 20 GB/hour.

Windows Easy Transfer includes a wizard that helps you to transfer your files, folders, and settings to a new computer or to a clean installation of Windows 7 on an existing computer. This is the simplest method when only a few computers are affected or when users are individually responsible for migrating the user states on their own computers.

Found on the Windows 7 DVD-ROM in the Support\Migwiz folder, the wizard (migwiz.exe) helps you to transfer files and settings by collecting them at the old (source) computer and then transferring them to a new computer running Windows 7 (called the destination computer).

Using Windows Easy Transfer to Collect Files at the Source Computer

You can use the following procedure to collect files from any computer running Windows XP (SP2 or later), Vista, or Windows 7. The steps shown here are as they occur for a USB disk on a computer running Windows XP; they are somewhat different if you are using the Windows Easy Transfer Cable or a network connection:

Step 1.   At the source computer, insert the Windows 7 DVD.

Step 2.   If the Windows 7 installation wizard starts, cancel it.

Step 3.   If you receive an AutoPlay dialog box, select the **Open folder to view files** option. Otherwise, access the DVD in Windows Explorer, right-click, and choose **Open**.

Step 4.   Navigate to the Support\Migwiz folder and double-click **migsetup.exe.** This starts the Windows Easy Transfer Wizard, as shown in Figure 4-2.

Step 5.   The wizard provides the three choices shown in Figure 4-3 for storing the collected data. Click the desired choice.

Step 6.   On the next screen, confirm that you are at the old computer (if you are transferring from one Windows 7 computer to another one, this screen asks whether this is the old computer or the new one).

Step 7.   The wizard displays the screen shown in Figure 4-4 as it collects data from this computer. This process takes several minutes or even longer, depending on the amount of data to be transferred. When it is done, click **Next**.

Step 8.   On the Choose what you can transfer page, clear the check boxes for any users whose data you do not want to transfer, and then click **Next**.

Figure 4-2   Windows Easy Transfer presents a wizard that facilitates transferring files from an old computer running Windows XP or later.

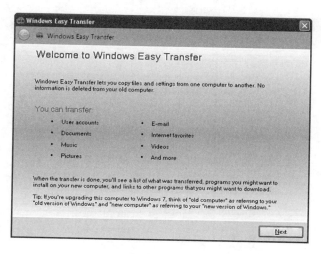

Figure 4-3   Windows Easy Transfer provides three choices for storing the collected data.

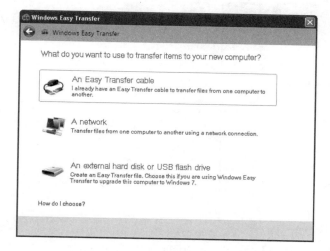

Step 9.   On the Save your files and settings for transfer page (see Figure 4-5), type and confirm a password that you will need to enter later at your new computer. Then click **Save** and confirm the filename provided or enter a new one and click **Save** again.

Step 10.   When informed that the files have been saved, click **Next**.

Step 11.   Click **Next** again, and then click **Close** to finish the wizard.

Figure 4-4   Windows Easy Transfer collects data from the user accounts stored on the old computer.

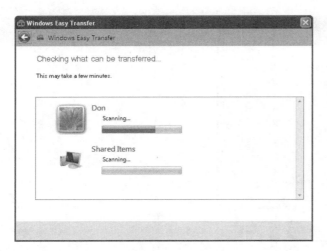

Figure 4-5   You must specify a password for the transfer to take place.

Using Windows Easy Transfer to Save Files at the Destination Computer

After you have installed Windows 7 plus any required applications on the destination computer, you can save the collected files by performing the following procedure:

Step 1.   At the destination computer, connect the USB drive and double-click the file containing the migrated information.

Step 2.   Windows Easy Transfer starts and displays the screen shown in Figure 4-6 asking you for the password you specified when you collected your files. Type this password and then click **Next**.

Figure 4-6   Type the password you specified at the old computer.

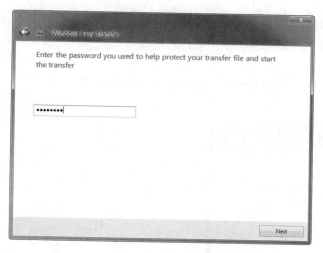

Step 3.   On the Choose what to transfer to this computer screen shown in Figure 4-7, deselect any users whose files and settings you do not want to transfer. If you want to map your user account to a different account on the new computer, or select a drive on the new computer to which you want to transfer files, click **Advanced Options** and make the appropriate choices.

Figure 4-7   Windows Easy Transfer enables you to choose what is transferred to the new computer.

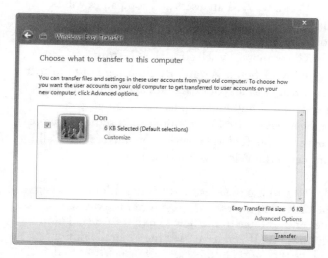

Step 4.   To begin the transfer, click **Transfer**.

Step 5. The wizard transfers the files and, when finished, informs you by means of the Your transfer is complete screen shown in Figure 4-8. Access the options on this screen to obtain more information on the transfer process and what programs you might want to install. When finished, click **Close**.

Figure 4-8   When the transfer is complete, you can obtain additional information about the results of the transfer.

Migrating Users from Previous Windows Versions

As you already know, Microsoft does not provide a direct path for upgrading computers running Windows XP to Windows 7. Many users and companies will be faced with performing upgrades of this nature in order to take advantage of the new features and capabilities of Windows 7. As explained in Chapter 2, you can install Windows 7 on a Windows XP computer by selecting the **Custom (Advanced)** option from the Windows 7 Setup Wizard. By choosing not to format your operating system partition during install, your data files and folders are preserved; in addition, operating system files and folders plus user settings from Windows XP are preserved in the `Windows.old` folder. Application settings are preserved in the `Windows.old\Program Files` folder; however, you must reinstall all applications after you have completed the Windows 7 installation.

NOTE   In some cases, you might want to use the Custom (Advanced) option when upgrading Windows Vista computers to Windows 7. If so, you can use the same procedures for migrating user files and settings to the new Windows 7 installation as used for a migration from Windows XP. If you have used the Upgrade option, these procedures are not required; furthermore, in this case, a `Windows.old` folder is not created.

> **CAUTION**   If you are using this upgrade option, make sure that you do *not* select the option to format your hard disk when installing Windows 7. If you do format your hard disk, the `Windows.old` folder will not be created.

Using the User State Migration Tool

As already discussed, USMT 4.0 is designed for use when large numbers of users must be migrated from older computers to new computers running Windows 7. You can also use this tool when you have upgraded these computers from Windows XP/Vista to Windows 7. After performing the upgrade, you can use a USB drive to hold the required commands for migrating user data from the `Windows.old` folder. Use the following procedure:

Step 1.   Download and install the Windows AIK as discussed earlier in this chapter.

Step 2.   Prepare an external USB drive by creating a `USMT` folder in the root directory. This folder should have `x86` and `amd64` subfolders for migrating 32-bit and 64-bit installations, respectively.

Step 3.   Copy the `Program Files\Windows AIK\Tools\USMT` folder from the computer on which you installed Windows AIK to the `USMT` folder in the USB drive.

Step 4.   Use Notepad to create a batch file for x86 file migrations. Microsoft suggests the following batch file:

```
@ECHO OFF
If exist D:\USMT\*.* xcopy D:\USMT\*.* /e /v /y C:\Windows\USMT\
If exist E:\USMT\*.* xcopy E:\USMT\*.* /e /v /y C:\Windows\USMT\
If exist F:\USMT\*.* xcopy F:\USMT\*.* /e /v /y C:\Windows\USMT\
If exist G:\USMT\*.* xcopy G:\USMT\*.* /e /v /y C:\Windows\USMT\
If exist H:\USMT\*.* xcopy H:\USMT\*.* /e /v /y C:\Windows\USMT\
If exist I:\USMT\*.* xcopy I:\USMT\*.* /e /v /y C:\Windows\USMT\
If exist J:\USMT\*.* xcopy J:\USMT\*.* /e /v /y C:\Windows\USMT\
If exist K:\USMT\*.* xcopy K:\USMT\*.* /e /v /y C:\Windows\USMT\
Cd c:\windows\usmt\x86
ScanState.exe c:\store /v:5 /o /c /hardlink /nocompress
   /efs:hardlink /i:MigApp.xml /i:MigDocs.xml
/offlineWinOld:c:\windows.old\windows
LoadState.exe c:\store /v:5 /c /lac /lae /i:migapp.xml
   /i:migdocs.xml /sf /hardlink /nocompress
:EOF
```

Step 5.   Save this file to the USB drive as `Migrate.bat`.

Step 6. Log on to the computer that has been upgraded using an administrative account.

Step 7. Insert the USB drive and copy the `Migrate.bat` file to the desktop.

Step 8. Right-click this file and then choose **Run as administrator**. If you receive a UAC prompt, click **Yes**.

Step 9. When the batch file finishes, access the `C:\Users` folder and confirm that all user files have been migrated to the appropriate file libraries.

This batch file locates USMT files and copies them to the `C:\Windows` folder so that the `ScanState.exe` command can create a hard-link migration store at `C:\Store` from the `Windows\old` folder. This hard-link migration process creates a catalog of hard links to files to be migrated. The `LoadState.exe` command then remaps the catalog of hard links to their appropriate locations in the Windows 7 installation. For AMD 64-bit machines, modify the batch file by changing the `x86` subfolder references to `amd64`.

> **NOTE**   For more information on this process, refer to "Building a USB Drive to Store USMT 4.0 Files and Simple Commands" at http://technet.microsoft.com/en-us/library/dd940094(WS.10).aspx.

Using Windows Easy Transfer

Windows Easy Transfer facilitates the transfer of settings from a Windows XP installation to an upgrade to Windows 7 on the same computer. Proceed as follows:

Step 1. Use an external USB hard disk or flash drive to collect the items to be transferred as described earlier in this chapter and illustrated in Figures 4-2 to 4-5.

Step 2. Install Windows 7 as a clean installation without formatting the hard disk, and then reinstall all applications.

Step 3. Complete the transfer procedure as illustrated in Figures 4-6 to 4-8. You can also click the link from Figure 4.8 that suggests additional programs you might want to install to verify that you have installed all required applications.

Side by Side Versus Wipe and Load

USMT supports the following two types of migration:

- **Side by Side:** Refers to copying data from an old computer to a new one.

- **Wipe and Load:** Refers to saving data from a computer, followed by performing a clean install of Windows 7, including formatting the computer's hard disk. Finally, the saved data and settings are reloaded onto the new Windows 7 installation.

Side by Side Migration

In side by side migration (also known as *Replace Computer*), an administrator uses ScanState.exe to collect user settings and data from the source computers and store this data in a file server used for intermediate storage, as shown in Figure 4-9. He then uses LoadState.exe to restore user settings and data to new computers on which Windows 7 has been preinstalled.

Figure 4-9   The side by side process transfers user files and settings from an old computer to a new one.

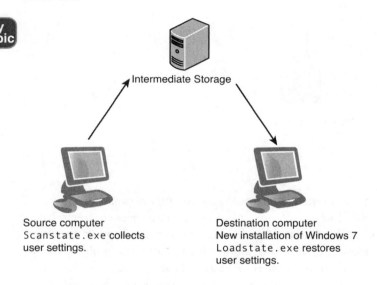

Intermediate Storage

Source computer
Scanstate.exe collects
user settings.

Destination computer
New installation of Windows 7
Loadstate.exe restores
user settings.

For example, a company has received a shipment of new Windows 7 computers for users in a particular department. The computers already in this department are to be donated to a charitable organization that refurbishes them and supplies them to the local school board for student use. The administrator would run ScanState.exe on the old computers, storing the data in the file server, and then run LoadState.exe on each of the new computers to restore each user's data and settings to the computer assigned to that particular employee. This procedure enables users to start working immediately on the new computers with all their settings and data intact and minimal user downtime involved.

Wipe and Load Migration

In a wipe and load migration (also known as *Refresh Computer*), an administrator uses ScanState.exe to collect user settings and data from the users' computers and stores this data in a file server, as shown in Figure 4-10. She installs Windows 7 as a clean installation on the same computers and then uses LoadState.exe to restore user settings and data to these computers.

Figure 4-10 The wipe and load process collects user settings from computers, upgrades those computers to Windows 7, and restores the collected settings.

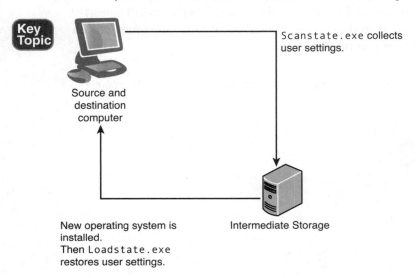

Scanstate.exe collects user settings.

Source and destination computer

New operating system is installed.
Then Loadstate.exe restores user settings.

Intermediate Storage

For example, a company has a series of relatively new computers running Windows XP Professional. These computers meet all the hardware requirements for installing Windows 7. After running ScanState.exe on each computer, the administrator installs Windows 7 Professional along with all corporate applications and then uses LoadState.exe to restore user settings and data to these computers. This procedure repurposes the same computers for use by the same users with the new operating system.

TIP It is possible to use the local computer disk as the USMT store in this scenario. Use a disk partition separate from that on which the operating system is to be restored or ensure that the setup process does not format the local hard disk.

Exam Preparation Tasks

Review All the Key Topics

Review the most important topics in the chapter, noted with the key topics icon in the outer margin of the page. Table 4-2 lists a reference of these key topics and the page numbers on which each is found.

Table 4-2   Key Topics for Chapter 4

Key Topic Element	Description	Page Number
Paragraph	Describes the USMT	112
Paragraph	Describes the Windows Easy Transfer	115
Figure 4-9	Side by side migration process	123
Figure 4-10	Wipe and load migration process	124

Definitions of Key Terms

Define the following key terms from this chapter, and check your answers in the glossary.

Windows Easy Transfer, Windows Automated Installation Kit (AIK), User State Migration Tool (USMT), LoadState.exe, ScanState.exe, source computer, destination computer, side by side migration, wipe and load migration

This chapter covers the following subjects:

- **Planning a Windows 7 Deployment:** This section introduces concepts and technologies used in Windows deployments and shows you how to create answer files.

- **Capturing a System Image:** This section shows you how to use Sysprep to prepare a reference computer for capture, and to use ImageX to capture the contents of the computer for deployment to new computers.

- **Preparing System Images for Deployment:** This section shows you how to use Deployment Image Servicing and Management to configure Windows images, including insertion and removal of applications, drivers, and updates.

- **Deploying Windows System Images:** This section introduces new Windows Deployment Services capabilities and shows you how to use this tool for automated computer deployment. It also shows you how to use Diskpart to set up a disk configuration and copy an image, and then use ImageX to apply this image manually to the new computer.

- **Troubleshooting an Unattended Installation:** This section introduces some of the problems you might encounter with answer files and Sysprep installations.

CHAPTER 5

Deploying Windows 7

Manual installation of Windows 7 is fine when you have only a few computers that need to be installed, but what would you do if you had several hundred (or thousand!) computers on which you needed to install Windows 7? Microsoft provides several automated deployment tools that facilitate large-scale Windows 7 rollouts and expects you to know how to use these tools for the 70-680 exam. You need to know how to capture and prepare system images for the deployment process, as well as performing the actual deployment using tools such as Windows Deployment Services (WDS) and the System Preparation Tool (Sysprep.exe, or Sysprep for short).

"Do I Know This Already?" Quiz

The "Do I Know This Already?" quiz enables you to assess whether you should read this entire chapter or simply jump to the "Exam Preparation Tasks" section for review. If you are in doubt, read the entire chapter. Table 5-1 outlines the major headings in this chapter and the corresponding "Do I Know This Already?" quiz questions. You can find the answers in Appendix A, "Answers to the 'Do I Know This Already?' Quizzes."

Table 5-1   "Do I Know This Already?" Foundation Topics Section-to-Question Mapping

Foundations Topics Section	Questions Covered in This Section
Planning a Windows 7 Deployment	1–4
Capturing a System Image	5–7
Preparing System Images for Deployment	8–10
Deploying Windows System Images	11–13
Troubleshooting an Unattended Installation	14–15

1. Which of the following best describes the purpose and use of a .wim file?

   a. This is an image file that contains the Windows 7 operating system after using Sysprep.

   b. This is a compressed file that contains answers to questions asked during Windows 7 Setup.

   c. This is an image file used in deploying Windows 7 operating systems to multiple computers.

   d. This is a library of compressed files used with Component-Based Servicing (CBS).

2. What tool would you use to create or edit answer files used to deploy Windows 7?

   a. Windows SIM

   b. Windows PE

   c. Windows AIK

   d. ImageX

   e. Sysprep

3. What tool would you use to capture, modify, and apply file-based disk images during Windows 7 deployment?

   a. Windows SIM

   b. Windows PE

   c. Windows AIK

   d. ImageX

   e. Sysprep

4. Which of the following is the default answer file used for unattended installation of Windows 7?

   a. Unattend.txt

   b. Unattend.xml

   c. Install.wim

   d. Sysprep.inf

5. Which parameter of Sysprep would you use to remove system-specific information such as the SID from a Windows installation that you are imaging?

   a. /audit

   b. /oobe

   c. /generalize

   d. /unattend

6. You are using Sysprep to prepare a Windows 7 image for deployment. You want to verify proper hardware and retain the ability to add drivers and applications to the image. Which parameter should you use?

   a. /audit

   b. /oobe

   c. /generalize

   d. /unattend

7. What tool would you use to capture the contents of a reference computer for deployment to new computers?

   a. Sysprep /generalize

   b. Sysprep /oobe

   c. ImageX /export

   d. ImageX /capture

8. Which of the following can you perform with Deployment Servicing and Management (DISM)? (Choose three.)

   a. Capture the contents of a Windows 7 installation for deployment to new computers

   b. Add, remove, and enumerate packages and drivers

   c. Copy Windows 7 images across the network for access by new computers

   d. Change the language, locale, fonts, and input settings within a Windows 7 image

   e. Upgrade a Windows installation to a higher edition

9. Which DISM command would you use to add application packages and updates to the mounted Windows image?

   a. /Get-AppInfo

   b. /Get-Apps

   c. /Add-package

   d. /Check-apps

10. What tool would you use to add system components to a Windows 7 image?

    a. ImageX /config

    b. OCSetup

    c. DISM /Add-package

    d. DISM /Get-AppPatches

11. Which of the following are new technologies first offered with WDS in Windows 7 and Windows Server 2008 R2? (Choose two.)

   a. The ability to deploy new computers in a workgroup environment

   b. The ability to install Windows 7 computers at a remote location across a wide area network (WAN)

   c. Support for Windows PE and the .wim format

   d. The ability to deploy virtual hard disk (.vhd) images during an unattended installation

12. You are planning to deploy 10 new computers on your network, which is configured as a workgroup. What technology should you use to simplify your task?

   a. ImageX and DISM

   b. Remote Installation Services (RIS)

   c. Windows Deployment Services (WDS) in Transport Server mode

   d. Windows Deployment Services (WDS) in Deployment Server mode

13. You are deploying Windows 7 to a series of target computers, and you want the installation to start at each computer when a user turns it on, without the need to press any keys or enter data. What should you do? (Choose two.)

   a. Specify the PXE Boot Policy option in the Boot tab of the WDS server's Properties dialog box.

   b. Ensure that the target computer's BIOS has a hard disk boot option.

   c. Specify a default boot image that will be deployed from the Boot tab of the WDS server's Properties dialog box.

   d. Copy the Default.wim file to a shared network location accessible by each target computer.

14. The `Unattend.xml` file you are using for unattended installation of Windows 7 contains a syntax error that you failed to detect when proofreading. Which of the following is most likely to occur when you attempt to install the first computer with this file?

   a. The computer selects a default installation option.

   b. The computer displays a screen from the Setup wizard, asking the user to enter the desired option.

   c. The computer reboots at the point where the syntax error occurs and Windows installation does not proceed further.

   d. The computer hangs at the point where the syntax error occurs and Windows installation does not proceed further.

15. You are the desktop technician for a company that operates an Active Directory Domain Services (AD DS) domain. You are using a domain computer to prepare a Windows 7 deployment image with Sysprep. What happens?

   a. The computer is automatically removed from the domain before the image is prepared.

   b. Sysprep asks if you want to remove the computer from the domain.

   c. Sysprep returns an error and the process halts.

   d. Image preparation proceeds as usual without problems.

Foundation Topics

Planning a Windows 7 Deployment

Whatever the size of the organization you work for, it can be a daunting task if you are faced with the prospect of installing or upgrading Windows 7 on each computer in the company. Before you begin to capture and deploy system images, you must understand the tools and concepts Microsoft makes available to facilitate the deployment process, whether you are rolling out a few dozen or several thousand computers.

A deployment process begins with the creation of answer files (Unattend.xml or Autounattend.xml), which are files that customize the components of installation within a single file. Microsoft provides the Windows System Image Manager (Windows SIM), which facilitates the process of creating an answer file. Table 5-2 introduces the core Windows deployment technologies that are discussed in this chapter.

Table 5-2   Windows Deployment Technologies

Tools	Description
Windows SIM	A tool that facilitates the creation or editing of answer files used to deploy Windows 7. The computer on which you install Windows SIM is normally termed the technician computer.
Answer file	An XML file that scripts the answers normally provided for questions asked by the Setup Wizard during Windows installation. The Windows 7 answer file is normally called Unattend.xml.
Windows image	A compressed file in the .wim format that includes the files and folders required to duplicate a Windows installation on a disk volume. A .wim file can include multiple Windows images.
Windows Automated Installation Kit (AIK)	A series of tools and documentation provided by Microsoft that facilitates the customization and deployment of computers running Windows 7 or Windows Server 2008 R2.
Windows Preinstallation Environment (Windows PE)	A minimal operating system that assists you in preparing a computer for installing and deploying Windows. This is the primary image installation agent used with the Windows AIK.
Windows Deployment Services (WDS)	A server-based deployment tool that helps you to set up remote client computers without the need to be physically present at each computer.

Table 5-2   Windows Deployment Technologies

Tools	Description
ImageX	A command-line tool that copies .wim files and assists their use in other technologies such as WDS. This tool assists original equipment manufacturers (OEMs) and companies in capturing, modifying, and applying file-based disk images during the deployment process.
Sysprep	The tool that images a Windows computer for deployment purposes. Sysprep removes system-specific information such as the security identifier (SID) so that you can capture and deploy the Windows image.
Windows Recovery Environment (Windows RE)	A diagnostic and recovery tool included with Windows PE. You can also use Window RE to build a custom system recovery solution.

NOTE   In most cases, the answer file is called Unattend.xml. Some answer files can include destructive actions including disk partitioning. In these cases, you must rename the answer file as Autounattend.xml in the windowsPE and offineServicing configuration passes. Typically, you would use Autounattend.xml when using the Windows 7 DVD-ROM together with an answer file supplied on a USB flash drive or floppy disk. For more information on using answer files with Windows Setup, refer to "Methods for Running Windows Setup" at http://technet.microsoft.com/en-us/library/cc749415(WS.10).aspx.

NOTE   For more information on Windows AIK and deployment of Windows images, refer to "Step-by-Step: Basic Windows Deployment for IT Professionals" at http://technet.microsoft.com/en-us/library/dd349348(WS.10).aspx.

Understanding Windows Images

First introduced with Windows Vista, a Windows image file is a compressed file with a .wim extension that is used in the deployment of Windows 7 operating systems to multiple computers. These files use compression and single-instance storage to reduce the file size significantly, thereby optimizing their storage and network transport capabilities. The single-instance storage feature ensures that only one physical copy of each file is stored for each instance of that file in the image. A single .wim file can contain multiple images so that you can deploy customized Windows installations from the same file.

As shown in Figure 5-1, a .wim file can contain the following six types of information:

Figure 5-1   The structure of a `.wim` file containing two images.

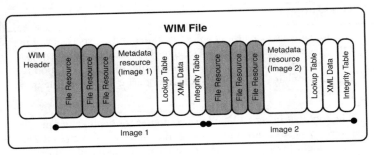

- **WIM Header:** Defines the file's contents, with pointers to the locations of other components as well as file attributes, including version, size, and compression types.

- **File Resources:** A series of packages containing captured data (such as source files).

- **Metadata Resource:** Contains file metadata such as directory structure and file attributes. Each image in the `.wim` file contains its own metadata resource.

- **Lookup Table:** Points to the memory location of metadata resource files.

- **XML Data:** Contains additional data regarding the image.

- **Integrity Table:** Contains a security hash that verifies an image's integrity when it is applied.

NOTE   For further information on `.wim` files, refer to Windows Imaging File Format (WIM) at http://www.microsoft.com/downloads/details.aspx?FamilyId=184706A3-6E05-4D9D-A034-830F4290EE42&display-lang=en.

Understanding Windows PE

Prior to Vista, Windows used MS-DOS as the preinstallation environment that initialized the computer and presented the initial setup screens at the beginning of installation. Windows Vista and Windows 7, along with Windows Server 2008 R2, employ Windows PE as a startup environment that boots the computer and displays the initial graphical user interface (GUI) that asks for initial input. Windows PE is a minimal version of a 32-bit operating system designed to facilitate the deployment of a Windows 7 image to multiple computers. Windows PE also enables the Preboot eXecution Environment (PXE) that enables a computer to access an image across the network for installation purposes. Furthermore, you can use Windows PE to access the Startup Repair Tool and other diagnostics testing if a Windows 7 computer is unable to start properly. We discuss the Startup Repair

Tool and these diagnostics in Chapter 18, "Configuring System and File Recovery."

You can get Windows PE from the Windows PE kit. It is also included with the Windows Automated Installation Kit (AIK) and the Windows OEM Preinstallation Kit. Windows PE includes separate 32-bit and 64-bit Windows 7 versions. Ensure that you have the latest edition of Windows 7 versions.

Windows PE enables access to partitions formatted with the FAT or NTFS file systems, and it enables communication to devices on the network. Windows PE also detects and installs Plug and Play (PnP)–compatible hardware devices. Table 5-3 describes several of the more important command-line tools available with Windows PE.

Table 5-3   Windows PE Command-Line Tools

Tools	Purpose
BCDBoot	Initializes the boot configuration data (BCD) store, enabling you to copy boot environment files to the new computer.
Bootsect	Creates and configures boot sectors and enables switching between BOOTMGR and NTLDR.
DiskPart	Creates and configures disk partitions and volumes.
DISM	Enumerates, installs, uninstalls, configures, and updates system images. You can use this tool to apply updates, drivers, and language packs to a Windows image.
Drvload	Installs and manages drivers.
ImageX	Captures and applies Windows images.
Net	Enables network communication and manages users and services.
Netcfg	Configures network access.
Wpeinit	Initializes Windows PE at boot time.

To use Windows PE, you first need to create a CD/DVD that enables you to capture an image of the master computer to be stored on a shared folder accessible to the target computers. The process involves creating a CD/DVD from which you can start Windows PE, using this CD to start Windows PE, using ImageX to capture the installation image, and then copying this image to a network share. The following steps show you how to complete these tasks:

Step 1.   At the technician computer, run the following commands to create a local Windows PE build directory:

```
cd \Program Files\Windows AIK\Tools\PETools
Copype.cmd arch destination
```

where *arch* refers to x86, amd64, or ia64, and destination is the path to a local folder; for example:

```
Copype.cmd x86 c:\WinPE_x86
```

Step 2.   Copy additional tools as required to the local folder, for example:

```
Copy "C:\Program files\Windows AIK\Tools\x86\imagex.exe"
C:\WinPE_x86\iso\subfolder
```

where *subfolder* refers to whatever subfolder structure is required for supporting the tools.

Step 3.   Use Notepad or other text editor to create a configuration file named wimscript.ini, which instructs ImageX to exclude specific files during the capture procedure. This file contains the following statements:

```
[ExclusionList]
ntfs.log
hiberfil.sys
pagefile.sys
"System Volume Information"
RECYCLER
Windows\CSC
[CompressionExclusionList]
*.mp3
*.zip
*.cab
\WINDOWS\inf\*.pnf
```

Step 4.   Save this file to the same location specified in step 2. This enables ImageX to detect this file automatically.

Step 5.   Use the Oscdimg.exe tool to create an ISO image file, for example:

```
cd \Program Files\Windows AIK\Tools\PETools
Oscdimg -n -bc:\winpe_x86\etfsboot.com c:\winpe_x86\ISO
c:\winpe_x86\winpex86.iso
```

Step 6.   Use the Windows CD-writing wizard or a third-party CD burning application to burn the ISO image file to a blank CD-ROM.

Having created the Windows PE CD-ROM, you can now start the master computer and copy its image to a network share for deployment by following these steps:

Step 1.   At the master computer, insert the Windows PE CD-ROM and restart the computer.

Step 2.   Windows PE opens a command prompt. To capture an image of the master installation, type the following:

```
D:\Tools\Imagex.exe /compress fast /capture C: C:\Myimage.wim "my
    Windows 7 Install" /verify
```

Step 3. On the network server, create and share a folder to hold the image, for example:

```
\\Server1\Windows_installation\Images
```

Step 4. At the master computer, type the following to copy the image to the share:

```
net use z: \\Server1\Windows_installation\Images
copy c:\Myimage.wim z:
```

You can use this image when deploying Windows 7 manually to other computers. This procedure is covered later in this chapter.

> **NOTE** Some of these tools are also available in a default Windows installation. Several additional tools are available. For more information, refer to "Command-Line Tools Technical Reference" at http://technet.microsoft.com/en-us/library/dd799280(WS.10).aspx. ImageX includes a large set of subcommands, which are described at "ImageX Command-Line Options" at http://technet.microsoft.com/en-us/library/cc749447(WS.10).aspx. For additional information on Windows PE overall, refer to "Windows PE Technical Reference" at http://technet.microsoft.com/en-us/library/cc749538(WS.10).aspx and "What is Windows PE?" at http://technet.microsoft.com/en-us/library/cc766093(WS.10).aspx.

Understanding Answer Files

Typically called `Unattend.xml` or `Autounattend.xml` (as explained earlier in this chapter), the answer file was first used with Windows Vista and replaces the `Unattend.txt` file that was used with Windows XP and older operating systems. You can include setup options (such as partitioning and formatting of disks), which Windows image to install, and the product key that should be used. You can also include installation-specific items (such as usernames, display settings, and Internet Explorer favorites).

Windows System Image Manager (SIM) enables you to create answer files from information included in a Windows image (`.wim`) file and a catalog (`.clg`) file. You can also include component settings and software packages to be installed on the computers with Windows 7. The following are several actions you can accomplish using SIM:

- Create new answer files and edit existing ones

- Validate the information in an answer file against a `.wim` file

- View and modify the component configurations in a `.wim` file

- Include additional drivers, applications, updates, or component packages in the answer file

You can use SIM to create unattended answer files. You should have two computers, as follows:

- A computer from which you install SIM and create the answer files. Microsoft refers to this computer as the *technician computer*.

- A computer without an operating system but equipped with a DVD-ROM drive, network card, and floppy drive (or USB support). Microsoft refers to this computer as the *reference computer*.

Understanding Configuration Passes

When you use an unattended installation answer file for installing Windows, settings are applied at various stages of the setup process that Microsoft calls *configuration passes*. Table 5-4 describes the different configuration passes used in setting up Windows 7 and Windows Server 2008 R2.

Table 5-4 Configuration Passes

Configuration Pass	Description
1 Windows PE	Configures Windows PE options and basic Windows Setup options. Use this configuration pass to add any drivers required for Windows PE to access the local or network hard drive. Also use this configuration pass to add any basic information such as a product key.
2 offlineServicing	Applies updates including packages, software fixes, language packs, and security updates to the Windows image.
3 specialize	Creates and applies system-specific information such as network, domain, and international settings.
4 generalize	Used only when running the sysprep /generalize command, enables you to configure this command for removing system-specific settings such as the SID.
5 auditSystem	Used only when booting to Audit mode after running sysprep, processes unattended Setup settings before a user logs on.
6 auditUser	Used only when booting to Audit mode after running sysprep, processes unattended Setup settings after a user logs on.
7 oobeSystem	Applies Windows settings before Windows Welcome starts.

NOTE For more information on configuration passes and their usage, refer to "How Configuration Passes Work" at http://technet.microsoft.com/en-us/library/cc749307(WS.10).aspx.

Creating an Answer File

To use SIM to create the files required for performing unattended installations, you first need to download and install the Windows AIK from Microsoft and copy the appropriate files from the Windows 7 DVD-ROM. You should perform these steps on a computer running Windows XP Service Pack 2 or later, Windows Server 2003 Service Pack 1 or later, Windows Vista, or Windows 7. Use the following steps to download and install the AIK.

Step 1.   Open Internet Explorer, navigate to http://www.microsoft.com/downloads/en/confirmation.aspx?familyId=696dd665-9f76-4177-a811-39c26d3b3b34&displayLang=en, and follow the instructions provided to save the Windows AIK image file to an appropriate location on your hard drive. You can also search for "automated installation kit" from Microsoft Live Search.

> **CAUTION**   AIK is a large download. If you do not have a high-speed Internet connection, be prepared for an overnight download.

Step 2.   Use third-party DVD-burning software or the native software included with Windows 7 to burn the image file to a blank DVD-ROM disc.

Step 3.   Insert the DVD-ROM disc into the technician computer. The AutoPlay program should appear. Click **Run StartCD.exe**. If not, navigate to the DVD-ROM folder and double-click the `StartCD.exe` file.

Step 4.   You should receive a User Account Control dialog box. Click **Continue** to display the Welcome screen shown in Figure 5-2.

Figure 5-2   Installing the Windows Automated Installation Kit.

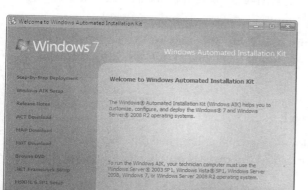

Step 5.   Select **Windows AIK Setup** from the list of options on the left side of this window.

Step 6.   The Windows Automated Installation Kit Setup Wizard starts with a Welcome page. Click **Next**.

Step 7.   On the License Agreement page, click **I Agree** and then click **Next**.

Step 8.   On the Select Installation Folder page, accept the folder provided or type the path to an appropriate folder and then click **Next**.

Step 9.   On the Confirm Installation page, click **Next** and then wait while the AIK is installed. This process takes several minutes.

Step 10.   When the completion page appears, click **Close**.

After you have installed the AIK, a folder is present on the technician computer, from which you can create answer files. To create an answer file based on the default Windows image found on the Windows 7 DVD, use the following procedure:

Step 1.   Insert the Windows 7 DVD-ROM. If you receive an Install Windows screen, click **Cancel**.

Step 2.   If you receive an AutoPlay window, click the **Open folder to view files** option. If not, open a Computer (or My Computer on a Windows XP or Windows Server 2003 computer) window, navigate to the Windows 7 DVD-ROM, right-click, and select **Open**.

Step 3.   Open the Sources folder, navigate to the install.wim file, right-click, and then choose **Copy**.

Step 4.   Open a Computer (or My Computer) window, navigate to a suitable location, and create a folder to hold the installation files; for example, C:\Windows_Install.

Step 5.   Open this folder and use Ctrl-V to paste the install.wim file into it. This will take several minutes.

Step 6.   Click **Start > All Programs**. In the program list that appears, click **Microsoft Windows AIK** and then click **Windows System Image Manager**.

Step 7.   In Windows System Image Manager shown in Figure 5-3, click **File > Select Windows Image**.

Step 8.   In the Select a Windows Image dialog box shown in Figure 5-4, navigate to the folder you copied the install.wim file to, select this file, and then click **Open**.

Step 9.   In the Select an Image dialog box shown in Figure 5-5, select the edition of Windows 7 that you want to create an answer file for.

Figure 5-3   You need to select a Windows image file to create an answer file.

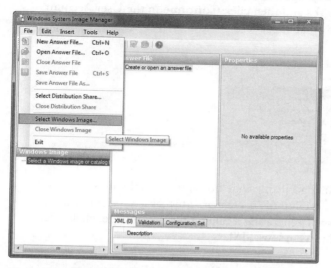

Figure 5-4   Selecting the **install.wim** file.

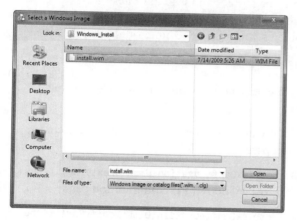

Figure 5-5   Selecting a Windows 7 image.

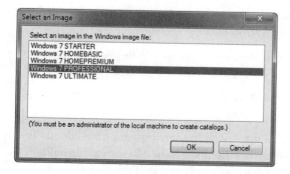

Step 10.   SIM displays the message shown in Figure 5-6, asking you to create a catalog file. Click **Yes** and then click **Continue** in the User Account Control dialog box that appears.

Figure 5-6   You are asked to create a catalog file.

Step 11.   A Generating Catalog File message box appears as the files are processed and the catalog file is created. This takes several minutes. When the process of generating a catalog file is complete, click **OK**. You are returned to Windows SIM.

NOTE   If you receive a message that Windows SIM was unable to generate a catalog, refer to "Understanding Windows Image Files and Catalog Files" at http://technet.microsoft.com/en-us/library/dd744249(WS.10).aspx. This page contains information on some of the problems you might encounter and possible workarounds.

Step 12.   In the Windows Image pane, expand the Component node to display the available components.

Step 13.   Right-click each of the following components in turn and add them to the indicated configuration pass:

— `Microsoft-Windows-Setup\DiskConfiguration\Disk\CreatePartitions\Create Partition`; add to 1 Windows PE configuration pass.

— `Microsoft-Windows-Setup\DiskConfiguration\Disk\ModifyPartitions\Modify Partition`; add to 1 Windows PE configuration pass.

— `Microsoft-Windows-Setup\ImageInstall\OSImage\InstallTo`; add to 1 Windows PE configuration pass.

— `Microsoft-Windows-Setup\UserData`; add to 1 Windows PE configuration pass.

— `Microsoft-Windows-Shell-Setup\OOBE`; add to 7 oobeSystem configuration pass.

Step 14.   The Answer File pane should display all the settings you have added. To complete the creation of an answer file for a basic Windows 7 installation, select and configure the settings contained in Table 5-5.

Table 5-5   Windows Settings for a Basic Answer File

Component	Value
`Microsoft-Windows-Setup\` `DiskConfiguration`	`WillShowUI = OnError`

`Microsoft-Windows-Setup\`
`DiskConfiguration\Disk`
	`DiskID = 0`
	
	`WillWipeDisk = True`

`Microsoft-Windows-Setup\`
`DiskConfiguration\Disk\`
`CreatePartitions\CreatePartition`
	`Extend = False`
	`Order = 1`
	`Size = 50,000` (creates a 50 GB partition)
	`Type = Primary`

`Microsoft-Windows-Setup\`
`DiskConfiguration\Disk\`
`ModifyPartitions\ModifyPartition`
	`Active = True`
	`Extend = False`
	`Format = NTFS`
	`Label = OS_Install`
	`Letter = C`
	`Order = 1`
	`PartitionID = 1`

`Microsoft-Windows-Setup\` `ImageInstall\OSImage\`	`WillShowUI = OnError`
`Microsoft-Windows-Setup\` `ImageInstall\OSImage\InstallTo`	`DiskID = 0` `PartitionID = 1`
`Microsoft-Windows-Setup\UserData`	`AcceptEula = True`
`Microsoft-Windows-Setup\UserData\` `ProductKey`	`Key = <product_key>` `WillShowUI = OnError`

`Microsoft-Windows-Shell-Setup\OOBE`	`ProtectYourPC = 1`
	
	`NetworkLocation = Work`

`Microsoft-Windows-Deployment\Reseal`	`ForceShutdownNow = false`
	
	`Mode = Audit`

Table 5-5   Windows Settings for a Basic Answer File

Component	Value
Microsoft-Windows-Shell-Setup\ AutoLogon	Enabled = true
	LogonCount = 5
	Username = Administrator

Step 15.   Validate the settings you have configured by selecting **Validate Answer File** from the Tools menu.

Step 16.   If you receive an error message, double-click the message in the Messages pane, correct the error, and then repeat step 15.

Step 17.   When all errors have been corrected, click **File > Save Answer File**. Save the answer file as `Autounattend.xml` and then copy this file to a removable flash drive or floppy disk.

CAUTION   It is possible to edit an answer file by using a text editor, such as Notepad. However, you must take care when editing answer files. When using Notepad to edit the answer file or UDF file, you must ensure that you follow the rules of syntax exactly; otherwise, unattended installations will either fail or prompt the user for additional information.

Using the Answer Files to Perform an Unattended Installation

Having created the answer files as described in the previous procedure, it is easy to run the automated installation of Windows 7 on a new computer (often called the *target computer*) without an operating system, as shown in the following steps:

Step 1.   Start the target computer and insert the Windows 7 DVD-ROM and the flash drive or floppy disk you created in the previous procedure.

Step 2.   To run `Setup.exe`, press **Ctrl-Alt-Delete**. The computer restarts and searches the flash drive or floppy disk for the `Autounattend.xml` file.

Step 3.   Setup should proceed automatically and install Windows 7 with all customizations you have previously configured.

NOTE   If you start the computer from a floppy disk, do not forget to remove it before the first restart; otherwise, you will receive an error message. If an error message appears, remove the disk and press **Ctrl-Alt-Delete**.

Capturing a System Image

The process of capturing system images utilizes the Sysprep utility that prepares an installed computer so that it can be duplicated as an image. This tool removes the original SIDs from the image, as well as other machine-specific information such as event logs and user settings.

Unlike the situation in Windows XP, the Windows 7 DVD already contains an image suitable for deployment to any computer. You can either deploy this image as-is or prepare an image of the computer you installed in the previous section for deployment to the destination computers.

Such a procedure can save considerable time when you are performing a large rollout. In addition, should you encounter problems with a computer at a later time, you can re-image the computer from the disk image that you originally created to return the computer to a baseline configuration.

Understanding the System Preparation Tool

When you first install Windows 7, Sysprep is automatically installed into the Windows\System32\Sysprep folder. To use Sysprep, you begin with a reference computer on which you have installed Windows 7 together with any applications and updates that you want to deploy to the destination computers.

NOTE   Computers using the newer 64-bit ia64 or amd64 architecture possess a %systemroot%\sysWOW64 folder that contains 64-bit version of all the various tools and drivers. When using a 64-bit computer, make sure you access the versions contained in this folder because these computers contain both a system32 and a sysWOW64 folder; if you are using a 32-bit computer, only the system32 folder is present.

Certain situations are *not* supported for the use of Sysprep. In these instances, you might be able to use WDS if your network meets the requirements for using WDS, as discussed later in this chapter:

- **Upgrades:** You cannot use Sysprep for upgrading computers running older versions of Windows to Windows 7. You also cannot use Sysprep for creating an image of a computer that was upgraded to Windows 7.

- **Production Environment:** Use of Sysprep for creating an image of a computer that has been used in a production environment is not recommended. In other words, you should use a freshly installed version of Windows 7 when preparing the computer to be imaged.

- **OEM Installation Image:** Microsoft does not support the use of Sysprep for imaging a computer that was originally set up from original equipment manufacturer installation images or media.

- **Default User Profile Has Been Overwritten:** You should not use Sysprep if you have copied another user profile over the default user profile.

Table 5-6 describes the optional switches provided with Sysprep.

Table 5-6   Sysprep Parameters

Parameter	Purpose
/audit	Runs Sysprep.exe in audit mode, which enables you to add drivers and applications as required for deployment. You can also verify proper hardware and software installation.
/quiet	Runs Sysprep.exe without user interaction.
/generalize	Removes system-specific information such as the security identifier (SID) and product activation information so that these items become unique on each newly installed computer.
/oobe	Runs Windows Welcome and the oobeSystem configuration pass on the next reboot. This is the default option, and should be used for deploying the image to end users.
/reboot	Forces the computer to reboot after completion of disk imaging.
/unattend: file_name	Specifies the name of an answer file, whose settings will be applied at the next reboot.
/shutdown	Forces the computer to shut down after Sysprep completes.

Using Sysprep to Prepare a System for Capture

Creation of the image for Sysprep deployment involves preparation of the computer and running the Sysprep.exe utility, followed by shutting down the system and running the disk-imaging program. You can run Sysprep from either the command line or in GUI mode. To use GUI mode, proceed as follows:

Step 1.   On the computer you installed in the previous section, navigate to the %systemroot%\system32\sysprep folder and double-click **Sysprep.exe**. Sysprep displays the dialog box shown in Figure 5-7.

Figure 5-7   The Sysprep dialog box presents options for system cleanup and shutdown.

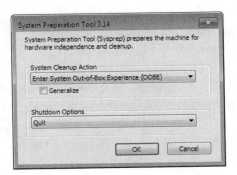

Step 2.   Choose one of the following cleanup actions. Also choose the **Generalize** option if needed to remove the SID, event logs, and product activation information:

—   **Enter System Out-of-Box Experience (OOBE):** Enables the computer to start in welcome mode. This is how users should receive the deployed computer.

—   **Enter System Audit Mode:** Enables the computer to start in audit mode so that you can add drivers or applications. You can also use this mode to test the installation before deploying it. On rebooting, Sysprep restarts automatically.

Step 3.   Choose one of the following shutdown options:

—   **Quit:** Closes Sysprep without shutting down the computer

—   **Reboot:** Reboots the computer after running Sysprep

—   **Shutdown:** Shuts the computer down after running Sysprep, but does not reboot it

Step 4.   Click **OK**. You receive a message that Sysprep is working. When finished, this message disappears if you have selected the **Quit** option. Otherwise, the computer is shut down or rebooted.

If you run Sysprep from the command line, you can use the parameters previously defined in Table 5-6 to perform the same actions. For example, to enable the computer to restart in welcome mode after removing the SID and activation information, and shut the computer down automatically after imaging, you would use the following command:

```
C:\Windows\System32\Sysprep.exe /oobe /generalize /shutdown
```

You can store the image created by this procedure on a CD-ROM, DVD-ROM, USB thumb drive, or a shared folder that is accessible to the target computers. It is also good practice to perform a test deployment and ensure that the operating system and all applications are properly installed and configured before deploying the image to production computers. Should any problems occur, you can reconfigure the source computer and re-create the image.

When you reboot the computer after having run Sysprep, The Set Up Windows Wizard steps you through the process of setting up your computer, similar to that of a new Windows installation as discussed in Chapter 2, "Installing Windows 7." You are asked to select your language, time, currency, and keyboard format. You are also asked to accept the license terms, and then you are asked to provide the same information requested after the final reboot during a clean installation as previously illustrated in Figures 2-5 to 2-8.

> **NOTE**   For more information on Sysprep and its available options, refer to "Sysprep Technical Reference" at http://technet.microsoft.com/en-us/library/dd744263(WS.10).aspx.

Creating a WIM File

You have already seen how to copy a default WIM file for use in creating an answer file. You can also use the ImageX command to create a WIM file containing one or more Windows images that can even include both 32- and 64-bit images within the same WIM file. However, you should create separate architecture-specific WIM files for different system architectures; for example, x64-based and Itanium-based 64-bit images should be in separate WIM files. To create a WIM file that includes both 32- and 64-bit images, follow these steps:

Step 1.   Copy the entire 32-bit Windows distribution files from the Windows 7 DVD-ROM to a temporary folder on your computer.

Step 2.   Copy the 64-bit `Install.wim` file to a separate temporary folder on your computer.

Step 3.   From a command prompt, use the `ImageX /export` command to export each 64-bit Windows image to the `Install.wim` file in the Windows distribution.

Step 4.   Repeat this command for each Windows image to be added to the `Install.wim` file.

For example, you would use the following command to copy the distribution to `C:\WindowsDist` and the 64-bit `Install.wim` file to `C:\Windows64`, you would execute the following command:

```
Imagex /export "C:\windows64\install.wim" 1
"C:\windowsdist\sources\install.wim" "Pearson 64-bit Image"
```

In this command, the first file path specifies the file path that contains the image to be copied, the number that follows references a specific volume within the WIM file (recall from Figure 5-1 that each WIM file can include separate installation images), the second file path specifies the WIM file that receives the image copy, and the final parameter provides a name for the image that users will see. Note that it is important to name this image so that users know that it is a 64-bit image.

Automated Image Capture

After you have used Sysprep to prepare your reference computer for capture, you can use ImageX to capture the contents of the generalized image for deployment to new computers. You can use Windows PE or another system partition for this task. Use the following command:

```
Imagex /capture image_path image_file "name" {"description"} {/boot ¦ /check
```

```
¦ /compress[type] ¦ /config ¦ /flags "EditionID" ¦ /norpfix ¦ /scroll ¦
/verify}
```

Table 5-7 describes the parameters used by the ImageX /capture command.

Table 5-7   ImageX /capture Parameters

Parameter	Purpose
image_path	Specifies the name and location of the volume image to be captured.
image_file	Specifies the name and location of the new .wim file.
"name"	Specifies the name of the new .wim file. This value, including the quote marks, is required.
"description"	An optional descriptor text for the new .wim file. The quote marks are required.
/boot	Marks a volume image as bootable. Available only for Windows PE images. Within a single .wim file, you can mark only one volume image as bootable.
/check	Checks the integrity of the .wim file.
/compress[type]	Specifies the type of compression used during capture. Specify maximum for the best compression (but takes the longest time), fast for faster compression but with larger files, or none for no compression (but fastest capture rate).
/config	Specifies the name and location of the configuration file (.ini).
/flags "EditionID"	Specifies the version of Windows to be captured.
/norpfix	Disables reparse point tag fixup.
/scroll	Scrolls output for redirection.
/verify	Checks file resources for errors and duplications, for verification purposes.

For example, use the following command syntax to capture a file-based image of Windows 7 Ultimate named ult.wim and located on the e: drive. The capture is to be stored in the f:\images folder and named Drive E. It is to include maximum compression, integrity checking, and verification.

```
Imagex /capture e: f:\images\ult.wim "Drive E" /verify /compress maximum
/flags "Ultimate" /check
```

NOTE To obtain more information on the ImageX command, open a command prompt and type **imagex /?.**

Manual Image Capture

After you have prepared the system using Sysprep as described earlier in this chapter, you can capture the image for manual deployment. Follow these steps to capture the image manually:

Step 1. Use bootable Windows PE media to start the computer on which you used Sysprep. For Unified Extensible Firmware Interface (UEFI)–based computers, you must use the EFI boot-mode option to start Windows PE.

Step 2. At the Windows PE command prompt, type **diskpart.**

Step 3. At the Diskpart prompt, type **list disk** and then note the number of the disk to be used.

Step 4. Type **select disk** *n*, where **n** is the desired disk number obtained in the previous command.

Step 5. Type **list volume.** Note the partition information provided. If any partition to be captured doesn't have a drive letter, use the **select volume** and **assign letter** subcommands to assign an appropriate drive letter.

Step 6. Type **cd c:\windows\system32** to change to the folder containing the ImageX utility.

Step 7. Capture images for each customized partition. For example, if the Windows partition is on drive c: and the system partition is on drive d:, you would use the following commands:

```
imagex /capture c: c:\win-partition.wim "Windows partition"
imagex /capture d: c:\sys-partition.wim "System partition"
```

Step 8. Use the **Net Use** command to connect to the distribution share and then copy the WIM files to the network share. For example, if the distribution share is called **Dist** and is stored on a server named **Server1**, you would use the following commands:

```
net use z: \\server1\dist
copy c:\win-partition.wim z:\
copy c:\sys-partition.wim z:\
```

Use the following steps to apply the images you have captured:

Step 1. Use bootable Windows PE media to start the computer. For UEFI-based computers, you must use the EFI boot-mode option in the EFI shell to start Windows PE.

Step 2. Connect to the network share containing images being deployed. For example, you can type **net use z: \\server1\dist**.

Step 3. From the Windows PE command prompt, type **diskpart**.

Step 4. At the Diskpart prompt, type **select disk 0**.

Step 5. Type **list volume** and note the partition information displayed. If any partition to be captured doesn't have a drive letter, use the **select volume** and **assign letter** subcommands to assign an appropriate drive letter.

Step 6. Type **cd c:\windows\system32** to change to the folder containing the ImageX utility.

Step 7. Use ImageX to apply the desired partition images. For example, if you have system and Windows partition images on the z: drive, you would use the following commands to apply the Windows partition to drive c: and the system partition to drive d:

```
imagex /apply c: z:\win-partition.wim 1 c:
imagex /apply d: z:\sys-partition.wim 2 d:
```

Step 8. Restart the computer and log on.

> **NOTE** WDS also provides the Image Capture Wizard, which enables you to capture a Windows 7 installation, including installed applications, to a .wim file that you can deploy to target computers. We discuss WDS in detail later in this chapter.

Preparing System Images for Deployment

After you have created your system images, you might need to perform other tasks before deploying the images. These tasks can include inserting applications, drivers, and updates into the images, and configuring tasks that will run after the image has been deployed to the target computers.

Understanding the Deployment Image Servicing and Management Utility

Deployment Image Servicing and Management (DISM) is a command-line utility that enables you to configure Windows images before deploying them. It enables you to install, configure, enumerate, update, and uninstall applications, drivers, Windows features, and international settings. However, it does not enable you to capture new Windows images. You can also use subsets of the DISM commands for working with a running operating system. Furthermore, you can use DISM to service Windows PE images or virtual hard disk (VHD) images. We look at the use of DISM for servicing VHD images in Chapter 6, "Configuring Virtual Hard Disks."

DISM is installed with Windows 7 and distributed in Windows OEM Preinstallation Kit (Windows OPK) and Windows AIK. Besides Windows 7, you can use DISM to service Windows Vista (SP1 or later), Windows Server 2008, or Windows Server 2008 R2 images.

The following are some of the tasks you can do with DISM:

- Add, remove, and enumerate packages and drivers.

- Enable or disable Windows features.

- Apply changes based on the `offlineServicing` section of an `unattend.xml` answer file.

- Configure international settings.

- Upgrade a Windows image to a higher edition.

- Prepare a Windows PE image.

- Take advantage of better logging.

- Service all platforms (32-bit, 64-bit, and Itanium), service a 32-bit image from a 64-bit host, and service a 64-bit image from a 32-bit host.

- Utilize old Package Manager Scripts.

NOTE   For more information about the DISM program, refer to "Deployment Image Servicing and Management Technical Reference" at http://technet.microsoft.com/en-us/library/dd744256(WS.10).aspx and references contained therein.

DISM utilizes various platform technologies that are generally associated with actions taken to update or configure an offline Windows image. In a few cases, they might even perform configuration actions with an online (running) Windows operating system. Table 5-8 summarizes these technologies.

Table 5-8   DISM Technologies

Purpose	Technology
Adding, removing, or enumerating driver `.inf` files	Device Management and Installation (DMI).
Adding, removing, or enumerating `.cab` or `.msu` installation package files	A `.cab` file is a library of compressed files stored as a single package. These files are used with Component Based Servicing (CBS) packages.
	Microsoft Update Standalone Package (MSU) files are associated with the Windows Update Stand-Alone Installer technology.

Applying settings in an unattended answer file DMI and CBS.	Settings Management Infrastructure (SMI).
Modifying Windows image **.wim** files	Windows Image File Format (WIM).
Creation and modification of Windows PE images	PEimg technology (a depreciated Windows Vista command-line tool).
Changing the language, locale, fonts, and input settings within a Windows image	Intlcfg technology (a depreciated Windows Vista command-line tool).
Upgrading Windows to a higher edition	CBS and Windows Anytime Upgrade.
Checking the applicability of an application update	Microsoft Windows Installer and Anytime Upgrade.

Working with DISM

DISM contains a large range of command-line options, the most important of which are covered here and in the sections to come. The basic syntax for a DISM command is as follows:

```
DISM {/image:image_path ¦ /online} [dism_options] {servicing_command}
[servicing_argument]
```

In this command, *image_path* specifies the path to the Windows image being worked on, */online* specifies servicing a running computer. [dism_options] specifies optional parameters for items such as output format, log paths, suppressing automatic reboots, and so on. The {servicing_command} [*servicing_argument*] section of the command specifies the action(s) to be taken, along with any arguments associated with these actions.

Before you can perform any action on a Windows image file, you must mount it. Table 5-9 summarizes the DISM options associated with mounting an image.

Table 5-9 DISM Mounting Options

Option	Description
/Mount-Wim	Mounts a WIM image. Specify the path to the WIM image and the index number and directory to which the image will be mounted.
/Commit-Wim	Saves changes to the mounted image without unmounting it.
/Unmount-Wim	Unmounts a mounted WIM image. Use the /Commit keyword with this command to save changes, or the /Discard keyword to discard the changes.

`/Remount-wim`	Remounts a mounted WIM image that has become inaccessible.
`/Cleanup-wim`	Deletes resources from corrupted WIM images.
`/Get-WimInfo`	Provides information on images in a WIM file.
`/Get-MountedWimInfo`	Provides information on mounted WIM images.

NOTE   For additional information and examples of these mounting options, refer to "Deployment Image Servicing and Management Command-Line Options" at http://technet.microsoft.com/en-ca/library/dd744382(WS.10).aspx.

Inserting Applications into System Images

You can use the `/add-package` command of DISM to add application packages and updates to the mounted Windows image. Specify the package path that includes the `.cab` or `.msu` package file to be added to the Windows image. You can add multiple packages on the same command line. The basic command syntax for adding application packages is as follows:

`DISM /image:`*image_path* `/Add-Package /PackagePath:`[*path_to_.cab_file*]

Specify the path to the package file at [*path_to_.cab_file*].

You can also remove packages by using the `/Remove-Package` option in place of `/Add-Package`. Table 5-10 summarizes the more common application packages that you can add using this command.

Table 5-10   Common Application Packages

Package	Description
`WinPE-FONTSupport-Language.cab`	Installs fonts for several international languages. For *language*, specify `ja-jp`, `ko-kr`, `zg-cn`, `zh-hk`, or `zh-tw`.
`WinPE-HTA.cab`	Installs HTML application support.
`WinPE-LegacySetup.cab`	Installs the legacy setup package.
`WinPE-MDAC.cab`	Installs Microsoft Data Access Component (MDAC) support.
`WinPE-Scripting.cab`	Installs Windows Script Host (WSH) support.
`WinPE-Setup.cab`	Installs the main setup package.
`WinPE-SetupClient.cab`	Installs the client setup package, after you've installed the main setup package.
`WinPE-SetupServer.cab`	Installs the server setup package, after you've installed the main setup package.
`WinPE-SRT.cab`	Installs the Windows Recovery Environment component.

Table 5-10 Common Application Packages

Package	Description
WinPE-WDS-Tools.cab	Installs the Windows Deployment Services tools package.
WinPE-WMI.cab	Installs support for Windows Management Instrumentation (WMI).

DISM also provides application servicing commands that check the application status of Windows Installer application patch files (.msp files) of offline images. You can also query these images about installed applications and patch files.

The basic command syntax for servicing applications is as follows:

```
DISM /image:image_path [/Check-AppPatch ¦ /Get-AppPatchInfo ¦ /Get-AppPatches
¦ /Get-AppInfo ¦ Get-Apps]
```

Table 5-11 describes the common application servicing options.

Table 5-11 Common Application Servicing Options

Option	Description
/Check-AppPatch / PatchLocation:<path_to_patch.msp>	Displays information only if the MSP patches are applicable to the offline image. You must specify the path to the patch file. You can specify multiple patch files.
/Get-AppPatchInfo: [/PatchCode:<patch_code_GUID>] [/ProductCode:<product_code_GUID>]	Displays detailed information about installed MSP patches filtered by <patch_code_GUID> and <product_code_GUID>.
/Get-AppPatches: [/ProductCode:<product_code_GUID>]	Displays basic information about all applied MSP patches installed on the offline image.
/Get-AppInfo: [/ProductCode:<product_code_GUID>]	Displays detailed information about a specific Windows Installer application installed within the image.
/Get-Apps	Displays basic information about all Windows Installer applications in the offline image.

Note that the /Get-AppPatches and /Get-AppPatchInfo options apply only to installed .msp patch files. For additional information and examples of these commands, refer to "Application Servicing Command-Line Options" at http://technet.microsoft.com/en-ca/library/dd744370(WS.10).aspx.

You can use the /get-features subcommand of DISM to display the features (applications, updates, and so on) included in the image being serviced and whether they are enabled or disabled in the image being serviced.

Inserting Drivers into System Images

You can use DISM driver servicing commands on an offline image to add and remove drivers based on their INF files. With an online (running) image, you can display a list of drivers added to the system.

The basic command syntax for servicing drivers is as follows:

```
DISM /image:image_path [/Get-Drivers ¦ /Get-DriverInfo ¦ /Add-Driver ¦
/Remove-Driver]
```

The basic command syntax for enumerating drivers on a running system is as follows:

```
DISM /online [/Get-Drivers ¦ /Get-DriverInfo]
```

Table 5-12 describes the driver servicing options.

Table 5-12   Common Driver Servicing Options

Option	Description
/Get-Drivers	Displays basic information about driver packages in the image. Add the /all parameter to display informaton about default drivers and third-party drivers.
/Get-DriverInfo /Driver:{installed_INF_ FileName ¦ path_to_driver.inf}	Displays detailed informaton about a specific driver package. Specify one or more drivers on the same command line, using the path to a driver that is not yet installed, or direct to an installed INF file.
/Add-Driver /Driver:path_to_driver.inf	Adds third-party driver packages to the offline Windows image. Specify the path to the desired driver; if you specify a folder, all driver files in that folder are added.
/Remove-Driver /Driver:path_to_Installed _driver.inf	Removes third-party driver packages from the offline Windows image.

NOTE   For additional information and examples of these commands, refer to "Driver Servicing Command-Line Options" at http://technet.microsoft.com/ en-ca/library/dd799258(WS.10).aspx.

CAUTION   Take care not to remove boot-critical driver packages when using the /Remove-Driver command. Doing so might make the offline image unbootable.

Inserting Updates into System Images

DISM enables you to update one edition of Windows 7 to a higher one. Each Windows 7 image already has packages for each potential target edition contained within it (referred to as *edition-family images*). This enables you to service a single image, and updates will be applied to each edition within the image. Doing so can help reduce the number of images that you need to manage.

The base syntax for inserting updates is as follows:

```
DISM /image:image_path [/Get-CurrentEdition ¦ /Get-TargetEditions ¦ /Set-
Edition ¦ /Set-ProductKey:productKey]
```

Table 5-13 describes the common updating options.

Table 5-13   Common Update Options

Option	Description
/Get-CurrentEdition	Displays the edition of the specified image
/Get-TargetEditions	Lists the Windows editions that the image can be upgraded to
/Set-Edition: target_edition_ID {/ProductKey:product_key}	Upgrades the image to a higher edition, using the specified product key
/Set-ProductKey:product_key	Enters the product key for the current edition if you haven't entered it earlier when upgrading

Configuring Tasks to Run After Deployment

You can use the Windows Optional Component Setup tool (OCSetup.exe) to add system components to a Windows image. This tool installs or removes Component-Based Servicing (CBS) packages online by passing them to the DISM tool for installing or removal. You can also use OCSetup.exe to install or remove Microsoft System Installer (MSI) application packages or CBS or MSI packages that have custom .exe installer files associated with them.

The basic OCSetup.exe command syntax is as follows:

```
Ocsetup.exe component [log:file] [/norestart] [/passive] [/quiet]
[/unattendfile:file] [/uninstall] [/x:parameter]
```

Table 5-14 describes the parameters used with this command.

Table 5-14   OCSetup.exe Parameters

Parameter	Description
component	The name of the component being installed or uninstalled. This name is case sensitive. You can include multiple components separated with semicolons.
/log: file	Specifies a nondefault log file location. If not specified or an invalid path is used, the default log file location (which is the current directory for Windows 7 or Windows Server 2008 R2) will be used.
/norestart	Does not reboot the computer after component installation, even if required.
/passive	Unattended mode, which displays installation progress only.
/quiet	Quiet mode, which provides no user interaction.
/unattendfile: file	Specifies an unattended answer file.
/uninstall	Uninstalls the specified component.
/x:parameter	Additional configuration parameters used when installing a component that requires a custom installer. OCSetup.exe passes these parameters to the installer.

NOTE   For more information on the OCSetup.exe command, refer to "OCSetup Command-Line Options" at http://technet.microsoft.com/en-us/library/dd799247(WS.10).aspx.

TIP   For all commands displayed in this section, you can obtain additional information by typing the command (plus subcommand if necessary) followed by /? or /help.

Deploying Windows System Images

After you have created and customized Windows 7 images by using any of the procedures outlined in the previous sections, you can deploy Windows 7 to any number of computers on your network either manually using the Windows PE CD/DVD-ROM or automatically using MDT or WDS. In this section, we look at the procedures you can use.

Suggested Deployment Strategies

Microsoft recommends several deployment strategies from which you can choose, based on the number of computers being deployed and the amount of user interaction desired.

High-Touch with Retail Media

This strategy involves installing Windows 7 on each client computer with the Windows 7 installation DVD, followed by manual configuration of each computer. You can automate this deployment method with the use of an answer file, which is an XML file that includes answers to the questions typically asked by the Setup wizard during Windows installation. We discuss the answer file in further detail later in this chapter. Microsoft recommends this strategy for companies that do not have dedicated IT staff and utilize a small network containing fewer than 100 client computers. The strategy is not recommended for deploying a large number of client computers or for deploying multiple Windows versions.

Using this strategy, you can automate the following components of the installation process:

- **Partitioning the Hard Disk:** You can use either a single partition or a custom disk configuration.

- **Installing Device Drivers:** You can install drivers during Setup so that computers are ready for use immediately after deployment.

- **Installing Applications:** You can install applications during Setup by providing the appropriate instructions in the answer file.

- **Adding Updates:** You can install updates so that client computers have the highest security level immediately after deployment.

- **Configuring Settings:** The answer file enables you to customize many settings such as the computer name and the Internet Explorer home page.

- **Enabling and Disabling Features:** You can customize the installation by adding or removing Windows features as required.

- **Suppressing the Setup GUI:** By doing so, users do not need to interact with the Setup program, thereby minimizing user errors and enabling the use of less skilled personnel for installing the computers.

High-Touch with Standard Image

This strategy involves manual installation of Windows using volume-licensed media and answer files, plus manual installation of applications and configuration of computers to suit the needs of the organization. It is suitable for small organizations with 100–200 client computers on small, unmanaged networks. Unlike the High-Touch with Retail Media strategy, this strategy uses a standard configuration image.

To use this strategy, you need to utilize the Windows AIK as well as a reference computer where you create and customize the master image. You can use a removable device such as a USB flash drive for installing images. The benefits include the following:

- It creates a consistent configuration for all client computers, resulting in fewer problems and reduced needs for support.

- Images are deployed rapidly because they include settings, applications, and so on.

- Validation and testing time is reduced.

- You can add updates to the standard image without the need to recustomize the image.

Lite-Touch, High-Volume Deployment

The Lite-Touch Installation (LTI) strategy utilizes Microsoft Deployment Toolkit (MDT) 2010 to deploy Windows 7 to networks used by medium-sized organizations with 200–500 client computers on a server-based network. MDT 2010 is a solution accelerator that you can download from Microsoft and that contains code that provides a Windows deployment framework for these organizations. This strategy also makes use of the User State Migration Tool (USMT), the Application Compatibility Toolkit (ACT), and Windows AIK. You also need to have suitable media for starting client computers for deployment or a server configured with WDS, as well as a file server with a distribution share. You learned about USMT in Chapter 4, "Migrating Users and Applications to Windows 7," and you will learn more about WDS later in this chapter. Benefits of this strategy include the following:

- You can provide consistent configurations for all client computers, thereby reducing problems.

- MDT 2010 handles installation of all applications, device drivers, and updates, thereby facilitating medium-sized deployments.

- You can easily update applications, device drivers, and the operating system, so maintenance is smoother.

Zero-Touch, High-Volume Deployment

The Zero-Touch Installation (ZTI) strategy is similar to the Lite-Touch, High-Volume Deployment but is more suited to organizations with more than 500 client computers and a server-based network that includes AD DS. Besides MDT 2010, USMT, AIK, and ACT, this strategy utilizes Configuration Manager 2007 R2, which is a server-based tool that provides a comprehensive deployment strategy for operating systems, software, and updates, as well as remote administration and systems inventory. This strategy provides a fully automated deployment solution that includes the following benefits:

- Installation of client computers is fully automated without user interaction.

- Configuration of all client computers is consistent, thereby reducing support costs.

- Using Configuration Manager 2007 R2 for maintaining applications, device drivers, and updates enables streamlined maintenance.

> **NOTE** The Zero-Touch, High-Volume Deployment strategy requires considerable infrastructure as well as personnel with the required training and expertise. If your organization does not meet these needs, use the Lite-Touch, High-Volume Deployment strategy instead.

> **NOTE** More information on these deployment strategies can be found at "Choosing a Deployment Strategy" at http://technet.microsoft.com/en-ca/library/dd919185(WS.10).aspx, or from any certification book for Exam 70-686, Pro: Windows 7, Enterprise Desktop Administrator.

Using Microsoft Deployment Toolkit 2010 to Deploy Windows 7

As mentioned earlier in this chapter, MDT 2010 is an updated version of the Microsoft Solution Accelerator for deployment of operating systems and applications. A solution accelerator is a set of documents, scripts, job aids, and methodologies that assist IT professionals in designing, deploying, and maintaining Microsoft technologies.

MDT originated as Business Desktop Deployment (BDD) 2.0 and then was updated to BDD 2.5; BDD 2007; MDT 2008; and finally the current version, MDT 2010. The major component of MDT 2010 is the Deployment Workbench, which is the topic of discussion for the remainder of this section. MDT 2010 also includes an extension toolkit for Microsoft Configuration Manager 2007 as well as document libraries and release notes.

What's New with MDT 2010

Among the many new features of MDT 2010 are the following more important ones:

- **Support for New Deployment Shares:** You can create deployment shares, which include everything needed for Windows deployment such as operating systems and packages, applications, and device drivers. You can host deployment shares on local drives, network shares, and distributed file system (DFS) shares.

- **Improved Management Model:** Any computer on which the Deployment Workbench is installed can be used for management of MDT 2010 deployment shares. Further, multiple users can work simultaneously with MDT 2010.

- **Improved Performance Features:** When you add information to the MDT database such as new columns, these are automatically displayed as you add them. You can also open linked deployment shares in single-user mode, which also offers improved performance for replicating share content. Such linked deployment shares are specialized deployments you can create in an existing deployment share by using a selection profile. You can replicate the content of these shares any time the content in the source deployment share is modified.

- **Integration with Windows PowerShell:** MDT 2010 supports the use of Windows PowerShell cmdlets and script-based automation of deployment and management tasks.

- **Improved Support for Media-Based Deployments:** MDT 2010 enables you to create media for deploying Windows 7 from existing deployment shares. You can include WIM and ISO files for deployments to physical and virtual target computers.

- **Optimization of Task Sequence and Logging Capabilities:** Improvements have been incorporated into task sequence steps and scripts for such items as diagnostics output, logging, network recovery, and so on.

NOTE For more information on MDT 2010 and its new features, refer to "What's New in Microsoft Deployment Toolkit 2010," available for download at http://technet.microsoft.com/en-us/solutionaccelerators/dd407791.aspx, and "Deploying Windows 7 with MDT 2010—Basic Scenarios" at download.microsoft.com/documents/France/TechNet/2009/WIN7/MDT_2010.pdf. For additional details on use of MDT 2010 for Windows 7 deployment, refer to "Automated Installation to Upgrade to Windows 7: Step-by-Step Guide" at http://technet.microsoft.com/en-us/library/ee523213(WS.10).aspx.

Downloading and Installing MDT 2010

You can download the installation and documentation files for MDT 2010 from http://www.microsoft.com/downloads/details.aspx?FamilyID=3bd8561f-77ac-4400-a0c1-fe871c461a89&displaylang=en. This website enables you to download x64 and x86 versions of MDT 2010 as well as the What's New document, print-ready documentation, and release notes. Use the following procedure to install MDT 2010:

Step 1.   Download the appropriate version of MDT 2010 and save it to your computer.

Step 2.   When informed the download is complete, click **Run**, and then in the Security Warning message box that appears, click **Run** again.

Step 3.   The Setup Wizard starts. Click **Next**.

Step 4. On the End-User License Agreement page, accept the terms of the license agreement and then click **Next**.

Step 5. On the Custom Setup page shown in Figure 5-8, click the features you want to install (or accept the defaults) and then click **Next**.

Figure 5-8   The Custom Setup dialog box enables you to specify the features to be installed.

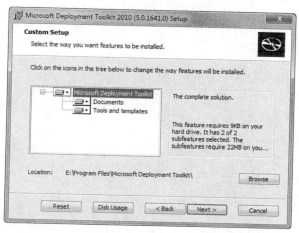

Step 6. On the Ready to Install page, click **Install**. If you receive a UAC prompt, click **Yes**.

Step 7. Windows displays a progress bar as the Setup Wizard installs MDT 2010. When informed the installation is completed, click **Finish**.

Using MDT 2010 Deployment Workbench to Create a Deployment Share

Having installed MDT 2010, you can now create a distribution share that will hold Windows images to be deployed. Proceed as follows:

Step 1. Click **Start > All Programs > Microsoft Deployment Toolkit > Deployment Workbench**. If you receive a UAC prompt, click **Yes** to accept it. This opens MDT to the Deployment Workbench.

Step 2. Right-click **Deployment Shares** and choose **New Deployment Share**. This starts the New Deployment Share Wizard as shown in Figure 5-9.

Step 3. Accept the Deployment share path provided (or enter one of your choosing) and then click **Next**.

Step 4. On the Share page, accept the deployment share name (or provide your own) and then click **Next**.

Step 5. On the Descriptive Name page, type a descriptive name for the share and then click **Next**.

Figure 5-9   Specify the local path for the deployment share you're creating.

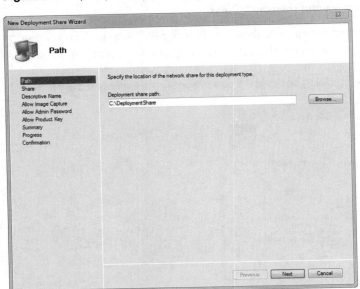

Step 6.   On the Allow Image Capture page shown on Figure 5-10, if you want to enable image capture, ensure that the check box labeled **Ask if an image should be captured** is selected. Click **Next**.

Figure 5-10   Specifying whether an image can be captured.

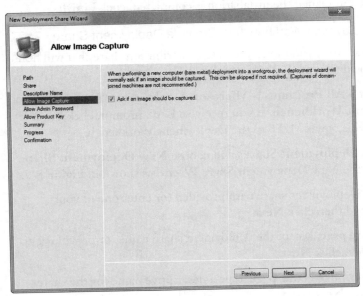

Step 7.   On the Allow Admin Password page shown in Figure 5-11, note the caution about setting the local Administrator password. If you want to enable the user to set this password, select the check box provided and then click **Next**.

Figure 5-11   Deciding whether a user is permitted to set the local administrator password.

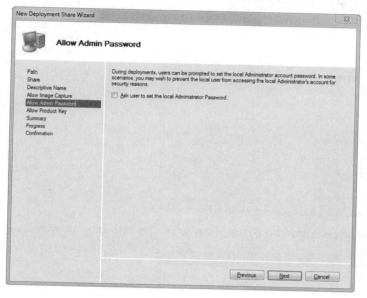

Step 8.   On the Allow Product Key page, if you want to enable the user to enter a product key, select the check box provided and then click **Next**.

Step 9.   The Summary page displays a list of the information you entered (see Figure 5-12). If you need to change any information, click **Previous** or select the required item from the list on the left side. When you're ready to proceed, click **Next**.

Step 10.   The Confirmation page shown in Figure 5-13 displays the actions performed. Click **Finish**. The deployment share is added to the list on the left side of the Deployment Workbench tool.

Adding Windows Images to the Deployment Share

Having created the deployment share, you can now add Windows images to this share so that Windows 7 or Windows Server 2008 R2 can be deployed to new computers. Use the following procedure:

Step 1.   Click **Start > All Programs > Microsoft Deployment Toolkit > Deployment Workbench.** If you receive a UAC prompt, click **Yes** to accept it. This opens MDT to the Deployment Workbench.

Figure 5-12   The Summary page enables you to review the information you've specified.

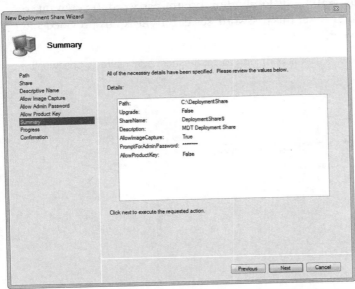

Figure 5-13   The Confirmation page provides details of the actions performed by the wizard.

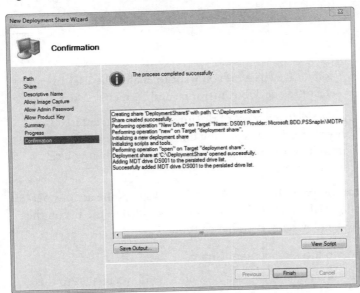

Step 2.   Insert the Windows 7 installation DVD and cancel the AutoPlay message that appears.

Step 3.   In Deployment Workbench, expand **Deployment Shares**, expand **MDT Deployment Shares**, and select **Operating Systems**.

Step 4.   Right-click **Operating Systems** and select **Import Operating System**. The Import Operating System Wizard starts with the OS Type page, as shown in Figure 5-14.

Figure 5-14   The Import Operating System Wizard provides choices for the type of operating system you want to add.

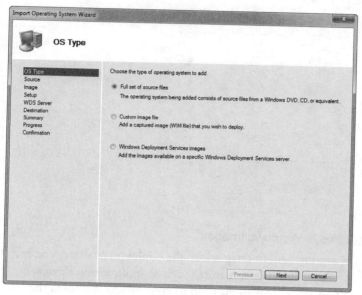

Step 5.   To import an image from the Windows 7 DVD, ensure that **Full set of source files** is selected and then click **Next**.

Step 6.   From the Source page, select the drive letter for the DVD-ROM drive and then click **Next**.

Step 7.   On the Destination page, specify the name of the folder that will hold the operating system files and then click **Next**.

Step 8.   Review the information presented on the Summary page and then click **Next** to perform the import.

Step 9.   The Progress page charts the progress of importing the operating system files. This takes several minutes. When informed that the import is completed, you will see the list of operating system images that have been imported, as shown in Figure 5-15. Click **Finish**.

Figure 5-15   This import action adds images of several editions of Windows 7 to the distribution share.

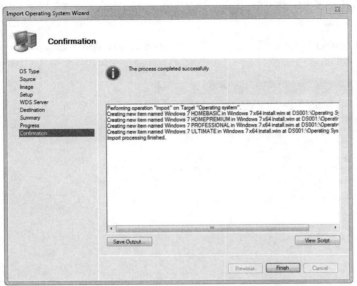

Adding Additional Features to Windows Images

After you've imported operating system images into the deployment share, you can customize the images by adding additional features such as applications, device drivers, and updates to them. To add an application to your images, perform the following steps:

Step 1.   Right-click Applications in the console tree of the Deployment Workbench and choose **New Application**. This starts the New Application Wizard, as shown in Figure 5-16.

Step 2.   To add an application from an installation CD or DVD, select **Application with source files**, insert the CD or DVD, and then click **Next**.

Step 3.   On the Details page, specify the application name and optional publisher, version, and language information. Click **Next**.

Step 4.   On the Source page, specify or browse to the location of the source files and then click **Next**.

Step 5.   On the Destination page, accept the destination name provided (or type one of your choice) and then click **Next**.

Step 6.   On the Command Details page, specify a quiet install command line and working directory (if not already provided) and then click **Next**.

Step 7.   Review the details in the Summary page and click **Next** to copy the installation files.

Figure 5-16   The New Application Wizard assists you in adding applications to your Windows images.

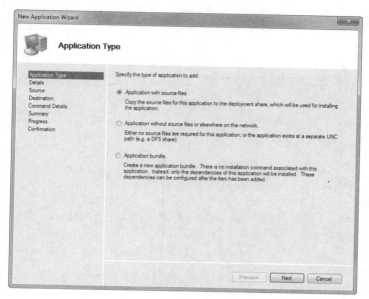

Step 8.   The Progress page charts the action of importing the application source files. This might take several minutes. When informed that the process has completed, click **Finish**. The application name is displayed in the details pane of the Deployment Workbench.

The process of adding device drivers is similar. To do so, right-click **Out-of-Box Drivers** in the console tree of Deployment Workbench and choose **Import Drivers**. To import drivers, follow the steps in the Import Driver Wizard shown in Figure 5-17.

The process of adding additional packages including hotfixes, language packs, or feature packs is similar to that for adding drivers or applications. Right-click **Packages** and choose **Import OS Packages**. Then follow the steps in the Import Package Wizard.

Using Task Sequences in MDT 2010

A task sequence enables you to run a predetermined set of tasks for deploying Windows images to multiple computers. Task sequences also enable you to auto-mate the addition of applications and packages such as updates and language packs to your images. Tasks in a task sequence will be run in sequence according to the order specified. You can include groups and subgroups of tasks in your sequence.

Figure 5-17   The Import Driver Wizard enables you to add device drivers to your operating system images.

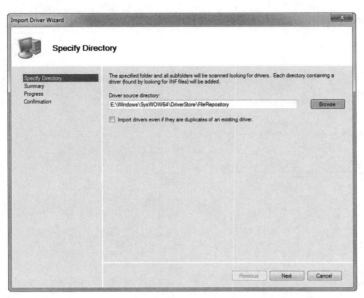

MDT 2010 provides the New Task Sequence Wizard to create a task sequence. Use the following steps to create a basic task sequence:

Step 1.   Right-click Task Sequences in the console tree of the Deployment Workbench and choose **New Task Sequence**. This starts the New Task Sequence Wizard with a General Settings page, as shown in Figure 5-18.

Step 2.   Specify an ID, a name, and an optional description. Click **Next**.

Step 3.   As shown in Figure 5-19, the Select Template page provides several templates that you can use in creating your task sequence. Select a template and then click **Next**.

Step 4.   On the Select OS page, choose an available operating system image and then click **Next**.

Step 5.   On the Specify Product Key page, select the appropriate option and then type your product key. If you want to specify the product key later, select the **Do not specify a product key at this time** option. Then click **Next**.

Step 6.   On the OS Settings page, specify any required settings and then click **Next**.

Step 7.   On the Admin Password page, type and confirm the Administrator password to be used and then click **Next**.

Figure 5-18   The New Task Sequence Wizard enables you to create task sequences.

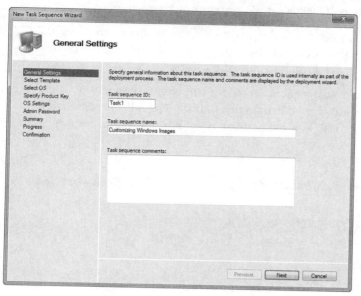

Figure 5-19   The New Task Sequence Wizard provides a series of predefined templates.

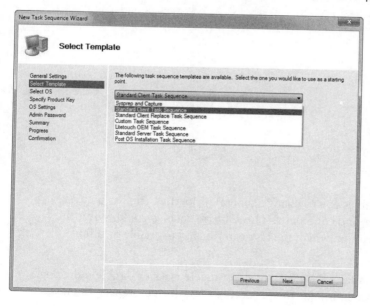

Step 8.   Review the information provided in the Summary page and make any needed changes. Click **Next** to create the task sequence.

Step 9.   The Progress page charts the progress of task sequence creation, and then the Confirmation page informs you that the process has completed successfully. Click **Finish** to close the wizard.

After you've created your task sequence, you can edit your task sequence. Right-click the task sequence and choose **Properties** to bring up its Properties dialog box, as shown in Figure 5-20. You can perform the following actions from the tabs of this dialog box:

Figure 5-20   You can edit your task sequence by using the Customizing Windows Images Properties dialog box.

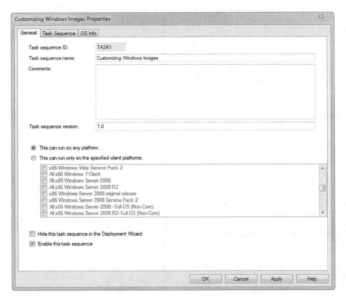

- **General Tab:** Enables you to change general properties, such as the task sequence ID, name, and comments. This tab also enables you to select the Windows platforms on which the task can run and to enable or disable the task sequence.

- **Task Sequence Tab:** Enables you to add or delete tasks or disable individual tasks. You can also customize the properties of individual steps in the task sequence.

- **OS Info Tab:** Provides a description and build number of the operating system serviced by this task sequence and enables you to use Windows SIM to edit the Unattend.xml file associated with this task.

NOTE   For additional information on creating and editing task sequences, refer to "Operating System Deployment: Task Sequence Editor" at http://technet. microsoft.com/en-us/library/bb680396.aspx. For a detailed procedure you can use in creating a task sequence for installing Windows 7, refer to "Automated Installation to Upgrade to Windows 7: Step-by-Step Guide" at http://technet.microsoft.com/en-us/library/ee523213(WS.10).aspx.

Using Deployment Points

You can use Deployment Workbench to set up a deployment point, which defines the operating system files and updates that can be applied to a given target computer and how they can be accessed by the target computer. The deployment point includes a subset of the files in the distribution share; it defines the files in the share to be distributed for a given deployment, as well as how a target computer will access them. You can create one or more of each of the following three types of deployment points:

- **Lab or Single-Server Deployment:** The simplest type of deployment point, this type shares the contents of the entire distribution folder as a hidden share.

- **Separate Deployment Share:** This is a shared folder usually created on a network file server. One or more deployment shares can be used for redundancy and load-balancing purposes.

- **Removable Media:** Useful for deploying Windows 7 to destination computers that are not on the network. You can use a DVD or place the deployment files on a USB hard drive or flash drive.

NOTE   Deployment Workbench provides a wizard that assists you in the task of creating these deployment points. For more information on deployment points, refer to "Preparing the Deployment Environment" at http://technet.microsoft.com/ en-us/library/bb978351.aspx.

Using MDT 2010 to Distribute Images to Multiple Computers

We have already introduced the Lite-Touch, High-Volume Deployment strategy that is designed for medium-sized organizations with generally about 200–500 client computers and an IT staff. You can use MDT 2010 to deploy computers within such an organization from a single file server. Besides MDT 2010, you should have the User State Migration Toolkit (USMT), Application Compatibility Toolkit (ACT), Windows AIK, and either deployment media (as discussed earlier in this chapter) or a WDS server (as discussed in the next section). The other tools mentioned here are introduced in various chapters of this *Cert Guide*.

NOTE For additional information on using this strategy to deploy Windows 7 computers within the organization, refer to "Lite-Touch, High-Volume Deployment" at http://technet.microsoft.com/en-us/library/dd919179(WS.10).aspx.

Automated Deployment of Windows 7 by Using Windows Deployment Services

WDS is the replacement for Remote Installation Services (RIS), which was first introduced with Windows 2000 to provide a means of performing on-demand, image-based installation of operating systems across a network connection from a server to the computer on which the operating system is to be installed, without the need to be physically present at the destination computer and without using installation media. You can install WDS on a server running either Windows Server 2003 or Server 2008/ R2 and use it to install Windows Vista/7 or Windows Server 2008/R2 on destination computers.

Understanding WDS

WDS provides several advantages to the administrator who needs to install Windows 7/Server 2008 R2 on a large number of computers, including the following:

- WDS enables you to install Windows 7 on computers at a remote location across a wide area network (WAN).

- WDS provides native support for Windows PE and the WIM file format.

- WDS reduces the complexity associated with large deployments, thereby reducing total cost of ownership (TCO).

- WDS simplifies the duties associated with management of an installation server.

- WDS simplifies the procedures required to recover an installation from system failures that occur during installation.

You can create installation images of Windows 7 or Windows Server 2008 R2 that include complete computer configurations, including such items as applications and desktop settings, and use WDS to push these images out to client computers on the network. WDS provides the following capabilities:

- Enables users to install an operating system on demand. On starting a client computer that is equipped with a PXE-enabled NIC, the computer connects to a WDS server, which then installs the operating system across the network without the need for a CD or DVD.

- Provides images of the operating system complete with specific settings and applications, such as those required by a corporate workstation policy. You can designate the group of users provided with a certain image or series of images.

- Creates images that enable the automated installation of Windows 7 or Windows Server 2008 R2.

In Windows 7 and Windows Server 2008 R2, WDS includes the following new features:

- **Dynamic Driver Provisioning:** You can add driver packages to boot images before deployment and add these packages to client computers during installation.

- **Virtual Hard Disk Deployment:** WDS adds the ability to deploy virtual hard disk (.vhd) images during an unattended installation. We discuss configuring VHD images in Chapter 6.

- **Additional Multicasting Functionality:** You can separate image transmissions into multiple streams according to client speeds. You can also use multicasting on IPv6 networks.

- **Use of Transport Server for Image Deployment:** Transport Server is a Windows Server 2008 R2 role service that can be installed on a standalone server. An included PXE provider enables you to perform network booting and multicasting on a network that does not require AD DS or Domain Name System (DNS).

- **Support for EFI:** Extensible Firmware Interface (EFI) enables network booting of x64-based computers, and includes auto-add functionality, the use of Dynamic Host Configuration Protocol (DHCP) to refer computers to a specific PXE server, and the use of multicasting to deploy Windows PE images.

NOTE   For further information on new features of WDS in Windows Server 2008 R2 and a comparison of features available in previous Windows Server editions, refer to "Windows Deployment Services: What's New" at http://technet.microsoft.com/en-ca/library/dd348499(WS.10).aspx.

Setting Up WDS

In Windows Server 2008/R2, you can install WDS in either of two modes: Deployment Server or Transport Server. If you are using the Deployment Server role, the following server components must be available on the WDS server or on another server available to the WDS server:

- **DHCP:** Provides TCP/IP configuration parameters that enable the client computer to create its own network connection.

- **DNS:** Provides name resolution services so that the client computer can locate the WDS server by name.

■ **AD DS:** WDS Deployment Server mode operates only in an Active Directory-enabled domain environment. You cannot use WDS Deployment Server mode in a workgroup environment.

In addition, you must be a member of the Local Administrators group to install either the Deployment Server or Transport Server mode. For the Deployment Server mode, you must also be a member of the Domain Users group. If you are using the Transport Server mode for network booting of client computers, DHCP must be available. You must also have the Windows AIK media available either on the WDS server or at an accessible location as well as a separate partition on the WDS server that is formatted with the NTFS file system.

You can install WDS on a server running Windows Server 2008 R2 by using Server Manager, the Initial Configuration Wizard, or the command line. Select the Windows Deployment Services server role. As shown in Figure 5-21, the installation wizard provides the Deployment Server and Transport Server options. To install the Deployment Server option, you must ensure that both Deployment Server and Transport Server are selected; clear the Deployment Server check box to install the Transport Server option.

Figure 5-21 WDS in Windows Server 2008 R2 gives you a choice of Transport Server or Deployment Server installation modes.

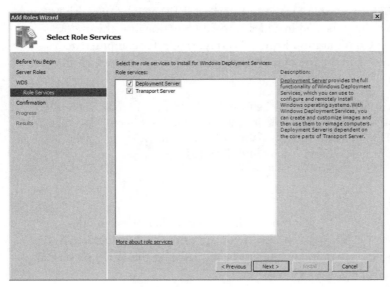

The WDS server role installation process creates a shared folder into which you can place the files required for PXE boot, the files for booting Windows PE, Windows PE boot images, and then install images. You also need to configure the PXE listener to control how the server will service incoming client boot requests.

After you have installed WDS, you are ready to add install and boot images. WDS uses the following two basic image types, both of which use the WIM file format:

- Install images are the operating system images that you deploy to the client computer. You can either create a custom install image or use the `install.wim` file from the Windows 7 product DVD.

- Boot images are Windows PE images used by client computers to perform an operating system installation. The `boot.wim` file can be copied from the Windows product DVD and contains Windows PE and WDS client components.

NOTE   Detailed procedures for installing and configuring WDS on the server are beyond the scope of the 70-680 exam. For details on the procedures involved, refer to "Windows Deployment Services Getting Started Guide" at http://technet.microsoft.com/en-us/library/cc771670(WS.10).aspx.

Using WDS to Perform an Automated Deployment of Windows 7

Client computers must meet the proper design specification to be installed with WDS. This includes the capability for remote booting, which is usually accomplished by adding a network interface card (NIC) that is equipped with a PXE ROM-enabled chip, along with support in the BIOS for booting the computer from this NIC. In addition, the client computer can have only a single disk partition. (Any additional partitions are destroyed when the operating system is installed, and the entire disk is formatted as a single NTFS partition.)

Enabling Automatic Network Boot

When a user is present at the target computer when deploying Windows 7, she can perform a network boot by pressing **F12** when prompted immediately after starting the computer. To enable this action to occur, configure the BIOS so that this option is higher in the boot order than the hard drive (if an active partition exists on the hard drive). If no active partition exists, simply ensure that a network boot option is found in the BIOS boot sequence.

For fully automatic Windows 7 deployment, you must enable all client computers to boot without the need for pressing **F12** at startup. To do so, set the default for the server in Windows Server 2008 R2 by accessing the Boot tab of the server's Properties dialog box in the WDS Microsoft Management Console (MMC) snap-in and specifying the PXE Boot Policy option.

CAUTION   If you have configured the computer to boot from the network at a higher priority, it might end up in a boot loop, where the computer repeatedly reboots from the network rather than the hard drive. A Windows 7 installation would then be unable to complete. You should disable any active partitions and then configure the BIOS boot sequence to boot first from the hard drive and then from the network. You can also configure the client to require pressing **F12** on subsequent boots for a network boot; to do this, run the command `wdsutil /set-server /resetbootprogram:yes` from an administrative command prompt at the WDS server. This command erases the boot path on a client that has booted without requiring an F12 key press.

A user at the target computer needs to select the boot image to be applied to the computer. When more than one boot image is available, WDS will display a menu at the target computer that enables the user to select a boot image. If he does not select a boot image within a timeout interval, the default boot image is automatically applied. The Boot tab of the WDS server's Properties dialog box shown in Figure 5-22 enables you to specify the default boot image deployed automatically to each client at startup.

Figure 5-22   Specifying the default boot image.

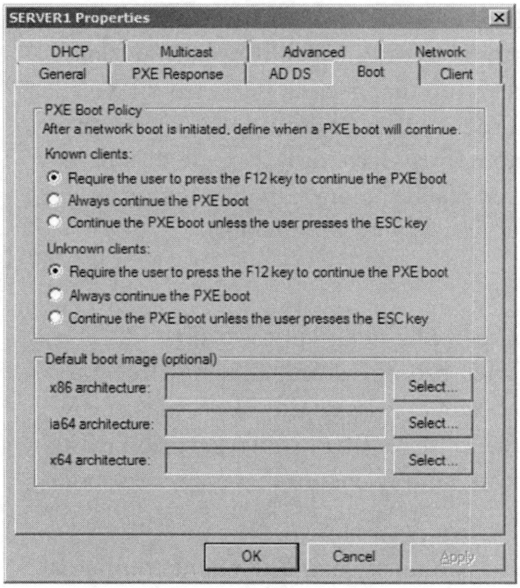

Automating the Setup Process

So that the target computer can install a Windows 7 image automatically when a user starts the computer, copy the proper `Unattend.xml` file to the `RemoteInstall\WDSClientUnattend` folder on the WDS server. This client unattend file automates the WDS client user interface screens for tasks such as entering credentials, choosing an install image, and configuring the disk, thereby allowing these actions to proceed without user intervention. You can create this file by using Windows SIM, saving it to a known location and then associating it with the required Windows 7 image using the image management tools.

> **NOTE**   Refer to "Automating Setup" at http://technet.microsoft.com/en-ca/library/cc730695(WS.10).aspx and "Performing an Unattended Installation" at http://technet.microsoft.com/en-ca/library/dd637990(WS.10).aspx for more information and step-by-step procedures. For sample unattended installation files, refer to "Sample Unattend Files" at http://technet.microsoft.com/en-ca/library/cc732280(WS.10).aspx.

Manually Deploying a Customized Image

It is easy to manually deploy a customized Windows 7 image to any number of computers. You can use the Windows PE CD/DVD-ROM that you created earlier in this chapter. Use the following steps to perform this action:

Step 1.   At the target computer, insert the Windows PE CD-ROM and restart the computer.

Step 2.   At the Windows PE command prompt, use the `Diskpart` command to create the appropriate disk configuration, for example:

```
diskpart
select disk 0
clean
create partition primary size=50000
select partition 1
active
format
exit
```

Step 3.   Type the following commands to copy the installation image to the local hard drive:

```
net use z: \\Server1\Windows_installation\Images
copy z:\image_name.wim c:
```

Step 4.   Type the following command to use ImageX from the Windows PE media to apply the image to the local hard drive:

```
D:\Tools\Imagex.exe /apply c:\image_name.wim c:
```

Step 5.   This deploys the Windows 7 image to the destination computer, ready for delivery to the end user.

> **NOTE**   If you want to redeploy the image to the computer you imaged earlier in this chapter, override the default boot order to boot the computer from the CD/DVD-ROM drive using the appropriate function key to access the BIOS program.

You can also manually deploy a computer using WDS, after the prerequisites covered earlier in this chapter have been satisfied. Simply start the computer and press **F12** to initiate a PXE network boot. The computer uses DHCP to obtain an IP address and connect to the WDS server, which responds and loads the `boot.wim` file to the client's RAM. From the WDS menu displayed, select a boot image. Installation of Windows 7 then proceeds without additional intervention. The boot image appears when you have configured either of the following:

- Two or more Windows PE boot images are added to the WDS server.

- A boot image and a capture image are both available on the WDS server.

Troubleshooting an Unattended Installation

A standard image of Windows 7 reduces implementation and maintenance costs. The implementation savings are obvious because you do not need to have a network administrator watch each installation and input information, which takes a lot of time. Ongoing maintenance costs of a standard configuration are less expensive because network administrators are thoroughly familiar with the configuration of the computer they are helping an end user troubleshoot, saving time and effort.

Because the method of setup for an unattended installation is different from an attended installation, you can expect that some of the problems you encounter are also different. You can encounter many of the same problems that you might have had in an attended installation, but you will also have unique problems associated with an unattended method of installation.

Problems with Answer Files

You can use answer files to automate a Windows 7 installation whether the computer is installed from a DVD or across a network. Nearly always, answer files are used with network installations. The fact that you can use an answer file with a DVD installation can help you troubleshoot a computer that has difficulty connecting to the network.

Boot Disks

Because answer files are mainly used with network installations, the first dilemma usually stumbled into is booting to the network and accessing the distribution server files. You can use USB portable drives or floppy boot disks, or you can execute the installation from a command line on a computer while it is running a different operating system. The only requirement you have of any existing operating system is that it has access to the network and that you are logged in with a user ID that has permissions to read the i386 folder structure on the distribution server. If you use a boot disk to access the network, you need to have the correct NIC driver for the computer already installed on the floppy disk. When you try to boot a computer with a boot disk that has drivers for one type of NIC while the computer has a different NIC, you will not be able to access the network. Depending on the computer's configuration, you might not even see an error on the screen.

Switches

The `Setup.exe` program used for installing Windows 7 utilizes a variety of switches to control how the Setup program runs. Table 5-15 displays the syntax used for `Setup.exe` switches. An incorrectly used switch can cause some of the errors you can encounter during an unattended installation. For example, you might need to specify an answer file for unattended installation. If you do not supply the proper path to the answer file, Setup will be unable to locate it and will ask for information otherwise included in the answer file.

Table 5-15   Syntax for **Setup.exe**

Switch	Results
`/1394debug:channel`	Enables kernel debugging across an IEEE 1394 port.
`/debug<port>` `[/baudrate:baudrate]`	Enables kernel debugging across a COM port.
`/emsport:[port¦usebiossettings ¦ off ¦[/emsbaudrate:baudrate]`	Enables or disables Emergency Management Services (EMS) and specifies the baud rate to use while transferring data. Used for x86 systems only.
`/noreboot`	Tells `Setup.exe` not to reboot after copying files. Subsequent reboots are not suppressed.
`/m:folder_name`	Tells `Setup.exe` where to find replacement files to be copied.
`/tempdrive:drive_letter`	Tells `Setup.exe` to put temporary Setup files on the root of the specified drive.
`/unattend:[answerfile]`	Specifies the answer file for the unattended installation.
`/usbdebug:[target_name]`	Enables kernel debugging across a USB 2.0 port.

Answer File Specifications

The answer file that you use is an XML file that's structured considerably differently from those used with Windows installations prior to Vista. Like its predecessors, it contains headings, parameters, and values. If you don't include a heading, a parameter, and a value for a specific item that you want to install a certain way, Windows 7 uses the default installation values for that item. Although the SIM program creates valid XML coding, it is possible to edit the answer file using a text editor (such as Notepad). Typos, incorrect headings, incorrect parameter names, or incorrect values cause errors or unexpected results during installation. Spelling counts!

A spelling error in an answer file usually does not cause a Windows 7 installation to fail unless the error is specifically related to a driver. Most people use SIM to create an answer file. When SIM creates the file, it does not always customize the features that you want to customize. Therefore, you likely must edit the file directly. The best way to troubleshoot your answer file is to make certain that you save your original answer file created by SIM and save each subsequent version of the answer file. By doing this and by testing the answer file with each individual customization as you make them, you will be able to pinpoint the specific problem with the file.

Problems with Sysprep Installations

As already discussed, Sysprep creates a snapshot of a Windows 7 workstation and strips out the unique information for that workstation so that the image can be stamped on another. Sysprep can not only prepare an image of Windows 7, it can include unusual settings, applications, special application configurations, and even additional files. After preparing the image with Sysprep, you can then use a third-party utility to transfer the image to a target computer. The process is quick and easy to repeat. This is called *cloning* and can be either the best thing since sliced bread to your company or its worst nightmare.

The problem with cloning is that software image information is often intertwined with hardware information in odd places. When you attempt to clone a source computer onto a target computer that is not identical to the source, the image might function perfectly well, but it also might have results in a few configuration errors or even fail to start. It depends on what is different between the source and target computers and whether Sysprep strips out that particular information or the target computer has true Plug and Play devices.

Another issue you might experience with Sysprep is the version of the tool that you are using. Microsoft has been known in the past to include updated deployment tools with service packs and will likely continue to do so with Windows 7 and Windows Server 2008 R2. When you create a source location that incorporates a service pack, you should also use the version of Sysprep that comes with that same service pack.

> **NOTE**   Note that Sysprep does not work on a computer that is a member of a domain. It works only on a computer that is a member of a workgroup. If you run Sysprep on a computer that has already joined a domain, Sysprep removes it from the domain before preparing the image.

If you try to copy encrypted files using the Encrypting File System (EFS) on an NTFS-formatted partition as part of your Sysprep image, you will fail because the Sysprep process makes encrypted files unreadable. The only way to encrypt the files is to execute the encrypting command after the image has been transferred to the target computer.

Whenever you use Sysprep, you should ensure that the computer functions properly. Use the following steps to test some basic computer functions:

Step 1.   Boot the computer and log on as a user.

Step 2.   Access the local hard drive and open a file.

Step 3.   Open all critical applications.

Step 4.   Run `chkdsk c: /r` to verify that the hard drive has no errors.

Step 5.   Click **Start > Network** and then view other machines located on the network.

Step 6.   Print a file to a network printer.

Step 7.   Send an email.

Step 8.   Look through Event Viewer logs for errors.

Step 9.   Review the Setup Error log.

Use cloning when you have hundreds of computers that have identical hardware and need identical software and operating system configurations. If you have a large number of different hardware configurations and/or software and operating system configurations, you should consider using answer files instead.

Exam Preparation Tasks

Review All the Key Topics

Review the most important topics in the chapter, noted with the key topics icon in the outer margin of the page. Table 5-16 lists a reference of these key topics and the page numbers on which each is found.

Table 5-16   Key Topics for Chapter 5

Key Topic Element	Description	Page Number
Table 5-2	Introduces the various Windows 7 deployment technologies	132
Figure 5-1	Structure of a .wim file	134
Table 5-3	Windows PE command-line tools	135
List	Using Windows AIK to create an answer file	140
Table 5-5	Sysprep parameters	143
List	Using an answer file to perform an unattended installation of Windows 7	144
Table 5-6	ImageX capture parameters	146
Table 5-7	Technologies included with DISM	149
List	Performing a manual image capture	150
List	Capabilities and new features of WDS	174
List	Requirements for using WDS in Deployment Server mode	175
Paragraph	Using WDS for automated computer deployment	177

Complete the Tables and Lists from Memory

Print a copy of Appendix C, "Memory Tables," (found on the CD), or at least the section for this chapter, and complete the tables and lists from memory. Appendix D, "Memory Tables Answer Key," also on the CD, includes completed tables and lists to check your work.

Definitions of Key Terms

Define the following key terms from this chapter, and check your answers in the glossary.

Answer file, Microsoft Deployment Toolkit (MDT), Windows Deployment Services (WDS), System Image Manager (SIM), Windows Preinstallation Environment (Windows PE), System Preparation Tool (Sysprep), ImageX, Windows Recovery Environment (Windows RE), Windows image (`.wim`) file, Deployment Image Servicing and Management (DISM), Windows Optional Component Setup tool (`OCSetup.exe`), Deployment Server, Transport Server, PreBoot eXecution Environment (PXE)

This chapter covers the following subjects:

■ **Understanding VHDs:** This section introduces VHDs and describes new developments in VHD technology as related to Windows 7 and Windows Server 2008 R2. It also briefly describes the types of VHDs and the tools used to work with them.

■ **Creating and Deploying VHDs:** This section discusses the procedures you need to be familiar with to create, mount, deploy, and boot a computer from VHDs.

■ **Offline Servicing and Updating VHDs:** This section introduces the procedures you can use to perform servicing and updating actions on a native-boot VHD while offline.

CHAPTER 6

Configuring Virtual Hard Disks

A virtual hard disk (VHD) is a special type of image file that contains all the operating system files, applications, and data that might be found on a typical hard disk partition, encapsulated in a single file. Using VHD technology, Microsoft has expanded the field of client virtualization (also known as *desktop virtualization*) to provide powerful new means of management for desktops in a corporate environment. It is even now possible to utilize servers with lots of RAM and several powerful processors with a series of virtual machines installed on these servers and accessed by users from their own desktop. Users can communicate with these virtual desktops by means of a client device that supports protocols such as Remote Desktop Protocol (RDP).

You can use methods described in the previous chapter to deploy a Windows 7 image in `.wim` format to the VHD, and you can copy this file to multiple virtual computer instances. You can perform almost any task you would normally perform on your computer from a VHD; in fact, nearly all the screen shots in this book were created by the author using VHDs.

"Do I Know This Already?" Quiz

The "Do I Know This Already?" quiz enables you to assess whether you should read this entire chapter or simply jump to the "Exam Preparation Tasks" section for review. If you are in doubt, read the entire chapter. Table 6-1 outlines the major headings in this chapter and the corresponding "Do I Know This Already?" quiz questions. You can find the answers in Appendix A, "Answers to the 'Do I Know This Already?' Quizzes."

Table 6-1 "Do I Know This Already?" Foundation Topics Section-to-Question Mapping

Foundations Topics Section	Questions Covered in This Section
Understanding VHDs	1–2
Creating and Deploying VHDs	3–9
Offline Servicing and Updating VHDs	10–12

1. Which of the following are valid types of VHDs in Windows 7? (Choose three.)

   a. Basic

   b. Fixed

   c. Dynamic

   d. Updating

   e. Differencing

2. Which of the following tools can be used to create a new VHD? (Choose two.)

   a. DiskPart

   b. Bcdedit

   c. Sysprep

   d. ImageX

   e. Disk Management

3. After you create your new VHD, you attempt to format it, but are unable to do so. Then you notice that the VHD is described as Unknown. What must you do first to fix this problem?

   a. Mount the VHD.

   b. Initialize the VHD.

   c. Partition the VHD.

   d. Assign the VHD a drive letter.

4. You are creating a script that will be used for creating a series of VHDs for deployment to users in your company. What command do you use to mount the VHD?

   a. `Create`

   b. `Mount`

   c. `Active`

   d. `Attach`

5. You have created a VHD on one computer that you now want to use on a second computer on the network. What should you do next to accomplish this task?

   a. Mount the VHD.

   b. Partition the VHD.

   c. Format the VHD.

   d. Create a path to the VHD.

6. Which of the following steps must you perform to deploy a custom Windows image to multiple VHDs? (Choose all that apply.)

   a. Install Windows and configure all applications on a reference physical computer.

   b. Use Sysprep to generalize the image.

   c. Use ImageX to capture the image into a `.wim` file.

   d. Use Remote Installation Services (RIS) to deploy the images from a server.

   e. Use Bcdedit to configure each computer for booting from the VHD.

   f. Use DISM to add updates to each computer.

7. Which of the following are true about using a VHD file as if it were a normal hard disk for booting an older computer? (Choose all that apply.)

   a. This provides a convenient way to run Windows XP on any computer that supports this operating system.

   b. This provides a convenient way to run Windows 7 on a computer whose hardware is below the minimum hardware requirements.

   c. You cannot use NTFS compression on a native-boot VHD.

   d. You cannot use BitLocker encryption to encrypt the contents of the disk containing the VHD file.

   e. You must have Virtual PC or Virtual Server installed on the computer.

8. What command would you use to deploy Windows 7 to a previously created VHD?

   a. `dism /apply`

   b. `ImageX /create`

   c. `ImageX /apply`

   d. `Bcdedit /copy`

9. You want to boot Windows 7 from a native-boot VHD you have deployed to a computer running Windows XP. What command (or commands) should you use?

   a. `Notepad boot.ini`

   b. `Ntldr`

   c. `Bcdedit`

   d. `Bcdboot` followed by `Bcdedit`

10. You are running Windows 7 on your computer from a native-boot VHD, and you realize that you want to add a Windows feature that is not included. What should you do?

    a. From a command prompt on the running computer, execute the `DISM /image:c:\ /Get-Feature /FeatureName:<name>` command.

    b. From a command prompt on the running computer, execute the `DISM /image:c:\ /Enable-Feature /FeatureName:<name>` command.

    c. Mount the VHD as drive e: on another computer, and then execute the `DISM /image:e:\ /Get-Feature /FeatureName:<name>` command.

    d. Mount the VHD as drive e: on another computer, and then execute the `DISM /image:e:\ /Enable-Feature /FeatureName:<name>` command.

11. What command would you use to add a driver to a previously created VHD?

    a. `DISM /image:<letter>:\ /Add-Driver:<path_to_driver>`

    b. `ImageX /image:<letter>:\ /Add-Driver:<path_to_driver>`

    c. `DISM /image:<letter>:\ /Get-Driver:<path_to_driver>`

    d. `ImageX /image:<letter>:\ /Get-Driver:<path_to_driver>`

12. You use the `/Get-TargetEditions` command to view the editions you can upgrade your native-boot VHD to. However, this command does not provide any upgrading options. What is the most likely reason?

    a. The native-boot VHD is running Windows Vista.

    b. The native-boot VHD is running the Windows 7 Ultimate edition.

    c. You have used the wrong command. You should be using the `/Get-Edition` command instead.

    d. You have used the wrong command. You should be using the `/Apply-Edition` command instead.

Foundation Topics

Understanding VHDs

The virtual hard disk (VHD) specification consists of a single file that includes all the files and folders that would be found on a hard disk partition—hence the term *virtual hard disk*. This file is capable of hosting native file systems and supporting all regular disk operations. Windows 7 (Enterprise and Ultimate) and Windows Server 2008 R2 (all editions except Foundation Edition) natively support the use of VHDs without the need for a hypervisor (an additional layer of software below the operating system for running virtual computers). These operating systems enable you to create, configure, and boot physical computers directly from VHDs, and they provide administrators and developers with the following capabilities:

- You can standardize image formats and toolsets used within the company.

- You can reduce the quantity of images that must be cataloged and supported.

- Developers can test applications on multiple operating systems; if applications break operating systems, developers can restore the operating system with minimal lost time and cost.

- You can have a common image format that runs on both physical and virtual machines.

- VHDs enable you to improve server utilization, with consequent energy savings.

Older Windows operating systems require you to install the Windows Server 2008 Hyper-V role, Microsoft Virtual Server, or Windows Virtual PC.

What's New in Virtual Hard Disks?

Windows 7 and Windows Server 2008 offer several new capabilities in the use of VHDs:

- You can deploy the VHD to designated hardware as the running operating system without the need for another parent operating system. This type of VHD is referred to as a *native-boot* VHD.

- You can create a VHD using common disk management utilities.

- You can deploy a Windows 7 image in .wim format to the VHD.

- You can configure the boot manager in Windows 7 to enable a native or physical boot of the Windows image contained within the VHD.

- You can connect the VHD file to a virtual machine used with the Hyper-V role in Windows Server 2008 R2.

These new capabilities help you to simplify the cataloging, management, and maintenance of images. In addition, native-boot VHDs ease the transition between physical and virtual environments because the same master image can be deployed to both virtual and physical machines. Furthermore, you can use the deployment tools in the Windows Automated Installation Kit (Windows AIK) to apply Windows images and updates to the VHD files. Although you would need to install the Hyper-V server role on a computer running Windows Server 2008 R2, this action is not required for Windows 7 computers.

Types of Virtual Hard Disks

Windows 7 and Windows Server 2008 offer three types of VHDs: fixed, dynamic, and differencing. Table 6-2 explains how these types differ.

Table 6-2   Types of VHDs

Tool	Description
Fixed	Describes a VHD with a fixed size. For example, if you create a fixed VHD of 30 GB size, the file size will always be about 30 GB (some space is used for the internal VHD structure) regardless of how much data is contained in it.
Dynamic	The VHD is only as large as the data contained in it. You can specify the maximum size. For example, if you create a dynamic VHD of 30 GB size, it starts out at around 80 MB but expands as you write data to it. It cannot exceed the specified maximum size. Fixed VHDs are recommended over dynamic because they offer the highest I/O performance; also, as a dynamic disk expands, the host volume could run out of space, causing write operations to fail.
Differencing	Also known as a child VHD, this VHD contains only the modified disk blocks of the parent VHD with which it is associated. The parent VHD is read-only, and all modifications are written to the differencing VHD. The parent VHD can be any of these three VHD types and multiple differencing VHDs are referred to as a *differencing chain*. A differencing VHD is useful in a test environment; when a developer performs tests, all updates are made on the differencing VHD. To revert to the clean state of the parent VHD, you need only delete the differencing VHD and create a new one.

CAUTION   If you are using differencing VHDs, you should not modify the parent VHD. If you do so, the block structure between the parent and differencing VHD will no longer match, resulting in corruption of the differencing VHD. Furthermore, you must keep both the parent and differencing VHDs within the same folder on a local volume for native-boot scenarios. Otherwise, the differencing

VHD will not boot. If the differencing VHD is not used for native-boot, the VHDs can be on different folders or volumes.

Tools Used with Virtual Hard Disks

Microsoft provides a large selection of tools that you can use for configuring and managing VHDs. Table 6-3 introduces VHD management tools included with Windows 7. You were introduced to some of these tools in Chapter 5, "Deploying Windows 7." We discuss the use of these tools in later sections of this chapter.

Table 6-3   Tools Used with VHDs

Tool	Description
Disk Management	A Microsoft Management Console (MMC) snap-in that enables you to manage VHDs, including creating, attaching, detaching, expanding, and merging VHDs.
DiskPart	A command-line tool that enables you to perform VHD management activities similar to those available with Disk Management. You can script these actions using DiskPart.
Bcdedit	A command-line tool that enables you to manage boot configuration data (BCD) stores.
Bcdboot	A command-line tool that enables you to manage and create new BCD stores and BCD boot entries. You can use this tool to create new boot entries when configuring a system to boot from a new VHD.
Deployment Image Servicing and Management (DISM)	A command-line tool that enables you to apply updates, applications, drivers, and language packs to a Windows image, including a VHD.
Sysprep	A utility that enables you to prepare an operating system for imaging and deployment by removing user and computer-specific data.
ImageX	A command-line tool that enables you to capture, create, modify, and apply Windows images.

All these tools are included with Windows 7 and Windows Server 2008 R2 except ImageX, which is included with the Windows AIK. Also included with Windows Server 2008 R2, but not with Windows 7, is the Windows Hyper-V Manager, which is an MMC snap-in that enables you to create VHD images, including the ability to install Windows from installation media or an ISO image file.

Creating and Configuring VHDs

For the 70-680 exam, you need to be familiar with the different methods available for creating and configuring VHDs, including installing Windows 7 on the VHD, deploying a Windows 7 VHD to other machines, and booting from the VHD.

Creating VHDs

In contrast to previous Windows versions, Windows 7 and Windows Server 2008 R2 enable you to manage virtual disks directly in the disk management tools without the need to install the Hyper-V Server role or the Hyper-V Manager console. You can use either the Disk Management MMC snap-in or the command line-based DiskPart tool to create and configure VHDs. We look at each in turn here.

Using Disk Management

The Disk Management snap-in contains all the utilities necessary to create and configure disks and partitions. We look at this snap-in in detail in Chapter 15, "Disk Management." Use the following procedure to create a VHD:

Step 1.   Click **Start**, right-click **Computer**, and then choose **Manage**. This opens the Computer Management snap-in, which contains Disk Management as a component snap-in.

Step 2.   In the console tree, click **Disk Management** to make its contents visible in the details pane.

Step 3.   Right-click **Disk Management** and choose **Create VHD**. This displays the Create and Attach Virtual Hard Disk dialog box, as shown in Figure 6-1.

Figure 6-1   The Create and Attach Virtual Hard Disk dialog box enables you to create a new VHD.

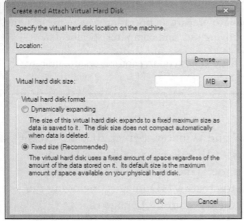

Step 4.   Type a path and filename for the VHD in the Location text box or click the **Browse** button to browse to a suitable location.

Step 5.   Specify a size in the Virtual hard disk size text box, select from the choices available under Virtual hard disk format.

- **Dynamically expanding:** Creates a dynamic VHD, as described in Table 6-2.

- **Fixed size (Recommended):** Creates a fixed VHD.

Step 6.   After you've made your choice, click **OK**.

Step 7.   The disk is created and attached and appears as an unknown disk in Disk Management. This might take several minutes, particularly for a VHD large enough to hold a Windows 7 installation.

Step 8.   Right-click the unknown disk in Disk Management and choose **Initialize Disk**. In the dialog box shown in Figure 6-2, keep the default partition style and then click **OK**.

Figure 6-2   Initializing the VHD.

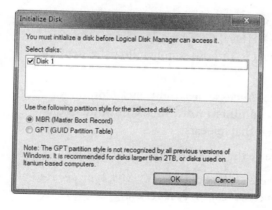

Step 9.   You can perform any actions described in Chapter 15 on the disk after it is initialized. To format it as a single partition, right-click in the empty space beside the disk label and choose **New Simple Volume**.

Step 10.   Click **Next**, accept the volume size as given, and then click **Next** again.

Step 11.   On the Assign Drive Letter or Path page, accept the defaults (or change the drive letter if desired) and then click **Next**.

Step 12.   On the Format Partition page shown in Figure 6-3, you should in most cases accept the defaults (type a different volume label if desired). Click **Next** and then click **Finish**.

Figure 6-3   Formatting the VHD.

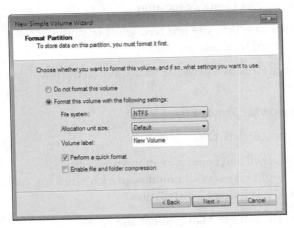

Step 13.   The volume is formatted and made ready for use. An AutoPlay dialog box appears, enabling you to view files in the volume.

Using DiskPart to Create a VHD

The DiskPart utility enables you to create a VHD from the command line. You can script this action to create multiple VHDs if necessary. We discuss the DiskPart commands in detail in Chapter 15; for now, simply follow the steps as provided here:

Step 1.   Click **Start > All Programs > Accessories**, right-click **Command Prompt**, and choose **Run as administrator**. Click **Continue** in the User Account Control prompt that appears.

Step 2.   Type **diskpart**. You will receive the **DISKPART** command prompt.

Step 3.   To create a fixed VHD of size 20 GB and named w7.vhd, type **create vdisk file="c:\w7.vhd" maximum=20000 type=fixed**.

Step 4.   When you are informed that DiskPart has successfully created the file, type **attach vdisk**.

Step 5.   When DiskPart informs you that the disk was attached, type **list disk** to show that the disk is present and online. This command also provides the disk number that you must enter in the next step of the procedure.

Step 6.   To create a partition on the VHD, type **select disk** *n*, press **Enter**, type **create partition primary**, and then press Enter again. In this command, *n* is the disk number you obtained from the previous step.

Step 7.   To perform a quick format on the partition using the NTFS file system, type **format fs=ntfs quick**.

Step 8.   To assign the drive letter e: to the new partition, type **assign letter=e.**

Step 9.   To mark the partition as active, type **active.**

These steps complete the creation of a VHD on drive e: that is suitable for installing a virtual copy of Windows 7. Figure 6-4 shows how these steps appear at the console, with the exception of the list disk command (omitted to conserve space). Table 6-4 outlines the parameters of the vdisk command that are most useful for creating and working with VHDs.

Figure 6-4   Using DiskPart to create, format, and assign a VHD

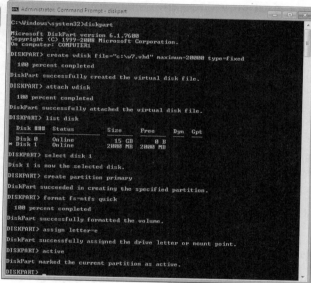

Table 6-4   DiskPart Commands Used in Creating VHDs

Command	Purpose
create vdisk file="*filename*" maximum=*size* type=*type*	Creates a VHD with name of filename, maximum size stated in MB, and type = fixed, expandable, or differencing.
attach	Attaches (mounts) the VHD.
list disk	Shows all disks (physical and virtual) attached to the system, together with their size and identifying number.
Select disk=*n*	Selects the VHD so that it can be partitioned and formatted, where *n* is the number of the disk as shown by the list disk command.

Table 6-4 .DiskPart Commands Used in Creating VHDs

Command	Purpose
`create partition primary`	Creates a primary partition on the VHD using the maximum available space. If you want to use only a portion of the VHD, include the keyword `size=nnnn`, where *nnnn* is the partition size in MB.
`format fs=filesystem`	Formats the partition using the file system *filesystem* (which can be `fat`, `fat32`, or `ntfs`). Add the keyword `quick` to perform a quick format.
`assign letter=letter`	Assigns a drive letter to the partition.
`active`	Marks the selected partition as active.

Mounting VHDs

The act of creating a VHD in the previous section also mounts the VHD automatically so that it is accessible to the physical machine as a distinct drive with its own drive letter. It is also possible to create a VHD on one computer, make copies of it, and use these copies on other computers. To do so, you must *mount* the VHD on each new computer. Simply put, this is the virtual analog of opening the computer, installing and connecting a new hard disk, closing the computer back up, and rebooting it. Use the Disk Management console to mount a VHD, as described in the following steps:

Step 1.   Open an administrative command prompt as previously described under Creating a VHD.

Step 2.   Right-click **Disk Management** and choose **Attach VHD**.

Step 3.   In the Attach Virtual Hard Disk dialog box shown in Figure 6-5, type or browse to the location of the VHD and then click **OK**.

Figure 6-5   Mounting a VHD from Disk Management.

You can also mount a VHD from the DiskPart command-line tool, as the following steps demonstrate:

Step 1.   Click **Start > All Programs > Accessories**, right-click **Command Prompt**, and then choose **Run as Administrator**. In the User Account Control prompt that appears, click **Continue**.

Step 2.   Type **diskpart.** You receive the **diskpart** command prompt.

Step 3.   Type **select vdisk file=**"*path*" where *path* is the complete path to the VHD file to be mounted.

Step 4.   Type **attach vdisk.** You will receive a message informing you that DiskPart successfully attached the virtual disk file. See Figure 6-6.

Figure 6-6   Using DiskPart to mount a VHD.

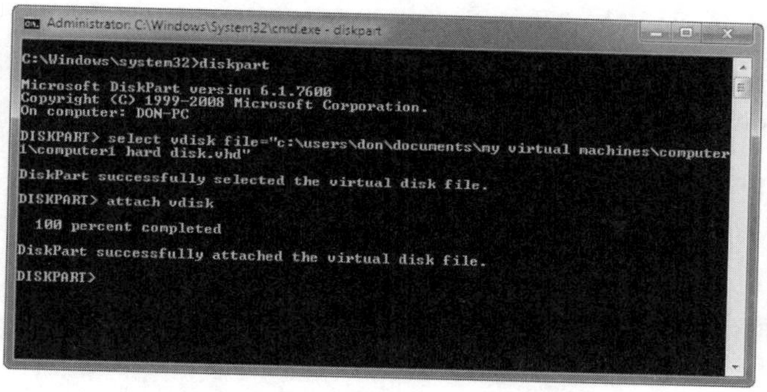

You can also dismount a VHD from either of these two utilities. In Disk Management, right-click the VHD in the details pane and choose **Detach VHD**. In DiskPart, select the VHD and then type **detach vdisk.**

TIP   You can even mount a VHD located on another computer across the network, provided you have proper access permissions to its location. In Disk Management, click **Browse**, click **Network**, and browse to the proper network location. In DiskPart, type the Universal Naming Convention (UNC) path to the shared location for *path* in step 3 of the preceding procedure.

Deploying VHDs

As mentioned earlier in this chapter, a native-boot VHD enables you to deploy Windows 7 to a computer as its native operating system. This enables you to deploy Windows 7 to older computers whose hardware does not meet the Windows 7 hardware requirements. You can treat such Windows 7–based VHD files similarly to .wim files with regards to offline image servicing and image-based setup.

This feature, also known as *VHD Boot*, enables you to use the VHD file as a normal hard disk; unlike using Virtual PC, the machine is actually booted physically from the VHD file and has the full power of the computer's processor, RAM, and cache. After you've created the bootable VHD file, you can use Sysprep (as discussed in Chapter 5) to strip user- and machine-specific data from the file and simply copy this file to as many machines as required. You can even use differencing VHD files (as discussed earlier in this chapter) by creating a single-base VHD file containing the operating system plus incremental VHD files for each virtual computer you create.

Preparing a Custom Windows Image

Use the following basic steps to prepare and deploy a custom Windows image to multiple VHDs:

Step 1.   Install Windows on a reference physical computer (as described in Chapter 2, "Installing Windows 7").

Step 2.   Customize this reference installation, including installation of all required applications.

Step 3.   Use Sysprep to generalize the image (as discussed in Chapter 5).

Step 4.   Use ImageX to capture the reference image into a .wim file on a shared folder location.

Step 5.   Deploy this image to a VHD file and initialize the VHD boot environment.

There are a few minor disadvantages to using VHD boot:

- This procedure results in a small performance decrease—about 3%.

- You can only run Windows 7 or Windows Server 2008 R2 in this fashion. You cannot run older Windows operating systems.

- You cannot use NTFS compression on a native-boot VHD.

- You cannot use BitLocker to encrypt the contents of the disk containing the VHD file. However, you can use BitLocker within the guest operating system.

- You cannot use the Hibernate function to save power; consequently, use of this procedure is of limited value on mobile computers.

- Windows Experience Index does not work on the VHD file.

Best Practices for Using Native-Boot VHDs

Microsoft recommends the following best practices for using native-boot VHDs:

- **Store mission-critical data outside the native-boot VHDs:** This facilitates recovery of the data should the VHD become corrupted.

- **Use fixed VHDs in production environments:** You can use any of the three VHD types; however, you should use fixed VHDs in production environments for reasons mentioned earlier. You can use dynamic or differencing VHDs in development and test scenarios.

- **Use a maximum size that is larger than the minimum disk requirements for Windows:** The VHD holds additional information about the virtual disk; furthermore, Windows updates take up disk space as they are added.

- **Ensure that sufficient space Is available on the host volume for the page file (pagefile.sys):** The page file is created on the host volume outside the VHD. You can use another physical volume for optimum performance.

- **Use Sysprep to generalize the image before using the VHD for native boot on a different computer:** As discussed in Chapter 5, Sysprep prepares the image for copying to additional computers. When you do so, Windows detects hardware devices and initializes properly for running on another computer.

Creating a Native-Boot VHD

You can use ImageX to deploy Windows 7 to a previously created VHD. The following procedure assumes that you have downloaded and installed the Windows AIK to its default location of C:\Program Files\Windows aik\tools*arch*, where *arch* is *x86*, amd64, or ia64 (as described in Chapter 5).

Step 1.   Open an administrative command prompt.

Step 2.   Navigate to the default Windows AIK location.

Step 3.   Type **imagex /info c:<*install_folder*>\install.wim**, where <*install_folder*> is the folder to which you copied the install.wim file (as described in Chapter 5). Note in Figure 6-7 the image count value of 5. This corresponds to the number of Windows images in the install.wim file. Then scroll the output and find the image index number corresponding to the edition of Windows 7 you want to deploy.

Figure 6-7   Obtaining the index number of the **install.wim** file.

CAUTION   Ensure that you select an index value corresponding to an installation of the Enterprise or Ultimate editions of Windows 7 or any edition of Windows Server 2008 R2 except the Foundation Edition. Otherwise, you will be unable to boot the VHD properly (you will receive a message that this edition of Windows does not support VHD boot).

Step 4.   Type **imagex /apply c:**<*install_folder*>\install.wim /check *n* <*drive_letter*>, where the **check** keyword instructs ImageX to validate the image, *n* is the index number obtained in the previous step, and <*drive_letter*> is the drive letter you assigned to the VHD when you created it.

Step 5.   This process will take several minutes, after which you are informed that the image was successfully applied (see Figure 6-8). If you navigate to the drive letter of the VHD, you will notice the files created for a new Windows installation are present (PerfLogs, Program Files, Users, and Windows).

Figure 6-8   Applying the **install.wim** file to create a virtual Windows 7 installation.

After you have deployed Windows 7 to the VHD as described here, you can dismount the VHD as described in the previous section. This enables you to set up the computer for booting from the VHD, as described in the next section. It also enables you to copy the VHD file to a network share or USB hard drive, as desired.

For additional information on VHDs in Windows 7, refer to "Frequently Asked Questions: Virtual Hard Disks in Windows 7" at http://technet.microsoft.com/en-us/library/dd440865(WS.10).aspx. For additional information on the deployment process, refer to "Walkthrough: Deploy a Virtual Hard Disk for Native Boot" at http://technet.microsoft.com/en-us/library/dd744338(WS.10).aspx.

NOTE   You cannot install Windows 7 or Windows Server 2008 R2 directly from the installation DVD to a VHD file. You must deploy Windows as described here.

TIP You can use Windows Deployment Services (WDS) to deploy the VHD image to large numbers of computers. WDS in Windows Server 2008 R2 includes the capability to add VHD image files to its image catalog, making them available to target computers using PXE boot. These computers copy the VHD file locally and configure booting from the VHD. On first boot, the computer configures Windows for the physical devices and performs the usual mini-setup. Using WDS in this manner facilitates rapid deployment of Windows to many computers. You can also script the use of WDS by using the command-line tool, WDSUTIL.

TIP Another way to create the VHD file is by using an open-source tool called WIM2VHD, available from the MSDN code gallery at http://code.msdn.microsoft.com/wim2vhd. This is a scriptable command-line tool that converts the .wim file to a VHD that can be booted.

Booting VHDs

New to Windows 7, you can boot either Windows 7 or Windows Server 2008 R2 from a VHD. To do so, you must configure the boot loader from the default Windows installation using the Bcdedit command-line utility. This tool manages Boot Configuration Data (BCD) stores, which replace the Boot.ini file used in Windows versions prior to Vista. You can use Bcdedit for several purposes, including creating new stores, modifying existing stores, adding or removing boot menu options, and so on. Use the following procedure:

Step 1. Open an administrative command prompt.

Step 2. Type **bcdedit.** This starts the Windows Boot Loader utility and displays the default Windows boot information, as shown in Figure 6-9.

Figure 6-9 The Windows Boot Loader program provides default Windows boot information.

Step 3.   Type **bcdedit /copy {current} /d "Boot from VHD"**. This command copies the current Windows boot loader information, creating a new entry that you can modify for booting from the VHD.

Step 4.   Type **bcdedit** again. You will notice a duplicate entry, identified by the globally unique identifier (GUID) in the **identifier** line. Make careful note of this GUID.

Step 5.   Type **bcdedit /set {guid} device vhd=[*drive*:]*path_to_vhd_file*** where **guid** is as noted in step 4, drive is the drive on which the VHD file is located, and <*path_to_vhd_file*> is the location of the VHD file on its drive. For example:

```
bcdedit /set {35bbc226-7920-11de-b6f7-a0288f236347} device
VHD="[C:]\users\don\documents\my virtual machines\w7vhd.vhd"
```

Step 6.   Set the OS device by typing **bcdedit /set {guid} osdevice vhd=[*drive*:]*path_to_vhd_file***. The syntax of this command is identical to the previous one, except that **device** is replaced by **osdevice**.

Step 7.   Set the Detect Hal command by typing **bcdedit /set {guid} detecthal on**.

Step 8.   Provide a description for this boot by typing **bcdedit /set {guid} description *description***, where **description** is a description of the boot that will appear at startup. Enclose the description in double quotes if it contains spaces.

Step 9.   Verify your output by typing **bcdedit** again. You should see something similar to Figure 6-10, enabling you to boot either into the full, previously configured operating system or to the VHD file.

When you reboot your computer, you will see a boot loader with a choice for booting into the previously configured operating system or to the VHD file. When you boot to the VHD file, Windows will run a setup routine, setting up devices and drivers, and then ask you for parameters (such as date and time, user and password, license key, and so on). You should run **Sysprep /generalize** on this VHD file (as described in Chapter 5) before deploying it to multiple computers.

If you want to delete the entry, take note of the GUID listed in bcdedit and use the following command:

```
bcdedit /delete {GUID} /cleanup
```

Adding a Native-Boot VHD to an Older Computer

An older computer, such as one running Windows XP, does not have the same boot loader file; it has the older Boot.ini file, which is loaded by Ntldr at startup time. If you are adding a native-boot VHD to such a computer, you will need to

Figure 6-10   A portion of the **bcdedit** output, showing the boot loader for the VHD file.

update the system partition first by using the Bcdboot tool before editing the boot menu with Bcdedit. The following steps show you how to update a BIOS-based computer to include a Windows 7 boot menu:

Step 1.   Open an administrative command prompt.

Step 2.   Use DiskPart to attach the VHD file to this computer and assign it a driver letter, as already described.

Step 3.   Use bcdboot to copy the boot environment files and boot configuration data (BCD) configuration from the \Windows\System32 folder of the VHD to the system partition. For example, type

```
cd <letter>:windows\system32
bcdboot <letter>:\windows /s c:
```

In these commands, *letter* is the drive letter you assigned to the mounted VHD file and it is assumed that the system partition is on drive *c:*. After you have performed these steps, you can use bcdedit as already described to edit the boot loader files to enable booting from the VHD.

Offline Servicing and Updating VHDs

The term *offline servicing* refers to modification or updating of a Windows image offline without first booting it. You can perform offline servicing or updating by using the Deployment Image Servicing and Management (DISM) command-line tool. You can treat Windows 7-based VHD files similarly to `.wim` files with regards to offline servicing and setup actions. Tasks you can perform using DISM include adding or removal of drivers, language packs, or local packs; enabling or disabling Windows features; and upgrading the Windows image to a higher edition. By doing so, you can ensure that your images are kept up-to-date; furthermore, you can customize images for various deployment scenarios by copying the master image and making the appropriate changes to each copy.

The following steps outline the general procedure you would use for performing any of these actions:

Step 1. Use Disk Management or DiskPart to mount the VHD (as explained earlier in this chapter). Note the drive letter on which the VHD is mounted.

Step 2. Open an administrative command prompt.

Step 3. Navigate to the folder in which the DISM tool is located (normally `C:\Program Files\Windows AIK\Tools\Servicing`).

Step 4. Type `dism /image:<letter>:\ /command /parameter:<path_to_file>`. In this command, `<letter>` is the drive letter to which the VHD is mounted and `/parameter:<path_to_file>` is the required parameter as outlined in Table 6-5. Specify the full path to the driver or other file as required. For most commands, you can enter multiple parameters to perform more than one similar action at a time.

Step 5. Repeat this step to perform additional servicing actions as required.

Step 6. When finished, use Disk Management or DiskPart to dismount the VHD (as explained earlier in this chapter).

Table 6-5 summarizes the DISM commands used for servicing offline VHD images and their parameters. Additional commands and options for other DISM actions are not included but can be found at "Deployment Image Servicing and Management Command-Line Options" at http://technet.microsoft.com/en-us/library/dd744382(WS.10).aspx.

Table 6-5   DISM Commands for Servicing Offline VHD Images

Command	Parameters	What It Does
/Add-Driver	/driver:<*path_to_driver*>	Adds a driver. You can specify multiple drivers.
/Remove-Driver	/driver:<*driver_name*>	Removes the specified driver(s).
/Add-Package	/PackagePath:<*path_to_package*>	Adds a package or language pack. You can specify multiple packages, as required.
/Remove-Package	/PackagePath:<*path_to_package*>	Removes a package or language pack.
/Get-Packages	None	Lists all packages added to the image.
/Get-Features	None	Lists all available Windows features and whether they are enabled. You can also output the list to a text file named featurelist.txt by using the parameter >featurelist.txt. This is helpful because this command returns a long list of features.
/Get-FeatureInfo	/FeatureName:<*name*>	Provides additional information about the stated feature. The feature name should be the same as that provided by the /Get-Features command.
/Enable-Feature	/FeatureName:<*name*>	Enables the stated feature.
/Disable-Feature	/FeatureName:<*name*>	Disables the stated feature.

You can also change all international language settings in the mounted offline image to match the Microsoft defaults for a given language. At the administrative command prompt, type

```
dism /image:letter: /Set-SKUIntlDefaults:language
```

In this command, *language* is the value defined for each language as enumerated in "Language Pack Default Values" at http://technet.microsoft.com/en-us/library/dd799301(WS.10).aspx (for example, en-US for United States English).

NOTE   You can add multiple drivers from the same folder by simply specifying the folder without a driver name for *path_to_driver*. To install an unsigned driver, include the /ForceUnsigned parameter in the command specified here. We discuss driver signing in Chapter 7, "Configuring Devices and Updates."

CAUTION   Ensure that you do not remove boot-critical drivers. If you do so, the Windows image might become unbootable.

Upgrading a Windows Image to a Higher Edition

You can upgrade the Windows edition from the administrative command prompt by using the following steps in place of step 4 in the previous procedure:

Step 1.   To display the current edition of a Windows image on a VHD mounted on drive *letter:*, type **dism /image:*letter*:\ /Get-CurrentEdition**.

Step 2.   To find which editions of Windows you can upgrade the image to, type **dism /image: *letter*:\ /Get-TargetEditions**.

Step 3.   To upgrade the Windows edition, type **dism /image:*letter*:\ /Set-Edition:*edition***, where **edition** is the desired edition (for example, Ultimate).

NOTE   You cannot downgrade a Windows image to a lower edition. Lower editions will not appear when you use the /Get-TargetEditions option. If the current edition is Ultimate, no editions will appear when you use this option.

Using an Answer File to Service an Offline VHD

You can use an answer file for servicing an offline VHD by typing the following command:

```
dism /image:letter: /Apply-Unattend:path_to_answer_file
```

In this command, *path_to_answer_file* is the full path to the XML answer file. For additional information about using answer files to service Windows images, refer to "Unattended Servicing Command-Line Options" at http://technet.microsoft.com/en-us/library/dd744522(WS.10).aspx.

Exam Preparation Tasks

Review All the Key Topics

Review the most important topics in the chapter, noted with the key topics icon in the outer margin of the page. Table 6-6 lists a reference of these key topics and the page numbers on which each is found.

Table 6-6   Key Topics for Chapter 6

Key Topic Element	Description	Page Number
Table 6-2	Lists types of VHDs	192
Table 6-3	Lists tools used for configuring VHDs	193
List	Shows how to create a VHD using Disk Management	194
Figure 6-1	Using the Create and Attach Hard Disk dialog box	194
List	Shows how to create a VHD using DiskPart	196
Figure 6-4	Using Diskpart to create, assign, and format a VHD	197
List	Steps used to prepare and deploy a custom Windows image	200
List	Steps used to create a native-boot VHD	201
List	Shows how to edit the boot loader for booting a VHD	203
Table 6-5	DISM commands for servicing offline VHD images	207

Complete the Tables and Lists from Memory

Print a copy of Appendix C, "Memory Tables" (found on the CD), or at least the section for this chapter, and complete the tables and lists from memory. Appendix D, "Memory Tables Answer Key," also on the CD, includes completed tables and lists to check your work.

Definitions of Key Terms

Define the following key terms from this chapter, and check your answers in the glossary.

Virtual hard disk (VHD), hypervisor, fixed VHD, dynamic VHD, differencing VHD, Bcdedit, Bcdboot

This chapter covers the following subjects:

- **Installing and Configuring Device Drivers:** This section teaches you how to install device drivers and use Device Manager for configuring and Windows Update for updating drivers.

- **Maintaining Device Drivers:** This section introduces the concept of driver signing and checking for valid driver signatures. It also discusses permissions for installing drivers and settings that you can configure from a driver's Properties dialog box.

- **Troubleshooting Device Drivers:** This section discusses the use of Device Manager to resolve driver problems, including conflicts, and to roll back problematic drivers.

- **Configuring Updates to Windows 7:** Windows Update provides a one-stop service for all types of updates available to Windows 7 users. This section shows you how to configure Windows Update, including Group Policy settings that determine how Windows Update works in an enterprise environment.

CHAPTER 7

Configuring Devices and Updates

When you first install Windows 7, it performs an inventory of all devices it finds on the computer and records information about them in the Registry under HKEY_LOCAL_MACHINE\Hardware. Each device is associated with a software program called a *driver*. This program enables the device to communicate properly with the operating system. Typically, a driver is in the form of an .inf file (for example, Mydevice.inf). These files are typically located in the hidden subfolder %systemroot%\inf. Device manufacturers frequently issue driver updates that improve device functionality or solve problems that users have reported. In addition, Microsoft issues updates at least once a month. For the 70-680 exam, Microsoft expects you to know how to use Device Manager to ensure that your devices are installed and working properly and to use Windows Update to provide the proper updates to drivers, software programs, and operating system files.

"Do I Know This Already?" Quiz

The "Do I Know This Already?" quiz enables you to assess whether you should read this entire chapter or simply jump to the "Exam Preparation Tasks" section for review. If you are in doubt, read the entire chapter. Table 7-1 outlines the major headings in this chapter and the corresponding "Do I Know This Already?" quiz questions. You can find the answers in Appendix A, "Answers to the 'Do I Know This Already?' Quizzes."

Table 7-1 "Do I Know This Already?" Foundation Topics Section-to-Question Mapping

Foundations Topics Section	Questions Covered in This Section
Installing and Configuring Device Drivers	1–4
Maintaining Device Drivers	5–7
Troubleshooting Device Drivers	8–10
Configuring Updates to Windows 7	11–13

1. Which of the following are possible locations from which drivers for Plug and Play (PnP) devices can be installed? (Choose all that apply.)

   a. Windows system files

   b. Windows Update

   c. CD-ROM or floppy disks

   d. Device manufacturer websites

2. You are looking in Device Manager to determine whether any hardware devices are disabled. What icon should you look for?

   a. A black downward-pointing arrow

   b. A red "X"

   c. A yellow question mark

   d. A blue "i" on a white field

3. You want to obtain information on the IRQ lines, DMA channels, and I/O ports being used by a device. Where should you look? (Choose two.)

   a. Type `msinfo32`, and then select the **Hardware Resources** node from the System Information dialog box.

   b. Type `msinfo32`, and then select the **Components** node from the System Information dialog box.

   c. Access the General tab of the device's Properties dialog box.

   d. Access the Details tab of the device's Properties dialog box.

   e. Access the Resources tab of the device's Properties dialog box.

4. You are removing an old device from your computer and are not planning on replacing it in the immediate future. You want to ensure that its drivers are permanently removed. What should you do?

   a. Use Device Manager to disable the driver.

   b. Use Device Manager to uninstall the driver.

   c. Use Device Manager to roll back the driver.

   d. Use Windows Update to update all drivers on your computer.

5. You are planning to stage a new driver package that was signed by an untrusted publisher. What is the prime benefit of performing this action?

   a. This allows all computers accessing the package to automatically update their drivers.

   b. This sends the package to Microsoft so that it can be signed by a trusted authority.

   c. This allows only selected administrative users to install the driver package.

   d. This enables standard users to install the driver package.

6. What program would you use to determine whether any unsigned drivers are present on your computer?

   a. `sfc.exe`

   b. `sigverif.exe`

   c. `msinfo32.exe`

   d. `gpedit.exe`

7. You install an updated driver for your network adapter card, and now the card does not work. What should you do to get the card working again?

   a. Update the driver.

   b. Roll back the driver.

   c. Uninstall the driver.

   d. Disable the driver.

8. You want to configure Device Manager so that it displays all devices present according to their IRQ, DMA, and memory addresses. What view should you use?

   a. Devices by type

   b. Devices by connection

   c. Resources by type

   d. Resources by connection

9. You install a new Blu-ray disc writer on your computer. When you restart your computer, you discover that not only does this device not work, but also you are unable to access the Internet. What should you be looking for?

   a. A resource conflict

   b. Insufficient power from your computer's power supply

   c. Outdated device drivers

   d. Unsigned device drivers

10. Which of the following tools enables you to view device-related problems but does not provide any tools to correct these problems?

   a. Device Manager

   b. `sigverif.exe`

   c. Action Center

   d. System Information

11. Microsoft has packaged a set of updates designed to fix problems with specific Windows components or software packages such as Microsoft Office. What is this package known as?

   a. A critical security update

   b. An optional update

   c. An update roll-up

   d. A service pack

12. You have a computer that is also used by an individual who has caused problems with an older computer in the past. You would prefer that this user be unable to install critical updates from the Windows Update website, and you have configured a nonadministrative user account for her. What additional step should you do?

   a. Clear the check box labeled **Allow all users to install updates on this computer**.

   b. Clear the check box labeled **Give me updates for Microsoft products and check for new optional Microsoft software when I update Windows**.

   c. Clear the check box labeled **Show me detailed notifications when new Microsoft software is available**.

   d. You do not need to perform any additional steps. By default, the non-administrative user is not permitted to install updates.

13. You have installed Windows Server Update Services on a server on your network, and you want to ensure that computers on the network do not attempt to access the Internet for downloading updates. What policy should you configure?

   a. **Allow Automatic Updates immediate installation**

   b. **Turn on Software Notifications**

   c. **Specify intranet Microsoft update service location**

   d. **Enable client-side targeting**

14. You want to check whether your computer has received a critical update from the Microsoft Windows Update website. Where should you look?

   a. Device Manager

   b. System Information

   c. The Windows Update Control Panel applet

   d. The Resources tab of each device's Properties dialog box

Foundation Topics

Installing and Configuring Device Drivers

Device drivers are software utilities that enable hardware components to communicate with the operating system. All components that you see in Device Manager utilize drivers, including disk drives, display adapters, network interface cards, removable media (floppy, CD-ROM, DVD-ROM, and so on) drives, keyboards, mice, sound cards, USB controllers, and so on. External components such as printers, scanners, and so on also use drivers. With each new version of the operating system, it becomes necessary for hardware manufacturers to produce new drivers. Drivers written for older operating systems such as Windows 2000, XP, and Windows Vista might work with Windows 7 but can result in reduced device functionality or might not work at all. You need to be able to install, configure, and troubleshoot drivers for various components for the 70-680 exam and for real-world computer support tasks.

When you first install or upgrade your computer to Windows 7, the operating system searches for hardware devices attached to your system and loads drivers required for these devices to function. In most cases, this process occurs automatically without the user even knowing that it's taking place. It is only when the operating system is unable to locate the proper drivers for a device that you really become aware that a problem might exist.

Windows 7 offers several major improvements in the process of locating, installing, and updating drivers:

- Searches are more automatic than before. All locations are searched including the Internet and drivers are automatically downloaded if necessary.

- Driver installation from Windows Update takes place automatically, without the need for a UAC prompt or a wizard. This process works even if no user is logged on.

- Searches are more accurate, with Windows Update being searched first, thereby ensuring that the most up-to-date driver is installed, even if a driver exists in the local computer driver store. Status information has been improved.

- Performance has been improved and users can cancel the download if it is lengthy. In special cases, you can configure certain devices not to search Windows Update.

In addition to driver installation, Windows Update offers updates to software applications installed on your computer as well as the operating system itself. Also available from time to time are optional updates that improve the functionality of your computer and its devices or add additional features. We look at Windows Update in greater depth later in this chapter.

Installing Devices and Drivers

Plug and Play (PnP) refers to the ability of a computer system to automatically configure hardware devices connected to expansion cards or external ports. You should be able to plug in a device and play with it without worrying about setting hardware components such as DIP switches or jumpers. If you connect USB, IEEE 1394 (FireWire), and SCSI devices to your computer, Windows 7 will automatically detect these devices. This is also true when you install a PnP expansion card in a PCI or AGP slot and turn on the computer. If Windows 7 does not have a driver available for the device, you will be prompted to provide a disk or path to the driver.

Installing hardware devices typically takes three steps:

Step 1. **Adding the device:** For internal devices such as hard drives or network adapters, you need to shut down your computer and, for some devices, open the case and insert it in the appropriate expansion slot or bay. For a USB or FireWire device, you simply plug it into a connector located somewhere on the computer.

Step 2. **Locating appropriate device drivers for the device:** Windows detects the device at startup and displays a message on the taskbar that it is installing device driver software (see Figure 7-1). In most cases, this message goes away within a few seconds and your device is ready for use.

Figure 7-1 Windows normally detects PnP devices and automatically installs driver software.

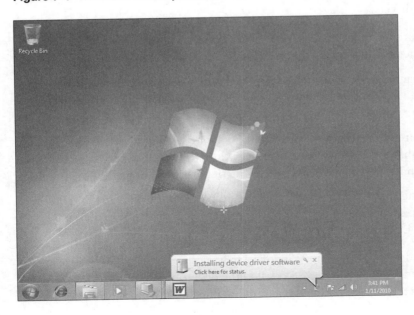

Step 3.   **Configuring device settings:** For PnP devices, this generally happens automatically. If Windows is unable to locate the driver, it requests any needed information, including any manufacturer-supplied CD-ROM or floppy disk. You might also be able to locate hardware drivers from the Microsoft Windows Update website.

Device Stage

Device Stage is a new Windows 7 application that provides a single location from which you can manage all devices that have been properly installed on your computer, as shown in Figure 7-2. You can access Device Stage by clicking **Devices and Printers** from the Start menu or the Control Panel Hardware and Sound category. When you connect a device, Device Stage attempts to add it automatically with the aid of an XML-based definition file provided by the manufacturer. If the device is not automatically detected, you can click **Add a device** to start a wizard that searches for devices that might be attached to your computer. Ensure that your device is properly plugged in and turned on. The wizard should display a selection of device types, from which you can select the appropriate device. Click **Next** and follow the remaining steps presented to install your device.

Figure 7-2   Windows normally detects PnP devices and automatically installs driver software.

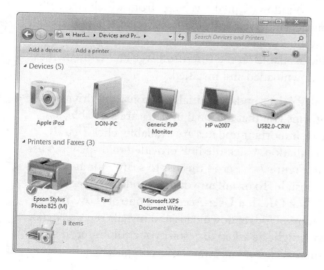

> **TIP**   If you do not want Windows to automatically download drivers for new hardware devices, you can modify this behavior. Access the Hardware tab of the System Properties dialog box and click the **Device Installation Settings** command button. On the dialog box that appears, click **No, let me choose what to do.** Select the desired option from those displayed in Figure 7-3, and then click **Save Changes.**

Figure 7-3   You can modify the default driver installation behavior if you want.

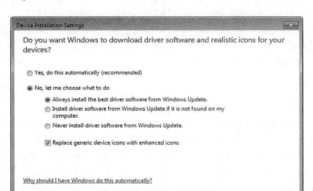

Updating Drivers

Windows Update provides a seamless, automatic means of updating all the device drivers on your computer. Click **Start > Control Panel > System and Security > Windows Update** (or type `Windows Update` into the Search box in the Start menu). This connects you to the Windows Update website, from which ActiveX controls compare the drivers on the computer with the latest updates and display a list of available updates. This method works by comparing the hardware IDs of installed devices with drivers made available on the Microsoft website. Only if an exact match is found is the driver downloaded and installed.

Windows Update does not display driver updates initially. It considers driver updates optional in nature and informs you that optional updates are available, as shown in Figure 7-4. If critical or important updates are available, click **Install updates** to proceed with the installation. Click the link provided to display the list of optional updates, as shown in Figure 7-5. Scroll this list to search for any driver updates that you might want to install. To install any desired updates, select them from the list in Figure 7-5 and click **OK**. If a User Account Control (UAC) prompt appears, click **Yes**. Windows Update downloads and installs the update(s). After installation is finished, you might be asked to restart your computer; if so, close any open programs and then click **Yes** to restart your computer.

Microsoft places these drivers on the Update site only if they are digitally signed, meet certain web publishing standards, and have passed the testing requirements for the Windows 7 Logo Program for Hardware. These procedures verify that drivers included on the site are certified to do what they are supposed to do.

Figure 7-4   Windows Update informs you whether any updates are available for your computer.

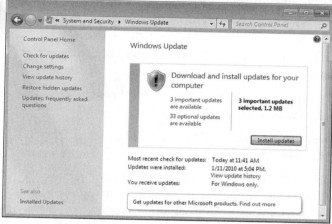

Figure 7-5   Windows Update enables you to select optional updates from this list.

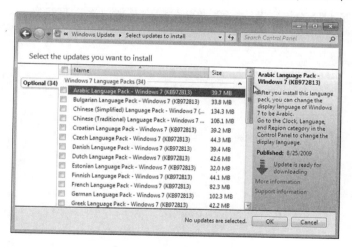

Using Device Manager

The majority of the work involving device implementation, management, and troubleshooting for many types of hardware devices is done in the Device Manager utility. You can run Device Manager either as a standalone Microsoft Management Console (MMC) snap-in or as a component of the Computer Management snap-in.

You can access Device Manager in any of the following ways:

- Click **Start**, right-click **Computer**, and select **Manage**. This opens the Computer Management console, from which you can open Device Manager by clicking its icon in the console tree.

- Click **Start**, right-click **Computer**, and select **Properties**. From the System applet, click **Advanced system settings** to display the System Properties dialog box. Click the **Hardware** tab, and then click the **Device Manager** command button.

- Access the Hardware and Sound category in Control Panel and then select **Device Manager** under the Devices and Printers heading.

- Click **Start**, right-click **Computer**, and select **Properties**. From the System applet, select the **Device Manager** link.

- Click **Start** and type `Device Manager` in the Search box. Then select **Device Manager** from the list that appears.

As shown in Figure 7-6, Device Manager displays a list of all types of hardware components that might be installed on your computer. Click the triangles on the various device categories to expand them and display the actual devices that are present (as shown for monitors and network adapters).

Figure 7-6 Device Manager enables you to configure and troubleshoot all hardware devices on your computer.

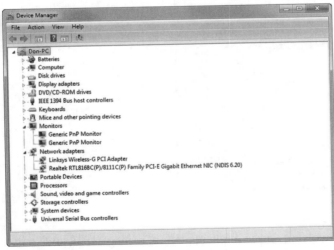

After you determine that a hardware device is installed correctly and is listed in the Windows 7 Logo Program for Hardware, you should check Device Manager for its listing to see whether the device is detected by Windows 7 and is functioning. Devices shown in Device Manager might display icons that indicate their status. These include the following:

- If a device is disabled, an icon with a black downward-pointing arrow appears over the device icon. A disabled device is a device that is physically present in the computer and is consuming resources but does not have a protected-mode driver loaded.

■ A red "X" appearing over the device icon indicates that the device is not functioning.

■ A yellow question mark icon appearing next to the device icon indicates that a device is functioning but experiencing problems.

■ A blue "i" on a white field (for information) indicates that the device has forced resource configurations.

When you right-click a device, a shortcut menu similar to the one displayed in Figure 7-7 appears. You can select to update the driver or uninstall or disable the device. You can also scan the device for hardware changes or access the device's properties. When you open the device's Properties dialog box, you can put a variety of configurations into effect, as well as disable or enable the device.

Figure 7-7   The right-click menu in Device Manager provides several configuration options.

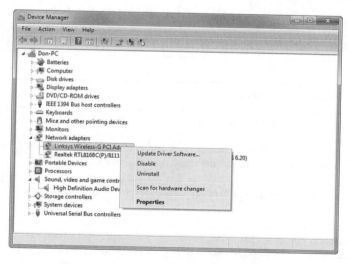

Every device has its own Properties dialog box (see Figure 7-8), specific to its device type and sometimes specific to the manufacturer and model (depending on the installed driver). Table 7-2 describes the standard tabs found in any device's Properties dialog box (not all these tabs are found for every device and manufacturers might add additional tabs not included here).

Figure 7-8 Each device in Device Manager has a Properties dialog box that enables you to configure a wide range of device properties.

Table 7-2 Tabs Found in a Device's Properties Dialog Box

Tool	Description
General	Displays the device's description and status.
Advanced	Provides additional configurable properties.
Driver	Displays the current device driver's information and enables you to perform several configuration options. We discuss these options later in this chapter.
Details	Displays the device's specifications. You can choose from a long list of device properties.
Resources	Displays the system resources being consumed, including interrupt requests (IRQs), input/output (I/O) ports, direct memory access (DMA) channels, and physical memory range. Displays whether these resources are in conflict with any others being used in the system.
Power Management	Provides options to allow the computer to turn off the device when not in use to save power and allow the device to wake the computer from sleep mode.

Using Device Manager to Uninstall Drivers

When you uninstall a device driver, the driver is completely removed from the computer. To uninstall a driver, right-click the device in Device Manager and choose **Uninstall**. In the Confirm Device Uninstall dialog box shown in Figure 7-9, select the **Delete the driver software for this device** check box if desired and then click **OK**. Note that Windows will redetect the device at the next restart (if the device is still attached to the computer) and attempt to reinstall it.

Figure 7-9   Uninstalling a driver.

Using Device Manager to Disable Drivers

Rather than uninstalling the device completely, you can disable the driver. The hardware configuration is not changed. Right-click the device in Device Manager and choose **Disable**. You receive a message box similar to that shown in Figure 7-10. Click **Yes** to disable the driver. The device appears in Device Manager with a small black arrow indicating that it is disabled. To reenable the device, right-click it again and choose **Enable**. The device is reenabled without any further prompts.

Figure 7-10   Disabling a driver.

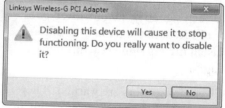

Maintaining Device Drivers

Manufacturers often release updated drivers for their devices, which provide new features or improve the functionality of their device. Occasionally an updated driver will not function properly on a particular machine. At times, you might need to download an updated driver from Microsoft or the manufacturer's website to fix problems with device functionality caused by poorly written drivers or by changing technology. You need to know how to maintain device drivers to ensure that all the computers in your responsibility function properly and individuals using these computers can get their work done.

Managing and Troubleshooting Drivers and Driver Signing

Driver signing is a process that Microsoft follows to validate files that a third-party manufacturer creates for use in a Windows 7 computer. A manufacturer submits its drivers to Microsoft, and after Microsoft completes a thorough quality assurance testing process, Microsoft signs the files digitally. This digital signature is an electronic security mark that indicates the publisher of the software and information that can determine whether a driver has been altered. Driver signing is an extra assurance of the quality of the software installed on the computer.

Device drivers included on the Windows 7 installation DVD or downloaded from the Microsoft Update website include a Microsoft digital signature. If you have problems installing a driver or a device is not working properly, you should check with the Microsoft Update website and visit the device manufacturer's support website to obtain an up-to-date digitally signed driver for your device.

What's New with Driver Signing in Windows 7

Microsoft has initiated the following new driver signing requirements for Windows 7:

- Standard (nonadministrative) users can install only drivers signed by either a Windows publisher or trusted publisher. These drivers are placed in a protected location on the computer called the *driver store*. Microsoft implemented this requirement because drivers run as a part of the operating system with unrestricted access to the entire computer. Therefore, it is critical that only properly authorized drivers be permitted.

- Standard users cannot install unsigned drivers or drivers that have been signed by an untrusted publisher; you cannot modify this policy in Windows 7.

- Administrators can install drivers that have been signed by an untrusted publisher, and they can also add the publisher's certificate to the trusted certificates store, thereby enabling standard users to install drivers signed by this publisher. This is known as *staging* driver packages.

- If drivers are unsigned or have been altered, administrators are warned. They can proceed in a manner similar to how they would if the drivers were from an untrusted publisher.

NOTE You cannot install a driver that lacks a valid digital signature, or one that was altered after it was signed, on x64-based versions of Windows.

If you install a device, Windows 7 looks for the driver signature as a part of System File Protection, which is a feature that prevents applications from replacing critical Windows files by creating and maintaining backups of many critical program files. When it fails to find one, Windows 7 notifies you that the drivers are not signed and prompts you to continue or stop the installation, provided you have administrative privileges. Otherwise, the installation attempt fails. If you continue with the installation, Windows 7 automatically creates a restore point, which facilitates returning to the previous configuration. Restore points are discussed in more depth in Chapter 18, "Configuring System and File Recovery."

NOTE   For more details on signing and staging device drivers, refer to "Device Management and Installation Step-by-Step Guide: Signing and Staging Device Drivers in Windows 7 and Windows Server 2008 R2" at http://technet.microsoft.com/en-us/library/dd919230(WS.10).aspx.

Checking Drivers for Digital Signatures

Dynamic-link libraries (DLLs) and other files are often shared by programs. Sometimes a program overwrites files that were originally installed by a digitally signed driver. If a device behaves oddly, you might want to verify that its driver still has the signature. You can check to validate the driver by looking in Device Manager. Double-click the device and click the **Driver** tab of its Properties dialog box. You should see the statement `Digital Signer: Microsoft Windows Hardware Compatibility Publisher`.

You can check individual files further by clicking the **Driver Details** button. Signed files have an icon of a sealed certificate, which appears to the left of the name (see Figure 7-11). Files that have not been digitally signed do not have a green check mark icon next to the filename.

Figure 7-11   Each digitally signed file is displayed with an icon for easy identification. Unsigned files are indicated as such.

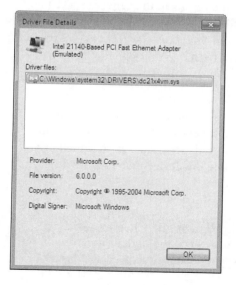

If you want to verify device drivers throughout the system, you can run the sigverif application. To do so:

Step 1. Click **Start** and type **sigverif** in the Search field. Then click **Sigverif.exe.**

The File Signature Verification program starts, as shown in Figure 7-12.

Figure 7-12   The File Signature Verification program checks all drivers for digital signatures.

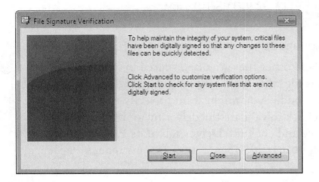

Step 2. Click the **Advanced** button and verify that sigverif will log the results and save them to a file.

Step 3. Click **OK** and then click **Start**.

After the program has completed its check, the program displays any files that were not signed in a window, plus you can see the results in the Sigverif.txt file. If the program does not detect any unsigned files, it displays a message box with the message Your files have been scanned and verified as digitally signed. Otherwise, it displays a list of files that have not been digitally signed.

Unsigned drivers might not cause a problem. If you are having problems with a device that has an unsigned driver, you should disable the driver. If you are having unspecified problems, such as the computer does not go into sleep mode, you should determine which devices have unsigned drivers, disable them one at a time, and then test to see whether the problem is resolved. To disable an unsigned driver that has already been installed, you should disable the device that uses the driver, uninstall the driver, or rename the driver files.

TIP   When in doubt, check the system files. The System File Checker, which is executed from the command line with sfc.exe, can check the digital signature of system protected files. With other uses, such as repopulating the DLLCACHE folder and replacing system files that are missing or incorrect, sfc.exe can be executed from a batch program or script. This program has several options; the /scannow option is one of the most useful, scanning the integrity of all protected system files and performing repairs where possible. This process takes several minutes. To view information on all available options, run sfc.exe /?. Note that in Windows 7, as was the case in Vista, you must run this command as an administrator; right-click the **Command Prompt** option, select **Run as administrator**, and then click **Continue** in the User Account Control dialog box.

Driver Installation Permissions in Windows 7

In previous versions of Windows, only users with administrative privileges could install drivers. Consequently, many enterprises provided their users with local administrative rights; this enables users to perform these tasks, but they also allowed users to undertake actions that could compromise security or configure the computer such that it would not run properly. These actions resulted in increased support costs and demands on the help desk.

In Windows 7, an administrator can implement a policy that prevents the installation of a driver according to its device ID or device setup class. If such a policy is present, Windows will not install devices forbidden by these policies. An administrator can also permit standard users to install devices drivers that are members of specified device setup classes.

Configuring Driver Settings

The Driver tab of a device's Properties dialog box enables you to configure several driver settings, as shown in Figure 7-13. The following options are available:

- **Driver Details:** Provides details about the driver in use, including the certificate icon already mentioned.

- **Update Driver:** Starts the Update Driver Software Wizard, which enables you to search automatically for updated drivers (including those located on the Internet) or to browse your computer for drivers. The latter option enables you to insert a CD or floppy disk containing drivers, if you have one.

- **Roll Back Driver:** Enables you to remove an updated driver and return the last functioning driver, should you experience problems after updating your driver. This option is available only if you have updated your driver previously.

- **Disable:** Disables the driver, as available from the right-click menu shown in Figure 7-7.

- **Uninstall:** Uninstalls the driver, as available from the right-click menu shown in Figure 7-7.

Figure 7-13   The Driver tab of a device's Properties dialog box enables you to configure several driver settings.

Troubleshooting Device Drivers

Even with all the improvements Microsoft has made in device and driver management in Windows 7, problems still do occur. Drivers use system resources, including IRQ lines, I/O ports, DMA channels, and physical memory addresses. If two hardware components attempt to use the same location of any of these resources, a conflict results and these components will not work. For example, you install a new scanner and discover that your network adapter does not work. Such a situation happens more often when using a non-PnP device. In such a situation, you should check resource assignments for conflicts. It is frequently necessary to modify settings on the non-PnP device, for example, with the aid of jumpers or DIP switches. Reconfigure the device with the aid of manufacturer instructions, which might be located on a label placed on the device. In this section, we look at troubleshooting these problems.

Resolving Driver Conflicts

You can use Device Manager to determine whether a resource conflict exists by changing the view. Device Manager offers several view types that assist in monitoring, as described in Table 7-3.

Table 7-3 Device Manager Views

View	What It Displays
Devices by type	Displays devices by the type of installed device, such as monitor or mouse. This is the default view. If you have multiple monitors, for example, you see each of the monitors displayed below the Monitor node.
Devices by connection	Displays devices according to the type of connection. For example, all the disk drives and CD or DVD drives connected to the IDE controller are displayed under the IDE connection node.
Resources by type	Displays devices according to resource type. Resources include DMA, I/O, IRQ, and memory. For example, Figure 7-14 shows devices listed in the order of the I/O resources it uses.
Resources by connection	Displays resources according to their type of connection. This also serves to indicate which resources are currently available.

Figure 7-14 Device Manager provides an organized view of devices by the I/O resources they consume.

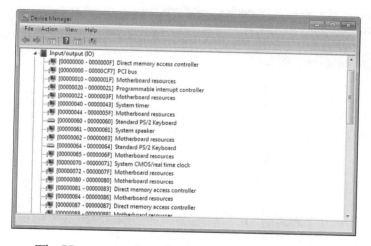

The View menu also offers two customization options that affect what you see. To expand the views to show non-PnP devices, select **Show hidden devices**. To modify what items Device Manager shows, select **Customize**. This displays the Customize View dialog box shown in Figure 7-15, which enables you to select which items are shown by Device Manager.

To view resources being used by a specific device, access the Resources tab of the device's Properties dialog box. As shown in Figure 7-16, this tab displays a list of all resources in use and reports conflicts that might be occurring. To change resource settings, clear the **Use automatic settings** check box and then click **Change Setting**. In the dialog box that appears, select a setting that does not conflict with other settings. Device Manager will inform you if these settings conflict with any other devices; if so, modify the settings so that no conflicts occur and then click **OK**.

Figure 7-15   You can select which items are displayed in the Device Manager window.

Figure 7-16   The Resources tab of a device's Properties dialog box displays all resources in use and informs you of any conflicts that might be occurring.

Use of the Action Center to View Device-Related Problems

The new Windows 7 Action Center also offers information on device-related problems. This is a primarily security-related application that replaces the

Windows Vista Security Center. As shown in Figure 7-17, the Maintenance section of Action Center replaces the Vista Problem Reports and Solutions Control Panel applet. Problems that have occurred on your computer are reported here; you can click the problems displayed to obtain additional information. A user is notified if there is a solution to a device-related problem that has been submitted to Action Center. A web link is supplied and notification is suppressed after the user has installed the application.

Figure 7-17 The Windows 7 Action Center includes a Maintenance section that displays device-related problems.

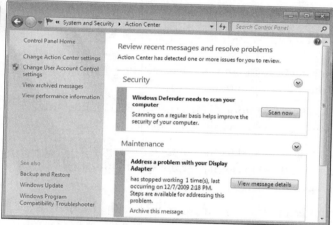

Use of System Information to View Device-Related Problems

The System Information utility is another place you can check devices and locate potential problems. Click **Start**, type **msinfo32** in the Search field, and then click **msinfo32.exe**. Expand the Hardware Resources category to obtain information. Note that the information displayed in the Conflicts/Sharing subnode does not necessarily indicate problems because some resources can be shared without creating a problem. Also note the Forced Hardware node, which displays information about devices whose default configuration has been modified by the user. Information in this node can be useful when troubleshooting resource conflicts.

Using Windows 7 Rollback to Resolve a Problem Driver

If you update an existing driver to a new version and then you experience system problems, you should roll back the driver to the previous version. In versions of Windows prior to Windows XP, this was almost impossible to do. As was the case in Windows XP and Vista, Windows 7 maintains a copy of the previous driver each time a new one is updated. If, at any time, you want to restore the previous version, simply roll back the driver. To do this, open Device Manager and double-click the device to open its Properties dialog box. Click the **Driver** tab and then click the **Roll Back Driver** button. When prompted with the question `Are you sure you would like to roll back to the previously installed driver software?`, click **Yes**. After the previous version is restored, click the **Close** button.

> **TIP**   It is usually helpful to create a restore point before installing the new driver. This enables you to restore your computer to its status as of before the driver installation by using the System Restore feature. Use of System Restore for performing these actions is covered in Chapter 18.

You can roll back all device drivers except for printers. You might receive a User Account Control prompt before either updating a driver or rolling it back to a previous version.

In some cases, your computer might not even start after installing a problem driver and rebooting. You can try the following options:

- Use the Last Known Good configuration, which starts the computer with Registry settings that worked prior to installing the device.

- If Last Known Good does not work, start the computer in safe mode, which disables all drivers except for those necessary for the system to start. Then use Device Manager to roll back the driver.

- You can also use System Restore from safe mode to restore the computer's configuration to a previous point. This is especially helpful if you have created a restore point in advance.

We discuss these and other startup options in Chapter 18.

Configuring Updates to Windows 7

Chapter 2, "Installing Windows 7," introduced Windows Update briefly with regards to receiving the most recent installation files at the beginning of installation. This section takes a closer look at the options available in Windows Update and using a server running Windows Server Update Services (WSUS) to receive and distribute updates to Windows 7 computers on a network.

Windows Update enables you to maintain your computer in an up-to-date condition by automatically downloading and installing critical updates as Microsoft publishes them. By default, your computer automatically checks for updates at the Windows Update website. Critical updates are automatically installed on a daily basis, and you are informed about optional updates that might be available. The following are several key features of Windows Update:

- Windows Update scans your computer and determines which updates are applicable to your computer. These updates include the latest security patches and usability enhancements that ensure your computer is kept as secure and functional as possible.

- Updates classified by Microsoft as High Priority and Recommended can be downloaded and installed automatically in the background without interfering with your work. At the same time, Windows Update can inform you about optional updates and Windows Ultimate Extras.

- Windows Update informs you if a restart is required to apply an update. You can postpone the restart so that it does not interfere with activities in progress. Should an update apply to a software program with files in use, Windows 7 can save the files and close and restart the program.

In Windows 7, Windows Update supports the distribution and installation of the following types of updates:

- **Critical security updates:** Updates that Microsoft has determined are critical for a computer's security. These are typically distributed on the second Tuesday of each month, which has become known as "Patch Tuesday." In general, they fix problems that intruders can exploit to perform actions such as adding administrative accounts, installing rogue software, copying or deleting data on your computer, and so on.

- **Optional updates:** Potentially useful updates that are not security-related. These might include software and driver updates, language packs, and so on.

- **Update roll-ups:** Packaged sets of updates that fix problems with specific Windows components or software packages such as Microsoft Office.

- **Service packs:** Comprehensive operating system updates that package together all updates published since the launch of the operating system or issuance of the previous service pack. In many cases, service packs also include new features or improvements to existing features.

Configuring Windows Update Settings

The System and Maintenance category in Control Panel includes the Windows Update applet, which enables you to configure and work with the various options offered. Use the following procedure to work with Windows Update:

Step 1. Click **Start > Control Panel > System and Security > Windows Update**. This opens Windows Update, as previously shown in Figure 7-4. You can also type `windows update` into the Start Menu search box and then select **Windows Update** from the list displayed.

Step 2. To perform a manual check for updates, click **Check for updates**. Windows Update checks on the Microsoft website. After a minute or two, it informs you of any available updates and offers to install them.

Step 3.   To modify the way Windows Update performs automatic checking and installation of updates, click **Change settings**.

Step 4.   This action displays the Choose how Windows can install updates page shown in Figure 7-18. From the Important updates drop-down list, select one of the following options:

Figure 7-18   The Choose how Windows can install updates page enables you to configure options related to downloading and installation of updates.

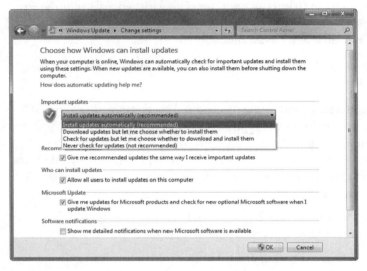

— **Install updates automatically (recommended):** Automatically downloads and installs updates at the day and time specified in the drop-down list boxes provided. You should ensure that your computer is on and connected to the Internet at the time you specify. This is the default setting.

— **Download updates but let me choose whether to install them:** Downloads updates when they are available and informs you by means of an icon in the notification area. You can select which updates should be installed by clicking this icon and choosing **Install**.

— **Check for updates but let me choose whether to download and install them:** Provides an icon in the notification area to inform you that updates are available from the Windows Update website. You can download these updates by clicking this icon and choosing **Start Download**. After the updates are installed, you can select **Install** to install them.

— **Never check for updates (not recommended):** You are not informed of any available updates and you must access the Windows Update website regularly to check for updates. You can do this by means of the link provided.

Step 5.   By default, Windows Update checks for both critical and recommended updates including drivers as well as updated definition files for Windows Defender. To limit the check to critical updates only, clear the check box labeled **Give me recommended updates the same way I receive important updates**.

Step 6.   If you don't want nonadministrative users to install updates, clear the check box labeled **Allow all users to install updates on this computer**.

Step 7.   If you don't want to receive new optional software from Microsoft or updates for other Microsoft Products such as Microsoft Office, clear the check box labeled **Give me updates for Microsoft products and check for new optional Microsoft software when I update Windows**. This check box is selected by default.

Step 8.   If you want to receive notifications of new Microsoft software, select the check box labeled **Show me detailed notifications when new Microsoft software is available**.

Step 9.   Click **OK** to return to Windows Update.

Step 10.   Updates can become hidden if you have asked Windows not to notify you or install updates automatically. To view and restore any hidden updates that might be available, select **Restore hidden updates**. On the page that appears, select the updates to be installed and then click **Restore**.

Step 11.   When you are finished, click **OK**.

Using a WSUS Server with Windows 7

WSUS is a server-based component that enables you to provide update services to computers on a corporate network without the need for individual computers to go online to the Microsoft Windows Update website to check for updates. It saves valuable bandwidth because only the WSUS server actually connects to the Windows Update website to receive updates, whereas all other computers on the network receive their updates from the WSUS server. Furthermore, WSUS provides network administrators with the ability to test updates for compatibility before enabling computers on the network to receive the updates, thereby reducing the chance of an update disrupting computer or application functionality across the network.

You can download WSUS 3.0 Service Pack (SP) 2 from Microsoft and install it on a computer running Windows Server 2003 or Windows Server 2008 R2. This most recent release of WSUS supports new Windows Server 2008 R2 and Windows 7 machines. Configuration of the WSUS server is beyond the scope of the Windows 7 exams and is not discussed here.

Configuring Windows Update Policies

Group Policy in Windows 7 provides a series of policies that govern the actions performed by Windows Update. To view and configure these policies, open the Group Policy Object Editor by clicking Start and typing **gpedit.msc** in the Search dialog box. If you receive a UAC prompt, click **Yes.** Navigate to the **Computer Configuration\Administrative Templates\Windows Components\ Windows Update** node to obtain the policy settings shown in Figure 7-19.

Figure 7-19   Group Policy in Windows 7 provides a series of settings that govern the operation of Windows Update.

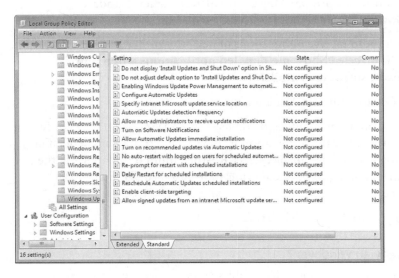

To use Group Policy to specify the behavior of automatic updates, double-click the **Configure Automatic Updates** policy setting (shown in Figure 7-19) to receive the Configure Automatic Updates properties dialog box shown in Figure 7-20. Select **Enabled** and then choose one of the following settings from the Configure automatic updating drop-down list:

- **2–Notify for downloading any updates and notify again before installing them:** Windows Update notifies you when updates are available by displaying an icon in the notification area and a message stating that updates are available for download. The user can download the updates by clicking either the icon or the message. When the download is complete, the user is informed again with another icon and message; clicking one of them starts the installation.

Figure 7-20   The Configure Automatic Updates dialog box offers four choices for configuring automatic updating of Windows 7 computers.

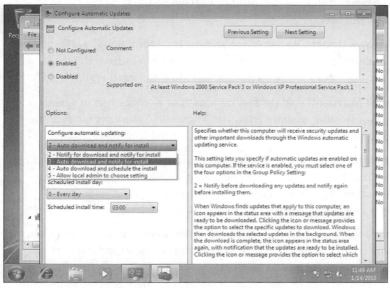

- **3–Download the updates automatically and notify when they are ready to be installed:** Windows Update downloads updates in the background without informing the user. After the updates have been downloaded, the user is informed with an icon in the notification area and a message stating that the updates are ready for installation. Clicking one of them starts the installation. This is the default option.

- **4–Automatically download updates and install them on the schedule specified below:** Windows Update downloads updates automatically when the scheduled install day and time arrive. You can use the drop-down lists on the left side of the dialog box to specify the desired days and times, which, by default, are daily at 3:00 a.m.

- **5–Allow local administrators to select the configuration mode that Automatic Updates should notify and install updates:** Enables local administrators to select a configuration option of their choice from the Automatic Updates control panel, such as their own scheduled time for installations.

The following describes several of the other more important available policy settings shown in Figure 7-19:

- **Do not display "Install Updates and Shut Down" option in Shut Down Windows dialog box:** Prevents the appearance of this option in the Shut Down Windows dialog box, even if updates are available when the user shuts down his computer.

- **Do not adjust default option to "Install Updates and Shut Down" option in Shut Down Windows dialog box:** When enabled, changes the default shut down option from Install Updates and Shut Down to the last shut down option selected by the user.

- **Enabling Windows Update Power Management to automatically wake up the system to install scheduled updates:** Uses features of Windows Power Management to wake computers up from hibernation to install available updates.

- **Specify intranet Microsoft update service location:** Enables you to specify a WSUS server for hosting updates from the Microsoft Windows Update site (as described in the previous section).

- **Automatic Updates detection frequency:** Specifies the length of time in hours used to determine the waiting interval before checking for updates at an intranet update server. You need to enable the Specify Intranet Microsoft Update Service Location policy to have this policy work.

- **Allow non-administrators to receive update notifications:** Enables users who are not administrators to receive update notifications according to other Automatic Updates configuration settings.

- **Turn on Software Notifications:** Enables you to determine whether users see detailed notification messages that promote the value, installation, and usage of optional software from the Microsoft Update service.

- **Allow Automatic Updates immediate installation:** Enables Automatic Updates to immediately install updates that neither interrupt Windows services nor restart Windows.

- **Turn on recommended updates via Automatic Updates:** Enables Automatic Updates to include both important and recommended updates.

- **No auto-restart with logged on users for scheduled automatic updates installations:** Prevents Automatic Updates from restarting a client computer after updates have been installed. Otherwise, Automatic Updates notifies the logged-on user that the computer will automatically restart in five minutes to complete the installation.

- **Re-prompt for restart with scheduled installations:** Specifies the number of minutes from the previous prompt to wait before displaying a second prompt for restarting the computer.

- **Delay Restart for scheduled installations:** Specifies the number of minutes to wait before a scheduled restart takes place.

- **Reschedule Automatic Updates scheduled installations:** Specifies the length of time in minutes that Automatic Updates waits after system startup before proceeding with a scheduled installation that was missed because a client computer was not turned on and connected to the network at the time of a scheduled installation, as previously specified by option 4 from the Configure Automatic Updating drop-down list.

- **Enable client-side targeting:** Enables you to specify a target group name to be used for receiving updates from an intranet server such as a WSUS server. The group name you specify is used by the server to determine which updates are to be deployed.

- **Allow signed updates from an intranet Microsoft update service location:** Enables you to manage whether Automatic Updates accepts updates signed by entities other than Microsoft when the update is found on an intranet Microsoft Update location.

For more information on these policies, consult the Help information provided on the right side of each policy's Properties dialog box.

Reviewing Update History and Rolling Back Updates

The Windows Update applet enables you to review your update history and roll back problematic updates, as described in the following procedure:

Step 1.   Open the **Windows Update Control Panel** applet, as previously described.

Step 2.   From the list of options on the left side of this page, select **View update history**. The Review your update history page shown in Figure 7-21 displays a list of the updates installed on your computer, including definition updates for Windows Defender. This page also indicates whether updates were successfully installed.

Figure 7-21   The Review your update history page displays all updates installed on your computer.

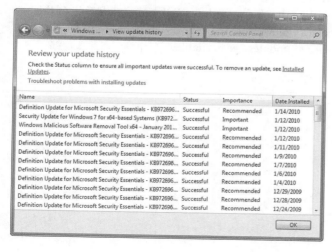

Step 3.   Double-click any update to provide detailed information, as shown in Figure 7-22.

Figure 7-22   Windows Update provides information on all updates it has installed, as well as links to websites that you can refer to.

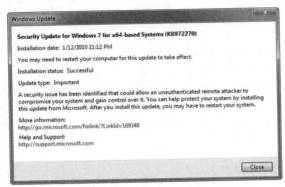

Step 4.   If an update is causing problems and you want to remove it, click the **Installed Updates** link (shown in Figure 7-21). On the Uninstall an Update page that appears, right-click the update you want to uninstall and select **Uninstall**. Confirm your intentions by clicking **Yes** in the message box that appears.

Checking for New Updates

As already stated, Windows 7 checks for new updates automatically according to the settings already described that you have configured. As previously shown in Figure 7-4, the Windows Update Control Panel applet displays the time at which the most recent check for updates took place. It is easy to perform a manual check for new updates—simply click the **Check for updates** link on the left side of this applet. Windows Update accesses the Microsoft Update website and informs you whether any important or optional updates are available.

Exam Preparation Tasks

Review All the Key Topics

Review the most important topics in the chapter, noted with the key topics icon in the outer margin of the page. Table 7-4 lists a reference of these key topics and the page numbers on which each is found.

Table 7-4 Key Topics for Chapter 7

Key Topic Element	Description	Page Number
List	Shows procedure for installing hardware devices	216
Figure 7-4	Windows Update shows available updates	219
Figure 7-6	Device Manager lists all hardware devices	220
Table 7-2	Describes tabs on a device's Properties dialog box	222
Figure 7-9	Uninstalling a device driver	223
Figure 7-10	Disabling a device driver	223
Table 7-3	Describes available view options in Device Manager	229
Figure 7-17	Using Action Center to view suggested maintenance actions	231
List	Describes types of updates handled by Windows Update	233
List	Describes ways of configuring download and installation of updates	234
Figure 7-20	Configuring automatic update properties	237

Complete the Tables and Lists from Memory

Print a copy of Appendix C, "Memory Tables" (found on the CD), or at least the section for this chapter, and complete the tables and lists from memory. Appendix D, "Memory Tables Answer Key," also on the CD, includes completed tables and lists to check your work.

Definitions of Key Terms

Define the following key terms from this chapter, and check your answers in the glossary.

Device driver, driver signing, `sigverif.exe`, Plug and Play (PnP), FireWire, Device Manager, Windows Update, Microsoft Management Console, interrupt request (IRQ), direct memory address (DMA), input/output (I/O) port address, Action Center, `msinfo32`, update roll-up, service pack (SP), Windows Server Update Services (WSUS), Group Policy

This chapter covers the following subjects:

- **Configuring Application Compatibility:** Many applications currently in use today were originally written for Windows XP or older versions of Windows. Some of these might not work properly with Windows 7. This section describes methods you can use to make these applications work properly.

- **Configuring Application Restrictions:** A lot of time can be lost over users running inappropriate applications or malicious websites downloading and installing inappropriate software. This section looks at methods you can use to limit what software can run.

- **Configuring Internet Explorer:** Internet Explorer has made significant improvements in security and browsing capability. This section shows you how to configure Internet Explorer for secure browsing under various situations. It also describes new usability enhancements such as add-ons, accelerators, and InPrivate browsing.

CHAPTER 8

Configuring Applications and Internet Explorer

We have finished looking at configuration and troubleshooting of hardware devices attached to or included with your computer. Having done so, it is now time to turn to the software applications installed on the computer. With each new version of Windows comes updated applications including Internet Explorer, now in version number 8. However, organizations and individuals have invested big money in applications that were run on older computers running operating systems such as Windows 2000, XP, and Vista. A new operating system brings with it the potential for compatibility issues, in which software written for older operating systems might not run properly, or stop responding (hang), or not even begin to start. For the 70-680 exam, it is important that you know how to configure applications so that they work properly on Windows 7.

Users often like to download software from the Internet. Such programs can bring malware such as viruses, Trojan horses, and spyware with them, thereby resulting in downtime and support calls. Other software (such as games) can result in users being distracted from important work objectives. Microsoft provides tools that limit user access to software programs that can either damage computers and network access or distract users from important work objectives; it is important that you are able to configure these tools to maximize user productivity.

Internet Explorer 8 brings new and improved browsing and security features that enhance the user experience and help to protect users from malicious websites and the software they might place on their machines. You are expected to know how to configure these features of Internet Explorer for the 70-680 exam and for assisting users in the real world.

"Do I Know This Already?" Quiz

The "Do I Know This Already?" quiz enables you to assess whether you should read this entire chapter or simply jump to the "Exam Preparation Tasks" section for review. If you are in doubt, read the entire chapter. Table 8-1 outlines the major headings in this chapter and the corresponding "Do I Know This Already?" quiz questions. You can find the answers in Appendix A, "Answers to the 'Do I Know This Already?' Quizzes."

Table 8-1   "Do I Know This Already?" Foundation Topics Section-to-Question Mapping

Foundations Topics Section	Questions Covered in This Section
Configuring Application Compatibility	1–4
Configuring Application Restrictions	5–7
Configuring Internet Explorer	8–15

1. You are working with a financial application your company has used successfully on Windows XP computers for over eight years. The application does not respond when accessed on a Windows 7 Professional computer. What compatibility option should you try in order to get this program working?

   a. **Run this program in compatibility mode for (and select Windows XP).**

   b. **Run in 256 colors.**

   c. **Disable visual themes.**

   d. **Disable display scaling on high DPI settings.**

   e. **Run this program as an administrator.**

2. You have obtained a minor compatibility fix that is designed to enable an engineering program to work with Windows 7 while the developers update the program as a more permanent solution. What is this compatibility fix generally known as?

   a. Compatibility Mode

   b. Filter

   c. Shim

   d. Hotfix

3. Your Windows 7 Professional computer has 4 GB RAM and a processor capable of hardware virtualization. You download and install Windows XP Mode and Virtual PC and restart your computer. However, Windows XP Mode will not start. Which of the following is the most likely reason for this problem?

   a. You need at least 6 GB RAM for Windows XP Mode to work.

   b. You need to enable virtualization in your computer's BIOS Setup program.

   c. You should install Windows Virtual Server rather than Windows Virtual PC.

   d. You need to upgrade your operating system to Windows 7 Ultimate.

4. Several customers accessing your company's website using new Windows 7 Home Premium computers have reported that the website does not appear properly in their browsers. You want to obtain information that would help you redesign the site so that it displays properly. What tool should you use?

   a. Windows XP Mode

   b. Internet Explorer Compatibility Test Tool

   c. Application Compatibility Mode

   d. SmartScreen Filter

5. Which of the following are types of rules you might configure in Software Restriction Policies? (Choose all that apply.)

   a. Certificate Rule

   b. Operating System Version Rule

   c. Hash Rule

   d. Internet Zone Rule

   e. Path Rule

6. Which of the following represent improvements that can be obtained through use of AppLocker rather than Software Restriction Policies? (Choose two.)

   a. You can specify any of Disallowed, Basic User, and Unrestricted rule settings.

   b. You can gather advanced data on software usage by implementing audit-only mode.

   c. You can lock down applications on a domain basis using Group Policy.

   d. You can create multiple rules at the same time with the help of a wizard.

7. With which editions of Windows 7 can you use AppLocker to specify the applications users are permitted to run? (Choose all that apply.)

   a. Home Basic

   b. Home Premium

   c. Professional

   d. Enterprise

   e. Ultimate

8. Which of the following are new features of Internet Explorer 8 that were not included in Internet Explorer 7? (Choose three.)

   a. Protected Mode

   b. Compatibility View

   c. Pop-Up Blocker

   d. InPrivate Mode

   e. SmartScreen Filter

9. Into what security zone are all websites placed by default in Internet Explorer 8?

    a. Trusted Sites

    b. Internet

    c. Local Intranet

    d. Restricted

10. You want to configure the Pop-up Blocker settings in Internet Explorer, so you open the Internet Options dialog box. On which tab do you find the option to configure these settings?

    a. Security

    b. Privacy

    c. Content

    d. Advanced

11. You want to configure additional search providers that you can access from the Search field on the Internet Explorer 8 address bar. Which menu option should you access? (Each answer represents a complete solution. Choose two.)

    a. **Tools > Manage Add-ons**

    b. **Toolbars**

    c. **All Accelerators**

    d. **Tools > Internet Options**

12. Which of the following are items that the Manage Add-ons dialog box lets you configure in Internet Explorer 8? (Choose three.)

    a. Search Providers

    b. Accelerators

    c. InPrivate Filtering

    d. SmartScreen Filter

13. You receive an email from your bank asking you to confirm your account data, so you access the linked website. You are afraid you might be duped into supplying information to an unauthorized website and want Internet Explorer 8 to display a warning if this is so. Which feature should you ensure is turned on?

    a. Protected Mode

    b. Pop-up Blocker

    c. InPrivate Browsing

    d. SmartScreen Filter

14. Your Internet connection has failed, and it will take several days before a repair can be completed. You must submit a report by tomorrow morning so you drive to an Internet café on the other side of town. You want to ensure that no traces of your activities are left behind on this computer. Which feature should you ensure is activated?

   a. Protected Mode

   b. Pop-up Blocker

   c. InPrivate Browsing

   d. SmartScreen Filter

15. You are purchasing books from an Internet bookstore and want to ensure that your credit card information is encrypted and cannot be viewed by intruders. What should you look for when you are on the bookstore's checkout pages?

   a. The browser address displays an InPrivate label.

   b. The browser address displays a gold padlock icon.

   c. A message displays stating that Protected mode is on.

   d. The browser tab is green in color.

Foundation Topics

Configuring Application Compatibility

As noted in Chapter 2, "Installing Windows 7," when you move to a new operating system, you should look at software compatibility while you are in the development and testing phase of the new operating system. Windows 7 is no different in this matter. Many applications originally developed for Windows 2000 or Windows XP might not run properly on Windows 7; antivirus applications developed for older Windows operating systems in particular are often incompatible.

Configuring Application Compatibility Mode

As in previous Windows versions, Windows 7 provides the Application Compatibility mode that assists you in troubleshooting applications that do not run properly in Windows 7. In general, applications originally written for Windows Vista work in Windows 7. Applications written for Windows XP or older might not run properly, stop responding (hang), or refuse to start at all. If these applications worked properly in previous Windows versions, this might indicate a compatibility issue with Windows 7. Application Compatibility mode emulates the environment found on versions of Windows as far back as Windows 95 and Windows NT 4.0. This mode also provides several other options that might enable a program to run. Use the following procedure to configure Application Compatibility mode:

Step 1. Right-click the desktop shortcut to the program and choose **Properties**.

Step 2. Select the **Compatibility** tab to display the options listed in Table 8-2 and shown in Figure 8-1.

Table 8-2   Application Compatibility Options

Option	Description
Run this program in compatibility mode for	Select the Windows version from the drop-down list that you know the program works properly on.
Run in 256 colors	Uses a limited set of colors to run the program. Some older programs are designed to run in this color space.
Run in 640 × 480 screen resolution	Runs this program in a smaller window. Try this option if the graphical user interface (GUI) appears jagged or is rendered poorly.
Disable visual themes	Disabling themes might help if problems occur with the menus or buttons on the program's title bar.

Table 8-2 Application Compatibility Options

Option	Description
Disable desktop composition	Shuts off advanced display features such as Aero Glass. Try this setting if windows movement appears erratic or other display problems occur.
Disable display scaling on high DPI settings	Shuts off automatic font resizing if you are using large-scale font sizes. Try this option if large-scale fonts interfere with the program's appearance.
Run this program as an administrator	Some programs require administrator mode to execute properly. You will receive a User Account Control (UAC) prompt when this option is selected. This option is not available to nonadministrative users.
Change settings for all users	Enables you to choose settings that will apply to all users on the computer.

Figure 8-1 The Compatibility tab of an application's Properties dialog box.

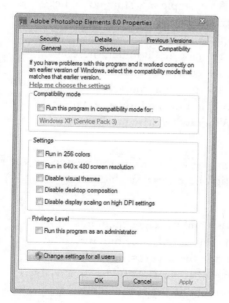

Step 3. Select one or more of these options and then click **Apply**.

Step 4. Test the program to see if it works properly. If necessary, repeat steps 3 and 4 until the program does work properly.

CAUTION   You should not use the Program Compatibility options with older antivirus programs, disk utilities, or system programs. Such programs might cause data loss or create a security risk.

Implementing Shims

A *shim* is a minor system compatibility fix that assists in enabling applications originally written for older Windows versions to work with a newer operating system such as Windows 7. Applications communicate with Windows by calling functions built in to the operating system via an internal structure called the *import address table*. As the Windows operating system evolves from one version to the next (and even with updates to the same version), modification of these functions to suit all applications in use could limit the ability to improve Windows functionality or require considerable additional software code. This could lead to a bloated operating system.

By using a shim, the import address table redirects application programming interface (API) calls to the shim, whose code implements modifications that enable the application to work properly with Windows 7. An example of a shim could be modifying the program to not require administrative privileges to run (or to demand administrative privileges). Another example would be the redirection of application output to a user-specific folder rather than a general folder, thereby enabling you to configure a more restrictive access control list (ACL) than would be otherwise needed. You can also use shims to locate system files that have been moved to a new location because of a change in Windows architecture. However, you cannot use a shim to circumvent built-in Windows security mechanisms.

CAUTION   You should regard shims as a temporary fix for your applications, to be used only until an updated version of the application becomes available.

Microsoft creates shims on a per-application basis and packages them in custom shim database files with the `.sdb` extension. You can install these files using the `sdbinst.exe` command-line tool, which is found in the `%systemroot%\system32` folder on a 32-bit computer and in the `%systemroot%\sysWOW64` folder on a 64-bit computer. Open an administrative command prompt and type the following:

```
Sdbinst filename.sdb [-?] [-q] [-u filepath] [-g GUID] [-n "name"]
```
In this command, the parameters are as follows:

- `filename.sdb`: The path and name of the shim database you are installing

- `[-?]`: Displays help information

- `[-q]`: Quiet mode (automatically accepts prompts)

- **[-u _filepath_]:** Uninstalls the database specified by the file path
- **[-g _GUID_]:** Specifies the database to be installed using a GUID
- **[-n _"name"_]:** Internal name of file (for uninstall only)

The workflow recommended by Microsoft for implementing shims includes the following steps:

Step 1. Create a new compatibility database (*.sdb) using the Compatibility Administrator, which is a component of the Application Compatibility Toolkit (ACT).

Step 2. Select the application and then select the required compatibility fixes or shims.

Step 3. Test the application with the compatibility fix or shim.

Step 4. Save the compatibility database and deploy using the sdbinst.exe command.

NOTE For more information on using shims, refer to "Managing Shims in an Enterprise" at http://technet.microsoft.com/en-ca/library/dd837648(WS.10).aspx.

Using the Application Compatibility Toolkit

ACT is a Microsoft resource that helps administrators identify the compatibility of their applications with Windows Vista and Windows 7, thereby helping organizations to produce a comprehensive software inventory. It also identifies which applications might require additional testing or the use of shims. You can also test the compatibility of web applications and websites with new releases and security updates to Internet Explorer. You can download ACT 5.6 from http:// www.microsoft.com/downloads/details.aspx?displaylang=en&FamilyID=24d a89e9-b581-47b0-b45e-492dd6da2971. Follow the instructions on this page to download the Application Compatibility Toolkit.exe file, and then click **Run** to run the installation wizard. As shown in Figure 8-2, the Compatibility Administrator comes loaded with fixes and settings for hundreds of applications that Microsoft has tested. You can apply compatibility fixes and compatibility modes to any application and then save the information you've configured to a SQL database. You can set up this database by using the ACT Configuration Wizard (see Figure 8-3), which is a component of the Application Compatibility Manager included with ACT.

Details of the usage and configuration of ACT are beyond the scope of the 70-680 exam and will not be included here. You can obtain comprehensive information on use of the ACT from the ACT Deployment Guide, which you can download from the same page from which you download ACT itself.

Figure 8-2   The Compatibility Administrator helps you to configure the compatibility of hundreds of applications originally written for older Windows versions.

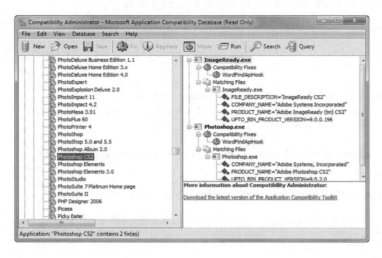

Figure 8-3   You can use the ACT Configuration Wizard to set up a SQL database and share for holding the compatibility data you've obtained.

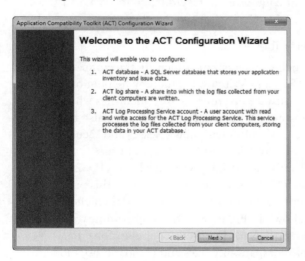

NOTE   You can also obtain information on ACT from "Using the Compatibility Administrator" at http://technet.microsoft.com/en-us/library/cc749034(WS.10).aspx and "Windows 7 Application Compatibility Toolkit 5.5" at http://blogs.technet.com/springboard/archive/2009/04/03/windows-7-application-compatibility-toolkit-5-5-interview-with-Jeremy-Chapman.aspx.

Windows XP Mode

For about seven years, Windows XP was the latest version of the Microsoft operating system. Hence, a very large number of applications were written for Windows XP. Although most of these applications will run on Windows 7, many do not. Another method of running these applications is to use Windows XP Mode to run them in a virtualized Windows XP environment on the Windows 7 desktop.

Windows XP Mode provides a fully functional, licensed copy of Windows XP SP3 sitting on top of the Windows 7 desktop, enabling you to access peripherals such as your CD/DVD drive, install programs, save files, and perform any task that you would normally do on a Windows XP computer. It uses Microsoft Virtual PC as a runtime engine. An application that you install in Windows XP Mode appears in both the Windows XP Start Menu Programs list and the Windows 7 All Programs list, so you can run the program directly from Windows 7.

To run Windows XP Mode, your computer must meet the following requirements:

- You must be running Windows 7 Professional, Enterprise, or Ultimate. You should also have at least 2 GB RAM and 15 GB of additional hard drive space to hold the virtual Windows XP files.

- Your processor must be capable of hardware virtualization (Intel-VT or AMD-V virtualization).

- Your BIOS must support virtualization, and you must enable virtualization in the BIOS Setup program.

To download and install Windows XP Mode, perform the following steps:

Step 1. Access the Download Windows XP Mode page at www.microsoft.com/windows/virtual-pc/download.aspx.

Step 2. Select your Windows 7 edition and desired language and then follow the instructions to download Windows XP Mode and Windows Virtual PC.

Step 3. When the download of Windows XP Mode completes, click **Run** and then accept the UAC prompt (if displayed).

Step 4. Windows XP Mode Setup starts with a Welcome page. Click **Next**.

Step 5. Specify the installation location for the virtual hard disk file and then click **Next**. If you receive a UAC prompt, click **Yes**.

Step 6. The installation of Windows XP mode takes several minutes. When you are informed that the installation has completed, click **Finish**.

Step 7. Return to the Download Windows XP Mode web page and click to download Windows Virtual PC.

Step 8.   When you are asked if you want to install the Windows software update KB958559, click **Yes**.

Step 9.   Click **I Accept** to accept the license terms. If you click **I Decline**, the installation wizard closes.

Step 10.   You are informed when installation is complete. Click **Restart Now** to restart your computer. Configuration of Virtual PC and Windows XP Mode takes several minutes.

Use the following steps to set up Windows XP Mode:

Step 1.   From Windows 7, click **Start > All Programs > Windows Virtual PC > Windows XP Mode**.

Step 2.   The Setup Wizard starts and displays the license terms. Click **I Accept the License Terms** and then click **Next**.

Step 3.   On the Installation Folder and Credentials page, accept the default location displayed for Windows XP Mode files or choose the desired location, and then click **Next**.

Step 4.   Type and confirm a password and then click **Next**.

Step 5.   On the Help Protect Your Computer page, select the option to turn on automatic updates and then click **Next**.

Step 6.   Click **Start Setup**.

Step 7.   When Setup is finished, Windows XP Mode opens in its own window, similar to the desktop appearance of a physical computer running Windows XP Professional.

Use the following steps to install an application to Windows XP Mode:

Step 1.   From Windows 7, click **Start > All Programs > Windows Virtual PC > Windows XP Mode**.

Step 2.   Insert the program's installation disc or browse to the program's installation file. Alternatively, open Internet Explorer to the program vendor's website and follow its instructions to download the installation files.

Step 3.   Open the installation file and follow the instructions provided by the application's installation wizard.

Step 4.   Click **Close** from the top of the Windows XP Mode window.

Step 5.   You can now run the program from Windows 7. To do so, click **Start > All Programs > Windows Virtual PC > Windows XP Mode Applications** and then click the desired program.

CAUTION   The prime purpose of Windows XP Mode is to assist organizations in their move from Windows XP to Windows 7. Windows XP Mode is not optimized for graphic-intensive programs such as 3D games. It is not well suited for programs using intensive hardware needs such as TV tuners.

Internet Explorer Compatibility Issues

ACT 5.5 includes the Internet Explorer Compatibility Test Tool, which collects issues with your company's websites and web-based applications in Internet Explorer versions 7 and 8. This tool uploads the data to the ACT Log Processing Service and displays the results in real time.

Use the following procedure to obtain Internet Explorer compatibility data:

Step 1.   Close any Internet Explorer windows that might be open.

Step 2.   Click **Start > All Programs > Microsoft Application Compatibility Toolkit > Developer and Tester Tools > Internet Explorer Compatibility Test Tool**.

Step 3.   On the Microsoft Internet Explorer Compatibility Test Tool dialog box shown in Figure 8-4, click **Enable**. This button changes to **Disable**.

Figure 8-4   The Microsoft Internet Explorer Compatibility Test Tool reports potential issues with your website.

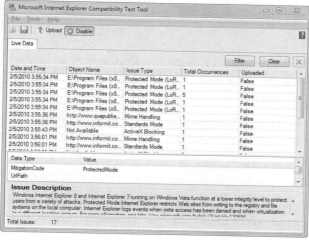

Step 4.   Open Internet Explorer to the website you want to check. As shown in Figure 8-4, the test tool displays potential compatibility issues.

Step 5.   When you are finished, click **Disable**.

Step 6.   To view a brief description of any issue, select it and read the text under Issue Description at the bottom of the Test Tool dialog box.

Step 7.   To filter the issue results, click **Filter**.

Step 8.   In the Issues Filter dialog box shown in Figure 8-5, type the name of the object that you want to view. If you want to find only those objects that match your criteria exactly, select the **Find Exact Match** check box.

Figure 8-5   The Issues Filter dialog box enables you to filter the issues according to object name and issue type.

Step 9.   Select the check boxes for the types of issues you want to view and then click **OK**. The information on the main Test Tool dialog box updates to display only those issues that match the search criteria.

Step 10.   You can repeat your search by clicking **Filter** again and typing the name of the desired object or clearing this space to view all objects.

Step 11.   To save the issue results as a report, click the **Save** icon at the top-left corner of the dialog box. Browse to a desired location and then click **Save**.

Step 12.   To view a previously collected issue report, click **File > Open**, browse to the location where you saved the file, select it, and then click **Open**.

Step 13.   To upload the issue results to the ACT database, click **Upload**. The Collecting Data message box appears as data is collected. When done, browse to the parent level of your ACT log file folder and then click **Save**. This saves the results as a cabinet (.cab) file.

NOTE To properly evaluate your websites and web applications, you should be using the version of Internet Explorer that users will be viewing these sites with. Run Internet Explorer 7 to test your websites and web applications if users at Windows XP machines will be using this version of Internet Explorer to access your sites; otherwise, run Internet Explorer 8. If necessary, repeat the evaluation with both versions of Internet Explorer.

NOTE For more information on the Internet Explorer Compatibility Test Tool, refer to "Testing and Mitigating Issues by Using the Development Tools" at http://technet.microsoft.com/en-us/library/cc766461(WS.10).aspx.

Configuring Application Restrictions

Application restrictions enable you to limit the types of software that run on computers to which the policy applies. For individual computers running Windows 7 Professional, Enterprise, or Ultimate, or those that belong to a homegroup or workgroup, you can set these policies by using the Local Security Policy tool. On an Active Directory Domain Services (AD DS) a domain, you can use Group Policy to configure these policies at a site, a domain, or an organizational unit (OU) level.

Windows 7 and Windows Server 2008 R2 include two types of application restrictions: software restriction policies and application control policies.

- Software restriction policies are the same policies that were included in Windows XP/Vista/Server 2003/2008 and can be used to limit application installation and use on these computers, as well as Windows 7 computers.

- Application control policies are new to Windows 7 and enable you to create separate rules for Windows Installer files, executable files, and script files. The new AppLocker feature enables you to restrict applications according to *publisher rules*, which limit application execution according to the application's digital signature. This even enables you to specify which versions are permitted; for example, you could allow Microsoft Office 2007 or later, while preventing use of older versions of Office.

Configuring application restrictions provides you with the following benefits:

- **Control which programs can run on computers on your network:** You can allow only those programs that users require to do their jobs properly, and you can restrict the use of other programs such as games. You can also limit the downloading of ActiveX controls and ensure that only digitally signed scripts can be run. This also helps to prevent viruses, Trojan horses, and other malware programs from executing.

- **Control which programs users on multiuser computers can run:** When more than one user can access a computer, you can set user-specific policies that prevent users from accessing programs only needed by other users of the same computer.

- **Control whether software restriction policies apply to all users:** You can specify whether software restriction policies apply to administrators.

- **Prevent email attachments from executing:** If you are concerned about users receiving viruses through email, you can apply policies that restrict files with certain extensions from executing.

Setting Software Restriction Policies

Local Security Policy and Group Policy both enable you to set software restriction policies and application control policies. You can choose to set policies according to security levels, and you can also configure additional rules. Security Level rules enable you to set a default policy and create exceptions. You can choose from the following security levels:

- **Disallowed:** Does not allow any software to run, regardless of a user's access rights. Four Registry path rules that allow system software to run are specified in the Additional Rules folder, preventing users from being completely locked out of the computer.

- **Basic User:** Enables the user to run applications as a normal user only. This privilege level was introduced in Windows Vista and is not supported on Windows 7 or Windows Server 2008 R2 computers.

- **Unrestricted:** Allows software to run according to a user's access rights. This is the default policy level.

Use the following steps to configure software restriction policies at the local computer level:

Step 1.   Click **Start** and type `Local Security Policy` in the Search box. Then click **Local Security Policy** to open this snap-in.

Step 2.   Right-click the **Software Restriction Policies** node and choose **New Software Restriction Policies**. This creates a default set of software restriction policies, which are displayed in the details pane as shown in Figure 8-6.

Step 3.   To specify either the **Basic User** or **Disallowed** security level, right-click the desired level and choose **Set As default**. You are warned that the default level you selected is more restrictive than the current security level (see Figure 8-7). Click **Yes** to continue.

Figure 8-6   Enabling software restriction policies.

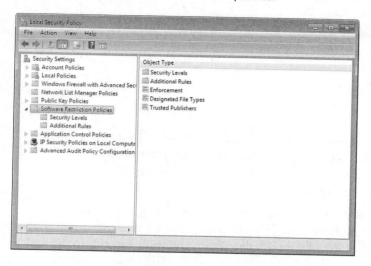

Figure 8-7   This message warns you that the chosen security level is more restrictive than the current security level.

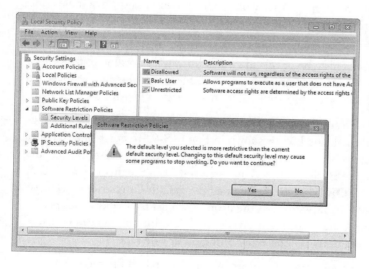

Step 4.   To specify rules that govern exceptions to the security level you specified, right-click **Additional Rules** and choose one of the following four rules, as shown in Figure 8-8.

Figure 8-8 You can configure four types of new rules in the Additional Rules folder.

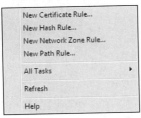

— **Certificate Rule:** This type of rule identifies software according to its signing certificate. You can use a certificate rule to specify the source of trusted software that should be allowed to run without prompting a user.

— **Hash Rule:** A *hash* is a fixed-length series of bytes that uniquely identifies an application or file. The policy uses a hash algorithm to calculate the hash of a specified program and compares this to the hash of a program that a user attempts to run, to determine whether the application or file should run.

— **Network Zone Rule:** This type of rule identifies software according to an Internet Explorer network zone. We discuss the available zones later in this chapter. You can specify zone rules only for Windows Installer software packages.

— **Path Rule:** This type of rule identifies software according to its local or Universal Naming Convention (UNC) file path. This rule enables you to grant access to software located in a specific folder for each user.

Step 5. For example, to specify a path rule, select **New Path Rule** to display the New Path Rule dialog box, as shown in Figure 8-9. To create an exception to the Disallowed security level, type the path to the applications that are allowed, choose **Basic User** or **Unrestricted** from the drop-down list, and then click **OK**. If you have retained the default Unrestricted security level, choose **Disallowed** from the drop-down list to disallow the specified software. You can also type an optional description. You can follow a similar procedure to designate any of the other rule types.

Step 6. If required, specify rules for enforcement, designated file types, and trusted publishers by clicking **Software Restriction** in the console tree to display these items in the details pane, as shown previously in Figure 8-6. The following describes the functions of these items:

— **Enforcement:** You can determine the scope of software restriction policies, as shown in Figure 8-10. This capability is useful for exempting local administrators from software restriction policies or for ignoring certificate rules.

— **Designated File Types:** This option determines what file types, in addition to standard file types such as `.exe`, are considered as executable code and subject to software restriction policies.

— **Trusted Publishers:** This option enables you to determine which users can select trusted publishers and to check for revoked certificates.

Figure 8-9 The New Path Rule dialog box enables you to specify the path to software defined by an additional rule.

Figure 8-10 You can modify the scope of software restriction policies from the Enforcement Properties dialog box.

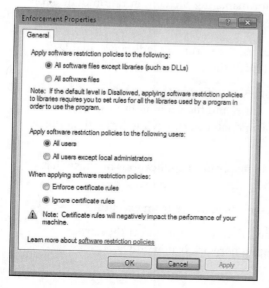

CAUTION Use caution when selecting the Disallowed security level. This security level prevents all applications from running except those you have specified using additional rules.

Application Control Policies

Windows 7 improves on the older Software Restriction Policies by introducing Application Control Policies, which includes the AppLocker feature. AppLocker provides new enhancements that enable you to specify exactly what users are permitted to run on their desktops according to unique file identities. You can also specify the users or groups permitted to execute these applications. Users are allowed to run the applications and scripts required for them to be productive while still providing the operational, security, and compliance benefits provided by application standardization.

NOTE You can use AppLocker on computers running Windows 7 Enterprise or Ultimate, or Windows Server 2008 R2 Standard, Enterprise, Datacenter, or Itanium-based. You can also use a computer running Windows 7 Professional to create AppLocker rules, but you cannot enforce these rules on a Windows 7 Professional computer.

NOTE For detailed information on AppLocker, refer to "AppLocker" and links cited therein at http://technet.microsoft.com/en-us/library/dd723678(WS.10).aspx.

Capabilities of AppLocker

AppLocker provides enhanced options for managing the configuration of desktop computers. It enables you to perform actions such as the following:

- Specify the types of applications that users can run, including executables, scripts, Windows Installer files, and DLL files.

- Define rules according to file attributes specified in the digital signature, such as the publisher, product name, filename, and file version. For example, you can allow Adobe Acrobat Reader 9.0 and later to run, while forbidding the use of an older version.

- Prevent the execution of unlicensed, unapproved applications or those that destabilize machines and increase help desk support calls.

- Prevent unauthorized applications such as malware from executing.

- Prevent users from running programs that needlessly affect the corporate computing environment by consuming network bandwidth.

- Enable users to run approved applications and software updates while maintaining the requirement that only administrative users are permitted to install applications and software updates.

- Specify rules that apply to a given user or security group.

- Ensure that your computers are in compliance with licensing and corporate requirements.

Table 8-3 provides a comparison of AppLocker with Software Restriction Policies.

Table 8-3   Comparing AppLocker to Software Restriction Policies

Feature	AppLocker	Software Restriction Policies
Rule scope	Specific users or groups	All users
Rule conditions	File hash, path, and publisher	File hash, path, certificate, Registry path, and Internet zone
Rule types	Allow and deny	Disallowed, Basic User, and Unrestricted
Default rule action	Implicit denial	Unrestricted
Audit-only mode	Yes	No
Wizard for creating multiple rules at the same time	Yes	No
Policy import or export	Yes	No
Rule collection	Yes	No
Support for PowerShell	Yes	No
Custom error messages	Yes	No

Basic Configuration of AppLocker Policies

As with Software Restriction Policies, you can configure AppLocker policies for the local computer in the Local Group Policy or Local Security Policy snap-in. You can also configure policies for an AD DS domain from the Group Policy Object Editor. Use the following procedure to configure default AppLocker rules on a local computer:

Step 1.   In the Local Security Policy snap-in, expand Application Control Policies to reveal AppLocker. AppLocker displays information and configurable links in the details pane as shown in Figure 8-11.

Step 2.   Click **Configure rule enforcement**. In the AppLocker Properties dialog box shown in Figure 8-12, select the check boxes against the three rule types that you want to configure. From the drop-down lists, select **Enforce rules** to create rules you want to enforce or **Audit only** to test rules for future use. Then click **OK**.

Figure 8-11 You can configure AppLocker from the Application Control Policies node of Local Security Policy.

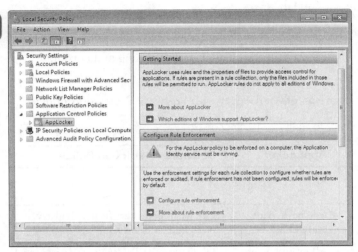

Figure 8-12 You can choose to enforce AppLocker rules or select Audit only to gather information.

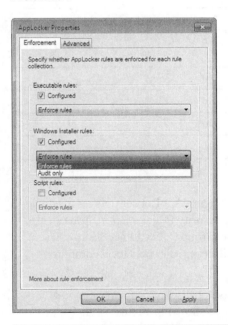

TIP The Audit only option enables you to determine who is using which applications in your company, without enforcing the rules you have specified. When a user executes an application specified in the rule, information about that use is written into the AppLocker event log.

Step 3.   In the console tree, expand AppLocker to reveal subnodes for each of these three rule types.

Step 4.   For each of the rule types you want to configure, create a default set of rules by right-clicking the rule type and choosing **Create Default Rules**. This adds the three rules (all set to Allow) indicated in Table 8-4 to each specified rule type.

Table 8-4   Default AppLocker Rules

Default Group	Executable Rule	Windows Installer Rule	Script Rule
Everyone	All files located in the Program Files folder	All digitally signed Windows Installer files	All scripts located in the Program Files folder
Everyone	All files located in the Windows folder	All Windows Installer files in `%systemdrive%\Windows\Installer`	All scripts located in the Windows folder
BUILTIN\Administrators	All files	All Windows Installer files	All scripts

Step 5.   If you want to delete any of these default rules, right-click the desired rule and choose **Delete**. Then click **Yes** in the confirmation dialog box that appears.

Creating Additional AppLocker Rules

AppLocker provides wizards that assist you in creating application-specific rules and policies. Before you begin creating these rules, ensure that you have installed the required applications or scripts and created any required security groups. You can automatically generate AppLocker rules for executables, Windows Installer, or scripts; the procedure is similar for each of these items. The following example describes a procedure that applies to creating a rule for the Adobe Photoshop CS4 executable:

Step 1.   In the Local Security Policy snap-in, right-click the desired subnode of AppLocker and choose **Automatically Generate Rules**. This starts a wizard with the Folder and Permissions page, as shown in Figure 8-13.

Step 2.   Type or browse to the folder containing the executable files.

Step 3.   Specify the user or security group to which the rule will apply. Click

Select to display the Select User or Group dialog box, from which you can select the desired user or group. The wizard supplies a name based on the folder containing the executable. If you want to change this name, do so.

Figure 8-13 Creating AppLocker rules to be applied to Adobe Photoshop CS4.

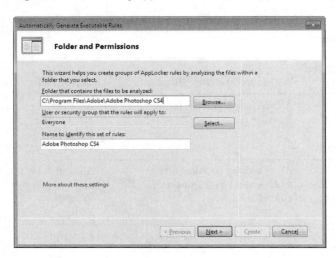

Step 4. Click **Next** to display the Rule Preferences page shown in Figure 8-14, and then specify the following options:

Figure 8-14 Specifying the types of rules to be created.

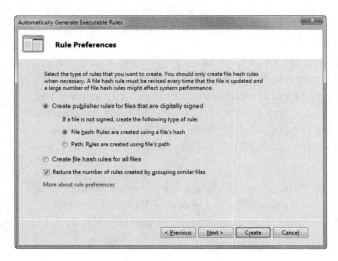

— **Create publisher rules for files that are digitally signed:** Specifies that rules are created according to the publisher for digitally signed files. If the file is not digitally signed, you can specify the rule is created according to either a file hash or a path.

— **Create file hash rules for all files:** Specifies that the file hash will be used for all files, regardless of whether the files are digitally signed.

— **Reduce the number of rules created by grouping similar files:** Selected by default, this option helps you to organize AppLocker rules by creating single publisher, path, or file hash condition according to files that have the same publisher, product name, subfolder of the specified folder, or file hash.

Step 5.   Click **Next** and review the information provided on the Review Rules page.

Step 6.   If you need to change any rule types, click **Previous**. When finished, click **Create** to create the rules and close the wizard.

AppLocker also includes a wizard that you can use to create granular rules according to any of the available options. To use this wizard, proceed as follows:

Step 1.   In the Local Security Policy snap-in, right-click the desired subnode of AppLocker and choose **Create New Rule**. This starts the wizard with a Before You Begin page that describes preliminary steps you should take.

Step 2.   Click **Next** to display the Permissions page. On this page, specify the **Allow** or **Deny** action and then click the **Select** button to display the Select User or Group dialog box, which enables you to select the desired user or group.

Step 3.   Click **Next** to display the Conditions page, from which you can select **Publisher**, **Path**, or **File Hash**.

Step 4.   If you select **Publisher**, you receive the page shown in Figure 8-15. Click **Browse** to browse to the desired publisher, as shown (for example) for Adobe Photoshop CS4. This page also enables you to choose how specific you want the rule to become, by moving the slider provided. For example, to create a rule that applies to all Adobe products, you would move the slider up to the Publisher line.

Step 5.   Click **Create** to create your rule, or click **Next** to specify exceptions. These include any publisher or path you want to exclude from the rule.

Figure 8-15   Creating a publisher-based executable file rule.

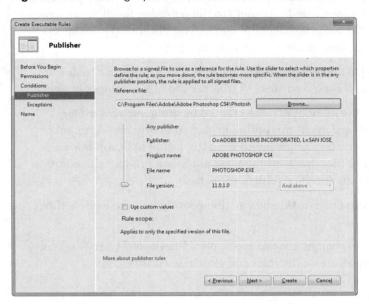

Step 6.   The wizard creates a name for the rule automatically. Click **Next** to modify this name and add an optional description. When finished, click **Create** to create the rule. This creates the rule and adds it to the list in the details pane of the Local Security Policy or Group Policy Object Editor snap-in.

At step 3 of this procedure, you can also choose **Path** and then browse to or type a local or UNC path to the executable file(s) the rule is to cover. Or you can select **File Hash** and then browse to the folder or file containing the file hash. You can specify any number of folders containing hashes to be covered by this rule.

You can also edit the properties of any rule you've created by any of the methods described here. To do so, right-click the rule in the details pane and click **Properties**. This displays the dialog box shown in Figure 8-16, which enables you to modify the properties described in Table 8-5: Note that not all tabs listed will appear; the type of rule being configured determines whether you see the Path, Publisher, or File Hash tab.

Figure 8-16 You can modify the properties of any AppLocker rule from the rule's Properties dialog box.

Table 8-5 Configurable AppLocker Properties

Tab	Description
General	Enables you to modify the action (allow or deny) and select a different group to apply the rule to.
Path	Enables you to change the path to the files or folders to which the rule should apply. This tab appears only for rules that have path conditions. (It is not shown in Figure 8-16.)
Publisher	Enables you to change the publisher, product name, filename, and file version. This tab appears only for rules that have publisher conditions.
File Hash	Enables you to add or remove files to be included in a file hash rule. This tab appears only for this type of rule. (It is not shown in Figure 8-16.)
Exceptions	Enables you to add, edit, or remove exceptions to the rule, according to publisher, file path, or hash.

Configuring Internet Explorer

Browsers are fast becoming a ubiquitous interface to every type of resource—from Hypertext Markup Language (HTML) files, Extensible Markup Language (XML) data, and FTP files, to network shares, network and local printers, local files and folders, and more. For the 70-680 exam, you are expected to have the skills to configure and troubleshoot various aspects of Internet Explorer 8, including tabbed browsing, pop-ups, add-ons, and InPrivate mode; you are also expected to know how to access a variety of network resources using Internet Explorer. Table 8-6 lists the methods you should know.

Table 8-6   Accessing Resources Via a Browser

Command	Sample URL	Usage
`http://`	`http://www.microsoft.com`	Downloads HTML files from Internet web servers and displays the file within the browser
`http://`	`https://www.microsoft.com`	Downloads HTML files using Secure Sockets Layer (SSL) so that the information exchanged is secured
`ftp://`	`ftp://ftp.microsoft.com`	Downloads a file from an FTP server
`File://`	`File://server/share/` `folder/file`	Opens the file specified from a network server
`http://`	`http://printserver/printers`	Displays a list of the printers that are being shared by a computer configured with IIS for sharing printers
`http://`	`http://printserver/printer`	Opens the printer page for the printer

TIP   Handling passwords when using FTP can be tricky. When you open a file using FTP, for example, you might need a password. Because Internet Explorer doesn't support password prompting, you need to supply that password within your URL. In this example, the correct syntax is `ftp://user:password@ftpserver/url-path`.

Although Microsoft made a great leap in improving Internet Explorer 7 compared to its predecessors, the improvements introduced with Internet Explorer 8 are more subtle. Microsoft has improved Protected Mode by restricting its privileges to reduce the capability of an attack that installs malicious code on a user's computer or an attack that modifies or destroys a user's data. The SmartScreen filter enhances the antiphishing and antimalware tools introduced with Internet Explorer 7 by comparing website addresses to a database that is continuously updated. Internet Explorer 8 also highlights the domain name within the Address bar in bold so that you can notice inappropriate websites more easily. InPrivate browsing enables you to protect your privacy by filtering your browsing information (such as history, passwords, cookies, and temporary Internet files) so that others cannot access them.

At the same time, Internet Explorer 8 is more user friendly, with improved visual search capabilities that suggest search terms as you type into the Search box. A new feature called *accelerators* enables you to locate additional information by right-clicking text and selecting an option that includes items such as mapping, dictionaries, translation, and blogs. The address bar suggests websites from your Favorites, History, and Really Simple Syndication (RSS) feeds as you type, thereby helping you locate the desired information. The Web Slices feature helps you to obtain up-to-date information without the need to navigate repeatedly to websites as they update their content. Should Internet Explorer 8 crash, it retains all tabs and information so that you can resume browsing with minimal data loss.

TIP If your organization uses intranet applications that were designed for Internet Explorer 6, it is possible that these applications might not operate properly with Internet Explorer 8. In most cases, Compatibility mode will enable these applications to work properly; however, it is recommended that you test these applications to ensure that they function as desired. Another possible solution to this problem is to utilize Internet Explorer 6 running under Windows XP Mode. As discussed earlier in this chapter, users can then run Internet Explorer 6 directly from the Windows 7 Start menu.

Configuring Compatibility View

The Compatibility View feature enables websites designed for earlier versions of Internet Explorer to display properly in Internet Explorer 8. Internet Explorer 8 displays the Compatibility View button in the address bar when it recognizes a non-compatible website. Simply click this button to turn Compatibility View on. You can also click **Compatibility View** from the **Tools** menu button. Doing so causes the website to display as if you were using an older version of Internet Explorer.

To configure Internet Explorer to add or remove websites displayed in Compatibility View, click **Tools > Compatibility View Settings**. This displays the Compatibility View Settings dialog box shown in Figure 8-17, with the current website displayed in the Add this website text box. Click **Add** to specify that this website will be displayed in Compatibility View. This adds the website to the list under Websites you've added to Compatibility View. You can also modify Compatibility View settings by configuring the following three options available at the bottom of this dialog box.

Figure 8-17 The Compatibility View Settings dialog box enables you to specify which websites are displayed in Compatibility View.

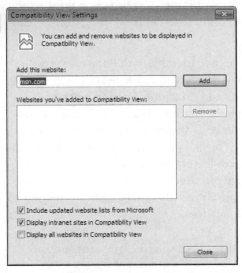

- **Include updated website lists from Microsoft:** Microsoft provides lists of websites that function better in Compatibility View. Selecting this check box enables these lists to be downloaded and used. This check box is selected by default.

- **Display intranet sites in Compatibility View:** Select this check box if your company's intranet websites were designed for older versions of Internet Explorer. This check box is selected by default.

- **Display all websites in Compatibility View:** Selecting this check box forces Compatibility View to always be used. This check box is cleared by default.

You can also use Group Policy to configure Compatibility View in an AD DS domain. From either the Computer Configuration or User Configuration section of the Group Policy Object Editor, access the **Administrative Templates\ Windows Components\Internet Explorer\Compatibility View** node. This provides the following policies shown in Figure 8-18.

- **Turn on Internet Explorer 7 Standards Mode:** Forces all websites to display in a mode compatible with Internet Explorer 7.

- **Turn off Compatibility View:** Prevents users from using the Compatibility View feature or the Compatibility View Settings dialog box.

Figure 8-18   Group Policy in Windows 7 contains a series of settings that control the use of Compatibility View.

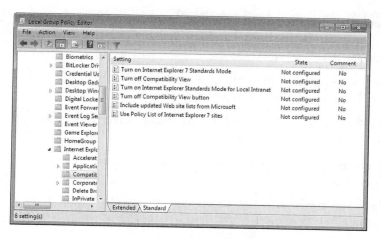

- **Turn on Internet Explorer Standards Mode for Local Intranet:** Controls the display of local intranet websites so that they appear in a mode compatible with Internet Explorer 7. Enable this setting if your company's intranet websites do not display properly in Internet Explorer 8.

- **Turn off Compatibility View button:** Prevents users from using the Compatibility View button on the toolbar.

- **Include updated Web site lists from Microsoft:** Enables the browser to use the compatible website lists provided by Microsoft. These websites will automatically display in Compatibility View.

- **Use Policy List of Internet Explorer 7 sites:** Enables users to add specific sites that will display in Compatibility View.

Configuring Security Settings

Each iteration of Internet Explorer has added additional security features that help protect your security and privacy when browsing online. Security features in Internet Explorer 8 include the following:

- **Information bar:** Internet Explorer displays an information bar at the top of the page under certain circumstances to alert you of possible security problems. These include attempts by a website to install an ActiveX control, open a pop-up window, download a file, or run active content. You will also see an information bar if your security settings are below recommended levels, if you access an intranet web page without turning on intranet address checking, or if you access a website whose address contains native language letters or symbols.

You can obtain additional information or take action by clicking the information bar message.

- **SmartScreen Filter:** Helps protect you from fraudulent websites that masquerade as legitimate sites (such as banks) and attempt to hijack your password and account information.

- **Protected Mode:** Helps protect you from websites that attempt to install malicious software or data files on your computer.

- **Pop-up blocker:** Blocks most pop-up windows that display advertising or attempt to entice you to visit malicious websites.

- **Add-on Manager:** Enables you to disable or allow browser add-ons or undesired ActiveX controls.

- **Notification:** Displays a message if a website attempts to download software or files to your computer.

- **Digital signatures:** Ensures that a file has been verified and notifies you if the file was altered since it was signed.

- **Secure Sockets Layer (SSL) 128-bit encryption for using secure websites:** Enables Internet Explorer to create a secure connection to e-commerce websites.

You can configure your Internet Explorer's security settings from the Internet Properties dialog box, which you can access by either of the following methods:

- Click **Start> Control Panel > Network and Internet** and then select **Internet Options**.

- In Internet Explorer, select **Tools > Internet Options**.

Configuring Internet Explorer Security Zones

The Security tab of the Internet Options dialog box displays a list of website types called *Internet zones*, as shown in Figure 8-19.

By default, all websites are included in the Internet zone. To move a website to another zone, select the desired zone and click **Sites**. On the dialog box that appears, type or copy the URL to the text box provided (if it is not already present), click **Add**, and then click **Close**. You can return a site to the Internet zone by selecting it and clicking **Remove**. You can also limit the Local intranet and Trusted sites zones to secured sites whose URLs start with https: by selecting the check box labeled **Require server verification (https:) for all sites in this zone**.

Figure 8-19 You can establish security settings separately to each type of website location.

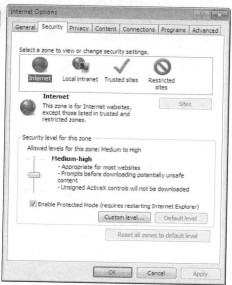

CAUTION The default security for the Trusted sites zone is considerably lower than that for any of the other zones. Be absolutely certain that you trust a website implicitly before adding the site to this zone. If you are uncertain, you should leave the site in the Internet zone until you have investigated it thoroughly.

To configure the security settings for a zone, click the desired zone to select it and then click the **Custom level** button. The Security Settings dialog box opens, as shown in Figure 8-20, where you can select each individual security setting or set an Internet zone to a predefined group of security settings, including Low, Medium-low, Medium, Medium-high (default), and High. Note that the default Internet zone does not include the Low and Medium-low options.

To establish the privacy settings, click the **Privacy** tab. Here you can select a preset level for handling cookies. If you click the **Sites** button, you can block or allow privacy information to be exchanged with specific websites. To establish a different method for handling cookies in the Internet zone, click the **Advanced** button and select your preferred settings.

For security settings that govern specific behaviors in Internet Explorer, click the **Advanced** tab and scroll down the window to the **Security** category. Here, you can set options such as reducing problems caused by software downloaded and installed from the Internet (do this by clearing the **Allow software to run or install even if the signature is invalid** check box; this check box is cleared by default).

Figure 8-20   Individual security settings apply to an Internet zone for a custom security definition.

TIP   Another way that you can secure Internet Explorer is to ensure that it is updated with the latest patches and service packs available. Access Windows Update as described in Chapter 7, "Configuring Devices and Updates," and ensure that security and optional updates to Internet Explorer are downloaded.

Configuring Protected Mode in Internet Explorer

First introduced with Internet Explorer 7 in Windows Vista and continued with Internet Explorer 8 in Windows 7, *Protected Mode* provides enhanced levels of security and protection from malware. Protected Mode prevents websites from modifying user or system files and settings or downloading unwanted software unless you provide your consent. It displays a prompt similar to those available with UAC, asking you to confirm any action that attempts to download something to your computer or launch a program. The user can ensure that these actions are desired and that they prevent any harmful action that might otherwise occur. You can stop any such type of action and confirm the trustworthiness of the website before proceeding. Protected Mode also prevents Internet Explorer from writing data to any location except the Temporary Internet Files folder unless you provide consent (such as during a desired download).

Protected Mode is enabled by default on all Internet zones except the Trusted Sites zone, and Internet Explorer confirms this fact by displaying the message Protected Mode: On in the status bar. If this message does not appear, you can turn Protected Mode on by selecting the check box labeled **Enable Protected Mode** on the Security tab (shown previously in Figure 8-19) and then restarting Internet Explorer. Internet Explorer might also display an information bar informing you that Protected Mode is turned off in this instance.

TIP   Internet Explorer runs in protected mode by default and informs you of this fact with a message in the status bar at the bottom of the browser window. You should not turn this mode off; if it is turned off by mistake, you can reenable it by resetting Internet Explorer to default settings.

Configuring the SmartScreen Filter

The SmartScreen Filer in Internet Explorer 8 enhances the capabilities of the phishing filter first introduced with Internet Explorer 7. Besides checking websites against a list of reported phishing sites, this filter checks software downloads against a list of reported malware websites. The practice of *phishing* refers to the creation of a fake website that closely mimics a real website and contains a similar-looking URL, intending to scam users into sending confidential personal information such as credit card or bank account numbers, birthdates, Social Security numbers, and so on. The attacker sends email messages that appear to originate from the company whose website was spoofed so that users connect to the fake website and provide this type of information. The attacker can use this information for identity theft and other nefarious purposes.

Microsoft built the SmartScreen Filter into Internet Explorer 8 to check websites for phishing activity using the following methods:

- Comparing website addresses visited by users with dynamically updated lists of reported legitimate sites saved on your computer.

- Comparing website addresses against lists of dynamically updated lists of sites reported as downloading malicious software to your computer.

- Analyzing website addresses against characteristics (such as misspelled words) used by phishing sites.

- Comparing website addresses with those in an online service that Microsoft operates for immediate checking against a list of reported phishing sites. This list is updated several times each hour using material gathered by Microsoft or other industries or reported by users. Other global databases of known phishing sites are also used.

If the SmartScreen Filter detects a known phishing or malware site, Internet Explorer displays the address bar in red and replaces the website with a message informing you of the risks. You receive options to close the website or continue to it. If the site is not a known phishing or malware site but behaves in a similar manner to such a site, the address bar appears in yellow and a warning message appears. The user can report the site to the Microsoft SmartScreen Filter list or gather further information to report a false positive if the site turns out to be legitimate.

If you suspect that a website you are visiting is a phishing site (whether the address bar has turned yellow or not), you can check the following items:

- **The URL appearing in the address bar:** A spoofed domain name will appear similar to the authentic one but contain misspelled or additional words. Internet Explorer 8 makes this easier to check by displaying all domain names in bold.

- **URLs associated with page links:** Although some of these might point to the authentic site, others might point to the phisher's site. Check the address that appears in the bottom-left corner of the status bar when you hover your mouse over the link.

- **Advertisements or other content not associated with the legitimate site:** Many phishers use free web-hosting services that might add advertising or other content to the fake site.

- **Failure to use a secure (https) connection:** Legitimate sites use secure connections for transmitting all sensitive data. Internet Explorer displays a gold lock icon in the address bar for all `https` connections. If this icon does not appear, you are most likely dealing with a phishing site.

- **Addresses used for submitting forms:** In general, the phisher site will contain a form that you are asked to fill out with your personal information and include a button that says **Submit** or something similar. To check this address, select **View > Source** and then locate the value of the `<form>` tag's `Action` attribute. If this is a nonlegitimate address, you know you are on a phishing site.

Use the following procedure to configure the SmartScreen Filter:

Step 1.   Open **Internet Explorer** to a website that you suspect might be a phishing site.

Step 2.   On the Safety menu, select **SmartScreen Filter** and then select one of the following options:

— **Check This Website:** Checks the current website. Click **OK** in the SmartScreen Filter message box that appears to receive a message informing you of the result.

— **Turn On SmartScreen Filter:** Displays the dialog box shown in Figure 8-21, which enables you to turn the filter on or off as desired. This menu item appears as Turn off SmartScreen Filter when the filter is already on.

— **Report Unsafe Website:** Enables you to report a phishing website or remove an authentic site that has been flagged as a phishing one.

Figure 8-21   The Microsoft SmartScreen Filter dialog box enables you to turn the automatic phishing filter on or off.

Privacy Tab Settings

The Privacy tab of the Internet Properties dialog box, shown in Figure 8-22, enables you to configure cookie handling, the pop-up blocker, and InPrivate browser settings. We discuss the InPrivate browser mode later in this chapter.

Handling Cookies

Cookies are small files that websites place on your computer to facilitate improved browsing or advertisement display on future visits to the same website. Information you provide on a form displayed by the website is placed in the cookie to be sent to the web server when you next visit the website, which then customizes the page sent to you with items such as your name and interests. You can choose from the following options:

■ **Block All Cookies:** Prevents all websites from storing cookies on your computer and from reading existing cookies.

Figure 8-22   The Privacy tab enables you to configure cookie settings and the pop-up blocker.

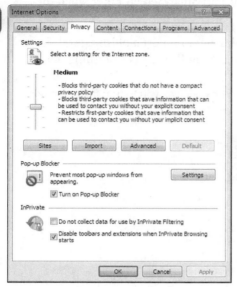

- **High:** Prevents websites that do not have a compact privacy policy from storing cookies on your computer. This is a condensed computer-readable privacy statement. Websites are also prevented from storing cookies that use personally identifiable information without your consent.

- **Medium High:** Prevents websites that do not have a compact privacy policy from storing cookies on your computer. Also blocks third-party cookies that use personally identifiable information without your explicit consent or first-party cookies that use personally identifiable information without implicit consent.

- **Medium:** Prevents websites that do not have a compact privacy policy from storing cookies on your computer. Limits websites that place first-party cookies that save information but use identifiable information without your implicit consent.

- **Low:** Allows websites to place cookies on your computer, including those that do not have a compact privacy policy or that use personally identifiable information without your explicit consent.

- **Accept All Cookies:** Allows all websites to place cookies on your computer and allows websites that create cookies to read them.

The Content tab, which is described in the next section, also enables you to specify which websites are allowed or prevented from using cookies regardless of their privacy policy. Click **Sites** to access the Per Site Privacy Actions dialog box to specify these websites. You can also choose the manner in which first- or third-party cookies are handled in the Internet zone. Click **Advanced** to specify whether these cookies are accepted or blocked, or whether you receive a prompt for these cookies.

You can view privacy statements provided by many websites. This policy informs you of the types of information collected and stored by the website. You should be concerned with information such as your name, email address, and so on. You can view a website's privacy policy by clicking **Safety > Webpage Privacy Policy** from the Internet Explorer toolbar. In the Privacy Policy dialog box that appears, click **Summary**. This page also enables you to determine how cookies from the website should be handled, including an option to never allow the site to use cookies.

Blocking Pop-ups

Initially included with Internet Explorer 6 on Windows XP with SP2, the Pop-up Blocker eases the frustrations of many Internet users. Pop-ups are additional windows that appear while browsing the Internet. Advertisers often use these to display ads to Internet users. Some pop-ups even deploy malware and are displayed in such a way that the only possible way to close the pop-up without installing the malware is to use the Task Manager to force the window to close. Users who do not know how to do this often end up with huge amounts of pop-up traffic, viruses, spy software, and other problems.

You can configure how the Pop-up Blocker feature functions by opening the **Tools** menu, selecting the **Pop-up Blocker** submenu, and then clicking **Pop-up Blocker Settings**. The Pop-up Blocker Settings dialog box opens, as shown in Figure 8-23. (This option is not available if the Pop-up Blocker is currently off.) The other option in the Pop-up Blocker submenu is to **Turn Off Pop-up Blocker** (if it is turned on) or **Turn On Pop-up Blocker** (if it is turned off).

To allow pop-ups from a certain website, type the URL in the Address of website to allow text box and then click the **Add** button. You can select whether to display the information bar and whether to play a sound when a website's pop-up is blocked. The Blocking level list box enables you to select whether to block all pop-ups (High: Block all pop-ups [Ctrl+Alt to override]), most pop-ups (Medium: Block most automatic pop-ups), or just the pop-ups that are from nonsecure sites (Low: Allow pop-ups from secure sites).

Figure 8-23   You can allow pop-ups from certain websites by editing the Pop-up Blocker
Settings.

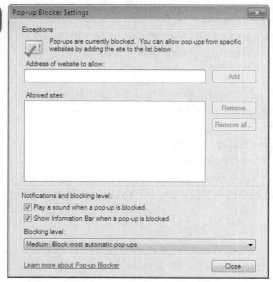

When Internet Explorer blocks a pop-up, it displays an information bar beneath
the line of tabs. You can click this bar to temporarily allow pop-ups, always allow
pop-ups from this site, or configure additional pop-up settings including suppressing the information bar.

Content Tab Settings

The Content tab includes the following security-related options:

- **Parental Controls:** Links to the Parental Controls feature that enables you to
  control the types of content your children are permitted to access.

- **Content Advisor:** Enables you to control the Internet content that users can
  view on the computer. You can specify ratings that filter websites according to
  their content as established by various rating boards.

- **Certificates:** Controls the behavior of certificates used for encrypted connections and identification. We discuss the use of certificates later in this chapter.

- **Auto Complete:** Stores information from previously visited web pages and tries
  to complete entries you make on web addresses, forms, usernames, passwords,
  and so on. Click **Settings** to specify the types of entries that Auto Complete is
  used for. You can delete Auto Complete history from the General tab of the
  Internet Properties dialog box.

- **Feeds and Web Slices:** Enables you to configure settings for Really Simple Syndicated (RSS) feeds and web slices, which enable you to receive up-to-date information on the Internet at times that are convenient for you.

Advanced Tab Settings

The Advanced tab of the Internet Properties dialog box contains a large range of settings that you can configure in the subjects of accessibility, browsing, HTTP 1.1, international, multimedia, printing, searching, and security. Figure 8-24 shows most of the security settings available from this tab.

Figure 8-24   The Advanced tab contains a series of settings that affect the security of Internet Explorer 8.

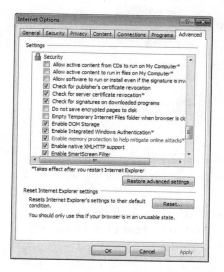

From this tab, you can click **Restore advanced settings** to reset all settings to their defaults, or you can click **Reset** to reset all Internet Explorer settings to their defaults.

Configuring Providers

By default, Internet Explorer uses Bing as its search provider when you first open it (note "Bing" in Figure 8-25). Use the following procedure to change the default search provider or add additional search providers to this box.

Figure 8-25   The Add Search Provider dialog box enables you to add search providers and set a default provider.

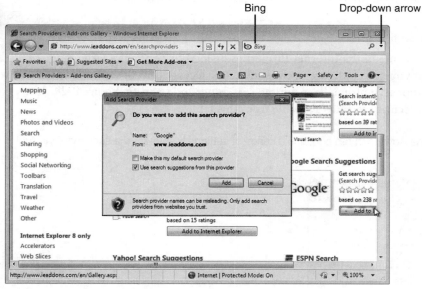

Step 1.   In Internet Explorer 8, click the small drop-down arrow immediately to the right of the Search field. From the pop-up menu that appears, select **Find More Providers**.

Step 2.   Internet Explorer 8 opens a new tab displaying the Add-ons Gallery: Search Providers Web page. Click the **Add to Internet Explorer** command button beside the desired search provider.

Step 3.   The Add Search Provider dialog box shown in Figure 8-25 appears. If you want to use this provider as your default, select the check box provided. Then click **Add**.

Step 4.   To change or remove search providers, select **Manage Search Providers** from the pop-up menu. In the Manage Add-ons dialog box shown in Figure 8-26, select the desired search provider and click **Set as default** to make it the default search provider. Or you can remove this provider from the list by clicking **Remove**. When finished, click **Close**.

Figure 8-26   You can specify your default search provider or remove search providers from the Manage Add-ons dialog box.

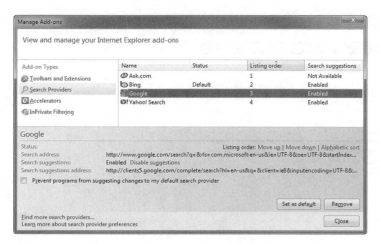

After you have added search providers, it is simple to perform a search with an alternative provider. Simply click the same small drop-down arrow shown in Figure 8-25 and select the desired search provider. This procedure enables you to change the search provider temporarily without changing the default provider.

Managing Add-ons

Add-ons are optional additional features that you can install in Internet Explorer to provide additional functionality. They generally come from sources on the Internet and are sometimes installed without your knowledge. At other times, the Internet source will ask you for permission to install an add-on before proceeding. However, if you deny this permission, the web page might not display as intended by its creators.

TIP   You can run Internet Explorer without any add-ons by clicking **Start> All Programs > Accessories > System Tools > Internet Explorer (No Add-ons)**. Internet Explorer opens and displays a page including an information bar that informs you that all add-ons are turned off.

Internet Explorer enables you to manage add-ons in several ways. Use the following procedure to manage add-ons:

Step 1.   In Internet Explorer 8, click **Tools > Manage Add-ons**. The Manage Add-ons dialog box shown in Figure 8-27 opens.

Figure 8-27   You can view and manage Internet Explorer add-ons from the Manage Add-ons dialog box.

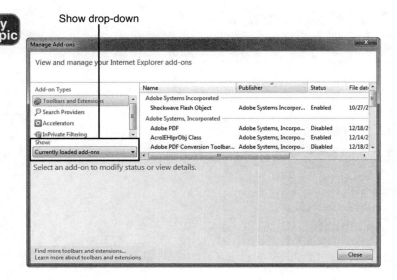

Step 2.   Select one of the following options from the Show drop-down list:

— **All add-ons:** Lists all add-ons that have been downloaded to Internet Explorer at any time since you installed Windows plus those that were preapproved by Microsoft or your computer manufacturer.

— **Currently loaded add-ons:** Displays only those add-ons used by a currently or recently viewed web page. This list appears by default when you first open the Manage Add-ons dialog box.

— **Run without permission:** Displays all add-ons that were preapproved by Microsoft, your computer manufacturer, or your Internet service provider (ISP). These add-ons have generally been digitally signed and run without displaying any permissions message box. Any unsigned add-ons carry the message (Not verified) in the Publisher column.

— **Downloaded controls:** Displays 32-bit ActiveX controls only. Although these controls add functionality to Internet Explorer, malicious software writers often use them for undesirable purposes.

Step 3.   If an add-on appears to be causing problems or preventing a web page from displaying properly, select it and click **Disable**. In the Disable Add-on dialog box that appears, select or deselect other related add-ons that are displayed and then click **Disable** to disable the chosen add-on.

Step 4.   To disable an ActiveX control, select **Downloaded controls** from the **Show** drop-down list. Then select the desired control and click **Disable**. Note that you cannot delete preinstalled ActiveX controls or other types of add-ons; you can only disable them.

Step 5.   To locate additional add-ons for Internet Explorer, click the small drop-down arrow immediately to the right of the Search field. From the pop-up menu that appears, select **Find More Providers**. From the list on the left side of the Search Providers web page, select the desired add-on type. In the web page that appears (for example, Finance is shown in Figure 8-28), click the **Add to Internet Explorer** button beside the desired add-on. Confirm your choice in the dialog box that appears.

Using Accelerators

An *accelerator* is a special type of add-on that enables users to perform actions against text they have selected from a website without leaving the website. Internet Explorer provides a default selection of accelerators. You can choose additional accelerators from an online list that is frequently updated.

Figure 8-28   You can add additional add-ons from many categories from the Add-ons Gallery.

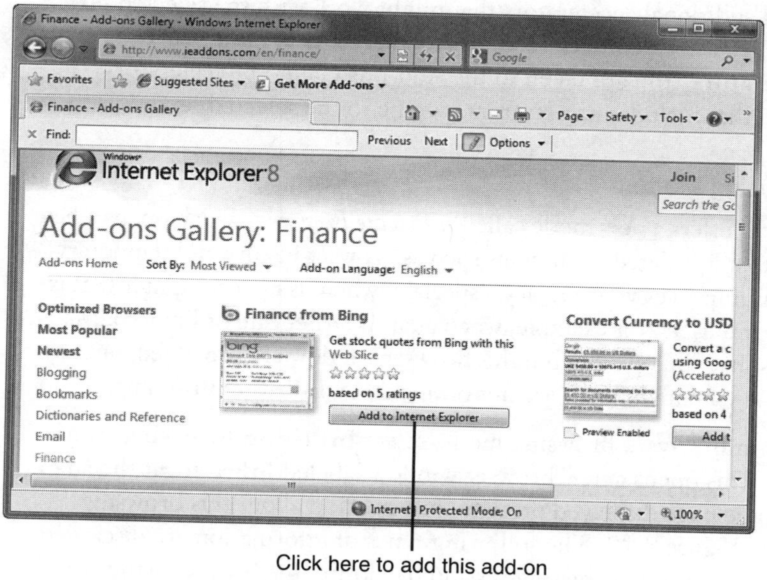

Click here to add this add-on

Microsoft offers the following default types of accelerators:

- **Blog:** Enables you to post the selected text directly to your blog
- **Email:** Pastes the selected text into a new email message, which you can then send to a recipient
- **Map:** Uses an online mapping service to locate an address included in the selected text
- **Search:** Uses your default search engine to locate additional information about the selected text
- **Translate:** Enables you to use an online translation service to translate the selected text into another language

Proceed as follows to use accelerators:

Step 1.   Open **Internet Explorer 8** to the desired website.

Step 2.   Select the text that you want to use with an accelerator.

Step 3.   Right-click the text, select **All Accelerators**, and then choose the desired accelerator from the fly-out list. You can also click the small blue button that appears next to the selected text.

Step 4.   To find additional accelerators that might work with the selected text, right-click the text and choose **All Accelerators > Find More Accelerators**. You are taken to the Add-ons Gallery: Accelerators website that includes accelerators specific to the selected text.

Using InPrivate Browsing Mode

Internet Explorer 8 offers a new mode called *InPrivate Browsing*, which opens a new browser window that is isolated from items such as browser history and temporary Internet files. This improves your privacy, especially when using a computer that is shared among several users (for example, when at an Internet café or library kiosk machine). All tabs that you open within this browser window are protected, but any additional windows you might open are not protected by InPrivate Browsing.

To start a session in InPrivate Browsing mode, select **InPrivate Browsing** from the Safety menu. This opens a new browser window labeled InPrivate at the address bar. The home page displayed provides information about this browsing mode, as shown in Figure 8-29. The following types of information are discarded when you end your InPrivate browsing session by closing the browser window:

- Cookies and temporary Internet files (stored in memory during the browsing session only so that pages work properly)
- Website browsing history

Figure 8-29   Enabling InPrivate Browsing.

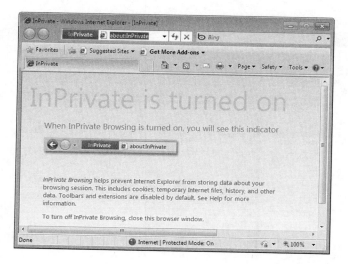

- Information you supply on form pages including passwords
- AutoComplete and address bar information
- Automatic Crash Restore information that would normally restore browser tabs if Internet Explorer should crash

The InPrivate Browsing mode also provides a capability called *InPrivate Filtering*, which blocks providers of additional website information from being sent to these providers. For example, advertisement content is generally provided by a third party. When you visit websites bearing such content, some information is usually sent to the third party, enabling this party to develop a profile of your browsing tendencies. This party uses this profile to send you specific advertisements based on your browsing history. By enabling InPrivate Filtering, you can block third parties from receiving information on your browsing activities.

To enable InPrivate Filtering, click **Safety> InPrivate Filtering**. The Safety list displays a check mark against InPrivate Filtering to show that it is enabled. To configure the settings used by InPrivate Filtering, choose **InPrivate Filtering Settings** from the **Safety** menu. This displays the InPrivate Filtering settings dialog box (see Figure 8-30), which enables you to perform the following actions:

Figure 8-30   The InPrivate Filtering settings dialog box enables you to configure which providers are blocked or allowed.

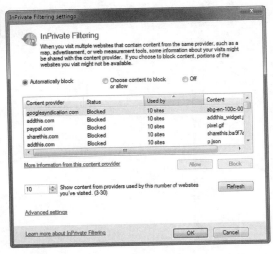

- **Perform selective blocking of content providers:** Click the **Choose content to block or allow** radio button to select any content provider, and then click the **Allow** or **Block** command buttons as desired.

- **Disable InPrivate Filtering:** Click the Off radio button to disable InPrivate Filtering.

- **Manage your add-ons:** If you click the **Advanced Settings** link, you are taken to the Manage Add-ons dialog box previously shown in Figure 8-27. Because an InPrivate Browsing window disables toolbars and extensions, you can use this option to enable any toolbars or extensions you want to use during an InPrivate session.

- **Modify the number of providers displayed:** Use the list box provided to determine the number of websites visited that is required to include the provider in this list, and then click **Refresh**. You can also click **Refresh** at any time to update the list according to websites you have visited during your browsing session.

InPrivate Browsing Group Policies

Group Policy enables you to configure several policies that govern the behavior of InPrivate Browsing and InPrivate Filtering. From either the Computer Configuration or User Configuration section of the Group Policy Object Editor, access the **Administrative Templates\Windows Components\Internet Explorer\ InPrivate** node. This provides the following policies (shown in Figure 8-31):

Figure 8-31   Group Policy provides these policies that govern the behavior of InPrivate Browsing and InPrivate Filtering.

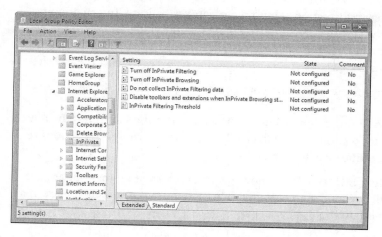

- **Turn off InPrivate Filtering:** When enabled, InPrivate Filtering is disabled.

- **Turn off InPrivate Browsing:** When enabled, InPrivate Browsing is disabled.

- **Do not collect InPrivate Filtering data:** Disables the collection of data on third-party providers used by InPrivate Filtering.

- **Disable toolbars and extensions when InPrivate Browsing starts:** When disabled, toolbars and browser helper objects are loaded by default during an InPrivate Browsing session (these items are normally disabled by InPrivate Browsing).

- **InPrivate Filtering Threshold:** Determines the number of websites that can reference a third-party provider before it appears on the blocked list previously shown in Figure 8-30.

Certificates for Secure Websites

The Internet has become an increasingly popular business resource in recent years. You can do your banking, pay bills, and order a large variety of items from e-commerce websites. These websites use a system of certificates to provide a secure identification and verification, as well as to protect and encrypt user information such as credit card data sent across the Internet. A website that uses the `https://` prefix is secured with Hypertext Transfer Protocol Secure (HTTPS), which in turn uses a combination of HTTP with Secure Sockets Layer (SSL)/Transport Layer Security (TLS) to encrypt all information transmitted across the website. SSL uses a public key/private key encryption system to encrypt data.

When you visit a website that uses the `https://` prefix, you should see a gold lock icon displayed in the address bar that informs you that the connection is secure. Click this icon to view information about the website's certificate. Information provided will indicate the certification authority (CA) that provided the certificate and inform you that the connection is encrypted. Click **Should I trust this site** to display help information that assists you in determining whether to trust the website.

To view the list of certificates stored on your computer, perform the following steps:

Step 1.   Open the Internet Options dialog box and select the **Content** tab. The Certificates section of this tab enables you to perform several actions related to certificate management.

Step 2.   Click **Clear SSL state** to remove personal information that might have been collected on your computer. This action is useful when you are at a public computer.

Step 3.   Click **Publishers** to view information on trusted and untrusted publishers.

Step 4.   Click the **Certificates** button to display the Certificates dialog box as shown in Figure 8-32. This dialog box enables you to view certificates issued to yourself or others on the computer. You can also view certificates issued by trusted root CAs or intermediate CAs, import new certificates, and configure certificate purposes.

Figure 8-32   The Certificates dialog box enables you to view available certificates.

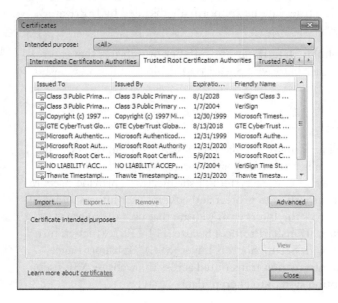

Step 5. Click **Advanced** to display the Advanced Options dialog box, which enables you to select the certificate purposes displayed on the various tabs of the Certificates dialog box.

Step 6. Click **Import** to start the Certificate Import Wizard, which enables you to copy certificates, certificate trust lists, and certificate revocation lists from your disk to a certificate store.

Step 7. When finished with the Certificates dialog box, click **Close**. You are returned to the Content tab where you can perform other actions if desired. When finished, click **OK**.

Should a problem occur when you access a secure website, Internet Explorer displays a warning message and blocks navigation to the site. In this case, you receive a page informing you of the error that occurred and offering options to close the web page or continue to the website (not recommended). You should not access the website unless you can obtain independent validation of its authenticity. Certificate errors that can be displayed include the following:

- **Website address does not match address in certificate:** Indicates that the website is using a certificate that was originally issued to a different website address. This might happen if a website has changed its address and the certificate has not been updated.

- **Website certificate has been revoked:** Indicates that the certificate was revoked for a reason such as having been obtained fraudulently.

- **Website certificate is out of date:** Indicates that the validity period for the certificate has expired.

- **Website certificate is not from a trusted source:** Indicates that the certificate was obtained from a source that is not trusted by Internet Explorer. Often this indicates that you have accessed a phishing or malware website. However, you might receive this error on an intranet website that has set up its own certification hierarchy using the Certificate Server role in Windows Server 2003/2008 R2.

- **Problem found with security certificate:** Indicates an error that is not covered by any of the other categories. You might receive this error if the certificate is corrupted or has been tampered by an unauthorized individual.

Exam Preparation Tasks

Review All the Key Topics

Review the most important topics in the chapter, noted with the key topics icon in the outer margin of the page. Table 8-7 lists a reference of these key topics and the page numbers on which each is found.

Table 8-7   Key Topics for Chapter 8

Key Topic Element	Description	Page Number
Table 8-2	Describes available application compatibility options	248
Paragraph	Describes Windows XP Mode	253
Figure 8-4	Shows the Internet Explorer Compatibility Test Tool	255
List	Introduces available application restriction policies	257
Figure 8-8	Shows available new Software Restriction Policy rules	260
List	Describes AppLocker capabilities	262
Figure 8-11	Accessing AppLocker	264
Table 8-4	Describes AppLocker default rules	265
Table 8-5	Describes configurable AppLocker properties	269
Figure 8-17	Configuring Compatibility View settings	272
Figure 8-19	Shows the available security zones in Internet Explorer	275
Figure 8-22	Shows available cookie and pop-up blocker settings in Internet Explorer	280
Figure 8-23	Configuring the Pop-up Blocker	282
Figure 8-25	Adding search providers	284
Figure 8-27	Managing add-ons	286
List	Describes items that are discarded when an InPrivate browsing session ends	288
Figure 8-30	Configuring InPrivate Filtering	290
Paragraph	Viewing certificates	291

Complete the Tables and Lists from Memory

Print a copy of Appendix C, "Memory Tables" (found on the CD), or at least the section for this chapter, and complete the tables and lists from memory. Appendix D, "Memory Tables Answer Key," also on the CD, includes completed tables and lists to check your work.

Definitions of Key Terms

Define the following key terms from this chapter, and check your answers in the glossary.

Application compatibility, Application Compatibility Toolkit (ACT), shim, Application Compatibility Manager, Windows XP Mode, Internet Explorer Compatibility Test Tool, Software Restriction Policies, AppLocker, add-ons, pop-up windows, Content Advisor, Local Security Policy, phishing, Compatibility View, Information bar, Protected Mode, SmartScreen Filter, Add-on Manager, Secure Sockets Layer (SSL), InPrivate browsing, InPrivate filtering, certificate

This chapter covers the following subjects:

- **Understanding the TCP/IP Protocol:** TCP/IP is the primary protocol used by computers connecting with each other and the Internet. This section introduces you to the important components of the TCP/IP protocol stack that you must be familiar with for the 70-680 exam.

- **Configuring TCP/IP Version 4:** Version 4 of the TCP/IP protocol has been used for many years and is still common today. This section describes IPv4 address classes and shows you how to configure your computer for addressing and name resolution.

- **Configuring TCP/IP Version 6:** With the increasingly large number of computers and other devices that connect to the Internet, TCP/IPv4 is running out of addresses. The 128-bit TCP/IP version 6 was developed to alleviate this problem. In this section you are introduced to the various types of IPv6 addresses that are available. You then learn how to configure your computer with IPv6 and connect to other computers running either IPv4 or IPv6.

- **Resolving IPv4 and IPv6 Network Connectivity Issues:** Many factors can result in an inability to access other computers on the network or can result in intermittent connectivity. This section introduces common troubleshooting techniques you should be aware of when your computer cannot connect to others.

CHAPTER 9

Configuring TCP/IP

Connectivity between Windows 7 computers and other networks (inclusive of the Internet and other computers) is provided in a variety of ways, all based upon the older version 4 or the newer version 6 of the TCP/IP networking protocol stack. Windows 7 improves on the Network and Sharing Center that was first introduced with Windows Vista. This tool consolidates many of these applications and utilities into one convenient location from which you can create and manage different types of network connections as well as file and print sharing. In this chapter, you study versions 4 and 6 of the TCP/IP protocol suite. You then look at the Network and Sharing Center and its use for configuring and troubleshooting network connections.

Not only do you explore each of these components in this chapter, but you also look at their features and dependencies as they exist within the Windows 7 operating system.

"Do I Know This Already?" Quiz

The "Do I Know This Already?" quiz enables you to assess whether you should read this entire chapter or simply jump to the "Exam Preparation Tasks" section for review. If you are in doubt, read the entire chapter. Table 9-1 outlines the major headings in this chapter and the corresponding "Do I Know This Already?" quiz questions. You can find the answers in Appendix A, "Answers to the 'Do I Know This Already?' Quizzes."

Table 9-1 "Do I Know This Already?" Foundation Topics Section-to-Question Mapping

Foundations Topics Section	Questions Covered in This Section
Understanding the TCP/IP Protocol	1
Configuring TCP/IP Version 4	2–6
Configuring TCP/IP Version 6	7–10
Resolving IPv4 and IPv6 Network Connectivity Issues	11–14

1. Which of the following are component protocols contained within TCP/IP? (Choose three.)

   a. User Datagram Protocol (UDP)

   b. Internet Control Messaging Protocol (ICMP)

   c. Dynamic Host Configuration Protocol (DHCP)

   d. Address Resolution Protocol (ARP)

2. You need to ensure that your IPv4-enabled computer can access other subnets on your company's network, as well as the Internet. Which addressing component should you ensure is specified properly?

   a. IP address

   b. Subnet mask

   c. Default gateway

   d. DNS server address

   e. WINS address

3. Your computer is configured with the IP address 131.107.24.5. To which class does this IP address belong?

   a. A

   b. B

   c. C

   d. D

   e. E

4. Your company is making use of the 192.168.21.0/24 network. This network address is an example of what type of address notation?

   a. Windows Internet Naming System (WINS)

   b. Unicast

   c. Multicast

   d. Classless Inter-Domain Routing (CIDR)

5. Your network is configured to use DHCP for assignment of IP addresses and DNS servers. Which of the following options should you ensure are selected in the Internet Protocol Version 4 (TCP/IPv4) Properties dialog box? (Choose two.)

   a. **Obtain an IP address automatically**

   b. **Use the following IP address**

   c. **Obtain DNS server address automatically**

   d. **Use the following DNS server addresses**

6. Your computer is configured to use the IPv4 address 169.254.183.32. What system is being used by your computer?

   a. Dynamic Host Configuration Protocol (DHCP)

   b. Automatic Private Internet Protocol Addressing (APIPA)

   c. Private IPv4 network addressing

   d. Alternate IP configuration

7. Your company has transitioned to using the IPv6 protocol, and you are responsible for configuring Internet servers that need direct access to the Internet. Which of the following types of IPv6 addresses should you use for this purpose?

   a. Global unicast

   b. Link-local unicast

   c. Site-local unicast

   d. Multicast

   e. Anycast

8. Your computer is using an IPv6 address on the fe80::/64 network. What type of IPv6 address is this?

   a. Global unicast

   b. Link-local unicast

   c. Site-local unicast

   d. Teredo

9. Your computer is using an IPv6 address that includes the 32-bit prefix of 2001::/32. What type of IPv6 address prefix is this?

   a. Global unicast

   b. Link-local unicast

   c. Site-local unicast

   d. Teredo

10. You have configured your Windows 7 computers located on a small subnet to obtain IPv6 addressing information automatically, but the subnet does not have a DHCP or DNS server. You notice that, despite not having these servers on the local subnet, they are able to locate each other by name. What type of addressing is in use?

   a. Automatic Private IP addressing (APIPA)

   b. Link-local multicast name resolution (LLMNR)

   c. Windows Internet Naming Service (WINS)

   d. Address Resolution Protocol (ARP)

11. Your computer is configured to use DHCP on the IPv4 network 192.168.4.0 but is unable to connect to other computers. You run `ipconfig /all` and notice that the computer is using the address 169.254.231.98. You must try again immediately to connect to other network computers. Which parameter of the `ipconfig` command should you use?

   a. `/release`

   b. `/renew`

   c. `/flushdns`

   d. `/displaydns`

12. Which two TCP/IP utilities provide information on the route taken by packets from your computer when connecting to a remote host? (Choose two.)

   a. Route

   b. Netstat

   c. Ping

   d. Tracert

   e. Pathping

13. You are troubleshooting the inability of your computer to connect to others on the network, so you are planning to run several TCP/IP utilities. Arrange the following in the sequence in which you should perform them.

   a. Ping the computer's own IP address.

   b. Ping a host that is on another subnet.

   c. Ping 127.0.0.1 or ::1.

   d. Run `ipconfig /all`.

   e. Ping the default gateway.

14. Computers on your network are configured to use static IP addresses. Your computer has been able to connect to the network most mornings when you start up, but one morning when you do not arrive until 9:30 a.m., your computer is unable to connect. Which of the following is the most likely reason for this problem?

   a. Your computer is using APIPA.

   b. Your computer is configured with an incorrect subnet mask.

   c. Your computer is configured with an IP address that is a duplicate of another one that has started up first.

   d. Your computer is configured with an alternative IP address and is using the alternative.

Foundation Topics

Understanding the TCP/IP Protocol

The Transmission Control Protocol/Internet Protocol (TCP/IP) protocol suite is the default protocol for all editions of Windows 7. With the omnipresent Internet, the usage of proprietary network protocol suites has diminished greatly in favor of seamless integration with the Internet, which requires TCP/IP. Since its introduction of Active Directory in Windows 2000, Microsoft has made TCP/IP the protocol required for Windows networks that use Active Directory. This is largely because of the Active Directory's dependence on Domain Name System (DNS) to provide the name and address resolution for all Active Directory resources.

TCP/IP is a suite of protocols that govern the transmission of data across computer networks and the Internet. The following is a brief description of the major protocols that you should be aware of:

- **Transmission Control Protocol (TCP):** Provides connection-oriented, reliable communication between two hosts, typically involving large amounts of data. Note that a *host* includes any device on the network (such as a computer or router) that is configured for TCP/IP. This kind of communication also involves acknowledgements that data has been correctly received.

- **User Datagram Protocol (UDP):** Used for fast, nonconnection-oriented communications with no guarantee of delivery, typically small short bursts of data. Applications using UDP data transmission are responsible for checking their data's integrity.

- **Internet Protocol (IP):** Handles, addresses, and routes packets between hosts on a network. It performs this service for all other protocols in the TCP/IP protocol suite.

- **Internet Control Messaging Protocol (ICMP):** Enables hosts on a TCP/IP network to share status and error information. It is specifically responsible for reporting errors and messages regarding the delivery of IP datagrams. It is not responsible for error correction. Higher-layer protocols use information provided by ICMP to recover from transmission problems. The ping command uses ICMP to check connectivity to remote computers.

- **Address Resolution Protocol (ARP):** Used to resolve the IP address of the destination computer to the physical or Media Access Control (MAC) address, which is a unique 12-digit hexadecimal number that is burned into ROM on every network adapter card.

These are only a few of the many protocols that make up the TCP/IP protocol suite. If you need additional information on these protocols and details on the other protocols that make up TCP/IP, refer to any book that specializes in computer internetworking.

By default, previous versions of Windows have used version 4 of the IP protocol, simply known as IPv4. With its 32-bit address space, this version has performed admirably well in the over 25 years since its initial introduction. However, with the rapid growth of the Internet in recent years, its address space has approached exhaustion and security concerns have increased. Consequently, the Internet Engineering Task Force (IETF) introduced version 6 of the IP protocol with Request for Comment (RFC) 1883 in 1995 and added RFCs 2460, 3513, and 4193 in more recent years. Simply known as IPv6, this protocol provides for 128-bit addressing, which allows for a practically infinite number of possible addresses, as well as the following benefits:

- **An efficient hierarchical addressing scheme:** IPv6 addresses are designed to enable an efficient, hierarchical, and summarizable routing scheme, making way for multiple levels of Internet service providers (ISPs).

- **Simpler routing tables:** Backbone routers on the Internet are more easily configured for routing packets to their destinations.

- **Stateful and stateless address configuration:** IPv6 simplifies host configuration with the use of stateful address configuration (configuring IP addresses in the presence of a Dynamic Host Configuration Protocol [DHCP] server) or the use of stateless address configuration (configuring IP addresses in the absence of a DHCP server). Stateless address configuration enables the automatic configuration of hosts on a subnetwork according to the addresses displayed by available routers.

- **Improved security:** IPv6 includes standards-based support for IP Security (IPSec). In fact, IPv6 requires IPSec support. You can configure IPSec connection security rules for IPv6 in the same fashion as with IPv4. IPSec is discussed further in Chapter 10, "Configuring Network and Firewall Settings."

- **Support for Link-Local Multicast Name Resolution (LLMNR):** This enables IPv6 clients on a single subnet to resolve each other's names without the need for a DNS server or using NetBIOS over TCP/IP.

- **Improved support for Quality of Service (QoS):** IPv6 header fields improve the identification and handling of network traffic from its source to destination, even when IPSec encryption is in use.

- **Extensibility:** You can add extension headers after the IPv6 packet header, which enable the inclusion of new features as they are developed in years to come.

By using a TCP/IP implementation known as the Next Generation TCP/IP stack (first included with Windows Vista), Windows 7 enables a dual IP layer architecture enabling the operation of both IPv4 and IPv6 at the same time. Unlike with

Windows XP and older Windows versions, Windows 7 does not require you to install a separate IPv6 component; IPv6 is installed and enabled by default.

NOTE For more introductory information on IPv6, refer to "Microsoft's Objectives for IP Version 6" at http://technet.microsoft.com/en-us/library/bb726949.aspx.

Configuring TCP/IP Version 4

Much of TCP/IPv4 is transparent to users and to administrators. The administrator might have to configure the address information applied to the network interface. Table 9-2 describes this address information:

Table 9-2   IPv4 Addressing Components

Addressing Component	Description
IP address	The unique, logical 32-bit address, which identifies the computer (called a *host* or *node*) and the subnet on which it is located. The IP address is displayed in dotted decimal notation (each decimal represents an octet of binary ones and zeroes). For example, the binary notation of an address may be 10000000.00000001.00000001.00000011, which in dotted decimal notation is written as 128.1.1.3.
Subnet mask	The subnet mask is applied to an IP address to determine the subnetwork address and the host address on that subnet. All hosts on the same subnet must have the same subnet mask for them to be correctly identified. If a mask is incorrect, both the subnet and the host address will be wrong. (For example, if you have an IP address of 128.1.1.3, and an incorrect mask of 255.255.128.0, the subnet address would be 128.1.0 and the host address would be 1.3. If the correct subnet mask is 255.255.255.0, the subnet address would be 128.1.1 and the host address would be 3.)
Default gateway	The address listed as the default gateway is the location on the local subnet to which the local computer will send all data meant for other subnets. In other words, this is the IP address for a router capable of transmitting the data to other networks.

Table 9-2   IPv4 Addressing Components

Addressing Component	Description
DNS server address	The place where names of IP hosts are sent so that the DNS server will respond with an IP address. This process is called *name resolution*. DNS is a distributed database of records that maps names to IP addresses and vice versa. A HOSTS file that maps names to IP addresses can be placed on the local computer and used instead of DNS, which renders this an optional setting, although it is rare that a network is small enough to make a HOSTS file more efficient than a DNS server. When a user types in a DNS name such as JacksPC.mydomain.local, the computer sends the name to the DNS server. If the name is one that the DNS server knows, it sends back the IP address. Otherwise, the DNS server sends the name request to a higher-level DNS server and this recursive process continues until either the IP address is found and returned to the original requestor or until all avenues have been exhausted and the original requestor is notified that the name cannot be found.
Windows Internet Naming Service (WINS) address	The WINS server address is the location where network computers send requests to resolve NetBIOS names to IP addresses. WINS is used on Microsoft Windows networks where older Windows computers or applications require NetBIOS naming. When a user types in a NetBIOS name, such as JACKSPC, the computer sends the name to the WINS server. Because WINS is a flat-file database, it returns an IP address or a Name not found message. WINS server addresses, like DNS server addresses, are optional. A computer can use a local LMHOSTS file to map the NetBIOS names to IP addresses rather than use WINS.

Static IPv4 Addressing

IP addresses indicate the same type of location information as a street address within a city. A building on a street has a number, and when you add it to the street name, you can find it easily because the number and the street will be unique within that city. This type of address scheme—an individual address plus a location address—allows every computer on the Internet to be uniquely identified.

A static IP address is one that is permanently assigned to a computer on the network. Certain computers (such as routers or servers) require static IP addresses because of their functions. Client computers are more often assigned dynamic addresses because they are more likely to be moved around the network or retired and replaced. DSL and cable modem users are usually given a static IP address, whereas dial-up users are provided with dynamic addresses.

As discussed earlier, IP addresses consist of two parts: one that specifies the network and one part that specifies the computer. These addresses are further categorized with classes, as described in Table 9-3.

Table 9-3   IPv4 Address Classes

Class	Dotted Decimal Hosts per Range	First Octet Binary	Usage	Number of Networks	Number of Hosts per Network
A	1.0.0.0–126.255.255.255	0xxxxxxx	Large networks /ISPs	126	16,777,214
B	128.0.0.0–191.255.255.255	10xxxxxx	Large or mid-size ISPs	16,382	65,534
C	192.0.0.0–223.255.255.255	110xxxxx	Small networks	2,097,150	255
D	224.0.0.0–239.255.255.255	1110xxxx	Multicasting	N/A	N/A
E	240.0.0.0–254.255.255.255	1111xxxx	Reserved for future use	N/A	N/A
Loopback	127.0.0.1–127.255.255.255	01111111	Loopback testing	N/A	N/A

NOTE   The concept of loopback testing is the usage of a predefined IP address that a computer can dial itself up to see whether the TCP/IP stack is properly set up. If TCP/IP is configured, you should be able to run the `ping 127.0.0.1` command when troubleshooting a connectivity problem.

The portion of the address that decides on which network the host resides varies based on the class, and, as you will see further on, the subnet mask. In the following list, the uppercase *N*s represent the part of the IP address that specifies the network, and the lowercase *C*s represent the part of the address that specifies the computer. This explains why there are differing numbers of networks per class and different numbers of hosts per network, as listed in Table 9-3:

- **Class A:** NNNNNNNN.cccccccc.cccccccc.cccccccc

- **Class B:** NNNNNNNN.NNNNNNNN.cccccccc.cccccccc

- **Class C:** NNNNNNNN.NNNNNNNN.NNNNNNNN.cccccccc

These address portions coincide with the default subnet masks for each address class. A Class A subnet mask is 255.0.0.0, a Class B subnet mask is 255.255.0.0, and a Class C subnet mask is 255.255.255.0.

Subnet masks enable you to reconfigure what constitutes the network portion and what constitutes the computer portion. When you apply the subnet mask to the IP address by using a bitwise logical AND operation, the result is a network number. A bitwise logical AND operation adds the bit, whether 1 or 0, to the corresponding bit in the subnet mask. If the subnet mask bit is a 1, the corresponding IP address bit is passed through as a result. If the subnet mask bit is a 0, a zero bit is passed through. For example, if the IP address is 141.25.240.201, you will have the following:

- **IP Address:** 10001101.00011001.11110000.11001001

- **Subnet Mask:** 11111111.11111111.00000000.00000000

- **Result from Bitwise Logical AND**

- **Network:** 10001101.00011001.00000000.00000000

This shows the network address as 141.25.0.0 and the host address to 0.0.240.201. If you add bits to the mask, you will be able to have additional subnetworks when you perform a bitwise logical AND and each subnetwork will have fewer hosts because fewer bits are available for the host portion of the address. If you use the same address and five bits to the subnet mask, you would receive the following:

- **IP Address:** 10001101.00011001.11110000.11001001

- **Subnet Mask:** 11111111.11111111.11111000.00000000

- **Result from Bitwise Logical AND**

- **Network:** 10001101.00011001.11110000.00000000

In this case, the subnet mask changes the network address to 141.25.240.0. The host address changes to 0.0.0.201. Other IP addresses that are under the default Class B subnet mask that would otherwise be part of the same network (such as 140.25.192.15 and 140.25.63.12) are now on different subnets.

For an organization with a large number of physical networks where each requires a different subnet address, you can use the subnet mask to segment a single address to fit the network. You can easily calculate how many subnets and hosts you will receive when you subnet a network. The formula is 2^n-2, where n is the number of bits. 2^n is the number 2 raised to the power of the number of bits, and that result minus 2 (the addresses represented by all 1s and all 0s) equals the available subnets or hosts. Therefore, if you have a subnet of 5 bits (as previously shown), you are able to achieve $2^5-2 = 32-2 = 30$ subnets. Because there are 11 bits left for host addresses, each subnet will have $2^{11}-2 = 2048-2 = 2,046$ hosts.

Classless Inter-Domain Routing

When you multiply 2046 by 30, you will see that you have 61,380 addresses available for network hosts and that you lost 4,154 addresses. This is the problem that Classless Inter-Domain Routing (CIDR) solves.

When you consider that a Class A address has over 16 million host addresses and that no organization with a Class A address has managed to utilize each of those addresses, you realize the use of classful addressing (an IP addressing system that does not segment the network into smaller subnetworks) is extremely wasteful. CIDR was developed to prevent the Internet from running out of IP addresses by reusing some of the unused addresses and expanding the addresses available when subnetting.

With CIDR, a subnet mask is not considered separate from the network portion of the mask. Instead, whatever portion of the mask is used for the network determines how many networks there are. This means that a company can supernet two (or more) Class C addresses to put more than 254 hosts on a single physical network. *Supernetting* is the process of subtracting bits from the default subnet mask. This adds bits to the host portion, increasing the number of hosts available.

CIDR notation enables you to simply specify the number of bits used for a mask after the IP address. For example, 192.168.1.0 with a subnet mask of 255.255.255.0 is written as 192.168.1.0/24. If the address were supernetted, it could be 192.168.1.0/22.

Private IPv4 Networks

IPv4 specifications define sets of networks that are specified as *private IPv4 networks*. The private IP address classes are used on private networks that utilize Network Address Translation or proxy services to communicate on the Internet. Internet routers are preconfigured to not forward data that contains these IP addresses. Table 9-4 describes these networks.

Table 9-4   Private IPv4 Network Addresses

Class	Dotted Decimal Hosts per Range	First Octet Binary	Number of Networks	Number of Hosts per Network
A	10.0.0.0–10.255.255.255	00001010	1	16,777,214
B	172.16.0.0–172.16.255.255	10101100	1	65,534
C	192.168.0.0–192.168.255.255	11000000	254	254

Dynamic IP Addressing

Dynamic IP addresses are provided to a computer when it needs to be connected to the network. The provider is the DHCP server. When the computer is disconnected, the IP address becomes available for use by another computer. The address does not become available immediately, however. It is leased for a specified period of time (the administrator specifies this time period when configuring the DHCP server), and when the lease is up, the IP address is placed back in an IP address pool and can be delivered to another computer.

Before DHCP was developed, network administrators were forced to manually assign a separate IP address to each computer on the network. If a user left for a two-month vacation and the computer was off the entire time, the IP address was unusable by anyone else. If the administrator (yes, to err is human) forgot to reuse an IP address for a computer that was retired, the number of IP addresses available was also reduced. Other administrative errors included assigning duplicate IP addresses to computers on the network and misconfiguring the subnet mask, default gateway, and DNS server addresses. DHCP resolves these problems.

NOTE   DHCP has a set communication process that is used to lease an IP address to a DHCP client. This process occurs each time a client starts up or when it requires a new IP address lease (typically after 50% of the lease period has expired or when a user issues the `ipconfig /renew` command):

1. Client boots up and broadcasts a DHCPDiscover packet.
2. Server responds with a DHCPOffer packet containing an IP address, subnet mask, and often including the default gateway and DNS server addresses.
3. Client replies with a DHCPRequest packet as a broadcast, requesting verification that it is okay to use the address. This notifies any other DHCP servers that they do not need to hold a reservation of an IP address for the client if they also responded to the original DHCPDiscover packet.
4. Server responds with a DHCPACK acknowledgement packet, and the client begins using the address.

On a Windows 7 computer, you can configure any network connection to be a DHCP client by selecting the option to **Obtain an IP Address automatically**, which is configured in the Internet Protocol (TCP/IP) Properties dialog box. If you change from a manual address to a dynamic one, you need to clear out the manual IP addressing information first.

Connecting to a Network

First introduced in Windows Vista and continued in Windows 7, the Network and Sharing Center, shown in Figure 9-1, brings all networking tasks together in a single convenient location. The diagram at the top indicates your connections to the network and the Internet and graphically indicates when a connection is unavailable. You can configure connections to other computers and networks; share folders, printers, and media; view devices on your network; set up and manage network connections and troubleshoot problems from this location.

Figure 9-1   The Network and Sharing Center provides a centralized location for configuring network properties.

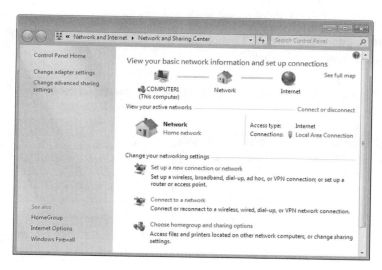

You can open the Network and Sharing Center by using any of the following methods:

- Click **Start**, right-click **Network**, and then click **Properties**.

- Click **Start** and click **Network**. At the top of the Network window, click **Network and Sharing Center**.

- Click Start and type **network and sharing** in the Search text box. Then select **Network and Sharing Center** from the Programs list.

- Click **Start > Control Panel**. On the Control Panel home page, click **Network and Internet** and then click **Network and Sharing Center** or **View network status and tasks**.

Using the Network and Sharing Center to Set Up a TCP/IP v4 Connection

You can configure TCP/IP version 4 on a Windows 7 computer either manually or dynamically. The default method is to dynamically configure TCP/IP. If the infrastructure includes DHCP services that deliver IP addresses to network computers, a Windows 7 computer can connect at logon with the default configuration of the network adapter. However, if you need to apply a static IPv4 address and other parameters, your only option is to manually configure the network adapter. Manually configuring one computer is time-consuming and error-prone. Multiply that by hundreds of computers and you can see why dynamic configuration has become so popular. Use the following procedure to configure a network adapter with a static IPv4 address:

Step 1. Open the **Network and Sharing Center** by any of the methods described in the previous section.

Step 2. From the Tasks list on the left side of the Network and Sharing Center, click **Change adapter settings**. This opens the Network Connections dialog box, as shown in Figure 9-2.

Figure 9-2 The Network Connections dialog box displays the network connections configured for your computer.

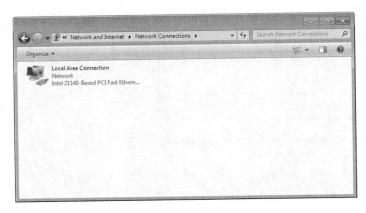

Step 3. Right-click the connection that represents the adapter you are going to configure and select **Properties**. If you receive a User Account Control (UAC) prompt, click **Yes**. The Local Area Connection Properties dialog box opens, as shown in Figure 9-3.

Step 4. Click to select **Internet Protocol Version 4 (TCP/IPv4)**. (You might need to scroll through other services to reach this item.) Click **Properties**. The Internet Protocol Version 4 (TCP/IPv4) Properties dialog opens, as shown in Figure 9-4.

Step 5. To use DHCP services, you should make certain that **Obtain an IP address automatically** is selected, and if the DHCP server provides extended information—including the DNS server information—you would also select **Obtain DNS server address automatically**. To manually configure the IP address, you should click **Use the following IP address**.

Step 6. In the IP address box, type the address that will function on the current network segment. For example, if the network segment uses a Class C address 192.168.1.0 with a subnet mask of 255.255.255.0, and you've already used 192.168.1.1 and 192.168.1.2, you could select any node address from 3 through 254 (255 is used for broadcasts), in which case you would type **192.168.1.3**.

Figure 9-3   The network adapter is considered a network connection.

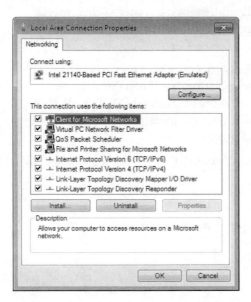

Figure 9-4   The Internet Protocol Version 4 (TCP/IPv4) Properties dialog box lets you define manual or dynamic IPv4 address information.

Step 7.   In the Subnet mask box, type the subnet mask. In this case, it would be
`255.255.255.0.`

Step 8.   In the Default gateway box, type the IP address that is assigned to the router interface on your current segment that leads to the main network or the public network. In this case, the IP address of the router on your segment is 192.168.1.1 and the IP address of the router's other interface is 12.88.54.179. In the Default gateway box, you would type **192.168.1.1.**

Step 9.   To configure an alternate IP address on a computer configured to use DHCP, click the **Alternate Configuration** tab. Then enter the required IP address, subnet mask, default gateway, and DNS and WINS server information. This is useful if your computer must connect to different networks such as work and home.

Step 10.   Click the **Advanced** button. The Advanced TCP/IP Settings dialog box opens, as shown in Figure 9-5.

Figure 9-5   The Advanced TCP/IP Settings dialog box enables you to control granular IP addressing options.

Step 11.   If you require more than one IP address for a computer, such as for hosting two different websites, you can configure the additional IP addresses in this dialog box by clicking the **Add** button. You cannot configure any additional IP addresses if you are using DHCP.

Step 12.   If your network segment is connected to more than one router leading to the main or outside networks, you can configure these gateway addresses in the Default Gateways section by clicking the **Add** button.

Step 13.   When finished, click **OK** until you're returned to the Network
Connections dialog box.

TIP   Many hardware routers, including those used when connecting home networks
to high-speed Internet connections, include DHCP functionality. If you are using
one of these, simply leave the defaults selected in step 5 of the preceding procedure.

Configuring IPv4 Name Resolution

As previously noted, Windows 7 uses DNS as its primary name resolution service.
For purposes of backward compatibility with networks running Windows NT or
9x machines, Windows 7 can also use WINS. DNS is the name resolution service
used by all servers on the Internet; when you type a URL into the address box in
Internet Explorer or any other browser, DNS resolves this URL into an IP address
so that you can obtain the desired website.

NOTE   If your network includes a DNS server, this server is used directly for any
name resolution requirements within the network. When a client requests an
Internet resource such as http://www.microsoft.com, an iterative name resolution
process occurs in which the local DNS server access a series of Internet DNS
servers to obtain the IP address of the requested resource. Each server that is
accessed knows the locations of one level of servers within the hierarchical DNS
namespace (in other words, is authoritative for this level by possessing in its database what is known as an A [address] resource record, which holds the hostname
to IPv4 address mapping). For example, the following happens when you type
`http://www.Microsoft.com` into your web browser.

1. The local DNS server checks with a root server on the Internet to locate the IP
   address of a server that is authoritative for `.com` addresses.

2. The `.com` server on the Internet locates the IP address of a server that is authoritative for `Microsoft.com` addresses.

3. The `Microsoft.com` server on the Internet locates the IP address of the
   `www.Microsoft.com` web server.

4. These servers return the required IP address to the client, whose browser then
   displays the home page of the requested website.

The Local Area Connection Properties dialog box enables you to configure your
computer to access a DNS server, as outlined in the following procedure:

Step 1.   Use the procedure outlined in the previous section to access the
Internet Protocol Version 4 (TCP/IPv4) Properties dialog box.

Step 2.   If your network is configured to use DHCP to automatically configure
client computers with the address of the DNS server, you need only

ensure that the **Obtain DNS server address automatically** option is selected.

Step 3. If your network is not configured with DHCP, click the **Use the following DNS server addresses** option and type the IP address for at least one DNS server.

Step 4. Click **Advanced** to bring up the Advanced TCP/IP Settings dialog box previously shown in Figure 9-5.

Step 5. Click the **DNS** tab to display the settings shown in Figure 9-6.

Figure 9-6 The DNS tab of the Advanced TCP/IP Settings dialog box enables you to configure additional DNS settings to be used by your network connection.

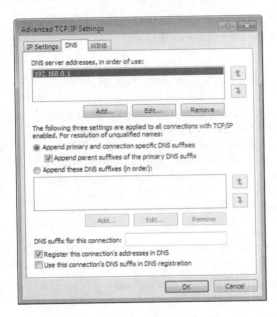

Step 6. To specify additional DNS servers, click the **Add** button under the DNS server addresses section, type the IP address to the additional DNS server, and then click **Add**.

Step 7. The lower section of the DNS tab applies to the fully qualified domain name (FQDN) of resources. Users sometimes use a simple name for a computer or printer. This section enables you to configure the last portion of the domain name that will be appended to the simple name to create an FQDN. For example, if you have configured `mydomain.local` and `jubilee.local` in this box and the user typed in **server,** the computer automatically attempts to contact `server.mydomain.local`. If that fails, the computer then attempts to contact `server.jubilee.local`.

Click the **Append these DNS suffixes (in order)** option. Then click the **Add** button to configure the DNS suffixes.

Step 8. For a DNS server that provides Dynamic DNS, and when you want to share files or printers from your computer, you should register your computer's DNS name and IP address in the DNS database. To do so, select the **Register this connection's addresses in DNS** check box.

Step 9. Click the **WINS** tab. WINS provides resolution for NetBIOS names to IP addresses on Windows networks. If you use legacy networks, or have applications that require NetBIOS names, you should configure the address for a WINS server on the network.

> **TIP** You can also use the `netsh.exe` tool to configure IPv4 from the command line. This tool enables you to perform almost any network configuration action from the command prompt. For example, the command `netsh interface ip set address "Local Area connection" static 192.168.0.2 255.255.255.0 192.168.0.1` configures the computer's local area connection with the static IP address 192.168.0.2, subnet mask 255.255.255.0, and default gateway 192.168.0.1. For more information, refer to "Netsh Overview" at http://technet.microsoft.com/en-us/library/cc732279(WS.10).aspx.

Implementing APIPA

The Automatic Private Internet Protocol Addressing (APIPA) system provides an alternate configuration to DHCP for automatic IP addressing in small networks. When a computer uses APIPA, Windows 7 assigns itself an IP address and then verifies that it is unique on the local network. To work effectively, APIPA is useful only on a small local area network (LAN) or as a backup to DHCP.

When a Windows 7 computer begins its network configuration, it performs the following procedures:

Step 1. It checks to see whether there is a manually configured (or static) IP address.

Step 2. If there is none, it contacts a DHCP server with a query for configuration settings. A response from a DHCP server leases—or validates the lease of—an IP address, subnet mask, and extended IP information such as DNS server, default gateway, and so on.

Step 3. If there is no DHCP server response within six seconds, Windows 7 looks to see whether an alternate configuration has been applied by the administrator.

Step 4. If there is no alternate configuration, Windows 7 uses APIPA to define an IP address unique on the LAN.

APIPA defines its IP addresses in the range of 169.254.0.1 to 169.254.255.254. The subnet mask on these addresses is configured as 255.255.0.0. You do have administrative control over APIPA. When Windows 7 selects an address from this range, it then performs a duplicate address detection process to ensure that the IP address it has selected is not already being used, while continuing to query for a DHCP server in the background. If the address is found to be in use, Windows 7 selects another address. The random IP selection occurs recursively until an unused IP address is selected, a DHCP server is discovered, or the process has taken place ten times.

Configuring TCP/IP Version 6

The 128-bit addressing scheme used by IPv6 enables an unimaginably high number of 3.4×10^{38} addresses, which equates to a total of 6.5×10^{23} addresses for every square meter of the Earth's surface. Consequently, this is a complicated addressing scheme, as described in the following sections.

IPv6 Address Syntax

Whereas IPv4 addresses use dotted-decimal format as already explained earlier in this chapter, IPv6 addresses are subdivided into 16-bit blocks. Each 16-bit block is portrayed as a four-digit hexadecimal number and is separated from other blocks by colons. This addressing scheme is referred to as *colon-hexadecimal*.

For example, a 128-bit IPv6 address written in binary could appear as follows:

0011111111111110 1111111111111111 0010000111000101
0000000000000000 0000001010101010 0000000011111111
1111111000100001 0011101000111110

The same address written in colon-hexadecimal becomes 3ffe:ffff:21a5:0000:00ff:fe21:5a3e. You can remove any leading zeros, converting this address to 3ffe:ffff:21a5::ff:fe21:5a3e. This process is known as *zero compression*. In this notation, note that the block that contained all zeros appears as :: (which is called *double-colon*).

IPv6 Prefixes

Corresponding to the network portion of an IPv4 address is the prefix, which is the part of the address containing the bits of the subnet prefix. IPv6 addresses do not employ subnet masks; they use the same CIDR notation used with IPv4. For example, an IPv6 address prefix could be 3ffe:ffff:21a5::/64, where 64 is the number of bits employed by the address prefix.

Types of IPv6 Addresses

IPv6 uses the following three types of addresses:

- **Unicast:** Represents a single interface within the typical scope of unicast addresses. In other words, packets addressed to this type of address are to be delivered to a single network interface. Unicast IPv6 addresses include global unicast, link-local, site-local, and unique local addresses. Two special addresses are also included: unspecified addresses (all zeros, equivalent to the IPv4 address of 0.0.0.0) and the loopback address, which is 0:0:0:0:0:0:0:1 or ::1, which is equivalent to the IPv4 address of 127.0.0.1.

- **Multicast:** Represents multiple interfaces to which packets are delivered to all network interfaces identified by the address. Multicast addresses have the first eight bits set to 1s so they begin with "ff".

- **Anycast:** Also represents multiple interfaces. Anycast packets are delivered to a single network interface that represents the nearest (in terms of routing hops) interface identified by the address.

Table 9-5 provides additional details on the IPv6 classes and subclasses.

Table 9-5 IPv6 Address Classes and Subclasses

Class	Address Prefix	Additional Features	First Binary Bits	Usage
Global unicast	2000::/3	Use a global routing prefix of 45 bits (beyond the initial 001 bits), which identifies a specific organization's network, a 16-bit subnet ID (which identifies up to 54,536 subnets within an organization's network), and a 64-bit interface ID (which indicates a specific network interface within the subnet).	001	Globally routable Internet addresses that are equivalent to the public IPv4 addresses.
Link-local unicast	fe80::/64	Equivalent to APIPA-configured IPv4 addresses in the 169.254.0.0/16 network prefix.	1111111010 00	Used for communication between neighboring nodes on the same link. These addresses are assigned automatically when you configure automatic addressing in the absence of a DHCP server.

Table 9-5   IPv6 Address Classes and Subclasses

Class	Address Prefix	Additional Features	First Binary Bits	Usage
Site-local unicast	fec0::/10	Equivalent to the private IPv4 address spaces mentioned previously in Table 9.4. Prefix followed by a 54-bit subnet ID field within which you can establish a hierarchical routing structure within your site.	1111111011 00	Used for communication between nodes located in the same site.
Unique local IPv6 unicast	fc00::/7	Prefix followed by a local (L) flag, a 40-bit global ID, a 16-bit subnet ID, and a 64-bit interface ID.	11111100	Provide addresses that are private to an organization but unique across all the organization's sites.
Multicast	ff	Use the next 4 bits for flags (Transient[T], Prefix [P], and Rendezvous Point Address[R]), the following 4 bits for scope (determines where multicast traffic is forwarded), and the remaining 112 bits for a group ID.	11111111	Multiple interfaces to which packets are delivered to all network interfaces identified by the address.
Anycast	(From unicast addresses)	Assigned from the unicast address space with the same scope as the type of unicast address within which the anycast address is assigned.	(Varies)	Only utilized as destination addresses assigned to routers.

> **NOTE**   Site-local IPv6 addresses are equivalent to the private IPv4 addresses mentioned in Table 9-4. You can access site-local addresses only from the network in which they are located; they are not accessible from external networks such as the Internet.

Compatibility Between IPv4 and IPv6 Addresses

To assist in the migration from IPv4 to IPv6 and their coexistence, several additional address types are used, as follows:

- **IPv4-compatible addresses:** Nodes communicating between IPv4 and IPv6 networks can use an address represented by 0:0:0:0:0:0:w.x.y.z, where w.x.y.z is the IPv4 address in dotted-decimal.

- **IPv4-mapped address:** An IPv4-only node is represented as ::ffff:.w.x.y.z to an IPv6 node. This address type is used only for internal representation and is never specified as a source or destination address of an IPv6 packet.

- **Teredo address:** Teredo is a tunneling communication protocol that enables IPv6 connectivity between IPv6/IPv4 nodes across **network address translation** NAT interfaces, thereby improving connectivity for newer IPv6-enabled applications on IPv4 networks. Teredo is described in RFC 4380. Teredo makes use of a special IPv6 address that includes the following components in the sequence given:
  — A 32-bit Teredo prefix, which is 2001::/32 in Windows Vista/7 and Windows Server 2008 R2
  — The 32-bit IPv4 address of the Teredo server involved in creating this address
  — A 16-bit Teredo flag field and an obscured 16-bit UDP port interface definition
  — An obscured external IPv4 address corresponding to all Teredo traffic across the Teredo client interface

- **6-to-4 address:** Two nodes running both IPv4 and IPv6 across an IPv4 routing infrastructure use this address type when communicating with each other. You can form the 6-to-4 address by combining the prefix 2002::/16 with the 32-bit public IPv4 address to form a 48-bit prefix. This tunneling technique is described in RFC 3056.

> **NOTE** More information on compatibility addresses and technologies used for transition to IPv6 is available in "Internet Protocol Version 6, Teredo, and Related Technologies in Windows 7 and Windows Server 2008 R2" at http://technet.microsoft.com/en-us/library/ee126159(WS.10).aspx.

Connecting to a TCP/IP Version 6 Network

You can let IPv6 configure itself automatically with a link-local address described previously in Table 9-5. You can also configure IPv6 to use an existing DHCP server or manually configure an IPv6 address as required. Configuration of IPv6 addresses is very similar to the procedure used with configuration of IPv4 addresses, as the following procedure shows:

Step 1.   Open the Network and Sharing Center by any of the methods previously described.

Step 2.   From the Tasks list on the left side of the Network and Sharing Center, click **Change adapter settings**. This opens the Network Connections dialog box, as previously shown in Figure 9-2.

Step 3. Right-click the connection that represents the adapter you are going to configure and select **Properties**. If you receive a UAC prompt, click **Yes**.

Step 4. Click to select **Internet Protocol Version 6 (TCP/IPv6)**. (You might need to scroll through other services to reach this item.) Click **Properties**. The Internet Protocol Version 6 (TCP/IPv6) Properties dialog opens, as shown in Figure 9-7.

Figure 9-7 The Internet Protocol Version 6 (TCP/IPv6) Properties dialog box lets you define manual or dynamic IPv6 address information.

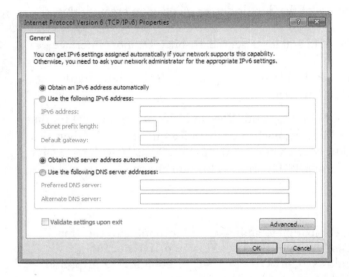

Step 5. To use DHCP, ensure that the **Obtain an IPv6 address automatically** radio button is selected. If the DHCP server provides DNS server information, ensure that the **Obtain DNS server address automatically** radio button is also selected. You can also select these options to configure IPv6 automatically with a link-local address using the address prefix fe80::/64 previously described in Table 9-5.

Step 6. To manually configure an IPv6 address, select **Use the following IPv6 address**. Then type the IPv6 address, subnet prefix length, and default gateway in the text boxes provided. For unicast IPv6 addresses, you should set the prefix length to its default value of 64.

Step 7. To manually configure DNS server addresses, select **Use the following DNS server addresses**. Then type the IPv6 addresses of the preferred and alternate DNS server in the text boxes provided.

Step 8.   Click **Advanced** to display the Advanced TCP/IP Settings dialog box shown in Figure 9-8.

Figure 9-8   The Advanced TCP/IP Settings dialog enables you to control granular IPv6 addressing options.

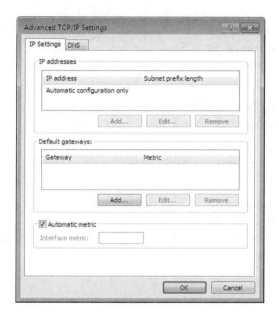

Step 9.   As with IPv4, you can configure additional IP addresses if you are not using DHCP. Click **Add** and type the required IP address in the dialog box that appears.

Step 10.   As with IPv4, if your network segment is connected to more than one router, configure additional gateway addresses in the Default gateways section by clicking the **Add** button.

Step 11.   When finished, click **OK** until you're returned to the Network Connections dialog box.

TIP   You can also use the `netsh.exe` tool with the `interface IPv6` subcommand to configure IPv6 from the command line. For example, `netsh interface IPv6 set address "local area connection 2" fec0:0:0:ffee::3` sets the IPv6 address of the second local area connection to the specified address. For more information, refer to "IPv6 Configuration Information with the `Netsh.exe` Tool" at http://technet.microsoft.com/en-us/library/bb726952.aspx#EBAA.

Configuring TCP/IPv6 Name Resolution

You can configure name resolution with IPv6 in much the same way as done with IPv4, as the following steps demonstrate:

Step 1.   Use the procedure outlined in the previous section to access the Internet Protocol Version 6 (TCP/IPv6) Properties dialog box.

Step 2.   If your network is configured to use DHCP to automatically configure client computers with the address of the DNS server, you need only ensure that the **Obtain DNS server address automatically** option is selected.

Step 3.   If your network is not configured with DHCP, click the **Use the following DNS server addresses** option and type the IPv6 address for at least one DNS server.

Step 4.   Click **Advanced** to bring up the Advanced TCP/IP Settings dialog box previously shown in Figure 9-8.

Step 5.   Click the **DNS** tab to display the settings shown in Figure 9-9. These settings are similar to those found in the DNS tab for IPv4 described previously. Click **Add** under the DNS server addresses section to add the IPv6 addresses of additional DNS servers, as required.

Figure 9-9   You can configure DNS options from the DNS tab of the Advanced TCP/IP Settings dialog box.

Step 6. To specify additional DNS servers, click the **Add** button under the DNS server addresses section, type the IPv6 address to the additional DNS server, and then click **Add**.

Step 7. As was the case with IPv4, if you need additional DNS suffixes to specify the FQDN of resources, click the **Append these DNS suffixes (in order)** option. Then click the **Add** button to configure the DNS suffixes.

Step 8. For a DNS server that provides Dynamic DNS, and when you want to share files or printers from your computer, you should register your computer's DNS name and IP address in the DNS database. To do so, select the **Register this connection's addresses in DNS** check box.

Step 9. Click **OK** until you're returned to the Local Area Connection Properties dialog box.

NOTE   DNS name resolution in IPv6 operates in a manner similar to that previously mentioned for IPv4, except that DNS servers use AAAA resource records to hold the hostname to IPv6 address mapping.

Disabling IPv6

You cannot remove IPv6 from a Windows 7 computer. However, you can disable IPv6 on a specific connection. From the Local Area Connection Properties dialog box shown previously in Figure 9-3, clear the check box beside **Internet Protocol Version 6 (TCP/IPv6)** and then click **OK**. You can do this selectively for each network connection on your computer.

NOTE   You can also selectively disable IPv6 components. This is a more complex procedure that involves editing the Registry and is beyond the scope of this book. For more details, refer to "How to disable certain Internet Protocol version 6 (IPv6) components in Windows Vista, Windows 7, and Windows Server 2008" at http://support.microsoft.com/kb/929852.

Link-Local Multicast Name Resolution

The concept of Link-Local Multicast Name Resolution (LLMNR) refers to the capability of computers running IPv6 on the local subnet to resolve each other's names without the need for a DNS server. Recall from Table 9-5 that a link-local address is configured in the absence of a DHCP server, exists solely on its own network, and cannot be referenced across an external network such as the Internet. Enabled by default in Windows Vista and Windows 7, each computer sends multicast DNS name queries rather than unicast queries. These computers listen for multicast LLMNR queries, thereby eliminating the need to perform name resolution on the local subnet by means of NetBIOS over TCP/IP in the absence of a DNS server. LLMNR is defined in RFC 4795.

NOTE   To configure address resolution by means of LLMNR, you must edit the Registry. For more information, refer to "Host Name Resolution for Dual Stack (IPv4/IPv6)" at http://msdn.microsoft.com/en-us/library/ms881910.aspx.

Resolving IPv4 and IPv6 Network Connectivity Issues

With any type of computer network, connectivity problems can and do occur whether you have configured your network to use IPv4, IPv6, or both. You should be aware of the types of problems that you might encounter and the steps to use for determining the source of the problem and the means to correct it.

Windows 7 Network Diagnostics Tools

Windows 7 provides several tools that are often useful in troubleshooting network and Internet connectivity failures. These tools provide wizards that ask questions as to what problems might exist and suggest solutions or open additional troubleshooters.

The Network and Sharing Center provides a comprehensive networking problem troubleshooter. Click **Troubleshoot problems** from the Change your networking settings list to obtain the Troubleshoot problems–Network and Internet dialog box shown in Figure 9-10. Clicking any of the options on this dialog box takes you to a wizard that attempts to detect a problem associated with the selected option. If the wizard is unable to identify a problem, it suggests additional options that you might explore.

Figure 9-10   You can open a wizard that attempts to troubleshoot problems with any of these network and printing categories.

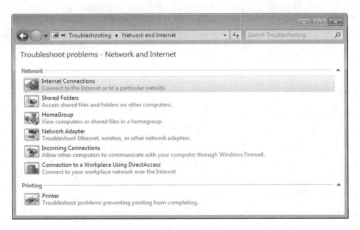

You can also check the status of a LAN connection from the Network Connections dialog box previously shown in Figure 9-2. Right-click your connection icon and choose **Status** to display the Local Area Connection Status dialog box shown in Figure 9-11. This dialog box provides information on your LAN connectivity. To obtain details on your LAN connection, click **Details**. The Network Connection Details dialog box shown in Figure 9-12 provides a subset of the information also provided by the `ipconfig` command discussed in the next section. To view or configure the properties of the connection, click the **Properties** button shown in Figure 9-11. This takes you to the same Local Area Connection Properties dialog box discussed earlier in this chapter and shown in Figure 9-3.

Figure 9-11   The Local Area Connection Status dialog box provides information on the connectivity of your LAN connection.

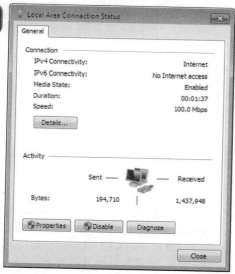

If you suspect a problem, click the **Diagnose** button shown in Figure 9-11 to open a troubleshooter. You will be informed of any problem that exists, such as a disconnected network cable or malfunctioning network adapter card.

Using TCP/IP Utilities to Troubleshoot TCP/IP

The TCP/IP protocol suite includes a number of tools that can help you isolate the source of connectivity problems. Windows 7 incorporates these tools as command-line executables. Each tool is different in what information it provides and when you might want to use it.

When you are troubleshooting a connectivity problem, remember that sometimes the problem is the hardware—a failed network adapter, a failed port on the hub, a failed switch, and so on. If the communication is between two different physical segments, it could be a problem with the router between them. And if you were able to communicate in the past but now cannot, the most likely suspect is a configuration change on one of the computers and the second most likely is that a piece of equipment has failed. To check whether there is an adapter failure, look at Device Manager.

Figure 9-12   The Network Connection Details dialog box provides IPv4 and IPv6 configuration information.

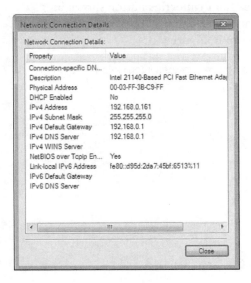

ARP

After data reaches the segment on which the IP address resides, it needs to discover the Media Access Control (MAC) address of the machine. The Address Resolution Protocol (ARP) is the protocol in the TCP/IP suite that resolves IP addresses to MAC addresses by creating an Address Resolution table in each host that transmits data on the network segment. The TCP/IP suite provides a utility called Arp that can check the table for errors. You should use the Arp utility when data is sent to an incorrect computer unexpectedly.

FTP and TFTP

File Transfer Protocol (FTP) and Trivial File Transfer Protocol (TFTP) are not considered troubleshooting tools. Sometimes you need to make certain that a protocol is able to move data from one network segment to another and these two utilities can help out in a pinch because they verify TCP and UDP specifically as well as all the protocols down to the Physical layer of the stack.

If you want to verify whether the Transport Control Protocol (TCP) is functioning across a router, you can use FTP to download a file from an FTP server on another subnet. If you want to verify whether the User Datagram Protocol (UDP) is functioning across a router, you can use TFTP to download a file from a TFTP server on another subnet.

Ipconfig

Windows 7 uses the Ipconfig utility without any additional parameters to display summary information about the IP address configuration of its network adapters. When you are experiencing a problem with connectivity, this is the first thing you should check (besides the link lights on the network adapter). If you are using DHCP, you can see whether the adapter was able to obtain an IP address lease. If you are using a static IP address, you can verify and validate whether it has been configured correctly. You can use Ipconfig with the following switches:

- **Ipconfig /all**: Displays a comprehensive set of IPv4 and IPv6 address data for all network adapters including IPv6 Teredo interfaces, as shown in Figure 9-13. Use this command to see whether an adapter has been misconfigured or if the adapter did not receive a DHCP lease. You can also determine whether the IP address the computer is using has been provided by APIPA; check the Autoconfiguration Enabled line of this output. If this line states Yes and the IP address is 169.254.0.1 through 169.254.255.254, you are using an APIPA address.

Figure 9-13   The **ipconfig /all** command provides a comprehensive set of TCP/IP configuration information.

- **Ipconfig /release**: Releases the current DHCP lease. Use this command to remove an IP address that is misconfigured or when you have moved from one network to another and the wrong IP address is still leased to the adapter.

- **Ipconfig /release6**: Same as the /release switch for IPv6.

- **Ipconfig /renew**: Renews (or tries to renew) the current DHCP lease. Use this command to see whether the computer can contact the DHCP server.

- **Ipconfig /renew6**: Same as the /renew switch for IPv6.

- **Ipconfig /displaydns**: Displays the contents of the DNS cache. Use this command when the computer connects to the wrong network.

- **Ipconfig /flushdns**: Flushes the contents of the DNS cache. Use this command when the computer connects to the wrong network and you see incorrect entries after using the ipconfig /displaydns command.

- **Ipconfig /registerdns**: Renews (or tries to renew) all adapters' DHCP leases and refreshes the DNS configuration. Use this command when the network has temporarily disconnected and you have not rebooted the PC.

- **Ipconfig /showclassid *adapter***: Shows the DHCP class ID. If you use the asterisk (*) in place of *adapter*, you see the DHCP class ID for all adapters.

- **Ipconfig /setclassid *adapter***: Changes the DHCP class ID for an adapter. If you use the asterisk (*) in the place of *adapter*, you set the DHCP class ID of all adapters.

Nbtstat

The Nbtstat utility is used on networks that run NetBIOS over TCP/IP. This utility checks to see the status of NetBIOS name resolution to IP addresses. You can check current NetBIOS sessions, add entries to the NetBIOS name cache, and check the NetBIOS name and scope assigned to the computer.

Netstat

The Netstat command-line tool enables you to check the current status of the computer's IP connections. If you do not use switches, the results are port and protocol statistics and current TCP/IP connections. You should use Netstat to look for the services that are listening for incoming connections if you have already checked the IP configuration and, although it is correct, the computer still displays a connectivity problem.

Nslookup

Name Server Lookup, or Nslookup, is a command-line utility that communicates with a DNS server. There are two modes to Nslookup: interactive and noninteractive. The interactive mode opens a session with a DNS server and views various records. The noninteractive mode asks for one piece of information and receives it. If more information is needed, a new query must be made.

ping

Packet InterNet Groper (ping) is a valuable tool for determining whether there is a problem with connectivity. The ping command uses an Echo packet at the Network layer—the default is to send a series of four echoes in a row—transmitting the packets to the IP address specified. The Echo returns an acknowledgment if the IP address is found. The results are displayed in the command window. If an IP address is not found, you see only the response Request timed out. You see similar results to those shown in Figure 9-14, where the first address that was pinged was found and the second address was not found. The ping command indicates how long each packet took for the response. You can use the ping command to determine whether a host is reachable and to determine whether you are losing packets when sending/receiving data to a particular host.

Figure 9-14   The **ping** command displays its results in a command window.

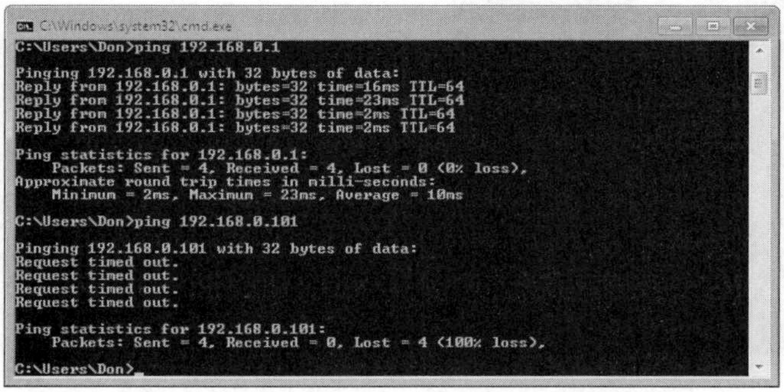

You can use the ping command to determine whether the internal TCP/IP protocol stack is functioning properly by pinging the loopback testing address. The command for IPv4 is

```
ping 127.0.0.1
```
For IPv6, the command is

```
ping ::1
```

NOTE   Firewall settings can prevent you from receiving responses from pinged hosts. In Windows 7, by default you cannot ping other computers on your network. We look at configuring firewall settings and policies in Chapter 10.

tracert

When you have a problem communicating with a particular host, yet you have determined that your computer is functioning well, you can use tracert (Trace Route) to tell you how the data is moving across the network between your computer and the one that you are having difficulty reaching. The tracert command offers a somewhat higher level of information than ping. Rather than simply tell you that the data was transmitted and returned effectively, as ping does, tracert logs each hop through which the data was transmitted. Figure 9-15 shows the results of a tracert command. Keep in mind that some network routers strip out or refuse to reply to tracert requests. When this happens, you see Request timed out messages.

Figure 9-15 The **tracert** command provides detailed information about the path that data travels between two IP hosts.

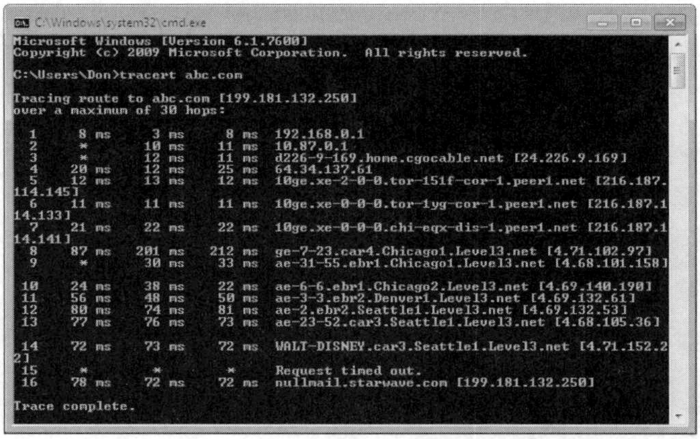

pathping

The pathping command combines the actions of the ping and tracert utilities into a single command that tests connectivity to a remote host and maps the route taken by packets transmitted from your computer to the remote host. It also provides data on packet loss across multiple hops, thereby providing an estimate of the reliability of the communication links being used.

Troubleshooting IPv4 and IPv6 Problems

Many problems can result in your inability to reach other hosts on your local subnet, other subnets on your local network, or the Internet. The 70-680 exam presents you with scenarios in which you must figure out the cause of and solution to problems with IPv4 and IPv6 connectivity failures. We cover the use of the TCP/IP troubleshooting tools already presented to test connectivity and follow this up with additional suggestions you can use for troubleshooting connectivity problems, both on the 70-680 exam and in the real world.

A Suggested Response to a Connectivity Problem

Microsoft recommends a troubleshooting procedure for TCP/IP connectivity problems similar to the following:

Step 1. Verify the hardware is functioning.

Step 2. Run `Ipconfig /all` to validate the IP address, subnet mask, default gateway, and DNS server, and whether you are receiving a DHCP leased address.

Step 3. Ping 127.0.0.1 or ::1, the loopback address, to validate that TCP/IP is functioning.

Step 4. Ping the computer's own IP address to eliminate a duplicate IP address as the problem.

Step 5. Ping the default gateway address, which tells you whether data can travel on the current network segment.

Step 6. Ping a host that is not on your network segment, which shows whether the router will be able to route your data.

Additional possible troubleshooting steps you can use include the following:

■ FTP a file from an FTP server not on your network, which tells you whether higher-level protocols are functioning. TFTP a file from a TFTP server on a different network to determine whether UDP packets are able to cross the router.

■ Check the configuration of routers on a network with multiple subnets. You can use the `tracert` and `pathping` commands to verify connectivity across routers to remote subnets. Also use the `route print` command to check the configuration of routing tables in use.

■ Clear the ARP cache by opening a command prompt and typing **netsh interface ip delete arpcache.**

■ Check the computer's DNS configuration. You can also clear the DNS client resolver cache by using the `ipconfig /flushdns` command.

Many LAN connection problems can be traced to improper TCP/IP configuration. Before looking at the use of TCP/IP utilities for troubleshooting these problems, this section reviews briefly some of the problems you might encounter:

Network Discovery

Network Discovery is a tool that is enabled by default on Windows 7 computers. For computers to be able to connect to one another, ensure that Network Discovery has not been turned off at either the source or destination computer. To check this setting, access the Network and Sharing Center and click **Change advanced sharing settings**, found in the list on the left side. As shown in Figure 9-16, you can configure a series of sharing options for different network profiles. Ensure that the **Turn on network discovery** option is selected and then click **Save changes**.

Figure 9-16   Checking the network discovery setting.

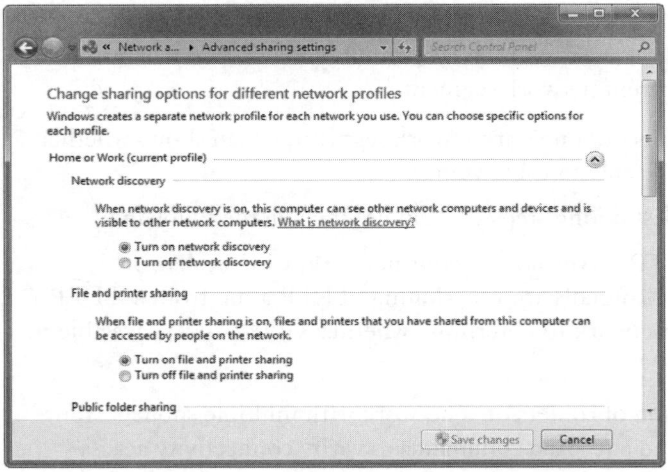

Incorrect IPv4 Address or Subnet Mask

Recall from earlier in this chapter that the subnet mask determines the number of bits assigned to the network portion of the IP address and the number of bits assigned to the host portion. Be aware of the fact that the network portion of the IP address must match properly on all computers within a network segment and that the subnet mask must be configured appropriately to ensure that the computer is able to determine whether the computer to which it is attempting to connect is on the same or different subnet.

For example, suppose that you are at a computer configured with an IP address of 192.168.1.2 with a subnet mask of 255.255.255.0. If you want to reach a computer with the IP address of 192.168.2.1, the subnet mask indicates that this computer is located on a different subnet. Connection will take place across a router. Should the computer you are at be configured with the same IP address but a subnet mask of 255.255.248.0, this would indicate that the destination computer with the IP address of 192.168.2.1 is on the same subnet. If in fact this computer is located across a router on another subnet, you will fail to connect to it.

Router problems could also cause a failure to access a computer on another subnet. These problems are beyond the scope of the 70-680 exam. For further information, consult any reference on computer networking.

Unable to Connect to a DHCP Server

If you configure your computer to automatically receive an IPv4 address and the DHCP server is down, the computer assigns itself an APIPA address as already described. If you notice this when using `ipconfig /all`, check the connectivity to the DHCP server or contact an administrator responsible for this server.

Duplicate IP Address

If your computer is using an IP address that duplicates another computer on the network, you will be unable to connect to any computer on the network. When this happens, the first computer on the network performs properly but receives a message when the second computer joins the network. Ping your computer's IP address to check for this problem. This problem cannot occur if you are using DHCP to obtain an IP address automatically, or if your computer is configured for an IP address using APIPA.

Unable to Configure an Alternate TCP/IPv4 Configuration

The Alternate Configuration tab of the TCP/IPv4 Properties dialog box (refer to Figure 9-4) enables you to configure an alternate IPv4 address, which is useful in situations where you need to connect to a second network (for example, when you are using a portable computer and traveling to a branch office of your company). However, to use the alternate configuration, your primary connection must be set to obtain an IP address automatically. If this is not the case, this tab does not appear.

Using Event Viewer to Check Network Problems

One of Windows 7's standard troubleshooting tools is Event Viewer, which is incorporated into the Computer Management console. You can rely on this utility to be
able to see errors and system messages. The ones that would be of most concern for
a network problem are in the System Event log. You learn about Event Viewer in
more detail in Chapter 16, "Managing and Monitoring System Performance."

Additional Troubleshooting Hints When Using IPv6

When verifying IPv6 network connectivity, you might have to specify a zone ID for
the sending interface with the `ping` command. The zone ID is a locally defined
parameter that you can obtain from the `ipconfig /all` command or the `netsh
interface ipv6 show interface` command. Using this zone ID, to verify
connectivity with a machine whose IPv6 address is fe80::b3:00ff:4765:6db7, you
would type **`ping fe80::b3:00ff:4765:6db7%12`** at a command prompt (if the
zone ID is 12).

Before using `ping` to check IPv6 network connectivity, clear the neighbor cache on
your computer. This cache contains recently resolved link-layer IPv6 addresses. To
view this cache, open an administrative command prompt and type **`netsh interface
ipv6 show neighbors`**; to clear it, type `netsh interface ipv6 delete neighbors`.

NOTE   For further suggestions with regard to troubleshooting IPv6 network connectivity, refer to "The Cable Guy–March 2005" at http://technet.microsoft.com/
en-us/library/bb878005.aspx.

Exam Preparation Tasks

Review All the Key Topics

Review the most important topics in the chapter, noted with the key topics icon in the outer margin of the page. Table 9-6 lists a reference of these key topics and the page numbers on which each is found.

Table 9-6   Key Topics for Chapter 9

Key Topic Element	Description	Page Number
Table 9-2	Describes important addressing components of TCP/IP version 4	303
Table 9-3	Describes the various IPv4 address classes	305
Paragraph	Explains how to use subnet masks to separate the network and machine portions of an IPv4 address	305
Table 9-4	Describes private IPv4 networks	307
List	Explains how to configure a network adapter with a static IPv4 address	310
List	Explains how to configure your computer to access a DNS server on IPv4	313
Table 9-5	Explains IPv6 address classes and subclasses	317
List	How to configure your computer to connect to an IPv6 network	319
List	How to configure your computer for IPv6 name resolution	322
Figure 9-11	Using the Local Area Connection Status dialog box to check LAN connection status	325
Figure 9-13	Use of the `ipconfig /all` command	327
List	Describes a procedure that tests your computer's IP connectivity	331

Complete the Tables and Lists from Memory

Print a copy of Appendix C, "Memory Tables" (found on the CD), or at least the section for this chapter, and complete the tables and lists from memory. Appendix D, "Memory Tables Answer Key," also on the CD, includes completed tables and lists to check your work.

Definitions of Key Terms

Define the following key terms from this chapter, and check your answers in the glossary.

anycast IPv6 address, Automatic Private IP Addressing (APIPA), Classless Inter-Domain Routing (CIDR), default gateway, Domain Name System (DNS), Dynamic Host Configuration Protocol (DHCP), global unicast IPv6 address, host, IP version 4 (IPv4), IP version 6 (IPv6), IP address, link-local IPv6 address, multicast IPv6 address, Network and Sharing Center, site-local IPv6 address, subnet mask, Internet Control Naming Protocol (ICMP), Address Resolution Protocol (ARP), Link-Local Multicast Name Resolution (LLMNR), Teredo, Ipconfig

This chapter covers the following subjects:

- **Configuring Networking Settings:** In this section, you learn about the various settings in Windows that enable you to connect to wired or wireless networks, including the Internet. You are also introduced to the wireless networking protocols used by Windows 7 and the available security settings that help protect your connection.

- **Configuring Windows Firewall:** Windows Firewall is a comprehensive stateful packet-filtering application that is enabled by default in Windows 7. This section introduces you to the Windows Firewall Control Panel applet and the Windows Firewall with Advanced Security Microsoft Management Console snap-in, both of which you can configure to specify what types of traffic will be allowed into and out of your computer and network.

CHAPTER 10

Configuring Network and Firewall Settings

Connectivity between Windows 7 computers and other networks (inclusive of the Internet and other computers) is provided in a variety of ways. Windows 7 computers utilize a variety of tools, applications, and protocols for connecting to networks. Chapter 9, "Configuring TCP/IP," introduced you to the Network and Sharing Center, which consolidates many of these applications and utilities into one convenient location from which you can create and manage different types of network connections as well as file and print sharing. This chapter continues our discussion of networking by introducing additional networking components, including how to install, configure, or manage them:

- Dial-up networking

- Wireless networking

- Windows Firewall

Not only do you explore each of these components in this chapter, you also look at their features and dependencies as they exist within the Windows 7 operating system.

"Do I Know This Already?" Quiz

The "Do I Know This Already?" quiz enables you to assess whether you should read this entire chapter or simply jump to the "Exam Preparation Tasks" section for review. If you are in doubt, read the entire chapter. Table 10-1 outlines the major headings in this chapter and the corresponding "Do I Know This Already?" quiz questions. You can find the answers in Appendix A, "Answers to the 'Do I Know This Already?' Quizzes."

Table 10-1 "Do I Know This Already?" Foundation Topics Section-to-Question Mapping

Foundations Topics Section	Questions Covered in This Section
Configuring Networking Settings	1–7
Configuring Windows Firewall	8–13

1. When setting up networking for a new Windows 7 computer, which of the following network types can you specify from the Set Network Location dialog box? (Choose all that apply.)

   a. Home

   b. Work

   c. Private

   d. Public

   e. Domain

2. You would like to ensure that others connecting to a shared folder on your computer have a valid username and password. What option should you enable?

   a. **Network discovery**

   b. **Public folder sharing**

   c. **File sharing connections**

   d. **Password protected sharing**

3. You are a computer consultant who has been asked by a small dental office to configure their network so that all computers can access the Internet via a Windows 7 computer that has two network adapter cards, one of which has a dedicated high-speed Internet connection. What feature should you enable?

   a. Network Address Translation (NAT)

   b. Internet Connection Sharing (ICS)

   c. Dynamic Host Configuration Protocol (DHCP)

   d. Wired Equivalent Privacy (WEP)

4. Which of the following are wireless security options that you can configure for protecting data sent from a Windows 7 computer? (Choose all that apply.)

   a. Temporal Key Integrity Protocol (TKIP)

   b. Advanced Encryption Standard (AES)

   c. Wired Equivalent Privacy (WEP)

   d. Wi-Fi Protected Access (WPA and WPA2)

   e. Service Set Identifier (SSID)

5. You want to select a wireless networking protocol that will enable you to transmit data at a rate of up to 150 Mbps while offering high resistance to interference from other electronic devices. Which of the following should you choose?

   a. 802.11a

   b. 802.11b

   c. 802.11g

   d. 802.11n

6. You are configuring security for your company's wireless network. You want to enable a security protocol that uses Advanced Encryption Service (AES) encryption by default; users should be required to type a security key or passphrase to access the network. What protocol should you choose?

   a. WPA-Personal

   b. WPA2-Personal

   c. WPA-Enterprise

   d. WPA2-Enterprise

7. You want to set up a wireless network profile for your computer that contains the settings available to specific users of the computer. What type of profile should you set up?

   a. Per-Computer Profile

   b. All-Computer Profile

   c. Per-User Profile

   d. All-User Profile

8. You want to configure Windows Firewall settings on your notebook computer so that others are unable to access anything on your computer. Which type of network location should you enable?

   a. Work

   b. Home

   c. Public

   d. Private

9. Which of the following actions can you perform from the Windows Firewall Control Panel applet on your Windows 7 computer? (Choose three.)

   a. Specify ports allowed to communicate across the Windows Firewall.

   b. Specify programs allowed to communicate across the Windows Firewall.

   c. Set the firewall to block all incoming connections, including those in the list of allowed programs.

   d. Configure logging settings for programs that are blocked by the firewall.

   e. Specify a series of firewall settings according to the type of network to which you are connected.

10. You open the Windows Firewall with the Advanced Security snap-in and notice that a large number of firewall rules have already been preconfigured. Which of the following rule settings types does *not* include any preconfigured firewall rules?

   a. Inbound rules

   b. Outbound rules

   c. Connection security rules

   d. Monitoring rules

11. You want to configure Windows Firewall so that Windows Media Player can receive data only from connections that have been authenticated by IPSec. What setting should you configure?

   a. Run the New Inbound Rule Wizard, specify the path to Windows Media Player on the program page, and then specify the **Allow the connection if it is secure** option.

   b. Run the New Outbound Rule Wizard, specify the path to Windows Media Player on the program page, and then specify the **Allow the connection if it is secure** option.

   c. Run the New Connection Security Rule Wizard, specify the path to Windows Media Player on the program page, and then specify the **Allow the connection if it is secure** option.

   d. Merely select **Windows Media Player** from the Allowed Programs and Features list in the Windows Firewall Control Panel applet.

12. You have configured a new inbound rule that limits connections by a specific application on your computer to only those connections that have been authenticated using IPSec. The next day when you start your application, you realize that you should have configured this rule as an outbound rule. What should you do to correct this error with the least amount of effort?

   a. Access the Scope tab of the Properties dialog box for your rule, and change the scope from Inbound to Outbound.

   b. Access the Advanced tab of the Properties dialog box for your rule, and change the interface type from Inbound to Outbound.

   c. Select the rule from the list of inbound rules in the left pane of Windows Firewall with Advanced Security, and drag the rule to the Outbound Rules node in the console tree.

   d. Deactivate or delete the inbound rule you configured, and then use the New Outbound Rule Wizard to set up a new rule that is specific to your application.

13. You want Windows Firewall with Advanced Security to display a notification when a program is blocked from receiving inbound connections. What should you do?

   a. Right-click Windows Firewall with Advanced Security at the top of the console tree and choose **Properties**. From the tab corresponding to the required profile, click **Customize** under Settings. Then ensure that the Display a notification drop-down list is set to **Yes**.

   b. Right-click the Inbound Rules node in the console tree and choose **Properties**. From the tab corresponding to the required profile, click **Customize** under Settings. Then ensure that the Display a notification drop-down list is set to **Yes**.

   c. Right-click the Monitoring node in the console tree and choose **Properties**. From the tab corresponding to the required profile, click **Customize** under Settings. Then ensure that the Display a notification drop-down list is set to **Yes**.

   d. Right-click the Firewall subnode below the Monitoring node in the console tree and choose **Properties**. From the tab corresponding to the required profile, click **Customize** under Settings. Then ensure that the Display a notification drop-down list is set to **Yes**.

Foundation Topics

Configuring Networking Settings

Windows 7 simplifies the process of connecting to diverse types of networks, including wired and wireless networks. In Chapter 9, you saw how to configure TCP/IP versions 4 and 6, and now you will learn about the different settings available from the Network folder and the Network and Sharing Center. Microsoft created the Network and Sharing Center in Windows Vista to make all networking settings available from one location; further, the networking improvements improved performance and provided an improved foundation for later enhancements. On Windows 7, most of the network connectivity items that you configure are similar to those on a Vista computer. The following are some of the major enhancements in Windows 7 networking:

- **Network and Sharing Center:** As already mentioned, this tool brings all networking configuration tasks together in a single interface. We introduced this tool in Chapter 9 and continue here to discuss additional available features.

- **Improved networking connectivity:** Starting in Windows Vista, it became possible to connect seamlessly to secure networks. Windows 7 adds the capability of automatically disabling unused network hardware (for example, a wired network adapter on a machine configured for wireless networking).

- **Network Explorer:** Introduced with Windows Vista and replacing the older Network Neighborhood and My Network Places applications, this tool simplifies your access to all computers, printers, projectors, media players, and other devices on your network.

- **Network Map:** Informs you how your computer is connected to other machines on the network. This tool can be a real time-saver in a complicated network that has been built up in bits and pieces, enabling you to see exactly how each device is connected to others.

- **HomeGroup sharing:** Brand new to Windows 7, HomeGroup sharing simplifies the process of sharing resources on small networks; you can still use older methods of sharing if you desire. We discuss various resource sharing capabilities, including HomeGroup, in Chapter 11, "Configuring Access to Local and Shared Resources."

Network Devices and Locations

When you first install Windows 7 (as covered in Chapter 2, "Installing Windows 7"), you receive the option to set your network location. You can configure new networks and network locations at any time from the Network and Sharing Center, as shown in Figure 10-1. You can change your network location at any time by clicking the active network; for example, **Work network** under View your active networks in Figure 10-1. Doing so displays the Set Network Location dialog box shown in Figure 10-2. Click the desired network location; the wizard informs you that the network location has been changed. Click **Close** to finish.

Figure 10-1   The Network and Sharing Center provides a one-stop location for configuring most of your networking settings.

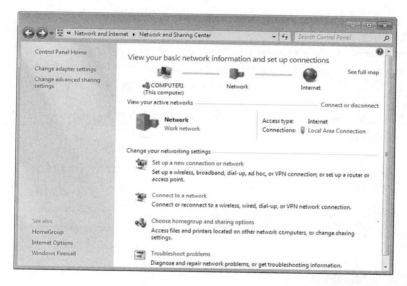

Figure 10-2   The Set Network Location dialog box enables you to change the location of a network that is already set up.

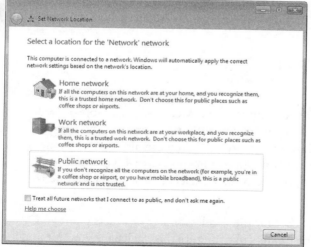

NOTE   Default networking settings for a Home or Work network are actually the same; both permit file sharing and discovery of other machines on the network, as well as discovery of your machine by others on the network. If you select **Public network** in Figure 10-2, network discovery and sharing becomes very restricted to protect your computer's security. Use this setting when you are using a portable computer at a location such as an airport or coffee shop. Other computers on the network cannot see your computer. This might impact the networking capabilities of some applications.

Setting Up New Network Connections

The Network and Sharing Center enables you to set up new networking connections. Click **Set up a new connection or network** (refer to Figure 10-1) to display the Set Up a Connection or Network Wizard shown in Figure 10-3 (note that this dialog box may not display all these options; the options vary according to the networking hardware attached to your computer). Select from the following options and then click **Next**:

Figure 10-3   The Set Up a Connection or Network Wizard offers several options for connecting your computer to networks.

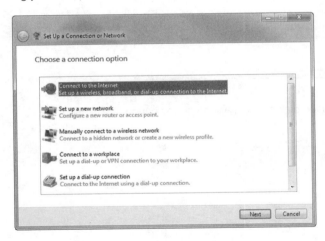

- **Connect to the Internet:** Detects any type of device (such as a cable or DSL broadband connection) and enables you to enter the username and password provided by your ISP, as shown in Figure 10-4. You can also enter a connection name that helps you to identify this connection later. If you want to enable other users on the computer to connect, select **Allow other people to use this connection**.

- **Set up a new network:** Searches for the wireless router or access point you want to configure and then attempts to configure this device for you. Although the wizard states that it might take up to 90 seconds to display unconfigured devices, this process can take considerably longer.

Figure 10-4 Enter your username and password to connect to the Internet.

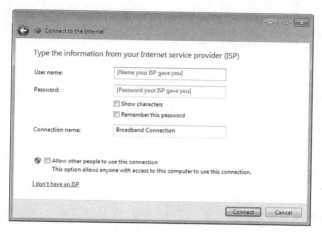

- **Manually connect to a wireless network:** Enables you to enter the wireless network information required for connecting to the network. We discuss wireless networking later in this chapter.

- **Connect to a workplace:** Enables you to connect by means of a virtual private network (VPN) connection across the Internet or to dial directly to the workplace network using a phone line without using the Internet. We discuss VPN connections in Chapter 14, "Configuring Remote Management and Remote Connections."

- **Set up a dial-up connection:** Detects a dial-up modem attached to the computer. You receive options similar to those displayed in Figure 10-4, plus the phone number required to dial in to the ISP.

- **Set up a wireless ad hoc (computer-to-computer) network:** Enables you to connect directly to another wireless-enabled computer without the need for wireless access point. If you do set up a connection of this type, you are disconnected from other wireless networks.

Connecting to Existing Networks

The Connect to a Network option in the Network and Sharing Center enables you to manage connections to networks you have previously set up. When you click this option, Windows displays the message box shown in Figure 10-5 informing you which network you are connected to and which networks are available. Select a desired network and then click **Connect**. To disconnect from a network, select it and then click **Disconnect**.

Figure 10-5   You are informed which network you are connected to.

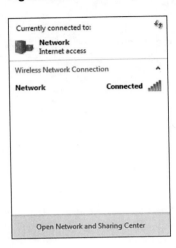

Setting Up Network Sharing and Discovery

You can access additional sharing and network discovery options from the Network and Sharing Center. Click **Change advanced sharing settings**, found in the left side of the Network and Sharing Center. As shown in Figure 10-6, the Advanced sharing settings dialog box enables you to configure the following additional networking options:

Figure 10-6   The Advanced Sharing Settings dialog box enables you to configure sharing options for different network profiles.

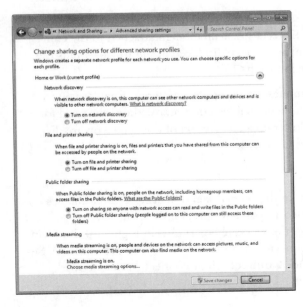

- **Network Discovery:** Enables your computers to see other network computers and devices and enables these machines to access your computer. This option is turned on by default if you have selected Home network or Work network from the Set Network Location dialog box previously shown in Figure 10-2. It is turned off if you have selected Public network from this dialog box.

- **File and printer sharing** and **Public folder sharing:** These options enable you to share files and printers on your computer that will be visible to other computers on the network. We discuss these options in Chapter 11.

- **Media streaming:** Enables machines on the network to access shared photos, videos, and music stored on your computer. Enables your computer to locate these types of shared information on other network computers.

- **File sharing connections:** Enables you to select the strength of encryption used for protecting file sharing connections with other machines on the network. By default, file sharing is enabled for machines that use 40- or 56-bit encryption, but you can choose to increase security by selecting 128-bit encryption. However, devices that do not support 128-bit encryption will be unable to access resources on your computer.

- **Password protected sharing:** Requires users attempting to access shared resources on your computer to have a user account with a password. Turn this option off if you want to enable users without a password to have access.

- **HomeGroup connections:** Enables you to determine whether Windows will utilize simple homegroup-based sharing or use the classic type of file sharing model employed by previous Windows versions. More information is provided in Chapter 11.

TIP   You can configure sharing options for two network profiles:

- Home or Work

- Public

This enables you to maintain these network profiles when switching between different network types, so that when you connect to a public network, more restrictive sharing options are automatically applied. The Home and Work settings use identical sharing options.

Using Internet Connection Sharing to Share Your Internet Connection

Quite often, it is not feasible for a small office or a home user to install a high-speed dedicated link to the Internet (such as a T1 line) or have each computer dial up to an ISP. Nowadays, home users can utilize a dedicated broadband link such as a reasonably priced cable or DSL link.

One of the growing trends for small office or home networks is to share an Internet connection with all the members of the network. Windows 7 contains a feature called Internet Connection Sharing (ICS), which enables a small office or home network to use one computer on the network as the router to the Internet.

Windows 7's ICS components consist of

- **Auto-dial:** A method of establishing the Internet connection when attempting to access Internet resources on a computer that does not host the Internet connection.

- **DHCP Allocator:** A simplified DHCP service that assigns IP addresses from the address range of 192.168.0.2–192.168.0.254, with a mask of 255.255.255.0 and default gateway of 192.168.0.1.

- **DNS Proxy:** Forwards DNS requests to the DNS server and forwards the DNS replies back to the clients.

- **Network Address Translation (NAT):** Maps the range of private Class C IPv4 addresses (192.168.0.1–192.168.0.254) to the public IP address, which is assigned by the ISP. NAT is a specification in TCP/IP that tracks the source private IP addresses and outbound public IP address(es), reformatting the IP address data in the header dynamically so that the source requests reach the public resources and the public servers can reply to the correct source-requesting clients.

NOTE   ICS is a simplified form of NAT, which is a protocol used on larger networks to hide internal IP addresses. NAT runs on a server or router and is capable of translating multiple external IP addresses to internal private IP addresses used on client computers. The NAT server/router can also be configured to provide DHCP services to the client computers. For more information on NAT, refer to "How NAT Works" at http://www.cisco.com/en/US/tech/tk648/tk361/technologies_tech_note09186a0080094831.shtml.

ICS can be used to share any type of Internet connection, although it must be a connection that is enabled for all users on the PC dial-up for sharing to be effective. To enable ICS, you need to make sure that the Internet-connected computer has been configured with connections for a modem and a network adapter. If you are using broadband, you need two network adapters: one to connect to the broadband device for the Internet and the other to connect to the network. Use the following procedure at the computer connected to the Internet to set up ICS:

Step 1.   From the Network and Sharing Center, click **Change adapter settings**, found on the left side. This opens the Network Connections dialog box shown in Figure 10-7.

Figure 10-7 The Network Connections dialog box displays all available network connections.

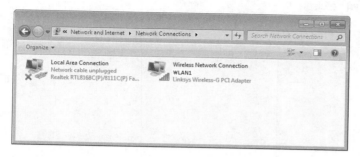

Step 2. Right-click the connection you want to share and choose **Properties**. If you receive a UAC prompt, click **Yes**.

Step 3. Select the **Sharing** tab and then select the check box labeled **Allow other network users to connect through this computer's Internet connection**.

Step 4. If desired, select the check box labeled **Allow other network users to control or disable the shared Internet connection**.

CAUTION   Before you configure ICS, you should ensure that no computers are currently assigned an IP address of 192.168.0.1 because the network adapter on the ICS computer is automatically assigned that address when ICS is configured.

After you have shared your connection, you need to configure the other computers to use this connection, as follows:

Step 1. In the bottom-left corner of the Network and Sharing Center, click **Internet Options**.

Step 2. On the Connections tab of the Internet Explorer Properties dialog box, ensure that **Never dial a connection** is selected.

Step 3. Click the **LAN Settings** command button.

Step 4. On the Local Area Network (LAN) Settings dialog box shown in Figure 10-8, clear the check boxes for **Automatically detect settings**, **Use automatic configuration script**, and **Use a proxy server for your LAN**. Then click **OK**.

Step 5. From the Network Connections dialog box previously shown in Figure 10-7, right-click the shared connection and choose **Properties**.

Step 6. Click **Internet Protocol Version 4 (TCP/IPv4)** or **Internet Protocol Version 6 (TCP/IPv6)** and then click **Properties**.

Figure 10-8   On an ICS client computer, the three check boxes in the Local Area Network
(LAN) Settings dialog box should be cleared.

Step 7.   On the Properties dialog box, select **Obtain an IP address automatically** or **Obtain an IPv6 address automatically**.

If you have problems with ICS, you should open Event Viewer and check out the
System log for any errors related to ICS. In addition you can view the NSW.LOG file
to look for errors. The following are several additional suggestions in case users
are unable to access the Internet from the client computers:

- Check the configuration of the client Internet browser. We mentioned client
  configuration earlier in this section.

- Ensure that the client can connect to the host computer. Check the connection by typing **ping 192.168.0.1**. If this ping is unsuccessful, check the physical network connections.

- Use ipconfig to check the client computer's IP configuration. Ensure that the
  client has an IP address on the proper subnet and that the default gateway is
  set to 192.168.0.1.

NOTE   For more information on ICS, including its use with IPv6, refer to
"Using Wireless Hosted Network and Internet Connection Sharing" at
http://msdn.microsoft.com/en-us/library/dd815252(VS.85).aspx.

Connecting to Wireless Networks

The recent advances in wireless networking technology have enabled individuals to
connect to networks from virtually anyplace a wireless access point is available.
Many offices are taking advantages of the ease of setup of wireless local area networks (WLANs), which allow for mobility and portability of computers and other
devices located within the office. And public access points in locations such as

restaurants and airports permit users to send and receive data from many places that would have been unthought-of not too many years ago. Along with this convenience comes an increased chance of unauthorized access to the networks and the data they contain.

Wireless networks are easy to install and use, and they are gaining tremendous popularity for small home and office networks. Security is still not perfected for wireless networks, so they have not made major inroads in corporate environments yet. Windows 7 supports the 802.11 protocols for wireless LANs and is capable of transparently moving between multiple wireless access points (WAPs), changing to a new IP subnet, and remaining connected to the network. Each time the IP subnet changes, the user is reauthenticated. In Windows 7, you can configure wireless networking in the Network and Sharing Center. This enables you to connect to wireless networks, configure an ad hoc connection or the use of a WAP, and manage your wireless networks.

Windows 7 provides similar wireless technologies to those of Vista, improving on the wireless support included with Windows XP so that wireless networking is as well integrated with the operating system as normal networking. Consequently, wireless network reliability, stability, and security are considerably enhanced over that of Windows XP. The following are some of the more important security improvements in Windows 7 wireless networking:

- Windows 7 minimizes the amount of private information, such as the service set identifier (SSID), that is broadcast before connecting to a wireless network.

- When users connect to an unencrypted public network (such as an airport or restaurant Wi-Fi hotspot), Windows 7 warns them of the risks so that they can limit their activities accordingly.

- Windows 7 supports a complete range of wireless security protocols, from Wired Equivalent Privacy (WEP) to Wi-Fi Protected Access (WPA and WPA2), Protected Extensible Authentication Protocol (PEAP), and its combination with Microsoft Challenge Handshake Authentication Protocol version 2 (MS-CHAP v2) and Extensible Authentication Protocol Transport Layer Security (EAP-TLS).

- Windows 7 uses WPA2-Personal for maximum security when communicating by means of an ad hoc wireless network (direct communication with another wireless computer without use of an access point). This helps to protect against common vulnerabilities associated with such unprotected networks.

- Administrators can use Group Policy settings to configure Single Sign On (SSO) profiles that facilitate wireless domain logon. 802.1x authentication precedes the domain logon and users are prompted for wireless credentials only if absolutely necessary. The wireless connection is therefore in place before the domain logon proceeds.

■ Windows 7 supports the three network location types (home, work, or public) together with their Windows Firewall settings for wireless networking. These settings are discussed later in this chapter.

Wireless Networking Protocols

Table 10-2 describes four wireless networking protocols available to Windows 7.

Table 10-2   Characteristics of Wireless Networking Protocols

Protocol	Transmission Speed	Frequency Used	Comments
802.11b	11 Mbps	2.4 GHz	The 2.4 GHz frequency is the same as that used by many appliances such as cordless phones and microwave ovens; this can cause interference. This technology also is limited in that it supports fewer simultaneous users than the other protocols.
802.11a	54 Mbps	5 GHz	Although it reduces interference from other appliances, this technology has a shorter signal range and is not compatible with network adapters, routers, and WAPs using the 802.11b protocol. However, some devices are equipped to support either 802.11a or 802.11b.
802.11g	54 Mbps	2.4 GHz	You can have 802.11b and 802.11g devices operating together on the same network. This standard was created specifically for backward compatibility with the 802.11b standard. The signal range is better than that of 802.11a, but this technology suffers from the same interference problems as 802.11a.
802.11n	Up to 150–600 Mbps depending on the number of data streams	2.4 or 5 GHz	This technology is compatible with devices using the older protocols at the same frequency. It also has the best signal range and is most resistant to interference, although it can have the same problems as 802.11b if using the 2.4 GHz frequency.

Setting Up a Wireless Network Connection

Windows 7 provides a wizard that simplifies the process of setting up various types of network connections and connecting to wireless and other networks. Use the following procedure to set up a wireless network connection:

Step 1. From the Network and Sharing Center, click **Set up a new connection or network**.

Step 2. Click **Set up a new network** and then click **Next**.

Step 3. When the wizard detects the required wireless router or WAP, select it and click **Next**.

Step 4. On the Give Your Network a Name page, type the network name and security key used by the required router or WAP. Choose the required security level and encryption type (more about these later in this chapter), and then click **Next**.

Step 5. The wizard configures your network. When done, click **Finish**.

You can connect to a network that you have previously set up by following these steps:

Step 1. From the Network and Sharing Center, click **Set up a new connection or network**.

Step 2. Click **Manually connect to a wireless network**, and then click **Next**.

Step 3. The wizard displays the Manually connect to a wireless network page shown in Figure 10-9. Enter the following information and then click **Next**.

Figure 10-9   The Manually connect to a wireless network page enables you to enter the information required for connecting to a wireless network.

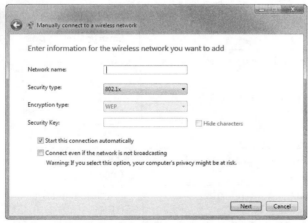

— **Network name:** The name (SSID) of the wireless network you are connecting to.

— **Security type:** Authentication method to be used in connecting to the wireless network. Table 10-3 lists the available security types.

— **Encryption type:** Select the method to be used for encryption of data sent across the wireless network. You can choose from 128-bit WEP, 128-bit Temporal Key Integrity Protocol (TKIP), or 128-bit Advanced Encryption Standard (AES) according to the security type chosen (refer to Table 10-3).

— **Security Key:** Enter the security key required by the security type selected (the WEP key for the WEP security type), the WPA pre-shared key (for the WPA-Personal security type), or the WPA2 pre-shared key (for the WPA2-Personal security type). Clear the Hide characters check box to view the information typed here.

— **Start this connection automatically:** When selected, Windows 7 automatically connects to the network when you log on. When cleared, you must use the Connect to a network option from the Network and Sharing Center to connect to the network.

— **Connect even if the network is not broadcasting:** Specifies whether Windows will attempt to connect even if the network is not broadcasting its name. This can be a security risk because Windows 7 sends Probe Request frames to locate the network, which unauthorized users can use to determine the network name. Consequently, this check box is not selected by default.

Table 10-3   Available Wireless Security Types

Security Type	Description	Available Encryption Types
No authentication (open)	Open system authentication with no encryption	None
WEP	Open system authentication using WEP	WEP
WPA-Personal	Wi-Fi Protected Access (WPA) using a preshared passphrase or key	TKIP (default) or AES
WPA2-Personal	Version 2 of WPA using a preshared passphrase or key	TKIP or AES (default)
WPA-Enterprise	WPA using IEEE 802.1x authentication	TKIP (default) or AES
WPA2-Enterprise	Version 2 of WPA using IEEE 802.1x authentication	TKIP or AES (default)
802.1x	IEEE 802.1x authentication using WEP (also known as dynamic WEP)	WEP

Step 4. The wizard informs you that it has successfully added the network you specified. Click the link specified to connect to the network, or click the **Close** button to finish the wizard without connecting.

NOTE WPA2-Enterprise security provides the highest level of wireless networking authentication security. It requires authentication in two phases: first, an open system authentication and, second, authentication using EAP. It is suitable for domain-based authentication and on networks using a Remote Authentication Dial-In User Service (RADIUS) authentication server. In environments without the RADIUS server, you should use WPA2-Personal security.

The wireless network you configured is visible in the Network and Sharing Center, from which you can connect later if you have not chosen the **Start this connection automatically** option.

TIP On the 70-680 exam, you might be asked to choose between the four available types of WPA wireless security. You should select **WPA** (either Personal or Enterprise) to use TKIP encryption by default or **WPA2** (either Personal or Enterprise) to use AES encryption by default. In addition, if you are required to type a security key or passphrase, you should select one of the **Personal** options. If you are not required to type a security key or passphrase, you should select one of the **Enterprise** options.

Managing Wireless Network Connections

After you have configured one or more wireless network connections, you can manage them from the Manage Wireless Networks dialog box shown in Figure 10-10. You can access this dialog box by selecting **Manage wireless networks** from the task list in the Network and Sharing Center. This dialog box enables you to add new wireless networks, view or modify the properties of a wireless network connection, modify the sequence of preferred connection to these networks, or choose the type of profile to be applied to a network. We discuss wireless network profiles later in this section.

To modify the order in which Windows attempts to connect to the wireless networks, select the network to be connected first and drag it to the top of the list. To modify the properties of the wireless network connection, right-click it and choose **Properties**. This displays the dialog box shown in Figure 10-11. (This dialog box is also available from the completion page of the Manually Connect to a Wireless Network Wizard by selecting **Change connection settings**.)

From this dialog box you can modify the options previously selected to connect automatically or connect even if the network is not broadcasting. You can also choose to connect to a more preferred network if you have configured one and it is

Figure 10-10   The Manage Wireless Networks dialog box displays the various wireless networks you have configured on your computer.

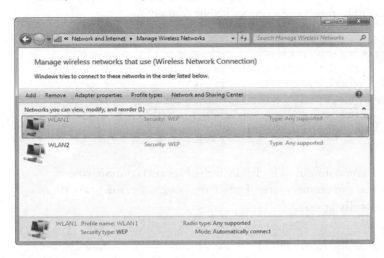

Figure 10-11   The Wireless Network Properties dialog box enables you to modify the properties of your wireless network connection.

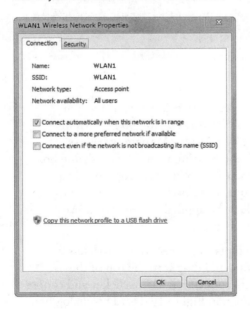

available (this option is unavailable if you have configured only one wireless network). You can also copy the network profile to a USB flash drive by clicking the link provided. This enables you to set the network up quickly later if you have to re-create the connection for any reason. The Security tab of this dialog box enables you to change the security and encryption types according to the types given previously in Table 10-3. From this tab you can also change the network security key if you have chosen a security type that requires this key.

Wireless Network Profiles

The Manage Wireless Networks dialog box (refer to Figure 10-10) also enables you to manage wireless network profiles. Simply put, a wireless network profile is a set of wireless networks available to a given user on a Windows 7 computer. The profile contains the SSID, the security settings as configured earlier in this section, and whether the network is an infrastructure or ad hoc network. There are two types of wireless network profiles:

- **Per-user profiles:** These profiles apply to specific users of the computer and are connected when that user logs on to the computer. Note that these profiles can cause a loss of network connectivity when logging off or switching between users.

- **All-user profiles:** These profiles apply to all users of the computer and are connected regardless of which user is logged on to the computer.

To configure the type of profile, click **Profile types** in the task list of the Manage Wireless Networks dialog box previously shown in Figure 10-10. From the Wireless Network Profile Type dialog box shown in Figure 10-12, select the desired profile type and then click **Save**.

Figure 10-12 The Wireless Network Profile Type dialog box enables you to choose the type of profile to be assigned.

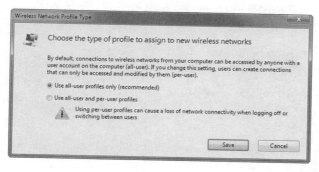

In addition to using the Manage Wireless Networks dialog box, you can use the netsh command to manage wireless network profiles. You can also use Group Policy to deploy or maintain wireless network profiles.

NOTE For more information, refer to "Netsh Commands for Wireless Local Area Network (WLAN) in Windows Server 2008 R2" at http://technet.microsoft.com/en-us/library/dd744890(WS.10).aspx.

Configuring Location Aware Printing

Location Aware Printing is a new feature of Windows 7 Professional, Enterprise or Ultimate that enables you to automatically print to a printer on the network your computer is currently connected to. For example, if you have a portable computer that you use both at home and in the office, you can print to the office computer when you are at work. Returning home in the evening, you print a document and this print job automatically goes to the home printer without your having to change the default printer, thereby simplifying this task and reducing problems from attempting to print to the wrong printer.

Location Aware Printing in Windows 7 obtains network names from several sources, including the Active Directory Domain Services (AD DS) domain name at work and the SSID of your home wireless network. The Manage Default Printers dialog box then enables you to associate a default printer with each network to which you connect and Windows 7 will automatically specify the assigned printer as the default when you connect to its network.

Use the following procedure to set up Location Aware Printing:

Step 1.   Click **Start > Devices and Printers**.

Step 2.   From the Devices and Printers Control Panel applet, select a printer and then click **Manage default printers** from the menu bar.

Step 3.   From the Manage Default Printers dialog box shown in Figure 10-13, select **Change my default printer when I change networks**.

Figure 10-13   The Manage Default Printers dialog box enables you to select a default printer that will be used at each network location.

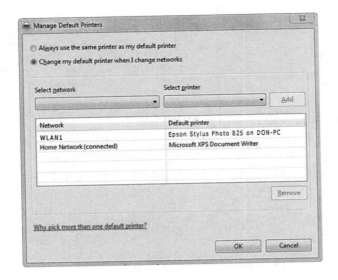

Step 4. For each network shown in the Select network drop-down list, select a printer from the Select printer drop-down list and then click **Add**.

Step 5. When finished, click **OK**.

Configuring Security Settings in Windows Firewall

Originally called the Internet Connection Firewall (ICF) in Windows XP prior to SP2, Windows Firewall is a personal firewall, stopping undesirable traffic from being accepted by the computer. Using a firewall can avoid security breaches as well as viruses that utilize port-based TCP or UDP traffic to enter the computer's operating system. For computers that use broadband Internet connections with dedicated IP addresses, Windows Firewall can help avoid attacks aimed at disrupting a home computer. When you take your laptop to a Wi-Fi–enabled public location such as an airport, hotel, or restaurant, the firewall protects you from individuals who might be probing the network to see what they can steal or infect. Even people with dial-up Internet connections can benefit from added protection. The Windows Firewall is enabled by default when you install Windows 7, as it was in Windows Vista.

Windows Firewall is a stateful host-based firewall that you can configure to allow or block specific network traffic. It includes a packet filter that uses an access control list (ACL) specifying parameters (such as IP address, port number, and protocol) that are allowed to pass through. When a user communicates with an external computer, the stateful firewall remembers this conversation and allows the appropriate reply packets to reach the user. Packets from an outside computer that attempts to communicate with a computer on which a stateful firewall is running are dropped unless the ACL contains rules permitting them.

Windows Vista introduced considerable improvements to its original implementation in Windows XP SP2, including outbound traffic protection, support for IP Security (IPSec) and IP version 6 (IPv6), improved configuration of exceptions, and support for command-line configuration. In Windows 7, Microsoft has improved Windows Firewall even further. The following are some of the important new features in the Windows 7 implementation:

- Support for multiple active profiles. If your computer is connected to more than one network, you can have each network adapter assigned to a different profile (public, private, or domain).

- Additional rules are available from the Windows Firewall with Advanced Security tool, including more specific disabling of its features.

- The ability to selectively disable features that might be in conflict with components of a third-party firewall.

- You can use Windows Firewall with Advanced Security to specify port numbers or protocols in connection security rules, as well as ranges of port numbers. In previous versions of Windows Firewall, you had to use the `netsh` command-line tool to perform this action.

- Creation of IPSec connection security rules has been simplified with the use of dynamic encryption.

- When securing tunnel-mode connections, you can specify the authorized users and computers that can set up an inbound tunnel to an IPSec gateway server.

- You can exempt DHCP traffic from IPSec requirements.

- You can specify that an outbound allow rule can override block rules when secured with an IPSec connection security rule.

- Additional options have been added for configuring authentication for an IPSec tunnel-mode rule.

- A new main mode configuration capability includes additional configuration options for specific origin and destination IP addresses or network location protocols. Network connections matching a main mode rule use these settings rather than the global defaults or those specified in connection security rules.

You can perform basic configuration of Windows Firewall from a Control Panel applet; you can also perform more advanced configuration of Windows Firewall, including the use of security policies from a Microsoft Management Console (MMC) snap-in. We shall look at each of these in turn.

Basic Windows Firewall Configuration

The Windows Firewall Control Panel applet, found in the System and Security category and shown in Figure 10-14, enables you to set up firewall rules for each of the same network types introduced earlier in this chapter for configuring network settings.

NOTE   If your computer is joined to an AD DS domain, an additional location called Domain Networks is added in Figure 10-14. Settings in this location are configured through domain-based Group Policy and cannot be modified here.

You can enable or disable the Windows Firewall separately for each connection. In doing so, you are able to use Windows Firewall to protect a computer connected to the Internet via one adapter and not use Windows Firewall for the adapter connected to the private network. Use the following instructions to perform basic firewall configuration:

Figure 10-14 You can configure basic firewall settings for different network locations from the Windows Firewall Control Panel applet.

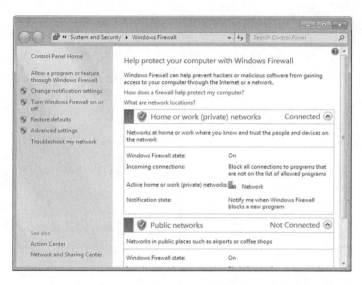

Step 1. Open the Windows Firewall applet by using any of the following methods:

— Click **Start > Control Panel > System and Security > Windows Firewall**.

— Click **Start** and type **firewall** in the Search field. From the list of programs displayed under Control Panel, click **Windows Firewall**.

— Click **Start**, right-click **Network**, and then click **Properties**. Select **Windows Firewall** from the bottom-left corner of the Network and Sharing Center.

Step 2. From the left pane of the Windows Firewall applet, select **Turn Windows Firewall on or off**. If you receive a UAC prompt, click **Yes**. This displays the **Customize settings for each type of network** dialog box, shown in Figure 10-15.

Step 3. If you are connected to a corporate network with a comprehensive hardware firewall, select **Turn off Windows Firewall (not recommended)** under the Home or Work (Private) Network Location Settings section. If you connect at any time to an insecure network, such as an airport or restaurant Wi-Fi hot spot, select the **Block all incoming connections, including those in the list of allowed programs** option under Public network location settings. This option disables all exceptions you've configured on the Exceptions tab.

Figure 10-15 The Customize settings for each type of network dialog box enables you to turn the firewall on or off and to block incoming connections.

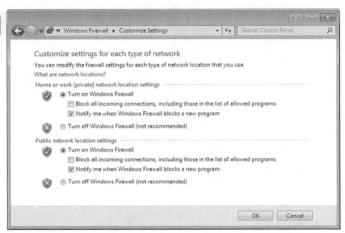

> **CAUTION** Don't disable the firewall unless absolutely necessary, even on the Home or Work (Private) Network Location Settings section. Never select the **Off** option in Figure 10-15 unless you're absolutely certain that your network is well protected with a good firewall. The only exception should be temporarily to troubleshoot a connectivity problem; after you've solved the problem, be sure to re-enable the firewall immediately.

Step 4. To configure program exceptions, return to the Windows Firewall applet and click **Allow a program or feature through Windows Firewall**.

Step 5. From the list shown in Figure 10-16, select the programs or ports you want to have access to your computer on either of the Home/Work (Private) or Public profiles. Table 10-4 describes the more important items in this list. Clear the check boxes next to any programs or ports to be denied access, or select the check boxes next to programs or ports to be granted access.

Step 6. To add a program not shown in the list, click **Allow another program**. From the Add a Program dialog box shown in Figure 10-17, select the program to be added and then click **Add**. If necessary, click **Browse** to locate the desired program. You can also click **Network location types** to choose which network type is allowed by the selected program.

Figure 10-16   The Allow programs to communicate through Windows Firewall dialog box enables you to specify which programs are allowed to communicate through the firewall.

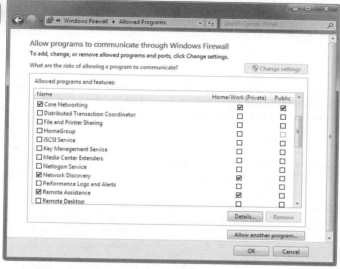

Figure 10-17   The Add a Program dialog box enables you to allow specific programs access through the Windows Firewall.

Step 7.   In the Allow programs to communicate through Windows Firewall dialog box (refer to Figure 10-16), to view properties of any program or port on the list, select it and click **Details**.

Step 8.   To remove a program from the list, select it and click **Remove**. You can do this only for programs you have added using step 6.

Table 10-4   Windows Firewall Configurable Exceptions

Exception	Description	Enabled by Default?
Core Networking Network Discovery	Each option works with the other to enable your computer to connect to other network computers or the Internet.	Yes; network discovery for home or work only
Distributed Transaction Co-ordinator	Coordinates the update of transaction-protected resources such as databases, message queues, and file systems.	No
File and Printer Sharing	Enables your computer to share resources such as files and printers with other computers on your network.	Yes
HomeGroup	Allows communication to other computers in the homegroup.	Yes, for home or work only when joined to a homegroup.
iSCSI Service	Used for connecting to iSCSI target servers and devices.	No
Key Management Service	Used for machine counting and license compliance in enterprise environments.	No
Media Center Extenders	Allows Media Center Extenders to communicate with a computer running Windows Media Center.	No
Netlogon Service	Maintains a secure channel between domain clients and a domain controller for authenticating users and services.	Only on a computer joined to an Active Directory domain
Network Discovery	Allows computers to locate other resources on the local network.	Yes, for home or work only
Performance Logs and Alerts	Allows remote management of the Performance Logs and Alerts service.	No
Remote Assistance	Enables an expert user to connect to the desktop of a user requiring assistance in a Windows Feature.	Yes, for home or work only
Remote Desktop	Enables a user to connect with and work on a remote computer.	No

Table 10-4   Windows Firewall Configurable Exceptions

Exception	Description	Enabled by Default?
Remote (*item*) Management	Enables an administrator to manage items on a remote computer, including event logs, scheduled tasks, services, and disk volumes.	No for all these tasks
Routing and Remote Access (RRAS)	Enables remote users to connect to a server to access the corporate network (used on RRAS server computers only).	No
Windows Easy Transfer	Enables a user to copy files, folders, and settings from an old computer running Windows 2000 or later to a new Windows 7 computer.	Yes
Windows Remote Management	Enables you to manage a remote Windows computer.	No

Step 9.   If you need to restore default settings, return to the Windows Firewall applet previously shown in Figure 10-14 and click **Restore defaults**. Then confirm your intention in the Restore Default Settings dialog box that appears.

Step 10.   If you are experiencing networking problems, click **Troubleshoot my network** to access the troubleshooter previously shown in Figure 9-10.

Step 11.   When you are finished, click **OK**.

TIP   When allowing additional programs to communicate through Windows Firewall, by default these programs are allowed to communicate through the Home/Work network profile only. You should retain this default unless you need a program to communicate through the Internet from a public location. From the Public column of the dialog box shown in Figure 10-16, you should select the boxes next to any connections that link to the Internet; you should clear the boxes next to any connections to a private network.

Using the Windows Firewall with Advanced Security Snap-in

First introduced in Windows Vista and enhanced in Windows 7, the Windows Firewall with Advanced Security snap-in enables you to perform a comprehensive set of configuration actions. You can configure rules that affect inbound and outbound communication, and you can configure connection security rules and the monitoring of firewall actions. Inbound rules help prevent actions such as unknown access or configuration of your computer, installation of undesired software, and so on. Outbound rules help prevent utilities on your computer performing certain actions, such as accessing network resources or software without your knowledge. They can also help prevent other users of your computer from downloading software or inappropriate files without your knowledge.

To access the snap-in, type **firewall** in the Search field of the Start menu and then select **Windows Firewall with Advanced Security** from the Programs list. You can also click **Advanced settings** from the task list in the Windows Firewall applet. After accepting the UAC prompt (if you receive one), you receive the snap-in shown in Figure 10-18.

Figure 10-18 The Windows Firewall with Advanced Security snap-in enables you to perform advanced configuration options.

When the snap-in first opens, it displays a summary of configured firewall settings. From the left pane, you can configure any of the following types of properties:

- **Inbound Rules:** Displays a series of defined inbound rules. Enabled rules are shown with a green check mark icon. If the icon is dark in appearance, the rule is not enabled. To enable a rule, right-click it and select **Enable Rule**; to disable an enabled rule, right-click it and select **Disable Rule**. You can also create a new rule by right-clicking **Inbound Rules** and selecting **New Rule**. We discuss creation of new rules later in this section.

- **Outbound Rules:** Displays a series of defined outbound rules, also with a green check mark icon for enabled rules. You can enable or disable rules, and create new rules, in the same manner as with inbound rules.

- **Connection Security Rules:** By default, this branch does not contain any rules. Right-click it and choose **New Rule** to create rules that are used to determine limits applied to connections with remote computers.

- **Monitoring:** Displays a summary of enabled firewall settings and provides links to active rules and security associations. This includes a domain profile for computers that are members of an AD DS domain. The following three links are available from the bottom of the left pane:
  - **Firewall:** Displays enabled inbound and outbound rules
  - **Active Connection Security Rules:** Displays enabled connection security rules that you have created
  - **Security Associations:** Displays IPSec main mode and quick mode associations

Configuring Multiple Firewall Profiles

A *profile* is simply a means of grouping firewall rules so that they apply to the affected computers dependent on where the computer is connected. The Windows Firewall with Advanced Security snap-in enables you to define different firewall behavior for each of the following three profiles:

- **Domain Profile:** Specifies firewall settings for use when connected directly to an AD DS domain. If the network is protected from unauthorized external access, you can specify additional exceptions that facilitate communication across the LAN to network servers and client computers.

- **Private Profile:** Specifies firewall settings for use when connected to a private network location, such as a home or small office. You can open up connections to network computers and lock down external communications as required.

- **Public Profile:** Specifies firewall settings for use when connected to an insecure public network, such as a Wi-Fi access point at a hotel, restaurant, airport, or other location where unknown individuals might attempt to connect to your computer. By default, network discovery and file and printer sharing are turned off, inbound connections are blocked, and outbound connections are allowed.

To configure settings for these profiles from the Windows Firewall with Advanced Security snap-in, right-click **Windows Firewall with Advanced Security** at the top-left corner and choose **Properties**. This opens the dialog box shown in Figure 10-19.

Figure 10-19   The Windows Firewall with Advanced Security on Local Computer Properties dialog box enables you to configure profiles that are specific for domain, private, and public networks.

You can configure the following properties for each of the three profiles individually from this dialog box:

- **State:** Enables you to turn the firewall on or off for the selected profile and block or allow inbound and outbound connections. For inbound connections, you can either block connections with the configured exceptions or block all connections. Click **Customize** to specify which connections you want Windows Firewall to help protect.

- **Settings:** Enables you to customize firewall settings for the selected profile. Click **Customize** to specify whether to display notifications to users when programs are blocked from receiving inbound connections or allow unicast responses. You can also view but not modify how rules created by local administrators are merged with Group Policy–based rules.

- **Logging:** Enables you to configure logging settings. Click **Customize** to specify the location and size of the log file and whether dropped packets or successful connections are logged (see Figure 10-20).

In addition, you can configure IPSec settings from the IPSec Settings tab (refer to Figure 10-19), including defaults and exemptions. IPSec authentication rules enable you to configure bypass rules for specific computers that enable these computers to bypass other Windows Firewall rules. Doing so enables you to block certain types of traffic while enabling authenticated computers to receive these types of traffic. Configuring IPSec settings is beyond the scope of the 70-680 exam and will not be further discussed here.

Figure 10-20   You can customize logging settings for each of the Windows Firewall profiles.

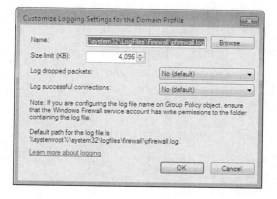

Configuring New Firewall Rules

By clicking **New Rule** under Inbound Rules or Outbound Rules in the Windows Firewall with Advanced Security snap-in (refer to Figure 10-18), you can create rules that determine programs or ports that are allowed to pass through the firewall. Use the following procedure to create a new rule:

Step 1.   Right-click the desired rule type in the Windows Firewall with Advanced Security snap-in and choose **New Rule**. This starts the New (Inbound or Outbound) Rule Wizard, as shown in Figure 10-21. (We chose a new inbound rule, so our example shows the New Inbound Rule Wizard.)

Step 2.   Select the type of rule you want to create:

— **Program:** Enables you to define a rule that includes all programs or a specified program path.

— **Port:** Enables you to define rules for specific remote ports using either the TCP or UDP protocol.

— **Predefined:** Enables you to select from a large quantity of predefined rules covering the same exceptions described previously in Table 10-4 and shown in Figure 10-16. Select the desired exception from the drop-down list.

— **Custom:** Enables you to create rules that apply to combinations of programs and ports. This option combines settings provided by the other rule-type options.

Figure 10-21   The New (Inbound or Outbound) Rule Wizard starts with a Rule Type page, which enables you to define the type of rule you want to create.

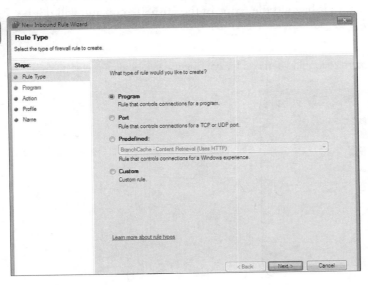

Step 3.   After you've selected your rule type, click **Next**.

Step 4.   The content of the next page of the wizard varies according to which option you've selected. On this page, define the program path, port number, and protocol, or the predefined rule that you want to create, and then click **Next**.

Step 5.   On the Action page, specify the action to be taken when a connection matches the specified conditions, as shown in Figure 10-22.

Step 6.   If you choose the **Allow the Connection if it is secure** option, click **Customize** to display the dialog box shown in Figure 10-23. From this dialog box, select the required option as explained on the dialog box and click **OK**. If you desire that encryption be enforced in addition to authentication and integrity protection, select the **Require the connections to be encrypted** option and also select the check box provided if you want to allow unencrypted data to be sent while encryption is being negotiated.

Step 7.   Click **Next** to display the Profile page. On this page, select the profiles (**Domain**, **Private**, and **Public**) to which the rule is to be applied. Then click **Next**.

Step 8.   On the Name page, specify a name and optional description for your new rule. Click **Finish** to create the rule, which will then appear in the right pane of the Windows Firewall with Advanced Security snap-in.

Figure 10-22 The Action page enables you to specify the required action type.

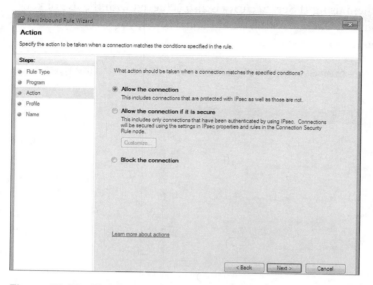

Figure 10-23 The Customize Allow if Secure Settings dialog box enables you to select additional actions to be taken for packets that match the rule conditions being configured.

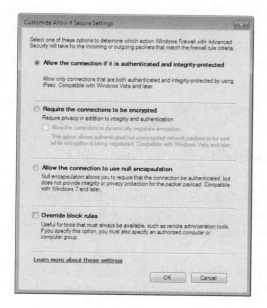

Creating a new connection security rule is similar to that for inbound or outbound rules, but the options are slightly different. From the Windows Firewall with Advanced Security dialog box previously shown in Figure 10-18, right-click **Connection Security Rules** and choose **New Rule** to display the New Connection Security Rule Wizard (see Figure 10-24). Connection security rules manage authentication of two machines on the network and the encryption of network traffic sent between them using IPSec. Security is also achieved with the use of key exchange and data integrity checks. As shown in Figure 10-24, you can create the following types of connection security rules:

Figure 10-24   The New Connection Security Rule Wizard enables you to create five types of connection security rules.

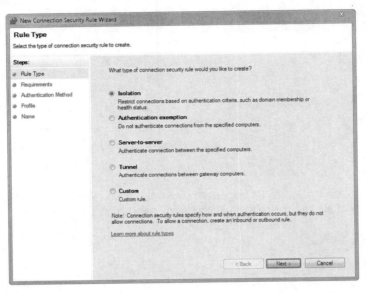

- **Isolation:** Enables you to limit connections according to authentication criteria that you define. For example, you can use this rule to isolate domain-based computers from external computers such as those located across the Internet. You can request or require authentication and specify the authentication method that must be used.

- **Authentication exemption:** Enables specified computers, such as DHCP and DNS servers, to be exempted from the need for authentication. You can specify computers by IP address ranges or subnets, or you can include a predefined set of computers.

- **Server-to-server:** Enables you to create a secured connection between computers in two endpoints that are defined according to IP address ranges.

- **Tunnel:** Enables you to secure communications between two computers by means of IPSec tunnel mode. This encapsulated network packets that are routed between the tunnel endpoints. You can choose from several types of tunnels; you can also exempt IPSec-protected computers from the defined tunnel.

- **Custom:** Enables you to create a rule that requires special settings not covered explicitly in the other options. All wizard pages except those used to create only tunnel rules are available.

Modifying Rule Properties

You can modify any Windows Firewall rule from its Properties dialog box, accessed by right-clicking the rule in the center pane of the Windows Firewall with Advanced Security snap-in and choosing **Properties**. From the dialog box shown in Figure 10-25, you can configure the following properties:

Figure 10-25   The Properties dialog box for a firewall rule enables you to modify rules criteria for rules you have created or default rules supplied in Windows Firewall with Advanced Security.

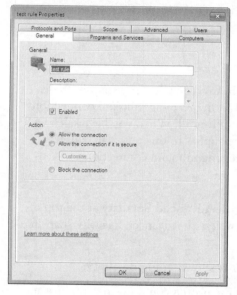

- **General tab:** Enables you to edit the name and description of the rule or change the action.

- **Programs and Services tab:** Enables you to define which programs and services are affected by the rule.

- **Computers tab:** Enables you to specify which computers are authorized to allow connections according to the rule or enables you to specify computers for which the rule will be skipped.

- **Protocols and Ports tab:** Enables you to specify the protocol type and the local and remote ports covered by the rule.

- **Scope tab:** Enables you to specify the local and remote IP addresses of connections covered by the rule. You can specify Any Address or select a subnet or IP address range.

- **Advanced tab:** Enables you to specify the profiles (domain, private, or public) to which the rule applies. You can also specify the interface types (local area network, remote access, and/or wireless) and whether edge traversal (traffic routed through a NAT device) is allowed or blocked.

- **Users tab:** Enables you to specify which users or groups are authorized to allow connections according to the rule or enables you to specify users or groups for which the rule will be skipped.

> **NOTE** For additional information on all aspects of using the Windows Firewall with Advanced Security snap-in, refer to "Windows Firewall with Advanced Security Getting Started Guide" at http://technet.microsoft.com/en-us/library/cc748991(WS.10).aspx and "What's New in Windows Firewall with Advanced Security" at http://technet.microsoft.com/en-us/library/cc755158(WS.10).aspx.

Configuring Notifications

You can configure the Windows Firewall with Advanced Security snap-in to display notifications when a program is blocked from receiving inbound connections according to the default behavior of Windows Firewall. When you have selected this option and no existing block or allow rule applies to this program, a user is notified when a program is blocked from receiving inbound connections.

To configure this option:

Step 1. Right-click **Windows Firewall with Advanced Security** at the top of the left pane in the Windows Firewall with Advanced Security snap-in and then choose **Properties**.

This opens the dialog box previously shown in Figure 10-19.

Step 2. Select the tab that corresponds to the profile you want to configure and then click the **Customize** command button in the Settings section.

Step 3. From the Customize Settings for the (selected) Profile dialog box shown in Figure 10-26, select **Yes** under Display a Notification and then click **OK** twice.

Group Policy and Windows Firewall

Group Policy in Windows Firewall enables you to configure similar policies to those configured with the Windows Firewall with Advanced Security snap-in. Use the following procedure to configure Group Policy for Windows Firewall:

Step 1. Click **Start**, type `gpedit,` and then click `gpedit.msc` in the Programs list. If you receive a UAC prompt, click **Yes**.

Figure 10-26   Configuring Windows Firewall to display notifications.

Step 2.   Navigate to the **Computer Configuration\Windows Settings\ Security Settings\Windows Firewall with Advanced Security\ Windows Firewall with Advanced Security – Local Group Policy Object** node. The right pane displays the Windows Firewall with Advanced Security settings, as shown in Figure 10-27.

Figure 10-27   You can use Group Policy to configure Windows Firewall with Advanced Security options.

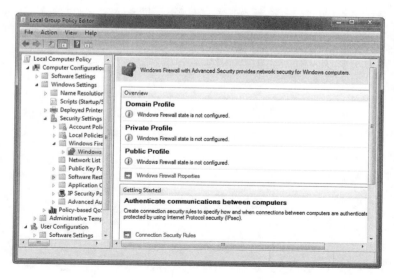

Step 3.   Scroll the right pane to select links for inbound rules, outbound rules, and connection security rules. These links open subnodes in the console tree.

Step 4.   Unlike the Group Policy with Windows Firewall snap-in, no default rules are present. To add rules, right-click in the details pane and select **New Rule**. This starts the New Rule Wizard, which enables you to create rules using the same options already discussed in this section.

After you have added firewall rules in Group Policy, you can filter the view according to profile (domain, private, or public) or by state (enabled or disabled).

TIP   A Group Policy feature first introduced in Windows Vista and continued in Windows 7 enables you to configure common policy settings for all user accounts on a computer used by more than one user. This includes Windows Firewall as discussed here, as well as UAC and all other policy settings. In addition, you can configure separate policies for administrators or nonadministrators. If necessary, you can even configure local group policies on a per-user basis.

Exam Preparation Tasks

Review All the Key Topics

Review the most important topics in the chapter, noted with the key topics icon in the outer margin of the page. Table 10-5 lists a reference of these key topics and the page numbers on which each is found.

Table 10-5 Key Topics for Chapter 10

Key Topic Element	Description	Page Number
Figure 10-2	Selecting network location types	345
List	Lists types of available network connections	346
Table 10-2	Describes available wireless networking protocols	354
List	Describes how to set up a wireless network connection	355
Figure 10-9	Manually connecting to a wireless network	355
Table 10-3	Describes available wireless security types	356
List	Shows how to perform basic Windows Firewall configuration	363
Figure 10-15	Customizing Windows Firewall settings for each network type	364
Figure 10-16	Allowing programs to communicate through Windows Firewall	365
List	Describes available Windows Firewall rule types	369
List	Describes types of available Windows Firewall profiles	369
Figure 10-21	Creating new firewall rules of different types	372
Figure 10-24	Shows different types of firewall connection security rules	374

Complete the Tables and Lists from Memory

Print a copy of Appendix C, "Memory Tables" (found on the CD), or at least the section for this chapter, and complete the tables and lists from memory. Appendix D, "Memory Tables Answer Key," also on the CD, includes completed tables and lists to check your work.

Definitions of Key Terms

Define the following key terms from this chapter, and check your answers in the glossary.

Internet Protocol Security (IPSec), Service Set Identifier (SSID), virtual private network (VPN), Windows Firewall, Wired Equivalent Privacy (WEP), Wi-Fi Protected Access (WPA), Network Address Translation (NAT), Internet Connection Sharing (ICS), wireless network profile, ad hoc network, firewall rule, wireless access point (WAP), firewall profile

This chapter covers the following subjects:

■ **Configuring Shared Resources:** Windows 7 provides two ways of sharing resources such as folders and printers on your computer so that users on other computers can access them. This section shows you how to configure your computer to share the public folder and how to set up a standard set of permissions and enable the sharing of individual folders and printers.

■ **Configuring Security Permissions:** Windows 7 enables you to secure files and folders on your computer so that you can determine who can access them and what level of access they are granted or denied. This section shows you how to configure these permissions and how they interact with shared folder permissions.

■ **Configuring Data Encryption:** Windows 7 enables you to encrypt files and folders using the Encrypting File System (EFS). This provides an additional layer of security in situations where an unauthorized user might be able to access confidential data by other means. This section shows you how to encrypt these items and ensure that authorized individuals can decrypt them.

CHAPTER 11

Configuring Access to Local and Shared Resources

One of the major reasons for connecting computers in a network is to share resources such as folders, files, and printers among them. Resources can exist on computers that are not connected to a network; these resources might need to be secured, protected, and accessed by different users as well. Windows 7 comes with a host of tools designed to secure and manage resources wherever they might be found.

In a modern workplace, workers require access to information created by others in the company and work they produce must be made available to their coworkers and superiors. Therefore, such resources must be shared so that others can access them. But lots of confidential information is also out there, and it must be protected from access by those who are not entitled to view it. At home, family members need to share things like photos, videos, and music. But parents have sensitive information, such as family finances, that must be protected as well.

From the earliest version of Windows NT right up to the present, Windows has had a system of access permissions in place that determine who has access to what and what can they do to it. More recent versions of Windows have enabled users to protect data even further with encryption methods that can help to prevent those who might have circumvented other access controls from viewing or modifying confidential information. This chapter looks at methods of sharing and protecting resources on computers and their networks.

"Do I Know This Already?" Quiz

The "Do I Know This Already?" quiz enables you to assess whether you should read this entire chapter or simply jump to the "Exam Preparation Tasks" section for review. If you are in doubt, read the entire chapter. Table 11-1 outlines the major headings in this chapter and the corresponding "Do I Know This Already?" quiz questions. You can find the answers in Appendix A, "Answers to the 'Do I Know This Already?' Quizzes."

Table 11-1   "Do I Know This Already?" Foundation Topics Section-to-Question Mapping

Foundations Topics Section	Questions Covered in This Section
Configuring Shared Resources	1–6
Configuring Security Permissions	7–13
Configuring Data Encryption	14–15

1. You want users at other computers on your network to be able to access folders located in the libraries of your Windows 7 computer without the need to perform additional sharing tasks, so you open the Advanced Sharing Settings dialog box. Which option should you enable?

   a. **File and printer sharing**

   b. **Public folder sharing**

   c. **Password protected sharing**

   d. **Media streaming**

2. Which of the following are true about hidden administrative shares? (Choose three.)

   a. These shares are suffixed with the $ symbol and are visible in any Explorer window.

   b. These shares are suffixed with the $ symbol and are visible only in the Shares node of the Computer Management snap-in.

   c. These shares are suffixed with the $ symbol and can be accessed from the Network and Sharing Center.

   d. You can access these shares by entering the UNC path to the share in the Run command.

   e. These shares are created by default when Windows 7 is first installed and cannot be removed.

3. Which of the following are valid permissions you can set for shared folders? (Choose three.)

   a. Full Control

   b. Modify

   c. Change

   d. Read & Execute

   e. Read

4. Which of the following best describes the function of a library on a Windows 7 computer?

   a. It is a set of virtual folders that is shared by default with other users of the same computer.

   b. It is a set of virtual folders that is shared by default with all users of Windows 7 computers on the network.

   c. It is a single folder into which you can copy documents to be shared with other users of the same computer.

   d. It is a single folder into which you can copy documents to be shared with all users of Windows 7 computers on the network.

5. You have shared your printer so that others can access it on the network. You want Kristin, who works at another computer on the network, to be able to pause, resume, restart, and cancel all documents, but you do not want her to be able to modify printer properties or permissions. What printer permission should you grant her user account?

   a. Print

   b. Manage this printer

   c. Manage documents

   d. Full control

6. You attempt to join your Windows 7 Professional computer to a homegroup, but the option for joining the homegroup is not available. Which of the following is a valid reason for the inability to join a homegroup?

   a. Your computer is joined to an Active Directory Domain Services (AD DS) domain.

   b. Your computer should be running the Home Premium version of Windows 7.

   c. The homegroup you want to join has no password configured.

   d. Your network location is set to Work.

7. You are configuring security permissions for a folder on your Windows 7 computer, and you want other users to be able to view files and run programs in the folder, but you do not want these users to be able to edit or delete files in the folder. What permission should you assign?

   a. Full Control

   b. Modify

   c. Change

   d. Read

   e. Read & Execute

8. You have granted a user named Bob the Read NTFS permission on a folder named Documents. Bob is also a member of the Managers group, which has Full Control NTFS permission on the Documents folder. What is Bob's effective permission on this folder?

   a. Full Control.

   b. Modify.

   c. Read.

   d. Bob does not have access to the folder.

9. You have granted a user named Jim the Read NTFS permission on a folder named Documents. Jim is also a member of the Interns group, which has been explicitly denied the Full Control NTFS permission on the Documents folder. What is Jim's effective permission on this folder?

   a. Full Control.

   b. Modify.

   c. Read.

   d. Jim does not have access to the folder.

10. You have granted a user named Carol the Full Control NTFS permission on a shared folder named Documents on your Windows 7 computer, which also has the Read shared folder permission granted to Everyone. Carol will be accessing this folder across the network on her computer. What is Carol's effective permission on this folder?

   a. Full Control.

   b. Modify.

   c. Read.

   d. Carol does not have access to the folder.

11. You have granted a user named Sharon the Full Control NTFS permission on a shared folder named Documents on your Windows 7 computer, which also has the Read shared folder permission granted to Everyone. Sharon will be accessing this folder on your computer. What is Sharon's effective permission on this folder?

   a. Full Control.

   b. Modify.

   c. Read.

   d. Sharon does not have access to the folder.

12. You have granted the Managers group Full Control NTFS permission on a folder named Accounts, which is located within the C:\Documents folder, which has the Modify NTFS permission applied to it. You copy the Accounts folder into the D:\Confidential folder, to which the Managers group has been granted the Read permission. A user named Ryan accesses the D:\Confidential\Accounts folder. What effective permission does Ryan have to this folder?

   a. Full Control.

   b. Modify.

   c. Read.

   d. Ryan does not have access to the folder.

13. You have granted the Managers group Full Control NTFS permission on the C:\Documents\Projects.doc file. You move this file to the C:\Confidential folder, to which the Managers group has been granted the Read permission. A user named Jennifer accesses the C:\Confidential\Accounts folder. What effective permission does Jennifer have to this folder?

   a. Full Control.

   b. Modify.

   c. Read.

   d. Jennifer does not have access to the folder.

14. You want to encrypt the Confidential folder. This folder is located on the D:\ volume, which is formatted with the FAT32 file system. You access the folder's Properties dialog box and click the **Advanced** button. But the option to encrypt the folder is not available. What do you need to do in order to encrypt this folder? (Choose two; each choice is a complete solution to the problem.)

   a. Format the D:\ volume with the NTFS file system.

   b. Use the Convert.exe utility to convert the D:\ volume with the NTFS file system.

   c. Move the Confidential folder to the C:\ volume, which is formatted with the NTFS file system.

   d. Decompress the Confidential folder.

15. You are the desktop support specialist for your company. A user named Peter has left the company, and you have deleted his user account. Later you realize that he had encrypted his Work folder on his Windows 7 computer and you must regain access to this folder. What should you do?

   a. Log on to Peter's computer with your user account and decrypt the file.

   b. Log on to Peter's computer with the default administrator account and decrypt the file.

   c. Recreate Peter's user account, log on with this account, and decrypt the file.

   d. You cannot access this folder; it is permanently lost.

Foundation Topics

Configuring Shared Resources

Sharing is a basic concept of networking in any computer environment. Simply put, sharing means making resources available on a network. Typically this means a folder on one computer is made accessible to other computers that are connected to the first computer by a network. The purpose of sharing folders is to give users access to network applications, data, and user home folders in one central location. You can use network application folders for configuring and upgrading software. This serves to centralize administration because applications are not maintained on client computers. Data folders enable users to store and access common files, and user home folders provide a place for users to store their own personal information. You can also share other resources such as printers so that users can print to a printer not directly attached to their computer.

You can share folders according to either or both of two file-sharing models:

- **Public Folder Sharing:** The simplest means of sharing folders, this model involves the use of a shared folder located within each of the Windows libraries. However, you cannot limit access to items in these public folders; you can only enable or disable public folder sharing for all libraries from the Advanced Sharing Settings dialog box in the Network and Sharing Center, previously introduced in Chapter 10, "Configuring Network and Firewall Settings."

- **Standard Folder Sharing:** Enables you to utilize a standard set of permissions that determine user access to files and folders across the network, in a similar fashion to that used in previous Windows versions. More secure than public folder sharing, you can enable or disable standard folder sharing on a per-computer basis.

Using the Network and Sharing Center to Configure File Sharing

As introduced in Chapter 10, the Network and Sharing Center enables you to perform actions related to sharing of resources on your computer with others on the network. Click **Advanced sharing settings** to obtain the Advanced sharing settings dialog box shown in Figure 11-1. Among other networking options, you can specify the following file-sharing options:

- **File and printer sharing:** Enables the Standard Folder Sharing model, thereby allowing others on the network to access shared files on your computer and print from printers attached to your computer.

- **Public folder sharing:** Enables the Public Folder sharing model, thereby allowing others on the network to access files in your Public folders of each Windows library (Documents, Pictures, Videos, and Music).

Figure 11-1 The Advanced sharing settings dialog box enables you to configure several global file and folder sharing settings.

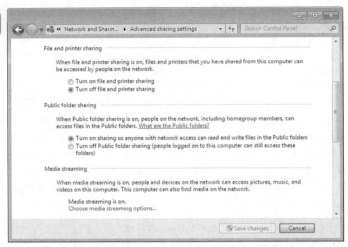

- **Password protected sharing:** Increases security by limiting access of shared files and printers to only those who have a user account and password on your computer.

- **Media streaming:** Enables others on the network to access shared music, pictures, and videos on the computer and enables your computer to access these types of shared information on the network.

Sharing Files, Folders, and Printers

Shared folders are folders on the local hard drive that other users on a network can connect to. For the exam, it is critical that you understand how to manage and troubleshoot connections to shared resources, how to create new shared resources, and how to set permissions on shared resources. The process that Windows 7 uses to share folders is that an administrator selects a folder, regardless of its location in the local folder hierarchy, and shares it through the Sharing tab of the folder's Properties dialog box. Shares can be managed through the Computer Management console snap-in.

Administrators might find that the Computer Management snap-in is helpful in file and folder security management. You can open Computer Management from within Administrative Tools, which is found in the System and Security category of Control Panel, or by right-clicking **Computer** and choosing **Manage**. To manage file and folder security, navigate to the Shared Folders node in the left pane. Double-click **Shares** to see the shared folders, as shown in Figure 11-2. The hidden administrative shares are followed by a dollar sign ($) and cannot be modified. From the remaining shared folders, select one to double-click and view the security settings on the folder.

Figure 11-2 You can view the shares on your computer from the Shared Folders node of the Computer Management snap-in.

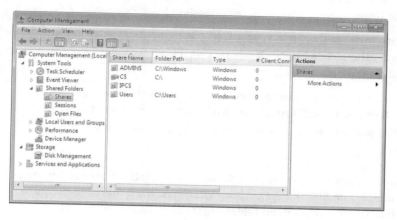

Aside from the Public folder (C:\Users\Public) and the default administrative shares, there are no folders that are automatically shared with the network. To share files with other users across the network, you must manually do so for each folder containing the files that you want to share. To share a folder with other network users, you can open any Explorer window and then use the following procedure:

Step 1.   In an Explorer window, navigate to the folder, right-click it, select **Share with,** and then click **Specific people**. The File Sharing dialog box opens, as shown in Figure 11-3.

Figure 11-3   The File Sharing dialog box enables you to choose those you want to share a file with.

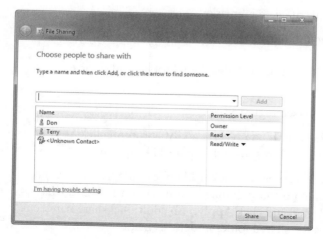

Step 2.   Type the name of a user with whom you want to share the folder and then click **Add**. The name appears in the Name list with a default permission level of Read.

Step 3.   To share with another user, repeat step 2 as many times as required. When finished, click **Share**. If you receive a User Account Control (UAC) prompt, click **Yes**.

Step 4.   To modify the permission assigned to a user, click that user and select either **Read** or **Read/Write**, as desired. To remove a user from the list, click the user and select **Remove**. When done, click **Share** to apply your changes.

To add people to the sharing list, repeat this procedure and select **Change Sharing Permissions** from the File Sharing dialog box. Then type the name of the required user and click **Add**. To remove a shared folder, right-click the folder and select **Share with > Nobody**.

Modifying Shared Folder Properties

Windows 7 shares folders to others with the Read permission, which means that the users you specify can view but not modify available files. The Advanced Sharing feature in Windows 7 enables you to modify these properties when necessary.

When granting full access to your local files to other users across a network, your computer becomes vulnerable to both unintentional and intentional attacks. Not only can the data simply be viewed for malicious purposes, such as corporate spying, it can be altered or destroyed on purpose or accidentally. For this reason alone, you should always grant the most restrictive permissions necessary for a network user to conduct work on those files. Granting just enough permission without being too lenient requires careful consideration. If you are too stringent, users can't get their jobs done. If you are too lenient, the data is at risk.

Use the following procedure to modify shared folder properties:

Step 1.   In an Explorer window, right-click the shared folder and choose **Properties**.

Step 2.   Click the **Sharing** tab (see Figure 11-4).

Step 3.   Click **Advanced Sharing.** If you receive a UAC prompt, click **Yes**. The Advanced Sharing dialog box shown in Figure 11-5 appears.

Step 4.   To add an additional share name, click **Add** under the Share name section. (If this command button is dimmed, ensure that the **Share this folder** option is selected and click **Apply**.) An additional share name enables users to access the shared folder under this name.

Figure 11-4 The Sharing tab of a folder's Properties dialog box enables you to modify shared folder properties.

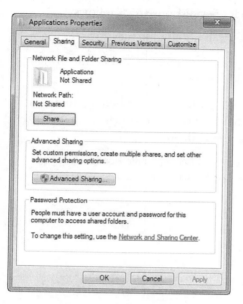

Figure 11-5 The Advanced Sharing dialog box enables you to configure several properties of shared folders.

Step 5. To change the maximum number of simultaneous users, type the required number or use the arrows to select a number. This number cannot be higher than 20 on a Windows 7 computer.

Step 6. To change shared folder permissions, click **Permissions**. This displays the Permissions for (*folder name*) dialog box shown in Figure 11-6. By default, the creator of the share receives Full Control permission and other users receive the Read permission. Click **Add** to add an additional user or group and then modify this user's permissions as desired. Click **OK** when finished. The available shared folder permissions are as follows:

— **Read:** Users are allowed to view but not modify files.

— **Change:** Users are allowed to view and modify files but not change the attributes of the shared folder itself.

— **Full Control:** Users are allowed to perform any task on the folder or its constituent files, including modifying their individual attributes and permissions used by others accessing them.

Figure 11-6   The Permissions for (folder name) dialog box enables you to configure permissions that apply to users accessing the folder across the network.

TIP   If you select permissions from the Deny column, you are explicitly denying access to that user or group. Such an explicit denial overrides any other permissions allowed to this group. Remember this fact if users experience problems accessing any shared resources across the network.

Step 7.   To modify settings that affect how users view and access shared folder contents, click **Caching** (as shown earlier in Figure 11-5) and configure the settings in the Offline Settings dialog box as required. We discuss these settings in Chapter 13, "Configuring Mobile Computing."

Step 8.   To set granular security permissions on the folder, click the **Security** tab and modify the settings in the dialog box shown in Figure 11-7 as required. These permissions apply to everyone accessing the folder either locally or across the network; more restrictive permissions configured here override those configured from the Sharing tab. We discuss these settings in detail later in this chapter.

Figure 11-7   The Security tab of a folder's Properties dialog box enables you to configure granular permissions for users and groups accessing the folder.

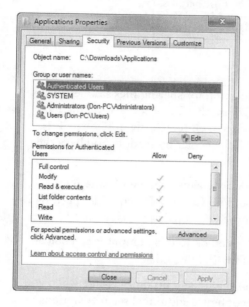

Step 9.   When you are finished, click **OK** to close the Properties dialog box. You can also click **Apply** to apply your changes and continue making modifications.

Table 11-2 summarizes the available shared folder options.

Table 11-2   Shared Folder Options in Windows 7

Option	Description
Share this folder	Click to start sharing the folder.
Share name	This is the folder name that remote users will employ to connect to the share. It will appear in a user's Explorer window, or the user can access it by typing **computername****sharename** at the Run command.
Comment	This information is optional and identifies the purpose or contents of the shared folder. The comment appears in the Map Network Drive dialog box when remote users are browsing shared folders on a server.
User limit	This sets the number of remote users who can connect to a shared resource simultaneously, reducing network traffic. For Windows 7, the limit is 20 (it was 10 on Windows Vista and older client versions of Windows).

Table 11-2 Shared Folder Options in Windows 7

Option	Description
Permissions	Permissions can be assigned to individual users, groups, or both. When a directory (folder) is shared, you can grant each user and each group one of the three types of permissions for the share and all of its subdirectories and files or choose to specifically deny them those permissions.
Caching	Enables offline access to a shared folder.

Use of the Public Folder for Sharing Files

Windows 7 provides the Public folder as a location for sharing files as a default. By default, public folder sharing is turned off. To use this folder for sharing files, access the Advanced Sharing Settings dialog box shown previously in Figure 11-1 and specify the desired option in the Public Folder Sharing section. You have the following options at `C:\Users\Public`:

- **Turn on sharing so anyone with network access can read and write files in the Public folders:** Shares the folder with Full Control shared folder permission. If password protected sharing is turned on, a password is required.

- **Turn off Public folder sharing (people logged on to this computer can still access these folders):** Disables sharing of the Public folder.

By default, this folder is located at `C:\Users\Public` and becomes visible when you select the Turn on sharing option. You can configure additional security options on this folder by accessing the Sharing tab of its Properties dialog box from this location and following the procedure outlined earlier in this section.

Mapping a Drive

Mapping a network drive means associating a shared folder on another computer with a drive letter available on your computer. This facilitates access to the shared folder. Proceed as follows to map a drive:

Step 1. Click **Start**, right-click **Network**, and then select **Map network drive**.

Step 2. In the Map Network Drive Wizard shown in Figure 11-8, select the drive letter to be assigned to the network connection for the shared resource. Drive letters being used by local devices are not displayed in the Drive list. You can assign up to 24 drive letters.

Step 3. Enter a UNC path to specify the network path to the computer and the shared folder. For example, to connect to the shared folder `Documents` on a computer named `Computer2`, type `\\Computer2\Documents`. You can also click **Browse** to find the shared folder and then select the desired path.

Figure 11-8   Mapping a network drive.

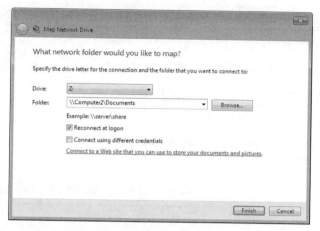

Step 4.   Select a connection option, as follows:

— **Reconnect At logon:** This option is enabled by default and creates permanent connections. It reconnects the user to the shared folder each time the user logs on unless the user manually disconnects from the resource.

— **Connect using different credentials:** Enables you to connect to a shared folder using a different user account. This option is useful if you are at another user's computer and need to connect to a resource to which the currently logged in user does not have the appropriate access.

Step 5.   Click **Finish**.

Command-Line Administration of Shared Folders

Windows 7 provides the `net share` command that you can use to manage shared resources. This is useful if you need to use scripts for automating administrative tasks. The syntax is as follows:

`net share` [*sharename*] [*/parameters*]

In this command, *sharename* is the name of the shared resource and */parameters* refers to any of a series of parameters that you can use with this command. Table 11-3 describes several of the more common parameters used with this command.

Table 11-3   Several Common Parameters Used with the **net share** Command

Parameter	Description
/users:*number*	Specifies the maximum number of users who can access the shared resource at the same time. Specify unlimited to allow the licensed limit of users.

Table 11-3   Several Common Parameters Used with the **net share** Command

Parameter	Description
/cache:*option*	Enables offline caching, according to the value of *option*:
	Documents: specifies automatic reintegration of documents
	Programs: specifies automatic reintegration of programs
	Manual: specifies manual reintegration
	None: advises the client that caching is inappropriate
/delete	Stops sharing the specified resource.
/remark:"*text*"	Adds a descriptive comment. Enclose the comment (*text*) in quotation marks.

Note that you can also use this command without any parameters to display information about all the shared resources on the local computer.

Password-Protected Sharing

When password-protected sharing is turned on, only users with a local user account and password on your computer can access shared files and printers, including the Public shared folder. To enable others to access shared resources, access the Password protected sharing section of the Advanced Sharing Settings dialog box and select the **Turn off password protected sharing** radio button. Then click **Save changes**.

Media Streaming

Turning media streaming on enable users and devices on the network to access music, pictures, and videos in Windows Media Player and from devices attached to the computer, such as digital cameras, personal data assistants (PDAs), cellular phones, and so on. In addition, the computer can locate these types of shared files on the network. To turn media sharing on, access the Media streaming section of the Advanced Sharing Settings dialog box and click **Choose media streaming options**. In the Choose media streaming options for computers and devices dialog box that appears, click **Turn on media streaming**. You can then customize media streaming options including selecting a media library and choosing what types of media will be accessible according to star ratings and parental control settings.

NOTE   For further information on media streaming, consult the Windows 7 Help and Support Center.

Folder Virtualization

Windows 7 introduces the concept of virtualized folders. In Windows 7, a *library* is a set of virtual folders that is shared by default with other users of the computer. By default, Windows 7 includes four libraries (Documents, Pictures, Music, and Videos), which you can access from the Start menu or from the task list on the left side of any Explorer window. Click **Libraries** to view the libraries on your computer, as shown in Figure 11-9. You can also see them when you open an Explorer window and navigate to `C:\Users\Public`. The subfolders you see here are actually pointers to the folder locations on the computer. You can also think of them as the results of search queries. From the Libraries folder, you can create a new library by clicking **New library** in the toolbar and providing a name for your new library.

Figure 11-9   Windows 7 creates these four default libraries.

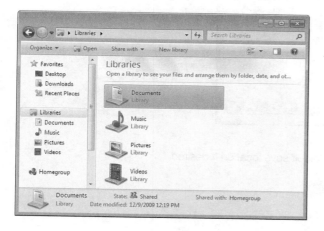

Each library contains a user-based subfolder, located by default at `C:\Users\%username%`, as well as a public subfolder from `C:\Users\Public` (see Figure 11-10). You can add additional folders by clicking the **Add** button and navigating to the desired folder; this can even include shared folders located on other computers on the network. You can also add folders to a library from any Explorer window by selecting the folder and clicking the **Add to Library** option in the Explorer toolbar.

To access additional properties of each library, right-click it from the Libraries folder and choose **Properties**. For example, Figure 11-11 shows the Documents Properties window. The check mark indicates the default save location used by programs such as Microsoft Office; to change this location, select the desired location and click the **Set save location** command button. You can add additional folders to the library by clicking **Include a folder** and selecting the desired folder, similar to that discussed in the previous paragraph. To remove a folder from the

library, select it and click **Remove**. To remove all added folders from the library
and reset it to its default settings, click the **Restore Defaults** button.

Figure 11-10   Each library by default contains a user subfolder and a public subfolder.

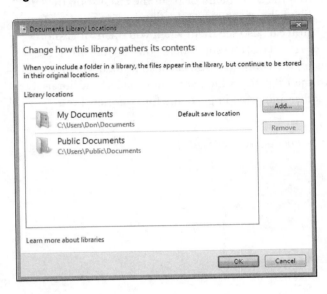

Figure 11-11   You can change the default save location if desired.

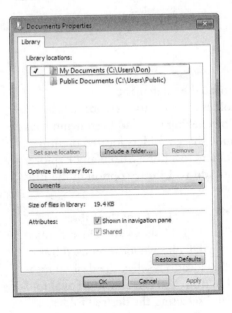

Sharing Printers

If you have turned on file and printer sharing from the Advanced Sharing Settings dialog box, you can share any printer attached to your computer so that others on the network can print documents to it. Use the following steps to share a printer:

Step 1. Click **Start > Devices and Printers**.

Step 2. In the Devices and Printers Control Panel applet, right-click your printer and choose **Printer properties**.

Step 3. Click the **Sharing** tab to display the dialog box shown in Figure 11-12.

Figure 11-12 Sharing a printer.

Step 4. Click **Share this printer** and either accept the share name provided or type a different name. This name identifies the printer to users on other computers.

Step 5. If users are running older Windows versions, click **Additional Drivers** to install drivers for these Windows versions. Select the required drivers from the Additional Drivers dialog box that appears and then click **OK**.

As with shared folders, you can assign share permissions for printers. Select the **Security** tab of the printer's Properties dialog box to configure the options shown in Figure 11-13. By default, the Everyone group receives the Print permission and the Administrators group receives the Print, Manage this printer, and Manage documents permissions. Table 11-4 describes the printer permissions, including Special permissions.

Figure 11-13   Configuring permissions for shared printers.

Table 11-4   Printer Permissions in Windows 7

Parameter	Description
Print	Users can connect to a given printer to print documents and control print job settings for their own documents only. This can include pausing, deleting, and restarting only their own documents in the print queue as needed.
Manage this printer	Users can assign forms to paper trays and set a separator page. In addition, they can change the printing order of documents in the queue; pause, resume, and purge the printer; change printer properties; and actually delete the printer itself or change printer permissions. Users with this permission can also perform all tasks related to the Manage documents permission.
Manage documents	Users can pause, resume, restart, and cancel all documents. They can also set the notification level for finished print jobs and set priority levels and specific printing times for documents to print.
Special permissions	Enables the assignment of granular permissions, including Read permissions, Change permissions, and Take ownership. To configure special permissions, click the **Advanced** button.

NOTE   For more information on configuring printer permissions, refer to "Assigning printer permissions" at http://technet.microsoft.com/en-us/library/cc773372(WS.10).aspx.

Configuring Homegroup Settings

New to Windows 7 is the concept of a homegroup, which is a small group of Windows 7 computers connected together in a home or small office network that you have designated in the Network and Sharing Center as a home network. Computers running any edition of Windows 7 can join a homegroup, but you must have the Home Premium, Professional, or Ultimate edition of Windows 7 to create a homegroup. Computers running Windows Vista or earlier cannot join a homegroup. To create or join a homegroup, your computer's network setting (discussed in Chapter 10) must be set to **Home**.

Creating a HomeGroup

You can create a homegroup from the HomeGroup applet, which is accessed from the Network and Internet category of Control Panel by clicking **HomeGroup**. You can also access this applet by clicking **Start** and typing `homegroup` in the Search field or by clicking **HomeGroup** from the Network and Sharing Center. From the Share with other home computers running Windows 7 dialog box shown in Figure 11-14, click **Create a homegroup**. As shown in Figure 11-15, the Create a Homegroup Wizard enables you to select the type of resources you want to share with other computers. After making your selections and clicking **Next**, the wizard provides you with a password that you can use to add other computers to the homegroup (see Figure 11-16). Make note of this password so that you can join other computers to the homegroup and then click **Finish**.

Figure 11-14   If your computer does not belong to a homegroup, you are provided with the option to create one.

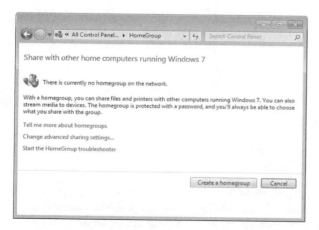

Joining a Homegroup

After you have created a homegroup, when you move to another Windows 7 computer on the network, the computer recognizes the homegroup and the Share with other home computers running Windows 7 dialog box informs you of this fact (see Figure 11-17). Click **Join now** to join the homegroup, select the libraries you want to share, and then type the homegroup password when requested.

Figure 11-15   Determining the type of resources you want to share on the homegroup.

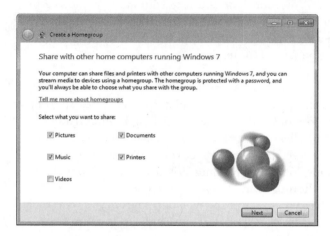

Figure 11-16   You are provided with a password that enables you to join other computers to the homegroup.

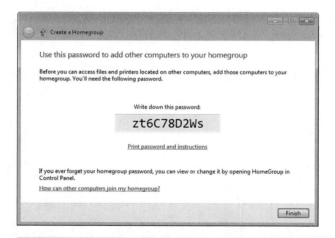

NOTE   If your computer is joined to a domain, you can still join a homegroup. However, you cannot share libraries or printers to the homegroup. This feature enables you to bring a portable computer home from work and access shared resources on your home network. Furthermore, it is possible to use Group Policy to prevent domain computers from being joined to a homegroup.

Figure 11-17   If a homegroup exists on the network, you are prompted to join it.

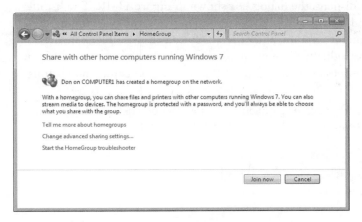

Modifying Homegroup Settings

After you've joined a homegroup, you receive the Change homegroup settings dialog box shown in Figure 11-18 when you access the HomeGroup option in the Control Panel Network and Internet category. From here, you can change the types of libraries and printers that are shared with other homegroup computers. You can also perform any of the other self-explanatory actions shown in Figure 11-18 under Other homegroup actions. Selecting the **Change advanced sharing settings** option takes you to the Advanced sharing settings dialog box previously shown in Figure 11-1.

Figure 11-18   The Change homegroup settings dialog box enables you to change which items you share on the homegroup or perform other configuration actions.

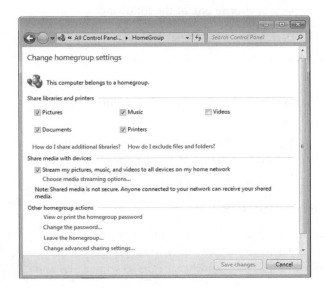

Selecting the **Stream my pictures, music, and videos to all devices on my home network** option displays the dialog box shown in Figure 11-19. The list includes all computers and other media devices found on the network including media players, electronic picture frames, and others. You can allow or block media access to each device individually by selecting the drop-down lists provided, or you can allow or block all devices by choosing from the appropriate command buttons provided.

Figure 11-19 The Choose media streaming options for computers and devices dialog box enables you to choose which devices are allowed to access shared media.

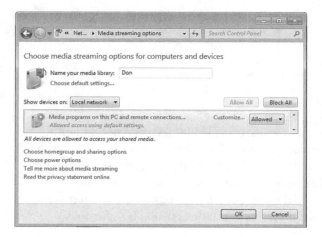

You can also modify the file-sharing options for subfolders located within any of your shared libraries. To do this, navigate to the desired library and select the folder. From the Share with menu option, choose one of the following:

- **Nobody:** Prevents all sharing of the selected file or folder.

- **Homegroup (Read):** Shares the file or folder with Read permission to all users in the homegroup.

- **Homegroup (Read/Write):** Shares the file or folder with Full Control permission to all users in the homegroup.

- **Specific people:** Displays the Choose people to share with dialog box shown in Figure 11-20. Type the name of the user with whom you want to share the folder and then click **Add**.

Configuring Security Permissions

The previous section introduced you to sharing folders and the permissions you can attach to shared folders. These permissions apply only when you access the folders across the network. Windows 7 provides another means to secure files and folders on the local computer. The New Technology File System (NTFS) that has existed since the early days of Windows NT enables you to secure and manage access to resources on both a network level and on a local level. These NTFS file and folder permissions are also known as *security permissions*; they can apply to both files and folders, and they apply on your computer to files and folders whether a folder is shared or not shared at all. Keep in mind, however, that although Windows 7 supports FAT and FAT32 partitions, NTFS permissions apply only on partitions that are formatted using NTFS. Because you are already familiar with shared folder permissions, we will use that as a jumping-off point to describe NTFS permissions.

Figure 11-20   You can use the Choose people to share with dialog box to share a file or folder with only specific individuals.

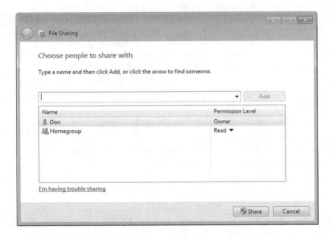

NTFS File and Folder Permissions

Like the shared permissions, which you can assign to users and groups, NTFS permissions for a folder control how users access a folder. Folders hold files. You access a folder to find out what it contains or to create, add, or delete its files. NTFS folder permissions are designed to control this kind of activity. If no explicit permissions are assigned to a folder, a user cannot access that folder at all.

Windows stores an access control list (ACL) with every file and folder on an NTFS partition. The ACL is a list of users and groups that have been granted access for a particular file or folder, as well as the types of access that the users and groups have been granted. Collectively, these kinds of entries in the ACL are called *access control entries* (*ACEs*). If you think of the ACL as a list, it isn't hard to conceive that a list contains entries of various kinds. Windows uses the ACL to determine the level of access a user should be granted when he attempts to access a file or folder.

NTFS file permissions control what users can do with files within a folder. More specifically, the permissions control how users can alter or access the data that files contain. Table 11-5 describes the standard NTFS file permissions in detail.

Table 11-5   NTFS File and Folder Permissions

Permission	What a User Can Do on a Folder	What a User Can Do on a File
Full control	Change permissions, take ownership, and delete subfolders and files. All other actions allowed by the permissions listed in this table are also possible.	Change permissions, take ownership, and perform all other actions allowed by the permissions listed in this table.
Modify	Delete the folder as well as grant that user the Read permission and the List Folder Contents permission.	Modify a file's contents and delete the file as well as perform all actions allowed by the Write permission and the Read and Execute permission.
Read & execute	Run files and display file attributes, owner, and permissions.	Run application files and display file attributes, owner, and permissions.
List folder contents	List a folder's contents, that is, its files and subfolders.	(n/a)
Read	Display filenames, subfolder names, owner, permissions, and file attributes (Read Only, Hidden, Archive, and System).	Display data, file attributes, owner, and permissions.
Write	Create new folders and files, change a folder's attributes, and display owner and permissions.	Write changes to the file, change its attributes, and display owner and permissions.

Applying NTFS Permissions

It is simple to apply NTFS permissions, as the following procedure shows:

Step 1.   Right-click a folder or file and choose **Properties**.

Step 2.   Select the **Security** tab of the Properties dialog box. Also known as the ACL Editor, the Security tab enables you to edit the NTFS permissions for a folder or file (see Figure 11-21).

Figure 11-21   The Security tab of a file or folder's Properties dialog box displays its security permissions.

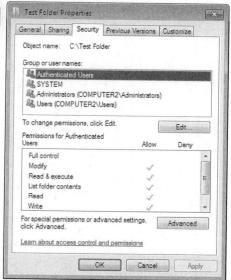

Step 3.   Click **Edit** to display the dialog box shown in Figure 11-22. You can configure the options described in Table 11-6.

Table 11-6   Security Tab Options

Option	Description
Group or user names	Start by selecting the user account or group for which you want to change permissions or that you want to remove from the permissions list.
Permissions for Authenticated Users	Select the **Allow** check box to allow a permission. Select the **Deny** check box to deny a permission.
Add	Click **Add** to open the Select Users or Groups dialog box to select user accounts and groups to add to the Name list.
Remove	Click **Remove** to remove the selected user account or group and the associated permissions for the file or folder.

Step 4.   When finished, click **OK** to return to the Security tab shown previously in Figure 11-21.

Figure 11-22   The Permissions for (file/folder name) dialog box enables you to configure security permissions.

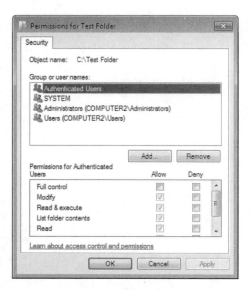

Step 5.   If you need to configure special permissions or access advanced settings, click **Advanced**. The next section discusses these permissions.

NOTE   You can also configure NTFS permissions from the command line by using the `icacls.exe` utility. This utility is useful for scripting permissions configuration. For more information on this utility, refer to "Icacls" at http://technet.microsoft.com/en-us/library/cc753525(WS.10).aspx.

Specifying Advanced Permissions

For the most part, the standard NTFS permissions are suitable for managing user access to resources. There are occasions where a more specialized application of security and permissions is appropriate. To configure a more specific level of access, you can use NTFS special access permissions. It isn't a secret, but it is not obvious in the Windows 7 interface that the NTFS standard permissions are actually combinations of the special access permissions. For example, the standard Read permission is comprised of the List folder/read data, Read attributes, Read extended attributes, and Read permissions special access permissions.

In general, you will use only the standard NTFS permissions already described. In exceptional cases, you might need to fine-tune the permissions further, and this is where the special access NTFS permissions come in. To configure special access permissions, use the following steps:

Step 1.   From the Security tab of the appropriate file or folder, click **Advanced** to access the Advanced Security Settings dialog box.

Step 2. Click **Change Permissions** to display the Advanced Security Settings dialog box shown in Figure 11-23.

Figure 11-23   The Advanced Security Settings dialog box displays information about the permissions currently assigned to the file or folder and enables you to add or edit permissions.

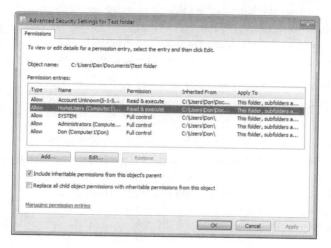

Step 3. Select the user or group account for which you want to apply special access permissions, and then click **Edit** to display the Permission Entry dialog box shown in Figure 11-24.

Figure 11-24   The Permission Entry dialog box enables you to configure advanced permissions.

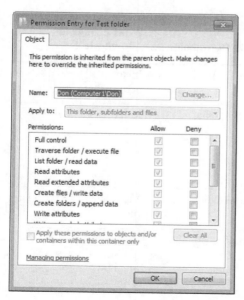

Step 4. Configure the following options as required:

— **Name:** The user account or group name appears in this dialog box, but you can select a different one in the scroll box by clicking the **Change** button.

— **Apply to:** You can adjust the level in the folder hierarchy at which the special permissions apply and are inherited. When permissions are not being inherited from a parent folder, you can choose between This folder, subfolders and files or any one or two of these components.

— **Permissions:** You can configure any one or more of the special access permissions by selecting their corresponding Allow or Deny check boxes.

— **Apply these permissions to objects and/or containers within this container only:** Here you can adjust a particular folder's properties so that files and subfolders inherit their permissions from the folder you are working on. Selecting this option propagates the special access permissions to files within and folders below your current location in a folder hierarchy.

— **Clear All:** You can clear all selected permissions.

Step 5. When finished, click **OK**.

Table 11-7 describes the special access file and folder permissions that you can configure from this location.

Table 11-7 NTFS Special Access Permissions

Folder Permission	What a User Is Allowed to Do	File Permission	What a User Is Allowed to Do
Full control	Includes all special access permissions.	Full control	Includes all special access permissions.
Traverse folder	Navigate through folders that a user normally can't access in order to reach files or folders that the user does have permission to access.	Execute file	Run executable files.
List folder	View files or subfolders.	Read data	View data in a particular file.
Read attributes	View folder attributes. These attributes are defined by NTFS.	Read attributes	View file attributes. These attributes are defined by NTFS.

Table 11-7   NTFS Special Access Permissions

Folder Permission	What a User Is Allowed to Do	File Permission	What a User Is Allowed to Do
Read extended attributes	View extended folder attributes. Extended attributes are defined by software and may vary.	Read extended attributes	View extended file attributes. Extended attributes are defined by software and may vary.
Create files	Create files within a folder.	Write data	Write changes to or overwrite a file.
Create folders	Create subfolders.	Append data	Make changes to the end of a file by appending data. Does not allow changing, deleting, or overwriting existing data.
Write attributes	Change the attributes of a folder, such as read-only or hidden. Attributes are defined by NTFS.	Write attributes	Change the attributes of a file, such as read only or hidden. Attributes are defined by NTFS.
Write extended attributes	Change the extended attributes of a folder. Extended attributes are defined by programs and may vary.	Write extended attributes	Change the extended attributes of a file. Extended attributes are defined by programs and may vary.
Delete subfolders and files	Delete subfolders, even if the Delete permission has not been granted on the subfolder.	Delete subfolders and files	Delete files, even if the Delete permission has not been granted on the file.
Delete	Delete a folder or subfolder.	Delete	Delete a file.
Read permissions	Read permissions for a folder, such as Full Control, Read, and Write.	Read permissions	Read permissions for a file, such as Full Control, Read, and Write.
Change permissions	Change permissions for a folder, such as Full Control, Read, and Write.	Change permissions	Change permissions for a file, such as Full Control, Read, and Write.
Take ownership	Take ownership of a folder.	Take ownership	Take ownership of a file.

Taking ownership is a very special type of access permission. In Windows 7, each NTFS folder and file has an owner. Whoever creates a file or folder automatically becomes the owner and, by default, has Full Control permissions on that file or folder. If that person is a member of the Administrators group, the Administrators group becomes the owner. The owner possesses the ability to apply and change permissions on a folder or file that he or she owns, even if the ACL does not explicitly grant them that ability. This does make it possible for the owner of a particular file or folder to deny Administrators access to a resource. But an administrator can exercise the optional right to take ownership of any resource to gain access to it, if this becomes necessary.

In Table 11-5, which describes the standard access permissions, you might have noticed that a standard permission such as Modify enables a user to do more than one thing to a file or folder. A special-access permission typically enables a user to do one thing only. All special permissions are encompassed within the standard permissions.

NTFS Permissions Inheritance

All NTFS permissions are inherited—that is, they pass down through the folder hierarchy from parent to child. Permissions assigned to a parent folder are inherited by all the files in that folder and by the subfolders contained in the parent folder as well. Unless you specifically stop the process of files and folders inheriting permissions from their parent folder, any existing files and subfolders and any new files and subfolders created within this tree of folders will inherit their permissions from the original parent folder. To use the fancy term, permissions are *propagated* all the way down the tree.

Windows 7 lets you modify this permissions inheritance sequence if necessary. To check whether permissions are being inherited and to remove permissions inheritance, use the following procedure:

Step 1. From the Advanced Security Settings dialog box previously shown in Figure 11-23, clear the check box labeled **Include inheritable permissions from this object's parent**.

Step 2. You receive the dialog box shown in Figure 11-25, which prompts you to specify one of the following permissions inheritance options:

— **Add:** Select **Add** to add existing inherited permissions assigned for the parent folder to the subfolder or file. This action also prevents subsequent permissions inheritance from the parent folder.

— **Remove:** Select **Remove** to remove existing inherited permissions assigned for the parent folder to the subfolder or file. Only permissions that you explicitly assign to the file or folder will apply.

Figure 11-25   If you choose to prevent permissions from being inherited, you will need to decide how they are going to be applied.

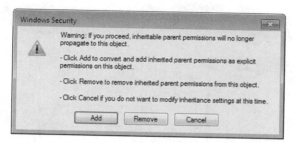

— **Cancel:** Select **Cancel** to abort the operation and restore the Allow inheritable permissions from parent to propagate to this object check box.

Step 3.   You are returned to the Advanced Security Settings dialog box. Click **OK** or **Apply** to apply your changes.

Taking Ownership of Files and Folders

In certain cases, you might need to grant the special Take Ownership permission to a user account. This can be valuable if a user is taking over responsibilities and resources from another individual. A user with the Full Control NTFS permission or the Take Ownership special permission can take ownership of a file or folder from the folder's Properties dialog box, as follows:

Step 1.   From the Security tab of the folder's Properties dialog box previously shown in Figure 11-21, click **Advanced**, and then click the **Owner** tab to display the dialog box shown in Figure 11-26.

Figure 11-26   The Owner tab of the Advanced Security Settings dialog box enables you to take ownership of a file or folder.

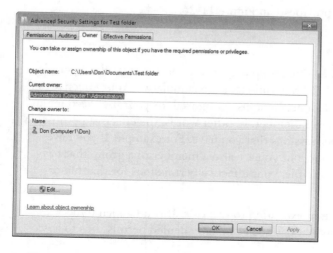

Step 2. Click **Edit** to display the Advanced Security Settings dialog box shown in Figure 11-27.

Figure 11-27   This dialog box enables you to select a new owner for the desired file or folder.

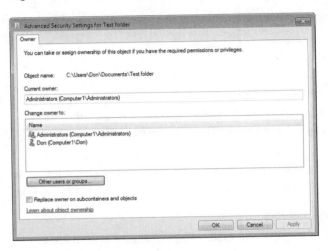

Step 3. Select the username of the desired owner from the list displayed. If the desired name does not appear, click **Other users or groups** to display the Select User or Group dialog box, from which you can select another user or group.

Step 4. Click **OK**. You are informed that if you have just taken ownership, you will need to close and reopen the object's Properties dialog box to view or change permissions.

Step 5. Click **OK** to accept this message, and then click **OK** again to close the dialog box shown previously in Figure 11-26.

Effective Permissions

Users who belong to more than one group may receive different levels of permission. Both shared folder and NTFS permissions are cumulative. Your effective permissions are a combination of all permissions configured for your user account and for the groups of which you are a member. In other words, the effective permission is the least restrictive of all permissions that you have. For example, if you have Read permissions for a given file, but you are also a member of a group that has Modify permissions for the same file, your effective permissions for that file or folder would be Modify.

However, there is one important exception to this rule. If you happen to be a member of yet another group that has been explicitly denied permissions to a resource (the permission has been selected in the Deny column), your effective permissions will not allow you to access that resource at all. Explicit denial of permission always overrides any allowed permissions.

Putting the two types of permissions together, the rules for determining effective permissions are simple:

- At either the shared folder or NTFS permissions level by itself, if a user receives permissions by virtue of membership in one or more groups, the *least restrictive* permission is the effective permission. For example, if a user has Read permission assigned to his user account and Full Control permission by virtue of membership in a group, he receives Full Control permission on this item.

- If the user is accessing a shared folder over the network and has both shared folder and NTFS permissions applied to it, the *most restrictive* permission is the effective permission. For example, if a user has Full Control NTFS permission on a folder but accesses it across the network where she has Read shared folder permission, her effective permission is Read.

- If the user is accessing a shared folder on the computer where it exists, shared folder permissions do not apply. In the previous example, this user would receive Full Control permission when accessing the shared folder locally.

- If the user has an explicit denial of permission at either the shared folder or NTFS level, he is denied access to the object, regardless of any other permissions he might have to this object.

TIP   It is important to remember that specifically denying permission to a file within a folder overrides all other file and folder permissions configured for a user or for a group that might contain that user's account. There is no real top-down or bottom-up factor to consider when it comes to denying permissions. If a user is a member of a group that has been denied a permission to a file or folder, or if a user's individual account has been denied a permission to a particular resource, that is what counts. If you are denied access to a folder, it does not matter what permissions are attached to a file inside the folder because you cannot get to it.

Viewing a User's Effective Permissions

Windows 7 enables you to view a user or group's effective permissions. This is most useful in untangling a complicated web of permissions received by a user who is a member of several groups. Use the following procedure:

Step 1.   From the Security tab of the folder's Properties dialog box previously shown in Figure 11-21, click **Advanced**, and then click the **Effective Permissions** tab to display the dialog box shown in Figure 11-28.

Figure 11-28   You can view a user or group's effective permissions to a resource from the Effective Permissions tab of the Advanced Security Settings dialog box.

Step 2.   Click **Select** to display the Select User or Group dialog box.

Step 3.   Select the appropriate user or group and then click **OK**.

Step 4.   You are returned to the Effective Permissions tab, which now displays the effective permissions for the user or group.

Copying and Moving Files and Folders

When you copy or move a file or folder that is configured with NTFS permissions, those NTFS permissions can change. The action that occurs depends on whether you are copying the file or folder or whether you are moving the file or folder.

Copying Files and Folders with NTFS Permissions

When you copy a file or folder that is configured with NTFS permissions, those NTFS permissions can change. If you are copying files and folders to a place where the NTFS permissions match exactly, the permissions will stay the same. There are no exceptions to this rule. The potential for change is always there, however, when you copy files and folders with NTFS permissions. To ensure that NTFS permissions are applied effectively on your computer, you will need to keep in mind how copying can change NTFS permissions. There are essentially three possible outcomes as outlined in Table 11-8.

Table 11-8   The Effect of Copying Files or Folders on Their NTFS Permissions

Action	Result
Copy a file or folder within the same partition	The copy inherits the NTFS permissions of the destination folder.

Table 11-8   The Effect of Copying Files or Folders on Their NTFS Permissions

Action	Result
Copy a file or folder from one NTFS partition to another NTFS partition	The copy inherits the NTFS permissions of the destination folder.
Copy a file or folder from an NTFS partition to a FAT or FAT32 partition	The copy of a file or folder loses its NTFS permissions completely. NTFS permissions cannot apply anywhere else but on an NTFS partition.

To copy files from an NTFS partition, you need to have at least the Read permission for the originating folder. To complete the copy operation so that the copied versions are written to disk, you need to have at least the Write permission for the destination folder.

CAUTION   A close look at Table 11-8 should alert you to the fact that copying a file or folder from an NTFS partition to a FAT or FAT32 partition will strip the file or folder of its NTFS permissions and make it fully available to all users at the local computer.

Moving Files and Folders with NTFS Permissions

Moving files with NTFS permissions might change those permissions. Depending on the circumstances, especially the destination of the move, the permissions might change or they might stay the same. As outlined in Table 11-9, there are also three possible outcomes.

Table 11-9   The Effect of Moving Files or Folders on Their NTFS Permissions

Action	Result
Move a file or folder within the same partition	The file or folder retains its NTFS permissions, regardless of the permissions that exist for the destination folder.
Move a file or folder from one NTFS partition to another NTFS partition	The file or folder inherits the NTFS permissions of the destination folder.
Move a file or folder from an NTFS partition to a FAT or FAT32 partition	The file or folder loses its NTFS permissions completely. NTFS permissions cannot apply anywhere else but on an NTFS partition.

To move files within an NTFS partition or between two NTFS partitions, you need to have at least the Modify permission for the originating folder. To complete the move operation so that the moved versions are written to disk, you need to have at least the Write permission for the destination folder. The Modify permission is required at the source so that source files and folders can be deleted after the files or folders are safely relocated to their new home.

> **NOTE**   When you have had time to think about how copying and moving files and folders affects NTFS permissions, there is an easy way to remember how all these possible outcomes will work. One simple sentence can serve to summarize what is going on: "Moving within retains." The only sure way to retain existing NTFS permissions during a copy or move operation is to move files within a single NTFS partition. All the other options hold a very real potential for altering NTFS permissions.

Using the Mouse to Copy or Move Objects from One Location to Another

Keep in mind the following facts about dragging objects between locations:

- When you use the mouse to drag an object from one folder to another on the *same* partition, you are *moving* that object.

- If you drag the object to a folder on *another* partition, you are *copying* that object.

- If you hold down the Ctrl key while dragging, you are *copying* the object, whether it is to the same or another partition.

- You can also right-drag the object. In this case, when you release the mouse button, you receive choices of copying the object, moving it, or creating a shortcut to the object in its original location.

Practical Guidelines on Sharing and Securing Folders

When you share folders, it is important to control how they are used. To control the use of shared folders, you should be aware of how shares are applied in Windows 7. The following facts should be kept in mind:

- **Denying permissions overrides all other shared permissions that may be applied to a folder:** If a user is part of a group that is denied permission to access a particular resource, that user will not be able to access that resource, even if you grant her user account access to the share.

- **Multiple permissions accumulate:** You may be a member of multiple groups, each with a different level of permissions for a particular shared resource. Your effective permissions are a combination of all permissions configured for your user account and the groups of which you are a member. As a user, you may have Read permissions for a folder. You may be a member of a group with Change permissions for the same folder. Your effective permissions for that folder would be Change. If you happen to be made a member of yet another group that has been denied permissions to a folder, your effective permissions will not allow you to access that folder at all. That is the one important exception to this rule.

- **Copying or moving a folder alters the shared permissions associated with that folder:** When you copy a shared folder, the original shared folder is still shared, but the copied folder is not. When you move a shared folder to a new location anywhere, that folder is no longer shared by anyone.

- **When you share a folder that is located on an NTFS volume, you will still need to consider the NTFS permissions that apply to that folder:** There might already be NTFS permissions in place on a folder that you are in the process of sharing. You will need to consider how your NTFS and shared folder permissions combine. (See the next item.) If there aren't any NTFS permissions on that folder, you might have to configure NTFS permissions for your shared folder or it is possible that no one will be able to access it.

- **When shared folder and NTFS file and folder permissions combine, the most restrictive permissions apply:** When both NTFS and shared folder permissions apply to the same folder, the more restrictive permission is the effective permission for that folder. Do not lose sight of the fact, however, that shared folder permissions have no effect on users that are logged in to the computer locally.

- **When a folder resides on an NTFS volume:** You will need at least the NTFS Read permission to be able to share that folder at all.

Configuring Data Encryption

You often hear news reports that mention thefts of laptop computers containing valuable data. In one such case, a computer stolen from a doctor's car in Toronto contained the records of thousands of patients, exposing them to misuse and potential identity theft. The computer was protected with a password, but the data was not encrypted. Windows 7 includes the following two systems of data encryption, designed to protect data not only on your laptop when you are in a place such as an airport or hotel where a thief can grab it when you're momentarily distracted, but also at any other place where an unauthorized individual might attempt to either connect to it across the network or physically access it.

- Introduced with Windows Vista, BitLocker Drive Encryption encrypts a computer's entire system partition. We take a look at BitLocker in Chapter 13, "Configuring Mobile Computing."

- First introduced with Windows 2000 and refined with each successive iteration of Windows, the Encrypting File System (EFS) can be used to encrypt files and folders on any partition that is formatted with the NTFS file system. The remainder of this chapter will be devoted to EFS.

EFS enables users to encrypt files and folders on any partition that is formatted with the NTFS file system. The encryption attribute on a file or folder can be toggled the same as any other file attribute. When you set the encryption attribute on a folder, all its contents—whether subfolders or files—are also encrypted.

The encryption attribute, when assigned to a folder, affects files the same way that the compression attribute does when a file is moved or copied. Files copied into the encrypted folder become encrypted. Files moved into the encrypted folder retain their former encryption attribute, whether or not they were encrypted. When you move or copy a file to a file system that does not support EFS, such as FAT or FAT32, the file is automatically decrypted.

For more information on the technology behind EFS, refer to "How EFS Works" at http://technet.microsoft.com/en-us/library/cc962103.aspx.

TIP   Remember that the file system must be set to NTFS if you want to use EFS, and no file can be both encrypted and compressed at the same time. On the exam, you might be presented with a scenario where a user is unable to use EFS or file compression on a FAT32 volume; the correct answer to such a problem is to convert the file system to NTFS, as described in the section "Preparing a Disk for EFS."

Encrypting File System Basics

EFS uses a form of public key cryptography, which utilizes a public and private key pair. The public key or digital certificate is freely available to anyone, whereas the private key is retained and guarded by the user to which the key pair is issued. The public key is used to encrypt data, and the private key decrypts the data that was encrypted with the corresponding public key. The key pair is created at the first time a user encrypts a file or folder using EFS. When another user attempts to open the file, that user is unable to do so. Therefore, EFS is suitable for data that a user wants to maintain as private but not for files that are shared.

Windows 7 has the capability to encrypt files directly on any NTFS volume. This ensures that no other user can use the encrypted data. Encryption and decryption of a file or folder are performed in the object's Properties dialog box. Administrators should be aware of the rules to put into practice to manage EFS on a network:

- Only use NTFS as the file system for all workstation and server volumes.

- Keep a copy of each user's certificate and private key on a floppy disk or other removable media.

- Remove the user's private key from the computer except when the user is actually using it.

- When users routinely save documents only to their Documents folder, make certain their documents are encrypted by having each user encrypt his own Documents folder.

- Use two recovery agent user accounts that are reserved solely for that purpose for each AD DS organizational unit (OU) if computers participate in a domain. Assign the recovery agent certificates to these accounts.

- Archive all recovery agent user account information, recovery certificates, and private keys, even if obsolete.

- When planning a network installation, keep in mind that EFS does take up additional processing overhead; plan to incorporate additional CPU processing power in your plans.

A unique encryption key is assigned to each encrypted file. You can share an encrypted file with other users in Windows 7, but you are restricted from sharing an entire encrypted folder with multiple users or sharing a single file with a security group. This is related to the way that EFS uses certificates, which are applicable individually to users, and how EFS uses encryption keys, which are applicable individually to files. Windows 7 continues the ability introduced with Windows Vista to store keys on smart cards. If you are using smart cards for user logon, EFS automatically locates the encryption key without issuing further prompts. EFS also provides wizards that assist users in creating and selecting smart card keys.

You can use different types of certificates with EFS: third-party–issued certificates, certificates issued by certification authorities (CAs)—including those on your own network—and self-signed certificates. If you have developed a security system on your network that utilizes mutual authentication based on certificates issued by your own CA, you can extend the system to EFS to further secure encrypted files. For more information on using certificates with EFS, refer to the Windows 7 Help and Support Center.

Preparing a Disk for EFS

Unlike versions of Windows prior to Vista, the system and boot partition in Windows 7 must be formatted with NTFS before you can install Windows 7, as you learned in Chapter 2, "Installing Windows 7." However, a data partition can be formatted with the FAT or FAT32 file systems. But you must ensure that such a partition is formatted with NTFS before you can encrypt data using EFS. If it is not, you can convert the hard disk format from FAT to NTFS or format the partition as NTFS. There are two ways to go about this:

- Use the command-line Convert.exe utility to change an existing FAT or FAT32 partition that contains data to NTFS without losing the data.

- Use the graphical Disk Management utility to format a new partition, or an empty FAT partition, to NTFS. If the volume contains data, you will lose it. (You can also use the command-line Format.exe utility to format a partition as NTFS.)

The Convert.exe utility is simple to use and typically problem-free, although you should make certain to back up the data on the partition before you convert it as a precaution. Perform the following steps to use this utility:

Step 1.   Log on to the computer as an administrator. Know which drive letter represents the partition that you plan to convert because only the partition that contains the encrypted files needs to be formatted with NTFS. For example, if users store all their data on drive D: and want to encrypt those files, you will convert drive D: to NTFS.

Step 2.   Click **Start**, type **cmd** in the Search box, and press **Enter.**

Step 3.   The Command Prompt window opens. At the prompt, type **convert d: /fs:ntfs**.

Step 4.   The conversion process begins. If you are running the Convert.exe utility from the same drive letter prompt as the partition you are converting, or a file is open on the partition, you are prompted with a message that states Convert cannot gain exclusive access to D:, so it cannot convert it now. Would you like to schedule it to be converted the next time the system restarts (Y/N)? Press Y at the message.

Step 5.   Restart the computer. The disk converts its format to NTFS. This process takes considerable time to complete, but at completion, you can click **Start > Computer** and then select the disk you've converted and note that it is formatted with the NTFS file system.

Encrypting Files

You can use either the `cipher` command-line utility or the advanced attributes of the file or folder to encrypt a file. To use the `cipher` utility for encrypting a file named `Myfile.txt` located in the `C:\mydir` folder, the full command to use is as follows:

```
cipher /e /s:c:\mydir\myfile.txt
```

To change the Advanced encryption attribute of a file, open Computer and navigate to the file. Right-click the file and select **Properties**. On the General tab, click the **Advanced** button in the Attributes section. The Advanced Attributes dialog box opens, as shown in Figure 11-29.

Figure 11-29   The Advanced Attributes dialog box enables you to either compress or encrypt a file.

Select the **Encrypt contents to secure data** check box and click **OK**. Then click **OK** again to close the file's Properties dialog box. You are given a warning dialog that lets you choose between encrypting just the file that you had selected or both the file and its parent folder. Select one of the options and click **OK**.

NOTE   Note that the compression and encryption attributes are mutually exclusive. In the Advanced Attributes dialog box, if you select the **Compress contents to save disk space** check box, the check mark disappears from the Encrypt contents to secure data check box. These two attributes are mutually exclusive—you can select only one.

After a file has been encrypted, you can view its encryption attribute details by again right-clicking the file, selecting **Properties**, and then clicking the **Advanced** button on the General tab. In the Advanced Attributes dialog box, click the **Details** button. The User Access to (*file*) dialog box opens, as shown in Figure 11-30.

Figure 11-30   After a file has been encrypted, you can add other users to access the file.

You can see who is able to open the encrypted file, and you can add other user accounts to share the encrypted file and view the designated data recovery agent, if any. Click the **Add** button to share the encrypted file. A dialog box listing all the EFS-capable certificates for users opens. If a user has never been issued a certificate, the user's account does not appear in this dialog box.

> **TIP**   If the desired user has not been issued an EFS certificate, she needs only to log on to the computer and encrypt a different file. This automatically creates a certificate that will be visible the next time you attempt to share an encrypted file.

After a file is encrypted, an unauthorized user attempting to open the file is given an error message that says the user does not have access privileges. If an unauthorized user tries to move or copy an encrypted file, the user receives an `Access is denied` error message.

Backing Up EFS Keys

What if a user were to encrypt a file using EFS and then the user's account were to become corrupted or be deleted for any reason? Or what if the user's private key were to become corrupted or lost? You would be unable to decrypt the file and it would be permanently inaccessible. Windows 7 offers the capability for backing up EFS certificates and keys to reduce the likelihood of this occurring. Use the following procedure to back up EFS keys:

Step 1.   From the User Access dialog box previously shown in Figure 11-30, click **Back up keys**.

Step 2.   The Certificate Export Wizard starts. Click **Next**.

Step 3.   On the Export File Format page, the Personal Information Exchange–PKCS #12 (.PFX) format is selected by default. If desired, select the **Include all certificates in the certification path if Possible** and **Export all extended properties** options and then click **Next**.

Step 4.   On the Password page, type and confirm a password. This is mandatory, and you should choose a hard-to-guess password that follows the usual complexity guidelines. Then click **Next**.

Step 5.   On the File to Export page, type the name of the file to be exported and then click **Next**. By default, this file is created in the user's Documents library with the .pfx extension.

Step 6.   Review the information on the completion page and then click **Finish**.

Step 7.   You are informed the export was successful. Click **OK**.

Step 8.   You should move this file to a location separate from the computer, such as a floppy disk or USB key that you store securely (such as in a locked cabinet).

Decrypting Files

The process of decryption is the opposite of encryption. You can either use the cipher command or change the Advanced attribute for encryption on the file.

To use the cipher command to decrypt the file, click **Start**, type **cmd** in the Search box, and then press **Enter**. At the command prompt, type **cipher /d /s:c:\my-folder\myfile.txt** and press **Enter**. The file will be decrypted.

To use the Advanced Attributes method, open Computer and navigate to the file. Right-click the file and select **Properties**. On the General tab, click the **Advanced** button. In the ensuing Advanced Attributes dialog box, clear the **Encrypt the Contents to Secure Data** check box. Click **OK** and then click **OK** again.

If you are not the person who originally encrypted the file, or if you are not the designated recovery agent, you will receive an error for applying attributes that says the access is denied.

EFS Recovery Agents

What if the user's keys, even though backed up, were to become lost or corrupted? Without some type of recovery capability, such a file would become permanently inaccessible. EFS in Windows 7 uses the concept of *recovery agents* as a means to recover encrypted data in such a situation.

Designated recovery agents are user accounts authorized to decrypt encrypted files. When a user account is designated as a recovery agent, you essentially are granting it a copy of the key pair. If you lose the key pair, or if they become damaged, and if there is no designated recovery agent, there is no way to decrypt the file and the data is permanently lost. By designating a recovery agent before a user first uses EFS, you can ensure that encrypted files and folders remain accessible by someone responsible for their maintenance.

Windows 7 can include two levels of EFS recovery agents:

- **Local computer:** By default, the local administrator account created when you first install Windows 7 is the recovery agent. Note that this account is not the account whose name you specify during Windows 7 installation; it is a built-in account that can be accessed from the Local Users and Groups node of the Computer Management snap-in. The account is disabled by default, but you can enable it from its Properties dialog box by clearing the **Account is disabled** check box.

- **Domain:** When you create an AD DS domain, the first domain administrator account is the designated recovery agent. If desired, you can use Group Policy to designate additional recovery agents and you can delegate the responsibility of EFS recovery to other users.

You can use Group Policy to designate additional recovery agents. A user must have an appropriate certificate before he can be designated as a recovery agent. Use the following procedure:

Step 1. Open Group Policy and navigate to the **Computer Configuration\ Windows Settings\Security Settings\Public Key Policies\ Encrypting File System** node.

Step 2. Right-click this node and choose **Add Data Recovery Agent**.

Step 3. The Add Recovery Agent Wizard starts with a Welcome page. Click **Next**.

Step 4. On the Select Recovery Agents page shown in Figure 11-31, select a user from the Recovery agents list and then click **Next**. (If necessary, click **Browse Folders** to locate a certificate for the desired user.)

Step 5. You are informed that you have successfully completed the wizard. Review the information about the designated recovery agents, and then click **Finish**.

Figure 11-31 The Add Recovery Agent Wizard enables you to designate additional users as EFS recovery agents.

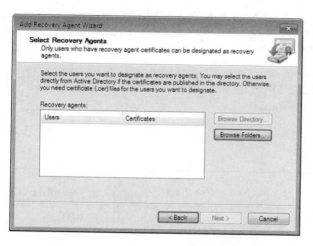

NOTE For more information on using EFS, backing up keys, and designating recovery agents, refer to "Protecting Sensitive Information from Theft on Windows XP Professional in a Workgroup" at http://www.microsoft.com/ smallbusiness/support/articles/efsxppro.mspx. Note that, although this article refers to Windows XP, information provided here is generally relevant to Windows Vista and Windows 7 as well.

Exam Preparation Tasks

Review All the Key Topics

Review the most important topics in the chapter, noted with the key topics icon in the outer margin of the page. Table 11-10 lists a reference of these key topics and the page numbers on which each is found.

Table 11-10   Key Topics for Chapter 11

Key Topic Element	Description	Page Number
Figure 11-1	Enabling global file-sharing options	390
Figure 11-5	Sharing a folder	393
Figure 11-6	Specifying shared folder permissions	394
Table 11-2	Describes available folder-sharing options	395
Paragraph	Introduces the concept of virtual folders in libraries	399
Table 11-4	Describes available printer permissions	402
Paragraph	Describes how to create a homegroup	403
Table 11-5	Describes NTFS file and folder security permissions	408
Figure 11-21	Shows how to configure security permissions	409
List	Describes how shared folder and security permissions interact with each other	417
Figure 11-29	Shows how to use EFS to encrypt files or folders	425
List	Shows how to back up EFS keys	427

Complete the Tables and Lists from Memory

Print a copy of Appendix C, "Memory Tables" (found on the CD) or at least the section for this chapter, and complete the tables and lists from memory. Appendix D, "Memory Tables Answer Key," also on the CD, includes completed tables and lists to check your work.

Definitions of Key Terms

Define the following key terms from this chapter, and check your answers in the glossary.

access control list (ACL), administrative shares, hidden shares, shared folder permissions, shared folders, NTFS permissions, virtual folders, library, encryption, Encrypting File System (EFS), decryption, certificate, private key, public key, Public folder sharing, homegroup, special access permissions, recovery agent

This chapter covers the following subjects:

- **Configuring User Account Control:** UAC is designed to enable all users, even administrators, to run with a standard access token. When a user requires administrative privileges for a task that can affect system properties, such as installing a program, the user receives a prompt that requests administrative credentials. UAC helps prevent unauthorized program installation and system modification. In Windows 7, you can modify the settings that determine when these prompts appear; you learn how to work with these settings in this section.

- **Configuring Authentication and Authorization:** All users on a Windows 7 computer must be authenticated to the operating system and authorized to perform certain tasks. This section shows you how to manage logon credentials using the new Credential Manager tool. You also look at the use of certificates and smart cards for purposes of authentication and authorization, as well as policies that govern passwords and account lockouts.

- **Configuring BranchCache:** In this section, you learn about BranchCache, which is a new Windows 7 feature useful in a corporate environment consisting of a head office and one or more branch offices. BranchCache enables branch office users to store copies of documents from head office servers locally on either client computers or a dedicated branch office server. You learn how to set up and configure BranchCache, and you take a quick look at network requirements and certificate usage.

CHAPTER 12

Configuring Access Controls

All users on Windows 7 computers must be known to the operating system—in other words, they must be authenticated to Windows and authorized to use resources on the local computer and across the network. In the last chapter, you learned how resources are shared across the network and how you can control access to files, folders, and printers. You learned how to specify who can do what with these items.

Now, we take these steps further by showing you how to configure authentication, authorization, and User Account Control (UAC). We also introduce a new Windows 7 feature called BranchCache that enables computers located in branch offices of a multilocation enterprise to retrieve documents from a locally hosted cache rather than having to connect across a wide area network (WAN) to access these documents, thereby reducing bandwidth requirements.

"Do I Know This Already?" Quiz

The "Do I Know This Already?" quiz enables you to assess whether you should read this entire chapter or simply jump to the "Exam Preparation Tasks" section for review. If you are in doubt, read the entire chapter. Table 12-1 outlines the major headings in this chapter and the corresponding "Do I Know This Already?" quiz questions. You can find the answers in Appendix A, "Answers to the 'Do I Know This Already?' Quizzes."

Table 12-1 "Do I Know This Already?" Foundation Topics Section-to-Question Mapping

Foundations Topics Section	Questions Covered in This Section
Configuring User Account Control	1–5
Configuring Authentication and Authorization	6–10
Configuring BranchCache	11–13

1. You have just migrated to a brand-new Windows 7 Professional computer after having worked on a Windows XP Professional computer for the past eight years. You are using an administrative user account but when you start to install Microsoft Office 2007, your screen dims and you are asked to confirm your intent. What happened and why?

   a. The media containing your Microsoft Office program has been compromised by an unknown entity, and Windows has discovered this problem.

   b. You need to check the Microsoft Office installation media for viruses or spyware before proceeding to install Office 2007.

   c. You have not configured your user account with the ability to install programs older than Windows 7, and you are being asked to configure the program for compatibility with Windows XP.

   d. This is normal behavior in Windows 7; UAC is asking you to provide administrative consent to install Microsoft Office 2007.

2. You right-click **Computer** and choose **Properties** to obtain system settings and perform some basic configuration activities on your Windows 7 computer. You notice a shield icon against several actions that you can access from here. What does this mean for a default configuration?

   a. When you select one of these actions, you will always receive a UAC prompt regardless of your user credentials.

   b. When you select one of these actions while running as a standard (non-administrative) user, you will receive a UAC prompt.

   c. When you select one of these actions while running as a standard (non-administrative) user, you will have to log off and log back on as an administrator.

   d. These icons merely warn you to be careful with the actions you're intending to perform, but you will be able to do them regardless of your user credentials.

3. You have downloaded an executable file from the Internet. When you attempt to run this program, you receive a UAC message box with a red title bar and red shield informing you that the program has been blocked. What does this mean, and what should you do to run this program?

   a. This program is an unsigned program from a verified publisher. Simply click **Yes** to run it.

   b. This program is an unsigned program from a nonverified publisher. Click **Yes** and reenter your password to run it.

   c. This program is a high-risk program from a nonverified publisher. Click **Yes** and reenter your password to run it.

    d. This program is a high-risk program that Windows has blocked completely. You cannot run it in its present form, and you should check the program's publisher on the Internet and locate a certified version that will run.

4. You sometimes use the built-in Administrator account on your Windows 7 computer, so you have configured this account with a strong username and password. You want to have this account display UAC prompts in the same fashion as other administrative accounts. What should you do?

    a. From the User Account Settings Control Panel applet, select the **Always notify** option.

    b. From the User Account Settings Control Panel applet, select the **Notify me only when programs try to make changes to my computer** option.

    c. In Group Policy, you should enable the **Admin Approval Mode for the Built-In Administrator account** policy.

    d. Do nothing. By default, this account works just like any other user account that belongs to the Administrators group.

5. You have had problems with users installing unapproved software on the Windows 7 computers in your small office. These users all have standard user accounts. You would like to configure UAC to block any programs that require elevated privileges in order to run the programs. So, you access the Group Policy editor. What policy should you enable?

    a. You should enable the **Behavior of the elevation prompt for standard users** policy and then select the **Prompt for credentials** option.

    b. You should enable the **Behavior of the elevation prompt for standard users** policy and then select the **Prompt for credentials on the secure desktop** option.

    c. You should enable the **Behavior of the elevation prompt for standard users** policy and then select the **Automatically deny elevation requests** option.

    d. You should enable the **Only elevate executables that are signed and validated** policy.

6. You have subscribed to a couple of websites that require user logons and passwords to control who has access to their sites. What Windows utility can you use to ensure that these usernames and passwords are always accessible to their respective sites?

    a. Credential Manager

    b. Certificate Manager

    c. The Security tab of the Internet Options dialog box

    d. The Content tab of the Internet Options dialog box

7. You have subscribed to a couple of websites from your office desktop computer that require user logons and passwords to access to those sites. You will be away from the office several weeks but will have your laptop computer with you. Both computers run Windows 7 Professional. What should you do to have these logons and passwords available, with the least amount of administrative effort?

   a. Use Windows Backup to back the credentials up from your desktop computer and then use Windows Restore on the laptop to restore these credentials.

   b. Use Credential Manager to back the credentials up from your desktop computer and then use Credential Manager on the laptop to restore these credentials.

   c. Manually copy the credentials from Credential Manager on the desktop to Credential Manager on the laptop.

   d. Log on to each website from the laptop and reenter the required credentials.

8. You have accessed the Properties dialog box for a certificate in your Personal certificate store. Which of the following properties can you modify from this location? (Choose all that apply.)

   a. Enable or disable purposes for the certificate.

   b. Specify additional cross-certificate download URLs.

   c. Modify the validity period for the certificate.

   d. Specify extended validation parameters.

   e. Specify Online Certificate Status Protocol (OCSP) download URLs.

9. What password policy actually weakens password security and is therefore not recommended for use by Microsoft?

   a. Enforce password history

   b. Minimum password age

   c. Maximum password age

   d. Complexity requirements

   e. Store passwords using reversible encryption

10. You want to grant Carolyn the ability to manage backups and restores on the Windows 7 client computers on your network. What is the best way to do this without granting her excessive privileges?

   a. Grant Carolyn the Back up files and directories user right and the Restore files and directories user right.

   b. Make Carolyn a member of the Administrators built-in group.

    c. Make Carolyn a member of the Backup Operators built-in group.

    d. Make Carolyn a member of the Power Users built-in group.

11. You are responsible for the Windows 7 computers in a small branch office in your company. The office is too small to justify installing a server computer locally. You would like to enable users in your office to access files and folders on a head office server while minimizing bandwidth requirements. What should you do?

    a. Configure BranchCache using the Distributed Cache mode.

    b. Configure BranchCache using the Hosted Cache mode.

    c. Configure a Windows 7 computer with a shared folder and copy the contents of the head office shared folder to this folder.

    d. Use the File Replication Service (FRS) to configure replication of the required files and folders to a Windows 7 computer in your office.

12. You are responsible for the Windows 7 computers in a small branch office in your company. The branch office has a Windows Server 2008 R2 server that is available to all users in the office. You would like to enable users in your office to access files and folders on a head office server while minimizing bandwidth requirements. What should you do?

    a. Configure BranchCache using the Distributed Cache mode.

    b. Configure BranchCache using the Hosted Cache mode.

    c. Configure the server with a shared folder and copy the contents of the head office shared folder to this folder.

    d. Use the File Replication Service to configure replication of the required files and folders to a Windows 7 computer in your office.

13. You are responsible for the Windows 7 computers in a small branch office in your company. A branch office computer running Windows Server 2003 R2 is available to all client computers. Client computers run either Windows Vista Business or Windows 7 Professional. You want to set up BranchCache to use Hosted Cache mode to facilitate access to content on head office servers that are already configured for BranchCache. Which of the following should you do? (Each answer represents part of the solution. Choose two.)

    a. Upgrade all client computers to Windows 7 Professional.

    b. Upgrade all client computers to Windows 7 Enterprise.

    c. Upgrade the server to Windows Server 2008.

    d. Upgrade the server to Windows Server 2008 R2.

    e. Install DNS on the server.

    f. Configure the server as a file and print server.

Foundation Topics

Configuring User Account Control

In versions of Windows prior to Vista, many users became frustrated with the inability to perform many common tasks and therefore ran their computers with an administrative user account, often the default Administrator account created when Windows was installed. These users received total system privileges as required for installing and configuring applications, modifying system configuration, running background system tasks, installing device drivers, and performing other system configuration actions. Such a practice left the computers open to many types of attacks by malware programs such as viruses, worms, rootkits, and others.

Administrators and technical support personnel in a corporate environment were often left in a dilemma. They could grant users administrative privileges, which can result in users changing settings, either accidentally or deliberately, that disrupted computer or network performance or compromised security. Or they could limit user privileges, which often limited productivity because users were unable to perform basic tasks such as connecting to a wireless network or installing a printer driver.

Beginning with Windows Vista, Microsoft addressed this problem by introducing a new feature called *User Account Control (UAC)*. Simply put, UAC requires users performing high-level tasks to confirm that they actually initiated the task. Members of the Administrators group are logged on with only normal user privileges and must approve administrative actions before such actions will run. Nonadministrative users must provide an administrative password. Providing administrative approval to run such tasks places the computer into *Admin Approval Mode*.

However, the implementation of UAC in Windows Vista generated large numbers of system prompts, even for such tasks as moving, renaming, or deleting files created or modified by a different user. I frequently experienced this problem in working with my extensive collection of photographic images, many of which had been originally copied onto an older computer running Windows XP. These annoying prompts contributed to the overall low consumer satisfaction of Vista and led many people to disable UAC completely, thereby negating its advantages. Microsoft has improved UAC in Windows 7, making it more user-friendly and less annoying while still providing protection against undesirable activities (such as installing unwanted software, unwittingly installing malware, and so on). You can now configure UAC to manage the extent of prompts provided, as will be discussed in the sections to come.

NOTE   For additional information on UAC improvements in Windows 7, refer to "What's New in User Account Control" at http://technet.microsoft.com/en-us/library/dd446675(WS.10).aspx.

Features of User Account Control

UAC requests approval before running administrative tasks on the computer. UAC redefines what a standard user is permitted to do. Such a user can perform many basic functions that pose no security risk; these functions previously required a user to have administrative privileges. In addition, UAC facilitates the act of providing administrative credentials when users need to perform higher-level tasks, such as installing an application or configuring system settings. Furthermore, UAC makes administrative accounts safer by limiting the types of tasks that can be performed without users providing additional consent. UAC still requests consent before allowing users to perform tasks that require higher privileges, such as system tasks.

Under UAC, all users (administrative or not) can perform the following tasks without supplying administrative credentials:

- Viewing the system clock and calendar and configuring the time zone (but users cannot change the system time)

- Modifying power management settings

- Installing printers and hardware devices that an administrator has allowed using Group Policy

- Interfacing portable devices (such as Bluetooth) with the computer

- Using Wired Equivalent Privacy (WEP) to connect to approved wireless networks

- Creating and configuring approved virtual private network (VPN) connections

- Installing ActiveX controls from sites that an administrator has approved

- Installing critical updates from Windows Update

TIP   The tasks summarized here are similar to those granted to members of the Power Users group in Windows versions prior to Vista. Windows 7 includes the Power Users group solely for backward compatibility purposes. You do not need to add users to this group to perform these functions. Add users to this group only if required for running noncertified or legacy applications. To grant this group all the privileges provided in Windows XP, you must apply a default security template that modifies default permissions on system folders and the Registry.

When authenticating a member of the Administrators group, Windows 7 issues two access tokens:

- **A full administrator token:** The administrator token is used only when administrative privileges are required.

- **A standard user token:** The standard token is used for all actions that do not require administrative privileges.

Windows 7 also marks tasks and programs as belonging to one of two integrity levels, which are implied levels of trust in these actions:

- **Low integrity:** A task or application (such as a web browser, email, or word processing program) that is less likely to compromise the operating system.

- **High integrity:** An action that performs tasks (such as installing applications) that have a higher potential for compromising the system. Applications running at low integrity levels cannot modify data in applications using a higher integrity level.

Windows 7 informs you when a task requires elevated (administrative) privileges by displaying shield icons such as those that appear in the left column of the System applet shown in Figure 12-1. On selecting one of these tasks, you receive a UAC prompt as shown in Figure 12-2. Click **Yes** to proceed with the task or **No** to cancel it. When you selected one of these tasks on a Windows Vista computer, the screen dimmed and a UAC prompt (also known as an *elevation prompt*) displayed. When you accepted the prompt, the administrative access token granted you elevated privileges, enabling you to perform the task you have selected. In Windows 7, this behavior depends on the UAC setting you've specified (as you will learn later in this section). The default setting enables administrators to perform most of the actions marked with shield icons without receiving UAC prompts; they receive prompts for performing tasks such as installing programs or running the Registry Editor or other programs that have a high potential for producing damaging effects.

Figure 12-1 Windows 7 uses a shield icon to inform you when a task requires administrative privileges.

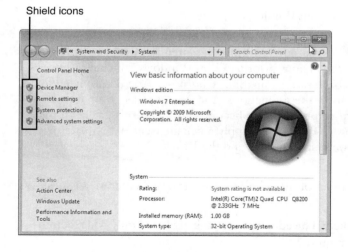

The dimmed screen indicates that the UAC prompt is running in *secure desktop mode* (such as when the Ctrl+Alt+Delete prompt appears when logging on to a domain-based computer). This means that you must either approve or cancel the UAC prompt before you can continue performing any other task on the computer.

Figure 12-2   User Account Control displays this prompt to ask for approval of an administrative task.

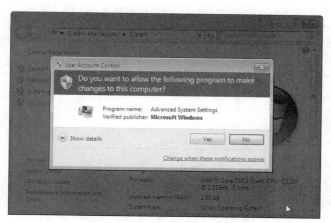

A user who is not a member of the Administrators group receives only the standard user token when access is authenticated. Such a user receives the UAC prompt shown in Figure 12-3, which requires that a password for an Administrator user account be entered. By default in Windows 7, a nonadministrative user receives this prompt for any action marked by a shield icon.

Figure 12-3   User Account Control requests that an administrative user password be entered when displayed from a nonadministrative user account.

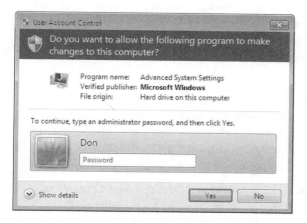

CAUTION   When you receive a UAC prompt, always ensure that the action that launches the prompt is the one you want to perform. This is especially true if a UAC prompt appears unexpectedly, which could indicate a malware program attempting to run. Should this happen, click **No** and the program cannot run. You should then scan your computer with one or more malware detection programs.

If a background application that is minimized to the taskbar requires elevated privileges, the UAC prompt appears on the taskbar and blinks to draw attention. An example of where this would happen is in the downloading of an application from the Internet. When the download completes and approval for installation is required, the user can click the prompt to approve it. This enables the user to continue performing other tasks, such as reading email, while the download is underway; the user can continue with these tasks without being interrupted by the dimming of her screen and a UAC prompt displaying onscreen.

Application Prompts

UAC causes some third-party applications to display prompts when you attempt to run them. This helps to secure your computer because the prompt informs you of the program that is attempting to run so that you can verify that it is a program you really want to run. Click **Yes** to run the program or **No** to exit. The type of shield icon depends on the security risk involved in running the program:

- **High-risk blocked program:** Windows displays a message box with a red title bar and red shield stating `This program has been blocked for your protection`. Such a program comes from a blocked publisher and cannot be run under any circumstances.

- **Program signed by Windows:** The UAC prompt includes a blue title bar and blue and yellow shield similar to that of Figure 12-2 for an administrative user. Click **Yes** to run the program. For a nonadministrative user, the prompt is similar to that shown in Figure 12-3. Provide an administrative password to run the program.

- **Unsigned program from a verified publisher:** When running with an administrative account, a program with a legitimate digital signature that includes its name and publisher will display a prompt similar to that shown in Figure 12-4. Click **Yes** to run the program. A nonadministrative user will receive a prompt that asks for an administrative password.

- **Unsigned program from a nonverified publisher:** If the third-party program does not have a digital signature that includes its name and publisher, the prompt that appears is a stronger caution. It uses a yellow title bar and yellow shield, as shown in Figure 12-5. Click **Yes** to run the program. Again, a nonadministrative user will receive a prompt that asks for an administrative password.

Figure 12-4   User Account Control displays a prompt similar to this when an administrative user starts a third-party program with a legitimate digital signature.

Figure 12-5   When a program that does not have a digital signature attempts to run, UAC displays this prompt to an administrative user.

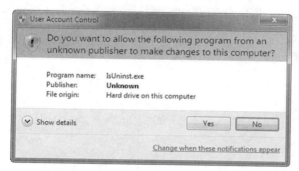

> **NOTE**   For more information on the various prompts that UAC can issue in Windows 7, refer to "UAC Processes and Interactions" at http://technet.microsoft.com/en-us/library/dd835561(WS.10).aspx.

Running Programs with Elevated Privileges

Microsoft has provided several means of configuring applications and tasks to run with elevated privileges. Use the following procedure to perform a task with elevated privileges:

Step 1.   Start the program or task displayed with a shield icon. The display dims and the UAC prompt appears, as previously shown in Figure 12-4.

Step 2.   Verify that the UAC prompt is requesting privileges for the task you're attempting to run (remember, some malware can deceive you here, so make certain the correct program or task is described in this prompt). If desired, click **Show details** for more information on the task.

Step 3.   If this is indeed the correct program or task, click **Yes** to start the task or application.

You can also mark an application to always run with elevated privileges. This situation might occur if the application developer has coded the program to access protected folders such as the `%ProgramFiles%` or `%Systemroot%` folders or requires access to the Registry. You can also configure a program to request administrative privileges from its shortcut properties. When you do this, the program always displays a UAC prompt when started from its shortcut. Use the following procedure to mark an application to always run with elevated privileges:

Step 1. Ensure that you are logged on to the computer as a member of the local Administrators group.

Step 2. If necessary, drag a shortcut to the desktop.

Step 3. Right-click the shortcut and choose **Properties**.

Step 4. On the Shortcut tab, click the **Advanced** button.

Step 5. On the Advanced Properties dialog box shown in Figure 12-6, select the **Run as administrator** check box and then click **OK**.

Figure 12-6   The Advanced Properties dialog box enables you to specify that the program always runs as an administrator.

Step 6. Click **OK** to close the shortcut Properties dialog box.

CAUTION   If you are logged on using the default Administrator account created when you installed Windows 7, you do not receive any UAC prompts. Do not use this account except under emergency conditions. Best practices recommend that this account remain disabled; it is disabled by default in Windows 7.

Configuring User Account Control

In Windows 7, as already mentioned, you can configure several levels of UAC that determine whether prompts are displayed and how they appear on the screen. Click **Start > Control Panel > System and Security** and then select **Change**

User Account Control settings under Action Center. Alternatively, you can type
`User Account Control` into the Start menu Search field and then select this option
from the search list. You receive the dialog box shown in Figure 12-7. Select from
the following options, click **OK**, and then accept the UAC prompt that appears:

Figure 12-7   The User Account Control Settings dialog box provides four settings for govern-
ing the behavior of UAC on your computer.

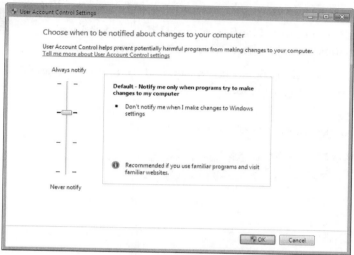

- **Always notify me when:** Windows displays a UAC prompt whenever you make
  changes to Windows settings or programs try to install software or make
  changes to your computer. This behavior is similar to that of Vista.

- **Default–Notify me only when programs try to make changes to my computer:**
  The default setting in Windows 7, this setting does not prompt you when you
  make changes to Windows settings. You are prompted on the secure desktop
  (that is, the desktop dims) when you perform higher-level actions, such as installing programs or accessing the Registry Editor.

- **Notify me only when programs try to make changes to my computer (do not
  dim my desktop):** Similar to the default setting, except that the desktop does
  not dim when a UAC prompt appears. With this setting, you can ignore the
  UAC prompt and continue performing tasks other than the task that is requesting approval.

- **Never notify me:** Disables UAC completely. This setting is not recommended;
  you should use it only when absolutely necessary to run a program that displays the red shield icon mentioned earlier in this section.

User Account Control Policies

Microsoft has provided a series of policies in Windows 7 Group Policy that govern the behavior of UAC. These policies are available from the Group Policy Management Editor snap-in or from the Local Security Policy snap-in in (available by typing **Local Security** from the Start menu Search field and then selecting the program from the list that appears). Use the following procedure to configure UAC policies:

Step 1.   Click **Start**, type **gpedit.msc** in the Search field, and then press **Enter**.

Step 2.   Navigate to the **Computer Configuration\Windows Settings\ Security Settings\Local Policies\Security Options** node.

Step 3.   Scroll to the bottom of the policy list to view and configure the available policies, as shown in Figure 12-8.

Figure 12-8   Group Policy provides a series of policies that govern UAC behavior.

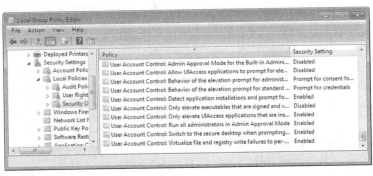

Step 4.   To configure a policy, right-click it and choose **Properties**. Choose **Enabled** or **Disabled** as required and click **OK**. Two of the policies offer options from a drop-down list, as shown in Figure 12-9. You can also click the **Explain** tab for further information on each policy.

Step 5.   When finished, click **OK**.

You can use this procedure to configure the following UAC policies:

- **Admin Approval Mode for the Built-in Administrator:** Governs the behavior of the built-in Administrator account. When enabled, this account displays the UAC prompt for all actions requiring elevated privileges. When disabled, this account runs all actions with full administrative privileges. This policy is disabled by default.

- **Allow UIAccess applications to prompt for elevation without using the secure desktop:** Determines whether User Interface Accessibility (UIAccess) programs can automatically disable the secure desktop with a standard user. When enabled, these programs (such as Remote Assistance) automatically disable the secure desktop for elevation prompts. When disabled, the application runs with UIAccess integrity regardless of its location in the file system. Note that UIAccess application programs and accessibility tools are used by developers to push input to higher desktop windows that require the uiAccess flag to be equal to true (that is, uiAccess=true). Also, the application program that wants to receive the uiAccess privilege must reside on the hard drive in a trusted location and be digitally signed. This policy is disabled by default.

Figure 12-9 You can configure each policy or obtain more information from its Properties dialog box.

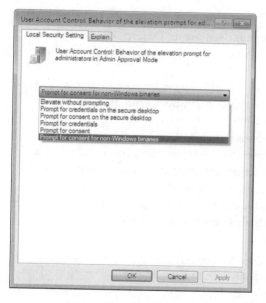

- **Behavior of the elevation prompt for administrators in Admin Approval Mode:** Determines the behavior of the UAC prompt for administrative users. This policy has the following options:
  - **Prompt for consent for non-Windows binaries:** Prompts a user on the secure desktop to select either **Permit** or **Deny** when a non-Microsoft program needs elevated privileges. Select **Permit** to run the action with the highest possible privileges. This option is the default setting.
  - **Prompt for consent:** Prompts a user to select either **Permit** or **Deny** when an action runs that requires elevated privileges. Select **Permit** to run the action with the highest possible privileges.
  - **Prompt for credentials:** Prompts for an administrative username and password when an action requires administrative privileges but does not display the secure desktop. When selected, administrative users receive the prompt previously shown in Figure 12-3 for nonadministrative users.

— **Prompt for consent on the secure desktop:** Prompts a user to select either **Permit** or **Deny** on the secure desktop when an action runs that requires elevated privileges. Select **Permit** to run the action with the highest possible privileges.

— **Prompt for credentials on the secure desktop:** Prompts for an administrative username and password on the secure desktop when an action requires administrative privileges. When selected, administrative users receive the prompt previously shown in Figure 12-3 for nonadministrative users.

— **Elevate without prompting:** Enables the administrator to perform the action without consent or credentials. In other words, the administrator receives Admin Approval Mode automatically. This setting is *not* recommended for normal environments.

■ **Behavior of the elevation prompt for standard users:** Determines the behavior of the UAC prompt for nonadministrative users. This policy has the following options:

— **Prompt for credentials:** Displays a prompt to enter an administrative username and password when a standard user attempts to run an action that requires elevated privileges. This option is the default setting.

— **Prompt for credentials on the secure desktop:** Displays a prompt on the secure desktop to enter an administrative username and password when a standard user attempts to run an action that requires elevated privileges.

— **Automatically deny elevation requests:** Displays an `Access is Denied` message similar to that shown in Figure 12-10 when a standard user attempts to run an action that requires elevated privileges.

Figure 12-10   When you have configured the policy to automatically deny elevation requests, nonadministrative users receive an error when they attempt to run a program requiring administrative credentials.

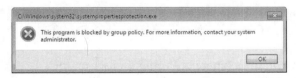

■ **Detect application installations and prompt for elevation:** When enabled, displays a UAC prompt when a user installs an application package that requires elevated privileges. When disabled, domain-based Group Policy or other enterprise-level technologies govern application installation behavior. This option is enabled by default in an enterprise setting and disabled by default in a home setting.

■ **Only elevate executables that are signed and validated:** When enabled, performs public key infrastructure (PKI) signature checks on executable programs that require elevated privileges before they are permitted to run. When disabled, no PKI checks are performed. This option is disabled by default.

- **Only elevate UIAccess applications that are installed in secure locations:** When enabled, runs applications with UIAccess integrity only if situated in a secure location within the file system such as %ProgramFiles% or %Windir%. When disabled, the application runs with UIAccess integrity regardless of its location in the file system. This option is disabled by default.

- **Run all administrators in Admin Approval Mode:** When enabled, enforces Admin Approval Mode and other UAC policies. When disabled, all UAC policies are disabled and no UAC prompts are displayed. In addition, the Windows Security Center notifies the user when disabled and offers the option to enable UAC. This option is enabled by default.

- **Switch to the secure desktop when prompting for elevation:** When enabled, displays the secure desktop when a UAC prompt appears. When disabled, the UAC prompt remains on the interactive user's desktop. This option is enabled by default.

- **Virtualize file and registry write failures to per user locations:** When enabled, redirects application write failures for pre-Windows 7 applications to defined locations in the Registry and the file system, such as %ProgramFiles%, %Windir%, or %Systemroot%. When disabled, applications that write to protected locations fail, as was the case in previous Windows versions. This option is enabled by default.

CAUTION If you disable the Run all administrators in Admin Approval Mode policy setting, you disable UAC completely and no prompts will appear for actions requiring elevated privileges. This leaves your computer wide open for attack by malicious software. Do *not* disable this setting at any time!

If you do disable this setting, note that the Windows Action Center will display a message from the notification area.

NOTE For information on problems you might encounter with UAC in Windows 7 and Windows Server 2008 R2, consult the links referenced in "User Account Control Troubleshooting Guide" at http://technet.microsoft.com/en-ca/library/ee844169(WS.10).aspx?ITPID=insider.

Configuring Authentication and Authorization

To use a Windows 7 computer, whether the computer belongs to a workgroup or HomeGroup or to an Active Directory Domain Services (AD DS) domain, a user must prove that she is who she says she is. This is what authentication is all about. Simply put, *authentication* is the process of a user or computer proving its identity on a network. *Authorization* is a process of the system giving appropriate resource access to a user who has been authenticated. These are important factors in any network, but they become even more important when applied to remote access communications through telephone lines or through the Internet. You will learn about remote access authentication in Chapter 14, "Configuring Remote Management and Remote Connections." Here we discuss authentication and authorization across the local network.

For years, companies have generally employed the simple means of usernames and passwords for authenticating users to their networks. In recent years with increased prevalence of password-guessing schemes and hacking software, companies have moved to multifactor authentication systems employing technology such as smart cards and biometric devices to improve the reliability of authentication. A smart card is a credit-card–sized device that includes information about the user and his rights and privileges; the user inserts the card in a reader attached to his computer and enters a personal identification number (PIN) to log on. Windows 7 supports the new Personal Identity Verification (PIV) smart card standards and policies that improve the security of this authentication method.

Controlling Windows Logon

By default, a Windows 7 computer that is not part of a domain displays the Welcome screen at startup, after a user has logged off and is attempting to log back on, and when a user has selected the **Switch User** option. This screen displays all enabled user accounts, allowing a user to select the appropriate account and enter the password if one has been specified. Although the Welcome screen is convenient, especially in a home environment, it does pose a security risk in a corporate environment, even in a small office. In an AD DS environment, Windows automatically uses the Classic Logon screen, at which a user must type a username and password. By default, this screen displays the username of the last user to log on, but you can configure it to not display this username.

You can use Group Policy to require the use of the Logon screen in a nondomain environment. Open the Local Group Policy Editor or Local Security Policy using methods described earlier in this chapter, navigate to the **Computer Configuration\Administrative Templates\Logon** node and then enable the Always use classic logon policy (see Figure 12-11). To remove the display of the last username, navigate to the **Computer Configuration\Windows Settings\Security Settings\Local Policies\Security Options** node and enable the Interactive logon: Do not display last user name policy.

Managing Credentials

Windows 7 provides the Credential Manager utility that stores credentials for user logon to resources such as websites, terminal servers, and applications. This utility stores credentials in an electronic Windows vault that makes them available for facilitated logon to these types of resources. If a user encounters problems logging on to these resources, you can use Credential Manager to create stored credentials for each resource a user needs to work with.

Figure 12-11   Requiring the use of the classic logon screen for logging on to Windows 7.

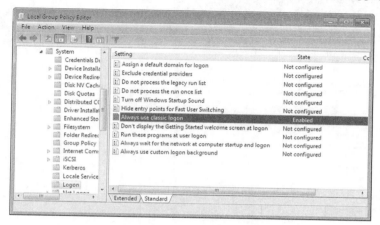

You can use the following three types of credentials in Credential Manager:

- **Windows credentials:** A credential used for standard Windows authentication by means of the Kerberos or NTLM protocols. It includes the username, password, and resource location.

- **Certificate-based credentials:** A credential that utilizes a certificate stored in the Certificate Manager's Personal store for authentication to the included resource location.

- **Generic credentials:** A customized credential that also includes the username, password, and resource location.

Adding, Editing, and Removing Credentials in Credential Manager

To access Credential Manager, click **Start > Control Panel > User Accounts and Family Safety > Credential Manager**. You can also type `credential` into the Start menu Search text box and select **Credential Manager** from the program list. You receive the Credential Manager applet, as shown in Figure 12-12.

To add a credential, select the desired type of credential. For a Windows or generic credential, you receive a screen similar to that shown in Figure 12-13. Enter the required server or network name, username, and password, and then click **OK**. You are returned to the Credential Manager where the added credential appears under the appropriate vault. You can now add additional credentials if needed.

Entering a certificate-based credential is slightly different. Enter the required server or network name, and then click **Select certificate** to locate a certificate that should be stored in the Personal store of Certificate Manager. When done, click **OK**.

Figure 12-12 The Credential Manager enables you to store three types of logon credentials.

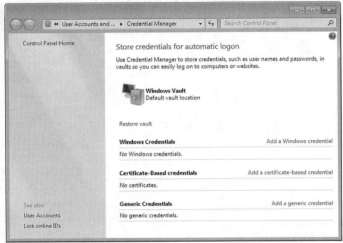

Figure 12-13 Entering a Windows credential into Credential Manager.

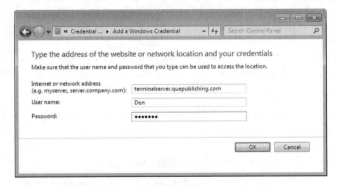

TIP Credential Manager automatically adds logon credentials to the Windows Credentials vault if you select the **Remember my credentials** check box found on the Logon dialog box displayed when first logging on to a server or website that requires authentication.

Credential Manager also enables you to modify or remove existing credentials. Click the arrow next to the stored credential to expand its entry, as shown in Figure 12-14. Clicking **Edit** takes you to the Edit Windows Credential screen, on which you can change the username and password or certificate. To delete a credential, click **Remove from vault** and then click **Yes** to confirm your intentions.

Figure 12-14 You can edit or remove credentials in Credential Manager.

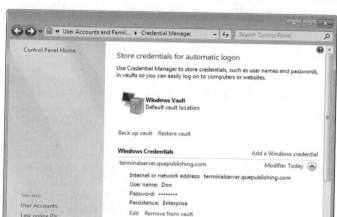

NOTE You cannot edit a server or website name associated with a credential in Credential Manager. If you need to do so, you must delete the improper credential and create a new credential with the correct resource location.

Backing Up and Restoring Credentials in Credential Manager

You can back up any of the three types of credentials from the Windows vault in Credential Manager. Perform the following steps:

Step 1. Click the **Back up vault** link under Windows Vault to display the Stored User Names and Passwords dialog box shown in Figure 12-15.

Figure 12-15 Backing up Windows credentials.

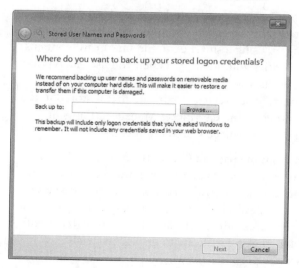

Step 2.   Type the path to the desired location (it is recommended that you use removable media) or click **Browse** to browse to an appropriate location. Then click **Next**.

Step 3.   As instructed, press **Ctrl+Alt+Delete**.

Step 4.   The desktop dims and you are asked to specify a password. Enter and confirm a secure password and then click **Next**. Credential Manager creates a backup file with the .crd extension.

Step 5.   You are informed that the backup was successful. Remove the media used and then click **Finish**.

You can also restore credentials to the Windows Vault. This provides a simple means of transferring credentials from one computer to another one (for example, when using a new computer). To restore credentials, use the following steps:

Step 1.   Click the **Restore vault** link under Windows Vault (refer to Figure 12-14).

Step 2.   On the dialog box that appears, type the path to the location of the backup file or click **Browse** to locate it. Then click **Next**.

Step 3.   As instructed, press **Ctrl+Alt+Delete**.

Step 4.   Type the password you supplied when creating the backup and then click **Next**.

Step 5.   You are informed that your logon credentials have been restored. Remove the media used and then click **Finish**.

Managing Certificates

When you use Credential Manager to store a certificate-based credential as discussed in the previous section, it looks for the certificate in the Personal store of Certificate Manager. When you log on using a smart card, the smart card contains a certificate with information that verifies your identity. When you use Encrypting File System (EFS) to encrypt a file as discussed in Chapter 11, "Configuring Access to Local and Shared Resources," you create a certificate that is stored in the same certificate store. Windows 7 provides the Certificate Manager Microsoft Management Console (MMC) snap-in to manage stored certificates.

You can open Certificate Manager from the page in Credential Manager that enables you to add a certificate-based credential or you can open this snap-in by typing `certmgr.msc` in the Start menu Search text box. Certificate Manager opens and displays a series of certificate stores, as shown in Figure 12-16. Expand any of these certificate stores and click the **Certificates** subnode to display any available certificates, as shown in the figure. Double-click a certificate to display its details, as shown in Figure 12-17. You can see the purposes for which the certificate is intended and the validity period. The Details tab includes information such as the serial number, signature hash algorithm, issuer, public key value, and so on.

Figure 12-16 Certificate Manager enables you to view and manage different types of certificates.

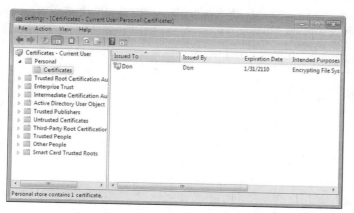

Figure 12-17 By double-clicking a certificate, you can view information about the certificate.

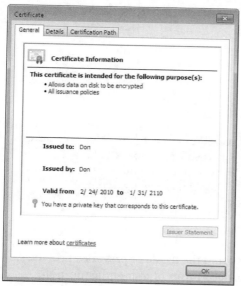

You can also view additional information and configure certificate properties by right-clicking the certificate and choosing **Properties**. From the (*Name*) Properties dialog box shown in Figure 12-18, you can modify the certificate purposes, specify cross-certificate download URLs, specify Online Certificate Status Protocol (OCSP) download URLs, and extend validation parameters. Using the

Friendly name field and the Description field in the General tab can help to differentiate among similar certificates. Cross-certificates are used to establish trust between separate certification authority (CA) hierarchies, such as those used on diverse networks. OCSP responders are used to verify certificate validity and check against certificate revocation lists issued by CAs. For more information about these certificate properties, click the Learn more about certificate properties link provided at the bottom of the Properties dialog box shown in Figure 12-18.

Figure 12-18   Configuring certificate properties.

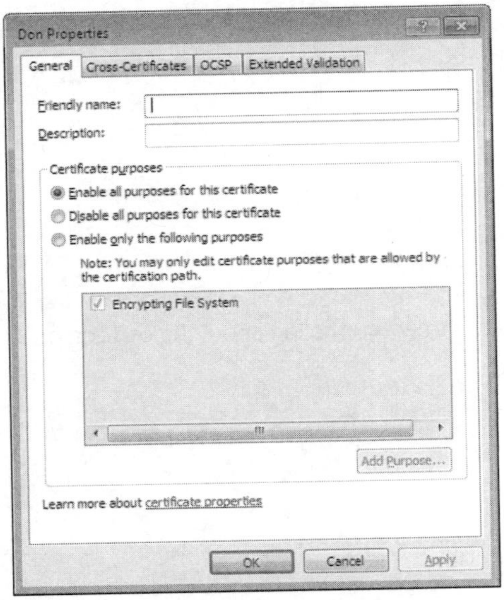

> **NOTE**   For more information on using Certificate Manager, refer to "Certificates: frequently asked questions" at http://windows.microsoft.com/en-us/windows7/Certificates-frequently-asked-questions and "View or manage your certificates" at http://windows.microsoft.com/en-US/Windows7/View-or-manage-your-certificates.

Using Smart Cards

To improve the security of user logons and avoid the hassle of password problems, organizations are turning toward more advanced forms of user authentication. Many companies have turned to using smart cards as an authentication mechanism, which helps to provide secure, tamperproof identification and authentication of users. They can be used for secure authentication of clients logging on to an AD DS domain as well as for those logging on remotely.

This system of authentication uses a smart card reader that attaches to a standard peripheral interface such as a USB port. Many manufacturers produce Plug-and-Play smart card readers that have been certified by Microsoft for use on computers running Windows XP/Vista/7/Server 2003/Server 2008 R2. Many of the newest portable computers even feature built-in smart card readers. You will also need one or more smart card writers for use during the enrollment process. You can use Active Directory Certificate Services (AD CS) in Windows Server 2008 R2 for enrolling certificates for smart cards that can be used for Windows 7 logons.

New to Window 7 is the ability to use the PIV standard from the National Institute of Standards and Technology (NIST). PIV-enabled smart cards can be used with drivers that are published through Windows Update; when a user inserts a PIV-enabled smart card into a reader attached to a Windows 7 computer, Windows downloads a driver from Windows Update. If an appropriate driver is not available, Windows uses a PIV-compliant minidriver included with the operating system. The following are several advantages of smart card support in Windows 7:

- **Ability to use BitLocker Drive Encryption:** You can use BitLocker to encrypt removable media such as USB drives. We discuss BitLocker in Chapter 13, "Configuring Mobile Computing."

- **Document and email signing:** You can sign and encrypt an email message or document, including XML Paper Specification (XPS) documents.

- **Use of the PKINIT protocol for domain logon:** You can use the smart card to authenticate to an AD DS domain without the use or configuration of additional middleware.

- **Use with line-of-business applications:** You can use the smart card with applications that employ Cryptography Net Generation (CNG) or CryptoAPI security protocols.

Smart Cards and Multifactor Authentication

Many organizations utilize multifactor authentication to improve their security and reduce the probability of unauthorized individuals gaining access to their networks. Multifactor authentication requires a user to provide two or more separate methods to complete authentication process. For example, a user might need to provide a username and password together with a smart card, or perhaps with a biometric device such as an iris scanner or fingerprint reader.

Smart Card Policies

You can use Group Policy to configure smart card policies. Navigate to the **Computer Configuration\Windows Settings\Security Settings\Local Policies\Security Options** node to access the following policies:

- **Interactive logon: Require smart card:** When enabled, users must employ a smart card to log on.

■ **Interactive logon: Smart card removal behavior:** Governs the action that occurs if a logged-on user removes her smart card. By default, no action takes place. You can also specify Lock Workstation, which locks the computer but retains the active session when the smart card is removed; Force Logoff, which automatically logs the user off; and Disconnect if a Remote Desktop Services Session, which disconnects a remote access session without logging the user off. With either the Lock Workstation or Disconnect if a Remote Desktop Services Session settings, the user can return to her session simply by reinserting the smart card.

NOTE   For more information on smart cards in Windows 7, refer to "PKI Enhancements in Windows 7 and Windows Server 2008 R2" at http://technet.microsoft.com/en-us/magazine/2009.05.pki.aspx?pr=blog.

Configuring Account Policies

Group Policy in Windows 7 includes the Account Policies node, which contains settings related to user accounts, including the password policy, account lockout policy, and Kerberos policy.

Password Policies

You can configure password policy settings that help to protect users of Windows 7 client computers. The options available in Windows 7 are similar to those found in previous Windows versions. Password policies are generally intended to make passwords more difficult for intruders to discover. Figure 12-19 shows the available password policies and their default settings.

Figure 12-19   Windows 7 provides default values for the available password policies.

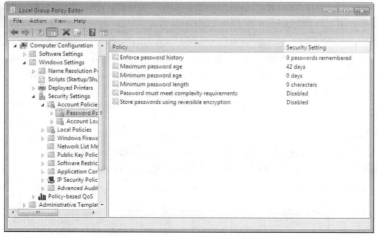

The following password policy settings are available:

- **Enforce password history:** Determines the number of passwords remembered by Windows for each user. Values range from 0 to 24. A user cannot reuse a password retained in the history list. A value of 0 means that no password history is retained and a user can reuse passwords at will.

- **Maximum password age:** Determines the number of days that a user can use a password before being required to specify a new one. Values range from 0 to 999. A value of 0 means that a user is never required to change his password. The default is 42 days.

- **Minimum password age:** Determines the minimum number of days a password must be used before it can be changed. Values range from 0 to 999 days and must be less than the maximum password age. The default value of 0 enables the user to immediately change a new password. This value enables a user to cycle through an entire history list of passwords in a short time; in other words, a user can repeatedly change a password in order to reuse his old password. This obviously defeats the purpose of enforcing password history, so you should configure this value to be at least one day.

- **Minimum password length:** Determines the minimum number of characters that can make up a password. Values range from 0 to 14. A value of 0 permits a blank password. Use a setting of 10 or higher for increased security.

- **Password must meet complexity requirements:** Stipulates that a password must meet complexity criteria, as follows: The password cannot contain the user account name or full name or parts of the name that exceed two consecutive characters. It must contain at least three of the following four items:
  — English lowercase letters
  — English uppercase letters
  — Numerals
  — Nonalphanumeric characters such as $; [ ] { } ! .

- **Store passwords using reversible encryption:** Determines the level of encryption used by Windows 7 for storing passwords. Enabling this option reduces security because it stores passwords in a format that is essentially the same as plain text. This option is disabled by default. You should enable this policy only if needed for clients who cannot use normal encryption, such as those using Challenge Handshake Authentication Protocol (CHAP) authentication or Internet Information Services (IIS) Digest Authentication.

To configure these policies, expand the **Computer Configuration\Windows Settings\Security Settings\Account Policies\Password Policy** node of the Local Group Policy Editor as shown in Figure 12-19. Right-click the desired policy and choose **Properties**. Then configure the appropriate value and click **OK**.

Each policy setting also has an Explain tab that provides additional information on the policy setting and its purpose.

Account Lockout

A cracked user account password jeopardizes the security of the entire network. The account lockout policy is designed to lock an account out of the computer if a user (or intruder attempting to crack the network) enters an incorrect password a specified number of times, thereby limiting the effectiveness of dictionary-based password crackers. The account lockout policy contains the following settings:

- **Account lockout duration:** Specifies the number of minutes that an account remains locked out. Every account except for the default Administrator account can be locked out in this manner. You can set this value from 0 to 99999 minutes (or about 69.4 days). A value of 0 means that accounts that have exceeded the specified number of failed logon attempts are locked out indefinitely until an administrator unlocks the account.

- **Account lockout threshold:** Specifies the number of failed logon attempts that can occur before the account is locked out. You can set this value from 0 to 999 failed attempts. A value of 0 means that the account will never be locked out. Best practices recommend that you should never configure a setting of 0 here.

- **Reset account lockout counter after:** Specifies the number of minutes to wait after which the account lockout counter is reset to 0. You can set this value from 1 to 99999.

When you configure this policy, Windows 7 sets default values for the account lockout settings. To configure an account lockout policy, right-click **Account lockout threshold**, choose **Properties**, and then specify a value of your choice. As shown in Figure 12-20, Windows suggests default values for the other two policy settings. Click **OK** to define the policy settings and set these defaults. If you want to change the other settings, right-click the appropriate settings, choose **Properties**, and then enter the desired value.

Unlocking an Account

When a user account is locked out because of too many incorrect attempts at entering a password, it is simple for an administrator or a user who is delegated the task to unlock it. Right-click the user account in the Local Users and Groups node of the Computer Management snap-in and choose **Properties**. On the General tab of the user's Properties dialog box, clear the **Account is locked out** check box and then click **OK** or **Apply**.

NOTE   You cannot lock out a user account by selecting this check box; it is provided for unlocking the account only. An account is locked out only by the user entering an incorrect password the specified number of times.

Figure 12-20 When you define an account lockout policy, Windows suggests defaults for the other two lockout policy settings.

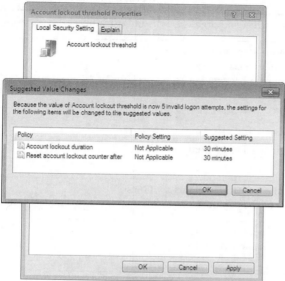

Configuring User Rights

User rights are defined as a default set of capabilities assigned to built-in local groups that define what members of these groups can and cannot do on the network. They consist of privileges and logon rights.

You can manage these predefined user rights from the Computer Configuration\Policies\Windows Settings\Security Settings\Local Policies\User Rights Assignment node in the Local Group Policy Editor. From this node, you can view the default rights assignments, as shown in Figure 12-21. To modify the assignment of any right, right-click it and choose **Properties**. In the Properties dialog box, click **Add User or Group**, and in the Select Users or Groups dialog box, type or browse to the required user or group. Then click **OK**.

In total, Windows 7 includes 44 user rights. For the purposes of the 70-680 exam, it is unlikely that you would need to know what these user rights actually involve. Although you can grant users these rights directly from the Local Group Policy Editor as explained here, the easiest way to do this in Windows 7 is to add the desired user to the appropriate default built-in local group. Table 12-2 summarizes the available built-in local groups.

Table 12-2   Default Built-in Local Groups in Windows 7

Local Group	Default Access	Default Members Locally
Administrators	Unrestricted access to the computer	Administrator
Backup Operators	Access to run Windows Backup and sufficient access rights that override other rights when performing a backup	N/A
Cryptographic Operators	Ability to perform cryptographic operations	N/A
Distributed COM Users	Launch, activate, and use Distributed COM objects	N/A
Guests	Limited only to explicitly granted rights and restricted usage of the computer	Guest
Network Configuration Operators	Access to manage the network configuration of the computer, such as TCP/IP properties	N/A
Performance Log Users	Ability to schedule logging of performance counters, enable trace providers, and collect event traces both locally and by means of remote access connection	N/A
Performance Monitor Users	Ability to access performance counter data locally and remotely	N/A
Power Users	Not used directly with Windows 7; included only for backward compatibility with Windows XP and older versions	N/A
Remote Desktop Users	Limited to accessing the computer via a remote desktop connection plus any explicitly granted rights and restricted usage of computer	N/A
Replicator	Used in a domain environment only for supporting AD DS replication	N/A
Users	Limited to use of the computer, personal files and folders, and explicitly granted rights	All newly created users NT Authority\Authenticated Users special built-in group NT Authority\Interactive special built-in group

Figure 12-21   Local Group Policy includes an extensive set of predefined user rights assignments.

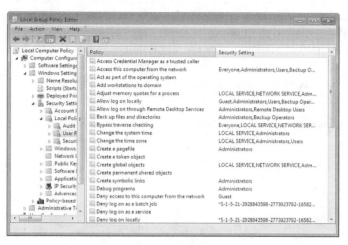

You can add users to these groups from the Local Users and Groups node of the Computer Management snap-in. Right-click the desired group in the Groups folder shown in Figure 12-22 and choose **Properties**. In the Properties dialog box that appears, click **Add**, type the desired username, and then click **OK**. Click **OK** again in the group's Properties dialog box to close it and add the user to the group.

NOTE   You can troubleshoot user rights using `whoami`, a command-line utility that is installed by default in Windows 7. To see the rights of a current user, type `whoami /all` at the command prompt. This utility displays all groups, even the built-in groups that do not appear under Member Of property sheets, which you can use to track down a misconfigured right.

Figure 12-22   Windows 7 contains a series of built-in local groups with defined user rights.

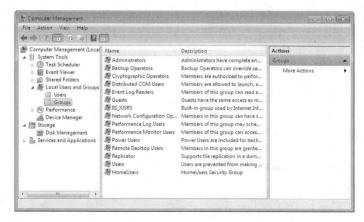

Resolving Authentication Issues

Users who are unable to log on for various reasons represent the major authentication issue that you will encounter in supporting Windows 7. Such users are unproductive until they can get back on to their computer, and they consume help-desk time in their efforts to log on. The major reason for logon failure is that they have forgotten their passwords. They might have been locked out because of entering an incorrect password too many times; you learned how to unlock a locked-out account earlier in this section.

If a user has forgotten his password, you can use either of two methods to get him back onto the network:

- Reset his password from Local Users and Computers.

- Use a password reset disk.

Resetting Passwords

Windows 7 makes it easy to reset a user's forgotten password. Access the Local Users and Groups node of the Computer Management snap-in, and click **Users** to display the list of users in the details pane. You must be a member of the local Administrators group to perform this action. Right-click the desired user and choose **Set Password**. You receive the warning shown in Figure 12-23 that the user might lose information if the password is reset; specifically, any files the user has encrypted using EFS will become inaccessible unless he has backed up his EFS keys or a recovery agent decrypts them. In addition, the user will lose access to certificates and credentials stored in the Windows Vault unless these have been backed up. Click **Proceed** to display the **Set Password for (*user*)** dialog box shown in Figure 12-24. Type and confirm the new password and then click **OK**.

Figure 12-23 You are warned that data loss might occur when you reset the password.

Figure 12-24 Resetting a user's password.

Best practices also recommend that you configure the user account so the user must change his password the next time he logs on. Right-click the user account and choose **Properties**; on the General tab, select the check box labeled **User must change password at next logon**. Doing so enables the user to select a password of his choice known only to himself.

Using a Password Reset Disk

A password reset disk enables a user to recover her password without losing encrypted data. The user can use either a floppy disk or USB thumb drive with the Forgotten Password Wizard to create her password reset disk. Proceed as follows:

Step 1. Click **Start**, type **password reset** in the Search text box, and then select **Create a password reset disk** from the program list.

Step 2. The Forgotten Password Wizard starts with a Welcome page as shown in Figure 12-25. Click **Next**.

Figure 12-25 The password reset disk enables you to log on if you've forgotten your password.

Step 3.   Select the drive on which you want to create the password reset disk and then click **Next**.

Step 4.   Ensure that the disk is in the selected drive and type the current password for the user account. Then click **Next**.

Step 5.   Windows displays a progress bar as the disk is created. Click **Next**.

Step 6.   You are informed that the password reset was created. Remove the disk and then click **Finish**.

> **CAUTION**   You must create the password reset disk in advance. If you've forgotten your password and haven't created the password reset disk, you must have an administrator reset your password as described in the previous section.

> **CAUTION**   The password reset disk can be used by anyone to log on to the account it protects. An intruder could use this disk to gain unauthorized access. You should store the disk in a secure place, such as a locked drawer, to prevent unauthorized access.

If the user has forgotten her password, she needs only to log on incorrectly once. When the logon screen reappears, she can click **Reset password**, insert the password reset disk, and then follow the instructions in the Password Reset Wizard to create a new password.

Configuring BranchCache

BranchCache is a new feature of Windows 7 Enterprise and Ultimate that enables users to rapidly access data from remotely located file and web servers. For example, users at a small branch office can cache copies of frequently accessed files from head office servers on a local computer. In doing so, users do not need to connect across the low-bandwidth wide area network (WAN) each time they need this content. Not only is access more rapid, bandwidth utilization across the WAN is optimized. When a second client requests the same data, the remote server sends metadata that includes a set of segment and block hashes computed with the use of the Secure Hash Algorithm (SHA)-256 hashing algorithm. The client can compare this hash with that contained in the locally cached version's metadata to check for changes. The client downloads a new version only if there are changes; otherwise, the user receives the content from the local cache. Servers hosting this content in the head office must be running Windows Server 2008 R2.

BranchCache utilizes the Background Intelligent Transfer Service (BITS) to perform its actions. It can work with web content transferred using Hypertext Transfer Protocol (HTTP), and with data files and documents transferred using Server Message Block (SMB).

NOTE   For more information on BranchCache, refer to "BranchCache Technical Overview" at http://www.microsoft.com/downloads/ details.aspx?displaylang=en&FamilyID=ee07308f-7c53-4c76-9ed9-670bc25a4c9d and "BranchCache Early Adopter's Guide" at http://technet.microsoft.com/ en-us/library/dd637762(WS.10).aspx.

Distributed Cache and Hosted Cache

You can operate BranchCache in either Distributed Cache mode or Hosted Cache mode.

- **Distributed Cache:** Each user's Windows 7 desktop computer hosts files cached from the remote server. This mode does not require a branch office server, thereby reducing hardware requirements in a small branch office that does not have the need for a server. This mode works on a branch office network containing a single subnet only with no more than 50 client computers. The client computer hosting the cached files must be available for other clients requesting the cached information; otherwise, the second client must download the files across the WAN.

- **Hosted Cache:** A server running Windows Server 2008 R2 located in the branch office hosts files cached from the remote server. You need to install the Hosted Cache server feature on this server using Server Manager. When users request these files, they are accessed from this server. Note that you do not require a dedicated server; the server running Hosted Cache can run other applications, such as a file and print server or web server. This enables all clients in the branch office to access a single cache location even if there is more than one subnet. Furthermore, it reduces the need for multiple downloads of hosted content because of client computers being offline or in sleep mode.

Configuring BranchCache Settings

You can use either Group Policy or the netsh command-line utility to configure BranchCache. With either tool, you need to enable BranchCache, select the required mode, and then configure the client firewall to pass the protocols used by BranchCache.

Using the **netsh** Command to Configure BranchCache

By default, BranchCache is disabled on Windows 7 client computers. It is simple to enable BranchCache in either mode and enable the firewall from an administrative command prompt, as follows:

Step 1.   Click **Start** and type **cmd** in the Search field. From the program list, right-click **cmd.exe**, choose **Run as administrator**, and then click **Yes** to accept the UAC prompt that appears.

Step 2.   To enable BranchCache in the required mode, type `netsh branchcache set options`.

In this command, *options* can have the following values:

- `service mode=DISTRIBUTED`: Enables BranchCache distributed mode.

- `service mode=HOSTEDCLIENT LOCATION=<fqdn>`: Enables BranchCache hosted mode; *<fqdn>* is the fully qualified domain name (FQDN) of the server hosting the cache.

- `service mode=local`: Enables the client to use local branch caching, where the client stores files retrieved across the WAN in a local cache but does not share its contents with any other branch office client computers. Multiple users on a single computer might find this mode beneficial. You can specify this alternative BranchCache mode only by using the `netsh` command.

- `cachesize size={default ¦ <number>} percent={true ¦ false}`: Specifies the size (*<number>*) of the local cache, either as a percentage of hard disk space (`true`) or as a number of bytes (`false`).

- `localcache directory=<filepath>`: Specifies the location of the local cache when using Hosted Cache mode, where *<filepath>* is the path to the local cache folder.

When you use `netsh` to configure BranchCache, this automatically configures the host computer firewall to pass BranchCache protocol packets.

NOTE   The `netsh` commands described here have several additional parameters. For more information, consult "Netsh Commands" at http://technet.microsoft.com/en-us/library/dd637805(WS.10).aspx.

Using Group Policy to Enable BranchCache

You can use Group Policy to enable BranchCache on all client computers located on the remote network. Create a Group Policy object (GPO) focused on the AD DS site for the remote network or to configure BranchCache for multiple branch offices in a single domain, create a GPO focused on the domain. Then open the Group Policy Management Editor and navigate to the **Computer Configuration\Administrative Templates\Network\Branch Cache** node. As shown in Figure 12-26, this node provides the following five policies:

- **Turn on BranchCache:** Enable this policy to enable BranchCache on all client computers affected by the GPO. You must enable this policy for any of the other policies to be effective.

- **Set BranchCache Distributed Cache mode:** Enable this policy to enable BranchCache Distributed Cache mode.

Figure 12-26   You can use Group Policy to configure these five BranchCache policies.

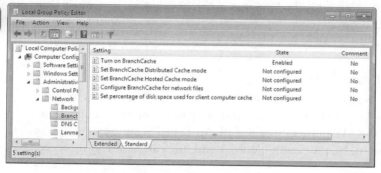

- **Set BranchCache Hosted Cache mode:** Enable this policy to enable BranchCache Hosted Cache mode. As shown in Figure 12-27, type the FQDN of the server hosting the cache in the space provided.

Figure 12-27   When enabling Hosted Cache mode, you must specify the FQDN of the hosting server.

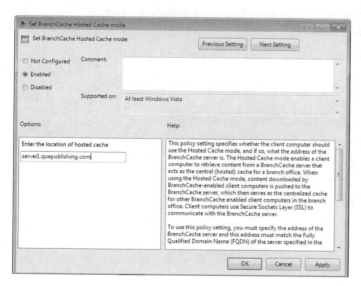

- **Configure BranchCache for network files:** Specifies the default round-trip network latency value in milliseconds above which network files must be cached. By default, this value is 80 milliseconds.

- **Set percentage of disk space used for client computer cache:** Specifies the percent of total client disk space on each client computer available for caching files with BranchCache. By default, this value is 5% of the client computer's total disk space.

> **TIP**   Although it is convenient to use site-based Group Policy for configuring BranchCache because it applies to all computers in the branch site, remember that domain-based and organizational unit (OU)-based policies override settings in a site-based GPO.

Specifying BranchCache Firewall Rules

When you use Group Policy to configure BranchCache, you must also configure firewall rules that permit BranchCache messages to pass to the client computers. You can do this by using Windows Firewall with Advanced Security, which we introduced in Chapter 10, "Configuring Network and Firewall Settings." Proceed as follows:

Step 1.   Open the Group Policy Management Editor focused on the same GPO used for enabling BranchCache.

Step 2.   Navigate to the **Computer Configuration\Windows Settings\ Security Settings\Windows Firewall with Advanced Security\ Inbound Rules** node.

Step 3.   Right-click **Inbound Rules** and choose **New Rule** to start the New Inbound Rule Wizard.

Step 4.   As shown in Figure 12-28, select the **Predefined** option.

Figure 12-28   Enabling an inbound firewall rule to pass BranchCache messages.

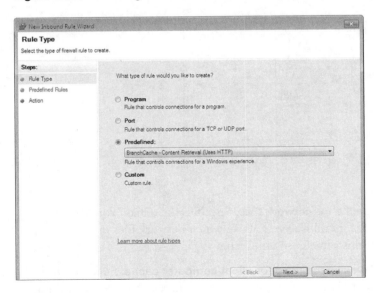

Step 5.   Ensure that the option reads **BranchCache–Content Retrieval (Uses HTTP)** and follow the remaining steps of the wizard, ensuring that the

Allow the Connection option is selected. If you are using HTTPS, ensure that the **Branch Cache–Hosted Cache Server (Uses HTTPS)** option is selected instead.

BranchCache Network Infrastructure Requirements

Because the client computer at the branch office needs to obtain the requested file only at the time of its first request, network infrastructure requirements are considerably reduced when you enable BranchCache. The BranchCache server in the head office sends a requested file in 64 KB blocks. When it sends the file, it also sends metadata (as mentioned earlier in this section). When another client computer requests the same file, the BranchCache server resends the metadata and the client computer compares the two sets of metadata to determine whether the contents of the requested file have changed. The BranchCache server resends the file only if changes have occurred; even then it might need to send only 64 KB blocks of data that have changed.

Because the metadata can be up to 2,000 times smaller than the file size, the bandwidth requirements are reduced by a factor of up to 2,000 when you enable BranchCache. This factor applies only when clients request files multiple times and the files are larger than 64 KB. Security is provided by the use of the Advanced Encryption Standard (aes) with a 128-bit key.

NOTE For more information on network optimization with BranchCache, refer to "End-to-End WAN Optimization with BranchCache" at http://technet.microsoft.com/en-us/magazine/ee914606.aspx.

Using BranchCache Across a Virtual Private Network

You can utilize BranchCache across remote access VPN connections that support split tunneling. If DirectAccess is being used for connections from your branch office computers to your head office, you must configure the firewall rules to support such a connection, as follows:

- If using Distributed Cache mode, you must configure IPSec firewall rules to allow the WS-Discovery (UDP multicast on port 3702) and HTTP (TCP port 80) protocols to pass between remote computers.

- If using Hosted Cache mode, you must configure IPSec firewall rules to allow HTTP (TCP port 80) protocols to pass between remote computers and the Hosted Cache server.

NOTE For more information about configuring a VPN, see Chapter 14, "Configuring Remote Management and Remote Connections."

Certificate Management with BranchCache

When using BranchCache with a Hosted Cache server, this server must be trusted by client computers to cache data that might be under access control. The client computers use Transport Layer Security (TLS) to communicate with the Hosted Cache server. Consequently, this server must have a certificate that clients can use to authenticate the server.

You can use Active Directory Certificate Services (AD CS) within an AD DS domain to issue a certificate to the Hosted Cache server that will verify this server's identity to client computers in the branch office accessing documents to be cached. In a nondomain environment, you can also use a server running Certificate Services as a standalone certification authority (CA).

The certificate is imported to the certificate store on the BranchCache server under the local computer account so that the client computers in the branch office can trust this server. If it is added under the administrator account, clients will be unable to use the certificate to access the Hosted Cache server. To import this certificate, use the Certificates snap-in at the server.

NOTE For further information on configuring a certificate on the BranchCache server, refer to "Hosted Cache Server Setup" at http://technet.microsoft.com/en-us/library/dd637793(WS.10).aspx and "Deploy a hosted cache mode design" at http://technet.microsoft.com/en-us/library/ee649239(WS.10).aspx.

Exam Preparation Tasks

Review All the Key Topics

Review the most important topics in the chapter, noted with the key topics icon in the outer margin of the page. Table 12-3 lists a reference of these key topics and the page numbers on which each is found.

Table 12-3   Key Topics for Chapter 12

Key Topic Element	Description	Page Number
Paragraph	Describes the workings of UAC	440
List	Describes the types of prompts issued by UAC	442
List	Configuring a program to always require elevated privileges	444
Figure 12-7	Specifying the levels of prompts that UAC can issue	445
Figure 12-8	Shows available UAC Group Policy settings	446
Figure 12-12	Using Credential Manager	452
Paragraph	Describes managing certificate-based credentials	454
Figure 12-19	Shows available password policies	458
Figure 12-23	Displays the caution about data loss when resetting passwords	464
List	Compares the two BranchCache modes	467
Figure 12-26	Shows available BranchCache Group Policy settings	469

Definitions of Key Terms

Define the following key terms from this chapter and check your answers in the glossary.

Admin Approval Mode, Group Policy object (GPO), Local group, Local Security Policy, built-in group, User Account Control (UAC), authentication, authorization, credential, Credential Manager, certificate, smart card, Personal Identity Verification (PIV), Password policy, user rights, BranchCache, Distributed Cache, Hosted Cache

This chapter covers the following subjects:

- **Configuring BitLocker and BitLocker To Go:** Microsoft has added to the BitLocker whole drive encryption scheme, first introduced in Windows Vista, by enabling you to encrypt data partitions. BitLocker To Go extends the BitLocker drive encryption to USB drives and portable hard drives.

- **Configuring DirectAccess:** This section introduces the new DirectAccess feature, which improves the reliability, ease, and security of access to corporate networks by users connecting from external locations.

- **Configuring Mobility Options:** This section introduces the mobility features found in Windows 7 that facilitate the use of portable computers. You will learn about the Windows Mobility Center and Offline Files as well as the new feature of transparent caching of offline files across a slow WAN link.

- **Configuring Power Options:** Microsoft provides several options for configuring power management on Windows 7 computers. This section introduces you to these options as well as configuring Group Policy for power management settings.

CHAPTER 13

Configuring Mobile Computing

Mobile computing has entered the mainstream of everyday business activity, with modern notebook or laptop computers presenting an unprecedented level of computing power. You can do almost as much on a notebook or laptop computer as on a desktop with the added convenience of portability to any workplace, client, hotel, or home situation as the demand requires. Along with the convenience of portability comes the risk of exposing valuable data to unauthorized access as a result of loss or theft of the computer. Microsoft has enhanced the BitLocker full drive encryption feature and added the new BitLocker To Go portable drive encryption feature.

Windows 7 introduces a completely new means of connecting to corporate networks from anywhere in the DirectAccess feature, which enables seamless access to the network without the need for a virtual private network. Microsoft has designed Windows 7 to accommodate a large range of mobile computer features such as the Windows Mobility Center, offline file access, improved power management, and presentation settings. This chapter introduces you to these portable computer features.

"Do I Know This Already?" Quiz

The "Do I Know This Already?" quiz enables you to assess whether you should read this entire chapter or simply jump to the "Exam Preparation Tasks" section for review. If you are in doubt, read the entire chapter. Table 13-1 outlines the major headings in this chapter and the corresponding "Do I Know This Already?" quiz questions. You can find the answers in Appendix A, "Answers to the 'Do I Know This Already?' Quizzes."

Table 13-1 "Do I Know This Already?" Foundation Topics Section-to-Question Mapping

Foundations Topics Section	Questions Covered in This Section
Configuring BitLocker and BitLocker To Go	1–4
Configuring DirectAccess	5–7
Configuring Mobility Options	8–9
Configuring Power Options	10–12

1. You are sure your Windows 7 Enterprise computer is equipped with a Trusted Platform Module (TPM), but when you go to enable BitLocker from the System and Security category of Control Panel, the BitLocker Drive Encryption option is not available. What do you need to do first?

   a. Upgrade your computer to Windows 7 Ultimate.

   b. Enable TPM in the BIOS.

   c. Configure TPM to use a startup key.

   d. Use Group Policy to enable TPM.

2. Which of the following are possible ways you can back up BitLocker recovery keys and passwords? (Choose all that apply.)

   a. Save the key to a USB flash drive.

   b. Save the key to a file on a portable drive.

   c. Save the key to Active Directory Domain Services (AD DS).

   d. Print the key.

3. Which of the following is something you should *not* do when enabling BitLocker and BitLocker To Go on your Windows 7 computer?

   a. Use BitLocker To Go to encrypt your USB flash drive containing the BitLocker recovery key.

   b. Use AD DS to save backup copies of your recovery keys.

   c. Use BitLocker without additional keys on a computer that is equipped with a TPM.

   d. Use Group Policy to enable BitLocker on a computer that is not equipped with a TPM.

4. You are using BitLocker To Go to protect portable hard drives in your organization. Users on Windows XP computers will need access to data on these hard drives. What do you need to do to ensure these users have access? (Choose two; each answer is part of the solution.)

   a. Copy the BitLocker To Go reader to the Windows XP computers.

   b. Select the **Require a startup key at every startup** option.

   c. Enable the **Configure use of passwords for fixed data drives** policy.

   d. Enable the **Allow access to BitLocker-protected fixed data drives from earlier versions of Windows** policy.

   e. Enable the **Allow data recovery agent** policy.

5. You want to set up DirectAccess to simplify access by mobile users to your company's network. Which of the following are required when setting up DirectAccess? (Choose three.)

   a. Client computers must be running either Windows Vista Enterprise or Ultimate, or Windows 7 Enterprise or Ultimate.

   b. Client computers must be running Windows 7 Professional or higher.

   c. Client computers must be running Windows 7 Enterprise or Ultimate.

   d. The DirectAccess server must be a domain controller and be running DNS.

   e. The DirectAccess server must be running the Web Server (IIS) server role and the DirectAccess Management Console server feature.

   f. The DirectAccess server must have two network adapters.

6. Some of your client computers that require DirectAccess connections to the network are set up to use Public IPv4 addresses. What technology should you use first to enable these computers to access the network?

   a. Unified Access Gateway (UAG)

   b. Teredo

   c. 6-to-4

   d. Secure Hypertext Transfer Protocol (HTTPS)

7. Which of the following are required on DirectAccess client computers to ensure that they can be authenticated on the network? (Choose two.)

   a. The clients must be joined to the domain and belong to a special security group configured on the DirectAccess server.

   b. The clients must be configured with IPv6 globally routable addresses.

   c. The clients must have installed a certificate that specifies the Client Authentication and Server Authentication certificate purposes.

   d. The clients must be equipped with a smart card reader that includes a certificate that specifies the Client Authentication and Server Authentication certificate purposes.

8. You have configured the Offline Files option on your Windows 7 computer and want to ensure that all available files on a network share are automatically cached to your computer. Which option should you enable?

   a. **Open Sync Center**

   b. **Disk usage**

   c. **Sync selected offline files**

   d. **Always available offline**

9. You want to enable client computers to temporarily cache all files obtained across a slow WAN link. What Group Policy setting should you enable?

   a. Configure Background Sync

   b. Enable Transparent Caching

   c. Administratively assigned offline files

   d. Configure slow link mode

10. You want to ensure that your Windows 7 laptop computer is ready to go within a few seconds and that your previous documents and applications are available to you immediately. You also want to ensure that your computer is protected with a password at this time. Which options should you enable?

    a. Standby mode and Password protection on wakeup

    b. Hibernation and BitLocker

    c. Sleep mode and Password protection on wakeup

    d. Sleep mode and BitLocker

11. You want to reduce the processor power being used so that you can watch a movie on your laptop computer while on a long flight without running out of battery power. What setting should you configure? (Choose two; each is a complete solution to this problem.)

    a. Balanced power plan

    b. Power saver power plan

    c. Processor power management advanced setting

    d. Sleep advanced setting

    e. Multimedia advanced setting

12. Which of the following tasks can you configure directly from the battery meter on a Windows 7 laptop computer? (Choose all that apply.)

    a. Choose a power plan

    b. Use presentation mode

    c. Adjust screen brightness

    d. Specify hard disk settings

    e. Open the Power Options dialog box

Foundation Topics

Configuring BitLocker and BitLocker To Go

First introduced with Windows Vista, BitLocker is a hardware-enabled data encryption feature that serves to protect data on a computer exposed to unauthorized physical access. Available on the Enterprise and Ultimate editions of Windows 7, BitLocker encrypts the entire Windows volume, thereby preventing unauthorized users from circumventing file and system permissions in Windows or attempting to access information on the protected partition from another computer or operating system. BitLocker even protects the data should an unauthorized user physically remove the hard drive from the computer and use other means to attempt access to the data.

New to Windows 7 is BitLocker To Go, which offers similar data encryption features to USB portable drives and external hard drives. BitLocker To Go creates a virtual volume on the USB drive, which is encrypted by means of an encryption key stored on the flash drive. BitLocker To Go also includes a Data Recovery Agent feature, which is modeled on the Encrypting File System (EFS) recovery agent that you learned about in Chapter 11, "Configuring Access to Local and Shared Resources."

BitLocker Drive Encryption

Available on the Enterprise and Ultimate editions of Windows 7, BitLocker utilizes the Trusted Platform Module (TPM) version 1.2 to provide secure protection of encryption keys and checking of key components when Windows is booting. A TPM is a microchip, built in to a computer, which is used to store cryptographic information such as encryption keys. Information stored on the TPM is more secure from external software attacks and physical theft. You can store keys and password on a USB flash drive that the user must insert to boot his computer. You can also employ an option that requires the user to supply a PIN code, thereby requiring multifactor authentication before the data becomes available for use. If an unauthorized individual has tampered with or modified system files or data in any way, the computer will not boot up.

On a computer that is equipped with a compatible TPM, BitLocker uses this TPM to lock the encryption keys that protect the contents of the protected drive; this includes the operating system and Registry files when you have used BitLocker to protect the system drive. When starting up the computer, TPM must verify the state of the computer before the keys are accessed. Consequently, an attacker cannot access the data by mounting the hard drive in a different computer.

At startup, TPM compares a hash of the operating system configuration with an earlier snapshot, thereby verifying the integrity of the startup process and releasing the keys. If BitLocker detects any security problem (such as a disk error, change to the BIOS, or changes to startup files), it locks the drive and enters Recovery mode. You can store encryption keys and restoration password on a USB flash drive or a separate file for additional data security and recovery capability. Should a user need to recover data using BitLocker's recovery mode, she merely needs to enter a recovery password to access data and the Windows operating system.

A user's computer does not need to be equipped with the TPM to use BitLocker. If your computer is equipped with TPM, you can use BitLocker in any of the following modes:

- **TPM only:** TPM alone validates the boot files, operating system files, and encrypted drive volumes during system startup. This mode provides a normal startup and logon experience to the user. However, if the TPM is missing or the integrity of the system has changed, BitLocker enters recovery mode, in which you will be required to provide a recovery key to access the computer.

- **TPM and PIN:** Uses both TPM and a user-supplied PIN for validation. You must enter this PIN correctly or BitLocker enters recovery mode.

- **TPM and startup key:** Uses both TPM and a startup key for validation. The user must provide a USB flash drive containing the startup key. If the user does not have this USB flash drive, BitLocker enters recovery mode.

- **TPM and smart card certificate:** Uses both TPM and a smart card certificate for validation. The user must provide a smart card containing a valid certificate to log on. If the smart card is not available or the certificate is not valid, BitLocker enters recovery mode.

If the computer does not have a TPM, BitLocker uses either a USB flash drive or smart card containing a startup key. In this case, BitLocker provides encryption, but not the added security of locking keys with the TPM.

NOTE Many newer computers are equipped with TPM, but TPM is not always activated. You might need to enter your BIOS setup system to enable TPM. The location of this setting depends on the BIOS in use but is typically in the Advanced section.

Preparing Your Computer to Use BitLocker

You can use a computer that does not have a TPM module if you have a USB flash drive to store the encryption keys and password. On such a computer, you need to enable BitLocker without a TPM from Group Policy, as the following procedure describes:

Step 1.   Click **Start**, type `gpedit.msc` in the Search field, and then press **Enter**. Accept the UAC prompt if you receive one.

Step 2. In the Local Group Policy Editor, navigate to **Computer Configuration\Administrative Templates\Windows Components\ BitLocker Drive Encryption\Operating System Drives**.

Step 3. Double-click **Require additional authentication at startup**, enable this policy, select the **Allow BitLocker without a compatible TPM** option, and then click **OK**.

Step 4. Close the Local Group Policy Editor.

Step 5. Click **Start**, type `Gpupdate /force` in the Search field, and then press **Enter**. This forces Group Policy to apply immediately.

After you've completed this procedure, you are ready to enable BitLocker as described next.

Enabling BitLocker

If your computer is equipped with a TPM, you can enable BitLocker directly without first accessing Group Policy. Use the following procedure to enable BitLocker on your operating system drive:

Step 1. Click **Start > Control Panel > System and Security > BitLocker Drive Encryption**. You receive the Help protect your files and folders by encrypting your drives dialog box, as shown in Figure 13-1. You can also access this utility by typing `bitlocker` into the Start menu search field and then selecting **BitLocker Drive Encryption** from the Programs list.

Figure 13-1   BitLocker offers to protect all available drives.

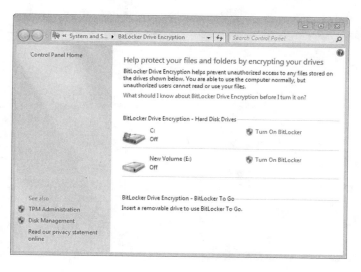

NOTE   If this dialog box is not available or the BitLocker Drive Encryption link does not appear in the Programs list, it means that the computer does not have a compatible TPM module. You will need to perform the procedure given in the previous subsection before you can enable BitLocker.

Step 2.   Opposite the drive you want to encrypt, click the **Turn On BitLocker** link. You can also right-click the desired drive in an Explorer window and choose **Turn On BitLocker**.

Step 3.   If you receive a UAC prompt, click **Yes** to proceed.

Step 4.   You receive a BitLocker Drive Encryption window, and after a few seconds, this window displays the Set BitLocker startup preferences page shown in Figure 13-2. Select from the following options:

— **Use BitLocker without additional keys:** Uses the TPM Only mode for validation, enabling the computer to start up without user interaction. If any hardware component has changed, BitLocker assumes the computer has been tampered with and locks up.

— **Require a PIN at every startup:** Enables the TPM and PIN option, requiring the user to enter a PIN at startup.

— **Require a Startup key at every startup:** Creates a startup key and writes it onto a USB flash drive. This is the only option available if your computer is not equipped with a TPM.

Figure 13-2   The BitLocker Drive Encryption applet in Control Panel enables you to encrypt your drive.

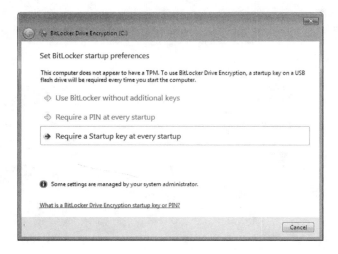

Step 5. If you have selected the **Require a Startup key at every startup** option, insert the USB drive when prompted and then click **Save**. If you have selected the **Require a PIN at every startup** option, enter and confirm the PIN and then click **Save**.

Step 6. The How do you want to store your recovery key? page provides the three options shown in Figure 13-3. Use one or more of these options to save the recovery password. If you print it, ensure that you save the printed document in a secure location. If you save it to a USB flash drive, you will see the dialog box shown in Figure 13-4. Click **Save** and then click **Next**.

Figure 13-3   You are given three options for storing your recovery key.

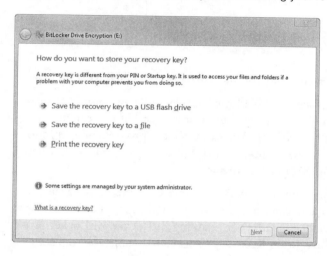

Figure 13-4   Select the appropriate USB drive for saving your password.

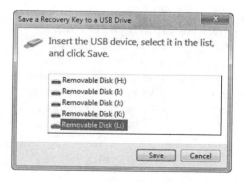

Step 7. You receive the Are you ready to encrypt this drive? dialog box shown in Figure 13-5. Ensure that the check box labeled **Run BitLocker system check** is selected and then click **Continue** to proceed.

Figure 13-5   Select Continue to encrypt your partition.

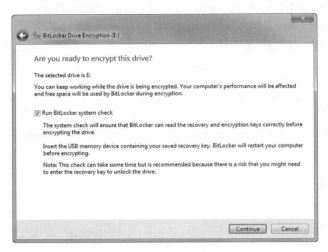

Step 8.   You will need to restart your computer to proceed. Click **Restart now**.

Step 9.   Encryption takes place and Windows 7 displays an icon in the notification area. This process can take an hour or longer, but you can use your computer while it is occurring. You can track the progress of encryption by hovering your mouse pointer over this icon. You are informed when encryption is complete. Click **Close**.

After you have completed this procedure, you must have the USB drive to start your computer. Alternatively, you can use the recovery mode and type the recovery password that was automatically created while enabling BitLocker. BitLocker provides the BitLocker Drive Encryption Recovery Console to enable you to insert the USB drive that contains the recovery password. Or press **Enter**, type the recovery password, and press **Enter** again.

> **CAUTION**   Ensure that you do not lose the recovery password. If you lose the recovery password, your Windows installation and all data stored on its partition will be permanently lost. You will need to repartition your hard drive and reinstall Windows. Consequently, you should create at least two copies of the password as described in the previous procedure and store them in a secure location. Do not leave the USB flash drive in your laptop bag; attach it to your key chain or store it elsewhere on your person.

Managing BitLocker

After you've encrypted your drive using BitLocker, the BitLocker applet shows additional options for the protected drive, as shown in Figure 13-6. The Manage BitLocker option enables you to save or print the recovery key again or to duplicate the startup key, thereby enabling you to recover these items while the system is running. You can also back this information up into Active Directory if your computer belongs to an Active Directory Domain Services (AD DS) domain.

Figure 13-6   The BitLocker applet displays a distinctive icon for the protected drive and provides several options for its management.

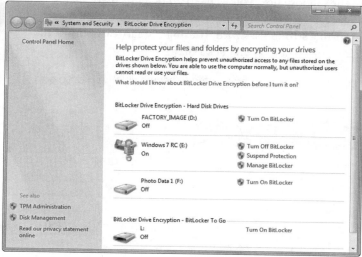

The Suspend Protection option enables you to temporarily disable BitLocker. Select this option and then click **Yes**. After doing so, this option changes to Resume Protection; click it to reenable BitLocker.

The Turn Off BitLocker option enables you to remove BitLocker protection. To do so, select **Turn Off BitLocker**. On the BitLocker Drive Encryption dialog box that appears, select **Decrypt Drive**. This procedure decrypts your volume and discards all encryption keys; it begins immediately without further prompts. You will be able to monitor the decryption action from an icon in the notification area.

BitLocker To Go

As already mentioned, BitLocker To Go extends the full volume encryption capabilities of BitLocker to USB flash drives and portable hard drives. You can protect all portable drives regardless of whether they are formatted with the FAT, FAT32, or NTFS file systems. Microsoft engineers modified BitLocker to overlay what it calls a *discovery volume* on top of the original physical volume on the portable drive. This volume includes a BitLocker To Go Reader that also enables use of the BitLocker To Go volume on computers running Windows XP and Vista. Users of these computers can download a reader from the Microsoft Download Center.

Use the following procedure to enable BitLocker To Go:

Step 1.   Click Start > **Control Panel > System and Security > BitLocker Drive Encryption** to display the screen previously shown in Figure 13-1.

Step 2.   Insert the USB drive and click **Turn On BitLocker** beside the drive icon.

Step 3.   You receive the Choose how you want to unlock this drive dialog box shown in Figure 13-7. If using a password, select this option and then type and confirm a strong password. If using a smart card, insert the smart card in your reader. Then click **Next**.

Figure 13-7   You can use either a password or smart card to secure your USB drive with BitLocker To Go.

Step 4.   Select an option to save the recovery password to a file or print it. Then click **Next**.

Step 5.   From the Encrypt the Drive page, select **Start Encrypting**.

Step 6.   You are returned to the BitLocker Drive Encryption applet, which tracks the progress of encrypting your drive and informs you when the drive is encrypted. Do not disconnect your drive until encryption is completed.

CAUTION   Do not enable BitLocker To Go on the USB drive containing your BitLocker startup key. Windows 7 currently does not permit this, although a future update or service pack might add this capability.

BitLocker Policies

Besides the policy already mentioned to enable BitLocker on a computer that is not equipped with a TPM, Group Policy has a series of settings that help you to manage BitLocker. You can access these polices from the **Computer Configuration\Administrative Templates\Windows Components\BitLocker Drive Encryption** node. This node has three subnodes: Fixed Data Drives, Operating System Drives, and Removable Data Drives, as well as several policies that affect all types of drives. Microsoft provides recommendations for many of these settings at "Best Practices for BitLocker in Windows 7" at http://technet.microsoft.com/en-us/library/dd875532(WS.10).aspx.

Operating System Drives

As shown in Figure 13-8, you can configure the following policies that govern BitLocker as used on operating system drives:

Figure 13-8   Group Policy provides these settings for BitLocker used on operating system drives.

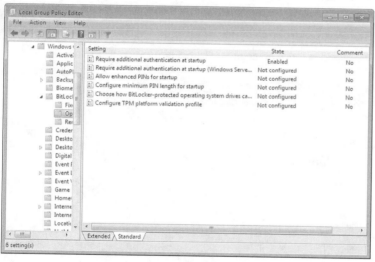

- **Require additional authentication at startup:** As mentioned earlier in this section, this setting enables you to use BitLocker on a computer without a TPM. By enabling this policy, you can also specify whether BitLocker requires additional authentication including a startup key and/or PIN.

- **Require additional authentication at startup (Windows Server 2008 and Windows Vista):** Enables similar settings for Windows Vista and Windows Server 2008 computers, except that you cannot utilize both a startup key and PIN.

- **Allow enhanced PINs for startup:** Enables the use of a PIN that contains additional characters, including uppercase and lowercase letters, symbols, numerals, and spaces.

- **Configure minimum PIN length for startup:** Specifies a minimum length for the startup PIN. You can choose a minimum length of anywhere from 4 to 20 digits.

- **Choose how BitLocker-protected operating system drives can be recovered:** Enables the use of a data recovery agent. We discuss this policy later in this section.

- **Configure TPM platform validation profile:** Enables you to specify how the TPM security hardware secures the BitLocker encryption key. The validation profile includes a set of Platform Configuration Register indices, each of which is associated with components that run at startup. You can select from a series of indices provided in the policy's options.

Fixed Data Drive Policies

As shown in Figure 13-9, you can configure the following policies that govern BitLocker used on fixed data drives (in other words, internal hard drive partitions containing data but not operating system files).

Figure 13-9   Group Policy provides these settings for BitLocker used on fixed data drives.

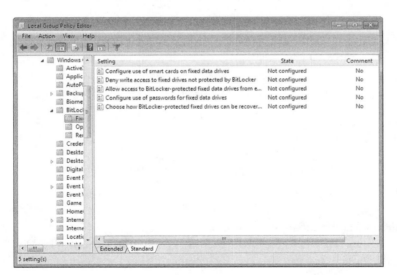

- **Configure use of smart cards on fixed data drives:** Enables you to specify whether smart cards can be used to authenticate user access to drives protected by BitLocker. You can optionally require the use of smart cards.

- **Deny write access to fixed drives not protected by BitLocker:** Enables you to require BitLocker protection on writable drives. If enabled, any drives not protected by BitLocker are read-only.

- **Allow access to BitLocker-protected fixed data drives from earlier versions of Windows:** Specifies whether drives formatted with the FAT or FAT32 file system can be unlocked and viewed on computers running earlier Windows versions (back to Windows XP SP2).

- **Configure use of passwords for fixed data drives:** Enables you to specify whether a password is required for unlocking BitLocker-protected fixed data drives. You can optionally specify that a password is required, and you can choose to allow or require password complexity and specify the minimum password length.

- **Choose how BitLocker-protected fixed drives can be recovered:** Similar to the corresponding operating system drives policy.

More information on all these policies is available from the Help field in each policy's Properties dialog box. These policies are also available for removable drives (BitLocker To Go) in the Removable Data Drives subnode of Group Policy.

Use of Data Recovery Agents

A data recovery agent (DRA) is a user account that is configured for recovering data encrypted with BitLocker in a manner analogous to the EFS recovery agent described in Chapter 11. The DRA uses his smart card certificates and public keys to accomplish this action.

To specify a DRA for a BitLocker-protected drive, you must first designate the recovery agent by opening the Local Group Policy Editor and navigating to the **Computer Configuration\Windows Settings\Security Settings\Public Key Policies\BitLocker Drive Encryption** node. Right-click this node and choose **Add Data Recovery Agent**. This starts a wizard that is similar to that used for creating EFS data recovery agents. You can browse for the required certificates or select them from AD DS in a domain environment.

After you've specified your data recovery agent, you need to access the **Computer Configuration\Administrative Templates\Windows Components\BitLocker Drive Encryption** node of Group Policy and enable the Provide the unique identifiers for your organization policy (see Figure 13-10). In the text boxes provided, specify a unique identifier that will be associated with drives that are enabled with BitLocker. This identifier uniquely associates the drives with your company or department and is required for BitLocker to manage and update data recovery agents. After doing so, this identifier will be automatically associated with any drives on which you enable BitLocker.

You can add this identifier to drives previously protected with BitLocker by opening an administrative command prompt and typing the following command:

```
manage-bde -SetIdentifier drive_letter
```

Figure 13-10   You need to provide a unique identifier to use a BitLocker DRA.

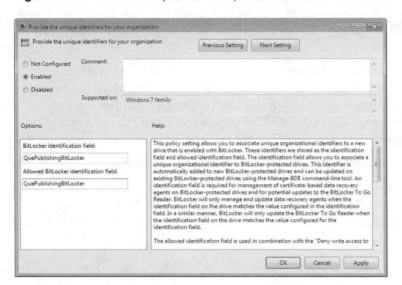

Where *drive_letter* is the drive letter for the BitLocker-protected drive. This utility sets the identifier to the value you've specified in Group Policy and displays a message informing you that this identifier has been set.

After you have specified a DRA and the unique identifiers, you can configure policies in each subnode of the **Computer Configuration\Administrative Templates\Windows Components\BitLocker Drive Encryption** node of Group Policy that choose how BitLocker-protected drives can be recovered. Each of the three subnodes contains a similar policy setting that is shown for operating system drives in Figure 13-11. Enable each of these policies as required and select the **Allow data recovery agent** check box. Then configure the following options as required:

- **48-digit recovery password:** This drop-down list provides choices to allow, require, or do not allow a 48-digit recovery password. Use of a 48-digit recovery password improves DRA security.

- **256-Bit recovery key:** This drop-down list provides choices to allow, require, or do not allow a 256-bit recovery key. Use of a 256-bit recovery key improves DRA security.

- **Omit recovery options from the BitLocker setup wizard:** Blocks the appearance of the recovery options previously shown in Figure 13-3; when enabled, these recovery options are determined by policy settings.

- **Save BitLocker recovery information to AD DS for operating system drives:** Enables you to choose the BitLocker recovery information that will be stored in AD DS.

Figure 13-11   Group Policy provides these data recovery options for operating system drives.

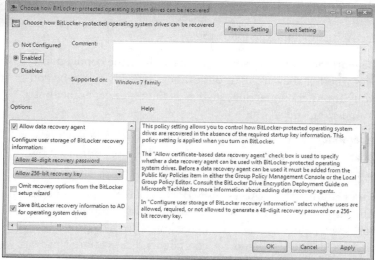

- **Configure storage of BitLocker recovery information to AD DS:** Determines how much recovery information is stored in AD DS when you have selected the preceding option. You can choose to store recovery passwords and key packages or to store recovery passwords only.

- **Do not enable BitLocker until recovery information is stored to AD DS for operating system drives:** When enabled, prevents users from enabling BitLocker unless the computer is attached to the domain and BitLocker recovery information can be backed up to AD DS.

Similar options are provided for fixed and removable data drives; the wording of the last policy setting changes to reflect the type of drive being configured.

NOTE   BitLocker provides several additional DRA management options, including verification of the identification field and listing of configured DRAs. For more information, refer to "Using Data Recovery Agents with BitLocker" at http://technet.microsoft.com/en-us/library/dd875560(WS.10).aspx. For additional information on BitLocker as a whole, refer to "BitLocker Drive Encryption in Windows 7: Frequently Asked Questions" at http://technet.microsoft.com/en-us/library/ee449438(WS.10).aspx.

Configuring DirectAccess

DirectAccess is a new feature of Windows 7 and Windows Server 2008 R2 that enables users to directly connect to corporate networks from any Internet connection. When enabled, a user can access network resources as though he were actually at the office. DirectAccess uses IPv6 over IPSec to create a seamless, bidirectional, secured tunnel between the user's computer and the office network, without the need for a virtual private network (VPN) connection.

The benefits of DirectAccess include the following:

- **Improved mobile workforce productivity:** Users have the same connectivity to network resources whether they are in or out of the office. Users can be connected through any Internet connection, such as a client's office, home, hotel, airport Wi-Fi connection, and so on.

- **Improved management of remote users:** You can apply Group Policy updates and software updates to remote computers whenever they are connected by means of DirectAccess.

- **Improved network security:** DirectAccess uses IPv6 over IPSec to enable encrypted communications and secured authentication of the computer to the corporate network even before the user has logged on. IPv6 also provides globally routable IP addresses for remote access clients. Encryption is provided using Data Encryption Standard (DES), which uses a 56-bit key, and Triple DES (3DES), which uses three 56-bit keys.

- **Access control capabilities:** You can choose to allow only specific applications or subnets of the corporate network or to allow unlimited network access by DirectAccess users.

- **Simplified network traffic:** Unnecessary traffic on the corporate network is reduced because DirectAccess separates its traffic from other Internet traffic. You can specify that DirectAccess clients send all traffic through the DirectAccess server.

Windows Server 2008 R2 includes the required server functionality to operate DirectAccess. Optionally, you can also include Microsoft Forefront Unified Access Gateway (UAG). This option provides enhanced security within and outside the corporate network, enabling DirectAccess for IPv4-only applications and resources on the network. Security is improved on the DirectAccess server, and built-in wizards and tools simplify deployment and reduce configuration errors.

NOTE   For more information on UAG, refer to "UAG and DirectAccess" at http://www.microsoft.com/Forefront/edgesecurity/iag/en/us/UAG-DirectAccess.aspx. For more information on all aspects of DirectAccess, refer to "DirectAccess Early Adopter's Guide" at http://technet.microsoft.com/en-us/library/dd637789(WS.10).aspx and "DirectAccess" at http://technet.microsoft.com/en-us/network/dd420463.aspx and links included in these documents.

Network Infrastructure Requirements

DirectAccess client computers must be running Windows 7 Enterprise or Ultimate edition. DirectAccess requires an AD DS domain with one or more DirectAccess servers that meet the following requirements:

- The server must be running Windows Server 2008 R2 and be a domain member server. This server needs to have the Web Server (IIS) server role installed.

- You need to install the DirectAccess Management Console server feature from the Server Manager Add Features Wizard to enable the server to act as a DirectAccess server.

- The server must be equipped with two network adapters: one connected directly to the network and one connected to the corporate intranet.

- The network adapter connected to the Internet must be configured with two consecutive IPv4 public addresses.

- The server requires digital certificates obtained from an Active Directory Certificate Services (AD CS) server configured as an Enterprise Certification Authority (CA). DirectAccess clients use certificates from the same CA; doing so enables both client and server to trust each other's certificates.

In addition, the domain must have at least one domain controller and DNS server that runs Windows Server 2008 SP2 or Windows Server 2008 R2. If UAG is not in use and connection to IPv4-only resources is required, you must have a Network Address Translation 64 (NAT64) device.

Using IPv6 with DirectAccess

DirectAccess requires using IPv6 in order that DirectAccess clients can have globally routable addresses. This technology extends network infrastructure that already is configured with IPv6 so that clients can still use IPv4 to access the Internet if desired. If the network infrastructure does not include IPv6, you can use the 6-to-4 and Teredo IPv6 technologies so that DirectAccess clients can connect to an intranet that includes IPv4 only. We introduced 6-to-4 and Teredo in Chapter 9, "Configuring TCP/IP."

Table 13-2 summarizes these network connectivity options.

Table 13-2   Options for Connecting DirectAccess Clients to the Network

Type of IP Address Assigned to the Client	Preferred Method of Connection
Globally routable IPv6 address	Globally routable IPv6 address
Public IPv4 address	6-to-4
Private (NAT) IPv4 address	Teredo
If unable to connect using these methods	IP-HTTPS

Use of Network Access Protection

You can use Network Access Protection (NAP) with DirectAccess so that DirectAccess clients must submit a health certificate for initial authentication with the DirectAccess server. This health certificate proves that the client is free of malware and is up-to-date with regard to security updates and antimalware definitions. Clients obtain this certificate from a Health Registration Authority on the Internet prior to initial connection to the DirectAccess server. NAP enables you to ensure that client computers do not spread malware to the internal network; noncompliant computers are restricted from connecting to compliant computers or network resources.

The DirectAccess Connection Process

Connecting to corporate resources involves the following process:

Step 1. The DirectAccess client computer connects to a network and determines whether it is connected to the corporate intranet. If it is already connected, it does not use DirectAccess; if it is external, it uses DirectAccess.

Step 2. The client computer uses IPv6 and IPSec to connect to the DirectAccess server via an intranet website on the server that is configured when the server is set up. If the client is not on an IPv6 network, it uses 6-to-4 or Teredo to encapsulate the IPv6 traffic into the IPv4 connection.

Step 3. If a firewall or proxy server prevents the client computer from using 6-to-4 or Teredo, the client computer tries to use IP over Secure Hypertext Transfer Protocol (IP-HTTPS) with Secure Sockets Layer (SSL) to encapsulate the IPv6 traffic.

Step 4. The DirectAccess client and server authenticate each other using their computer certificates, and the IPSec tunnel is set up. In addition, the DirectAccess server validates the client by means of group memberships configured in AD DS.

Step 5. If NAP is in use, the DirectAccess client submits its health certificate to a NAP health policy server, which determines whether the client is in compliance with system health requirements.

Step 6. The user logs on and the DirectAccess client establishes a second IPSec tunnel for access to the network resources.

Step 7. The DirectAccess server forwards traffic between the client and the corporate network resources according to the user's access permissions.

Typically, this process happens automatically without intervention from the user apart from the logon process.

Configuring DirectAccess Clients

Windows 7 Enterprise or Ultimate client computers must be joined to the AD DS domain and belong to a special security group that the server administrator configures when setting up the DirectAccess server. When connected to the internal network, a client receives its configuration via Group Policy. You also need to install a computer certificate on the client that enables DirectAccess authentication. As already mentioned, a Windows Server 2008 R2 computer running AD CS provides this certificate.

You can configure the required Group Policy settings in a GPO linked to the security group used for DirectAccess client computers. Figure 13-12 shows the available settings, which are found at the **Computer Configuration\Administrative Templates\Network\TCPIP Settings\IPv6 Transition Technologies** node. These settings enable you to configure settings for client computers using the 6-to-4, Teredo, or IP-HTTPS connection technologies. Consult the Help text for each policy for information on what each policy does.

Figure 13-12   Group Policy provides these settings for configuring DirectAccess client computers.

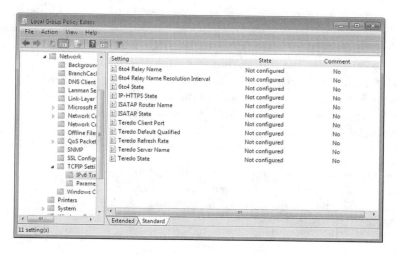

From within the same GPO, you need to configure the name resolution policy found at **Computer Configuration\Windows Settings\Name Resolution Policy**. As shown in Figure 13-13, this policy sets up a name resolution policy table that stores configuration settings for DNS security (DNSSEC) and DNS settings for DirectAccess. You can create or edit policy rules from this policy.

Figure 13-13   Group Policy provides these settings for configuring a name resolution policy.

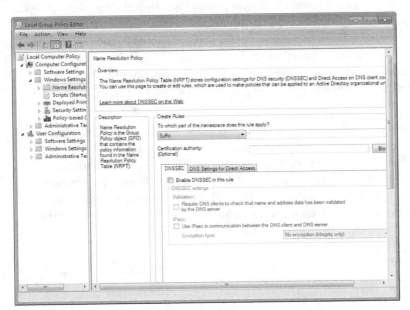

You can use the Certificates snap-in to verify that each client computer has received an appropriate certificate. Add this snap-in to a blank Microsoft Management Console (MMC) and configure it for the local computer account. You should see a certificate in the Personal\Certificates node of this snap-in and it should specify the Client Authentication and Server Authentication certificate purposes, as shown in Figure 13-14.

> **NOTE**   For a detailed procedure that sets up both servers and client computers for DirectAccess, refer to "Test Lab Guide: Demonstrate DirectAccess" at http://www.microsoft.com/downloads/details.aspx?displaylang=en&FamilyID=8d47ed5f-d217-4d84-b698-f39360d82fac.

Configuring Authentication

As already mentioned, DirectAccess authenticates the computer before the user logs on with the aid of the client computer and server certificates. This authentication provides access to DNS servers and domain controllers so that the user can log on with her username and password and be authenticated to AD DS.

Figure 13-14   The Certificates snap-in should show that your computer has received a certificate that specifies the Client Authentication and Server Authentication purposes.

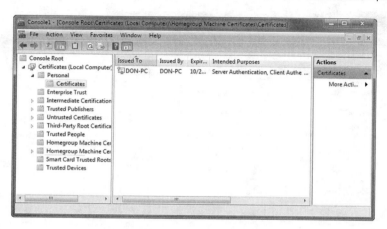

You can also implement two-factor authentication using a smart card as well as the username/password combination. The user must insert her smart card and then log on and provide her password; however, she can access Internet resources from her client computer without the smart card. This increases security by preventing an unauthorized user who has obtained the legitimate user's password but not the smart card from accessing the network (or the smart card but not the password).

Configuring Mobility Options

Windows 7 provides a feature-complete environment for all types of mobile computers, including laptops, notebooks, and Tablet PC devices. Included are features for connecting your portable computer with wired and wireless networks and sharing data with these networks in a secure fashion.

Control Panel

The Hardware and Sound category of Control Panel contains two applets of particular interest to mobile users. Open the **Control Panel** and select **Hardware and Sound** to display the window shown in Figure 13-15, which features the following applets among others:

- **Power Options:** Enables you to configure power use for specific conditions, including connecting your computer to an AC outlet or running it on battery power.

- **Windows Mobility Center:** Enables you to configure common mobile computer settings, such as display settings, speaker volume, and battery status.

Figure 13-15   The Hardware and Sound category of Control Panel on portable computers features the Windows Mobility Center for performing activities specific to mobile computing.

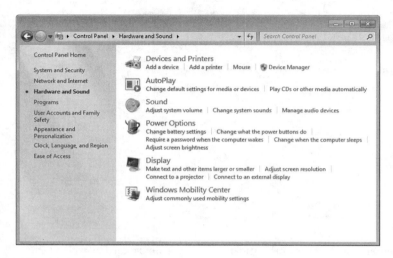

Windows Mobility Center

Windows versions prior to Vista required you to navigate to different locations in order to perform actions specific to portable computers (such as adjusting the display properties, power conservation, wireless networking, and so on). Windows 7 continues the Windows Mobility Center, which centralizes features important to mobile computing in a single location. This application enables you to configure a large range of features specific to notebook computers. Use the following procedure to access the Windows Mobility Center:

Step 1.   Click **Start,** type `mobility` in the Start Search text box, and then click **Windows Mobility Center** in the program list. You can also click **Start > Control Panel > Hardware and Sound > Windows Mobility Center.** The Windows Mobility Center opens, as shown in Figure 13-16.

Figure 13-16   Windows Mobility Center enables you to control several features related to portable computers.

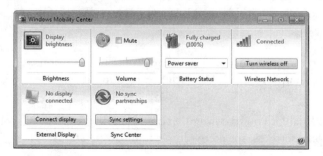

Step 2. Select the control provided by the appropriate applet. The following might be available, depending on the edition of Windows 7 and the capabilities of your computer:

— **Brightness:** Adjust the slider provided to control the brightness of your portable computer display.

— **Volume:** Adjust the slider to control your computer's speaker volume or select the **Mute** check box to turn it off.

— **Battery Status:** Displays the current charge level of your computer's battery. You can also select a power scheme from the drop-down list provided, which might include custom settings set up by the computer manufacturer if available. We discuss power options later in this chapter.

— **Wireless Network:** Provides the current connection status and signal strength. Select the command button provided to toggle the wireless network on or off. You learned about configuring wireless network settings in Chapter 10, "Configuring Network and Firewall Settings."

— **Screen Orientation:** Available on Tablet PC devices only, enables you to toggle the display orientation between horizontal (landscape) and vertical (portrait) modes.

— **External Display:** Enables you to connect an external monitor to your mobile computer or its docking station and configure its properties.

— **Sync Center:** Displays your current synchronization settings. Select the command button provided to view synchronization activities or modify the settings.

— **Presentation Settings:** Select the command button provided to turn on and modify settings for giving presentations.

NOTE Mobility Center controls depend on your computer's features. Windows 7 does not display modules associated with features not supported by your mobile computer. In addition, certain editions of Windows 7 do not support and therefore do not display certain portability features. Furthermore, computer manufacturers might add additional modules to the Mobility Center.

Using Offline Files

The Offline Files feature in Windows 7 originated with Windows 2000 and XP. It replaces the My Briefcase feature included with Windows 9x/NT and works only on Microsoft-based networks. The Offline Files feature enables a user to access and work with files and folders stored on a network share when the user is disconnected from that share. For example, such a situation could occur when the user is working from a laptop on the road or at home. This feature ensures that users are always working with the most recent version of their files.

When you enable Offline Files, the feature makes anything you have cached from the network available to you. It also preserves the normal view of network drives, as well as shared folder and NTFS permissions. When you reconnect to the network, the feature automatically synchronizes any changes with the versions on the network. Also, changes made to your files while online are saved to both the network share and your local cache.

Offline files are stored on the local computer in a special area of the hard drive called a *cache*. More specifically, this is located at `%systemroot%\CSC`, where `CSC` stands for client-side caching. By default, this cache takes up 10% of the disk volume space.

You need to configure both the client computer and the server to use the Offline Files feature. Keep in mind that, in this sense, the "server" refers to any computer that holds a shared folder available to users of other computers. This might be a computer running Windows 2000 or XP Professional; Vista Business, Enterprise, or Ultimate; Windows 7 Professional, Enterprise, or Ultimate; as well as a server running Windows 2000 Server, Windows Server 2003, or Windows Server 2008 R2.

> **NOTE**   For more information on new features of Offline Files in Windows 7 and Windows Server 2008 R2, refer to "What's New in Offline Files" at http://technet.microsoft.com/en-us/library/ff183315(WS.10).aspx.

Client Computer Configuration

By default, the Offline Files feature is enabled on the client computer. The following procedure shows you how to configure the available client options.

Step 1.   Click **Start**, type `offline` in the Start menu search box, and then select **Manage offline files** from the list that appears.

Step 2.   From the General tab of the Offline Files dialog box shown in Figure 13-17, select the following options as required:

— **Disable offline files:** Select this command button if you do not want to use Offline Files. You must accept a UAC prompt and then restart your computer to disable offline files. If Offline Files are disabled, this command button enables you to enable Offline Files.

— **Open Sync Center:** Opens the Sync Center.

Figure 13-17   You can configure offline files at the client computer from the Offline Files dialog box.

— **View your offline files:** Opens a Windows Explorer window displaying the contents of the Offline Files folder.

Step 3.   Select the **Disk Usage** tab to configure the amount of disk space currently used for storing offline files. Click **Change limits** to modify this setting. Click **Delete temporary files** to delete locally stored files.

Step 4.   Select the **Encryption** tab and then click **Encrypt** to encrypt offline files. This feature uses EFS to encrypt offline files, keeping them secure from unauthorized users. By default, offline files are not encrypted.

Step 5.   Select the **Network** tab to check for slow network connections. You can specify the number of minutes (five by default) at which Windows 7 checks for a slow connection.

Step 6.   When finished, click **OK** or click **Apply** (and then click **OK**).

When you have enabled your computer for Offline Files, copies of files and folders you access across the network are stored automatically in your cache area according to the server configuration parameters in effect. These parameters are discussed in the next section.

You can also automatically cache all available files from a network share to which you have connected. Right-click the shared folder icon and choose **Always available offline**, as shown in Figure 13-18. This automatically caches all available files without your having to open them first. You can also synchronize your cached files manually when you are connected to the network share. To do so, right-click the shared folder icon and choose **Sync > Sync Selected Offline Files**.

Figure 13-18 Caching files from a network share.

Server Configuration

To enable the caching of files stored on a shared folder, you need to configure the shared folder on the server and specify the type of caching available. The following procedure shows you how to perform these tasks on a Windows 7 computer.

Step 1.   Right-click the shared folder and choose **Properties**.

Step 2.   On the Sharing tab of the folder's Properties dialog box, click **Advanced Sharing**. If you receive a UAC prompt, click **Yes**.

Step 3.   On the Advanced Sharing dialog box, click **Caching** to open the Offline Settings dialog box shown in Figure 13-19.

Figure 13-19 The Offline Settings dialog box provides several options for enabling offline caching in Windows 7.

Step 4.   Select from the following options and then click **OK**:

— **Only the files and programs that users specify will be available offline:** Requires that a user connecting to the share specifically indicate the files to be made available for caching. This is the default setting.

— **No files or programs from the shared folder are available offline:** Effectively disables the Offline Files feature.

— **All files and programs that users open from the shared folder are automatically available offline:** Makes every file in the share available for caching by a remote user. When a user opens a file from the share, the file is downloaded to the client's cache and replaces any older versions of the file.

— **Optimized for performance:** Enables expanded caching of shared programs so that users can run them locally, thereby improving performance.

Step 5.   Click **OK** to close the Advanced Sharing dialog box and then click **Close** to close the Properties dialog box for the shared folder.

Use of the Sync Center

The Sync Center was first included in Windows Vista; it enables you to manage cached offline files and folders after you have configured them as described in the previous sections. Shown in Figure 13-20, the Sync Center enables you to perform the following actions:

Figure 13-20   The Sync Center enables you to view and manage file and folder synchronization.

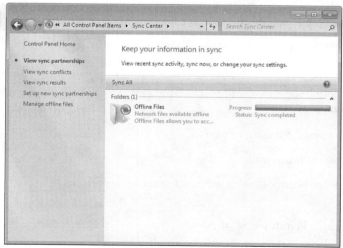

- **Synchronization with different device types:** The Sync Center enables you to synchronize data with other computers and with devices such as smart phones, digital media devices, personal data assistants (PDAs), and so on.

- **Multiple synchronization:** You can synchronize files and folders with a single device or all available devices.

- **Manage synchronization activities:** You can initiate manual synchronization, stop actions in progress, check device connectivity status, view the status of activities, and be notified about possible conflicts.

- **Conflict resolution:** If different users have performed conflicting edits on a file (such as a Word document), the Sync Center informs you and enables you to save multiple copies of the edited file for later analysis.

- **Sync partnerships:** Sync Center establishes sync partnerships for all shared folders that you have cached locally. You can configure these partnerships to specify how and when the folders are synced.

Use the following procedure to view sync partnerships and synchronize files:

Step 1.   Use one of the following methods to open the Sync Center:

— From the Windows Mobility Center, click **Sync Settings**.

— Click **Start** and type **sync** in the Search text box. Click **Sync Center** in the Programs list.

— From the Offline Files dialog box previously shown in Figure 13-17, click **Open Sync Center**.

Step 2.   In the task list on the left side of the Sync Center, click **View sync partnerships** to display configured partnerships.

Step 3.   To set up a new sync partnership, click **Set up new sync partnerships**.

Step 4.   To synchronize a specific network share, right-click its partnership and then click **Sync offline files**.

Sync Center also enables you to schedule synchronization activities to take place at any of the following actions:

- At a specified time and synchronization interval

- When you log on to your computer

- When your computer has been idle for a specified number of minutes (15 minutes by default)

- When you lock or unlock Windows

Use the following steps to create a schedule:

Step 1.   In Sync Center, right-click the required synchronization partnership and then click **Schedule for Offline Files**.

Step 2.   In the Offline Files Sync Schedule dialog box that appears, select the items to be synced on this schedule and then click **Next**.

Step 3.   To specify a time for the sync to begin, select **At a scheduled time**. To initiate synchronization when an event such as logging on to the computer occurs, select **When an event occurs** and then select the desired action or actions.

Step 4.   If you select **At a scheduled time**, Sync Center automatically provides the current date and time as a start time and a one-day repeat interval (see Figure 13-21). Accept these or specify a different date, time, and interval as required, and then click **Next**.

Figure 13-21   You can specify the date, time, and synchronization interval for your sync schedule.

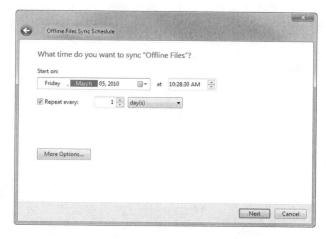

Step 5.   Specify a descriptive name for the scheduled synchronization and then click **Save schedule**.

After you have created a synchronization schedule, the Offline Files Sync Schedule dialog box provides additional options for viewing or editing an existing sync schedule or deleting the schedule.

If different users modify a synchronized file while working on different computers, a synchronization conflict occurs. Sync Center informs you when conflicts have occurred. To view information about sync conflicts, click **View sync conflicts** in the Tasks pane. As shown in Figure 13-22, Sync Center informs you about the file or files that are in conflict.

Figure 13-22   Sync Center informs you when synchronization conflicts occur.

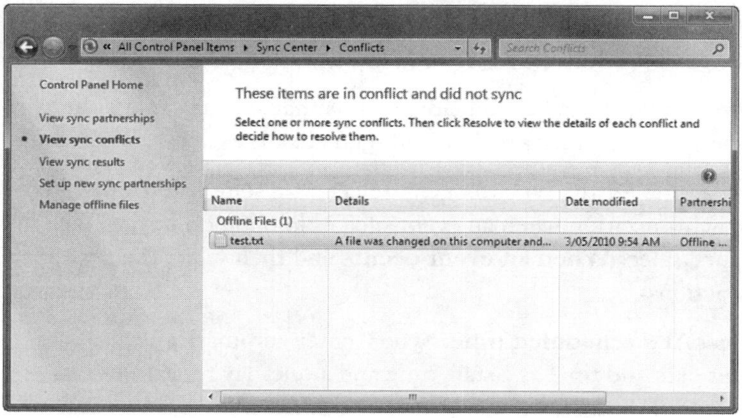

To resolve a conflict, select it and click **Resolve**. As shown in Figure 13-23, Sync Center enables you to keep either or both versions by using an altered filename, thereby allowing you to compare them and resolve differences later.

Figure 13-23   Sync Center enables you to decide which version of a file you want to keep or if you want to keep both versions.

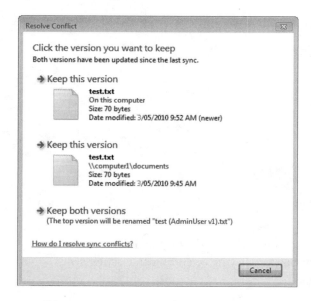

Offline File Policies

Group Policy makes available a series of policy settings. In Local Group Policy Editor or Group Policy Management Editor, navigate to **Computer Configuration\Administrative Templates\Network\Offline Files** to display the policy settings shown in Figure 13-24. Note that some of the policy settings available here are applicable to computers running older Windows versions only and are provided for backward compatibility purposes. Table 13-3 describes the more important policy settings relevant to Windows 7 and Windows Server 2008 R2 computers that you should be aware of.

Figure 13-24   You can configure a large number of policy settings related to the use of Offline Files.

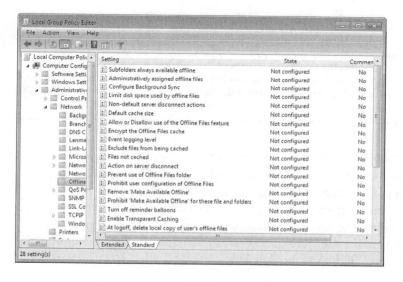

Table 13-3   Offline File Policies

Policy	Description
Administratively assigned offline files	Specifies network files and folders that are always available offline. Type the Universal Naming Convention (UNC) path to the required files.
Configure Background Sync	Enables you to control synchronization of files across slow links. You can configure sync interval and variance parameters, as well as blackout periods when sync should not occur.
Limit disk space used by offline files	When enabled, limits the amount of disk space in megabytes used to store offline files.
Allow or Disallow use of the Offline Files feature	Determines whether users can enable Offline Files. When enabled, Offline Files is enabled and users cannot disable it; when disabled, Offline Files is disabled and users cannot enable it.
Encrypt the Offline Files cache	When enabled, all files in the Offline Files cache are encrypted.

Table 13-3   Offline File Policies

Policy	Description
Exclude files from Being cached	Enables you to exclude file types according to extension from being cached. Specify the extensions to be excluded, separated by semicolons—for example, *.jpg; *.mp3.
Enable Transparent Caching	Controls caching of offline files across slow links. You can specify a network latency value above which network files are temporarily cached. More about this policy in the next section.
Configure slow-link mode	Controls background synchronization across slow links and determines how network file requests are handled across slow links.
Configure Slow link speed	Specifies the threshold link speed value below which Offline Files considers a network connection to be slow. Specify the value in bits per second divided by 100; for example, specify 1280 for a threshold of 128,000 bps.

Configuring Transparent Caching of Offline Files

New to Windows 7 is the concept of *transparent file caching*, which enables client computers to temporarily cache files obtained across a slow WAN link more aggressively, thereby reducing the number of times the client might have to retrieve the file across the slow link. Use of transparent caching also serves to reduce bandwidth consumption across the WAN link. Prior to Windows 7, client computers always retrieved such a file across the slow link.

The first time a user accesses a file across the WAN, Windows 7 retrieves it from the remote computer; this file is then cached to the local computer. Subsequently, the local computer checks with the remote server to ensure that the file has not changed and then accesses it from the local cache if its copy is up-to-date. Note that this type of file caching is temporary; clients cannot access these files when they go offline.

You can configure the Enable Transparent Caching policy shown in Figure 13-25 so that clients can perform transparent caching. Enable this policy and set the network latency value, which is the number of milliseconds beyond which the client will temporarily cache files obtained across the WAN.

Configuring Power Options

The chief issue with system performance for mobile users is that of managing power consumption on laptop computers when running on battery power. Microsoft provides the Control Panel Power Options applet for configuring several power management options that enable you to configure energy-saving schemes appropriate to your hardware.

Figure 13-25   Enable the Enable Transparent Caching policy setting so that clients can temporarily cache files obtained across a slow WAN link.

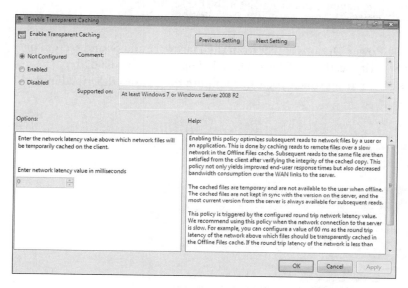

NOTE   Although designed with mobile users in mind, the power options discussed in this section are available to all users of Windows 7. Users of desktop computers can utilize these options to decrease electricity consumption in these days of ever-increasing electric utility bills.

Windows 7 uses sleep mode, which replaces the standby mode used in Windows versions prior to Vista and offers the following advantages compared to shutting down your computer:

- Windows 7 automatically saves your work and configuration information in RAM and turns off the computer's monitor, hard disk, and other system components. Should your battery run low, Windows 7 saves your work to the hard disk and turns off your mobile computer.

- Entering the sleep state is rapid: It takes only a few seconds.

- When you wake your computer, Windows 7 restores your work session rapidly. You don't need to wait for your computer to boot up and restore your desktop after logging on.

NOTE   Hibernation is available in Windows 7 as an advanced power management setting. This option saves configuration information and data to the hard disk and turns off all computer components. You need an amount of free hard disk space equal to the amount of RAM on the computer to save the entire contents of RAM.

Waking from hibernation takes more time than waking from sleep mode. You learn about advanced power management settings later in this section.

You can access the Power Options applet from the Hardware and Sound section or the System and Security section of Control Panel. This opens the dialog box shown in Figure 13-26, from which you can configure the options described in the following section.

Figure 13-26 The Power Options applet provides several options for configuring power management.

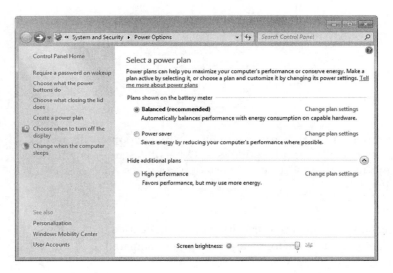

Power Plans

Microsoft has supplied three preconfigured power plans that help to strike a balance between usability and power conservation. The high-performance power plan optimizes the computer for performance at the expense of battery life and is suitable for individuals who run graphics-intensive or multimedia applications frequently. The power saver plan optimizes battery life by slowing the processor down and is suitable for those who use the computer primarily for purposes such as email, web browsing, and word processing. The balanced plan strikes a balance between these extremes. You can edit one of these power schemes or create a new one if the preconfigured power schemes do not fulfill your needs. Table 13-4 compares the three preconfigured power plans.

Table 13-4   Windows 7 Power Plans

Power Plan	When on Battery Power	When Plugged into AC Outlet
Balanced	Turns off display after 5 minutes	Turns off display after 20 minutes
	Sleeps after 15 minutes	Sleeps after 1 hour
	Display dims slightly	Displays at full brightness
Power Saver	Turns off display after 3 minutes	Turns off display after 20 minutes
	Sleeps after 15 minutes	Sleeps after 1 hour
	Display dims slightly	Displays at full brightness
High Performance	Turns off display after 20 minutes	Turns off display after 20 minutes
	Sleeps after 1 hour	Does not sleep
	Displays at full brightness	Displays at full brightness

CAUTION   Do not use sleep mode when on a commercial airplane. Airline regulations forbid the use of electronic devices during takeoff and landing. Because a computer can wake to perform a scheduled task or other action, you should turn off your computer completely at these times.

Additional Power Plan Options

Windows 7 enables you to perform additional power management actions that you can use to tailor your computer's power scheme to your needs.

Selecting any of the top three options on the task list in the Power Options applet previously shown in Figure 13-26 brings up the System Settings screen shown in Figure 13-27, which enables you to perform the following actions:

- **Power and sleep buttons and lid settings:** You can choose from do nothing, sleep mode, hibernation, and shut down for each of these actions on battery or AC power. The shut down option is not available for the sleep button.

- **Password protection on wakeup:** You can choose whether to require a password when the computer wakes from sleep mode.

You can also modify any of the existing power plans or create your own custom power plan. To do so, select the **Change plan settings** link under the desired power plan or any of the last three links on the left side of the Power Options applet previously shown in Figure 13-26. You receive the Edit Plan Settings dialog box shown in Figure 13-28, focused on the power plan currently in use or the plan whose link you selected.

Figure 13-27   The Define power buttons and turn on password protection dialog box enables you to define power lid actions and configure password protection.

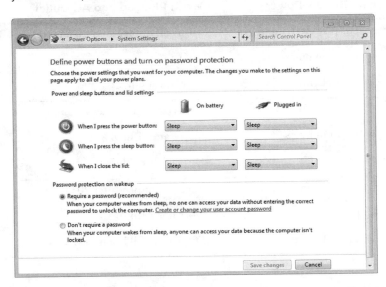

Figure 13-28   You can modify the settings for any of the predefined power plans.

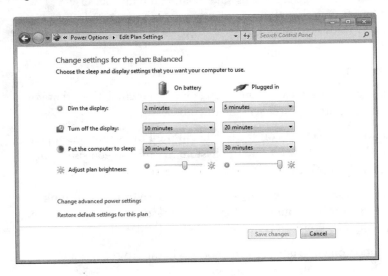

Advanced Power Settings

Click **Change advanced power settings** to bring up the dialog box shown in Figure 13-29 for the following additional options, each of which you can define separately for operation on battery power or plugged in:

- **Require a password on wakeup:** You can choose to require a password on waking from either battery power or plugged in.

Figure 13-29   The Power Options dialog box provides several options for configuring power management.

- **Hard disk:** You can specify the number of minutes of inactivity after which the hard disk is turned off.

- **Desktop background settings:** You can choose whether to make the background slide show available or to pause it.

- **Wireless adapter settings:** You can specify a maximum performance or low, medium, or maximum power saving for the adapter. The more power saving you specify, the poorer the signal throughput might become.

- **Sleep:** You can specify the number of minutes after which your computer enters sleep or hibernation mode. You can also turn on *hybrid sleep*, which saves all open documents to both memory and the hard disk. Should a power failure occur when in hybrid sleep, Windows can restore your data from the hard disk. If hybrid sleep is not enabled and a power failure occurs, your data is lost.

- **USB Settings:** You can enable *USB selective suspend setting*, which enables Windows 7 to turn off the USB root hub when not in use.

- **Power buttons and lid:** You can define the action that occurs when you close the lid or press the power or sleep buttons, in a manner similar to that described previously. You can also define the action (sleep, hibernate, or shut down) that occurs when you select the power off button from the Start menu.

- **PCI Express:** You can define the level of power savings for *link state power management*, which controls the power management state for devices connected to the PCI Express bus if present in the computer.

■ **Processor power management:** You can control the minimum and maximum power status of the processor, also known as *throttling the processor*. Reducing the processor power levels saves battery power at the expense of lengthening the time required to respond to keyboard and mouse actions.

■ **Display:** You can control the display brightness and the length of time before it is turned off. You can also enable *adaptive display*, which increases the waiting time before turning off the display if you wake the computer frequently.

■ **Multimedia settings:** You can control whether the computer enters sleep mode when sharing multimedia with other users. By setting this option to Prevent idling to sleep, the computer will not go to sleep if media is being shared with other computers or devices.

■ **Battery:** You can specify actions to take place when the battery power reaches a low or critical level, as well as the battery level at which these events occur. By default, low battery level is at 10% and produces a notification but takes no action. The critical level is at 5% and notifies you and puts the computer into hibernation when running on battery power.

> **TIP** Configure power plans to turn off components after a period of inactivity. If you set up a power plan to turn off components separately after an interval of nonuse, the computer progressively moves toward sleep mode. This should happen if a user is away from his laptop for 20 or 30 minutes. At the same time, a user doing presentations should not have her computer go into sleep mode. Remember that the user can enable presentation settings so that this and other actions do not occur.

You can customize a power plan to suit your needs if required. Use these steps to create a custom power plan.

Step 1. From the left pane of the Power Options window previously shown in Figure 13-26, click **Create a power plan**.

Step 2. On the Create a power plan dialog box that appears, select the default plan (balanced, power saver, or high performance) that is closest to your desired plan.

Step 3. Provide a descriptive name for the plan and then click **Next**.

Step 4. On the Change settings window, select the time interval after which the display is turned off and put to sleep, select the display brightness, and then click **Create**.

Step 5. You are returned to the main Power Options window. If you want to configure additional settings for the plan you just created, click **Change advanced power settings** to display the dialog box previously shown in Figure 13-29.

Battery Meter

Windows 7 uses the battery meter to help you keep track of remaining battery life. This is represented by a battery icon in the notification area, which also contains a plug icon when the notebook is plugged into AC power. Hover your mouse over this icon to view the percent battery power left and the power plan in use. To view the battery meter in full as shown in Figure 13-30, click the battery icon.

Figure 13-30   The battery meter informs you of the current battery charge level.

From the battery meter, you can also perform the following tasks:

- **Select a power plan:** Enables you to choose any of the default or custom power plans configured on your computer.

- **Adjust screen brightness:** Opens the Power Options applet as previously described and shown in Figure 13-26, where you can adjust the Screen brightness slider.

- **More power options:** Opens the Power Options applet as previously described and shown in Figure 13-26.

When the battery power drops below 25%, the notification area icon and the full battery meter display a yellow exclamation point triangle. When the power drops below 10% (or any other value configured in the Power Options dialog box), you receive a warning message informing you to either plug in your computer or shut it down and change the battery; the battery meter and icon display a red X icon. Some computers can sound an audible notification. You should plug your computer into a power outlet when this message appears.

Power Management and Group Policy

Windows 7 includes the capability for configuring power management settings in Group Policy. When you configure policies for power management, a nonadministrative user cannot modify the power settings.

Use the following procedure to use Group Policy to configure power management settings:

Step 1.   Click **Start** and type `gpedit.msc` in the Search text box. Then select **gpedit.msc** from the programs list.

Step 2.   Navigate to the **Computer Configuration\Administrative Templates\System\Power Management** node. You receive the policy groups shown in Figure 13-31.

Figure 13-31   Group Policy enables you to configure a large range of power management settings.

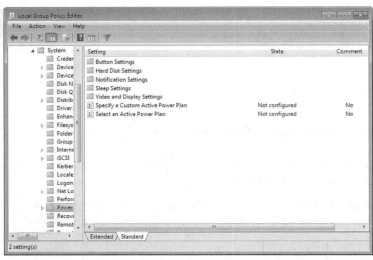

Step 3.   Configure the following groups of settings as required:

— **Button Settings:** Enables you to define the actions that occur when the power button, sleep button, or Start menu power button is pressed or the lid closed. You can define these separately for battery and AC power conditions.

— **Hard Disk Settings:** Enables you to specify when the hard disk will be turned off when the computer is plugged in and when the computer is running on battery.

— **Notification Settings:** Enables you to define the battery levels at which low and critical alarm notifications take place and the actions that will occur.

— **Sleep Settings:** Includes settings for controlling when and how the computer enters sleep mode and when and how it reawakens.

— **Video and Display Settings:** Enables you to specify how long the computer must be inactive before the display is turned off and whether the time interval is adjusted according to the user's keyboard and mouse usage.

— **Power plans:** Enables you to select either an active power plan or specify a custom power plan to be active on all computers controlled by the Group Policy object.

Step 4.   When finished, close the Group Policy Object Editor.

Exam Preparation Tasks

Review All the Key Topics

Review the most important topics in the chapter, noted with the key topics icon in the outer margin of the page. Table 13-5 lists a reference of these key topics and the page numbers on which each is found.

Table 13-5   Key Topics for Chapter 13

Key Topic Element	Description	Page Number
Paragraph	Describes how BitLocker functions	479
List	Shows how to enable BitLocker	481
Figure 13-6	Shows management options for BitLocker-encrypted drive	485
Figure 13-8	Shows BitLocker Group Policy settings	487
Figure 13-11	Configuring BitLocker Data Recovery Agent policy	491
Table 13-2	Describes DirectAccess connection options	493
List	Describes DirectAccess connection process	499
List	Configuring a client computer for using offline files	500
Figure 13-20	Using the Sync Center	503
Table 13-3	Describes Offline Files Group Policy settings	507
Table 13-4	Summarizes default Windows 7 power plans	511
Figure 13-29	Shows advanced power settings	513
Figure 13-31	Shows Power Options Group Policy settings	516

Complete the Tables and Lists from Memory

Print a copy of Appendix C, "Memory Tables" (found on the CD), or at least the section for this chapter, and complete the tables and lists from memory. Appendix D, "Memory Tables Answer Key," also on the CD, includes completed tables and lists to check your work.

Definitions of Key Terms

Define the following key terms from this chapter and check your answers in the glossary.

battery meter, cache, hibernation, Offline Files, power plans, Sleep mode, Sync Center, synchronization conflicts, synchronizing files, Windows Mobility Center, BitLocker, BitLocker To Go, Data Recovery Agent, DirectAccess, Microsoft Forefront Unified Access Gateway (UAG), Network Access Protection (NAP)

This chapter covers the following subjects:

- **Configuring Remote Management:** This section describes new and improved methods of managing computers remotely. You learn about time-saving management options that enable you to perform a large range of management tasks on remotely located computers directly from your Windows 7 computer.

- **Configuring Remote Connections:** Windows 7 enables you to make connections to remote computers in a variety of ways. This section shows you how to set up dial-up and VPN connections, as well as how to receive connections from other computers. You also learn about the use of Remote Desktop Gateway for accessing applications installed on specially configured Windows Server 2008 R2 computers.

CHAPTER 14

Configuring Remote Management and Remote Connections

Chapter 13, "Configuring Mobile Computing," introduced you to many tools and technologies employed by mobile users to access the network from external locations, as well as tools for keeping mobile users safe and secure. This chapter continues our discussion of remote computing to look at methods you can use to manage computers from afar and make connections to these computers from diverse locations. You will see that you can be in a distant location such as home or a hotel and perform almost anything that you could do directly from the computer console. When that emergency occurs late at night, you can diagnose many problems and perform fixes without the need to travel to the office.

"Do I Know This Already?" Quiz

The "Do I Know This Already?" quiz enables you to assess whether you should read this entire chapter or simply jump to the "Exam Preparation Tasks" section for review. If you are in doubt, read the entire chapter. Table 14-1 outlines the major headings in this chapter and the corresponding "Do I Know This Already?" quiz questions. You can find the answers in Appendix A, "Answers to the 'Do I Know This Already?' Quizzes."

Table 14-1 "Do I Know This Already?" Foundation Topics Section-to-Question Mapping

Foundations Topics Section	Questions Covered in This Section
Configuring Remote Management	1–5
Configuring Remote Connections	6–12

1. You are working from home on your Windows 7 computer and need to access your work computer, which is also running Windows 7 by means of your cable Internet connection. What tool should you use to make this connection?

    a. Terminal Services

    b. Remote Assistance

    c. Remote Desktop

    d. Virtual Private Network

2. You are working from home on your Windows 7 computer and experience a problem that you cannot fix. You want to contact a user on another Windows 7 computer that you believe can help you correct your problem. What tool should you use?

   a. Terminal Services

   b. Remote Assistance

   c. Remote Desktop

   d. Virtual Private Network

3. Yesterday evening, you worked on an important project from home on your Windows 7 Home Premium computer. Your children interrupted you and you forgot to upload your work to your work computer. The work computer runs Windows Vista Business. Needing the upgraded project files, you attempt to connect to your home computer but are unable to do so. What do you need to do to make this connection?

   a. Download the Remote Desktop Connection Software application from Microsoft and install it on your home computer.

   b. Upgrade your work computer to Windows 7 Professional or Ultimate.

   c. Upgrade your home computer to Windows 7 Professional or Ultimate.

   d. Use Remote Assistance to make the connection.

4. You are attempting to establish a Remote Assistance session with another user to obtain help in configuring several options, so you select the Easy Connect option to simplify the connection procedure. You phone this user and provide the session password. However, the other user reports that she has not received any invitation from you. Which of the following is a possible reason for this problem?

   a. The other user is situated at a Windows Vista computer.

   b. The other user is using a nonadministrative user account.

   c. You have not selected the **Allow this computer to be controlled remotely** option.

   d. You should have used Remote Desktop instead.

5. Which of the following are valid commands that you can enter at a PowerShell interface? (Choose all that apply.)

    a. `Get-process`

    b. `Value-output`

    c. `Select-object`

    d. `Format-data`

    e. `Folder-create`

6. Which of the following remote access protocols uses IPSec Tunnel Mode over UDP port 500 to create a secure connection?

    a. PPTP

    b. L2TP

    c. SSTP

    d. IKEv2

7. Which of the following remote access protocols does not provide data encryption on its own?

    a. PPTP

    b. L2TP

    c. SSTP

    d. IKEv2

8. Which of the following remote access authentication protocols should you avoid because it sends credentials in unencrypted form?

    a. PAP

    b. CHAP

    c. EAP

    d. MS-CHAPv2

9. You have created a VPN connection but now need to enable the use of File and Printer Sharing for Microsoft Networks so that you can print a report on the office network that your manager needs to have by 8:00 tomorrow morning. You right-click the VPN connection and choose **Properties**. Which tab contains the option that you must configure?

    a. General

    b. Options

    c. Security

    d. Networking

    e. Sharing

10. You are downloading a large file to your laptop at the airport Wi-Fi connection while waiting for your flight to be called. You are concerned that you might need to interrupt the download and want to be able to resume the download at your destination hotel room, so you have enabled VPN Reconnect. What protocol does this feature use?

    a. PPTP

    b. L2TP/IPSec

    c. SSTP

    d. IKEv2

11. You are responsible for ensuring the security of your company's internal network and want to ensure that computers connecting remotely do not bring viruses or spyware onto the network. What feature should you enable?

    a. VPN Reconnect

    b. NAP Quarantine Remediation

    c. Advanced Security Auditing

    d. L2TP/IPSec tunneling

12. You have set up a new Windows Server 2008 R2 computer on which you want to specify programs that users will access remotely through the RD Gateway server. What feature do you enable?

    a. VPN Reconnect

    b. NAP Quarantine Remediation

    c. RemoteApp

    d. Internet Connection Sharing

Foundation Topics

Configuring Remote Management

Microsoft has built several remote management tools into Windows 7 and Windows Server 2008 R2 that enable you to connect to computers located across the hall or across the continent. You can use these tools to save precious minutes out of a busy day, or an entire trip lasting days, to manage and troubleshoot resources located on these computers. Users in other locations can connect to your computer, and you can offer suggestions or train them in procedures that correct problems or make their day's work go more smoothly.

Windows 7 continues to improve on the Remote Desktop and Remote Assistance tools first introduced with Windows XP. The Remote Server Administration Tools for Windows 7 download enables you to manage roles and features installed on servers running Windows Server 2003 or later from your Windows 7 desktop. Also offered are the new Windows Remote Management service and (introduced with Vista) the Windows PowerShell command-line interface.

Remote Desktop

Windows 7 incorporates the Remote Desktop Protocol (RDP), which was originally introduced with Terminal Services and included with Windows XP Professional. The protocol enables any user to use the Remote Desktop application to run a remote control session of a Windows Terminal Server or of a Windows 7 computer that has been configured to provide Remote Desktop services. RDP also allows a remote session to be executed on a request basis so that an administrator can assist a user with a problem. This is called Remote Assistance, and it is located in the All Programs menu. We look at Remote Assistance in the next section.

When Windows 7 is configured to be a Remote Desktop host, there is a restriction for usage that does not apply to a Terminal Services computer. This restriction is that only one user can ever execute an interactive session on the computer at any one time. So, if you run a Remote Desktop session and a user is already logged on to the Remote Desktop server, that user will be logged off (at your request) for your own session to run. However, that user's session will be saved so that he can resume it later.

Establishing a Remote Desktop Connection with Another Computer

Any version of Windows 7 can be a Remote Desktop client. However, only the Professional, Enterprise, or Ultimate edition of Windows 7 can be a Remote Desktop host (server). You can run a Remote Desktop session with another computer running Windows XP, Vista, or Windows 7. Use the following instructions to make a Remote Desktop connection:

Step 1.   Click **Start > All Programs > Accessories > Remote Desktop Connection**. The Remote Desktop Connection dialog box opens, as shown in Figure 14-1. You can also access this dialog box by clicking **Start**, typing `remote` in the Start Menu Search field, and then selecting **Remote Desktop Connection** from the program list.

Figure 14-1   The Remote Desktop Connection dialog requires you to know the name and/or IP address of the target computer.

The Computer list shows only Windows Terminal Servers. Windows 7 computers do not advertise the Remote Desktop service, so you are required to know the full name or IP address of the computer.

Step 2.   Type the name of the Windows XP, Vista, or Windows 7 computer and click **Connect**.

You should see a message box informing you that you are connecting, followed by a remote session with a logon screen prompting you for a user ID and password.

Step 3.   Click the **Options** button. The General tab for the connection's Properties dialog box opens. You can save the current logon settings or open a file containing previously saved settings, as well as change the computer name in this dialog box.

Step 4.   Click the **Display** tab. If your session is running slowly, you can increase performance by reducing the number of colors and size of the screen.

Step 5.   Click the **Local Resources** tab. You can choose whether to map sounds, disk drives, printers, clipboard, and serial ports. You can also select how the key combination Alt+Tab works when executing that key combination while in the remote session. By clicking the **More** button, you can choose to use smart cards and specified ports on this computer to be used within the remote session.

Step 6.   Click the **Programs** tab. If you would like to configure a connection that starts a single application, rather than *all* the applications, you can type the command line in this screen so that it executes automatically.

Step 7.   Click the **Experience** tab. This tab enables you to enable or disable various display behaviors shown in Figure 14-2 to enhance the computer's performance.

Figure 14-2   The Experience tab of the Remote Desktop Connection dialog box enables you to select the performance options applicable to the remote session.

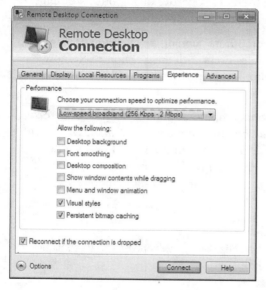

Step 8.   Click the **Advanced** tab. You can choose from three options that describe the behavior if authentication fails: **Warn me** (the default), **Connect and don't warn me**, or **Do not connect**. You can also configure Terminal Services Gateway settings that apply for connections to remote computers located behind firewalls.

Step 9.   Click the **Options** button to return to the original logon screen. Type the information for your username and password, and click **OK** to start the session.

Step 10.   If someone else is already logged on to the computer, you will be asked whether you should log off the existing user. Click **Yes**. The session begins.

Configuring the Server Side of Remote Desktop

The *server side* of the Remote Desktop connection refers to the computer to which you are making the connection. Before you can use Remote Desktop, you must enable the computer to which you want to connect to receive Remote Desktop connections. This computer must be running the Professional, Enterprise, or Ultimate edition of Windows 7. You can do this from the Remote tab of the System Properties dialog box, as follows:

Step 1. Click **Start,** right-click **Computer**, and then choose **Properties**.

Step 2. From the Control Panel System applet, click **Advanced system settings**. If you receive a User Account Control (UAC) prompt, click **Yes** to proceed.

Step 3. Select the **Remote** tab of the System Properties dialog box and then select one of the following options, as shown in Figure 14-3:

— **Allow connections from computers running any version of Remote Desktop (less secure):** Enables users with any version of Remote Desktop to connect to your computer, regardless of Windows version in use.

— **Allow connections only from computers running Remote Desktop with Network Level Authentication (more secure):** Enables users with computers running Remote Desktop with Network Level Authentication to connect to your computer. This is the most secure option if people connecting to your computer are running Windows 7.

Step 4. Click **OK** or **Apply**.

Figure 14-3   The Remote tab of the System Properties dialog box enables you to configure Remote Assistance and Remote Desktop settings.

You also need to specify the users that are entitled to make a remote connection to your computer. By default, members of the Administrators and Remote Desktop Users groups are allowed to connect to your computer. To add a nonadministrative user to the Remote Desktop Users group, click the **Select Users** button in the Remote tab previously shown in Figure 14-3. This opens the Remote Desktop Users dialog box shown in Figure 14-4. Click **Add**; in the Select Users dialog box that appears, type the name of the user to be granted access, and then click **OK**. The Select Users dialog box also enables you to add users from an Active Directory Domain Services (AD DS) domain if your computer is a domain member.

Figure 14-4   The Remote Desktop Users dialog box enables you to grant Remote Desktop access to nonadministrative users.

Selecting a Nondefault Port

You can configure the listening port, from the default TCP 3389, to another port of your choice. When you do so, only the people who specify the port can connect and then run a remote session. In Windows 7, you are able to adjust the port only by editing the Registry:

Step 1.   Open the Registry Editor, supply your UAC credentials, and navigate to the **HKEY_LOCAL_MACHINE\System\CurrentControlSet\Control\TerminalServer\WinStations\RDP-Tcp** key.

Step 2.   Select the **PortNumber** value, click the **Edit** menu, and then select Modify.

Step 3.   Click **Decimal** and type in the new port number.

Step 4.   Click **OK** and close the Registry Editor.

On the client computer, you then make a connection by opening the Remote Desktop Connection dialog box as previously described and shown in Figure 14-1. In the

Computer text box, type the name or IP address of the Remote Desktop host computer, concatenated with a colon and the port number. For example, if you edited the Registry of the host computer named NANC511 with an IP address of 192.168.0.8 and changed the port number to 4233, you would type either **NANC511:4233** or **192.168.0.8:4233** in the Computer text box of the Remote Desktop Connection dialog box.

Keep in mind that a Remote Desktop Connection functions across any TCP/IP link, whether dial-up, local, or otherwise. You can link to a host computer with older Windows versions—Windows 9x, Me, NT, 2000, XP, or Vista—but you need to have the client software to do so. You can download the client software to connect older computers from Microsoft at http://www.microsoft.com/windowsxp/downloads/tools/RDCLIENTDL.mspx. When you configure a host computer, be sure to add users to the Remote Desktop users group and to create an exception for Remote Desktop traffic for the Windows Firewall. You should also create the exception on the client computer as well.

Remote Assistance

First introduced with Windows XP, Remote Assistance enables a user running a Windows 7 computer on a network to request assistance online; it also enables an expert to offer assistance remotely. Regardless of how the session is initiated, the result is that the expert can remotely view the user's console and provide assistance to the user by taking control of the session, or can simply view the session and give the user specific directions on how to fix the problem the user is experiencing. New to Windows 7 is the Easy Connect option, which uses the Peer Name Resolution Protocol (PNRP) to send the Remote Assistance invitation across the Internet. Easy Connect provides a password that you must provide separately to the other individual (for example, by making a phone call).

The requirements for Remote Assistance are that both computers must be configured to use it. If using an AD DS domain, Group Policy for Remote Assistance must also allow the user to accept Remote Assistance offers and must list from which experts the users can accept offers. An Active Directory network also requires both users to be members of the same or trusted domains.

Windows Firewall can affect whether a user can receive Remote Assistance offers or use Remote Desktop. To configure Windows Firewall to use either or both of these features, do the following:

Step 1.   Click **Start > Control Panel > System and Security**.

Step 2.   In the System and Security Category program list, select **Allow a program through Windows Firewall** beneath Windows Firewall.

Step 3.   On the Allow programs to communicate through Windows Firewall dialog box shown in Figure 14-5, click **Change settings** and then select the

Remote Assistance and **Remote Desktop** check boxes under the Home/Work (Private) column.

Figure 14-5 You need to allow Remote Assistance and Remote Desktop to communicate through Windows Firewall.

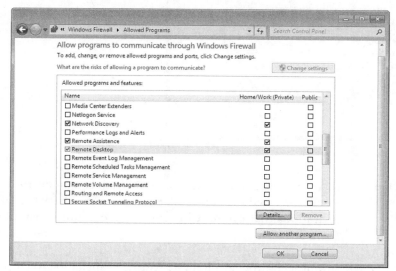

Select these options under the Public column only if you need to accept requests from individuals on public networks; deselect these options once you've completed the action. (If you have made changes to the port number of any service, you will need to use Windows Firewall with Advanced Security to enable a firewall rule allowing that port to pass. You learned how to do this in Chapter 10, "Configuring Network and Firewall Settings.")

Step 4. Click **OK** to close the applet.

Use the following steps to configure Windows 7 to accept Remote Assistance Offers:

Step 1. Click **Start,** right-click **Computer**, and choose **Properties**.

Step 2. From the Control Panel System applet, click **Advanced system settings**. If you receive a User Account Control (UAC) prompt, click **Yes** to proceed.

Step 3. Select the **Remote** tab of the System Properties dialog box, and select the **Allow Remote Assistance connections to this computer** option in the Remote Assistance section (refer to Figure 14-3).

Step 4. Click the **Advanced** button to display the Remote Assistance Settings dialog box shown in Figure 14-6 and select the **Allow this computer to be controlled remotely** check box.

Figure 14-6   Configuring Remote Assistance settings.

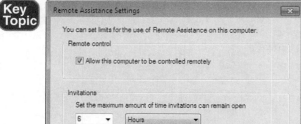

Step 5.   If you want to allow connections only from computers running Windows Vista/7 or Windows Server 2008 R2, select the check box labeled **Create invitations that can only be used from computers running Windows Vista or later.**

Use the following steps to send a Remote Assistance invitation to receive help from an expert user:

Step 1.   Click **Start > All Programs > Maintenance > Windows Remote Assistance.** You can also click **Start**, type **remote** in the Start menu Search field, and then select **Windows Remote Assistance** from the programs list.

Step 2.   From the Windows Remote Assistance dialog box shown in Figure 14-7, you can either ask for help or help someone else. To ask for help, click **Invite someone you trust to help you**.

Step 3.   Select one of the three options on the following page, shown in Figure 14-8:

— **Save the invitation as a file:** Creates an invitation file in the Microsoft Remote Control Incident (MsRcIncident) format. You can use this method with web-based email programs by sending it as an attachment.

— **Use e-mail to send an invitation:** Available only if you have installed Windows Mail or another email client.

— **Use Easy Connect:** Uses the Peer Name Resolution Protocol to send the invitation across the Internet. The other person must also be using a Windows 7 computer.

Figure 14-7   Windows Remote Assistance enables you to either ask for help or help someone else.

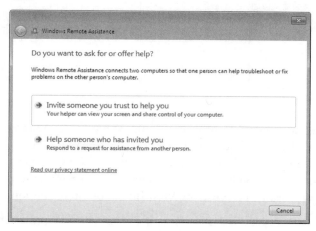

Figure 14-8   Remote Assistance enables you to send invitations three ways.

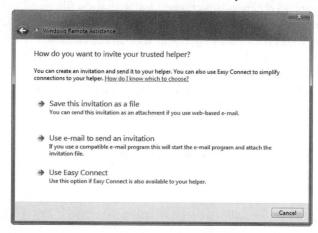

Step 4.   The next step depends on the option you've selected from Figure 14-8:

— If you save the invitation as a file, you are prompted for a name and location to save the file.

— If you use email, your email program opens and provides a prepared message including an invitation attachment. Supply the email address of the expert who will be helping, and then send the message.

— If you use Easy Connect, you receive a password, as shown in Figure 14-9, that you need to provide to the expert by another means such as by phone. You can also click Chat to start an online chat session.

Figure 14-9   Easy Connect provides a password that you need to provide to the expert.

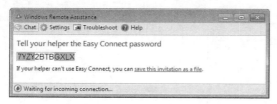

Depending on from whom you are requesting information and how you are request-ing it, you should make a selection that will best reach the expert user. Whichever method you select for use, you can password-protect the session; the Easy Connect option has already done that for you. If you have created an invitation for assistance and want to cancel it before it expires, you can use the View Invitation Status option and cancel the invitation.

After the expert receives the email or the invitation file, he can open Remote Assistance on his computer and select the **Help someone who has invited you** option previously shown in Figure 14-7. He can then open the invitation file that the other person has sent, or he can select the Use Easy Connect option if the other person has selected that option. In this case, the expert will receive the Remote Assistance dialog box shown in Figure 14-10, asking him to type the password that Remote Assistance provided to the other person. Using the supplied password, the expert can initiate the session and the user's computer validates the password and invitation before the user is prompted to start the session.

Figure 14-10   Provide the password to open the Remote Assistance session.

The expert sees a Remote Assistance Expert console that provides a real-time view of the user's session. This is called a *shadow session*. If remote control has been en-abled, the expert can click the Take Control button, notifying the user that the ex-pert is asking to share control of the keyboard and mouse. The user can prevent a remote control session by pressing the Esc key, pressing Ctrl+C, or clicking the Stop Control button in the chat window.

TIP   You can ask a user who is experiencing problems to make a recording of the steps she has taken. To do so, ask her to type psr into the Start Menu Search text box. This opens the Problem Steps Recorder shown in Figure 14-11. She can click Start Record, perform the steps that are creating the problem, and then click Stop Record when she's finished. At that time she can click Add Comment and then save the recording as a Zip file that she can attach to the email Remote Assistance request email message.

Figure 14-11   The Problem Steps Recorder enables a user to record the steps that created a problem.

Using Windows Remote Management Service

Microsoft has provided Windows Remote Management (WinRM) to assist you in managing hardware on a network that includes machines that run a diverse mix of operating systems. WinRM is the Microsoft implementation of the WS-Management Protocol, which was developed by an independent group of manufacturers as a public standard for remote computer management. You can use WinRM to monitor and manage remote computers.

WinRM is a series of command-line tools that operate from an administrative command prompt. You need to set up the Remote Management Service by clicking **Start > All Programs > Accessories**, right-clicking **Command Prompt**, and then choosing **Run as administrator**. After accepting the UAC prompt, type `winrm` `quickconfig`. You receive the output shown in Figure 14-12. Type y twice as shown in the figure to enable the granting of remote administrative rights to local users, create a WinRM listener on HTTP, and enable a firewall exception that allows WinRM packets to pass.

You can also configure WinRM by means of Group Policy. This enables you to enable WinRM for all computers in the same AD DS site, domain, or organizational unit (OU). Access the **Computer Configuration\Administrative Templates\ Windows Components\Windows Remote Management** node. This node contains two subnodes: WinRM Client and WinRM Service. The WinRM Client policies deal with permitted authentication methods and available trusted hosts, whereas the WinRM Service policies deal with how the service listens on the network for requests, as well as client authentication methods that it will accept and whether unencrypted messages are permitted. You can also enable or disable an HTTP listener. For more information on the available policies in each of these subnodes, double-click any policy and consult the Help text provided.

Figure 14-12   You can enable WinRM from an administrative command prompt.

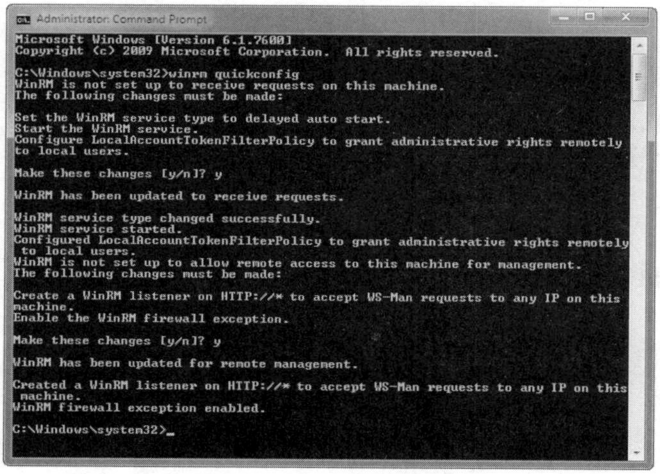

After you've set up WinRM, you are able to use either of two tools included in the Remote Management Service: Windows Remote Shell and Windows PowerShell. We take a quick look at each of these tools in turn.

> **NOTE**   For more information about Windows Remote Management, refer to "About Windows Remote Management" at http://msdn.microsoft.com/en-us/library/aa384291(VS.85).aspx.

Using Windows Remote Shell

Windows Remote Shell (WinRS) enables you to execute command-line utilities or scripts against a remote computer. For example, you can run the `ipconfig` command on a remote computer named Server1 by typing the following command:

`winrs –r:Server1 ipconfig`

You can specify the NetBIOS name of a computer located on the local subnet or the fully qualified domain name (FQDN) of a computer on a remote network. You can also specify user credentials under which the WinRS command will be executed, by using the following command:

`Winrs –r:Server1 –u:user_name -p:password command`

In this command, *user_name* is the username in whose context you want to run the command, *password* is the password associated with this username, and *command* is the command to be run. You can use this syntax to remotely execute any command that you can normally run locally using the `cmd.exe` command prompt. If you don't specify the password, Windows Remote Shell prompts you for the password. You can also use `http://` or `https://` against the computer name in the –r parameter to specify an HTTP or Secure HTTP connection to a remote computer specified by its URL or IP address.

NOTE   For more information on using WinRS, open a command prompt and type `winrs /?`.

Using Windows PowerShell

Windows PowerShell, currently in version 2.0, is a task-based command-line scripting interface that enables you to perform a large number of remote management tasks. PowerShell includes the Integrated Scripting Environment (ISE), which assists you in the task of writing, testing, and executing scripts. You can control and automate the administration of remote Windows computers and their applications. Installed by default in Windows 7 and Windows Server 2008 R2, PowerShell also enables you to perform automated troubleshooting of remote computers. You can even read from and write to the Registry as though its hives were regular drives; for example, HKLM for HKEY_LOCAL_MACHINE and HKCU for HKEY_CURRENT_USER.

NOTE   You can also download PowerShell 2.0 and install it on computers running Windows 2000/XP/Vista/Server 2003/2008. Any scripts you write using PowerShell 2.0 can then be run on computers using any of these operating systems.

Windows PowerShell borrows from the functionality of the object-oriented Microsoft .NET programming model. Objects used by this mode have well-defined properties and methods; for example, a file object has properties such as its size, modification date and time, and so on. All commands issued to PowerShell are in the form of a command-let, or *cmdlet*, which is an expression of the form *verb-object*, for example, `Get-process`. You can run a cmdlet on its own or build these tools into complex scripts that enable you to perform almost unlimited tasks against any computer on the network. The following are several verbs used in many cmdlets:

- **Get:** Retrieves data.

- **Set:** Modifies or establishes output data.

- **Format:** Formats data.

- **Select:** Selects specific properties of an object or set of objects. Also finds text in strings, files, or XML documents.

- **Out:** Outputs data to a specific location.

To start a PowerShell session, click **Start > All Programs > Accessories > Windows PowerShell > Windows PowerShell**. This starts a PowerShell command session, similar to that shown in Figure 14-13. Help functions are provided for all available cmdlets, similar to that shown in the figure. You can also type **help verb-*,** where *verb* is an available PowerShell verb, including (but not restricted to) those mentioned in the previous paragraph.

Figure 14-13   You can execute a large number of cmdlets from a PowerShell session.

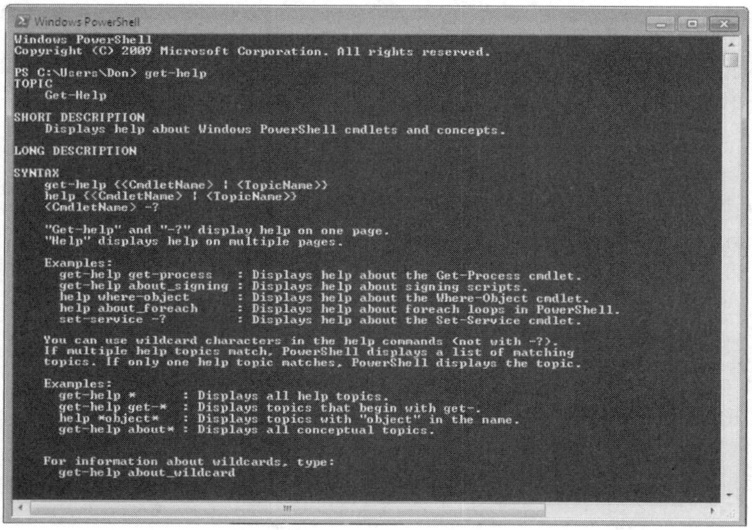

You can also get help on PowerShell objects by typing **help *-object,** where *object* is a PowerShell object. See the next paragraph for an example of obtaining help for the content object.

PowerShell 2.0 also includes the PowerShell ISE, which is a PowerShell graphical user interface (GUI) that enables you to run commands and write, edit, run, test, and debug scripts in the same window. Access this tool by clicking **Start > All Programs > Accessories > Windows PowerShell > Windows PowerShell ISE.** PowerShell ISE also includes debugging, multiline editing capabilities, selective execution, and many other components that aid you in writing and debugging complex scripts. An example of PowerShell ISE is shown in Figure 14-14.

Figure 14-14   You can write and debug complex scripts using Windows PowerShell ISE.

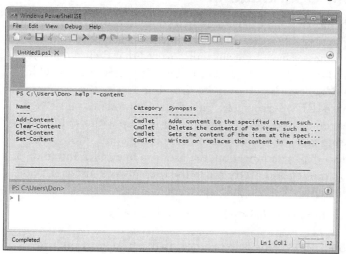

To run a PowerShell command against a remote computer, use the following command:

```
Icm computername {powershell-cmd}
```

In this command, `Icm` is the Invoke-Command cmdlet, `computername` is the name of the computer you are running the command against, and `{powershell-cmd}` is the command being run.

NOTE   For more information on all aspects of Windows PowerShell, refer to "Windows PowerShell" at http://msdn.microsoft.com/en-us/library/dd835506(VS.85).aspx and "What's New in Windows PowerShell" at http://technet.microsoft.com/en-us/library/dd367858(WS.10).aspx.

Configuring Remote Connections

Connectivity is the single most valuable capability in a computer. By connecting to other computers, a computer is able to access other information, applications, and peripheral equipment. Businesses have long since discovered that their employees will work longer hours and greatly increase their productivity when they are able to connect to the company's network from remote sites. For this reason, they provide Remote Access Service (RAS) servers with either dial-up modems or VPN servers and Internet connections. Windows 7 computers link up with the Internet or corporate networks using dial-up or broadband networking connections. After Windows 7 connects with a dial-up connection, the user can open files and folders, use applications, print to printers, and pretty much use the network just as if he or she were connected to the network through its network adapter.

Standard protocols are used to make dial-up network connections:

- **Point-to-Point Protocol (PPP):** A dial-up protocol that can support multiple networking protocols, such as TCP/IP and Internetwork Packet Exchange/ Sequenced Packet Exchange (IPX/SPX), and can be used with compression and encryption. Note that support for the older Serial Line Interface Protocol (SLIP) has been removed from Windows 7.

- **Point-to-Point Tunneling Protocol (PPTP):** A protocol used to transmit private network data across a public network in a secure fashion. PPTP supports multiple networking protocols and creates a secure VPN connection.

- **Layer 2 Tunneling Protocol (L2TP):** A protocol used to transmit private network data across a public network. L2TP supports multiple networking protocols. Used with IP Security (IPSec), it creates a secure VPN connection.

- **Secure Socket Tunneling Protocol (SSTP):** A tunneling protocol that uses Secure Hypertext Transfer Protocol (HTTPS) over TCP port 443 to transmit traffic across firewalls and proxy servers that might block PPTP and L2TP traffic. SSTP uses Secure Sockets Layer (SSL) for transport-level security that includes enhanced key negotiation, encryption, and integrity checking.

- **Internet Key Exchange version 2 (IKEv2):** A tunneling protocol that uses IPSec Tunnel Mode over UDP port 500. This combination of protocols also supports strong authentication and encryption methods.

NOTE   For more information on remote access protocols, refer to "VPN Tunneling Protocols" at http://technet.microsoft.com/en-us/library/ dd469817(WS.10).aspx.

Understanding Remote Access

Dial-up networking connections are used for any type of connection—between two different computers, between a computer and a private network, between a computer and the Internet, and from a computer through the Internet to a private network using a tunneling protocol. You can share a dial-up connection using Internet Connection Sharing (ICS). All these functions and features offer different ways of connecting computers across large geographical distances.

When a computer connects to a remote access server, it performs functions nearly identical to logging on locally while connected to the network. The major difference is the method of data transport at the physical level because the data is likely to travel across a rather slow telephone line for dial-up and Internet connections. Another difference between a local network user and a remote access user is the way that the user's identification is authenticated. If using Remote Authentication Dial-In User Service (RADIUS), the RADIUS server takes on the task of authenticating users and passing along their data to the directory service(s) in which the users' accounts are listed.

Don't confuse remote access with remote control. Remote access is the capability to connect across a dial-up or VPN link, and from that point forward, to be able to gain access to and use network files, folders, printers, and other resources identically to the way a user could do on a local network computer. Remote control, on the other hand, is the capability to connect to a network remotely, and then, through the use of features such as Remote Desktop or Remote Assistance discussed earlier in this chapter. Remote control also includes third-party applications (such as PCAnywhere or Citrix) that create a session with a host computer where the desktop for that host computer is displayed on your PC, often within the application's window, although most of these applications enable you to run the session "full screen."

Remote Access Authentication Protocols

Authentication is the first perimeter of defense that a network administrator can define in a remote access system. The process of authenticating a user is meant to verify and validate a user's identification. If the user provides invalid input, the authentication process should deny the user access to the network. An ill-defined authentication system, or lack of one altogether, can open the door to mischief and disruption because the two most common methods for remote access are publicly available: the Internet and the public services telephone network. Table 14-2 discusses the authentication protocols supported by Windows 7's dial-up network connections.

Table 14-2   Authentication Protocols for Remote Access

Acronym	Name	Usage	Security
CHAP	Challenge Handshake Authentication Protocol	Client requests access. Server sends a challenge to client. Client responds using MD5 hash value. Values must match for authentication.	One-way authentication. Server authenticates client.
MS-CHAPv2	Microsoft Challenge Handshake Authentication Protocol version 2	Requires both the client and the server to be Microsoft Windows based. Does not work with LAN Manager. Client requests access, server challenges, client responds with an MD5 hash value and piggybacks a challenge to server. If a match is found, server responds with a success packet granting access to client, which includes an MD5 hash response to the client's challenge. Client logs on if the server's response matches what client expects. Note that the older MS-CHAP authentication protocol is no longer supported in Windows 7.	Mutual (two-way) authentication.
EAP	Extensible Authentication Protocol	Developed for PPP and can be used with IEEE 802.1X. Is capable of heading other authentication protocols, so improves interoperability between RAS systems, RADIUS servers, and RAS clients. Used with MD5-Challenge, smart cards, and certificate authentication in Windows 7.	Provides additional authentication types based on plug-in modules, enables enhanced interoperability and efficiency of authentication process.
PEAP-TLS	Protected Extensible Authentication Protocol with Transport Layer Security	A highly secure password-based authentication protocol combination that utilizes certificate-based authentication.	Requires a computer certificate on the VPN server.
PAP	Password Authentication Protocol	Client submits a clear-text user identification and password to server. Server compares to information in its user database. If a match, client is authenticated.	Clear-text, one-way authentication. Least secure method.

Table 14-2 Authentication Protocols for Remote Access

Acronym	Name	Usage	Security
Smart cards	Certificates	User must have knowledge of PIN and possession of smart card. Client swipes card, which submits smart card certificate, and inputs PIN. Results are reviewed by server, which responds with its own certificate. If both client and server match, access is granted. Otherwise, error that credentials cannot be verified.	Certificate-based, two-way authentication.

NOTE   When using certificate authentication, the client computer must have a way of validating the server's certificate. To ensure absolutely that this validation will work, you can import the server's certificate into the client's Trusted Publishers list. If there is no way for a client to validate the server's certificate, an error displays stating that the server is not a trusted resource.

Remote Access Security

Windows 7 can be configured in an assortment of ways to ensure that your remote access services meet your organization's security criteria. Much of the configuration takes place on the server side of remote access. These security features are available on a Windows 7 computer when you configure it to receive remote access connections.

You can access the Local Security Policy snap-in through Administrative Tools under Control Panel's System and Security category or by typing `secpol.msc` in the Start menu Search field. The policies defined in this utility affect all users on the computer, unless the policies allow you to configure them on a per-user or per-group basis. This snap-in is shown in Figure 14-15.

Figure 14-15   You can configure security policies that affect remote access in the Local Security Policy snap-in.

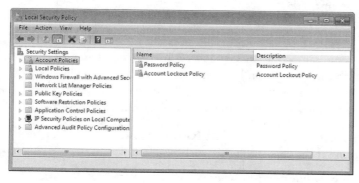

You can configure the Account Lockout Policy on the local computer to increase security. Under the Account Lockout Policy, you can configure how many bad passwords the computer will accept before it disables the user from logging on, how long the user will be locked out, and how long to wait before starting to count invalid logon attempts again. Remember that the Account Lockout Policy does not only affect remote access users, but all users who try to log on to the computer. We discussed account lockout settings in Chapter 12, "Configuring Access Controls."

You should always consider that because the default time periods are known quantities, an experienced hacker attempting to gain access to one of these accounts is likely to try again at intervals that will allow retries without locking the compromised account. To counter this, you should always set the Account lockout duration and Reset account lockout counter after policies to a longer duration than 30 minutes. If your computer is configured to accept VPN connections, you will probably want to establish IPSec settings. IPSec is a protocol used for authentication and encryption and is often used in VPNs in conjunction with L2TP.

Establishing VPN Connections and Authentication

We've already touched on VPN connections. The way a VPN works is rather interesting. The private network is connected to the Internet. An administrator sets up a VPN server that sits basically between the private network and the Internet. When a remote computer connects to the Internet, whether via dial-up or other means, the remote computer can connect to the VPN server by using TCP/IP. Then the PPTP or L2TP protocols encapsulate the data inside the TCP/IP packets sent to the VPN server. After the data is received at the VPN server, it strips off the encapsulating headers and footers and then transmits the packets to the appropriate network servers and resources.

The four tunneling protocols, although similar and all supported by Windows 7 and Windows Server 2008 R2 computers, act somewhat differently. PPTP incorporates security for encryption and authentication in the protocol by using Microsoft Point-to-Point Encryption (MPPE). SSTP encrypts data by encapsulating PPP traffic over the Secure Sockets Layer (SSL) channel of the HTTPS protocol. IKEv2 encapsulates datagrams by using IPSec ESP or AH headers. L2TP does not provide encryption on its own. Instead, you must use IPSec to secure the data.

To establish the VPN client connection on Windows 7, use the following procedure. To follow along with this exercise and to test it, you should have a client computer and a VPN server that can both connect to the Internet. These two computers should not be connected in any other way than through the Internet.

Step 1.   Click **Start > Network** and then select **Network and Sharing Center** from the options at the top of the Network applet.

Step 2.   Click **Set up a new connection or network**.

Step 3.   The Set Up a Connection or Network page shown in Figure 14-16 provides several connection options. Click **Connect to a workplace** and then click **Next**.

Figure 14-16   The Set Up a Connection or Network dialog box enables you to connect to several types of networks.

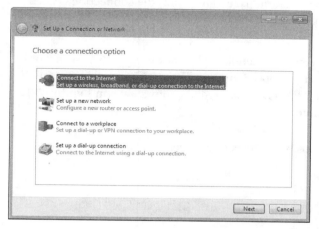

Step 4.   You are given the option for selecting a dial-up or a VPN connection. Click **Use my Internet connection (VPN)**.

Step 5.   On the Type the Internet address to connect to page (see Figure 14-17), type the name of the organization and the Internet address (FQDN, IPv4 address, or IPv6 address). Select the other options displayed on this page as required, and then click **Next**.

Figure 14-17   Type the Internet address and destination name of the network you want to access.

Step 6.   On the Type your user name and password page, type the username and password you will use to access the network. If this is a domain-based network, type the domain name. To remember the password for future access, select the **Remember this password** check box. Then click **Create**.

Step 7.   Windows 7 displays a creation page as it creates the connection. When completed, it informs you that the connection is ready. Click **Connect Now** to connect.

Step 8.   To connect later to your connection, right-click it in the Network Connections dialog box and choose **Connect**. Type the required information in the Connect VPN Connection dialog box shown in Figure 14-18 and then click **Connect**.

Figure 14-18   Type the username, password, and domain to connect to.

After you have set up a VPN connection, you can modify its properties if required. Right-click the connection in the Network Connections folder and choose **Properties**. The connection's Properties dialog box consists of the following tabs, each with different types of configurations:

- **General:** This tab enables you to specify the hostname or IP address of the destination and the need to connect to a public network such as the Internet before attempting to set up the VPN connection.

- **Options:** This tab provides the presentation features, such as prompting for a name, password, certificate, and phone number, as well as the Windows domain, and redialing options if the line is busy or the connection dropped. The PPP Settings button enables you to use link control protocol (LCP) extensions and software compression, or to negotiate multilink (use of multiple dial-up lines for increased transmission speed) for single-link connections.

- **Security:** As you can guess, the Security tab lets you select the type of VPN (automatic, PPTP, L2TP/IPSec, SSTP, or IKEv2), the security protocols to use, including EAP (for smart cards, certificates already on this computer, or trusted root certification authorities), CHAP, MS-CHAPv2, PAP, and so on. You can also configure encryption to be optional, required, or required at maximum strength.

- **Networking:** This tab enables you to specify the use of TCP/IPv4 and TCP/IPv6, as well as File and Printer Sharing for Microsoft Networks, and the Client for Microsoft Networks. Click **Install** to install additional features, including network clients, services, and protocols. To install these features, you should have an installation disk.

- **Sharing:** This tab lets you configure ICS to share the connection with other computers on your local network. You can also select options to establish dial-up connections when other computers attempt to access the Internet, or allow other users on the network to control or disable a shared connection. Click **Settings** to configure ICS.

VPN Connection Security

As already mentioned, any of PPTP, L2TP, SSTP, or IKEv2 enable you to set up a tunneled connection from a remote location across the Internet to servers in your office network and access shared resources as though you were located on the network itself. Recall that PPTP, SSTP, and IKEv2 include built-in security for encryption and authentication, whereas L2TP does not. You must use IPSec to secure data being sent across an L2TP connection.

An issue that you should be aware of concerns the encryption levels used by client and server computers when establishing a VPN connection. If these encryption levels fail to match, you might receive an error code 741 accompanied by the message stating that The local computer does not support the required encryption type or an error code 742 with the message The remote server does not support the required encryption type. This problem occurs if the server is using an encryption level different from that of your mobile computer. Servers running Windows 2000 Server or Windows Server 2003 use Rivest Cipher 4 (RC4) encryption at a level of either 40 bits or 56 bits. By default, Windows Vista and Windows 7 use 128-bit encryption. Use the following procedure to modify the encryption level:

Step 1. From the Network and Sharing Center, click **Change adapter settings** to access the Network Connections dialog box.

Step 2. Right-click the desired VPN connection and select **Properties**.

Step 3.   On the Security tab of the VPN Connection Properties dialog box shown in Figure 14-19, select **Maximum strength encryption (disconnect if server declines)** and then click **OK**.

Figure 14-19   The Security tab of the connection's Properties dialog box enables you to specify the level of encryption used in a VPN connection.

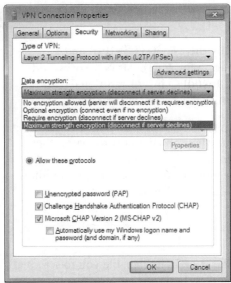

Enabling VPN Reconnect

New to Windows 7 is the VPN Reconnect feature, which utilizes IKEv2 technology to automatically reestablish a VPN connection when a user has temporarily lost her Internet connection. This avoids the need to manually reconnect to the VPN and possibly having to restart a download. VPN Reconnect can reestablish a connection as long as eight hours after the connection was lost. A user could be connected to an airport Wi-Fi connection when his flight is called for boarding; when he lands at his destination, he can reconnect and finish his download.

Use the following procedure to set up VPN Reconnect:

Step 1.   Access the Security tab of the connection's Properties dialog box as previously shown in Figure 14-19.

Step 2.   In the Type of VPN drop-down list, select **IKEv2** and then click **Advanced settings**.

Step 3.   In the Advanced Properties drop-down list shown in Figure 14-20, ensure that **Mobility** is selected and then select a value (30 minutes by default) in the Network outage time dialog box.

Figure 14-20   You can choose a reconnection time of up to eight hours from the Advanced Properties dialog box.

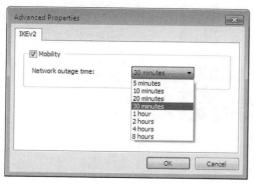

Step 4.   Click **OK** and then click **OK** again to close the connection's Properties dialog box.

> **NOTE**   For further information and a sample detailed procedure, refer to "Remote Access Step-by-Step Guide: Deploying Remote Access with VPN Reconnect" at http://www.microsoft.com/downloads/details.aspx?FamilyID= 7e973087-3d2d-4cac-abdf-cc7bde298847&displaylang=en.

Advanced Security Auditing

Windows 7 Group Policy provides a new set of advanced audit policy configuration settings that you can use to provide a high level of control over audit policies. Found in the Computer Configuration\Windows Settings\Security Settings\ Advanced Audit Policy Configuration\System Audit Policies node of Group Policy, the advanced audit policies provide a total of 53 policy settings within 10 categories as shown in Figure 14-21. These policy settings are available for Windows 7 Professional, Enterprise, and Ultimate, as well as all editions of Windows Server 2008 R2.

Previous versions of Windows supported basic audit policy settings. These settings are still available in Windows 7 but do not provide this granular level of audit policy configuration. For example, the basic audit policy setting for account logon provides a single audit setting, whereas advanced audit policy provides four settings. Enabling the basic setting is equivalent to enabling all the advanced settings. This provides greater control over auditing setting and enables you to control the size and detail provided by the security logs to a much greater extent.

To configure any of these settings, double-click the desired category in Figure 14-21 to display the available settings. Double-click the desired setting to display its **Properties** dialog box, select the **Configure the following audit events** check box, and then select **Success** and/or **Failure** as required. Audited events will be displayed in the Event Viewer Security log. For more information on each policy setting, click its **Explain** tab.

Figure 14-21   Advanced Audit Policy Configuration provides a comprehensive set of audit policies classified into 10 categories.

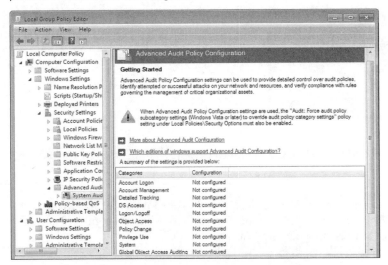

> **NOTE**   For more information on advanced audit policy settings as a whole, refer to "Advanced Security Audit Policy Settings" at http://technet.microsoft.com/en-us/library/dd772712(WS.10).aspx.

NAP Quarantine Remediation

Chapter 13, "Configuring Mobile Computing," introduced the Network Access Protection (NAP) as used with DirectAccess to require that authenticating clients submit a health certificate proving the client is free of malware and up-to-date with regard to security updates and antimalware definitions. You can use NAP in the same manner with Remote Access and VPN clients.

First introduced with Windows Vista and Windows Server 2008 and available in Windows 7 Professional, Enterprise, and Ultimate, NAP can address health criteria such as the following:

- Is the client's antivirus and antispyware software installed, enabled, and up-to-date?
- Is Windows Firewall enabled?
- Is automatic updating enabled?

- Are security updates installed according to a security severity rating in the Microsoft Security Response Center?

- Are all software updates installed and configured?

NAP utilizes system health validators (SHVs) to assess these criteria. Windows 7 and Windows Server 2008 enable you to use multiple SHV configurations. You can configure health policies in which you select one of these SHV configurations, such as one configuration for internal desktop computers and another one for portable computers that connect across the VPN.

You can check the status of the NAP security agent by accessing the Action Center from the System and Security category of Control Panel. Expand the Security section and scroll down to see the Network Access Protection listing as shown in Figure 14-22. If the service is not running, you can start it from the Services snap-in, accessed from the Computer Management snap-in, or by typing `Services` in the Start menu Search field.

Figure 14-22   Action Center informs you whether the Network Access Protection agent service is running.

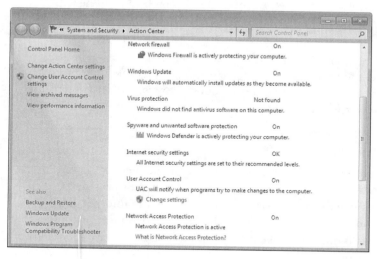

On the network, you can configure a health server to perform a process of remediation on client computers not meeting health requirements. This health validation server tests clients using VPN to connect to the corporate network. It redirects noncompliant clients to a remediation network where clients can be updated to become compliant with corporate standards. Only after the clients have been appropriately remediated can they connect to network resources. You can include services such as a Windows Server Update Services (WSUS) server that enables the client to receive operating system and software updates and an antivirus update server configured to provide updated antivirus and antimalware signatures.

Enforcement options against noncompliant clients in NAP include the following:

- **No enforcement:** Simply monitors the client's health state; can include auto remediation.

- **IPSec:** Unhealthy client connection requests can be rejected; compliant clients receive an X.509 health certificate.

- **802.1X:** Can provide strong network restrictions and can be applied to both wired and wireless connections. Unhealthy clients reach a restricted VLAN.

- **Terminal Services Gateway:** Limits access to limited set of resources for purposes of remediation; only compliant clients can reach terminal services applications.

- **VPN:** Uses IP filters enforced by VPN server to route unhealthy clients to remediation servers.

- **DHCP:** Can check clients when they request IP address assignment and restricts route to remediation servers.

- **DirectAccess:** Verifies client health before allowing an IPSec tunnel connection; rejects connections and requires new health certificates.

NOTE   For more information on NAP in Windows 7 and Windows Server 2008 R2, refer to "NAP Client Configuration" at http://technet.microsoft.com/en-us/library/cc754803.aspx and "Network Access Protection" at http://technet.microsoft.com/en-us/network/bb545879.aspx.

Configuring Dial-Up Connections

You can configure Internet connections identically to private network connections except that you must specify TCP/IP as the protocol. Most ISPs provide a CD-ROM with proprietary software to connect to and use the Internet. This software usually creates an Internet connection in the Network Connections applet for you. The reason ISPs do this is to make it very simple for a new user to configure a connection to her network.

To configure your own connection to an ISP, you use the same wizard used for creating other remote access connections, as described in the following procedure:

Step 1.   Start by accessing the Set Up a Connection or Network Wizard previously shown in Figure 14-16 and select **Set up a dial-up connection**.

Step 2.   As shown in Figure 14-23, the resulting dialog box enables you to enter the required connection parameters. Type the phone number of the ISP, the name and password that the ISP provided you, and provide a name for the connection. Select the option for whether you want other people to use this connection.

Figure 14-23   The Create a Dial-Up Connection Wizard enables you to enter the parameters required for making a dial-up connection.

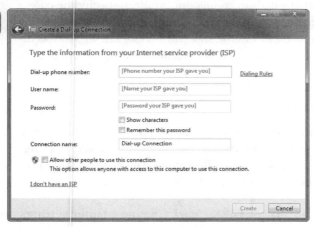

Step 3.   If you need to provide dialing rules information, click **Dialing Rules** to display the Location Information dialog box shown in Figure 14-24. Enter the required information for your connection and then click **OK**.

Figure 14-24   The Location Information dialog box enables you to enter dialing rules.

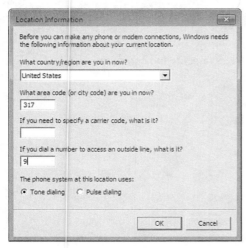

Step 4.   Click **Create** when you are finished. When you're informed that the connection is ready for use, click **Close**.

Step 5.   To connect, right-click the connection and click **Connect** to then open
up the Connect screen. If your ISP provided you with additional configuration information, you should click the **Properties** button to fine-
tune your connection.

After you have successfully created a dial-up connection, you can specify the configuration options to match those of your remote access server. Right-click the
connection icon and select **Properties** from the shortcut menu. The Properties dialog box for a dial-up connection is similar to that described in the previous section for VPN connections.

Accepting Incoming Connections

You can configure Windows 7 to receive incoming calls as a dial-up server. License
limitations allow only one user at a time to dial in to the computer. You can configure the inbound connection properties so that this user can gain access to the computer only, or the entire LAN, as described in the following procedure:

Step 1.   From the Network and Sharing Center, click **Change adapter settings**
to access the Network Connections dialog box.

Step 2.   Press **Alt** to access the menu bar and then click **File > New Incoming
Connection**.

Step 3.   The Allow connections to this computer Wizard presents the Who may
connect to this computer? page shown in Figure 14-25. Select the required user(s) and then click **Next**. If you need to add a user that does
not appear, click **Add someone**.

Figure 14-25   Choosing the users that are allowed to connect to the computer.

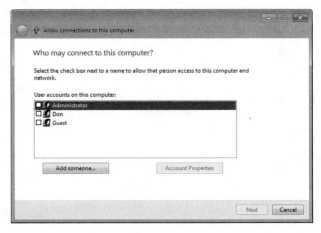

Step 4.   The How will people connect page enables you to receive incoming connections through the Internet or the dial-up connection that you have created. Select the required option and then click **Next**.

Step 5.   On the Networking software allows this computer to accept connections from other kinds of computers page shown in Figure 14-26, select the required types of networking software that you want to enable and then click **Allow access**.

Figure 14-26   Choosing the types of networking components that will be used for incoming connections.

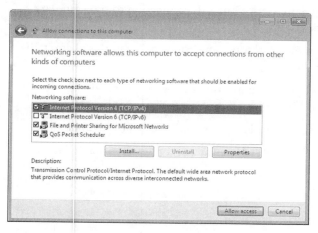

Step 6.   You are informed that the people you chose can now connect to your computer, and the information required for connection is given. Click **Close** to finish the wizard.

The new incoming connection is added to the Network Connections dialog box. If you need to modify the properties of the connection, including the parameters you specified while running the wizard, right-click it and choose **Properties**.

Published Applications on Remote Desktop

Windows 7 and Windows Server 2008 R2 offer a new application gateway that works with Remote Desktop, called Remote Desktop Gateway (RD Gateway), which replaces the Terminal Services feature included with older versions of Windows Server. RD Gateway enables you to connect to remote servers on the corporate network from any computer connected to the Internet. RD Gateway utilizes the Remote Desktop Protocol (RDP) together with HTTPS to enable a secure, encrypted connection to the internal servers through TCP port 443.

When using RD Gateway, you connect directly to a specially configured RD Gateway server on the internal network, which in turn allows connections to any computer that has been granted access. This server is a Windows Server 2008 R2 computer on which you have installed the RD Gateway server role through Server Manager. Advantages of using an RD Gateway server for accessing published applications include the following:

■ Connections to remote computers across firewalls are facilitated.

■ You do not need to set up a VPN connection to enable the RD Gateway connection.

■ You can share the network connection with other applications running on your computer, thereby enabling you to use your ISP connection to transmit data across the remote connection.

You learned how to set up a Remote Desktop connection earlier in this chapter. To use RD Gateway, proceed as follows:

Step 1. Access the Remote Desktop Connection dialog box as previously described and shown in Figure 14-1.

Step 2. Click **Options** to expand this dialog box and select the **Advanced** tab.

Step 3. Click **Settings** to open the RD Gateway Server Settings dialog box, as shown in Figure 14-27.

Figure 14-27   The RD Gateway Server Settings dialog box enables you to specify server settings.

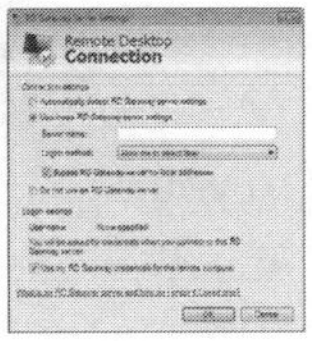

Step 4. Select **Use these RD Gateway server settings** and type the FQDN or IP address of the server to which you want to connect.

Step 5. Select one of the following available logon methods:

— **Allow me to select later:** Enables you to select a logon method when you connect.

— **Ask for password (NTLM):** Uses NT LAN Manager (NTLM) and prompts you for a password when you connect.

— **Smart card:** Prompts you to insert your smart card when you connect.

Step 6. If you need to prevent traffic to and from local network addresses from going through the RD Gateway server, select the **Bypass RD Gateway server for local addresses** check box (selected by default).

Step 7.   When finished, click **OK**. You can now connect to the RD Gateway server through the Remote Desktop Connection dialog box.

> **NOTE** For detailed information on setting up RD Gateway, including how to set up the RD Gateway server, refer to "Deploying Remote Desktop Gateway Step-by-Step Guide" at http://www.microsoft.com/downloads/en/confirmation.aspx?familyId= 6d146124-e850-4cec-9efa-33a5225e155d&displayLang=en.

RD Gateway Policies

You can use Group Policy to specify RD Gateway configuration. This enables you to set up uniform policy settings for all client computers that belong to an AD DS domain. Navigate to the User Configuration\Administrative Templates\Windows Components\Remote Desktop Services\RD Gateway node to receive the policies shown in Figure 14-28. You can configure the following policies:

- **Set RD Gateway authentication method:** Enable this policy to specify the authentication method to be used. You can allow users to change this setting, or you can specify that users will be asked for credentials using the Basic or NTLM method, locally logged-on credentials, or smart card.

- **Enable connection through RD Gateway:** When enabled, clients will attempt to connect to the remote computer through an RD Gateway server whose IP address is specified in the next policy.

- **Set RD Gateway server address:** Specifies the IP address of the RD Gateway server to which clients will connect.

More information on each of these policies is available in the Help text of each policy setting's Properties dialog box.

Figure 14-28   Group Policy provides three policy settings that govern connections through RD Gateway.

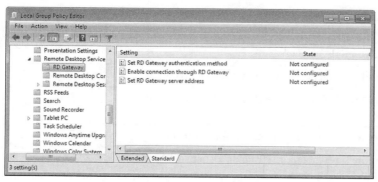

Using RemoteApp to Specify Applications

Remote Desktop Services in Windows Server 2008 R2 enables you to specify RemoteApp programs, which are the programs users can access remotely through the RD Gateway server. When a user accesses one of these programs, it appears on her desktop as though it were running locally. These programs are even available to the user on her computer's Start menu.

To configure RemoteApp and Desktop Connections, type `remoteapp` in the Start Menu Search field. Click **Set up a new connection with RemoteApp and Desktop Connections** and then specify the URL of the required connection. After you have configured this information, available programs appear directly in the Start menu. When a user connects, he simply needs to provide a password or smart card when requested unless the policy to use logged-on credentials has been enabled; in this case, he connects directly to the program.

NOTE   For more information on RemoteApp, refer to "RemoteApp and Desktop Connection" at http://technet.microsoft.com/en-us/library/dd560650(WS.10).aspx.

Exam Preparation Tasks

Review All the Key Topics

Review the most important topics in the chapter, noted with the key topics icon in the outer margin of the page. Table 14-3 lists a reference of these key topics and the page numbers on which each is found.

Table 14-3   Key Topics for Chapter 14

Key Topic Element	Description	Page Number
List	Outlines the procedure used for creating a Remote Desktop connection	526
Figure 14-3	Specifying incoming Remote Desktop connection options	528
Figure 14-6	Enabling Remote Assistance	532
List	Describes how to send a Remote Assistance invitation	532
List	Describes protocols used with Remote Access network connections	540
Table 14-2	Describes Remote Access authentication protocols	542
Figure 14-17	Shows options available for setting up a client VPN connection	545

Table 14-3 Key Topics for Chapter 14

Key Topic Element	Description	Page Number
Figure 14-19	Specifying available VPN data encryption methods	548
List	Describes available NAP enforcement and remediation options	
Figure 14-23	Shows information you must enter to create a dial-up connection	553
Figure 14-27	Configuring RD Gateway server settings	556

Complete the Tables and Lists from Memory

Print a copy of Appendix C, "Memory Tables" (found on the CD), or at least the section for this chapter, and complete the tables and lists from memory. Appendix D, "Memory Tables Answer Key," also on the CD, includes completed tables and lists to check your work.

Definitions of Key Terms

Define the following key terms from this chapter, and check your answers in the glossary.

Virtual Private Network (VPN), Point-to-Point Protocol (PPP), Point-to-Point Tunneling Protocol (PPTP), Layer 2 Tunneling Protocol (L2TP), Secure Socket Tunneling Protocol (SSTP), Internet Key Exchange version 2 (IKEv2), Remote Assistance, Remote Desktop, Windows Remote Management (WinRM) Service, Windows PowerShell, Password Authentication Protocol (PAP), Challenge Handshake Authentication Protocol (CHAP), Microsoft Challenge Handshake Authentication Protocol version 2 (MS-CHAPv2), Extensible Authentication Protocol (EAP), Protected Extensible Authentication Protocol-Transport Layer Security (PEAP-TLS), RemoteApp, Remote Desktop Gateway (RD Gateway)

This chapter covers the following subjects:

- **Managing Disks and Volumes:** Windows 7 enables you to create several types of disk volumes on your computer. This section introduces you to these volume types and shows you how to create, manage, and troubleshoot problems with disks.

- **Managing File System Fragmentation:** If you edit and delete a large number of files on your computer, new files can become fragmented—in other words, be stored in several noncontiguous portions of your disk. This section shows you how to defragment your disks so that performance is kept optimal.

- **RAID volumes:** Windows 7 enables you to create different types of RAID volumes, including striped, mirrored, and striped volumes with parity. This section introduces you to the benefits and drawbacks of each volume type and shows you how to create, manage, and troubleshoot these volumes.

- **Configuring Removable Drive Policies:** Removable drives can be a security risk to a company. You can configure Group Policy settings that limit what users can do with various types of removable drives.

CHAPTER 15

Disk Management

Storage needs for computers have changed significantly over time. You could feed the data of hundreds of computers from just 10 years ago into a single computer today and still not fill its hard disk. Part of the reason is that today's data is much different than that of 10 years ago. It includes multimedia files, 20-plus megapixel images, extended attributes, complex formulas, and WYSIWYG (What You See Is What You Get) formatting. The result is that the size of a single file can be hundreds of megabytes (MB) or even several gigabytes (GB). So, although storage space has grown, the demand for storage space has increased along with it.

"Do I Know This Already?" Quiz

The "Do I Know This Already?" quiz enables you to assess whether you should read this entire chapter or simply jump to the "Exam Preparation Tasks" section for review. If you are in doubt, read the entire chapter. Table 15-1 outlines the major headings in this chapter and the corresponding "Do I Know This Already?" quiz questions. You can find the answers in Appendix A, "Answers to the 'Do I Know This Already?' Quizzes."

Table 15-1 "Do I Know This Already?" Foundation Topics Section-to-Question Mapping

Foundations Topics Section	Questions Covered in This Section
Managing Disks and Volumes	1–6
Managing File System Fragmentation	7–8
RAID volumes	9–10
Configuring Removable Drive Policies	11

1. Your hard disk is configured as a basic disk, and you do not want to convert it to dynamic storage because you want to enable dual-booting. Which of the following partition types can you configure on the disk? (Choose all that apply.)

   a. Simple volume

   b. Primary partition

   c. Extended partition

   d. Spanned volume

   e. Mirrored volume

   f. Striped volume

   g. Logical drive

   h. RAID-5 volume

2. You have added a new 5 TB hard disk to your Windows 7 computer and initialized it. You now want to create a single volume that uses the entire space on the disk, so you start the DiskPart tool from an administrative command prompt. On attempting to create the volume, you receive an error. Which of the following commands should you execute first?

   a. `convert basic`

   b. `convert dynamic`

   c. `convert gpt`

   d. `convert mbr`

3. You want to add additional space to your D: partition so that you can store a large number of digital images. You do not want to add an additional drive letter, so you run the Extend Volume Wizard. What type of volume are you creating?

   a. Simple volume

   b. Spanned volume

   c. Mirrored volume

   d. RAID-5 volume

4. Which tab of a volume's Properties dialog box enables you to check the volume for errors?

   a. General

   b. Tools

   c. Hardware

   d. Quota

   e. Customize

5. You have moved a hard disk containing several years' worth of digital images from your old computer running Windows XP to your new Windows 7 computer. On starting Disk Management, you notice that the disk status is listed as Unknown. What should you do?

   a. Right-click the disk and choose **Initialize**.

   b. Right-click the disk and choose **Resynchronize**.

   c. Right-click the disk and choose **Properties**. Then check the disk for errors and perform corrective actions according to the output.

   d. Right-click the disk and choose **Format**. Then restore all the images from backup.

6. Your computer is configured for dual-booting between Windows 7 Professional and Windows XP Professional. While running Windows 7, you convert your hard disk to dynamic storage. You attempt to start the computer in Windows XP, but it will not boot. What do you need to do to boot Windows XP?

   a. In Disk Management, right-click your computer's disk and choose **Convert to Basic**.

   b. In Disk Management, right-click the Windows XP volume and choose **Convert to Basic**.

   c. Boot your computer with the Windows XP CD-ROM and select the Recovery Console option. Then select the option to repair your installation.

   d. In Windows 7, first back up all your data. Then boot your computer with a floppy disk, use the `fdisk` utility to delete all volumes on the disk, and create a new partition. Then install Windows XP, install Windows 7, and finally restore all your data from backup.

7. One morning, you start the Disk Defragmenter to defragment your `c:` drive. This drive is 75 GB in size with a free space of 6 GB. After lunch, the defragmenter is still running and you start to wonder what else you should do to optimize disk usage. Which of the following can you do to improve the rate of disk response? (Choose all that apply.)

   a. Run the Disk Cleanup utility.

   b. Back up old data and then delete this data from the drive.

   c. Uninstall several applications whose files are on this drive.

   d. Just let the Disk Defragmenter run overnight.

8. Your computer has three volumes, `C:`, `D:`, and `E:`. You want to defragment the `C:` and `D:` volumes only from the command line. What command will do this? (Choose two; each is a complete solution.)

   a. `defrag c: d:`

   b. `defrag /e:`

   c. `defrag /E e:`

   d. `defrag /E c: d:`

9. Which of the following RAID technologies are fault tolerant? (Choose all that apply.)

   a. Spanning

   b. Striping

   c. Mirroring

   d. Striping with parity

10. You have four hard disks in your computer and want to create a RAID-5 volume. The amount of free space on the disks is as follows: Disk 0, 60 GB; disk 1, 80 GB; disk 2, 40 GB; disk 3, 100 GB. What is the maximum size of RAID-5 volume that you can create?

   a. 120 GB

   b. 160 GB

   c. 180 GB

   d. 280 GB

11. You want to ensure that your Windows 7 computer will always boot, so you decide that you want to implement fault tolerance on your system and boot volumes. Your computer has two hard disks. You start the DiskPart command and select the system/boot volume. What command should you use?

   a. `create volume stripe disk=0,1`

   b. `create volume mirror disk=0,1`

   c. `create volume raid disk=0,1`

   d. `add disk 1`

12. You would like to prevent users from writing potentially confidential information onto iPods, iPhones, and similar portable devices. What policy should you enable?

   a. CD and DVD: Deny write access

   b. Custom Classes: Deny write access

   c. Removable Disk: Deny write access

   d. WPD Devices: Deny write access

Foundation Topics

Managing Disks and Volumes

Windows 7 offers several tools and utilities that assist you in working with disks and volumes, including removable disks. We discuss configuring policies with removable disks later in this chapter. You can use the Computer Management Microsoft Management Console (MMC) snap-in or the DiskPart command-line utility to manage disks. We introduced these tools in Chapter 6, "Configuring Virtual Hard Disks," with regard to their use in creating virtual hard disks (VHDs); here we discuss them in detail.

The Computer Management tool, shown in Figure 15-1, enables you to manage disks and other storage devices in Windows 7. To open Computer Management, right-click **Computer** and select **Manage** from the shortcut menu. Computer Management offers the following tools and utilities, many of which are discussed in other chapters of this book:

Figure 15-1   The Computer Management tool contains the main administration utilities for disk devices.

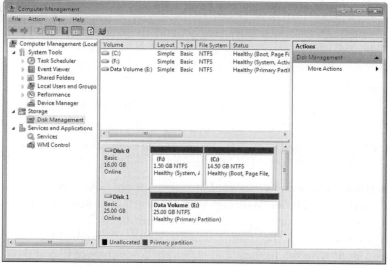

- **Task Scheduler:** Used for configuring programs and utilities to run at predetermined times and repeated schedules.

- **Event Viewer:** Used for troubleshooting errors.

- **Shared Folders:** Used for managing shares and connections to your computer.

- **Local Users and Groups:** Used for managing local users and groups on the computer.

- **Performance:** Used for troubleshooting errors as well as optimizing performance.

- **Device Manager:** Used for configuring devices, updating or uninstalling device drivers, rolling back device drivers, enabling and disabling devices, and troubleshooting.

- **Disk Management:** Used for viewing and managing volume and disk configuration.

- **Services:** Used for starting and stopping services related to a device.

- **WMI Control:** Used for turning error logging on or off or backing up the Windows Management Instrumentation (WMI) repository (in most cases, you will not use this tool).

The following list summarizes the major actions you can perform from the Disk Management snap-in:

- **Create Dynamic Disks:** Disks can be either basic (the default) or dynamic. You can convert a basic disk to a dynamic disk, but you cannot change back. Your only avenue to reverting to a basic disk is by deleting all volumes on the dynamic disk, losing the data, creating a new basic volume, and restoring the data from a backup.

- **Create Volumes:** You can create several types of volumes on a dynamic disk. Microsoft provides a wizard to assist you in creating these volumes.

- **Extend Volumes:** You can add additional unallocated space on a disk to an existing volume. Windows 7 provides the Extend Volume Wizard to assist you in this action.

- **Shrink Volumes:** You can reduce the size of a volume to generate unallocated space for creating or extending a different volume.

- **Display Properties of Disks and Volumes:** For disks, you can obtain the same information as provided by Device Manager. For volumes, you can obtain information about free space and device properties. This feature also lets you defragment the volume, share the volume, configure an access control list (ACL), back up all files on the volume, and create shadow copies of files and folders within the volume.

Basic and Dynamic Disks

When you first install Windows 7, the hard disk on which you install Windows is set up as a *basic disk*. When you add a brand-new hard disk to your computer, this disk is also recognized as a basic disk. This disk type is the one that has existed ever since the days of MS-DOS. Starting with Windows 2000, Microsoft offered a new type of disk called a *dynamic disk*. This disk type offers several advantages over the basic disk, including the following:

- You can create specialized disk volumes on a dynamic disk, including spanned, striped, mirrored, and RAID-5 volumes. Basic disks are limited to primary and extended partitions, and logical drives.

- You can work with and upgrade disk volumes on the fly, without the need to re-boot your computer.

- You can create an almost unlimited number of volumes on a dynamic disk. A basic disk can hold a total of only four primary partitions, or three primary plus one extended partitions.

Dynamic disks have their disadvantages, however:

- The disk does not contain partitions or logical drives and therefore can't be read by another operating system.

- On a multiboot computer, the disk might not be readable by operating systems other than the one from which the disk was upgraded. You cannot read a dynamic disk using Windows NT or 9x.

- Laptop computers do not support dynamic disks.

Besides a disk type, all disks have one of two partition styles:

- **Master Boot Record (MBR):** Uses a partition table that describes the location of the partitions on the disk. The first sector of an MBR disk contains the master boot record plus a hidden binary code file that is used for booting the system. This disk style supports volumes of up to 2 terabytes (TB) with up to four primary partitions or three primary partitions plus one extended partition subdivided into any number of logical drives.

- **GUID Partition Table (GPT):** Uses extensible firmware interface (EFI) to store partition information within each partition and includes redundant primary and backup partition tables to ensure structural integrity. This style is recommended for disks larger than 2 TB in size and for disks used on Itanium-based computers. Not all previous Windows versions can recognize this disk style, however.

When you add a new disk of less than 2 TB in size, it is added as an MBR disk. You can convert an MBR disk to a GPT one using either Disk Management or the DiskPart tool, provided there are no partitions or volumes on the disk. To use Disk

Management, right-click it and choose **Convert to GPT Disk**. To use DiskPart, proceed as follows:

Step 1. Open an administrative command prompt, type `DiskPart`, and accept the User Account Control (UAC) prompt. You receive the DiskPart command window.

Step 2. Type `list disk` to get the disk number of the disks on your system.

Step 3. Type `select disk n` where *n* is the number of the disk you want to convert.

Step 4. Type `convert gpt`. DiskPart informs you that it has successfully converted the selected disk to GPT format.

If you want to convert a GPT disk back to MBR, the procedures are the same. You must back up all data and delete all volumes on the disk before performing the conversion. In Disk Management, right-click the disk and choose **Convert to MBR Disk**. In DiskPart, use the same steps and type `convert mbr` in the last one.

Working with Basic Disks

When you first install Windows 7 on a new computer or add a new disk to an existing Windows 7 computer, the disk appears in Disk Management as a basic disk. Windows 7 enables you to create a new partition (AKA a simple volume) from the free space on a new or existing disk. This partition can be a primary, extended, or logical volume. Keep in mind that a single basic disk can contain up to four primary partitions or three primary partitions plus an extended partition; the extended partition can contain any number of logical drives. Use the following procedure to create a partition:

Step 1. Right-click **Computer** and select **Manage** from the shortcut menu.

Step 2. Select **Disk Management** in the left pane.

Step 3. Locate the disk in the right pane that contains the unallocated space where the new volume will reside.

Step 4. Right-click the unallocated space of the disk, and select **New Simple Volume** from the shortcut menu.

Step 5. The New Simple Volume Wizard starts. Click **Next**.

Step 6. On the Specify Volume Size page, type the size of the partition in megabytes and then click **Next**.

Step 7. On the Assign Drive Letter or Path page shown in Figure 15-2, accept the drive letter provided or use the drop-down list to select a different letter. Then click **Next**.

Figure 15-2   You can assign a drive letter to your partition or mount it in an empty NTFS folder.

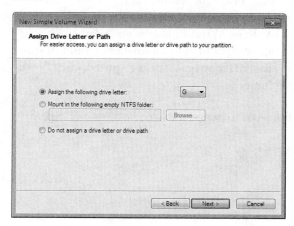

Step 8.   On the Format Partition page shown in Figure 15-3, choose the file system (FAT, FAT32, or NTFS) to format the partition. Provide a volume label name or accept the default of New Volume (this name will appear in the Computer window). If formatting with NTFS, you can modify the allocation unit size and/or enable file and folder compression. When done, click **Next**.

Figure 15-3   You are given several choices for formatting a new partition.

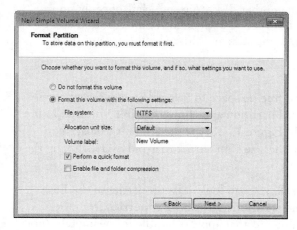

Step 9.   Review the information provided on the completion page and then click **Finish**. Windows 7 creates and formats the partition and displays its information in the Disk Management snap-in.

On a basic disk, Disk Management also enables you to perform several other management activities. You can extend, shrink, or delete volumes as necessary. Extending a volume adds any unallocated space to the volume. Right-click the volume and choose **Extend Volume**. The Extend Volume Wizard informs you what space is available and enables you to add additional space or select a smaller amount of space, as shown in Figure 15-4. Modify the amounts in megabytes as required, click **Next**, and then click **Finish** to extend the volume.

Figure 15-4   The Extend Volume Wizard helps you to extend a volume on a basic or dynamic disk.

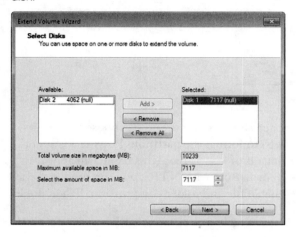

> **NOTE**   If you add additional space on another disk from the Available column in the Extend Volume Wizard, you will be creating a spanned volume. The wizard will ask you to convert the disks to dynamic storage. More about this later in this chapter.

Shrinking a partition enables you to free up space to be used on a different partition. To do so, right-click the desired partition and choose **Shrink Volume**. In the Shrink Volume dialog box shown in Figure 15-5, type the amount of space you want to shrink the volume by (note the size after shrink to avoid overshrinking the volume). Then click **Shrink**.

To view how a partition is configured, you can look at its properties in the Disk Management utility. Right-click the partition and select **Properties** from the shortcut menu. The Properties dialog box that appears has the following tabs (not all tabs will appear if the disk is not formatted with the NTFS file system):

■   **General:** As shown in Figure 15-6, this tab provides an immediate view of the space allocation on the disk in a pie chart. The General tab also enables you to type a volume name and to click a button that executes the Disk Cleanup graphical utility. This utility enables you to remove unnecessary files from your disk such as the Temporary Internet Files folder, downloaded program install files, and the Recycle Bin.

Figure 15-5 The Shrink Volume dialog box lets you shrink a partition or volume.

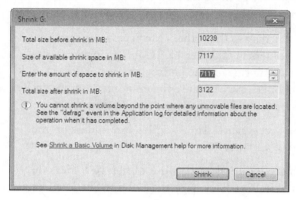

Figure 15-6 A volume's properties displays its space allocation.

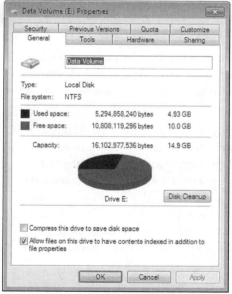

- **Tools:** This tab has the following three buttons. We discuss the first two later in this chapter and the Back Up Now option in Chapter 17, "Configuring Backups."

  — **Check now:** Executes the GUI version of Chkdsk.

— **Defragment now:** Executes the GUI version of Defrag.

— **Back up now:** Starts the Back Up or Restore Your Files program, which enables you to configure backup and restore options.

- **Hardware:** Displays the storage device hardware for the computer. You can obtain properties for any device, similar to that obtained from Device Manager, by selecting it and clicking **Properties**.

- **Sharing:** Enables you to share the disk so that others can access information on it, similar to that discussed for folders in Chapter 11, "Configuring Access to Local and Shared Resources." Doing this for the entire drive is not considered a good practice. It is generally unnecessary because the computer automatically generates an administrative share for each partition when Windows starts.

- **Security:** Enables you to assign access permissions to files and folders on the disk, similar to those discussed in Chapter 11.

- **Previous Versions:** Enables you to locate older versions of files or folders that might have been created from Windows Backup or the Volume Shadow Copy Service.

- **Quota:** Enables you to assign disk quotas to users on the disk. This lets you limit the amount of space used on the disk by an individual user, who will receive a Disk Full message if he attempts to use more space than assigned to his quota.

- **Customize:** Enables you to optimize folders on the disk for purposes such as general items, documents, pictures, music, or videos. You can also choose to display a different icon that will appear in the Computer window or to restore default settings.

You can delete a logical drive or partition easily from within the Disk Management utility. Simply right-click the logical drive and select **Delete Volume** from the shortcut menu, as depicted in Figure 15-7. A prompt appears to verify that you want to have the logical drive or partition deleted or if you want to back the data up. Click **Yes** to continue or **No** to first back the data up. When you click **Yes**, Windows 7 deletes the drive or partition. Windows 7 prevents you from deleting the system partition, the boot partition, or any partition that contains an active paging file. Extended partitions can be deleted only if they are empty of data and logical drives.

Converting Basic Disks to Dynamic

The process to convert a basic disk to a dynamic disk requires that you have a minimum of 1 MB of available space on the disk. Best practices state that when you make changes to a disk configuration, you should back up the data before starting, just in case you need to restore it after you are finished. Even so, converting a basic disk to a dynamic disk should not have any effect on your data.

Figure 15-7 The Disk Management utility enables you to delete a partition or logical drive.

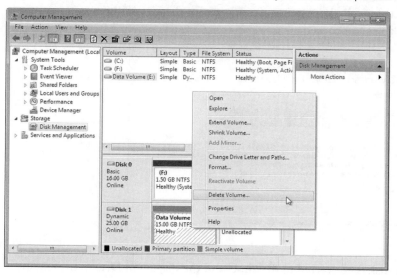

You can convert a basic disk to dynamic at any time. Any partitions on the disk are converted to simple volumes in this process. To perform a conversion, you must be logged on as an administrator of the computer.

Step 1. In Computer Management, right-click the disk to be converted to dynamic and choose **Convert to Dynamic Disk**.

Step 2. If more than one hard disk is present, you receive the dialog box shown in Figure 15-8. Select any additional disks that you want to convert to dynamic and then click **OK**.

Figure 15-8 You can convert any of or all your disks to dynamic storage at the same time.

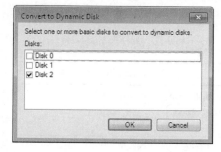

Step 3. The Disks to Convert dialog box shows you the disks that will be converted. Click **Convert** to proceed.

Step 4.   Disk Management warns you (see Figure 15-9) that you will be unable to start installed operating systems except the current boot volume. Click **Yes** to proceed.

Figure 15-9   You are warned that you will be unable to start other operating systems if you convert to dynamic storage.

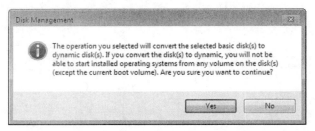

Step 5.   The disk is converted to dynamic, and the display in Disk Management is updated accordingly.

To convert a dynamic disk back to basic, you must first back up all data on the disk and delete all volumes. Then right-click the disk in Computer Management and choose **Convert to Basic Disk**. The conversion proceeds and the display in Disk Management is updated within a few seconds.

Working with Dynamic Disks

When you convert a basic disk to a dynamic disk, the existing partitions are converted to simple volumes and fault-tolerant volumes are converted into dynamic volumes. Dynamic volumes can be changed on the fly, as the name *dynamic* implies. A *dynamic volume* is a unit of storage initially created from the free space on one or more disks. Table 15-2 lists the volume types available on a dynamic disk.

Table 15-2   Dynamic Volume Types

Volume Type	Number of Disks	Configuration	Fault Tolerance
Simple	1	A single region or multiple concatenated regions of free space on a single disk.	None
Spanned	2–32	Two or more regions of free space on 2–32 disks linked into a single volume. Can be extended. Cannot be mirrored.	None

Table 15-2 Dynamic Volume Types

Volume Type	Number of Disks	Configuration	Fault Tolerance
Striped	2–32	Multiple regions of free space from two or more disks. Data is evenly interleaved across the disks, in stripes. Known as RAID Level 0.	None
Mirrored	2	Data on one disk is replicated on the second disk. Cannot be extended. Known as RAID Level 1.	Yes, with maximum capacity of the smallest disk
RAID-5	3–32	Data is interleaved equally across all disks, with a parity stripe of data also interleaved across the disks. Also known as striping with parity.	Yes, with maximum capacity of the number of disks minus one (if you have five 200 GB disks, your volume would be 800 GB)

Creating a simple volume on a dynamic disk proceeds exactly as already described for creating a partition on a basic disk. As with basic disks, you can also extend, shrink, or delete a volume. We look at the methods of creating and working with striped, mirrored, and RAID-5 volumes later in this chapter.

Dynamic volumes allow you to change their properties on an as-needed basis. If you have a computer that is, for example, running short of space, you can install an extra hard drive and extend an existing simple or spanned volume so that the new space is immediately available without directing the user to use drive J for this data, drive C for that data, drive Y for the network, and so on. Users find multiple drive letters confusing, so being able to keep it all under one letter is highly preferable. Unfortunately, you cannot extend a system volume or a boot volume. Because most computers are installed with a single volume, `C:`, which includes boot and system files, any volumes created on a new disk added to the computer must have a separate drive letter from the `C:` drive.

To increase the size of a simple volume, in Disk Management, right-click the existing volume and select **Extend Volume** from the shortcut menu. The Extend Volume Wizard starts and you are prompted to select the disk or disks that contain the free space you will be adding. After you specify the size of free space to add, you need to confirm your options and click **Finish**. The volume is extended and appears in the Disk Management window with new space allocated to it.

The Disk Management utility is fairly comprehensive, but it is not the only tool available in Windows 7 to configure or manage disks. Some of these tools hearken back to the days of DOS and Windows 3.x, yet they are still very useful, especially if there is a problem accessing the graphical user interface (GUI):

- **Chkdsk.exe**: A command-line utility that verifies and repairs FAT- or NTFS-formatted volumes. (For NTFS drives, use the CHKDSK C: /R command to automatically check and repair disk problems.)

- **Cleanmgr.exe**: Also known as Disk Cleanup, a GUI utility that deletes unused files.

- **Defrag.exe**: Also known as Disk Defragmenter, a command-line utility that rearranges files contiguously, recapturing and reorganizing free space in the volume. Optimizes performance.

- **DiskPart.exe**: A command-line utility that can run a script to perform disk-related functions. DiskPart's nearest GUI counterpart is the Disk Management utility.

- **Fsutil.exe**: A command-line utility that displays information about the file system and can perform disk-related functions.

Troubleshooting Disk Problems

An administrator should understand how to handle the errors that can plague a hard disk. Common problems are listed in Table 15-3. We look at the Windows 7 Startup Repair Tool in Chapter 18, "Configuring System and File Recovery."

Table 15-3   Troubleshooting Disk Errors

Error	Problem or Process	Possible Repairs
Non-System Disk or Disk Error	Basic Input Output System (BIOS) generates this error when the master boot record (MBR) or boot sector is damaged, or when a different device is configured as the boot device in the BIOS.	Check the BIOS and reconfigure, if necessary. Remove any nonsystem disks from the floppy or CD-ROM drives. Repair the boot volume with Windows 7 Startup Repair Tool. Reinstall Windows 7. Replace the hard disk.
There is not enough memory or disk space to complete the operation	Disk is full.	Free up space on the hard disk by deleting files, removing applications, or compressing files. Add another disk and extend the volume to span both disks.

Table 15-3   Troubleshooting Disk Errors

Error	Problem or Process	Possible Repairs
Missing Operating System	No active partition is defined.	Check the BIOS settings and configure if they incorrectly identify the boot disk.
		Boot up with a floppy. Use `Diskpart.exe` to mark the boot volume as active.
		Use Windows 7 Startup Repair Tool. Reinstall Windows 7.
Invalid Media Type	Boot sector is damaged.	Repair the boot volume with Windows Startup Repair Tool.
		Reinstall Windows 7.
		Replace the hard disk.
Hard disk controller failure	BIOS's disk controller configuration is invalid, or the hard disk controller has failed.	Check the BIOS and reconfigure controller.
		Replace the hard disk controller.

The volume properties of a disk as displayed in the graphical display in the Disk Management snap-in (refer back to Figure 15-1) provide you with a status display, which can help you in troubleshooting disk problems. The following volume statuses can appear:

- **Healthy:** This status is normal and means that the volume is accessible and operating properly.

- **Active:** This status is also normal. An *active partition* is a partition or volume on a hard disk that has been identified as the primary partition from which the operating system is booted.

- **Failed:** This status means that the operating system could not start the volume normally. Failed usually means that the data is lost because the disk is damaged or the file system is corrupted. To repair a failed volume, physically inspect the computer to see whether the physical disk is operating. Ensure that the underlying disk(s) has an Online status in Disk Management.

- **Formatting:** This status is temporary, appearing only while the volume is being formatted.

- **Unknown:** This status means that you've installed a new disk and have not created a disk signature or that the boot sector for the volume is corrupt, possibly because of a virus. You can attempt to repair this error by initializing the underlying disk by right-clicking the disk and selecting **Initialize** from the shortcut menu.

■ **Data Incomplete:** This status appears when a disk has been moved into or out of a multidisk volume. Data is destroyed unless all the disks are moved and imported on the new computer.

■ **Healthy (At Risk):** This status indicates I/O errors have been detected on an underlying disk of the volume, but that data can still be accessed. The underlying disk probably shows a status of Online (Errors) and must be brought back online for the volume to be corrected.

When you see a status other than Healthy for your volumes, or other than Online for your disks, you can attempt to repair by selecting the **Rescan Disks** option from the Action menu in Disk Management.

Managing File System Fragmentation

All disks, regardless of the file system in use (FAT16, FAT32, or NTFS), divide disk space into *clusters*, which are groups of disk sectors that are the smallest units of space available for holding files. The size of clusters depends on the file system in use and the size of the partition; for example, for NTFS-formatted volumes of more than 2 GB in size, the default cluster size is 4 KB.

A file is stored in the first available clusters on a volume or partition, and not necessarily in contiguous space. Thus if empty space has been left on the volume as a result of moving, editing, or deleting files, these small noncontiguous clusters will be used. Access to files fragmented in this way takes a longer time because extra read operations are required to locate and access all the pieces of the file. You can defragment your disks with either the Disk Defragmenter GUI tool or the command-line defrag.exe tool.

Disk Defragmenter

Windows 7 provides a tool called the Disk Defragmenter to locate and consolidate these fragmented files into contiguous blocks of space. Consequently, access time is improved. You can access the Disk Defragmenter by clicking **Defragment now** from the Tools tab of any partition's Properties dialog box or by clicking **Start > All Programs > Accessories > System Tools > Disk Defragmenter**. You can also access this tool by typing **defrag** into the Start Menu Search field and clicking **Disk Defragmenter** in the Programs list.

Any of these methods opens the newly redesigned Disk Defragmenter tool, as shown in Figure 15-10. This tool enables you to configure scheduled defragmentation or to analyze and defragment any disk volume immediately.

Figure 15-10   The Disk Defragmenter tool enables you to perform on-demand and scheduled defragmentation.

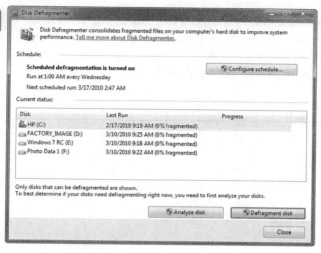

You can perform the following actions from the Disk Defragmenter:

- **Schedule Defragmentation:** Click **Configure schedule** to set up a schedule. By default, Windows 7 schedules defragmentation to take place on all disks every Wednesday at 1:00 AM, as shown in Figure 15-11. You can modify this schedule if desired by selecting options from the drop-down lists shown, or select disks to be defragmented by clicking the **Select disks** command button.

Figure 15-11   The Disk Defragmenter: Modify Schedule dialog box enables you to specify the schedule for defragmentation.

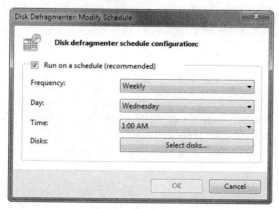

- **Analyze disk:** Select a disk and click **Analyze disk** to have the Disk Defragmenter check the current level of fragmentation. Although the dialog box says you need to first analyze your disks, they are first analyzed when you click **Defragment disk**.

■ **Perform an on-demand defragmentation:** Select a disk and click **Defragment disk**. Disk Defragmenter first analyzes the disk and then performs a multipass defragmentation, displaying its progress as shown in Figure 15-12. If you need to stop a defragmentation in progress, click **Stop operation**.

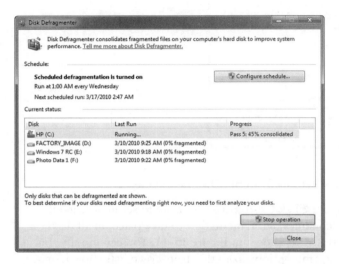

Figure 15-12   Disk Defragmenter displays the progress of disk defragmentation.

NOTE   It is recommended that you have at least 15% of free space on a disk volume before running the Disk Defragmenter. Otherwise, the defragmentation process will take much longer and might be incomplete. Use the Disk Cleanup tool first, if necessary, to optimize the amount of available free space.

TIP   Disks can become quite fragmented after you've uninstalled applications or deleted large files. Further, when installing large applications, the installation runs much better when plenty of contiguous space is available and the application will also run better later. It is a good idea to analyze your disk after deleting large files or before installing applications and then run the defragmentation if necessary.

The **Defrag.exe** Command-Line Tool

You can use Defrag.exe to defragment a volume from the command line. As with other command-line utilities, you can include it as part of a script to be executed when the disk is not in use. To do so, click **Start > All Programs > Accessories**, right-click **Command Prompt**, and choose **Run as administrator**. Click **Yes** to accept the UAC prompt and then type the following command:

```
Defrag <volume> ¦ /C ¦ /E <volume> [/A ¦ /X ¦ /T] [/H] [/M] [/U] [/V]
```

Table 15-4 describes the parameters of the Defrag command:

For example, the command defrag C: /X /V would defragment the C: volume, perform free space consolidation, and provide verbose output.

Table 15-4   Parameters Available with the **Defrag** Command

Parameter	Meaning
volume	The drive letter of the volume to be defragmented. You can specify more than one drive letter if needed.
/B	Optimizes boot files and applications but does not defragment the rest of the volume.
/C	Defragment all local volumes.
/E	Defragment all local volumes except those specified.
/A	Analyze the volume and display a report, but do not defragment.
/X	Perform free space consolidation.
/T	Track a defragmentation already in progress.
/H	Run the defragmentation at normal priority (by default, runs at low priority).
/M	Defragment multiple volumes simultaneously in parallel.
/U	Print the defragmentation process on the screen.
/V	Use verbose mode, which provides additional detailed information.

Error Checking

Occasionally, a volume might not appear in the Disk Defragmenter dialog box. This might happen because the disk contains errors such as bad sectors. You can check a disk for errors and repair problems by accessing the Tools tab of the disk's Properties dialog box and clicking **Check now**. You receive the Checking Disk dialog box shown in Figure 15-13. To proceed, select **Automatically fix file system errors**. If desired, also select the **Scan for and attempt recovery of bad sectors** option. Then click **Start**. If the disk is in use, Windows will ask you whether you want to dismount the disk, which will invalidate any opened references to the disk. Click **Force a dismount** to do so or **Cancel** to perform the disk check later. You can then schedule the disk check to take place on the next reboot. Note that this might slow down the startup significantly, especially if you've selected the **Scan for and attempt recovery of bad sectors** option.

Figure 15-13   Checking a disk for errors.

RAID Volumes

The acronym RAID refers to *Redundant Array of Independent (or Inexpensive) Disks*—it is a series of separate disks configured to work together as a single drive with a single drive letter. You have already seen three of the most common types of RAID arrays in Table 15-2: RAID-0 (disk striping), RAID-1 (mirroring), and RAID-5 (disk striping with parity). Other versions of RAID also exist but are generally unused; you are unlikely to see these referenced on the 70-680 exam.

When you use fault-tolerant volumes, a disk can fail and the operating system will continue to function. The failure can be repaired with no loss of data. Most Windows 7 computers do not have fault-tolerant volumes. An administrator should understand how to handle the errors that can plague a hard disk. Refer to Table 15-3 for common problems that can also plague fault-tolerant volumes.

> **CAUTION**   Don't confuse the RAID-5 or mirrored volumes that you can create within the Windows 7 operating system with RAID-5 or mirrored drives that are configured in a hardware storage array. A disk array produces a highly performing, fault-tolerant volume that appears in Windows 7 Disk Management as a simple volume. When you create mirrored or RAID-5 volumes in Windows 7, you achieve fault tolerance but lose some performance to disk management processes, especially if a disk fails.

Creating a RAID-0 Volume

A RAID-0 (striped) volume contains space on 2–32 separate hard disks. Data is written in 64-KB blocks (*stripes*) to each disk in the volume, in turn. A striped volume offers considerable improvement in read/write efficiency because the read/write heads on each disk are working together during each I/O operation. A striped volume offers a maximum amount of space equal to the size of the smallest disk multiplied by the number of disks in the volume. However, the striped volume does not offer fault tolerance; if any one disk is lost, the entire volume is lost. Note that the system or boot volume cannot be housed on a striped volume.

You can create a striped volume by using 2 to 32 separate hard disks in Disk Management. Use the following procedure:

Step 1.   In Disk Management, right-click any one disk to be made part of the striped volume and choose **New Striped Volume**.

Step 2.   The New Striped Volume Wizard starts and displays the Select Disks page shown in Figure 15-14. The disk you initially selected appears under Selected. Select the disks you want to use from the Available column and then click **Add**.

Figure 15-14   You need to select at least two disks to create a striped volume.

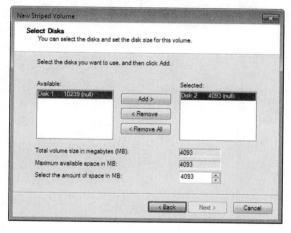

Step 3.   Disks you add appear in the Selected column. If you want to change the amount of space to be allocated, modify the value under **Select the amount of space in MB**. When done, click **Next**.

Step 4.   From the Assign Drive Letter or Path page shown in Figure 15-15, accept the default, choose another drive letter, or select the option to mount the volume in an empty NTFS folder if desired. Then click **Next**.

Step 5.   Choose the desired options in the Format Volume page shown in Figure 15-16 and then click **Next**.

Step 6.   Review the information on the completion page and then click **Finish**.

Step 7.   If any of the disks to be used in the volume are configured as basic disks, you receive the same message previously shown in Figure 15-9, warning you that you will be unable to boot other operating systems. To create your volume, you must click **Yes** and convert these disks to dynamic storage, as discussed earlier in this chapter.

Figure 15-15   Assigning a drive letter or mount path for a striped volume.

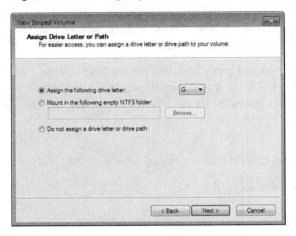

Figure 15-16   You have several options for formatting your volume.

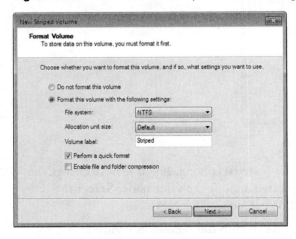

Step 8.   The volume is created and formatted and appears in the Disk Management snap-in display.

CAUTION   Remember that RAID-0 is *not* fault tolerant. As mentioned in Table 15-2, RAID-0 writes data in 64-KB blocks to each disk in the array sequentially, thereby improving read/write performance. However, if you lose any one of the disks in the array, all data is lost and you must restore the data from backup after replacing the lost disk and re-creating the array.

Creating a Spanned Volume

You can extend storage space on an existing volume to a new disk by creating a spanned volume. This is essentially a volume that spans two or more disks and enables you to add space without the need to specify a new drive letter. Note that the spanned volume is even less fault tolerant than a simple volume; if any one disk fails, all data is lost from all disks and must be restored from backup.

To create a spanned volume, right-click the desired volume and choose **Extend Volume**. From the Extend Volume Wizard, select the available disk(s) and complete the steps in this wizard, as previously described and shown in Figure 15-4.

Creating a Mirrored Volume

A mirrored volume contains two disks, each of which is an identical copy of the other, thereby providing fault tolerance at the expense of requiring twice the amount of disk space. You can use a mirrored volume to provide fault tolerance for the system and boot volumes, as well as any data volumes.

Creating a mirrored volume is similar to that of creating a striped volume. Use the following procedure:

Step 1.   In Disk Management, right-click any one disk to be made part of the striped volume and choose **New Mirrored Volume**.

Step 2.   Steps displayed by the New Mirrored Volume Wizard are similar to those of the New Striped Volume Wizard outlined in the previous procedure. When you have completed the procedure, the mirrored volume appears in the Disk Management display.

Creating a RAID-5 Volume

A RAID-5 volume is similar to a striped volume in that data is written in 64-KB stripes across all disks in the volume. However, this volume adds a parity stripe to one of the disks in the array, thereby providing fault tolerance. The parity stripe rotates from one disk to the next as each set of stripes is written. The RAID-5 volume offers improved read performance because data is read from each disk at the same time; however, write performance is lower because processor time is required to calculate the parity stripes. You cannot house the system or boot volumes on a RAID-5 volume.

Creating a RAID-5 volume is also similar; remember that you must have at least three disks to create this type of volume. Select **New RAID-5 Volume** from the right-click options and follow the steps presented by the New RAID-5 Volume Wizard.

NOTE   For more information on how RAID-5 volumes function, refer to "RAID-5 Volumes" at http://technet.microsoft.com/en-us/library/cc938485.aspx.

Using DiskPart to Create Striped, Mirrored, and RAID-5 Volumes

You can use the DiskPart command-line utility to create striped, mirrored, and RAID-5 volumes. To perform any of these tasks, first execute the following commands from an administrative command prompt:

```
Diskpart
List disk
Select disk=n
Convert dynamic
```

The List disk command returns the disk numbers on your computer that you use when entering the commands to create the desired volume. The Select disk command selects a disk you want to work with, and the Convert dynamic command converts the disk to a dynamic disk; repeat these two commands for each disk that needs to be converted to dynamic storage before beginning to create your volumes.

To create a mirror, you actually add a mirror to an existing simple volume. Use the Select volume command to select the volume to be mirrored, and then use the following command:

```
Add disk=n [noerr]
```

In this command, n is the disk number of the disk to be added to the current simple volume and noerr enables a script containing this command to continue processing even if an error has occurred. To obtain disk numbers used in this command, use the List disk command.

Use the following command to create a striped volume:

```
Create volume stripe [size=size] disk=n[,n[,...]] [noerr]
```

In this command, size is the number of MB used in each disk for the striped volume and n is the disk number (repeat from 2 to 32 times for each disk in the striped volume). If you do not specify a size, the size is assumed to be that of the smallest disk in the array. For example, if you specify three disks with unallocated space of 300, 400, and 500 GB and do not specify a size, DiskPart uses 300 GB per disk for a total striped volume size of 900 GB.

Creating a RAID-5 volume is similar to that of creating a striped volume. Use the following command:

```
Create volume raid [size=size] disk=n[,n[,...]] [noerr]
```

The parameters have the same meaning; in this case, repeat the disk number from 3 to 32 times. For the same example with three disks with unallocated space of 300, 400, and 500 GB and which do not specify the size parameter, DiskPart uses 300 GB per disk for a total RAID-5 volume size of 600 GB.

Managing and Troubleshooting RAID Volumes

Several things can go wrong with RAID volumes. Spanned and striped volumes are particularly vulnerable; as has already been mentioned, failure of any one disk in the volume renders the entire volume useless and data must be restored from backup. If one disk in a mirrored volume fails, you can break the mirror and use the data on the other disk as a simple volume. If one disk in a RAID-5 volume fails, the system reconstructs the missing data from the parity information and the volume is still usable, but without fault tolerance and with reduced performance until the failed disk is replaced. If more than one disk in a RAID-5 volume fails, the volume has failed and must be restored from backup after the disks have been replaced.

Besides the volume statuses already described for partitions on basic disks and simple volumes, Disk Management can display the following messages with RAID volumes:

- **Resynching:** Indicates that a mirrored volume is being reinitialized. This status is temporary and should change to Healthy within a few seconds.

- **Data Not Redundant** or **Failed Redundancy**: For a mirrored or RAID-5 volume, this status usually means that half of a mirrored volume was imported, or that half is unavailable, or that only part of the underlying disks of a RAID-5 volume were imported. You should import the missing disk(s) to re-create the volume. You can also break the mirror and retain the half that is functioning as a simple volume. If you have all but one of the underlying disks of a RAID-5 volume, you can re-create the RAID-5 volume by adding unallocated space of a different disk.

- **Stale Data:** This status is shown when you import a disk that contains a mirrored volume half, or a portion of a RAID-5 volume, with a status other than Healthy before it was moved. You can return the disk to the original PC and rescan the disk to fix the error.

Configuring Removable Drive Policies

Windows includes Group Policy settings that apply to removable drives. These are important because removable drives pose a significant security risk to companies. Users can copy confidential data to USB drives, CD-ROMs, DVD-ROMs, or cell phones and take it to a competing company. Users can also bring in undesirable software including viruses, spyware, and other types of malicious applications.

Group Policy contains a series of settings that you can use to limit what users can do with removable drives. You can configure these policies using the Local Group Policy Editor on a standalone computer, or you can use the Group Policy

Management Editor in an AD DS environment to apply policies to all computers in a site, domain, or organizational unit (OU).

Navigate to the **Computer Configuration\Administrative Templates\ System\Removable Storage Access** node to obtain the policy settings shown in Figure 15-17. By enabling specific policies, you can deny read, write, and execute access to the specified type of device; the WPD devices class refers to devices such as media players, cell phones, iPods, auxiliary displays, Windows CE devices, and so on (WPD stands for *Windows Portable Device*). Enabling the All Removable Storage classes: Deny all access policy denies read and write access to all types of removable storage devices, whereas enabling the All Removable Storage: Allow direct access in remote sessions policy enables access to these devices when connected by a remote access session only. Enabling these policies overrides settings that you can configure for individual drive types. The Custom Classes policy enables you to deny access to custom removable storage classes according to their class GUID. The Time (in seconds) to force reboot enables you to specify a time interval after which a computer will reboot to enforce a change that you've made to one of the other policies; if you have not configured this setting, the change will not take place until a user reboots her computer.

Figure 15-17 Windows provides policy settings that enable you to deny certain types of access to specific removable drive types.

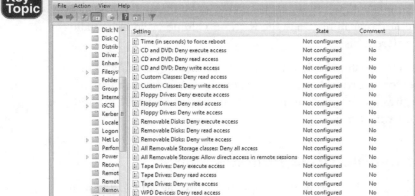

Exam Preparation Tasks

Review All the Key Topics

Review the most important topics in the chapter, noted with the key topics icon in the outer margin of the page. Table 15-5 lists a reference of these key topics and the page numbers on which each is found.

Table 15-5 Key Topics for Chapter 15

Key Topic Element	Description	Page Number
Figure 15-1	Shows the Computer Management snap-in and the tasks it can perform	565
List	Shows you how to create a basic disk partition	568
Figure 15-6	A volume's Properties dialog box can let you perform a large range of management tasks	571
Table 15-2	Describes the available dynamic volume types in Windows 7	575
Table 15-3	Describes common disk errors	576
Figure 15-10	Using the Disk Defragmenter	579
Table 15-4	Describes parameters available with the `defrag.exe` command line tool	581
List	Shows how to create a striped volume	583
Figure 15-17	Shows available removable drive policies	588

Complete the Tables and Lists from Memory

Print a copy of Appendix C, "Memory Tables" (found on the CD), or at least the section for this chapter, and complete the tables and lists from memory. Appendix D, "Memory Tables Answer Key," also on the CD, includes completed tables and lists to check your work.

Definitions of Key Terms

Define the following key terms from this chapter, and check your answers in the glossary.

Computer Management console, Disk Management snap-in, DiskPart, active partition, basic disk, dynamic disk, extended partition, logical drive, mirroring, partition, primary partition, striping, RAID-5, volume

This chapter covers the following subjects:

- **Windows System Monitoring Tools:** This section introduces you to the monitoring tools provided in Windows 7 and describes the options available from the Performance Information and Tools applet.

- **Configuring and Working with Event Logs:** This section shows you how to work with Event Viewer and configure event log subscriptions that enable you to collect events from multiple computers in one place.

- **Managing Computer Performance:** This section describes the capabilities of Performance Monitor. It introduces the concept of performance objects and counters and describes the more important objects and counters that you should be familiar with. It then shows you how to log information using data collector sets that can be stored for later analysis and display.

- **Configuring Additional Performance Settings:** This section introduces several other tools that you can use to configure settings that affect your computer's performance.

CHAPTER 16

Managing and Monitoring System Performance

When you first set up a brand-new Windows 7 computer with a baseline set of applications, you will generally find that it performs very capably. As you install additional applications, store data, and work with the computer, its performance can slow down. Factors that affect a computer's performance include memory, processor, disks, and applications. Windows 7 provides tools such as Event Viewer, Performance Console, Reliability Monitor, Action Center, and Task Manager to monitor and troubleshoot computer performance. This chapter looks at using these tools to troubleshoot system errors, monitor system performance, and optimize your computer to keeping it working at a level close to that observed when you first set it up.

"Do I Know This Already?" Quiz

The "Do I Know This Already?" quiz enables you to assess whether you should read this entire chapter or simply jump to the "Exam Preparation Tasks" section for review. If you are in doubt, read the entire chapter. Table 16-1 outlines the major headings in this chapter and the corresponding "Do I Know This Already?" quiz questions. You can find the answers in Appendix A, "Answers to the 'Do I Know This Already?' Quizzes."

Table 16-1 "Do I Know This Already?" Foundation Topics Section-to-Question Mapping

Foundations Topics Section	Questions Covered in This Section
Windows System Monitoring Tools	1
Configuring and Working With Event Logs	2–5
Managing Computer Performance	6–9
Configuring Additional Performance Settings	10–13

1. You access the Performance Information and Tools applet from the Control Panel and then click Advanced Tools. Which of the following tools can you access from this location? (Choose all that apply.)

   a. Performance Monitor

   b. Reliability Monitor

   c. Resource Monitor

   d. Task Manager

   e. System Information

   f. Disk Defragmenter

2. You open Event Viewer and want to access logs that store events from single components such as Distributed File Service (DFS) replication, hardware events, and Internet Explorer events. In which Event Viewer log should you look for this information?

   a. Application

   b. Security

   c. System

   d. Applications and Services Logs

3. You want to reduce the number of events viewed in the System log of Event Viewer because you've found that you waste a lot of time going through thousands of minor events when trying to locate important events that can pinpoint problems. What should you do?

   a. Filter the log to display only Critical, Warning, and Error events.

   b. Filter the log to display Error, Warning, and Information events.

   c. Configure the log to overwrite events after 48 hours.

   d. Create an event log subscription.

4. You are responsible for eight computers, located in a small medical office, that are configured as a workgroup. You want to collect event logs from all these computers onto a single computer so that you can spot problems more rapidly. What should you configure on this computer?

   a. A source-initiated event subscription

   b. A collector-initiated event subscription

   c. A filter that views logs by event source

   d. A filter that views logs by user and computer

5. Which of the following commands do you have to run on all computers involved in an event log subscription before setting up the subscription? (Choose two.)

   a. Winrm

   b. Wdsutil

   c. Wecutil

   d. Logman

6. You want to view a time trend of your computer's stability since you installed Windows 7, which is now almost a year ago. Which tool should you use?

   a. Reliability Monitor

   b. Resource Monitor

   c. Performance Monitor

   d. Task Manager

   e. Event Viewer

7. You are working at your computer and a program you're using has hung and you cannot exit the program. Which utility can you use to terminate the program? (Choose two; each is a complete solution.)

   a. Reliability Monitor

   b. Resource Monitor

   c. Performance Monitor

   d. Task Manager

   e. Event Viewer

8. You want to receive a message when your computer's processor time exceeds 85 percent. What feature of Performance Monitor should you configure?

   a. Event Trace Data Collector Set

   b. Event log

   c. Performance Counter Alert Data Collector Set

   d. System Diagnostics Data Collector Set

9. You think your computer might need more RAM, and you're wondering how much memory is committed to either physical RAM or running processes. What counter should you check in Performance Monitor?

   a. Memory\Pages/sec

   b. Memory\Available Bytes

   c. Memory\Committed Bytes

   d. Processor\% Processor Time

   e. System\Processor Queue Length

10. Your Windows 7 computer has been starting slowly as of late, and you'd like to see what items are causing this to happen, so you open the System Configuration Utility. You would like to selectively disable items that might be causing this behavior. What should you do?

    a. Access the General tab and select the **Diagnostic startup** option.

    b. Access the General tab and select the **Selective startup** option, and then clear the check boxes against items you do not want to start when your computer starts.

    c. Access the Boot tab and then clear the check boxes against items you do not want to start when your computer starts.

    d. Access the Startup tab and clear the check boxes against items you do not want to start when your computer starts.

11. Your computer is running a 64-bit version of Windows 7 Home Premium. You have an old 16-bit MS-DOS game that you'd like to use again after many years of nonuse. What do you need to do to enable this program to run?

    a. From the Compatibility tab of the program shortcut's Properties dialog box, select **Run this program in compatibility mode** and then select **Windows 95** from the drop-down list.

    b. From the Processes tab of Task Manager, right-click the process and choose **Set Affinity**. Then select one processor to run the program.

    c. From the Run dialog box, type `start /separate game.exe`, where `game.exe` is the game's executable file.

    d. You cannot run this game on a 64-bit computer; you must search the Internet for a newer version of the game running in either 32- or 64-bit space.

12. Which of the following items can you perform by accessing the Action Center in Windows 7? (Choose three.)

a. Check for possible security-related alerts

b. Check for solutions to possible maintenance problems

c. View alerts generated by data collector sets

d. Configure backup

e. Close unresponsive applications

13. You are considering disabling some services on your Windows 7 computer but want to ensure that you do not disable important services that other services depend on for their functionality. Where should you check for the required information?

a. The Dependencies tab of the service's Properties dialog box, accessed from the Services snap-in

b. The General tab of the service's Properties dialog box, accessed from the Services snap-in

c. The General tab of the System Configuration tool

d. The Services subnode of the Software Environment node in the System Information tool

Foundation Topics

Windows System Monitoring Tools

Windows 7 contains a large suite of system and performance monitoring tools that enable you to monitor system performance and diagnose problems that might be occurring, even very subtly, within your computer. Many of these tools can be found in the Computer Management console, which we introduced in Chapter 15, "Disk Management." Another location from which you can open many of these tools is the Performance Information and Tools Control Panel applet. To access this applet, open Control Panel and switch it to either the Large Icons or Small Icons view. You can also type **performance** in the Start Menu Search field. In either case, select **Performance Information and Tools** to obtain the window shown in Figure 16-1.

Figure 16-1   The Performance Information and Tools applet provides access to most of the available performance monitoring tools.

Prominent on this page is the Windows Experience Index, first introduced with Windows Vista. This is a performance scoring metric that assesses the capability of several hardware and software components on your computer. It includes such components as the processor, memory, graphics card, and hard disk and displays a base score that relates to the weakest performing component on your computer. Thus it suggests which component you should upgrade to improve your computer's overall performance.

The links on the left side of this page take you to additional monitoring and configuration tools that you can use to optimize your computer's performance according to installed hardware and uses to which you put your computer:

- **Adjust visual effects:** Shown in Figure 16-2, you can select from a large range of settings that affect the appearance of your computer's desktop. By default, Windows optimizes the effects as a balance between appearance and performance; you can choose to adjust for the best appearance, best performance, or select **Custom** to choose from among 20 different settings in the check boxes provided. The Advanced tab enables you to adjust processor scheduling to optimize processor use for programs or background services, and to change the location of the Windows paging file. The Data Execution Prevention tab enables you to choose between turning on Data Execution Prevention (DEP) for essential Windows programs and services only, or for all programs and services except those you can add to a list on this tab. DEP helps protect your computer against damages from viruses and other malware.

Figure 16-2   The Performance Options dialog box enables you to configure visual effects, processor scheduling, and DEP.

- **Adjust indexing options:** Enables you to modify which folders on your computer are indexed for quicker searching from the Start Menu Search field or the Windows Search folders.

- **Adjust power settings:** Opens the Power Options applet, which enables you to select a power plan and modify its settings. We discussed this applet and its controls in Chapter 13, "Configuring Mobile Computing."

- **Open disk cleanup:** Starts the Disk Cleanup tool, as discussed in Chapter 15.

- **Advanced tools:** Shown in Figure 16-3, the Advanced Tools applet enables you to run the system monitoring and optimization tools summarized in Table 16-2. Details of many of these tools are discussed in this chapter; some of them are discussed in other chapters of this book.

Figure 16-3   The Advanced Tools dialog box enables you to run a large number of performance monitoring and optimization tools.

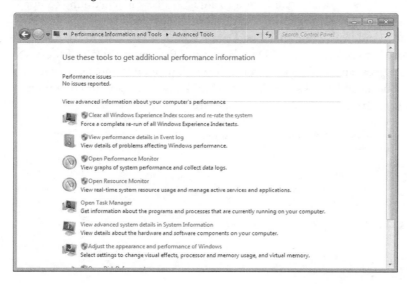

 Table 16-2   Tools Available from the Advanced Tools Window

Tool	Purpose
Clear all Windows Experience Index scores and rerate the system	Reevaluates the Windows Experience Index shown on the Performance Information and Tools applet.
View performance details in Event log	Opens the Event Viewer in its own console.
Open Performance Monitor	Opens the Performance Monitor in its own console, which provides a comprehensive set of performance counters for generating advanced system monitoring statistics.
Open Resource Monitor	Opens the Resource Monitor in its own console, which provides a quick view of processor, memory, disk, and network performance statistics.

Table 16-2 Tools Available from the Advanced Tools Window

Tool	Purpose
Open Task Manager	Opens the Task Manager to the Processes tab, which provides details on the processes currently running on the computer and enables you to end misbehaving processes.
View advanced system details in System Information	Opens the System Information dialog box, which provides summary information on hardware resources, system components, and the software environment.
Adjust the appearance and performance of Windows	Opens the same Performance Options dialog box already mentioned and shown in Figure 16-2.
Open Disk Defragmenter	Runs the Disk Defragmenter, as discussed in Chapter 15.
Generate a system health report	Creates a 60-second system diagnostics report that includes details on local hardware resources, system response times, and processes, as well as system information and configuration data. See Figure 16-4.

Figure 16-4 System Diagnostics provides a series of system health reports.

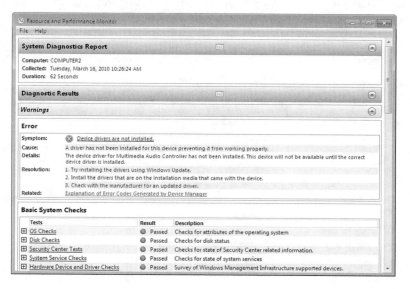

Configuring and Working with Event Logs

One of Windows 7's standard troubleshooting tools is Event Viewer, which is incorporated into the Computer Management console, as well as being available from the Advanced Tools window. You can rely on this utility to be able to see errors and system messages. This tool enables you to view events from multiple event logs on the local computer or another computer to which you can connect, save event filters as custom views for future usage, schedule tasks to run in response to events, and create and manage event log subscriptions.

You can open Event Viewer by using any of the following methods:

- Click **Start**, right-click **Computer**, and then select **Manage**. Select **Event Viewer** under System Tools in the Computer Management console.

- Click Start and type `msconfig` in the Start menu Search field. From the Tools tab of System Configuration, select **Event Viewer** and then click **Launch**.

- Click **Start > All Programs> Administrative Tools> Event Viewer**.

- Click **Start** and type `event` in the Start menu Search field. Select **Event Viewer** from the Programs list.

If you receive a User Account Control (UAC) prompt, click **Yes** or supply administrative credentials (this depends on the UAC settings discussed in Chapter 12, "Configuring Access Controls.") The Event Viewer snap-in opens and displays a summary of recent administrative events in the details pane, as shown in Figure 16-5.

Figure 16-5   Event Viewer records events that have occurred on your computer.

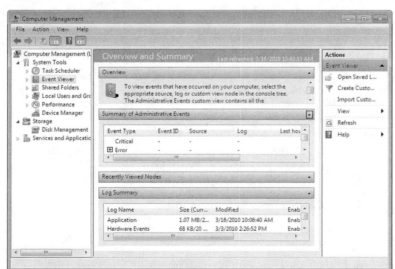

The following sections provide more detail with regard to several aspects of working with Event Viewer.

Viewing Logs in Event Viewer

To view the actual event logs, expand the Event Viewer node in the console tree and then expand the Windows Logs subnode. Windows 7 records events in the following types of logs:

- **Application:** Logs events related to applications running on the computer, including alerts generated by data collector sets.

- **Security:** Logs events related to security-related actions performed on the computer. To enable security event logging, you must configure auditing of the types of actions to be recorded.

- **Setup:** Logs events related to setup of applications.

- **System:** Contains events related to actions taking place on the computer in general, including hardware-related events. See Figure 16-6.

Figure 16-6 Most Event Viewer logs record errors, warning events, and informational events.

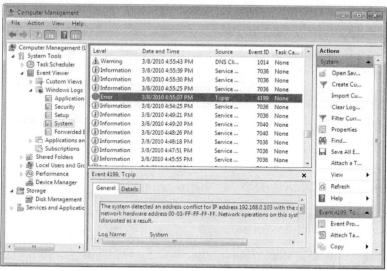

- **Forwarded events:** Contains events logged from remote computers. To enable this log, you must create an event subscription.

- **Applications and Services logs:** Contained in its own subnode, these logs store events from single applications or components, as opposed to events with potential systemwide impact. Logs might include categories such as Distributed

File Service (DFS) replication, hardware events, Internet Explorer events, Key Management service events, and Media Center events.

> **NOTE** If you are looking at Event Viewer on a server, you might observe additional event logs added by applications such as Active Directory and DNS. Installed applications on servers and even on Windows 7 might add additional event logs to Event Viewer.

Most logs in Event Viewer record the three types of events—errors, warnings, and informational events—as previously seen in Figure 16-6. Error messages are represented by a red circle with a white exclamation mark in the center. Information messages are represented by a balloon with a blue "i" in the center, and warning messages are represented by a yellow triangle with a black exclamation mark in the center. Although not always true, an error is often preceded by one or more warning messages. A series of warning and error messages can describe the exact source of the problem or at least point you in the right direction. To obtain additional information about an event, select it. The bottom of the central pane displays information related to the selected event. You can also right-click an event and select **Event Properties** to display information about the event in its own dialog box that can be viewed without scrolling.

Customizing Event Viewer

If you have selected a large number of auditable events, the Event Viewer logs can rapidly accumulate a large variety of events. Windows 7 provides capabilities for customizing what appears in the Event Viewer window. To customize the information displayed, right-click **Event Viewer** in the console tree and choose **Create Custom View**. This displays the Create Custom View dialog box shown in Figure 16-7.

Options available from this dialog box include the following:

- **Logged:** Select the time interval that you want to examine.

- **Event level:** Choose the type(s) of events you want to view. Select **Verbose** to view extra details related to the viewed events.

- **By log:** Select the Windows logs or Applications and Services logs you want to include.

- **By source:** Select from an extensive range of Windows services, utilities, and components whose logs you want to include.

- **Task category:** Expand the drop-down list and select the categories you want to view.

- **Keywords:** Select the keywords that you want to include in the customized view.

Figure 16-7 You can create custom views that filter event logs according to several categories.

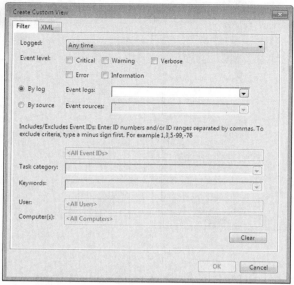

- **User and Computer(s):** Select the usernames of the accounts to be displayed and the names of the computers to be displayed. Separate the names in each list by commas.

- **XML tab:** Enables you to specify an event filter as an XML query.

When you have made your selections, click **OK** and type a name for the custom view in the **Save Filter to Custom View** dialog box that appears. After you have saved the custom view, you can see this view by expanding the Custom Views node in the console tree to locate it by the name you provided.

Creating Tasks from Events

Event Viewer in Windows 7 also enables you to associate tasks with events. Event Viewer integrates with Task Scheduler to make this action possible. To do so, right-click the desired event and choose **Attach Task To This Event**. Follow the instructions in the Create Basic Task Wizard that opens, as shown in Figure 16-8. Actions that you can take include starting a specified program, sending an email, and displaying a message.

NOTE For more information on Event Viewer, refer to "Event Viewer" and links contained therein at http://technet.microsoft.com/en-us/library/cc766042.aspx.

Figure 16-8 The Create Basic Task Wizard enables you to specify an action that will be taken each time a specific event takes place.

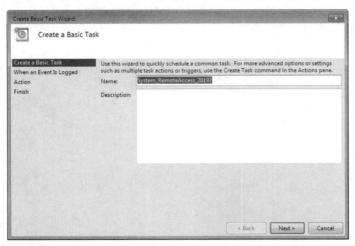

Using Event Log Subscriptions

Event Viewer includes a Subscriptions feature that enables you to collect event logs from a number of computers in a single, convenient location that helps you keep track of events that occur on these computers. You can specify the events that will be collected and the local log in which they will be stored. After activating the subscription, you can view these event logs in the same manner as already discussed for local event logs.

The Event Subscriptions feature works by using Hypertext Transfer Protocol (HTTP) or Secure HTTP (HTTPS) to relay specified events from one or more originating (source) computers to a destination (collector) computer. It uses the Windows Remote Management (WinRM) and Windows Event Collector (Wecsvc) services to perform these actions. To configure event log subscriptions, you must configure these services on both the source and collector computers.

You can configure Event Subscriptions to work in either of two ways:

- **Collector-initiated:** The collector computer pulls the specified events from each of the source computers. This type is typically used where there are a limited number of easily identified source computers.

- **Source-initiated:** Each source computer pushes the specified events to the collector computer. This type is typically used where there are a large number of source computers that are configured using Group Policy.

Configuring Computers to Forward and Collect Events

You need to run the `Winrm` and `Wecutil` commands at both the source and collector computers. To do so, log on to each source computer with an administrative user account (it is best to use a domain administrator account when configuring computers in an Active Directory Domain Services [AD DS] domain). Add the computer account of the collector computer to the local Administrators group on each source computer. In addition, type the following command at an administrative command prompt:

```
Winrm quickconfig
```

Also log on to the collector computer with an administrative account, open an administrative command prompt, and type the following command:

```
Wecutil qc
```

Having run these commands, the computers are now ready to forward and collect events. Note that in a workgroup environment, you can use only collector-initiated subscriptions. In addition, you need to perform the following additional steps:

- You must add a Windows Firewall exception for Remote Event Log Management at each source computer. We discussed configuring Windows Firewall in Chapter 10, "Configuring Network and Firewall Settings."

- You must add an account with administrative privileges to the Event Log Readers group at each source computer and specify this account in the Configure Advanced Subscription Settings dialog box mentioned in the next section.

- At a command prompt on the collector computer, type **winrm set winrm/ config/client @{TrustedHosts="<sources>"}.** In this command, <sources> is a list of the names of all workgroup source computers separated by commas.

> **NOTE**   For more information on the winrm and wecutil commands, refer to "Hardware Management Introduction" at http://technet.microsoft.com/en-us/ library/cc785056(WS.10).aspx.

Configuring Event Log Subscriptions

After you have completed the preceding procedures at all source and collector computers, you are ready to configure event log subscriptions at the collector computer by using the following procedure:

Step 1.   In the console tree of Event Viewer, right-click the type of log you want to configure a subscription for and choose **Properties**.

Step 2.   Select the **Subscriptions** tab of the Properties dialog box that appears.

Step 3.   Event Viewer displays the message box shown in Figure 16-9, asking you to start the Windows Event Collector Service. Click **Yes** to proceed.

Figure 16-9 You are asked to start the Windows Event Collector Service before you can create an event log subscription.

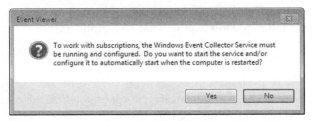

Step 4. Click **Create** to create your first event subscription. This displays the Subscription Properties dialog box shown in Figure 16-10.

Figure 16-10 The Subscription Properties dialog box enables you to configure an event log subscription.

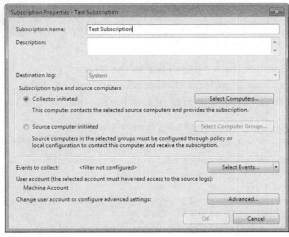

Step 5. Configure the following properties for your event log subscription and then click **OK** when finished.

— **Subscription name:** Provide an informative name that you will use to locate your event log subscription later. If desired, type an optional description in the field provided.

— **Destination log:** Displays the log type, according to the Windows log you right-clicked in step 1 of this procedure.

— **Subscription type and source computers:** Select **Collector initiated** and click the **Select Computers** button to specify the computers from which you want to collect event data. Or select **Source computer initiated** to specify groups of computers that have been configured through Group Policy to receive the subscription from the computer at which you are working. In either case you can also select computers from an AD DS domain.

— **Events to collect:** Click **Select Events** to display the Query Filter dialog box, which provides the same options as shown previously in Figure 16-7 and enables you to select the event types that will be included in the subscription.

— **Advanced:** Click **Advanced** to display the Advanced Subscription Settings dialog box shown in Figure 16-11, which enables you to select the user account that has access to the source logs and to optimize event delivery. To specify a user other than the one indicated, click **Specific User**, and then click the **User and Password** button and type the required user/password information. Choose **Normal** to provide reliable event delivery without conserving bandwidth. Select **Minimize Bandwidth** to control the use of bandwidth but reducing the frequency of event delivery. Select **Minimize Latency** to ensure the most rapid delivery of events.

Figure 16-11   Specifying user account and event delivery settings.

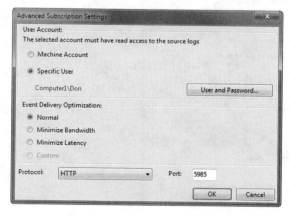

NOTE   If you select a different user account from the Advanced Subscription Settings dialog box, the account you select must be a member of the local computer's Event Log Readers group or the Administrators group.

NOTE   For more information on creating and managing event log subscriptions, refer to "Event Subscriptions" at http://technet.microsoft.com/en-us/library/cc749183.aspx and "Manage Subscriptions" at http://technet.microsoft.com/en-us/library/cc749140.aspx, plus the links contained therein.

Managing Computer Performance

Windows 7 includes several tools that are used for monitoring, optimizing, and troubleshooting performance. These include Reliability Monitor, Task Manager, Resource Monitor, and Performance Monitor.

Reliability Monitor

First introduced with Windows Vista, Reliability Monitor utilizes the built-in Reliability Analysis Component (RAC) to provide a trend analysis of your computer's system stability over time. As shown in Figure 16-12, Reliability Monitor provides the System Stability Chart, which correlates the trend of your computer's stability against events that might destabilize the computer. Events tracked include Windows updates; software installations and removals; device driver installations, updates, rollbacks, and removals, as well as driver failure to load or unload; application hangs and crashes; disk and memory failures; and Windows failures such as boot failures, crashes, and sleep failures. This chart enables you to track a reliability change directly to a given event.

Figure 16-12   Reliability Monitor provides a trend analysis of your computer's stability.

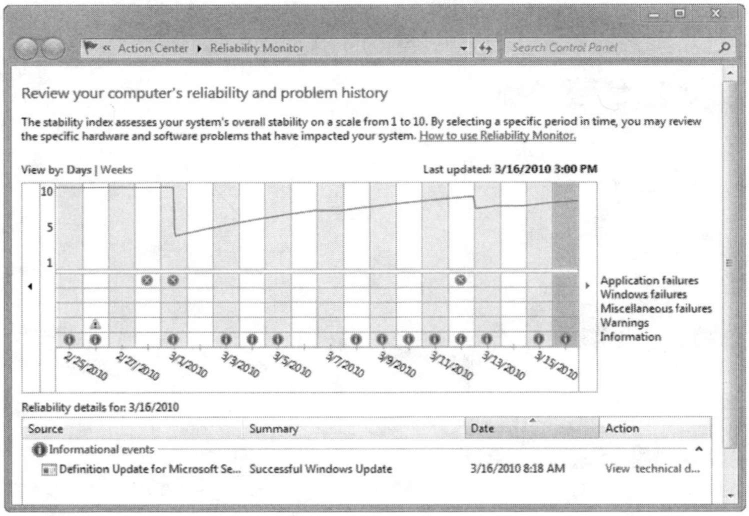

Windows 7 enhances Reliability Monitor by integrating it with Problem Reports and Solutions to improve the correlation of system changes, events, and possible problem resolutions.

NOTE   To display data in the System Stability Chart, you must run your computer for at least 24 hours after first installation of Windows 7. For the first 28 days, Reliability Monitor uses a dotted line on the Stability Chart graph, indicating that the data is insufficient to establish a valid baseline for this index.

Use the following steps to run Reliability Monitor:

Step 1. Ensure that you are logged on as an administrator or have administrator credentials available.

Step 2. Click **Start** and type `reliability` in the Start Search text box. Then click **View Reliability History** in the Programs list. If you receive a UAC prompt, click **Yes.**

Step 3. As shown previously in Figure 16-12, events that cause the performance index to drop are marked in one of the event rows. Click a date containing one of these marks and then expand the appropriate section to obtain more information for the following categories:

— **Application failures:** Software programs that hang or crash. Information provided includes the name of the program, its version number, the type of failure, and the date.

— **Windows failures:** Problems such as operating system crashes, boot failures, and sleep failures. Information provided includes the type of failure, the operating system and service pack version, the Stop code or detected problem, and the failure date.

— **Miscellaneous failures:** Other types of failures such as improper shutdowns. Information includes the failure type, details, and date.

— **Warnings:** Other problems such as unsuccessful application reconfiguration or update installation. Information includes the type of reconfiguration attempted.

— **Information:** Includes the successful installation of various updates and definition packs, as well as successful installation or uninstallation of software programs.

Step 4. To view a comprehensive list of problems, click the **View all problem reports** link at the bottom of the dialog box. The list displayed includes the various types of failures noted here.

Step 5. To export an XML-based reliability report, click **Save reliability history**, specify a path and filename, and then click **Save.**

Step 6. To check for solutions to problems, click **Check for solutions to all problems**. Reliability Monitor displays a Checking for solutions message box as it goes to the Internet and attempts to locate solutions to your problems. You might have to click **Send information** to send additional information to the Microsoft Error Reporting Service.

Task Manager

Task Manager provides data about currently running processes, including their CPU and memory usage, and enables you to modify their priority or shut down misbehaving applications.

You can use any of the following methods to start Task Manager:

- Click Start, type **taskmgr** in the Search box, and then select **taskmgr.exe** from the programs list.

- From the Advanced Tools applet previously shown in Figure 16-3, click **Open Task Manager**.

- Click Start and type **msconfig** in the Start menu Search field. From the Tools tab of System Configuration, select **Task Manager** and then click **Launch**.

- Press **Ctrl+Shift+Esc**.

- Press **Ctrl+Alt+Delete** and select **Start Task Manager** from the Windows Security dialog box.

- Right-click a blank area on the taskbar and then select **Start Task Manager**.

As shown in Figure 16-13, Task Manager has six tabs that perform the following tasks:

Figure 16-13 Task Manager enables you to troubleshoot applications currently running, including closing ones that are not responding.

- **Applications:** Displays all applications running on the computer. You can terminate an ill-behaved program by selecting it and clicking **End Task**.

- **Processes:** Provides information on resources consumed by processes running on the computer. The Description column provides a detailed description of each process running on your computer. You can modify the property of a running application or terminate an ill-behaved process or one that is consuming a large amount of processor time. To obtain additional information, select the **Select Columns** option from the View menu. This displays the Select Process Page Columns dialog box shown in Figure 16-14, from which you can choose to display a large number of variables associated with each process.

Figure 16-14   The Select Process Page Columns dialog box enables you to select the information that is displayed on the Process tab of Task Manager.

- **Services:** Provides information on services installed on the computer. You can view which services are running or stopped, the service group to which they belong, and descriptive information about each service. Click the **Services** command button to access the Services snap-in, which enables you to configure service startup type and properties. You can start a stopped service or stop a running service by right-clicking the service name and selecting **Start Service** or **Stop Service**. You can also determine whether a service is associated with a particular process by right-clicking the service name and selecting **Go to Process**. This opens the Processes tab and highlights the appropriate process.

- **Performance:** Provides a limited performance monitoring function, showing processor and physical memory usage statistics. This tab is ideal for providing a quick snapshot of computer performance. The memory graph now displays actual memory usage instead of the page file usage previously displayed in Windows XP. If your computer is equipped with multiple processors or a multicore processor, the CPU usage history graph is split to show the activity of all cores or processors. You can also access the Resource Monitor application described in the next section.

- **Networking:** Provides information on network utilization across the local area interface.

- **Users:** Displays the users that have sessions, active or disconnected, running on the local computer.

You can access additional options from the menu bar of Task Manager. In particular, you can start a new process from the File menu. Doing so is equivalent to using the Run dialog box and is useful if the Explorer process has terminated or is misbehaving. The Options menu enables you to keep the Task Manager window always visible on the desktop. The View menu enables you to adjust the refresh rate of the graphs on the Performance and Networking tabs. It also enables you to modify what data displays on the Processes, Networking, and Users tabs.

Configuring Application Priority

You can modify application behavior by adjusting its priority in Task Manager or by starting the application at a different priority. Windows 7 offers the following application priorities, arranged in decreasing order:

- **Realtime:** The highest priority level. Use extreme caution when selecting this priority because it can hang the computer.

- **High:** The highest useful priority level. Devotes a high level of priority to the application without disrupting essential services.

- **AboveNormal:** Runs the application at a priority slightly higher than default.

- **Normal:** The default priority. All processes run at this priority unless configured otherwise.

- **BelowNormal:** Runs the application at a priority slightly lower than default.

- **Low:** The lowest priority.

You can modify an application's priority in either of the following ways:

- **From Task Manager:** From the Processes tab, right-click the required process and choose **Set Priority**. Then select one of the priorities shown here. If you are unsure of the process associated with a given application, right-click the application in the Applications tab and select **Go To Process**. This switches you to the Processes tab, with the required process selected.

- **From a Command Prompt:** Type `Start /option executable_name`, where `option` refers to one of the priorities shown in the preceding list and `executable_name` refers to the program's name.

Resource Monitor

Resource Monitor provides a summary of CPU, disk, network, and memory performance statistics including mini-graphs of recent performance of these four components. In Windows Vista, Resource Monitor was combined with Performance Monitor in a single MMC snap-in; Windows 7 separates these two applications into their own interfaces. To run Resource Monitor, open Task Manager and click **Resource Monitor** from the Performance tab, or open the Advanced Tools dialog box previously shown in Figure 16-3 and click **Open Resource Monitor.** You can also open Resource Monitor by clicking **Start**, typing `resource` in the Start Menu Search Field, and then clicking **Resource Monitor** in the Programs list. Or by clicking Start, typing `msconfig` in the Start Menu Search Field, selecting **Resource Monitor** from the Tools tab of System Configuration, and then clicking **Launch.** Click the downward-pointing arrow to display additional information about a component similar to that shown for CPU in Figure 16-15.

Figure 16-15 You can expand each component in Resource Monitor to obtain a summary of its performance information.

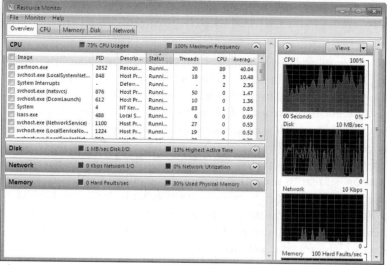

For each of the four components, the information provided on the Overview tab includes the application whose resource usage is being monitored (known as the *image*) and the process identifier number (PID) of the application instance. The following additional information is provided for each of the four components:

- **CPU:** A brief description of the monitored application, the number of threads per application, the CPU cycles currently used by each application instance, and the average CPU resulting from each instance as a percentage of total CPU usage.

- **Disk:** The file being read or written by each application instance, the current read and write speeds in bytes/minute, and the total disk input/output (I/O) in bytes/minute, the I/O priority level, and the response time in milliseconds.

- **Network:** The IP address of the network component with which the computer is exchanging data and the amount of data (bandwidth) in bytes per second (sent, received, and total) by each instance.

- **Memory:** Current hard faults per second and memory usage information in KB for committed, working set, sharable, and private memory components.

To filter the display of disk, network, and memory usage according to process, select the check box or boxes in the Image column of the CPU section, as previously shown in Figure 16-15. To change the size of the graphical displays on any tab, select **Large**, **Medium**, or **Small** from the Views drop-down list above the graphical displays.

By selecting the tab associated with each component, you can view additional details about the component selected.

CPU Tab

The CPU tab provides graphical displays of the total CPU percentage utilization, as well as values for each processor or core and the Service CPU Usage. If you want to display information for certain processors or cores only, you can do so by selecting **Monitor > Select Processors** and choosing the desired processor(s) from the dialog box that appears. Tabulated information includes CPU usage by all processes and services running on the machine. You can filter the display in the information tables of any tab by selecting the check boxes for the desired processes in the Processes section, similar to the action previously described for the Overview tab. When you are filtering the results on any tab, the graphical displays include an orange line that represents the proportion of each activity type represented by the selected processes; tabulated displays show an orange information bar that informs you which processes are included.

Memory Tab

The Memory tab provides graphical displays of the Used Physical Memory, Commit Charge, and Hard Faults/sec memory counters. Besides a tabular view of memory usage by processes running on the computer, this tab includes a bar graph representation that shows the relative amount of memory apportioned to Hardware Reserved, In Use, Modified, Standby, and Free. The amount of memory that's available to programs includes the total of standby and free memory. Free memory includes zero page memory.

Disk Tab

Graphs included on the Disk tab include total disk usage over a 60-second period plus the queue length for each disk as well as the total queue length. Processes with disk activity are tabulated, along with bytes/sec values for disk reads, writes, and total access. Disk activity by process and available storage by logical disk volume are also tabulated.

Network Tab

The Network tab includes a graphical display of network activity as well as the number of TCP connections and the percentage utilization of network connections across each network adapter in the computer. Tabulated information includes the processes with network activity, for which the number of bytes/sec sent, received, and total. Tables of network activity, TCP connections, and listening ports are also shown; similar to other tabs, you can filter these displays by selecting the check boxes in the top section of the tabular display.

TIP   You can use Resource Monitor to end unresponsive processes in a manner similar to that of Task Manager. Such a process is displayed in red in the top section of the Overview tab. Right-click the process in the tabular display and choose **End Process**. A message box warns you that you will lose any unsaved data, and that ending a system process might result in system instability. Click **End process** to end the process or **Cancel** to quit.

NOTE   For more information on using Resource Monitor, refer to "Resource Availability Troubleshooting Getting Started Guide" at http://technet.microsoft.com/en-us/library/dd883276(WS.10).aspx.

Performance Monitor

The Windows 7 Performance console includes the following monitoring tools:

- **Performance Monitor:** Provides a real-time graph of computer performance, either in the current time or as logged historical data.

- **Data Collector Sets:** Known as *Performance Logs and Alerts* in Windows 2000/XP, this component records computer performance information into log files. Data collectors are grouped into groups that you can use for monitoring performance under different conditions.

■ **Reports:** Included as the Report function of the System Monitor console in Windows 2000/XP, this component creates performance report data.

Performance Monitor, which is shown in Figure 16-16, provides a real-time graph of computer performance and enables you to perform tasks such as the following:

Figure 16-16   Performance Monitor displays a real-time graph of activity for selected objects and counters.

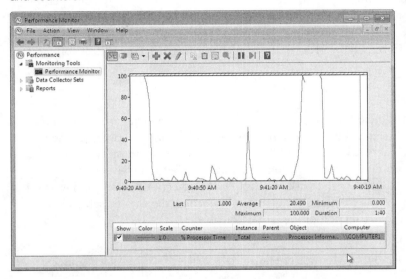

■ Identify performance problems such as bottlenecks

■ Monitor resource usage

■ Track trends over time

■ Measure the effects of changes in system configuration

■ Generate alerts when unusual conditions occur

Before you learn more about the Performance Monitor tool, you need to be familiar with the following terms, which are used in a specific manner when referring to performance metrics:

■ **Object:** A specific hardware or software component that the Performance Console is capable of monitoring. It can be any component that possesses a series of measurable properties. Windows 7 comes with a defined set of objects; applications such as Internet Information Services (IIS) installed on Windows 7 might add more objects to the available set.

■ **Counter:** One of a series of statistical measurements associated with each object.

■ **Instance:** Refers to multiple occurrences of a given object. For example, if your computer has two hard disks, two instances of the PhysicalDisk object will be present. These instances are numbered sequentially, starting with 0 for the first occurrence. An instance labeled "_Total" is also present, yielding the sum of performance data for each counter. Note that not all objects have multiple instances.

Information on objects and counters is displayed in the following format: *Object (_instance)\Counter*. For example, Processor (_0)\%Processor Time measures the %Processor time on the first processor. The instance does not appear if only a single instance is present.

Performance Monitor enables you to obtain a real-time graph of computer performance statistics. Use the following procedure:

Step 1. Click **Start** and type `performance` in the Start Search text box. Then click **Performance Monitor** in the Programs list. You can also start the Reliability and Performance console from the Computer Management console, accessed by right-clicking **Computer** and choosing **Manage,** or from the Advanced Tools applet previously shown in Figure 16-3 by clicking **Open Performance Monitor.**

Step 2. If you receive a User Account Control (UAC) prompt, click **Yes** or supply administrative credentials.

Step 3. In the Performance console, click **Performance Monitor.** As previously shown in Figure 16-16, Performance Monitor displays the Processor\%Processor Time counter.

Step 4. To add objects and counters, click the + icon on the toolbar.

Step 5. In the Add Counters dialog box that appears (see Figure 16-17), ensure that the Select counters from computer drop-down list reads `<Local computer>` for monitoring the local computer performance. Then select the desired object and instance from the lists directly below the Select counters list.

Step 6. Expand the desired object to display a list of available counters from which you can select one or more counters, as shown in Figure 16-18. To add counters to the graph, select the counter and click **Add.**

Step 7. Repeat steps 5 and 6 to add more counters. You learn about suitable counters in the following sections.

Step 8. When you are finished, click **OK.**

TIP   You can highlight individual counters in Performance Monitor. To highlight an individual counter in the Performance Monitor display, select it from the list at the bottom of the details pane and click the highlight icon (looks like a highlighter pen) in the taskbar. You can also press the **Backspace** key to highlight the counter. The high-lighted counter appears in a heavy line. You can use the up and down arrow keys to toggle through the list of counters and highlight each one in turn. This feature helps you to find the desired counter from a graph that includes a large number of counters.

Figure 16-17   You can select from a large number of objects from the Performance Object drop-down list in the Add Counters dialog box.

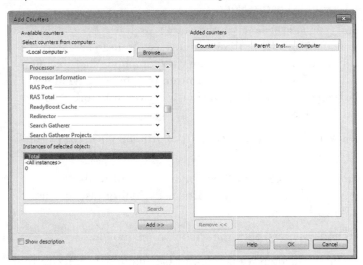

Figure 16-18   Expanding a performance object enables you to select from the available counters for that object.

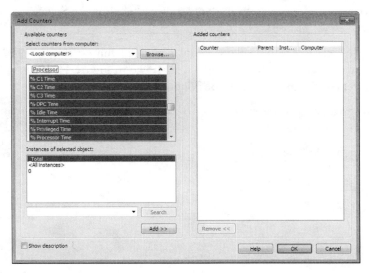

NOTE   For more information on Performance Monitoring, refer to "Performance Monitoring Getting Started Guide" at http://technet.microsoft.com/en-ca/library/dd744567(WS.10).aspx.

Data Collector Sets

A data collector set is a set of performance objects and counters that enables you to log computer performance over time while you are performing other tasks. Such logging is important because changes in computer performance often occur only after an extended period of time. Best practices state that you should create a *performance baseline*, which is a log of computer performance that you can save for comparing with future performance and tracking any changes that might have occurred over time. In this way you can identify potential bottlenecks in computer performance and take any required corrective measures. You can also monitor the effectiveness of any changes you make to a computer's configuration.

The Data Collector Sets feature was formerly known as Performance Logs and Alerts in previous Windows versions.

Creating Data Collector Sets

Data collector sets are binary files that save performance statistics for later viewing and analysis in the Performance Monitor snap-in; you can also export them to spreadsheet or database programs for later analysis. Windows 7 creates a series of data collector sets by default. The default data collector sets enable you to log default sets of performance counters for various purposes, including system diagnostics, LAN diagnostics, system performance, wireless diagnostics, event trace sessions, and startup event trace sessions. To view these sets, expand the branches under the Data Collector Sets node of the Reliability and Performance Monitor. Right-click any available data collector set and choose **Properties** to view information on the selected data collector set.

You can also create your own user-defined data collector set. Use the following procedure to create a data collector set:

Step 1.   In the console tree of the Performance Monitor snap-in, select and expand **Data Collector Sets**.

Step 2.   Select **User Defined**.

Step 3.   To create a new data collector set, right-click a blank area of the details pane and select **New > Data Collector Set**. The Create new Data Collector Set Wizard starts.

Step 4.   Provide a name for the new data collector set. Select either **Create from a template (Recommended)** or **Create Manually (Advanced)**, and then click **Next**. If you select the **Create Manually (Advanced)**

option, refer to the next procedure for the remainder of the steps you should perform.

Step 5.   If you select the **Create from a template** option, you receive the dialog box shown in Figure 16-19, which enables you to use one of the following templates:

— **Basic:** Enables you to use performance counters to create a basic data collector set, which you can edit later if necessary.

— **System Diagnostics:** Enables you to create a report that contains details of local hardware resources, system response times, and local computer processes. System information and configuration data are also included.

— **System Performance:** Enables you to create a report that provides details on local hardware resources, system response times, and local computer processes.

Step 6.   Select the desired template and click **Browse** to locate a template file (XML format) if one exists. Then click **Next**.

Step 7.   Select a location to which you would like the data to be saved (or accept the default location provided), and then click **Next**.

Step 8.   You receive the Create the data collector set? page shown in Figure 16-20. To run the set as a different user, click **Change** and then select the desired user. To start logging now or configure additional properties, select the option provided. Then click **Finish**.

Figure 16-19   The Create new Data Collector Set Wizard enables you to use several different templates.

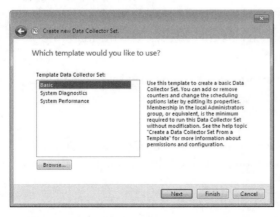

Figure 16-20   The Create the data collector set? page enables you to run the set as another user or configure the properties of the data collector set.

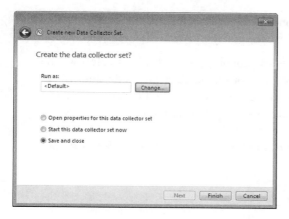

To create a custom data collector set, use the **Create manually (Advanced)** option in step 4 of the previous procedure and then use the following steps to complete the procedure:

Step 1.   After selecting the **Create manually (Advanced)** option and clicking **Next**, you receive the screen shown in Figure 16-21, which enables you to specify the following options:

Figure 16-21   You can create several types of logs or alerts from the Create Manually option in the Create new Data Collector Set Wizard.

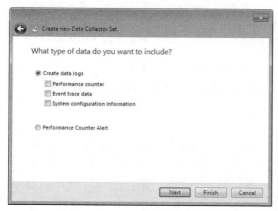

— **Performance counter:** Enables you to select performance objects and counters to be logged over time. Click **Next** to specify the perform- ance counters to be logged and the desired sampling interval.

— **Event trace data:** Enables you to create trace logs, which are similar to counter logs, but they log data only when a specific activity takes place, whereas counter logs track data continuously for a specified interval.

— **System configuration information:** Enables you to track changes in Registry keys. Click **Next** to specify the desired keys.

— **Performance Counter Alert:** Enables you to display an alert when a selected counter exceeds or drops beneath a specified value. Click **Next** to specify the counters you would like to be alerted for and the limiting value (see Figure 16-22 for an example).

Figure 16-22   You can create an alert that informs you when the Processor\% Processor Time value exceeds 80 percent.

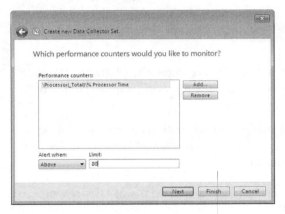

Step 2.   After clicking **Next**, you receive the same dialog box shown previously in Figure 16-20. Make any changes needed and then click **Finish**.

Using Performance Monitor to Create a Data Collector Set

Perhaps the simplest method to create a data collector set is to use a set of counters you have already configured in Performance Monitor. The following steps show you how:

Step 1.   After creating a performance graph as described earlier in this section, right-click **Performance Monitor** in the console tree and select **New > Data Collector Set**. The Create New Data Collector Set Wizard starts, as previously described.

Step 2.   Provide a name for the data collector set and then click **Next**.

Step 3.   Accept the location to which the data is to be saved, or type or browse to the location of your choice, and then click **Next**.

Step 4.   In the Create the data collector set? page, select any required options and then click **Finish**.

The data collector set is created and placed in the User Defined section. If you select the option to start the data collector set now, logging begins immediately and continues until you right-click the data collector set and choose **Stop**.

You can view data collected by the data collector set in Performance Monitor. From the view previously shown in Figure 16-16, select the **View Log Data** icon (the second icon from the left in the toolbar immediately above the performance graph). In the Source tab of the Performance Monitor Properties dialog box that appears, select the **Log files** option and click **Add**. Select the desired log file in the Select Log File dialog box that appears, click **Open**, and then click **OK**. This displays the selected log in the performance graph.

Optimizing and Troubleshooting Memory Performance

The Memory object includes counters that monitor the computer's physical and virtual memory. Table 16-3 discusses the most important counters for this object.

Table 16-3   Important Counters for the Memory Object

Counter	What It Measures	Interpretation and Remedial Tips
Pages/sec	The rate at which data is read to or written from the paging file	A value of 20 or more indicates a shortage of RAM and a possible memory bottleneck. To view the effect of paging file performance on the system, watch this counter together with LogicalDisk\% Disk Time. Add RAM to clear the problem.
Available Bytes	The amount of physical memory available	A value consistently below 4 MB indicates a shortage of available memory. This might be due to memory leaks in one or more applications. Check your programs for memory leaks. You might need to add more RAM.
Committed Bytes	The amount of virtual memory that has been committed to either physical RAM or running processes	Committed memory is in use and not available to other processes. If the amount of committed bytes exceeds the amount of RAM on the computer, you might need to add RAM.

Table 16-3 Important Counters for the Memory Object

Counter	What It Measures	Interpretation and Remedial Tips
Pool Nonpaged	The amount of RAM in the nonpaged pool system memory (an area holding objects that cannot be written to disk)	If this value exhibits a steady increase in bytes without a corresponding increase in computer activity, check for an application with a memory leak.
Page Faults/sec	The number of data pages that must be read from or written to the page file per second	A high value indicates a lot of paging activity. Add RAM to alleviate this problem.

In addition to these counters, the Paging File\% Usage counter is of use when troubleshooting memory problems. This counter measures the percentage of the paging file currently in use. If it approaches 100%, you should either increase the size of the paging file or add more RAM.

Lack of adequate memory can also have an impact on the performance of other subsystems in the computer. In particular, a large amount of paging, or reading/writing data from/to the paging file on the hard disk, results in increased activity in both the processor and disk subsystems. You should monitor counters in these subsystems at the same time if you suspect memory-related performance problems. You learn more about monitoring counters later in the section "Optimizing and Troubleshooting Processor Utilization."

The paging file is an area on the hard disk that is used as an additional memory location for programs and data that cannot fit into RAM (in other words, virtual memory). By default, the paging file is located at %systemdrive%\pagefile.sys and has a default initial size of the amount of RAM in the computer plus 300 MB and a default maximum size of three times the amount of RAM in the computer.

To improve performance on a computer equipped with more than one physical hard disk, you should locate the paging file on a different hard disk than that occupied by the operating system. You can also increase the size of the paging file or configure multiple paging files on different hard disks. Any of these configurations help to optimize performance by spreading out the activity of reading/writing data from/to the paging files. Note that you should retain a paging file on the system/boot drive to create a memory dump in case of a crash. This memory dump is useful for debugging purposes.

Use the following procedure to modify the configuration of the paging file:

Step 1.   Right-click **Computer** and choose **Properties,** and then select **Advanced system settings** from the Tasks list in the System applet.

Step 2.   On the Advanced tab of the System Properties dialog box, select **Settings** under **Performance**.

Step 3.   Select the **Advanced** tab of the Performance Options dialog box.

Step 4.   In the Virtual memory section of this tab, click **Change**.

Step 5.   As shown in Figure 16-23, the Virtual Memory dialog box displays the disk partitions available on the computer and the size of the paging file on each. To add a paging file to a drive, first clear the **Automatically manage paging file size for all drives** check box. Select the drive and choose **Custom size** to specify an initial and maximum size in MB or **System managed size** to obtain a default size. To remove a paging file, select the drive holding the file and click **No paging file**. Note that some programs might not work properly if you choose the **No paging file** option. Then click **Set**.

Figure 16-23   You can modify paging file properties from the Virtual Memory dialog box.

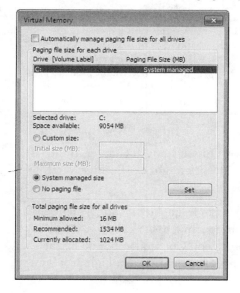

Step 6.   Click **OK** three times to apply your changes and to close the Performance Options and System Properties dialog boxes.

Step 7.   Click **Restart Now** to restart your computer if so prompted.

Optimizing and Troubleshooting Processor Utilization

The processor is the heart of the system because it executes all program instructions, whether internal to the operating system or in user-executed applications.

The Processor object contains counters that monitor processor performance. Table 16-4 discusses the most important counters for this object.

Table 16-4   Important Counters for the Processor Object

Counter	What It Measures	Interpretation and Remedial Tips
% Processor Time	The percentage of time the processor is executing meaningful actions (excludes the Idle process)	If this value is consistently greater than 85%, the processor could be causing a bottleneck. You should check the memory counters discussed previously; if these are high, consider adding more RAM. Otherwise, you should consider adding a faster processor (or an additional one if supported by your mother-board).
Interrupts/sec	The rate of service requests from I/O devices that interrupt other processor activities	A significant increase in the number of interrupts, without a corresponding increase in system activity, might indicate some type of hardware failure. Brief spikes are acceptable.

You should also look at the **System\Processor Queue Length** counter. If the value of this counter exceeds 2, a processor bottleneck might exist, with several programs contending for the processor's time.

As mentioned in Table 16-4, memory shortages can frequently manifest themselves in high processor activity. It is usually much cheaper and easier to add RAM to a computer than to add a faster or additional processor. Consequently, you might want to consider this step first when you are experiencing frequent high processor activity.

Optimizing and Troubleshooting Disk Performance

Disk performance is measured by two processor objects: The PhysicalDisk counters measure the overall performance of a single physical hard disk rather than individual partitions. LogicalDisk counters measure the performance of a single partition or volume on a disk. These counters include the performance of spanned, striped, or RAID-5 volumes that cross physical disks.

PhysicalDisk counters are best suited for hardware troubleshooting. Table 16-5 describes the most important counters for this object.

Table 16-5   Important Counters for the PhysicalDisk Object

Counter	What It Measures	Interpretation and Remedial Tips
% Disk Time	The percentage of time that the disk was busy reading or writing to any partition	A value of over 50% suggests a disk bottleneck. Consider upgrading to a faster disk or controller. Also check the memory counters to see whether more RAM is needed.
Avg. Disk Queue Length	The average number of disk read and write requests waiting to be performed	If this value is greater than 2, follow the same suggestions as for % Disk Time.
Average Disk Sec/Transfer	The length of time a disk takes to fulfill requests	A value greater than 0.3 might indicate that the disk controller is retrying the disk continually because of write failures.

LogicalDisk counters are best suited for investigating the read/write performance of a single partition. Table 16-6 describes the most important counters for this object.

Table 16-6   Important Counters for the LogicalDisk Object

Counter	What It Measures	Interpretation and Remedial Tips
% Disk Time	The percentage of time that the disk is busy servicing disk requests	A value greater than 90% might indicate a performance problem except when using a RAID device. Compare to Processor\% Processor Time to determine whether disk requests are using too much processor time.
Average Disk Bytes/Transfer	The amount of data transferred in each I/O operation	Low values (below about 20 KB) indicate that an application might be accessing a disk inefficiently. Watch this counter as you close applications to locate an offending application.
Current Disk Queue Length	The amount of data waiting to be transferred to the disk	A value greater than 2 indicates a possible disk bottleneck, with processes being delayed because of slow disk speed. Consider adding another faster disk.
Disk Transfers/sec	The rate at which read or write operations are performed by the disk	A value greater than 50 might indicate a disk bottleneck. Consider adding another faster disk.

Table 16-6 Important Counters for the LogicalDisk Object

Counter	What It Measures	Interpretation and Remedial Tips
% Free Space	Percentage of unused disk space	A value less than about 15% indicates that insufficient disk space is available. Consider moving files, repartitioning the disk, or adding another disk.

TIP You should log disk activity to a different disk or computer. The act of recording performance logs places an extra hit on performance for the disk on which logs are recorded. To obtain accurate disk monitoring results, record this data to a different disk or computer.

Command-Line Utilities

You can perform several tasks associated with performance monitoring and optimization from the command line. The following are several available tools:

- `Logman`: Manages data collector logs. You can start, stop, and schedule the collection of performance and trace data.

- `Relog`: Creates new performance logs from data in existing logs by modifying the sampling rate and/or converting the file format.

- `Typeperf`: Displays performance data to the command prompt window or to a log file.

You can also use the `Perfmon` command to start the Reliability and Performance Monitor from a command line. For information on running these tools, type the command name followed by `/?` at a command prompt.

Configuring Additional Performance Settings

Windows 7 contains several additional tools that you can use to manage your computer's performance. The exam objectives mention power plans and mobile computer performance. We looked at these items in Chapter 13. Most of the power plan settings discussed there are applicable to desktop computers as well. The paging file was discussed earlier in this chapter (refer to Figure 16-23).

Configuring the Hard Drive Cache

When Windows writes to a hard drive, high-speed volatile RAM is used for temporary storage of information being sent to the drive until these devices, which are typically slower, can write the information permanently. On a removable drive such as a USB hard drive or thumb drive, or a memory card, write caching speeds up writing but requires that you use the Safely Remove Hardware notification setting before disconnecting such a drive or risk data loss.

To modify this behavior, right-click the USB drive or memory card in Computer and choose **Properties**. Select the **Hardware** tab, select the device, and click **Properties**. Then click **Change settings** to obtain the dialog box shown in Figure 16-24. To disable write caching and enable removal of the device without using the Safely Remove Hardware notification icon, access the **Policies** tab and ensure that the **Quick removal (default)** setting is selected. If improved perform-ance is more of a concern, select the **Better performance** option. If you select this option, you must use the Safely Remove Hardware icon in your notification area to stop the device and ensure you can remove it without suffering data loss.

Figure 16-24   You can choose from two caching options for removable drives.

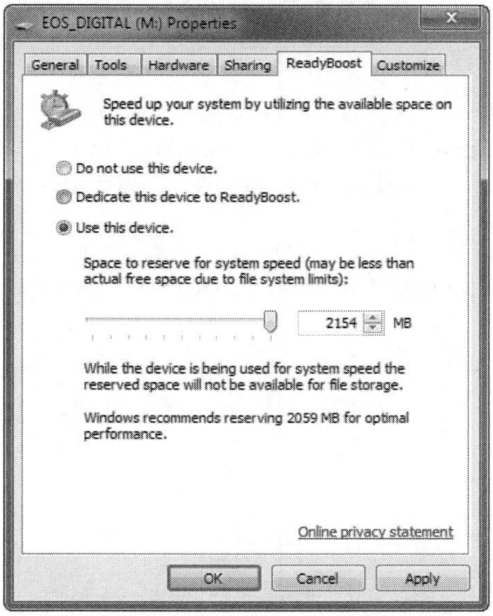

Windows ReadyBoost

Included with all versions of Windows 7, Windows ReadyBoost enhances your computer's performance without adding additional RAM. ReadyBoost enables you to use a USB flash drive or a Compact Flash or Secure Digital (SD) memory card as an additional source of memory (also known as a *cache*) to improve your com-puter's performance. The computer can access this cache more rapidly than it can access the paging file or other data on the hard drive. You can even use a portion of the flash drive for Windows ReadyBoost and the remainder for data storage. Microsoft recommends that you use one to three times the amount of RAM in your computer for optimum performance of Windows ReadyBoost.

Devices used by Windows ReadyBoost must be USB 2.0–capable and be of at least 256 MB capacity. The device must support a minimum read speed of 2.5 MB/s and a write speed of 1.75 MB/s. In addition, the USB host controller on the computer must accept the USB 2.0 standard. Windows ReadyBoost can use a cache of up to 4 GB in size.

It is simple to use Windows ReadyBoost, as described in the following steps:

Step 1.   Insert the USB flash drive into an available port. Windows displays an AutoPlay message box with an option to use Windows ReadyBoost.

Step 2.   To use Windows ReadyBoost, select the **Speed up my system** option. Windows tests the device to determine whether it can be used with ReadyBoost.

Step 3.   If you do not receive a prompt, or if you want to use a portion of the drive for data storage, open Computer. Right-click the USB drive and choose **Properties**.

Step 4.   On the ReadyBoost tab of the device's Properties dialog box shown in Figure 16-25, ensure that the **Use this device** option is selected and then drag the slider to select the amount of space to be used for Ready-Boost. Then click **OK**.

Figure 16-25   The ReadyBoost tab of a device's Properties dialog box enables you to select the space to be used by ReadyBoost.

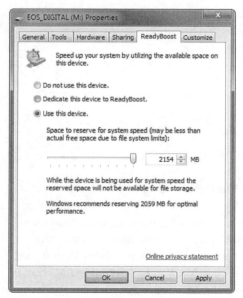

NOTE For more information on using ReadyBoost in Windows 7, refer to "ReadyBoost" at http://windows.microsoft.com/en-us/windows7/products/features/readyboost.

System Configuration Utility

Microsoft has enhanced the System Configuration Utility to improve its capabilities for identifying problems that can prevent Windows from starting properly. System Configuration Utility enables you to disable common services and startup programs to selectively troubleshoot which items are preventing a normal startup.

To start the System Configuration Utility, click **Start**, type `msconfig` in the Start menu Search field, and then press **Enter**. If you receive a UAC prompt, click **Yes** or supply administrative credentials. You receive the dialog box shown in Figure 16-26.

The following sections describe the functions available on each tab.

Figure 16-26 The System Configuration Utility enables you to troubleshoot problems that prevent Windows from starting normally.

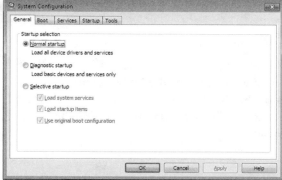

General Tab

Similar to the General tab on the Windows XP System Configuration tool, you can choose **Normal startup**, which loads all drivers and services configured to start automatically; **Diagnostic startup**, which loads basic drivers and services; or **Selective startup**, which enables you to select the following options:

- **Load system services:** Starts all services that are configured for automatic startup.

- **Load startup items:** Starts applications that have been configured to start at boot or logon time.

- **Use original boot configuration:** Remains selected unless you modify default settings on the Boot tab.

Boot Tab

Shown in Figure 16-27, the Boot tab has been completely modified compared to its previous function in Windows XP. On a multiboot computer, the display window contains entries for the different operating systems present. To choose which operating system boots by default, select the desired entry and click **Set as default**. You have the following boot options available:

- **Safe boot:** Provides four options for booting your computer into safe mode. The Minimal option brings up the Windows GUI with only critical system services loaded and networking disabled. The Alternate shell option boots to the command prompt and disables both the GUI and networking. The Active Directory repair option boots to the GUI and runs Active Directory as well as critical system services. The Network option boots to the Windows GUI with only critical services loaded and enables networking.

- **No GUI boot:** Starts Windows without displaying the Windows splash screen.

- **Boot log:** Boots according to the other options selected, and logs information from the boot procedure to `%systemroot%\Ntbtlog.txt`.

- **Base video:** Uses standard VGA drivers to load the Windows GUI in minimal VGA mode.

- **OS boot information:** Displays driver names as the boot process loads them.

In addition, the **Timeout** setting determines the number of seconds that the boot menu is displayed on a multiboot computer, and the **Make all boot settings permanent** option disables tracking of changes made in the System Configuration Utility. This option disables the ability to roll back changes by selecting the **Normal startup** option from the General tab.

Services Tab

The Services tab lists all Windows services available on the computer, including those installed by other applications running on the computer. You can enable or disable individual services at boot time when you think that running services might be causing boot problems. Clear the check box for those services you want to disable for the next boot, or click the **Disable all** command button to disable all nonessential services.

To show only services installed by non-Microsoft programs, select the **Hide all Microsoft services** check box. This enables you to more rapidly locate non-Microsoft services that might be contributing to boot problems.

CAUTION   Ensure that you do not disable essential services. You might encounter system stability problems or other malfunctions if you disable too many services. Ensure that services you disable are not essential to your computer's operation. The Disable all option does not disable secure Microsoft services required at boot time.

Startup Tab

The Startup tab lists all applications configured to start automatically when the computer starts up. Information provided includes the manufacturer name, the path to the file that starts the application, and the Registry key or shortcut that starts the application.

To prevent an application from starting on the next boot, clear its check box. To enable it to start on subsequent boots, select its check box or select the **Normal startup** option from the General tab.

Tools Tab

Shown in Figure 16-28, the Tools tab enumerates all diagnostic applications and other available tools. It provides a convenient location from which you can start a program; to do so, select the desired program and click **Launch**.

Figure 16-28   The Tools tab enables you to start a program from a comprehensive list of Windows diagnostic utilities.

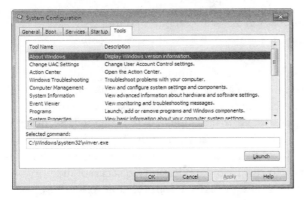

> **NOTE**   For more information on using the System Configuration Utility, refer to "Using System Configuration" at http://windows.microsoft.com/en-US/windows7/Using-System-Configuration.

Configuring the Relative Priority of Foreground and Background Tasks

Depending on your computer's usage, you might be able to improve computer performance by changing the relative priority of foreground and background applications. You can accomplish this action from the Advanced tab of the Performance Options dialog box by performing the following steps:

Step 1.   From the Advanced Tools applet previously shown in Figure 16-3, select the **Adjust the appearance and performance of Windows** option to open the dialog box previously shown in Figure 16-2.

Step 2.   Select the **Advanced** tab.

Step 3. Under Processor Scheduling, choose one of the following options:

— **Programs:** Assigns more processor resources to programs currently running in the foreground (active programs). This is the default.

— **Background services:** Assigns equal amounts of resources to all programs, including those such as disk backup or defragmentation that are running in the background.

Configuring Processor Scheduling

Windows 7 includes built-in capability for computers with two or more processors or cores. Under most conditions, dual-processor computers provide enhanced computing power; however, you should be aware of several considerations that exist with regard to dual-processor computers:

■ **Use of Task Manager:** As already mentioned, the Performance tab of Task Manager shows processor usage information for both processors by splitting the graph of CPU Usage History into two portions.

■ **Running 16-bit legacy applications:** On a 32-bit computer, Windows 7 uses a special 32-bit application called a Windows NT Virtual DOS Machine (Ntvdm.exe) to emulate the older 16-bit environment. You can have multiple instances of the Ntvdm.exe process on a single computer; however, by default Windows 7 runs all 16-bit applications in a single instance of Ntvdm.exe (also called a *single memory space*). This can cause two problems: First, if one application crashes or becomes unresponsive, all 16-bit applications are halted. Second, on a dual-processor computer, all 16-bit applications run on the same processor, thereby resulting in the possibility of this processor being overloaded while the other processor is underutilized. To run 16-bit applications in separate memory spaces, click **Start > Run** and type **start /separate *application.exe*,** where *application.exe* is the name of the 16-bit application.

On a 64-bit Windows 7 computer, Ntvdm.exe has been removed. Consequently, 16-bit applications will not run and you will need to replace these applications with 32- or 64-bit ones.

■ **You can configure processor affinity for each application:** This capability enables you to specify on which processor a given process will execute and can be utilized to distribute activity evenly across more than one processor. You can set processor affinity from Task Manager. Simply right-click the process from the Processes tab and choose **Set Affinity**. Then select the appropriate processor.

> **CAUTION** The 64-bit editions of Windows 7 do not support 16-bit DOS applications. If you are purchasing 64-bit computers, make sure that you have upgraded all such applications to at least 32 bits.

Action Center

New to Windows 7 is the Action Center, which replaces the Windows Vista Security Center and adds several maintenance and performance options. You can access Action Center by opening Control Panel to the System and Security category and selecting **Action Center**. You can open Action Center by selecting it in the Tools tab of the System Configuration utility and clicking **Launch**. You can also click **Start** and type `action` in the Start menu Search field. Then select **Action Center** from the programs list. Either of these options brings up the applet shown in Figure 16-29. Expand the Security section to configure the security options discussed in earlier chapters of this book. Take note of any messages appearing in the Maintenance section and click **Check for solutions** to send information to Microsoft that might provide resolution for these problems. To configure backup, click **Set up backup.** We discuss backup in Chapter 17, "Configuring Backups."

Figure 16-29   Action Center enables you to troubleshoot security, maintenance, and perform-ance issues.

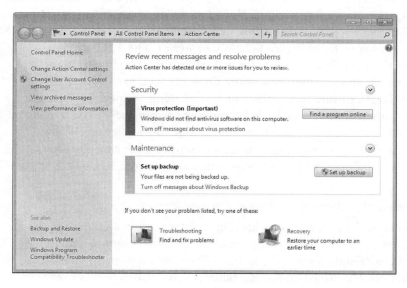

The links at the left side of the Action Center panel enable you to perform the following tasks:

- **Change Action Center settings:** Enables you to select the type of security and maintenance messages displayed by Action Center. You can also choose to participate in Microsoft's Customer Experience Improvement Program or modify problem reporting or Windows Update settings. We discussed Windows Update settings in Chapter 7.

- **Change User Account Control settings:** Enables you to change the behavior of UAC, as previously discussed in Chapter 12, "Configuring Access Controls."

- **View archived messages:** Enables you to view archived messages about computer problems previously reported to Microsoft.

- **View performance information:** Accesses the Rate and improve your computer's performance window previously shown in Figure 16-1.

Advanced Networking Performance Options

Networking performance depends to a considerable extent on the networking hardware available to the computer, including devices such as switches, routers, hubs, network interface cards (NICs), and network cables. Ensure that these are in optimal order and check the Device Manager if you suspect a problem with the NIC.

Internet connectivity can be affected by other options, as well. We looked at many settings that can impact on Internet and network performance in Chapter 8, "Configuring Applications and Internet Explorer," including firewall settings and options in the Internet Properties dialog box such as specifying cookie handling and the pop-up blocker (refer to Figure 8-22 in Chapter 8). The Advanced tab of the Internet Options tab offers several additional settings that can impact upon network performance. In particular, look at the Browsing section of this tab, as shown in Figure 16-30. Ensure that options such as disabling script debugging are enabled; disabling these options can degrade browsing performance. Even options such as Suggested Sites can slow down browsing; disable this when using a slow connection such as dial-up. Options such as smooth scrolling can slow the browsing experience on a computer with an underpowered video card.

Configuring Services and Programs to Resolve Performance Issues

We have seen in several past sections of this chapter how you can configure programs or stop them in case of performance problems. Windows services run in the background and enable significant and important functions on your computer—in fact, nearly all actions performed on the computer depend on one or more services. Many applications install their own services when you install them. Many of services are configured to start automatically at system startup; although many of these are essential to proper computer operation, having nonessential services starting can degrade computer performance noticeably.

We have shown how you can configure service startup from the System Configuration Utility. You can also configure service startup and properties from the Services snap-in. This tool is a component of the Computer Management snap-in and can also be accessed in its own console by typing **services** at the Start Menu Search field. This brings up the console shown in Figure 16-31, which lists all services installed on the computer and indicates their statuses and startup types.

Figure 16-30 Browsing settings in the Internet Options dialog box Advanced tab can affect browsing performance.

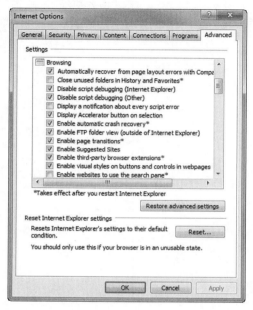

Figure 16-31 The Services console enables you to observe the status of services running on your computer.

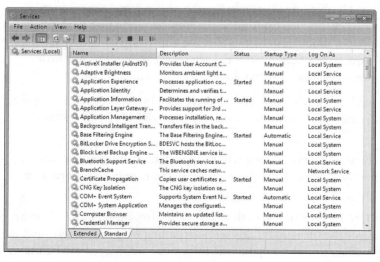

You can modify the properties of any service, including its startup type, as required. Right-click the desired service and choose **Properties** to bring up its Properties dialog box shown in Figure 16-32. This enables you to configure the following properties of each service:

Figure 16-32   You can configure service properties from each service's Properties dialog box.

- **General Tab:** You can set the startup type to Automatic, Automatic (Delayed Start), Manual, or Disabled. By disabling services that consume extra computer resources on startup, you can sometimes improve computer performance. Certain services should also be disabled for improving computer security. However, you must ensure that all essential services remain set to Automatic. Set nonessential services that perform useful tasks to Manual startup.

- **Log On Tab:** Enables you to change the account used by services when logging on. In nearly all cases, you should leave this set to its default Local System Account.

- **Recovery Tab:** Enables you to specify actions to be taken if the service fails, such as restarting the service, restarting the computer, running a program, or taking no action.

- **Dependencies Tab:** Lists the services that this service depends on as well as the system components that depend on this service running properly. There are no configurable options on this tab, but the information displayed can be useful in troubleshooting failures.

Exam Preparation Tasks

Review All the Key Topics

Review the most important topics in the chapter, noted with the key topics icon in the outer margin of the page. Table 16-7 lists a reference of these key topics and the page numbers on which each is found.

Table 16-7 Key Topics for Chapter 16

Key Topic Element	Description	Page Number
Table 16-2	Summarizes the monitoring and maintenance tools available from the Advanced Tools window	598
Figure 16-6	Viewing error and warning messages in Event Viewer	601
Figure 16-7	Filtering event logs	603
Figure 16-10	Creating an event log subscription	606
Figure 16-15	Using Resource Monitor to monitor your computer's performance	613
List	Shows you how to use Performance Monitor	617
List	Shows you how to create a data collector set	619
Table 16-3	Describes the important counters for the Memory performance object	623
Table 16-4	Describes the important counters for the Processor performance object	626
Figure 16-26	Displays the various diagnostic startup options available from System Configuration	631
List	Describes processor scheduling options	634

Complete the Tables and Lists from Memory

Print a copy of Appendix C, "Memory Tables" (found on the CD), or at least the section for this chapter, and complete the tables and lists from memory. Appendix D, "Memory Tables Answer Key," also on the CD, includes completed tables and lists to check your work.

Definitions of Key Terms

Define the following key terms from this chapter, and check your answers in the glossary.

alert, Event Viewer, Data Collector Sets, paging file, performance counter, Performance object, Performance Monitor, Reliability Monitor, Resource Monitor, System Configuration Utility, Task Manager, Windows Experience Index, Msconfig, event log subscription, Action Center

This chapter covers the following subjects:

- **Using Windows Backup to Protect Your Data:** Backups of operating system and data files are very important because you could lose much valuable information should your hard disk fail. This section describes the various types of backup that you can perform to protect your valuable data.

- **Creating a System Recovery Disk:** A system recovery disk enables you to boot your computer and perform a repair should your computer become nonfunctional. This section shows you how to create a system recovery (also known as system repair) disk.

CHAPTER 17

Configuring Backups

Backing up and restoring crucial data is an important responsibility for an individual charged with this duty. Without some sort of backup strategy in place, loss of critical data could threaten the very existence of an organization. At the very least, it can make a computer unusable. A good data backup program can make recovering from a disk crash or restoring a corrupted file a straightforward exercise. Backing up data will never be one of the more enjoyable tasks related to network administration. However, if you do not have backup copies of data stored on a computer, valuable data can be lost forever. Windows 7 provides a Backup tool that you can use to create backup copies of data on a variety of media including disk, CD-ROM, DVD, and shared network drives.

"Do I Know This Already?" Quiz

The "Do I Know This Already?" quiz enables you to assess whether you should read this entire chapter or simply jump to the "Exam Preparation Tasks" section for review. If you are in doubt, read the entire chapter. Table 17-1 outlines the major headings in this chapter and the corresponding "Do I Know This Already?" quiz questions. You can find the answers in Appendix A, "Answers to the 'Do I Know This Already?' Quizzes."

Table 17-1 "Do I Know This Already?" Foundation Topics Section-to-Question Mapping

Foundations Topics Section	Questions Covered in This Section
Using Windows Backup to Protect Your Data	1–7
Creating a System Recovery Disk	8

1. You want to back up the contents of your c: drive of your computer running
Windows 7 Home Premium to another computer on your network running
Windows XP Professional. However, you cannot find the option to back up to
the network. Which of the following is the most likely reason for this problem?

   a. You do not have a homegroup configured on your network.

   b. Your target computer is not running Windows 7.

   c. Windows Firewall is not set up to allow backup traffic.

   d. Your Windows 7 computer is not running the Professional or Ultimate
   edition of Windows 7.

2. You have selected the option to let Windows choose what will be backed up.
Which of the following are backed up using this option? (Choose all that apply.)

   a. Windows libraries

   b. Desktop folders

   c. Data folders on portable hard drives

   d. Windows system image

3. You completed your first backup of your Windows 7 computer a few days ago
but have been busy designing an important project for an upscale client. You
want to ensure this design is not lost, so you access the Backup and Restore applet and click the **Back up now** option. What type of backup does this perform?

   a. Normal

   b. Differential

   c. Incremental

   d. Copy

4. You have run a backup from the Backup and Restore applet, but a few days later
you realize that the backup does not include all the files and folders you should
have backed up. You return to the Backup and Restore applet and notice that
the Set up backup option is no longer available. What should you do?

   a. Click **Manage space** and add the required files and folders.

   b. Click **Change settings** and add the required files and folders.

   c. Select the **Create a system image** option.

   d. Select the **Back up computer** option.

5. You have configured Windows Backup to back your files and folders up on a monthly basis, but you decide you need to perform a weekly backup, so you access the Backup and Restore applet. You cannot find an option to change the backup schedule. What option should you select first?

a. **Turn off schedule**

b. **Manage space**

c. **Set up backup**

d. **Change settings**

6. Which of the following commands would you use to perform a backup of the C: drive to a portable hard drive configured as the E: drive?

a. `Ntbackup backup –backuptarget:e: -include:c:`

b. `Ntbackup backup –backuptarget:c: -include:e:`

c. `Wbadmin start backup –backuptarget:e: -include:c:`

d. `Wbadmin start backup –backuptarget:c: -include:e:`

7. You want to ensure that you can fully restore your computer to its operating system in the event of a hardware failure. Which of the following should you do to accomplish this objective with the least amount of administrative effort?

a. Create a system recovery disk

b. Create a system state backup

c. Create a system image

d. Create a Complete PC Backup

8. Which of the following actions can you perform by using a system repair disc?

a. Start the Windows Recovery Environment after a serious Windows error has occurred.

b. Restore critical data and applications from a backup.

c. Fully restore your computer in the event of a hardware failure.

d. Remove updates that have caused Windows errors.

Foundation Topics

Using Windows Backup to Protect Your Data

Microsoft has rewritten the backup program completely in Windows 7, updating Windows Vista's Backup and Restore Center in the form of a new Backup and Restore Control Panel applet that provides a comprehensive tool for performing all backup and restore actions. In this chapter, we look at the various backup options; restoration of files and folders is covered in Chapter 18, "Configuring System and File Recovery." As in Vista, the new Backup and Restore applet enables you to back up all data on a disk or a portion thereof to a variety of media, including tapes, shared network drives, CD-ROM drives, USB flash drives, and so on.

The available backup tools in Windows 7 depend on the version you are working with, as follows:

■ All editions of Windows 7 include file backup and restore capabilities, including the ability to create a complete system image backup and use this backup to restore the computer to its current condition. All editions also include the Previous Versions feature, which enables you to restore individual files to a previous condition.

■ In addition, the Professional, Enterprise, and Ultimate editions of Windows 7 enable you to perform backups to network locations.

Configuring Windows Backup for the First Time

Use the following steps to set up Windows Backup for first use:

Step 1.   Click **Start > Control Panel > System and Security > Backup and Restore**. You can also click **Start**, type `backup` in the Start Menu Search field, and then select **Backup and Restore** from the programs list. As shown in Figure 17-1, the Backup and Restore applet opens and informs you that Windows Backup has not been set up.

Step 2.   Click **Set up backup**. A Starting Windows Backup message box appears. After a few seconds, the Set up backup wizard starts with the Select where you want to save your backup page shown in Figure 17-2.

Step 3.   Select a suitable destination for your backup and then click **Next**. Microsoft recommends that this be on an external hard disk. Be aware that you might need a large number of DVD-ROM discs to back up a system configured with a large number of applications and data, should you select this option.

Figure 17-1   The Backup and Restore applet enables you to perform different types of backup procedures.

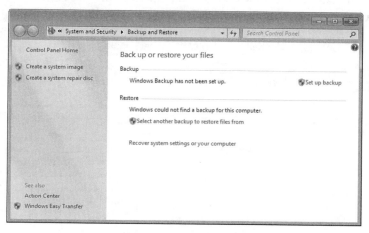

Figure 17-2   Selecting a location where your backup will be stored.

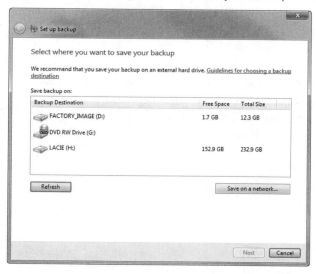

NOTE   The wizard alerts you if the selected drive does not have enough space to store a system image. If you receive this message, select a different backup destination. You can still back up selected files and folders to a disk that does not have sufficient space for a system image.

Step 4.   To back up to a network location, select **Save on a network**. From the Select a network location page shown in Figure 17-3, type the UNC path to the network share plus a username and password with administrative credentials on the remote share. Then click **OK**. If you are on an

Active Directory Domain Services (AD DS) domain and using an account with Domain Administrator or Backup Operator privileges, you should not need to enter any credentials here.

Figure 17-3   Specifying a location and credentials for a network-based backup.

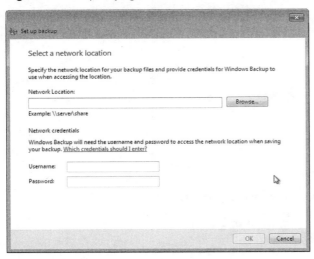

Step 5.   The What do you want to back up? page shown in Figure 17-4 enables you to choose what libraries and folders will be backed up, or you can select the default of **Let Windows choose**. This default backs up all personal data and creates a complete system backup. Make a choice and then click **Next**.

Figure 17-4   Choosing what Windows will back up.

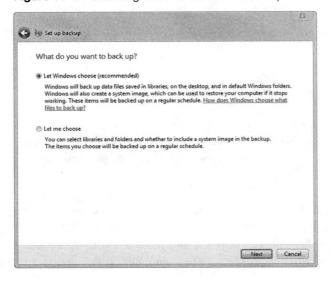

Step 6.   If you select the **Let me choose** option, you receive the page shown in Figure 17-5, from which you can select the libraries, folders, files, and drives to be backed up. You can expand any entry in this list to choose the specific items to be backed up. To create a system backup, select the check box labeled **Include a system image of drives**. When finished, click **Next**.

Step 7.   The Review your backup settings page summarizes the items you have selected for backup. If you need to make changes, click the back arrow in the top-left corner of the dialog box. If you want to change the backup schedule, which is every Sunday at 7:00 PM by default, click the link provided (we discuss scheduling backups later in this chapter). When finished, click **Save settings and run backup** to close the wizard and perform a backup.

Having set up your backup, the Backup and Restore applet now shows information about the backup and charts its progress, as shown in Figure 17-6.

Figure 17-5   Choosing the items to be backed up.

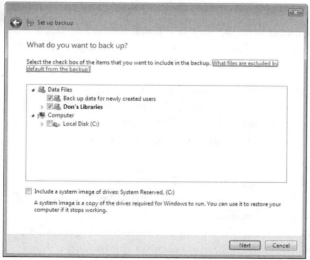

Figure 17-6   The Backup and Restore applet displays the progress of the current backup and enables you to view its details and to modify the backup settings.

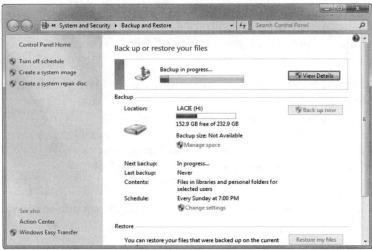

Managing and Troubleshooting Your Backups

After you have configured your initial backup, the Backup and Restore applet appears similar to that previously shown in Figure 17-6, enabling you to perform various management tasks, as follows:

- **Back up now:** Performs an incremental backup of files and folders according to settings you have configured in the Backup and Restore Wizard. An *incremental backup* procedure backs up only those files and folders that have changed since the previous backup. This procedure also marks these files as having been backed up.

- **Manage space:** Displays the Manage Windows Backup disk space dialog box shown in Figure 17-7. As shown, this dialog box provides a summary of the space used by backups. Click **Browse** to modify the backup location used. Click **View backups** to display the dialog box shown in Figure 17-8, which lets you delete older backups to free up space on the backup volume. Click **Change settings** to display the dialog box shown in Figure 17-9, which enables you to conserve disk space by keeping only the latest system image.

Figure 17-7 The Manage Windows Backup disk space dialog box enables you to configure several settings related to space used by Windows Backup.

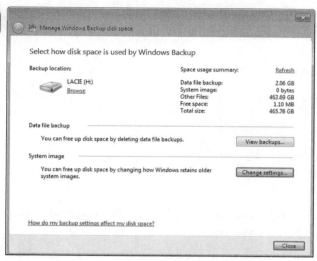

Figure 17-8 You can delete older backups if required to free up disk space for new backups.

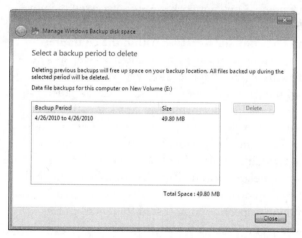

Figure 17-9   You can conserve disk space by choosing the option to keep only the latest system image.

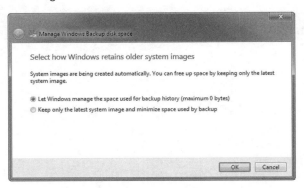

- **Change settings:** Restarts the Set up backup wizard so that you can modify all settings used by the default backup routine.

- **Restore my files:** Enables you to restore any or all files on your computer. We discuss restoring files in Chapter 18.

Within the backup volume you've specified, the Backup and Restore applet creates a folder named by your computer's name. On a network location accessed by more than one computer, you will see folders named for each computer. The Backup and Restore applet automatically creates a subfolder structure within the computer folder that contains a subfolder for each backup you've preformed, as well as a couple of system files. These subfolders are named Backup Set yyyy-mm-dd hhmmss, where yyyy-mm-dd hhmmss refers to the date and time (24-hour clock) at which the backup was performed. For example, a backup performed on April 26, 2010 at 3:13:30 PM created a folder named Backup Set 2010-04-26 151330. Each of these backup set subfolders contains a series of similarly named Zip files that hold the backed-up data plus a Catalogs folder that includes Windows Backup Catalog (.wbcat) files that contain pointers to the appropriate Zip files for each of the individual files backed up during this backup operation. If you like, you can actually locate backed up files directly from their respective compressed folders from this information without using the Backup and Restore applet directly.

Should a problem arise during backup, the Backup and Restore applet will inform you and provide options for resolution. The following are several problems that this applet will alert you to:

- **Insufficient backup disk space:** Backup and Restore will provide a Check Backup Disk Space message informing you that the disk your backups are saved on doesn't have enough free space.

- **Unavailable network location:** If the backup server is unavailable or offline, Backup and Restore will inform you. Check that the server is operational and that network connectivity is okay.

- **Open files might be skipped:** If Backup is unable to copy all files in the source locations, Backup and Restore will provide a Check Your Backup Results message that informs you some files were skipped.

To troubleshoot any of these messages, click **Options** to display a dialog box such as that shown in Figure 17-10, which provides one or more options for troubleshooting the problem. Click **Show Details** to obtain more information on the problem that occurred, and click any of the available options to troubleshoot the problem.

Figure 17-10   Windows provides troubleshooting options when a problem occurs during backup.

NOTE   For additional troubleshooting scenarios that you might encounter, refer to "Troubleshooting Backup and Recovery" at http://technet.microsoft.com/en-us/library/cc731602.aspx.

Scheduling Your Backups

By default, Windows 7 schedules your backup to take place every Sunday at 7 PM. After you have created your first backup using the procedure outlined in the previous section, you can modify the backup schedule by performing the following procedure:

Step 1.   Use the previous procedure to open the Backup and Restore Control Panel applet.

Step 2.   Click **Change settings** to reopen the Set up backup wizard.

Step 3. Click **Next** repeatedly until you reach the Review your backup settings page, and then click **Change schedule**.

Step 4. On the How often do you want to back up? page shown in Figure 17-11, select the desired options. If you select **Weekly**, select the desired day; if you select **Monthly**, select the desired day of the month from the drop-down list provided.

Figure 17-11 Selecting the day and time at which your backup will be performed.

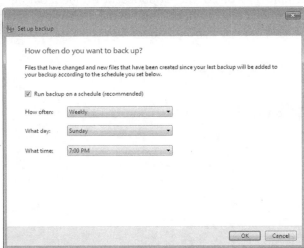

Step 5. From the What time drop-down list, select the hour at which the backup is to commence. Ensure that this is set to a time when your computer will be turned on.

Step 6. When finished, click **OK**. The Backup and Restore applet will display your configured day and time.

> **NOTE** If you do not want Windows to automatically perform scheduled backups, click the **Turn off schedule** link found on the left side of the Backup and Restore applet. This applet will now indicate that no schedule exists. Click the **Turn on schedule** link that appears to restore scheduled backups.

Using the Command Line to Perform a Backup

Microsoft has replaced the Ntbackup utility used by previous versions of Windows with the Wbadmin command. This command enables you to script the creation and management of backups on Windows 7 and Windows Server 2008 R2 computers. To use this command for performing a simple backup of your computer, click

Start > All Programs > Accessories. Then right-click **Command Prompt** and choose **Run as administrator**. Click **Yes** or supply administrative credentials in the User Account Control (UAC) prompt and then type the following command:

```
Wbadmin start backup –backuptarget:targetdrive: -include:sourcedrive:
```

In this command, *sourcedrive* is the drive whose contents you are backing up and *targetdrive* is the drive on which you are storing the backup. For example, to back up the contents of the C: drive to a portable hard drive in E:, you would type:

```
Wbadmin start backup –backuptarget:d: -include:c:
```

Table 17-2 describes the subcommands supported by Wbadmin:

Table 17-2   Wbadmin Subcommands

Subcommand	Purpose
Start backup	Performs a one-time backup
Stop job	Stops a currently running backup or restore operation
Get versions	Lists details of available backups at a specified location
Get items	Lists items currently backed up
Get status	Displays the status of a currently running backup operation

All these subcommands use a comprehensive list of parameters. To display available parameters for any subcommand, type **wbadmin** *subcommand* **/?**. You can also refer to the Wbadmin command-line reference at http://technet.microsoft.com/en-us/library/cc754015(WS.10).aspx for additional information.

Creating a System Image

The Backup and Restore applet provides an option to create a system image, which enables you to fully restore your computer in the event of a hardware failure. This procedure replaces the System State backup used in Windows 2000/XP and the Complete PC Backup procedure used in Windows Vista. You can also use this procedure to back up your data at the same time. Use the following procedure:

Step 1.   From the Backup and Restore applet, select the **Create a system image** option. If you receive a UAC prompt, click **Yes**.

Step 2.   The Where do you want to save the backup? screen shown in Figure 17-12 enables you to save the backup to a hard disk or to one or more DVDs. Make a selection and then click **Next**.

Figure 17-12   You can save a system image backup to a hard drive, a set of DVDs, or a network location.

Step 3.   The Which drives do you want to include in the backup? screen enables you to select the disks to be backed up. Select the required disks and then click **Next**.

Step 4.   The Confirm your backup settings page shows which disks will be backed up and to what location. Verify that these are correct and then click **Start backup** to perform the backup.

Step 5.   Windows displays a progress chart as the backup is performed. When the backup is completed, you are given the option to create a system repair disc. To do so, insert a blank CD or DVD and click **Create disc**. The procedure for creating this disc is discussed in the next section. Click **OK** and then click **Close**.

Step 6.   The Backup and Restore applet now displays the date and time that the complete Windows PC Backup was performed.

TIP   You can also create a system image at the same time as you perform regular Windows backups by ensuring that the check box labeled **Include a system image of drives: (*drive letter*)** in the What do you want to back up? page of the Set up backup wizard previously shown in Figure 17-5 is selected.

Creating a System Recovery Disk

You can use a system recovery disk, also known as a system repair disc, to boot your computer should you need to recover from a serious error or to restore Windows on your computer. Use of this disk enables you to access several options in the Windows Recovery Environment, which we discuss in more detail in Chapter 18.

Use the following procedure to create a system repair disc:

Step 1.   From the Backup and Restore applet, select the **Create a system repair disc** option. If you receive a UAC prompt, click **Yes**.

Step 2.   You receive the Create a system repair disc dialog box, as shown in Figure 17-13. Select the drive to be used, insert a blank CD/DVD disc, and then click **Create disc**.

Figure 17-13   Creating a system recovery disk.

Step 3.   The System Repair Disc utility charts the progress of creating the disc. This takes a minute or two and then you receive the message box shown in Figure 17-14, informing you that you can use the disc to access system recovery options. Click **Close**.

Figure 17-14   You are informed when the disc creation process is completed.

Exam Preparation Tasks

Review All the Key Topics

Review the most important topics in the chapter, noted with the key topics icon in the outer margin of the page. Table 17-3 lists a reference of these key topics and the page numbers on which each is found.

Table 17-3   Key Topics for Chapter 17

Key Topic Element	Description	Page Number
List	Describes how to set up Windows Backup for the first time	646
Figure 17-5	Selecting items to be backed up	649
Figure 17-7	Displays available backup management options	651
Figure 17-10	Displays typical backup troubleshooting options	653
Figure 17-11	Displays available backup scheduling options	654
Table 17-2	Summarizes command-line backup options	655
Figure 17-13	Creating a system repair disc	657

Complete the Tables and Lists from Memory

Print a copy of Appendix C, "Memory Tables" (found on the CD), or at least the section for this chapter, and complete the tables and lists from memory. Appendix D, "Memory Tables Answer Key," also on the CD, includes completed tables and lists to check your work.

Definitions of Key Terms

Define the following key terms from this chapter, and check your answers in the glossary.

Backup, Backup and Restore applet, incremental backup, normal backup, Wbadmin, system repair disc

This chapter covers the following subjects:

- **Restoring Files and Folders:** When a file or folder has become corrupted, improperly modified, or deleted, you can restore it from a backup to undo any harmful changes. This section describes the procedures available for restoring files and folders.

- **System Restore:** This feature enables you to restore your computer to a previous point in time. You need to know how to recover your computer from problems caused by improper configuration, malware, or other situations.

- **Recovering Your Operating System from Backup:** In this section, you learn how to use a system image backup to fully restore your computer in the event of a hardware failure.

- **Advanced System Startup Options:** Similar to previous versions of Windows, Windows 7 provides a comprehensive list of advanced startup options that can help you recover your computer from different types of problems. You are expected to know which option you should use under a given set of circumstances.

CHAPTER 18

Configuring System and File Recovery

You have just learned how to create backups of files, folders, and your operating system in Chapter 17, "Configuring Backups." It is time to now take a look at what to do with these backups—in other words, how to use them to restore components anywhere from a single damaged file to your entire operating system. At the same time, as a Windows 7 support technician, you must be able to perform various methods to recover a computer that does not start properly. Microsoft has provided a wide range of utilities that enable you to perform these recovery tasks, and expects you to know how to use them as part of the 70-680 exam.

"Do I Know This Already?" Quiz

The "Do I Know This Already?" quiz enables you to assess whether you should read this entire chapter or simply jump to the "Exam Preparation Tasks" section for review. If you are in doubt, read the entire chapter. Table 18-1 outlines the major headings in this chapter and the corresponding "Do I Know This Already?" quiz questions. You can find the answers in Appendix A, "Answers to the 'Do I Know This Already?' Quizzes."

Table 18-1 "Do I Know This Already?" Foundation Topics Section-to-Question Mapping

Foundations Topics Section	Questions Covered in This Section
Restoring Files and Folders	1–3
System Restore	4–5
Recovering Your Operating System from Backup	6–8
Advanced System Startup Options	9–10

1. You are unsure that the backup of your Windows 7 computer you created last week contains all the desired files. What is the best thing to do to check this backup?

   a. Restore the backup and watch for messages asking you whether you want to copy and replace files in the same location.

   b. Use the **In the following location** option to specify a different folder to save the restored files, and then check the contents of the folder you specified.

   c. Use the Search option and specify each file that you want to check.

   d. Simply browse the backed-up files and verify that all required files are present.

2. You need to restore Emily's profile because her account was accidentally deleted. You browse the backup to the `C:\Users\Emily` folder. Which of the following will be restored when you restore this folder? (Choose all that apply.)

   a. Emily's documents

   b. Emily's email messages

   c. Applications Emily has installed

   d. Application settings Emily has configured

   e. Files Emily has downloaded from the Internet

3. You are working on an important report that your boss needs first thing tomorrow morning and discover that an entire section that took you several days to prepare is missing. Your computer is running Windows 7 Professional. What should you do to get this section back with the least amount of effort and ensure that you do not lose your most recent changes?

   a. Access the Previous Versions tab of the report's Properties dialog box and select a version from a couple of days ago. Then click **Copy**.

   b. Access the Previous Versions tab of the report's Properties dialog box and select a version from a couple of days ago. Then click **Restore**.

   c. Restore from a backup created a couple of days ago. When prompted, select the **Copy but keep both files** option.

   d. Restore from a backup created a couple of days ago and select the option to restore to another location.

4. You have downloaded and installed an application that you thought would improve your productivity, but you discover that this application has overwritten several drivers and other essential files. You would like to return your computer to its status as of the day before you downloaded the application. What should you do to accomplish this task with the least amount of effort?

   a. Roll back the affected drivers.

   b. Restore your user profile to that of the most recent backup created before the application was downloaded.

   c. Restore your operating system from a system image backup.

   d. Use System Restore and specify the desired date.

5. An update that you downloaded from the Internet has resulted in your sound card not working. Checking Device Manager, you discover that the sound card is using a problematic driver. What should you do to correct this problem most rapidly?

   a. Roll back the affected driver.

   b. Download and install a new driver from the sound card manufacturer's website.

   c. Use System Restore and specify a date before the download occurred.

   d. Use a system repair disk to repair your computer.

6. You want to fully restore your computer to default functionality because of a virus infestation that has affected multiple locations on the hard drive. Which type of backup should you use for this restore?

   a. Windows Complete PC Backup

   b. System State Backup

   c. System Image Backup

   d. System Repair Disk

   e. System Restore

7. Your computer's hard disk has failed and you have installed a new 1.5 TB hard disk. You are lucky enough to have created a system image backup a week ago. What should you do to get your computer up and running again with the least amount of effort and without losing your installed applications?

   a. Start your computer with a system repair disk and choose the option to use a system image you created earlier to recover your computer.

   b. Start your computer with a system repair disk and choose the option to reinstall Windows.

   c. Start your computer with a system repair disk and choose the System Restore option.

   d. Start your computer with a Windows 7 DVD and perform an in-place upgrade of Windows.

8. You use a system repair disk to start your computer and choose the **Use recovery tools that can help fix problems starting Windows** option. Which of the following recovery options can you select to repair your computer? (Choose three.)

   a. Startup Repair

   b. System Restore

   c. System Image Recovery

   d. Device Driver Rollback

   e. Recovery Console

9. You install a new video driver and reboot your computer. The display shows a large number of horizontal lines and nothing is legible, so you are unable to log on. What should you do to correct this problem with the least amount of effort?

   a. Reboot your computer, press **F8**, and select **Safe Mode**. Then perform a device driver rollback.

   b. Reboot your computer, press **F8**, and access the **Last Known Good Configuration** option.

   c. Reboot your computer, press **F8**, and select **Enable low-resolution video (640x480)**. Then perform a device driver rollback.

   d. Use the system repair disk to reboot your computer and then select the **System Restore** option.

10. You install a new network card driver and reboot your computer. After entering your password, you attempt to access servers on your network but are unable to access any of them. A minute later, your display becomes garbled and you cannot access any recovery options. What should you do to correct this problem with the least amount of effort?

    a. Reboot your computer, press **F8**, and select **Safe Mode**. Then perform a device driver rollback.

    b. Reboot your computer, press **F8**, and access the **Last Known Good Configuration** option.

    c. Reboot your computer, press **F8**, and select the **System Restore** option.

    d. Use the system repair disk to reboot your computer and then select the **System Restore** option.

Foundation Topics

Restoring Files and Folders

Chapter 17 introduced you to the Backup and Restore Control Panel applet that enables you to perform various backup and restore options. We looked at backing up files and folders, creating a system image, and creating a system repair or recovery disc. Now we turn our attention to using this applet for restoring information that you have backed up.

Using Windows Backup to Recover Data

After you have performed a backup, the Backup and Restore Control Panel applet makes it simple to restore data in the event of a hardware or software failure of some kind. Use the following procedure to restore data:

Step 1.   Click **Start > Control Panel > System and Security > Backup and Restore**. You can also click **Start**, type `restore` in the Start Menu Search field, and then select **Backup and Restore** from the programs list. This brings up the Backup and Restore applet, as you learned in Chapter 17.

Step 2.   In the Restore section, click **Restore my files**. The Restore Files dialog box shown in Figure 18-1 appears.

Figure 18-1   The Restore Files dialog box enables you to locate the files and folders you want to restore.

Step 3.   To restore a file, click **Browse for files**, or to restore a complete folder, click **Browse for folders**. You receive the dialog box shown in Figure 18-2.

Figure 18-2   You can browse for the files or folders that you want to restore.

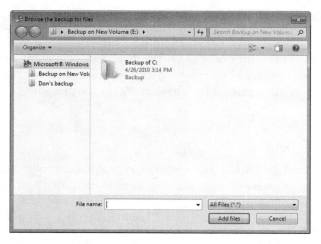

Step 4.   Browse this dialog box for the files or folders you want to restore, and then double-click the desired item(s). You are returned to the Restore Files dialog box with these item(s) added to the list in this dialog box.

Step 5.   If you do not know the name of an item you want to restore, or are unsure of its folder location, click **Search**, and then type all or part of the filename or folder name to search for it in the dialog box that appears. Select the desired item and click **OK** to return to the previous dialog box.

Step 6.   When finished selecting files or folders, click **Next**.

Step 7.   The Where do you want to restore your files? screen shown in Figure 18-3 enables you to select a location to save the restored files. Make an appropriate selection and then click **Restore** to restore the files.

Step 8.   If any file you are restoring already exists in the same location, you receive the message box shown in Figure 18-4. Select the appropriate option to resolve this conflict.

Step 9.   Windows displays a message box that charts the progress of file restoration. When completed, it informs you. Click **Finish**.

CAUTION   You should make a habit of testing your backups and restores. Ensure that you are creating valid backups by performing test restores on a regular basis. Use the In the following location option shown in Figure 18-3 to restore data to a different folder and to verify that the restored data is present. Otherwise, you might not realize something is wrong with your backups until it is too late.

Figure 18-3   The Where do you want to restore your files? screen enables you to select a location to save the restored files.

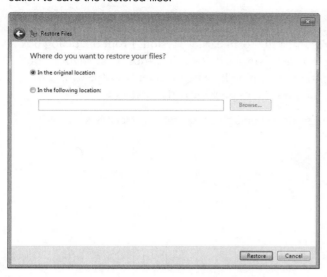

Figure 18-4   If a file already exists, you receive this message box, enabling you to either keep the current file or replace it.

Windows 7 also provides the following additional options for restoring files and folders:

- **Choose a different date:** Select this option from the dialog box shown previously in Figure 18-1 to restore a file to an earlier version. From the dialog box shown in Figure 18-5, select the desired date (the drop-down list enables you to choose several settings that determine how many older backups will be displayed). Then click **OK** and proceed as previously discussed.

Figure 18-5   You can choose from various available dates for restoring older versions of files or folders.

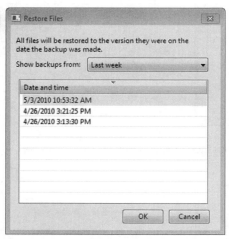

- **Restore all users' files:** Enables you to restore files belonging to other users of this computer.

- **Select another backup to restore files from:** Useful if you have backed up your computer to an additional drive. This is a recommended procedure for important data; by backing data up to an additional portable drive and storing this drive offsite, you are protected against disasters such as fire or flood. Connect the drive and select this option, and then select the backup location from the dialog box that appears.

> **NOTE**   The restore tool in the Windows 7 Backup and Restore utility is not compatible with the .bkf files created using the Windows NT/2000/XP/Server 2003 Ntbackup program. However, Microsoft makes a version of the Windows NT Backup and Restore utility available for download, should you need to restore backups created on an older Windows computer. To obtain details on using this utility and download a version that is appropriate for the edition of Windows 7 that you are running, access "Description of the Windows NT Backup Restore Utility for Windows 7 and for Windows Server 2008 R2" at http://support.microsoft.com/kb/974674.

Restoring User Profiles

When a user logs on to a Windows 7 computer, the operating system generates a *user profile*. This profile is comprised of desktop settings, files, application data, and the specific environment established by the user. For example, a user named Peter logs on to Windows 7, changes his desktop wallpaper to a picture of his dog, edits the user information in Microsoft Word, configures a dial-up connection to his Internet service provider (ISP), and adjusts the mouse so that it is easier to double-click. When Sharon logs on to the same computer using her own account, she sees the default settings for Windows 7, not Peter's settings. When Peter logs on next, Windows finds Peter's existing profile and loads his settings—the wallpaper, the Word data, the dial-up connection, and the mouse click settings.

When Windows 7 is connected to a Windows network, you can configure a user profile to roam the network with the user. Because the profile is stored in a subfolder in the Users folder on the %systemdrive% volume, you can configure the profile to be placed on a network drive rather than a local hard disk, thereby making it accessible to the user regardless of which computer she is using.

User profiles enable users to customize their own settings without impairing another user's configuration. User profiles were developed in response to organizations that routinely provided shared desktop computers. In cases where a user absolutely requires certain settings to use the computer comfortably, having to share a computer with another person who then removes the needed configuration can be frustrating, plus it causes a loss of productivity. Another advantage to user profiles is that, when used in conjunction with network storage of data, the desktop computer is easily replaceable—users can use any computer on the network without having to perform extra tasks to customize the computer to suit their needs.

You can restore a user profile in exactly the same fashion as already described for restoring files and folders. Simply select **Browse for folders** and browse to the Users folder. Double-click this folder and then select the username as shown in Figure 18-6 to restore this user's profile. Then select **Add folder** and follow the remainder of the procedure already described to complete restoring the user's profile. You can also restore a portion of a user's profile by double-clicking the username to open the profile and then selecting the subfolder or subfolders (such as Contacts, Documents, Downloads, and so on) you need to restore.

Using Shadow Copies to Restore Damaged or Deleted Files

First introduced with Windows XP Professional and continued in Windows 7 is the concept of *volume shadow copies*, which creates shadow copies of files and folders as you work on them so that you can retrieve previous versions of files that you might have corrupted or deleted.

Figure 18-6   Restoring a user's profile.

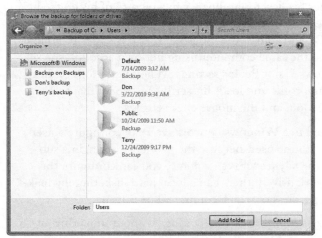

The shadow copy feature, first introduced with Windows XP and Windows Server 2003, is available in the Professional, Enterprise, and Ultimate editions of Windows 7, as well as all editions of Windows Server 2008 R2. This feature creates copies of files in real time as you work on them. It enables you to revert to a previous version of a file should you accidentally delete a file or save unsuitable modifications. In addition, this feature works with Windows Backup to enable the back up of all files, including those that an application might have open currently. Versions of Windows prior to XP skipped any open files, thereby risking incomplete backups. Data is then backed up from the shadow copy rather than from the original volume. Volume shadow copies enable users to work with files on the volume being backed up during the backup process, without the risk of having the backup program skip the open files. Using this technology removes the need for applications to be shut down to ensure a successful, complete backup.

To restore a file or folder, right-click it and choose **Restore previous versions**. This opens the Properties dialog box for the file or folder to the Previous Versions tab, as shown in Figure 18-7. Simply click the desired version and click **Restore** to restore the file or folder. You can also preview any version by selecting it and clicking **Open**; this helps you to choose the version you want to restore. To restore an older version of a file or folder without overwriting the current version, select it and click **Copy**. Then select the location to which you want to copy the previous version from the Copy Items dialog box that appears.

Figure 18-7   The Previous Versions tab of a file or folder's Properties dialog box enables you to restore the file or folder to a previous point in time.

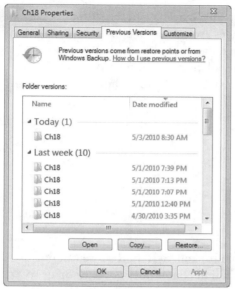

TIP   You can use the Copy function to restore multiple previous versions of a file; for example, if you need to track changes to a document that have been made by several individuals. From the Copy Items dialog box, select a folder to which you want to copy the document and then click **Make New Folder** to create a folder to which you want to copy the document. Repeat this process as often as required, creating new folders with descriptive names for each previous version you want to restore. You can also rename each previous version with an appropriate descriptive name as you restore it so that you do not need to create multiple folders.

CAUTION   Creation of shadow copies requires that the Volume Shadow Copy service be started. By default, this service is set for Manual startup, which means that the service will be started as required. If the service is set to Disabled, shadow copies will not be created. If you cannot find the expected previous versions of a folder or file, access the Services console and check the startup type for this service, and reset it to Manual if required.

System Restore

First introduced with Windows XP, System Restore enables you to recover from system problems such as those caused by improper system settings, faulty drivers, or incompatible applications. It restores your computer to a previous condition without damaging any data files such as documents and email. System Restore is useful when problems persist after you have uninstalled incompatible software or device drivers, or after downloading problematic content from a website, or when you are having problems that you cannot diagnose, but that have started recently.

During normal operation, System Restore creates snapshots of the system at each startup and before major configuration changes are started. It stores these snapshots and manages them in a special location on your hard drive. It also copies monitored files to this location before any installation program or Windows itself overwrites these files during application or device installation. These snapshots include backups of the following settings:

- Registry
- DLL Cache Folder
- User Profiles
- COM+ and WMI Information
- Certain Monitored System Files

System restore points are not the same as data backup. System Restore can restore applications and settings to an earlier point in time, but it does not back up or restore any personal data files. Use the Backup and Restore application to back up personal data files or recover any that have been deleted or damaged.

Running System Restore

You can run System Restore from the System Properties dialog box. The following steps show you how:

Step 1.   Click **Start**, right-click **Computer**, and then choose **Properties**.

Step 2.   On the left pane of the System applet, select **System protection**.

Step 3.   If you receive a UAC prompt, click **Yes**. This opens the System Protection tab of the System Properties dialog box, as shown in Figure 18-8.

Step 4.   Click **System Restore** to open the System Restore dialog box, as shown in Figure 18-9. You can also access this dialog box directly from the Start menu Search field by typing `restore` and clicking **System Restore**.

Step 5.   Click **Next** to display the Restore your computer to the state it was in before the selected event page shown in Figure 18-10.

Step 6.   Select a date and time to which you want to restore your computer, and then click **Next**.

Step 7.   In the Confirm your restore point dialog box, note the warning to save open files and then click **Finish** to perform the restore.

Figure 18-8   The System Protection tab of the System Properties dialog box includes a System Restore option.

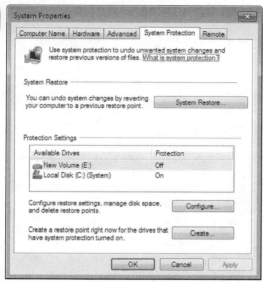

Figure 18-9   The System Restore dialog box enables you to restore system files and settings.

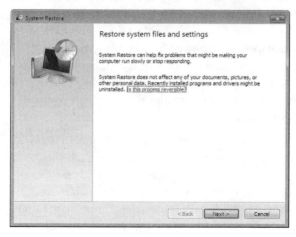

Step 8.   You receive a message box informing you that System Restore may not be interrupted and cannot be undone. Click **Yes** to proceed. The computer performs the restore and then shuts down and restarts.

Step 9.   Log back on as an administrator. You receive a System Restore message box informing you that the restore completed successfully. Click **Close**.

Figure 18-10 System Restore enables you to select the date and time to which you want to restore your computer.

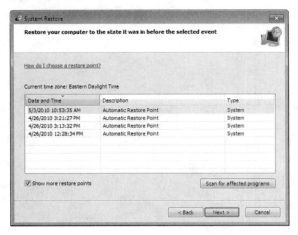

Configuring System Restore Properties

The System Protection tab of the System Properties dialog box previously shown in Figure 18-8 also lets you configure several settings related to its performance on any volume on your computer. From this tab, select the desired volume and click **Configure** to bring up the System Protection for (drive) dialog box shown in Figure 18-11. By default, System Protection is enabled for the %systemdrive% volume only. To configure System Protection for another volume, select either of the **Restore system settings and previous versions of files** or **Only restore previous versions of files** options as desired, and then adjust the slider under Disk Space Usage to specify the maximum amount of disk space that will be used. If you want to free up space for other uses, click **Delete** and then confirm your intention by clicking **Continue** in the message box that appears.

System Restore also enables you to create restore points. This is valuable in situations such as downloading or installing applications or other material from the Internet. Before downloading any problematic material, create a manual restore point first. From the System Protection tab of the System Properties dialog box, select **Create** and follow the instructions provided. Provide a descriptive name that helps you identify the restore point later.

TIP The Restore-Computer PowerShell cmdlet also enables you to restore your computer to a restore point that you specify as a parameter to this cmdlet. This command restarts the computer and then performs the restore. It is supported only on client operating systems including Windows 7, Windows Vista, and Windows XP. Fore more information including available parameters and options, refer to "Restore-Computer" at http://technet.microsoft.com/en-us/library/dd347740.aspx.

Figure 18-11   You can configure several options that govern how System Protection works on any given disk volume.

Device Driver Rollback

Windows 7 enables you to roll back a device driver to a previous version should you encounter problems with a device after updating an existing driver. Problems of this nature occasionally occur when a manufacturer releases a new driver that has not been thoroughly tested and Windows Update automatically downloads and installs the driver without your intervention.

Although you can use System Restore to restore your computer to a point prior to installation of the problematic driver, it is normally much simpler to roll back the driver. To do so, open Device Manager, right-click the device, and choose **Properties**. From the Driver tab of the device's Properties dialog box shown in Figure 18-12, click **Roll Back Driver** and then click **Yes** in the Driver Package rollback message box that appears. If this option is unavailable (dimmed), Windows does not have a previous version of the driver. If necessary, you can restart your computer in Safe Mode and then employ this procedure to roll back a troublesome driver. We discuss Safe Mode later in this chapter.

NOTE   For more information on device drivers, including updating and rollback, refer to Chapter 7, "Configuring Devices and Updates."

Figure 18-12   The Driver tab of a device's Properties dialog box enables you to roll back the driver.

Recovering Your Operating System from Backup

In Chapter 17, you learned how to create a system image backup. Recall that the system image includes all files necessary to fully restore your computer in the event of a hardware failure. The Recovery option in Control Panel enables you to use this backup to restore your computer if problems have occurred, or if you want to restore your settings to a different computer. Use the following steps:

Step 1.   Click **Start**, type **recovery** in the Start menu Search field, and then select **Recovery** from the Programs list. This starts the Control Panel Recovery applet.

Step 2.   Click **Advanced recovery methods** to display the Choose an advanced recovery method page shown in Figure 18-13.

Step 3.   Select the **Use a system image you created earlier to recover your computer** option.

Step 4.   The Do you want to back up your files? page shown in Figure 18-14 enables you to back up user files that might have changed since your last user file backup. Click **Back up now** to do so or **Skip**, as required.

Step 5.   If you choose **Back up now**, Windows Backup starts and enables you to perform a backup as described in Chapter 17.

Figure 18-13   You can either use a system image or reinstall Windows to recover your computer.

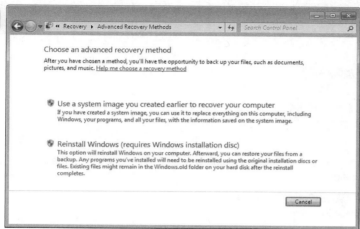

Figure 18-14   You receive an option to back up your files before proceeding.

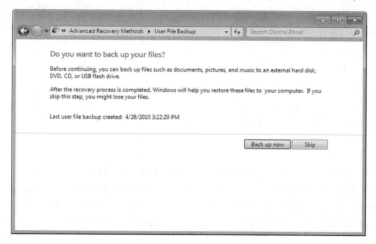

Step 6.   After the backup has completed (or immediately, if you choose **Skip** in step 4), you are prompted to restart your computer to continue the recovery. Click **Restart** to proceed.

Step 7.   The computer restarts and proceeds with the recovery. You receive the System Recovery Options dialog box shown in Figure 18-15. If necessary, make any needed changes and then click **Next**.

Step 8.   You receive the Select a system image backup dialog box shown in Figure 18-16. Specify the location of the most recent system image or choose the **Select a system image** option and then click **Next**.

Figure 18-15   Make any needed changes in the System Recovery Options dialog box.

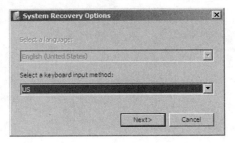

Figure 18-16   The Select a system image backup dialog box enables you to select the image to be used in the restore operation.

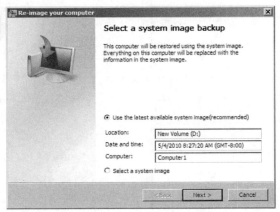

Step 9. From the Re-image your computer dialog box shown in Figure 18-17, click **Install drivers** if you need to reinstall drivers for required disks or **Advanced** to specify additional options for restarting the computer and checking for disk errors. When finished, click **Next** to continue.

Step 10. Review the options provided and click **Back** if you need to make any changes. Then click **Finish** to proceed with re-imaging your computer.

Step 11. You are warned that all data on the drives to be restored will be replaced with data from the image. Click **Yes** to continue.

Step 12. A message box charts the progress of re-imaging your computer, and then the computer restarts. After logging back on, a Recovery message box informs you that recovery has completed and offers an option to restore user files. Click **Restore my files** to do so or **Cancel** to quit.

Figure 18-17 The Re-image your computer dialog box provides several additional restore options.

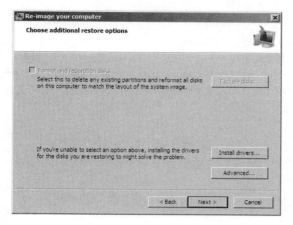

Using a System Repair Disk

In Chapter 17, we introduced the system repair disc, also known as a *system recovery disk*, which is a CD or DVD that contains the files needed to reboot your computer for recovering from a serious error.

The system repair disk attempts to automatically recover a computer that will not start normally by loading a Startup Repair routine that provides several recovery options. The following are some of the problems that Startup Repair can attempt to repair:

- Missing, corrupted, or incompatible device drivers

- Missing or corrupted system files or boot configuration settings

- Improper or corrupted Registry keys or data

- Corrupted disk metadata, such as the master boot table, boot sector, or partition table

Startup Repair provides a diagnostics-based, step-by-step troubleshooting tool that enables end users and tech support personnel to rapidly diagnose and repair problems that are preventing a computer from starting normally. When Startup Repair determines the problem that is preventing normal startup, it attempts to repair this problem automatically. If it is unable to do so, it provides support personnel with diagnostic information and suggests additional recovery options.

Use the following procedure to run the System Repair disk and invoke Startup Repair:

Step 1.   Insert the system repair disk and restart your computer. If necessary, press a key to boot the computer from the system repair disk as opposed to the hard disk.

Step 2. A `Windows is loading files` message appears and then the System Recovery Options dialog box previously shown in Figure 18-15 appears. Make any changes that might be needed and then click **Next**.

Step 3. The computer searches for Windows installations and then displays all operating systems found in the dialog box shown in Figure 18-18. Select the operating system to be recovered. If desired, select the option labeled **Restore your computer using a system image that you created earlier**. Then click **Next**.

Figure 18-18 You can recover any Windows operating system found on the computer or restore from a previously created system image.

Step 4. If you select the latter option, recovery continues in the same manner as described in the previous section. If you have selected a Windows Vista or Windows 7 installation option, you receive the System Recovery Options dialog box shown in Figure 18-19. Click **Startup Repair**.

Figure 18-19 The System Recovery Options dialog box provides five options for repairing an unbootable computer.

Step 5.   Startup Repair searches for problems and displays the message shown in Figure 18-20. If it does not detect any problem, it informs you and offers links to view diagnostic and repair details or advanced system recovery options. Select either of these links if desired; otherwise, click **Finish**.

Figure 18-20   Startup Repair checks your computer for problems.

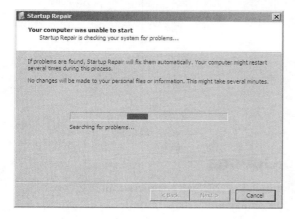

Step 6.   If Startup Repair detects and repairs a problem, it displays a message such as the one in Figure 18-21, informing you that it repaired the problem successfully. To see details of its actions, click the link provided. If it is unable to repair the problem, it offers additional information and links (see Figure 18-22).

Figure 18-21   When Startup Repair fixes a problem, it informs you of its actions.

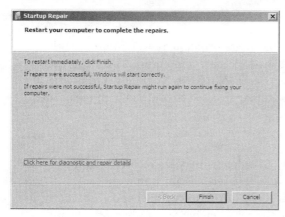

Step 7.   When you are finished, click **Finish** and then click **Restart** to restart your computer normally.

Figure 18-22   When Startup Repair is unable to repair the problem, it provides links to additional details and log files.

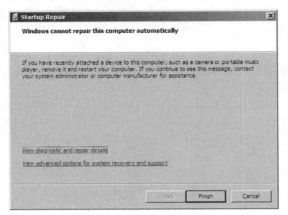

Advanced System Startup Options

Windows 7 provides several tools that help you recover from computer failures that prevent you from starting Windows normally. This section looks at several of these tools, including the Last Known Good Configuration, Safe Mode, and System Restore.

NOTE   The Recovery Console, which was used in Windows 2000/XP/Server 2003 to perform command-line–based recovery procedures, has been replaced by the command prompt option in System Recovery Options (refer to Figure 18-19 shown previously). For additional information on the actions you can perform using this option, refer to "Command-line reference for IT Pros" in Windows 7 Help and Support Center.

If Windows fails to start because of a hardware problem, power failure, or other serious problem, you might receive the message shown in Figure 18-23. For a simple problem such as a power failure, select **Start Windows Normally**. Otherwise, leave the default of **Launch Startup Repair** selected to proceed with repair options discussed earlier in this chapter.

Last Known Good Configuration

Every time a user logs on successfully, Windows 7 makes a recording of the current Registry settings known as a *control set*. These settings are stored under HKEY_LOCAL_MACHINE\SYSTEM\CurrentControlSet and are made available so that they can be used if the computer is unable to boot because of configuration changes such as installation of new device drivers or inappropriate modification of settings. For example, if configuration changes result in a computer displaying the Blue Screen of Death (BSOD) or modified display settings render the screen unreadable, you can revert to the previous settings by using the Last Known Good Configuration. Perform the following steps to use this configuration.

Figure 18-23 When Windows fails to start, you receive an option to run Startup Repair.

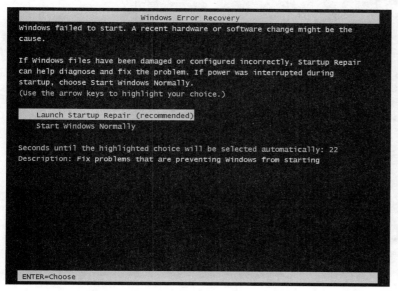

```
                        Windows Error Recovery
Windows failed to start. A recent hardware or software change might be the
cause.

If Windows files have been damaged or configured incorrectly, Startup Repair
can help diagnose and fix the problem. If power was interrupted during
startup, choose Start Windows Normally.
(Use the arrow keys to highlight your choice.)


    Launch Startup Repair (recommended)
    Start Windows Normally


Seconds until the highlighted choice will be selected automatically: 22
Description: Fix problems that are preventing Windows from starting




ENTER=Choose
```

Step 1. Restart the computer (use the reset button if necessary).

Step 2. Press **F8** as the boot sequence begins to display the Windows Advanced Boot Options menu as shown in Figure 18-24.

Step 3. Use the arrow keys to select **Last Known Good Configuration (Advanced)** and then press **Enter**. The computer proceeds to start from this configuration.

Step 4. When the logon screen appears, log on as usual.

CAUTION Using the Last Known Good Configuration is the easiest way to correct changes when you are unable to log on as a result of various problems. However, you can use this option only to correct changes made since the previous logon. If you are able to log on successfully and then encounter a problem caused by a previous configuration change, you are unable to use the Last Known Good Configuration because this configuration is overwritten at the successful logon. Under these circumstances you must select a different startup option.

NOTE You can use the **Repair Your Computer** option shown in Figure 18-24 to access the same repair options described in the section "Using a System Repair Disk."

Figure 18-24   Windows 7 provides several advanced startup options that you can use when unable to start normally.

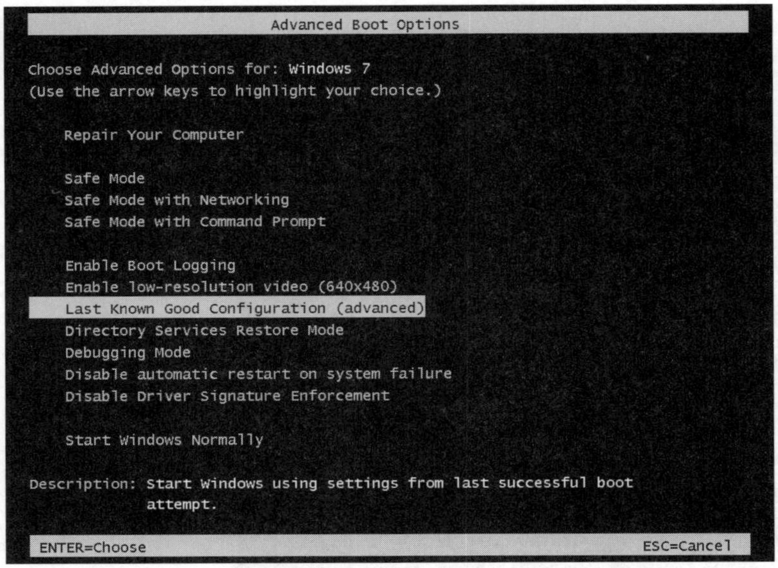

```
                        Advanced Boot Options

 Choose Advanced Options for: Windows 7
 (Use the arrow keys to highlight your choice.)

    Repair Your Computer

    Safe Mode
    Safe Mode with Networking
    Safe Mode with Command Prompt

    Enable Boot Logging
    Enable low-resolution video (640x480)
    Last Known Good Configuration (advanced)
    Directory Services Restore Mode
    Debugging Mode
    Disable automatic restart on system failure
    Disable Driver Signature Enforcement

    Start Windows Normally

 Description: Start Windows using settings from last successful boot
              attempt.


 ENTER=Choose                                    ESC=Cancel
```

Safe Mode

Safe Mode starts your computer with a minimal set of drivers (mouse, VGA, and keyboard) so that you can start your computer when problems with drivers or other software are preventing normal startup. The following are several problems with which you can use Safe Mode for recovering your computer:

- **The computer stops responding or runs very slowly:** You can start in Safe Mode and use various tools for diagnosing and correcting the problem. You can also uninstall software, roll back device drivers, or use System Restore to roll back the computer to an earlier point in time.

- **The computer display is blank or distorted:** After starting in Safe Mode, you can use the Control Panel Display applet to select appropriate display settings.

- **The computer fails to respond after new hardware or software is installed:** Use Safe Mode to uninstall software, disable hardware devices in Device Manager, roll back drivers, or restore the computer using System Restore.

To enter Safe Mode, follow the procedure outlined previously for Last Known Good Configuration and select **Safe Mode** from the options displayed in Figure 18-24. You can also select either of the following options:

- **Safe Mode with Networking:** Starts network drivers as well as the other basic drivers. This is useful if you need to copy files from a network location.

- **Safe Mode with Command Prompt:** Starts the computer to a command prompt. This can be useful if you cannot obtain a normal GUI.

NOTE You can use Safe Mode and System Restore together to correct problems. If you are unable to start your computer properly but are able to start in Safe Mode, you can perform a System Restore from Safe Mode to restore your computer to a functional state.

CAUTION Safe Mode has its limitations. Safe Mode does not repair problems caused by lost or corrupted system files or problems with basic drivers. In these cases, you might be able to use Startup Repair.

Boot Logging

The Enable Boot Logging option, selected from the options displayed previously in Figure 18-24, starts Windows 7 normally while creating the \windows\ntbtlog.txt file, which lists all drivers that load or fail to load during startup. From the contents of this file, you can look for drivers and services that are conflicting or otherwise not functioning. After using this mode, reboot to Safe Mode to read the ntbtlog.txt file and identify the problematic driver.

Low Resolution Video (640×480)

The low-resolution video option starts Windows 7 at the lowest video resolution with 16 colors. This is useful if you have selected a display resolution and refresh rate that is not supported by your monitor and video card, or if you have installed a driver that is incompatible with your video card. You can go to the Display Properties dialog box and select an appropriate video option and then reboot to normal mode.

Debugging Mode

Debugging mode provides advanced troubleshooting options for experienced developers and administrators. It sends kernel debug information to another computer via a serial cable.

Disable Automatic Restart on System Failure

The Disable Automatic Restart on System Failure option prevents Windows 7 from automatically restarting if a problem is causing your computer to enter an endless loop of failure, restart attempt, and failure again.

Disable Driver Signature Enforcement

The Disable Driver Signature Enforcement option permits you to install unsigned drivers or drivers that are improperly signed. After you reboot normally, driver signatures are again enforced but the unsigned driver is still used.

Exam Preparation Tasks

Review All the Key Topics

Review the most important topics in the chapter, noted with the key topics icon in the outer margin of the page. Table 18-2 lists a reference of these key topics and the page numbers on which each is found.

Table 18-2   Key Topics for Chapter 18

Key Topic Element	Description	Page Number
List	Shows you how to set up and run Windows Backup for the first time.	665
Figure 18-1	Locating files and folders to be restored.	665
Figure 18-5	Windows lets you restore files or folders from any previously performed backup.	668
Figure 18-7	Using Shadow Copy to restore a file to a previous version.	671
Figure 18-8	System Protection provides several options for restoring your operating system to a previous point in time.	673
Figure 18-13	You have two advanced system recovery methods for recovering your computer.	677
Figure 18-16	Restoring your computer from a system image.	678
Figure 18-19	You have five options for recovering your computer.	680
Figure 18-24	Windows provides a series of advanced boot options for starting a computer that will not start normally.	684

Complete the Tables and Lists from Memory

Print a copy of Appendix C, "Memory Tables" (found on the CD), or at least the section for this chapter, and complete the tables and lists from memory. Appendix D, "Memory Tables Answer Key," also on the CD, includes completed tables and lists to check your work.

Definitions of Key Terms

Define the following key terms from this chapter, and check your answers in the glossary.

Last Known Good Configuration, Safe Mode, Startup Repair, System Restore, Backup and Restore applet, user profile, shadow copies, System Protection

Practice Exam

1. You are a desktop support technician for your company. Management has asked you to implement smart cards as a secure authentication procedure for all computers in your company, and you must install smart card readers on all company computers. You have purchased a supply of the readers from an independent vendor. The shipment comes with a CD-ROM that includes drivers and support applications for Windows 7. Although the drivers are digitally signed, the support applications are not. You must ensure that the correct drivers and applications are installed.

   How should you proceed? (Each answer represents part of the solution. Choose two.)

   a. Insert the CD-ROM and install the drivers and applications before installing the reader.

   b. Insert the CD-ROM and install the drivers and applications after installing the smart card reader.

   c. Select **Update Driver** from the reader's properties in Device Manager to install the drivers and applications.

   d. Attach the smart card reader to the computer before inserting the CD-ROM.

   e. Attach the smart card reader to the computer after inserting the CD-ROM.

2. Joe is a landscape designer who travels extensively throughout his state working with residential and business clients to create award-winning gardens and beauty spots. He uses a Windows 7 Ultimate portable computer and needs to conserve power when traveling on the road. He has noticed that when he presses the power button on his computer, it does not fully turn off and continues to consume battery power with the result that he has occasionally lost work.

   Joe would like to ensure that the computer is always completely off when he presses the power button when on battery power. What should he do? (Each answer represents a complete solution. Choose two.)

a. From the Windows Mobility Center, select the **Power saver** option.

b. From the Power Options Control Panel applet, select **Change plan settings** under the current power plan, and then select **Change advanced power settings**. In the Power Options dialog box, expand the **Power buttons and lid** category, expand **Power button action**, and then select **Shut down**.

c. From the Power Options Control Panel applet, select **Change plan settings** under the current power plan, and then select **Change advanced power settings**. In the Power Options dialog box, expand the **Power buttons and lid** category, expand **Start menu power button**, and then select **Shut down**.

d. From the Power Options Control Panel applet, select **Choose what the power buttons do**, and then select **Shut down** under On Battery for When I press the power button.

e. From the Power Options Control Panel applet, select **Change plan settings** under the current power plan. Then change the Put the Computer to Sleep setting under On Battery to **Never**.

f. From the Power Options Control Panel applet, select the **Power saver** power plan.

3. You have upgraded your computer to Windows 7 Home Premium. After several of your friends experienced problems with unwanted software being installed on their Windows XP Home Edition computers, you want to ensure that Internet Explorer displays a warning should a web page attempt to install software or run programs on your computer. Which of the following should you do?

a. From the Safety menu in Internet Explorer, ensure that the SmartScreen Filter is enabled.

b. On the Privacy tab of the Internet Options dialog box, select the **Block All Cookies** option.

c. On the Privacy tab of the Internet Options dialog box, ensure that the pop-up blocker is enabled.

d. On the Security tab of the Internet Options dialog box, ensure that Protected mode is enabled for the Internet zone.

4. Shirley is a tech support technician for Que Publishing. In recent months, many users in her company have received new Windows 7 computers. A manager named Karen needs to access a website operated by a subsidiary company named Cert Guide. She reports that she receives the message `Your security settings prohibit the display of unsigned ActiveX controls` when she attempts to connect.

Que Publishing has a policy requiring that users can download unsigned ActiveX controls from approved Internet websites only. Shirley verifies that Karen's Internet Explorer settings are configured as the defaults.

What should Shirley do to enable Karen to access the website operated by Cert Guide? (Each answer represents part of the solution. Choose two.)

a. Add the Cert Guide website to the Local intranet zone.

b. Add the Cert Guide website to the Trusted sites zone.

c. In the Security Settings–Internet Zone dialog box, enable the **Download unsigned ActiveX controls** option.

d. In the Local Intranet dialog box, clear the **Include all sites that bypass the proxy server** check box.

e. In the Local Intranet dialog box, clear the **Require server verification (https:) for all sites in this zone** check box.

f. In the Trusted Sites settings, clear the **Require server verification (https:) for all sites in this zone** check box.

g. In the Security Settings–Internet Zone dialog box, enable the **Initialize and script ActiveX controls not marked as safe for scripting** option.

5. Alex has refurbished an older laptop computer by installing a new 2.5 GHz processor, a 300 GB hard disk, and 2 GB RAM. The computer has a CD-ROM drive that he has not replaced, but no DVD-ROM drive. Alex would like to install Windows 7 Home Premium on this computer but is concerned because the installation media is published on a DVD-ROM disc. Which of the following methods can he use to install Windows 7 on this computer? (Choose all that apply.)

a. A network share

b. A portable hard drive

c. Windows Deployment Service (WDS)

d. A USB thumb drive

6. You are a help desk administrator for Billbored's LLC. The company's network consists of an Active Directory Domain Services (AD DS) forest with an "empty" root domain and two child domains: one that houses user and desktop accounts and another that houses proprietary resources and the majority of administrative accounts. All employees are running Windows 7 Enterprise computers and receive IP addresses from DHCP servers. The company has implemented folder redirection so that computers can be moved about the network without affecting users' data. A new user calls the help desk because he cannot open his Documents folder. You ask him to open the Network folder, and he reports that the folder is empty. You then provide him with the instructions to run Ipconfig. He reports that the screen states:

```
Windows IP Configuration
Ethernet adapter Local Area Connection:
Media State ......................: Media disconnected
Connection-specific DNS Suffix: . :
IPv4 address ....................:192.168.0.88
Subnet Mask .....................:255.255.255.0
Default Gateway .................:
```

What should you instruct the user to do?

a. Click **Start,** type `cmd` in the Start menu Search field, and press **Enter**. At the command prompt, type `netstat -e` and press **Enter**.

b. Plug the cable into the wall outlet, and the other end into the Ethernet adapter of the computer, and if they are already connected then ensure the connection is not loose. When they are firmly connected, open the command prompt window and type `ipconfig/release,` and then follow that command with `ipconfig /renew`.

c. Plug the cable into the wall outlet, and the other end into the Ethernet adapter of the computer, and if they are already connected then ensure the connection is not loose. When they are firmly connected, access the Network and Sharing Center. Click **Manage network connections**. Then right-click the local area connection and choose **Diagnose**, and in the dialog box that appears, click **Reset the network adapter Local Area Connection**.

d. Click **Start,** type `cmd` in the Start menu Search field, and press **Enter**. At the command prompt, type `nbtstat -RR` and press **Enter**.

e. Click **Start** and in the Start Menu Search field, type `notepad c:\windows\system32\drivers\etc\hosts;` then press **Enter**. Add the IP address of the DHCP server to the end of the HOSTS file.

7. Abby is a graphics art designer for an advertising agency. She is using a Windows 7 Ultimate computer that contains three hard disks, two of 400 GB capacity and one of 200 GB capacity. The operating system and several design applications are installed on the 200 GB disk, which is configured as the `c:` drive. The applications access very large files and consume considerable disk I/O actions. She needs to configure the hard disks on her computer for optimum operation of these applications.

Which of the following actions should Abby take to accomplish this objective? (Each correct answer represents part of the solution. Choose two.)

a. Convert the two 400 GB disks to dynamic storage.

b. Convert all three disks to dynamic storage.

c. Create a spanned volume from the two 400 GB disks.

d. Create a spanned volume from all three disks.

    e. Create a striped volume from the two 400 GB disks.

    f. Create a striped volume from all three disks.

8. Peter is an office administrator and part-time technical support specialist for an insurance office that employs eight agents. The office runs a workgroup containing eight Windows 7 Professional computers and one Windows Server 2008 computer. Sarah creates an intranet website on her Windows 7 computer that includes current fees for services offered by the medical office.

Other users in the office attempt to access Sarah's website but are unable to access it. In fact, other users are unable to reach Sarah's computer using the `ping` command with either the name or IP address of her computer. But Sarah is able to reach personal files that are stored on the server.

How should Peter advise Sarah to enable other users to access her website? (Each answer represents part of the solution. Choose two.)

    a. Open the Windows Firewall with Advanced Security on Local Computer dialog box. On the Public Profile tab, select the **Allow** option under Inbound Connections.

    b. In the Windows Firewall Control Panel applet, click **Change notification settings**. In the Customize Settings for Each Type of Network dialog box that appears, click **Turn off Windows Firewall** under Home or work (private) network location settings.

    c. In the Windows Firewall Control Panel applet, click **Change notification settings**. In the Customize Settings for Each Type of Network dialog box that appears, clear the check box labeled **Block all incoming connections, including those in the list of allowed programs**.

    d. In the Windows Firewall Control Panel applet, click **Allow a program or feature through Windows Firewall**. In the Allow programs to communicate through Windows Firewall dialog box that appears, select **Remote Administration**.

    e. In the Windows Firewall Control Panel applet, click **Allow a program or feature through Windows Firewall**. In the Allow programs to communicate through Windows Firewall dialog box that appears, click **Change settings**, select **Add port**, and then add **TCP port 80 (Hypertext Transfer Protocol, HTTP)** to the exceptions list.

    f. Open the Windows Firewall with Advanced Security on Local Computer dialog box. From the left pane, right-click **Inbound Rules** and choose **New Rule**. From the New Inbound Rule Wizard, select **Port** and then specify **TCP** and **Specific local ports**. Type **80** in the text box and complete the remaining steps of the wizard.

9. Kevin is a consultant who is responsible for deploying 200 new Windows 7 Enterprise computers. The client firm has requested that Kevin use the

Deployment Workbench and ensure that the Windows 7 images he uses are placed on a distribution share and include all required device drivers, applications, and updates. Which deployment tool should Kevin use?

   a. Windows Deployment Services (WDS)

   b. Microsoft Deployment Toolkit (MDT) 2010

   c. Deployment Image Servicing and Management (DISM)

   d. Remote Installation Services (RIS)

10. Brendan is a desktop support technician for his company, which operates an Active Directory network consisting of a single domain. All client computers run Windows 7 Enterprise. No policies have been configured in the domain for use of BitLocker or data recovery.

A user named Olga has configured BitLocker Drive Encryption on her laptop, which is equipped with a Trusted Platform Module (TPM). While configuring BitLocker, Olga chose the option to print the recovery password. Olga contacts Brendan and informs him that she is unable to start the computer and cannot remember the recovery password or locate the document on which she printed it. What should Brendan do to enable access to the data?

   a. Access the BitLocker applet in Control Panel and select the **Turn Off BitLocker** option.

   b. Insert a USB flash drive.

   c. Access the BitLocker Drive Encryption Recovery Console.

   d. Reformat the laptop's hard drive and reinstall Windows 7. Then restore the data from backup.

11. Ethan is a desktop support specialist for a small company that operates a workgroup-based network. A Windows 7 Ultimate computer in his office contains several shared folders that users in the office must have access to. Ethan needs to ensure that only users with valid usernames and passwords can access the shared folders on this computer, including the Public folder. What should he do?

   a. Configure each shared folder with the usernames of the users who need access.

   b. In the Network and Sharing Center, enable the **Public folder sharing** option.

   c. In the Network and Sharing Center, disable the **Network discovery** option.

   d. In the Network and Sharing Center, enable the **Password protected sharing** option.

12. Tom is upgrading a computer from Windows Vista Ultimate to Windows 7 Ultimate. The computer is a 2.8 GHz Pentium IV and has 1 GB of RAM and a 250 GB hard disk. After the first restart, Tom is informed that the computer is infected with a master boot record virus. What should he do before continuing with the installation?

a. Reboot the computer to Windows Vista Ultimate, and scan and remove all viruses.

b. Remove or disable any antivirus software installed in Windows Vista.

c. Run the Check Compatibility Online option and follow any recommendations provided.

d. Run `fixmbr.exe` from the Windows 7 DVD-ROM.

e. Upgrade the computer to 2 GB of RAM.

13. Owen is a systems administrator for an engineering firm located in Dallas. The firm operates an Active Directory Domain Services (AD DS) domain in which servers run Windows Server 2008 R2 and client computers run Windows 7 Enterprise. Software developers have created two specialized applications that engineers use in their day-to-day work. These engineers have user accounts that belong to the Engineers global group. Some junior employees who do not need access to these applications have fooled around with them, wasting valuable time and jeopardizing vital corporate functions. These applications are not digitally signed, and it is not anticipated that this status will change. Owen's boss would like him to ensure that only authorized employees have access to these applications. Other applications should not be blocked. What should Owen do? (Each answer represents part of the solution. Choose two.)

a. In a GPO linked to the domain, configure an AppLocker path rule that blocks execution of the specialized applications.

b. In a GPO linked to the domain, configure an AppLocker publisher rule that blocks execution of the specialized applications.

c. In a GPO linked to the domain, configure an AppLocker file hash rule that blocks execution of the specialized applications.

d. Specify an exception that allows other programs covered by the rule to execute.

e. Specify an exception that allows members of the Engineers group to run the applications.

14. Wayne is a consultant who is preparing a bid for a multimillion dollar contract his company is hoping to land. After working all week on an important document for this bid, Wayne discovers one Friday that this document file has become corrupted. Wayne's computer runs Windows 7 Enterprise and has system protection enabled on all volumes.

Wayne's computer is configured with the default backup options. He must recover the latest version of this document so that he can complete the bid with minimal delay because the submission deadline is next Monday. What should Wayne do?

a. Use System Restore to restore the computer to its state of yesterday afternoon.

b. Use the Restore previous versions option.

c. Restore the document from the most recent backup.

d. Use a system repair disc.

15. Teresa is preparing a script that will create a virtual hard disk (VHD) on which she will be installing Windows 7. She opens an administrative command prompt and starts the DiskPart utility. Which of the following commands can she use to create a fixed VHD of size 40 GB and named w7.vhd?

a. `create vdisk file="c:\w7.vhd" maximum=40 type=fixed`

b. `create vdisk file="c:\w7.vhd" maximum=40000 type=fixed`

c. `create partition primary file="c:\w7.vhd" maximum=40 type=fixed`

d. `create partition primary file="c:\w7.vhd" maximum=40000 type=fixed`

16. Paul is using a computer that he has upgraded from Windows Vista Home Premium to Windows 7 Home Premium. He notices that whenever he starts many of his programs or attempts to access the properties of many Control Panel items, he is presented with a UAC prompt. Paul believes that he should not be receiving all these prompts but still would like to be prompted when he attempts to install a program or when websites attempt to make changes to his computer's configuration. What should Paul do?

a. Create shortcuts for the programs that should not receive UAC prompts. On these shortcuts, access the **Compatibility** tab and select the **Run this program as an administrator** option.

b. Access the User Account Control Settings dialog box and select **Always notify me when: Programs try to install software or make changes to my computer; I make changes to windows settings**.

c. Access the User Account Control Settings dialog box and select **Default–Notify me only when programs try to make changes to my computer**.

d. Access the User Account Control Settings dialog box and select **Never notify me when: Programs try to install software or make changes to my computer; I make changes to windows settings**.

17. Sheila is a help desk technician for White's Photographic Supply, a company that caters to digital photographic needs of camera stores and portrait studios. All desktop computers run either Windows XP Professional or Windows 7 Professional and receive TCP/IP configuration information from a DHCP server on the network.

One evening, several administrators shut down a file server named Server1 for some much-needed maintenance tasks. Several hours later they restart the server and move it to a different subnet. The next morning, Sheila receives calls from several users reporting that they cannot connect to shared folders on Server1. Which of the following commands should Sheila instruct the users to run on their computers?

a. `ipconfig /flushdns` and `ipconfig /registerdns`

b. `ipconfig /release` and `ipconfig /renew`

c. `ipconfig /displaydns`

d. `nbtstat -R`

e. `nslookup`

18. Nancy is a sales representative for a high technology firm that includes aerospace and defense firms as well as the U.S. military among its clients. She uses a notebook computer running Windows 7 during her visits to client locations. This computer holds confidential data for all clients including data that could provoke a national security incident should the notebook fall into the wrong hands.

Nancy decides to use BitLocker drive encryption to secure the contents of the notebook, which is not equipped with a TPM module. The computer already contains several folders with important data files. Which of the following does she need to do to enable BitLocker on her notebook without losing any existing data? (Each correct answer represents part of the solution. Choose two.)

a. Use a system repair disc to access the System Recovery Options dialog box and select the **Command prompt** option. Then repartition the hard drive in the notebook to hold a 40 GB Windows partition and a single partition that holds all data files.

b. Use a system repair disc to access the System Recovery Options dialog box and select the **Command prompt** option. Then repartition the hard drive in the notebook to hold a 1.5 GB system partition and a single partition that holds both operating system files and the data files.

c. In the Local Group Policy Editor, enable the **Choose how BitLocker-protected operating system drives can be recovered** policy.

d. In the Local Group Policy Editor, enable the **Require additional authentication at startup** policy and select the **Allow BitLocker without a compatible TPM** option.

e. Use a USB flash drive to hold the encryption keys and access password.

f. Use a floppy disk to hold the encryption keys and access password.

19. Colby is a network administrator for a company that operates an Active Directory Domain Services (AD DS) domain in which all servers run Windows Server 2008 R2. Client computers run a mix of Windows Vista Enterprise and Windows 7 Professional. Much employee time has been lost to users playing games on their computers during work hours, so Colby would like to create a policy that blocks execution of any games including those installed by default in Windows. He opens a Group Policy object (GPO) linked to the domain. Which of the following policies should he create and enable?

    a. He should create an AppLocker policy that specifies a path rule that blocks all games.

    b. He should create an AppLocker policy that specifies a hash rule that blocks all games.

    c. He should use Software Restriction Policies to create a policy specifying a path rule that blocks all games.

    d. He should use a Software Installation Policy that uninstalls all game software from affected computers.

20. Robert is using the User State Migration Tool (USMT) to migrate 100 users in his company from old Windows XP computers to newly purchased computers running Windows 7 Enterprise. He will be using a file server running Windows Server 2008 R2 as a storage location for user documents and settings during the course of the migration. He also wants to ensure that all data is encrypted and password-protected to minimize the possibility of unauthorized access during the migration. What migration strategy should Robert use?

    a. He should use a wipe-and-load migration utilizing a compressed migration store.

    b. He should use a side-by-side migration utilizing a compressed migration store.

    c. He should use a wipe-and-load migration utilizing a hard-link migration store.

    d. He should use a side-by-side migration utilizing a hard-link migration store.

21. Kristin has just purchased a new portable computer that runs Windows 7 Ultimate and is setting up a new wireless connection that will enable her to access her company's wireless access point, which uses the IEEE 802.1x authentication method and the TKIP encryption protocol.

Kristin accesses the Manually connect to a wireless network dialog box and enters the network name and passphrase. She needs to select a security type that will enable connection using the TKIP encryption protocol by default without the need to enter a preshared key or passphrase. Which security type should she select?

    a. **WPA-Personal**

    b. **WPA2-Personal**

    c. **WPA-Enterprise**

    d. **WPA2-Enterprise**

22. Lynn is responsible for performance management of 50 computers running Windows 7 Enterprise in her company's Active Directory Domain Services (AD DS) domain. She has configured Group Policy to assist her in collecting event logs from these computers onto a single Windows 7 Ultimate computer in her work cubicle so that she can identify problems rapidly and respond to users' concerns. Which of the following should she configure on this computer?

    a. A source-initiated event subscription

    b. A collector-initiated event subscription

    c. A filter that views logs by event source

    d. A filter that views logs by user and computer

23. George is using a computer that is equipped with a 100 GB hard disk containing three partitions. The first partition holds an installation of Windows XP Professional, the second partition holds data files, and the third partition is currently empty.

George would like to install Windows 7 on his computer but still have access to Windows XP. What should he do?

    a. Boot the computer with the Windows 7 DVD. Select the option to perform a clean installation, select the first partition, format this partition with the NTFS file system, and install Windows 7 on this partition.

    b. Boot the computer with the Windows 7 DVD. Select the option to upgrade Windows, and install Windows 7 on the first partition.

    c. Boot the computer with the Windows 7 DVD. Select the option to perform a clean installation, select the third partition, format this partition with the NTFS file system, and install Windows 7 on this partition.

    d. Boot the computer with the Windows 7 DVD. Select the option to perform a clean installation, format both the first and third partitions, install Windows 7 on the first partition, and then install XP on the third partition.

24. Mike uses a Windows 7 Home Premium computer for web browsing, word processing, and photo editing. One day, while on an interesting website, he is offered a new add-on for download. So, he downloads and installs this add-on and then restarts Internet Explorer. However, he is unable to access any websites even though Internet Explorer starts properly. What should Mike do?

    a. Reset Internet Explorer to default settings.

    b. Run Internet Explorer using the No Add-ons option.

    c. Uninstall the add-on from the Manage Add-ons dialog box.

    d. Uninstall the add-on from the Control Panel Programs applet.

25. Ross is the network administrator for Bones, LLC. He has configured a new Windows 7 Professional desktop computer that will be used to share files for a folder named FOLDER. Ross has set the security permissions to be as follows:

- Authenticated users—Allow Read

- Administrator—Allow Full Control

- Accounting—Allow Modify

Ross has set the shared folder permissions to be as follows:

- Everyone—Allow Read

- Accounting—Deny Full Control

- Administrators—Allow Full Control

Jill is a member of the Accounting group and the Administrators group. When Jill tries to access FOLDER from another computer on the network, what access rights will she have?

- **a.** Full Control
- **b.** Modify
- **c.** Read
- **d.** None

26. Ann is responsible for maintaining Windows 7 images for her company. Graphic artists use computers prepared from an image that includes Adobe Photoshop among other applications. This image currently includes Photoshop CS4, but Ann would like to update the image by replacing Photoshop CS4 with Photoshop CS5. What should she do? Each correct answer represents a complete solution. Choose two.

- **a.** Use DISM with the /Remove-Package option to remove Photoshop CS4, and then use DISM with the /Add-Package option to add Photoshop CS5 to the image.
- **b.** Use DISM with the /Remove-Package option to remove Photoshop CS4, and then use the New Application Wizard in MDT 2010 to add Photoshop CS5 to the image.
- **c.** Use DISM with the /Remove-Apps option to remove Photoshop CS4, and then use the New Application Wizard in MDT 2010 to add Photoshop CS5 to the image.
- **d.** Use DISM with the /Remove-Package option to remove Photoshop CS4, and then use DISM with the /Add-Apps option to add Photoshop CS5 to the image.

27. Louise is a computer consultant that provides assistance to several clients, working as much as possible from her home office, where she has a Windows 7 Professional desktop computer. She has just entered into a new contract to provide support to a client named DLJ Software, a software company that specializes in high-end computer games as well as complex mathematical and graphical art programs. The company's network is connected to the Internet through a firewall operated on a Windows Server 2003 computer.

An employee named Andrew sends Louise a Remote Assistance invitation. Louise accepts the invitation but cannot connect to Andrew's computer. Part of Louise's contract is the providing of assistance to users in DLJ Software's, clerical, human resources, and financial departments, most of whom are not very knowledgeable about advanced computer technologies.

What should Louise do so she can fulfill her tasks?

a. Ask Andrew to select the **Allow connections only from computers running Remote Desktop with Network Level Authentication (more secure)** option.

b. Ask Andrew to clear the **Allow this computer to be controlled remotely** option.

c. Ask Andrew to add Louise's domain user account to the Remote Desktop Users local group on his computer.

d. Request that a network administrator open TCP port 3389 on the company firewall.

28. Maria is responsible for a new Windows 7 computer. She has set up Windows Backup to back up her computer's system image and document files but after a few weeks realizes that an important folder containing images she has shot with her digital camera is not being backed up. So, she opens the Backup and Restore applet and it appears to her as seen in the exhibit. Which location should she select to modify the backup settings to include these digital images?

a. Create a system image

b. Create a system repair disc

c. Back up now

d. Manage space

e. Change settings

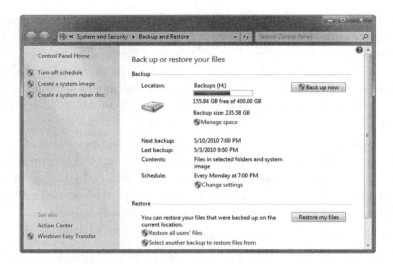

29. Brenda has experienced problems in the past with updates downloaded from the Microsoft website causing applications to fail unexpectedly. So, she has configured Windows Update on her computer to check for updates but to let her choose whether to download and install them.

   A few months later, Brenda realizes that an optional patch that her work colleagues have received is missing from her machine, and its performance has suffered as a consequence. What should she do to view and restore this update while retaining the option to let her choose whether to download and install future updates?

   a. From the Windows Update applet in Control Panel, click **Change settings**, and then select the check box labeled **Give me recommended updates the same way I receive important updates**.

   b. From the Windows Update applet in Control Panel, click **Change settings**, and then select the **Install updates automatically (recommended)** option.

   c. From the Windows Update applet in Control Panel, click **View update history**, select the update, and then click **Restore**.

   d. From the Windows Update applet in Control Panel, click **Restore hidden updates**, select the update, and then click **Restore**.

30. Bob is the desktop administrator of his company. A user named Emily installs a tax calculation application on her Windows 7 Professional computer. After she restarts her computer, she observes that the computer runs very slowly.

Emily uninstalls the tax calculation application and restarts her computer. However, the computer still runs very slowly. She asks Bob to return her computer to its previous condition as soon as possible while preserving her data and computer settings. What should Bob do?

a. Restart the computer with a system repair disc and use the most recent system image to restore the computer.

b. Restart the computer in safe mode and restore Windows 7 using the most recent system restore point.

c. Edit the Registry to remove all references to the tax calculation application.

d. Restart the computer in safe mode and use `Wbadmin.exe` to restore the most recent system image.

e. Restart the computer by using the Last Known Good configuration.

31. Kane is a desktop support specialist for his company. He is responsible for enforcing policies on a Windows 7 Ultimate computer that are designed to reduce the chance of outsiders hacking passwords on this computer, so he configures the password policy as shown in the exhibit.

The company security auditor comes around and looks at Kane's password settings. He informs Kane that one of these settings actually reduces the security of the computer's passwords from its default. Which setting should Kane modify?

a. Enforce password history

b. Minimum password age

c. Minimum password length

d. Password must meet complexity requirements

e. Store passwords using reversible encryption

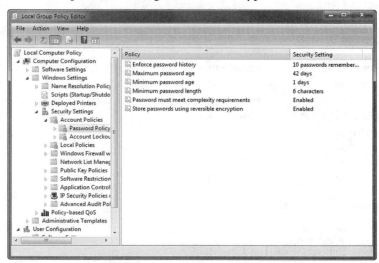

32. Erin is a temporary employee who is performing accounting tasks for a clothing company named Femme Fatale. The company operates an Active Directory Domain Services (AD DS) domain. The company has its own certification authority (CA) hierarchy hosted on three Windows Server 2008 R2 computers. The company also has a secured internal website named https://www.femmefatale.com/financial.

Erin needs to connect to this website to perform her job, but when she attempts to reach it from her computer running Windows 7 Ultimate, she receives a message that the website certificate is not from a trusted source. She checks with company employees and is assured that this is the correct website name. What should she do to connect successfully to the website?

a. From the Security tab of the Internet Options dialog box, change the security level of the Local Intranet zone to **Low**.

b. From the Advanced tab of the Internet Options dialog box, enable the Use **SSL 2.0** option.

c. From the Content tab of the Internet Options dialog box, install the website certificate to the Trusted Root Certification Authorities certificate store on her computer.

d. From the Security tab of the Internet Options dialog box, clear the **Enable Protected Mode** check box.

33. Judy has run System Image Manager to create an answer file that she intends to distribute to users on a USB flash drive that will be used for installing Windows 7 Professional from a DVD-ROM. She needs to ensure that the answer file has been given the proper name. Which name should this file have?

a. `Unattend.txt`

b. `Unattend.xml`

c. `Winnt.sif`

d. `Reminst.sif`

34. Phil is concerned with the performance of his Windows 7 computer because it does not appear to be responding as rapidly as it did a few months ago. He creates a data collector set and logs his performance over the period of a workday. Then he uses Performance Monitor to display the collected data and notices the following results:

- Memory\Pages/sec: 62

- Processor\% Processor Time: 71

- LogicalDisk\% Disk Time: 74

- PhysicalDisk\% Disk Time: 63

- System: Processor Queue Length: 3

Which of the following system upgrades should Phil do first?

a. Add a faster hard disk.

b. Add a larger hard disk.

c. Add additional memory.

d. Install a faster processor.

e. Install a second processor.

35. Jason has been using a computer running Windows XP Home Edition for several years. The computer has suited him well, especially with the several hardware upgrades he has performed over the years, but he is excited about all the new features available in Windows 7, so he purchases the upgrade to Windows 7 Home Premium.

Jason is unsure that all the hardware on his computer will work properly once he has installed Windows 7. What should he do first?

a. Run the Windows 7 Upgrade Advisor.

b. Run the Windows 7 Program Compatibility Wizard.

c. Run the Windows 7 Easy Transfer Wizard.

d. Access the Device Manager in Windows XP and upgrade the drivers on all hardware devices with the Windows 7–compatible ones.

36. Kim is responsible for maintaining the virtual hard disk images used on Windows 7 computers in her company. A VHD mounted on the `f:` drive of a computer contains an image of Windows 7 Home Premium. Kim would like to upgrade this VHD to Windows 7 Ultimate. Which command should she use for this purpose?

a. `dism /image:f:\ /Set-Edition:Ultimate`

b. `dism /image:f:\ /Get-Edition:Ultimate`

c. `wdsutil /image:f:\ /Set-Edition:Ultimate`

d. `wdsutil /image:f:\ /Get-Edition:Ultimate`

37. You are a tax preparer for Taxes in Texas. All your computers are configured with Windows 7 Enterprise. Because of recent privacy laws, you cannot allow anyone other than official tax preparers to have access to your tax preparation materials for clients. You store all client files in the CLIENTS folder on your NTFS-formatted `c:` drive, as do all other tax preparers in your workgroup. You have four staff persons who work in the office. They are in the STAFF group. All tax preparers are in the PREP local group. One of the STAFF group members is also a member of the local Administrators group on each computer. What can you do to configure your system to ensure the privacy laws are met?

    a. Delete all users and groups from your computer.

    b. Configure the PREP group to have full control of the C:\CLIENTS folder.

    c. Run `cipher /e` on the C:\CLIENTS folder. Add certificates for each tax preparer to the encryption attributes.

    d. Run `cipher /d` on the C:\CLIENTS folder. Add certificates for the STAFF group.

38. Evan is the systems administrator for his company. All desktop and portable computers in the company run Windows 7 Enterprise. Users in the Research department bring their portable computers to the conference room for a bi-weekly planning meeting. These users require a simple means of manually placing their computers in a low-power condition without using the Start menu. In addition, they need their computers to resume normal operating condition as rapidly as possible.

How should Evan configure the Power Options properties to accomplish these needs?

    a. Configure the computers to use the Power saver power plan.

    b. Configure the computers to use the High performance power plan.

    c. Configure the Critical battery alarm on the computers to enable sleep mode when the battery capacity drops to 5%.

    d. Configure the computers to enter sleep mode when the lid is closed.

    e. Configure the power button on each computer to enable hibernation.

39. Donna is a developer who needs to work with more than one operating system to assess how her applications behave in different conditions. Her computer has a 300 GB hard disk containing three partitions formatted with the FAT32 file system. Windows XP Professional is installed on the first partition. She wants to install Windows 7 Ultimate in a dual-boot configuration.

What should she do?

    a. While running Windows XP, insert the Windows 7 DVD-ROM and follow the prompts provided. When she receives the option to select the type of installation, select **Custom (advanced)**. Then select the second partition to install Windows 7, and format this partition with the NTFS file system.

    b. While running Windows XP, insert the Windows 7 DVD-ROM and follow the prompts provided. When she receives the option to select the type of installation, select **Upgrade**. Then select the second partition to install Windows 7, and format this partition with the NTFS file system.

    c. Do not reformat any partition. While running Windows XP, insert the Windows 7 DVD-ROM and follow the prompts provided. When she receives the option to select the type of installation, select **Custom (advanced)**. Then select the second partition to install Windows 7.

d. Do not reformat any partition. While running Windows XP, insert the Windows 7 DVD-ROM and follow the prompts provided. When she receives the option to select the type of installation, select **Upgrade**. Then select the second partition to install Windows 7.

40. Barbara has become frustrated as of late because she receives a large quantity of pop-up advertisements when she is browsing the Internet from her Windows 7 Home Premium computer. She would like to eliminate pop-up advertisements from appearing on all websites except http://www.myfavoritesite.com. What should she do? (Each answer represents part of the solution. Choose two.)

a. From the Pop-up Blocker Settings dialog box, select the **Low** blocking level.

b. From the Pop-up Blocker Settings dialog box, select the **Medium** blocking level.

c. From the Pop-up Blocker Settings dialog box, select the **High** blocking level.

d. From the Pop-up Blocker Settings dialog box, add the http://www.myfavoritesite.com website as an allowed website.

e. From the Security tab of the Internet Options dialog box, add the http://www.myfavoritesite.com website to the Trusted Sites zone.

41. Jim is deploying 150 new Windows 7 Professional computers to users in his company. These users have old computers running either Windows XP Professional or Windows Vista Business that are to be donated to a charity that refurbishes the computers for use by schoolchildren. Jim must ensure that documents, personal data, and settings for all users are copied from their old computers to their new computers. What should he do?

a. Run the Sysprep utility on each old computer. Use a third-party disk imaging utility to create an image of the hard disk. After installing Windows 7 Professional, apply each user's disk image to his or her new computer.

b. Use `Robocopy.exe` to copy all documents and personal data from each user's old computer to the new computer. Run the `Regedit` command to export the computer's Registry to a `.reg` file. In the installation script for each new computer, copy the documents and personal data to the computer, and import the `.reg` file.

c. Use the Recovery Console to start each old computer. Copy the Registry files, documents, and personal data to a network share. In the installation script for each new computer, copy the information from the network share to each new computer.

    d. Run the `Scanstate.exe` utility on each user's old computer. Save the information created by the utility to a network share. Run the `Loadstate.exe` utility in the installation script for each new computer, and specify the network share as the data source.

42. Leona is the domain administrator for an advertising agency, which operates an Active Directory Domain Services (AD DS) domain. There are 15 Windows Server 2008 computers, 75 Windows XP Professional computers, and 63 Windows 7 Professional computers. The company has just purchased a Plug and Play digital camera for use by the advertising designers, and Leona has installed this camera on a Windows 7 Professional computer.

Leona needs to verify that the drivers for the camera are signed, and she needs to view information about the signer of the drivers. What should she do?

    a. Run the `sigverif` utility.

    b. View the driver information from Device Manager.

    c. View the driver information from the Components node of the System Information tool.

    d. Verify that the device is listed on the latest version of the Windows 7 Logo Program for Hardware list.

43. John installs a new application on his computer. The computer immediately exhibits errors and shuts down with a Stop error. John doesn't know what to do and calls you before he restarts his computer. What do you tell John?

    a. Restart the computer with the Last Known Good Configuration.

    b. Restart the computer in safe mode and then use System Restore.

    c. Use a system image to restore the computer.

    d. Use the Startup Repair Tool to repair the computer's configuration.

44. You are the network administrator for a company that operates a network consisting of two subnets separated by a router, as shown in the exhibit.

The subnets are configured with IPv4 addresses according to the network ranges shown in the exhibit. The router interfaces are configured with the IP addresses 172.16.0.1 and 172.16.192.1, respectively, and all client computers are configured with static IP addresses.

A user named Evelyn reports that she is unable to access any computers on Subnet 2. She does not have any difficulty accessing computers and their shared resources on Subnet 1. You run `ipconfig` on her computer and notice that it is configured with the IP address 172.168.11.201, the subnet mask of

255.255.255.0, and the default gateway 172.16.0.1. How should you modify the configuration of Evelyn's computer so that she is able to reach computers on Subnet B?

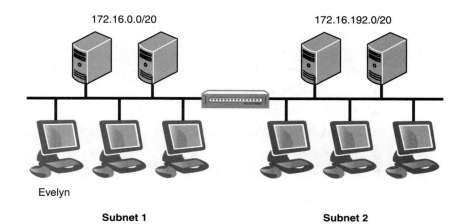

172.16.0.0/20   172.16.192.0/20

Evelyn

Subnet 1   **Subnet 2**

   a. Change the subnet mask on Evelyn's computer to 255.255.240.0.

   b. Change the subnet mask on Evelyn's computer to 255.255.255.0.

   c. Change the default gateway on Evelyn's computer to 172.16.192.1.

   d. Access the Advanced TCP/IP Settings dialog box on Evelyn's computer and configure an additional IP address on the 172.16.11.192/20 network.

45. Tara is working at her Windows 7 Ultimate desktop computer and wants to use PowerShell to obtain a list of processes running on a Windows Server 2008 R2 machine named Server8. Which of the following commands should she use?

   a. `icm server8 {get-process}`

   b. `icm server8 get-process`

   c. `winrs -r:server8 {get-process}`

   d. `winrs -r:server8 get-process`

   e. `winrm server8 {get-process}`

   f. `winrm server8 get-process`

46. Lawrence is a network administrator for the head office of a large bank. As part of a general systems upgrade, the bank has purchased 150 new 500 GB hard disks to be installed in Windows 7 Enterprise computers. These computers already have a single hard disk of 60 to 200 GB capacity, which is configured as a basic volume and formatted with the NTFS file system.

Lawrence needs to write a script that will automate the creation of a simple volume on a new hard disk and mount it to the `c:\mounted` folder on a Windows 7 Enterprise computer. From the list of commands given, choose the commands that he must include in the script and arrange them in the proper order.

a. `Convert basic`

b. `Convert dynamic`

c. `Create partition simple disk 1`

d. `Assign mount=c:\mounted`

e. `Select disk 1`

f. `Create volume simple disk 1`

g. `Add disk=1`

h. `Mount volume c:\mounted`

47. Stephanie is a tech support specialist for a company that operates an Active Directory Domain Services (AD DS) network with two domains in a single forest. She has installed Windows 7 Professional on a new computer with the aid of an answer file named `Unattend.xml`. The answer file instructs the computer to join one of the domains, but after the final reboot, Stephanie discovers that the computer has not joined the domain. Which of the following logs should she use to troubleshoot this problem?

a. `Setupapi.dev.log`

b. `Setuperr.log`

c. `Scesetup.log`

d. `Setupact.log`

e. `Netsetup.log`

48. Connie is using a Windows 7 Professional laptop computer to connect to her company's VPN server using Secure Sockets Tunneling Protocol (SSTP) to make the connection to a VPN server running Windows Server 2003. When she attempts to complete the connection, she receives an error code 741 accompanied by the message stating that `The local computer does not support the required encryption type`. What should Connie do to make a successful connection to the VPN server?

a. Access the Security tab of the VPN Connection Properties dialog box, select **No encryption allowed (server will disconnect if it requires encryption)**, and then click **OK**.

b. Access the Security tab of the VPN Connection Properties dialog box, select **Require encryption (disconnect if server declines)**, and then click **OK**.

   c. Access the Security tab of the VPN Connection Properties dialog box, select **Maximum strength encryption (disconnect if server declines)**, and then click **OK**.

   d. Reconfigure her VPN connection to use the Point to Point Tunneling Protocol (PPTP) instead.

49. Lisa installs a new device driver and reboots her Windows 7 Ultimate computer. Before the logon screen appears, the computer displays the Blue Screen of Death (BSOD) with the error IRQL_NOT_LESS_OR_EQUAL. Which of the following should she do first?

   a. Press **F8** to access the Advanced Startup Options menu. Select **Safe Mode**, roll back the device driver, and restart the computer.

   b. Press **F8** to access the Advanced Startup Options menu. Select **Last Known Good Configuration**.

   c. Use a system repair disc to restart the computer. From the System Recovery Options dialog box, choose **System Restore**.

   d. Use a system repair disc to restart the computer. From the System Recovery Options dialog box, choose **Command Prompt**, remove the device driver, and restart the computer.

50. Terri has used the DiskPart utility to create a VHD named `c:\w7.VHD` of size 50 GB on her computer. She now accesses the Disk Management snap-in and wants to create a partition on the VHD that she can use for installing a virtual copy of Windows 7. However, she cannot find the disk listed. What does she need to do before she can proceed further?

   a. She needs to format the disk.

   b. She needs to convert the disk to dynamic storage.

   c. She needs to mark the disk as active.

   d. She needs to mount the disk.

51. Harry is a tech support specialist for a consultant that operates an Active Directory Domain Services (AD DS) domain. Client computers run either Windows XP Professional or Windows 7 Enterprise. The consultant has landed a contract with a major engineering firm that runs a series of intranet websites containing material and project specifications. Employees of Harry's company running Windows XP Professional are able to access these intranet websites without problem but employees with Windows 7 computers report that the websites display with large portions of data missing. What should Harry do to ensure that the Windows 7 computers display the websites properly without the need for users to perform their own configuration actions?

a. Configure a Group Policy object (GPO) and enable the **Use Policy List of Internet Explorer 7 sites** policy. Then add the URLs of the engineering firm's intranet websites to the list in this policy.

b. Configure a GPO and disable the **Turn off Compatibility View** policy.

c. Configure a GPO and enable the **Turn on Internet Explorer Standards Mode for Local Intranet** policy.

d. Add the URLs of the engineering firm's intranet websites to the Local Intranet zone.

52. You are manually preparing a target computer for deployment-based installation of Windows 7 using Microsoft Deployment Toolkit (MDT) 2010 and need to use the DiskPart tool to format the computer's hard drive, which is currently blank. How should you boot this computer?

a. Use an MS-DOS floppy disk.

b. Use a Windows 7 installation DVD-ROM.

c. Use a Windows PE CD-ROM.

d. Use a Windows 7 system repair disc.

53. You are the administrator for Grapevines Magazine, a small company of 10 administrative users and four reporters. All the network computers run Windows 7 Professional as members of a workgroup. A reporter named Charles logs on to a computer, opens the System applet in Control Panel, and selects the **Advanced System Settings** link. He receives the message `This program is blocked by group policy. For more information, contact your system administrator` and asks you for assistance. On opening the Local Group Policy Object Editor snap-in to the Security Options subnode, you notice that policies are configured as shown in the exhibit.

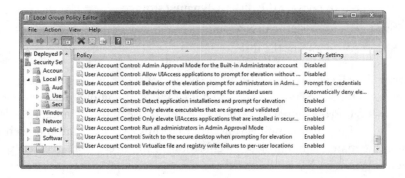

What should you do to enable Charles to access the System Properties dialog box without granting him excess privileges?

   a. Add Charles to the local Administrators group.

   b. Configure the **User Account Control: Behavior of the elevation prompt for standard users** policy to prompt for credentials.

   c. Enable the **User Account Control:** Only **elevate executables that are signed and validated** policy.

   d. Enable the **User Account Control: Switch to the secure desktop when prompting for elevation** policy.

   e. Disable the **User Account Control: Run all administrators in Admin Approval Mode** policy.

54. You have received a new computer running Windows 7 Home Basic. Wanting access to the Media Center and other media-based applications, you purchase and install the upgrade edition of Windows 7 Home Premium.

You want to access several of the old settings contained in the previous operating system files. Where should you look?

   a. `Windows.old` folder

   b. `Program Files` folder

   c. `Users` folder

   d. Software Explorer

55. Don is a technical support specialist for a company that has recently purchased 50 new computers running Windows 7 Professional. A user named Debbie has reported that she is unable to boot the computer, so Don takes a look and ends up completely reinstalling and rebuilding the system from scratch. Don would like to ensure that he can start any nonfunctioning Windows 7 computer and access repair options more rapidly in the future. He accesses the Backup and Restore applet and obtains the dialog box shown in the exhibit. Which option should he select to enable him to start any of these computers in the future?

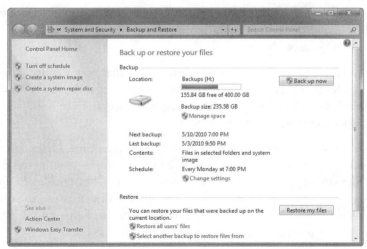

    a. Create a system image

    b. Create a system repair disc

    c. Back up now

    d. Manage space

    e. Change settings

56. Nolan is a network administrator for PQR Company, which operates an Active Directory Domain Services (AD DS) domain named pqr.com. He has set up a Windows Server 2008 R2 computer as a DirectAccess server to facilitate employee connections to the network from client locations. On this server he has created a security group named DA. He must now configure employee client computers for DirectAccess connections. Which of the following must he do? (Each answer represents part of the solution. Choose four.)

    a. Install a computer certificate on each client computer that enables DirectAccess authentication.

    b. Enroll each employee with a user certificate that enables DirectAccess authentication.

    c. Add the user account of each employee to the DA security group.

    d. Add the computer account of each client computer the DA security group.

    e. Configure a Group Policy object (GPO) linked to the domain that specifies IPv6 transition technologies for connection to the DirectAccess server.

    f. Configure a GPO linked to the domain that specifies Secure Sockets Layer (SSL) configuration settings for connection to the DirectAccess server.

    g. Configure a GPO linked to the domain that specifies a name resolution policy including WINS security and DirectAccess settings.

    h. Configure a GPO linked to the domain that specifies a name resolution policy including configuration settings for DNS security and DNS settings for DirectAccess.

57. Helen is a junior executive for an accounting firm that operates an Active Directory Domain Services (AD DS) domain. She uses a Windows 7 Enterprise laptop that is joined to the domain and frequently works from home to prepare briefing documents for top management.

One afternoon, after printing a draft document in the office, Helen left to pick up her children from daycare, and that evening she worked further on this document. She attempted to print her document at home, but nothing happened. Checking her settings, she realized that she sent the document to the office printer. What should Helen do to simplify the process of ensuring that the document is always printed wherever she is working at that time?

a. In the Devices and Printers applet, select both printers, right-click, and choose **Set as default printer** from the context menu.

b. From the Manage Default Printers dialog box, select **Always use the same printer as my default printer**.

c. From the Manage Default Printers dialog box, select **Change my default printer when I change networks**.

d. She cannot do anything other than ensure that the correct printer is selected from the Print menu of the application she is using.

58. Jorge uses a Windows 7 Home Premium computer that is configured to belong to a homegroup. There are two other Windows 7 computers on the network, as well as a home theater system. Jorge has downloaded an extensive collection of music and video files that he would like to play on the home theater system but does not want his children, who use the other two computers, to have access to these files on their computers. What should he do?

a. From the Change Homegroup Settings dialog box, select **Music** and **Videos** in the Share Libraries and Printers section.

b. From the Change Homegroup Settings dialog box, click **Choose media streaming options**. On the dialog box that appears, click **Allowed** opposite the entry for the home theater system and **Blocked** opposite the entry for the other two Windows 7 computers.

c. From the Change Homegroup Settings dialog box, click **Choose advanced sharing settings**. On the dialog box that appears, click **Allowed** opposite the entry for the home theater system and **Blocked** opposite the entry for the other two Windows 7 computers.

d. From the Change Homegroup Settings dialog box, click **Change advanced sharing settings**. Then select **Turn on media streaming**.

59. Sam is an administrator who has worked with Windows XP computers for the past eight years and has only recently become responsible for a shipment of new Windows 7 computers that his company is introducing for replacement of the oldest Windows XP machines. He needs to ensure that the Windows 7 computers continue to run at optimal performance levels and that he can obtain information on problems that might occur. He notices that these computers include a new Reliability Monitor program that logs specific types of events in graphical form. Which of the following types of events can he obtain information about by using this tool? (Choose all that apply.)

a. Application failures

b. Logon failures

c. Windows failures

    d. Improper shutdowns

    e. Sleep failures

60. Michelle is the system administrator for Acme Plumbing, which operates a network with 20 users. This network is configured as a workgroup. Michelle's manager has decided to replace all the computers in the company and at the same time to deploy a new application. He asks Michelle to install the 20 new computers identically using Windows 7 Professional. She is given access rights to the network installation point on a standalone server running Windows Server 2008 R2 and a product key for the volume licensing media. Michelle decides to automate the installation. She does not have any third-party tools or additional servers at her disposal, nor does she have any reference computer on which Windows 7 has already been installed. Which of the following methods should she select to perform the installation with the least amount of administrative effort?

    a. WDS using Deployment Server mode

    b. WDS using Transport Server mode

    c. Microsoft Deployment Toolkit (MDT) 2010

    d. Unattended installation using DVD media

61. Beth is in charge of keeping medical records for a major hospital up-to-date. She accidentally deleted a file for a current patient and emptied the recycle bin before realizing that this file contains important medication information that must be kept handy at all times. The most recent backup of her Windows 7 computer was performed three days ago, but these files have been continuously updated. What should Beth do to recover this file to its most recent state?

    a. Use Windows Backup to recover the file.

    b. Use the volume shadow copy feature to restore the file.

    c. Use the volume shadow copy feature to restore the folder in which the file was located.

    d. Use the System Restore feature.

62. You are the network administrator for Boxes Corp., a box manufacturer. The network consists of 4,000 Windows 2000 and Windows XP computers scattered across several sites, each with its own Windows Server 2008 domain controller. The company operates an Active Directory Domain Services (AD DS) network with a single domain in a single forest. You have been tasked with deploying Windows 7 Professional to a shipment of new computers that will replace the older Windows 2000 computers. To test the process, you have decided to install a new computer by running the Windows 7 Professional installation process across the network before setting up to begin the deployment. Which of the following steps should you perform? Put the steps you should follow in the correct order.

a. Run `Setup.exe`.

b. Boot the computer with a network boot disk.

c. Install Windows Deployment Services (WDS) on the server.

d. Check the client computer's hardware and BIOS for compatibility.

e. Create a network share on a server and copy the Windows 7 Professional Setup files to it.

f. Create a virtual hard disk (VHD) and copy the Windows 7 Professional Setup files to it.

g. Connect to the server's network share containing the Windows 7 Professional Setup files.

63. Fred would like to change the search engine in Internet Explorer 8 temporarily. What should he do?

a. Access the Privacy tab of the Internet Options dialog box and click **Settings**. Select the desired search provider and then click **Set Default**.

b. Access the General tab of the Internet Options dialog box and click **Settings** in the Search section. Select the desired search provider and then click **Set as default**.

c. Click the down arrow next to the Search area in the Internet Explorer address bar. From the menu displayed, select the desired search provider.

d. Click the down arrow next to the Search area in the Internet Explorer address bar. From the menu displayed, click **Manage Search Providers**. Right-click the desired search provider and then click **Set Default**.

64. Greg uses a computer that runs Windows XP Professional. The computer has a 600 GB hard drive configured with three partitions. Greg wants to explore the possibility of using Windows 7 Ultimate, so he installs this operating system on the second partition as a clean install. When he attempts to access the Internet from Windows 7 by means of the computer's PCI Express (PCIe) network

adapter, he is unable to reach any websites. He reboots the computer to Windows XP and is able to access the Internet. After rebooting the computer to Windows 7, he accesses Device Manager and notices a red X on the network adapter. What should he do?

a. Right-click the network adapter and select **Update Driver Software**.

b. Right-click the network adapter and select **Enable**.

c. Right-click the network adapter and select **Scan for hardware changes**.

d. Open Control Panel Windows Update and select the **Check for updates** option.

65. Keisha is a systems administrator for a company that operates an Active Directory Domain Services (AD DS) domain. The word-processing application in use on the network is configured so that all temporary files are created in the folder in which the document is located. A user named Ben is working on some highly confidential information that must receive a high level of protection from unauthorized users. Keisha creates a folder on Ben's Windows 7 Professional computer and moves the confidential files into it. She needs to ensure that only Ben has access to the confidential files and all temporary files created while he is working on them.

Which of the following should Keisha do? (Each answer represents part of the solution. Choose three.)

a. Assign the Users group the Deny–Full Control permission for the folder.

b. Assign Ben's user account the Allow–Full Control permission for the folder.

c. Encrypt the folder.

d. Encrypt the files.

e. Add Ben's user account to the list of users allowed to open the folder.

f. Designate Ben's user account as an EFS recovery agent.

66. You are the desktop administrator for a company that operates a Windows Server 2008 network. A group of researchers performs hardware and software testing and upgrades on computers located on a separate departmental network that is not connected to the company's main network.

A researcher named Matthew currently uses a Windows XP Professional computer. He has purchased a new computer running Windows 7 Professional, wants to transfer his data and settings to the new computer, and has asked you for help.

Which of the following should you advise Matthew to do?

a. Copy his user profile from the Windows XP computer's Documents and Settings folder to the new computer.

b. Use Windows Easy Transfer.

c. Use the Scanstate and Loadstate command-line tools.

d. Use the Files and Settings Transfer Wizard.

67. Ron is a scientist with a state government environmental agency who uses a Windows 7 Professional computer for modeling of pollutant transport in lakes and rivers. One morning, he turns on his computer and attempts to access a file server that stores data files required for his work. However, he is unable to connect to this server. He is also unable to connect to several other servers or to the Internet. Running the ipconfig /all command, he obtains the output shown in the exhibit.

He talks to several colleagues in the work unit and discovers that they are able to connect to network servers and the Internet as usual. What should he do to restore connectivity?

a. At a command prompt, type **ipconfig /renew**.

b. Go to the TCP/IP Properties dialog box, and specify the IP address of the default gateway as **169.254.0.1**.

c. Go to the TCP/IP Properties dialog box, and specify the IP address of the DNS server as **169.254.0.1**.

d. Shut down his computer, replace the network adapter card, and restart the computer.

68. You are the desktop security administrator for a company that operates several offices in different cities in Texas. You want to remotely manage Windows 7 client computers in the various offices from your home office in Austin by using a tool that utilizes Remote Procedure Call (RPC). How should you configure Windows Firewall on the client computers that you need to manage?

a. In the Windows Firewall Control Panel applet, click **Allow a program or feature through Windows Firewall**. In the Allow programs to communicate through Windows Firewall dialog box that appears, select **Remote Administration**.

b. In the Windows Firewall Control Panel applet, click **Allow a program or feature through Windows Firewall**. In the Allow programs to communicate through Windows Firewall dialog box that appears, select **Remote Assistance**.

c. In the Windows Firewall Control Panel applet, click **Allow a program or feature through Windows Firewall**. In the Allow programs to communicate through Windows Firewall dialog box that appears, select **Remote Desktop**.

d. In the Windows Firewall Control Panel applet, click **Allow a program or feature through Windows Firewall**. In the Allow programs to communicate through Windows Firewall dialog box that appears, click **Change Settings**, select **Add Port**, and then add **TCP port 135** for Remote Procedure Call to the exceptions list.

e. In the Windows Firewall Control Panel applet, click **Allow a program or feature through Windows Firewall**. In the Allow programs to communicate through Windows Firewall dialog box that appears, click **Allow another program**. Then select **Remote Procedure Call** and add this option.

69. You are the enterprise administrator for MoneyCard. The network consists of three sites—New York, London, and Phoenix—each connected to the other two sites by a high-speed link. Each site filters traffic using an access control list (ACL) on the routers between the sites to prevent proliferation of malicious traffic. You have flown to London to deploy Windows 7 Enterprise across the entire network. There is a Windows 2008 Server computer configured with Terminal Services in the New York office, and users are comfortable with using the Remote Desktop Connection application. One of the executives in London has had consistent errors on his computer, and you decide to enable Remote Desktop for your user account on his computer so that you can connect remotely and attempt to re-create the errors. Given the company's strict Internet usage policy, you edit the Registry key HKEY_LOCAL_MACHINE\System\Current ControlSet\Control\TerminalServer\WinStations\RDP-Tcp and edit the PortNumber value to set the Remote Desktop TCP port to 4322. All computers use DHCP and Dynamic DNS, and when you execute Ipconfig, you discover that the exec's current IP address is 192.168.33.82 and his DNS server's IP address is

192.168.33.2. You determine that the name of the exec's computer is
LON182-EX. What steps should you take to connect to the exec's computer
from the Phoenix office? (Choose all that apply.)

a. On each router between the sites, explicitly allow TCP port 4322 for both
incoming and outgoing traffic.

b. On your computer, open the Registry Editor and edit the `PortNumber` value
in the Registry key HKEY_LOCAL_MACHINE\System\
CurrentControlSet\Control\TerminalServer\WinStations\RDP-Tcp.

c. On your computer, open the System Properties dialog box, click the
Remote tab, and then click the **Advanced** button. On the dialog box that
appears, ensure that the **Create invitations that can only be used from
computers running Windows Vista or later** check box is cleared.

d. On the exec's computer, open the System Properties dialog box, click the
Remote tab, and then click the **Advanced** button. On the dialog box that
appears, ensure that the **Create invitations that can only be used from
computers running Windows Vista or later** check box is cleared.

e. On your computer, click **Start > All Programs > Accessories** and then select **Remote Desktop Connection**. In the text box, type `192.168.33.2` and
click the **Connect** button.

f. On your computer, click **Start > All Programs > Accessories** and then select **Remote Desktop Connection**. In the text box, type
`192.168.33.82:4233` and click the **Connect** button.

g. On your computer, click **Start > All Programs > Accessories** and then select **Remote Desktop Connection**. In the text box, type `LON182-EX:4322`
and click the **Connect** button.

h. On your computer, click **Start, > All Programs > Accessories** and then select **Remote Desktop Connection**. In the text box, type `LON182-EX` and
click the **Connect** button.

70. Gerry manages Windows deployment images for his company, which operates
an Active Directory Domain Services (AD DS) domain. He needs to ensure that
the images are kept up-to-date with regard to patches and other security fixes.
He has opened an administrative command prompt on his Windows 7 Ultimate
desktop computer, which includes a folder named `c:\mountedimages` for storing
mounted Windows 7 image files. Which command should he issue first so that
he can service an image named `image1.wim` that is currently located on a network share to which he has mapped the `x:` drive? (Each answer represents a
complete solution. Choose two.)

a. `dism /mount-wim /wimfile:x:\image1.wim /index:1`
   `/mountdir:c:\mountedimages`

b. `imagex /mountrw x:\image1.wim 1 c:\mountedimages`

c. `imagex/mount-wim /wimfile:x:\image1.wim /index:1`
   `/mountdir:c:\mountedimages`

d. `imagex /mount-wim x:\image1.wim 1 c:\mountedimages`

e. `dism/mountrw x:\image1.wim 1 c:\mountedimages`

f. `dism /mount-wim x:\image1.wim 1 c:\mountedimages`

71. Kingsley is responsible for ensuring that all Windows 7 computers in his company's Active Directory Domain Services (AD DS) domain receive all updates in a timely fashion. He has set up a Windows Server Update Services (WSUS) server to distribute updates from the Microsoft Windows Update website and must ensure that all computers access this server for their updates, rather than going across the Internet to the Windows Update website.

Kingsley sets up a Group Policy object (GPO) linked to the domain. Which of the following policies should he enable to accomplish this objective?

   a. **Configure Automatic Updates**

   b. **Turn on Software Notifications**

   c. **Enable client-side targeting**

   d. **Specify intranet Microsoft update service location**

72. Roberta is the network administrator for a company that operates an Active Directory Domain Services (AD DS) domain that includes a head office and two regional offices. The head office has domain controllers and member servers running Windows Server 2008 R2 and client computers running a mix of Windows Vista and Windows 7. Each regional office has two Windows Server 2003 R2 servers and 80 client computers running a mix of Windows Vista and Windows 7. These offices are organized into a network that includes two subnets in each office.

Roberta would like to set up BranchCache so that computers in the regional offices can easily access data on head office servers. Which of the following steps must she take? (Each answer represents part of the solution. Choose four.)

    a. Install BranchCache in Distributed Cache mode.

    b. Install BranchCache in Hosted Cache mode.

    c. Upgrade branch office servers to Windows Server 2008 R2.

    d. Upgrade Windows Vista head office client computers to Windows 7.

    e. Upgrade Windows Vista branch office client computers to Windows 7.

    f. Create a Group Policy object (GPO) that includes a predefined firewall rule that specifies **BranchCache–Content Retrieval (Uses HTTP)** and select the **Allow the connection** option.

    g. Create a Group Policy object (GPO) that includes a custom firewall rule that allows all local ports and select the **Allow the connection if it is secure** option.

73. You have copied a useful legacy program from your old computer running Windows XP to your new Windows 7 Home Premium computer. However, the program does not run properly when you attempt to start it. What should you do to run this program on Windows 7?

    a. Right-click the program and choose **Properties**. On the dialog box that appears, select the **Previous Versions** tab and select the option to run this program in compatibility mode for Windows XP (Service Pack 3).

    b. Right-click the program and choose **Properties**. On the dialog box that appears, select the **Compatibility** tab and select the option to run this program in compatibility mode for Windows XP (Service Pack 3).

    c. Download and install Windows XP Mode. Then install the legacy program to the Windows XP virtual machine.

    d. In the Appearance and Personalization section of Control Panel, select **Change the theme**. Then choose the **Windows Classic** theme and click **Apply**.

74. Laurie discovers that her new Windows 7 Home Premium laptop shuts itself down immediately after she receives the low battery warning. She does not have time to save her work before the shutdown occurs. What should she do?

    a. On the Change Settings for the Plan dialog box for the power plan in use, set the **Put the computer to sleep** setting to a higher value.

    b. From the battery meter, select the **Power saver** power plan.

    c. Access the Battery section of the Power Options dialog box and increase the **Low battery level** setting.

    d. Access the Battery section of the Power Options dialog box and increase the **Low battery notification** setting.

75. Lance is the team leader of a field research group for an environmental research company. The company is working on a new system for toxic contaminant removal from municipal sewage effluents. Researchers in his group have stored experimental data on a Windows 7 Professional laptop computer that they regularly take to the field when performing measurements at several sites. They record their measurements into a folder named Effluents. The network administrator at the company has created a group named Field and added the user accounts for Lance and the other field researchers to this group.

Lance's boss is concerned that the laptop could be stolen and the data could fall into the wrong hands. So, he decides to use EFS to encrypt the Effluents folder on the laptop. He needs to enable the other researchers in his group to access data on this folder while in the field. All researchers have valid certificates for using EFS. Lance right-clicks the data folder, chooses **Properties**, clicks the **Advanced** button, and then selects the **Encrypt contents to secure data** option.

What else does Lance need to do so that all users of the laptop can access the experimental data?

a. In the Advanced Attributes dialog box for the Effluents folder, click **Details**. In the Encryption Details dialog box that appears, click **Add** and add the other researchers individually to the list of users that can transparently access the folder.

b. In the Advanced Attributes dialog box for the Effluents folder, click **Details**. In the Encryption Details dialog box that appears, click **Add** and add the Field group to the list of users that can transparently access the folder.

c. Right-click each file in the Effluents folder and choose **Properties**. Click the **Advanced** button, and in the Advanced Attributes dialog box for the file, click **Details**. In the User Access to Effluents dialog box that appears, click **Add** and add the other researchers individually to the list of users that can transparently access the file.

d. Right-click each file in the Effluents folder and choose **Properties**. Click the **Advanced** button, and in the Advanced Attributes dialog box for the file, click **Details**. In the User Access to Effluents dialog box that appears, click **Add** and add the Field group to the list of users that can transparently access the file.

76. Brent's Windows 7 computer is running a large number of applications. On starting an additional application, the computer locks up and becomes totally unresponsive. Brent wants to continue working with the other applications, but they have become inaccessible because of the unresponsive application, so he wants to terminate this application without losing the other ones. Which tools should he use for this purpose? (Each answer represents a complete solution to this problem. Choose two).

   a. Task Manager

   b. Performance Monitor

   c. Resource Monitor

   d. Reliability Monitor

   e. Event Viewer

77. Ken wants to upgrade his computer from Windows Vista Business to Windows 7 Professional. He is concerned that his computer's hardware might be somewhat outdated and will not support the upgrade. Which of the following can he do to determine whether the computer will support Windows 7 Professional?

   a. Run the `setup /checkupgradeonly` command from the Windows 7 DVD-ROM.

   b. Run the `winnt32 /checkupgradeonly` command from the Windows 7 DVD-ROM.

   c. Download and run the Windows 7 Upgrade Advisor.

   d. Simply install Windows 7 and hope that everything is compatible.

78. Amanda is responsible for the Windows 7 deployment for a company that operates an Active Directory Domain Services (AD DS) network that includes servers running Windows Server 2008 R2. She is deploying Windows 7 Professional computers to branch offices where no tech-savvy personnel are available to assist users in setting them up. She is using Microsoft Deployment Kit (MDT) 2010 to perform this deployment. Which deployment method should she use in this scenario?

   a. Lite Touch Installation (LTI)

   b. Zero Touch Installation (ZTI)

   c. High Touch with Standard Image

   d. High Touch with Retail Media

79. Ellen is responsible for backups of data on 200 Windows 7 computers on her company's network. She is writing a script that she plans to use for automating these backups so that she does not need to spend hours configuring these computers individually. Which of the following commands should she include in her script?

a. Ntdsutil

b. Ntbackup

c. Wdsutil

d. Wbadmin

80. Mark is the network administrator for his company, which operates an Active Directory Domain Services (AD DS) domain. He has been tasked with rolling out Windows 7 to the 40 laptops for the sales team. After installing the operating system, one of the computers cannot join the domain. Which of the following should Mark do to begin troubleshooting the problem? (Choose all that apply.)

a. Reboot Windows 7 into safe mode and view the device settings.

b. Open the setupapi.log file to see whether there are any errors applicable to networking.

c. Open the netsetup.log file to see whether there are any errors applicable to networking.

d. Check the network adapter to see whether it is functioning.

e. Open a command prompt and enter **ipconfig /all**.

81. You are the network administrator for Oil of Alaska Yukon, a company that speculates for oil drilling. A team of employees is working at a promising site in the Yukon territory. They have a single telephone line available to the seven computers. Each Windows 7 Professional computer is configured with a network adapter, a modem, and a static IP address because you don't have a DHCP server available, and you have provided the team with a hub. The team requires access to email simultaneously, and they want to somehow be able to all connect to the phone line simultaneously. Which of the following should you do to help the team out? (Choose all that apply. Each answer presents part of the solution.)

a. Install a router that performs Network Address Translation (NAT).

b. Reconfigure each network adapter to use DHCP except for the computer connected to the modem.

c. Configure Internet Connection Sharing (ICS) on one computer.

d. Configure Windows Firewall on all the computers.

e. Configure ICS on all of the computers.

f. Reconfigure the modem connection properties to use a static IP address.

g. Right-click each computer's LAN connection and select **Bridge connections** from the shortcut menu.

82. You need to visit large numbers of potentially questionable websites during the performance of your job tasks. If you happen to visit websites that are not legitimate and might attempt to hijack your personal data, you must ensure that Internet Explorer warns you of this possibility and sends the address of the website to Microsoft. What should you do?

    a. On the Privacy tab of the Internet Explorer Properties dialog box, ensure that the pop-up blocker is enabled.

    b. From the Safety menu in Internet Explorer, ensure that the SmartScreen Filter is enabled.

    c. On the Security tab of the Internet Explorer Properties dialog box, ensure that Protected mode is enabled.

    d. On the Security tab of the Internet Explorer Properties dialog box, set the security level of the Internet zone to High.

83. Pauline uses a Windows 7 Home Premium laptop computer for her day-to-day activities that include word processing, website browsing, photo editing, and so on. She has accumulated a large number of photos and documents, and her computer is becoming slow. In addition, she wants to avail herself of the enhanced capabilities available with Windows 7 Ultimate, so she purchases a new desktop computer with a 1.5 TB hard drive.

Pauline has accumulated a large number of website logons and passwords and would like to transfer these to her new desktop computer so that she can access these websites without delay. What should she do?

    a. Use the Windows Backup and Restore applet to back up her logons and passwords and restore them to the desktop computer.

    b. Use Windows Easy Transfer to migrate the settings to her desktop computer.

    c. Use Credential Manager to back up the logons and password and restore them to the desktop computer.

    d. Access the Privacy tab of the Internet Options dialog box and click **Import**. Then import the logons and passwords to the desktop computer.

84. Christina is using a notebook computer running Windows 7 Professional to connect to her company's Active Directory Domain Services (AD DS) network. The network has a DirectAccess server running Windows Server 2008 R2 and configured with a security group named DA. She has obtained and installed a computer certificate on her notebook and joined the notebook to the domain. However, when she attempts to connect to her company's network by means of DirectAccess from a hotel in another city, she is unable to connect. Which of the following does Christina need to do so that she can connect to the server?

    a. Upgrade her computer to Windows 7 Ultimate.

    b. Obtain a user certificate and install this on her computer.

    c. Configure her computer with two consecutive IPv4 addresses.

    d. Ensure that her user account is included in the DA security group.

85. Rupert is responsible for keeping device drivers up-to-date and ensuring that only authorized drivers are available for users to install. He needs to enable ordinary users to install approved devices without the need for administrative credentials. What can he do to accomplish this task? (Each answer represents part of the solution. Choose two.)

    a. Add the publisher's certificate for each driver to the driver store.

    b. Add the publisher's certificate for each driver to the trusted certificates store.

    c. Deploy a Windows Server 2008 computer as a certificate server to generate certificates for unsigned drivers, and then add these certificates to the trusted certificates store.

    d. Ensure that the drivers have been signed by either a Windows publisher or trusted publisher, and then place the drivers in the `Windows\System32\Drivers` folder.

    e. Ensure that the drivers have been signed by either a Windows publisher or trusted publisher, and then place the drivers in the driver store.

86. Doug is responsible for security in his company, which operates an Active Directory Domain Services (AD DS) domain. All client computers run Windows 7 Enterprise. With the proliferation of smart phones, USB drives, and other removable storage devices, Doug needs to ensure that all employees of the company are unable to copy data from corporate computers to these devices. He also needs to ensure that users cannot copy programs, music, images, and other items from these devices to corporate computers.

Doug creates a Group Policy object (GPO) linked to the domain and navigates to the **Computer Configuration\Administrative Templates\System\ Removable Storage Access** node. Which of the following policies should Doug enable?

    a. **All Removable Storage classes: Deny all access** policy

    b. **All Removable Storage: Allow direct access in remote sessions**

    c. **Custom Classes: Deny read access**

    d. **Removable Disks: Deny read access**

87. Janet is responsible for transitioning her company's network from IPv4 to IPv6. She is aware that several transition technologies are in use for this purpose. On running `ipconfig` on a Windows 7 computer, she observes the IPv6 address `2002:0afe:fdfc::`. What technology is being used on this computer?

   a. Teredo

   b. 6-to-4

   c. IPv4-mapped address

   d. Link-local unicast

88. You have received a new computer running Windows 7 Ultimate and are plan-
    ning to give your current computer, which runs Windows 7 Home Premium, to
    your teenaged daughter. You have subscribed to a large number of websites and
    stored usernames and passwords for access to these sites in Internet Explorer, as
    well as several custom settings and preferences used by these sites.

    You do not want your daughter to have access to any of these websites, so you
    want to ensure that all these passwords, settings, and preferences are deleted
    from your current computer. What should you do? (Each answer represents
    part of the solution. Choose two.)

   a. Access the General tab of the Internet Options dialog box. Under Browsing
   history, click **Settings**, and then in the Temporary Internet Files and
   History Settings dialog box click **Delete all**.

   b. Access the General tab of the Internet Options dialog box. Under Browsing
   history, click **Delete**. In the Delete Browsing History dialog box that appears, select all the check boxes provided and then click **Delete**.

   c. Access the Content tab of the Internet Options dialog box. Click **Settings**
   in the Feeds and Web Slices section, and then clear the check box labeled
   Turn on feed reading now.

   d. Access the Security tab of the Internet Options dialog box. Change the security level for the Internet zone to **High**.

   e. Access the Content tab of the Internet Options dialog box. Click **Settings**
   in the AutoComplete section, and then clear the check box labeled **User
   names and passwords on forms**.

89. Wendy is responsible for managing the network configuration of Windows 7
    and Windows Server 2008 R2 computers on her company's network. She has
    opened an administrative command prompt on her Windows 7 Enterprise desk-
    top computer and wants to set up her computer for managing servers. Further,
    she wants to determine the media access control (MAC) address of a server
    named Server3. Which of the following commands should she execute from her
    desktop? (Each answer represents part of the solution. Choose two.)

   a. `winrm get server3`

   b. `winrm quickconfig`

   c. `winrs -r:Server3 ipconfig /all`

   d. `winrs ipconfig /all`

    e. `winrs -r:Server 3 arp -a`

    f. `winrs arp -a`

90. You are the systems administrator for your company. Bill is a manager who wants to share files from his Windows 7 computer with his assistant across the network. He has set permissions on a share named VOLT, which is the `C:\DATA\VOLT` directory on his hard drive. The assistant logs on to Bill's computer and can append data to the files locally. He can read the share from his own computer across the network, but he cannot make changes to the files from his computer. What should you do?

    a. Reset the NTFS permissions to allow Write.

    b. Reset the share permissions to deny Full Control.

    c. Reset the share permissions to allow Full Control.

    d. Reset the share permissions to deny Read.

91. Steve is an independent professional project planner who works in a small office 20 miles from his home. He has run the Set Up Backup Wizard to configure backup for his Windows 7 Professional computer, which is located in the office. He seldom visits the office on the weekend, preferring to spend quality time with his young family. His computer is always turned off when he is not in the office.

Several weeks later, Steve checks the backup folder on his computer and is surprised to discover that no backups have occurred beyond the initial one performed when he configured Backup. Which of the following is the most likely reason for this problem?

    a. Steve has not modified the default backup schedule.

    b. Steve has not specified the creation of a system image as part of the backup.

    c. Steve has not allocated sufficient space for creation of additional backups.

    d. Steve has left the default option of **Let Windows choose** selected.

92. You are the desktop administrator at the headquarters (HQ) for Billboreds, LLC. You have been called to assist Suzanne, a help desk administrator, whose Windows 7 Professional laptop is connected to the corporate network via an 802.11(g) wireless adapter. Company policy prevents users from running Windows Firewall on corporate network–connected computers because an Internet firewall is already in existence, and headquarters has a T-3 line to the Internet because a large number of bandwidth-intensive data transactions occur across an extranet VPN link with vendors and clients alike. Suzanne has developed a new application and wants to demonstrate it. The application runs on Suzanne's home computer, which uses Windows XP Professional SP3 and is connected to the Internet with a dedicated cable modem link and static IP address. Suzanne reports that when she is at work, she is unable to connect to her home computer to run a Remote Desktop Connection, which she needs to do to demonstrate the application. You have verified that Suzanne has enabled Windows Firewall on her home computer. What actions can you and Suzanne perform to enable the Remote Desktop Connection? (Choose all that apply.)

a. On Suzanne's home computer, open the Windows Firewall Properties dialog box from within Control Panel. Under the Exceptions tab, select the **Remote Desktop** check box.

b. On Suzanne's laptop, open the Windows Firewall Properties dialog box from within Control Panel. Under the Exceptions tab, select the **Remote Desktop** check box.

c. On the corporate router and firewall, verify that Remote Desktop protocol traffic for port TCP 3389 is enabled for both incoming and outgoing traffic.

d. On Suzanne's laptop, open the wireless network connection Properties dialog box, click the **Sharing** tab, and then select the check box labeled **Allow other network users to connect through this computer's Internet connection**.

e. On Suzanne's home computer, open the dedicated link to the Internet connection Properties sheet, click the **Advanced** tab, and enable Internet Connection Sharing.

f. On Suzanne's laptop, open the System Properties dialog box, click the **Remote** tab, and then click the **Advanced** button. On the dialog box that appears, ensure that the **Create invitations that can only be used from computers running Windows Vista or later** check box is cleared.

g. On Suzanne's home computer, open the System Properties dialog box, click the **Remote** tab, and select the **Allow users to connect remotely to this computer** check box. Click the **Select remote users** button and add Suzanne's user account.

93. You are using a Windows 7 Home Premium computer at home and a Windows 7 Professional computer in the office. You are working on a large, urgent project that needs to be completed by next week, but the weather office has issued a blizzard warning for tomorrow and the next day. Anticipating that you will be unable to go to the office, you use Windows Backup to back up all the folders required for the project to a DVD-ROM and take this DVD-ROM home.

Which of the following procedures should you follow to restore these folders to your home computer?

a. From the Backup and Restore Control Panel applet, select **Restore my files** and then select the option to save the files in the following location and choose an appropriate folder on your computer.

   b. From the Backup and Restore Control Panel applet, choose the option to select another backup to restore files from. Then follow the steps indicated to restore this backup.

   c. From the Backup and Restore Control Panel applet, select the option to create a restore point or change settings.

   d. From the Backup and Restore Control Panel applet, select the option to recover system settings or your computer.

94. Mary has created a virtual hard disk (VHD) on her computer and has downloaded and installed the Windows Automated Installation Kit (AIK). She has mounted the VHD as drive letter `p:`. She has also copied a Windows 7 Ultimate installation file, `install.wim`, to the `c:\Windows_Install` folder on her computer. This file contains a single image of Windows 7 Ultimate.

Mary now wants to deploy a copy of Windows 7 Ultimate to the VHD. Which of the following commands should she use?

   a. `dism /apply c:\Windows_Install \install.wim /check 1 p:`

   b. `wdsutil /apply c:\Windows_Install \install.wim /check 1 p:`

   c. `imagex /apply c:\Windows_Install \install.wim /check 1 p:`

   d. `dism /image:c:\Windows_Install\ /Set-Edition:Ultimate p:`

   e. `imagex /image:c:\Windows_Install\ /Set-Edition:Ultimate p:`

95. After a colleague of yours was forced to format his hard drive and reinstall Windows 7 because of an especially persistent malicious software program that he had inadvertently downloaded from the Internet, you are afraid of accessing sites on the Internet that might be infected. You have heard that Internet Explorer 8 can run in Protected mode to prevent malicious software from running.

What should you do to ensure that Internet Explorer 8 is running in Protected mode? (Each answer represents a complete solution. Choose all that apply.)

   a. Choose the option to reset Internet Explorer to default settings.

   b. Delete all browsing history options.

   c. Disable all add-ons.

   d. Check the status bar for a message informing you that Protected mode is on.

   e. Disable RSS feeds.

96. You are an independent consultant offering a service to install Windows 7 on users of home computers. A customer named Ted has purchased Windows 7 Home Premium from an electronics store and is attempting to install it on his home computer. Receiving an error message, Ted phones you for assistance.

At Ted's home, you check the hardware specifications of his computer and notice the following:

- 1.6 GHz processor

- 512 MB RAM

- 80 GB hard drive

- DirectX 9-capable video card with WDDM 1.0 driver and 128 MB video RAM

- 10/100 mbps integrated network card

Which of the following should you upgrade?

  a. Processor

  b. RAM

  c. Hard drive

  d. Video card

  e. Network card

97. Rachel is a desktop support specialist for her company, which operates an Active Directory Domain Services (AD DS) domain. Client computers run a mix of Windows XP Professional, Windows Vista Ultimate, and Windows 7 Ultimate. After the most recent Patch Tuesday updates, a user at a Windows 7 Ultimate computer reports that his computer is running more slowly than usual. On checking for the probable cause of this problem, Rachel discovers that one of the updates causes known issues with an important application used by this user. What should Rachel do?

  a. From the Windows Update Control Panel applet, select **View update history**. She should then select the **Installed Updates** link, and on the Uninstall an Update page that appears, right-click the problematic update and select **Uninstall**.

  b. From the Windows Update Control Panel applet, select **Change settings**. She should then clear the check box labeled **Allow all users to install updates on this computer**.

  c. From the Windows Update Control Panel applet, select **Change settings**. She should then select the **Download updates but let me choose whether to install them** option.

  d. From the Windows Update Control Panel applet, select **Change settings**. She should then right-click the problematic update and select **Uninstall**.

98. You are a consultant who has been hired to upgrade 20 computers running various older versions of Windows to Windows 7 Home Premium. Which of the following computers can you upgrade to Windows 7 Home Premium without the need to reinstall all applications and user settings? (Choose all that apply.)

   a. Computer1, which runs Windows 2000 Professional

   b. Computer2, which runs Windows XP Home Edition

   c. Computer3, which runs Windows XP Professional

   d. Computer4, which runs Windows Vista Home Premium

   e. Computer5, which runs Windows Vista Ultimate

   f. Computer6, which runs Windows 7 Home Basic

99. Bill is a technical support specialist employed at a branch office of a large national conglomerate. He has set up BranchCache in Hosted Cache mode on a Windows Server 2008 R2 computer in his office so that users can easily access documents located on servers in other offices. He needs to ensure that the server is trusted by client computers for caching data and realizes that a certificate of some sort is required. Which of these should Bill do?

   a. Import a certificate to the certificate store on the BranchCache server under the administrator account.

   b. Import a certificate to the certificate store on the BranchCache server under the local computer account.

   c. Import a certificate to the certificate store on each client computer under the administrator account.

   d. Import a certificate to the certificate store on each client computer under the local computer account.

100. You are the administrator for Seams Corp., which has implemented Internet Protocol version 6 (IPv6). The network uses a DHCP server on a Windows Server 2008 R2 computer to assign IPv6 addresses from the global unicast address range 2008::/64 to client computers. A user named Jean reports that she is unable to connect to any network resources from her Windows 7 Professional computer. On running `ipconfig` on her computer, you notice that her computer is configured with an address from the address range fe80::/64. What should you do first to correct this problem?

   a. On the Internet Protocol Version 6 (TCP/IPv6) Properties dialog box, select the **Use the following IPv6 address** option and manually specify an IPv6 address in the address range 2008::/64.

   b. On the Internet Protocol Version 6 (TCP/IPv6) Properties dialog box, select the **Alternate Configuration** tab and specify an IPv6 address in the address range 2008::/64.

•

c. On the Internet Protocol Version 6 (TCP/IPv6) Properties dialog box, click **Advanced** to access the Advanced TCP/IP Settings dialog box. Under IP Address, type an IPv6 address in the address range 2008::/64 and then click **Add**.

d. Check the network connectivity from her computer to the DHCP server and verify that the DHCP server is operating normally.

101. Kathy is responsible for configuring BitLocker policies for her company's Active Directory Domain Services (AD DS) domain. She wants to set up a data recovery agent (DRA) so that she can ensure that any data encrypted with BitLocker on domain computers can be recovered. She sets up a Group Policy object (GPO) linked to the domain and accesses the **Computer Configuration\ Administrative Templates\Windows Components\BitLocker Drive Encryption** node. Which of the following policies must she configure so that she can specify a DRA? (Each answer represents part of the solution. Choose two.)

a. **Provide the unique identifiers for your organization.**

b. **Choose how BitLocker-protected operating system drives can be recovered.**

c. **Save BitLocker recovery information to AD DS for operating system drives.**

d. **Choose default folder for recovery password**

102. Edward is using a Windows 7 Ultimate computer that is part of a homegroup that includes Windows 7 Home Premium computers used by his wife, Louise, and his two children, Eddy and Lara. He has configured homegroup sharing for the default libraries. Within his Documents library, he has created a folder named Financial that he would like to share with Louise but not with Eddy or Lara. Louise should have the capability to view and modify the files in this folder. All his family members should be able to view but not modify other folders in the Documents library. How should he set up sharing? (Each answer represents part of the solution. Choose three.)

a. Configure the Documents library with the Share with Homegroup (Read) option.

b. Configure the Documents library with the Share with Homegroup (Read/Write) option.

c. Configure the Documents library with the Share with Specific people option. Then add Louise with the capability to Read/Write.

d. Create a new library and move the Financial folder from the Documents library to this library.

e. Configure the new library using the Share with Homegroup (Read) option.

f. Configure the new library using the Share with Homegroup (Read/Write) option.

g. Configure the new library using the Share with Specific people option. Then add Louise with the capability to Read/Write.

103. You have been hired to deploy Windows 7 Enterprise to all the computers in a company with 500 desktops. The company provides a lab for research and development, which, because of its security settings, cannot be connected to the production network. You have performed the unattended installation on identical hardware from a network share for other computers. For the lab computers, you need to deploy Windows 7 using the DVD media. What must you do to ensure that the unattended installation completes properly?

a. Use Windows System Image Manager (SIM) to create a file named `Unattend.xml`. Place this file on a USB flash drive or floppy disk and insert the disk after you have inserted the Windows 7 DVD and started the computer.

b. Use SIM to create a file named `Unattend.txt`. Place this file on a USB flash drive or floppy disk and insert the disk after you have inserted the Windows 7 DVD and started the computer.

c. Use `Sysprep.exe` to create a file named `Unattend.xml`. Place this file on a USB flash drive or floppy disk and insert the disk after you have inserted the Windows 7 DVD and started the computer.

d. Use `Sysprep.exe` to create a file named `Unattend.txt`. Place this file on a USB flash drive or floppy disk and insert the disk after you have inserted the Windows 7 DVD and started the computer.

104. You are a help desk analyst for a company that operates an Active Directory Domain Services (AD DS) domain. All servers run either Windows Server 2003 or 2008 R2, and all desktop computers run either Windows XP Professional or Windows 7 Enterprise. Recently, a user named Kelly attempted to install beta hardware drivers on her Windows 7 Enterprise computer after having configured it with customized post-installation settings. After rebooting her computer and logging back on, problems occurred and her computer locked up. After another reboot, the computer would not even boot up properly.

What should you do to get Kelly's computer to boot successfully without losing her post-installation settings?

a. Boot her computer from a system repair disk and run the Startup Repair tool.

b. Press **F8** and select the **Last Known Good** configuration option.

c. Press **F8** and select **Safe Mode**. Then open Device Manager and roll back the problematic drivers.

d. Boot her computer from a system repair disk and select the **Recovery Console** option.

e. Reinstall Windows 7 Enterprise.

105. You are a road warrior who frequently accesses the Internet from various locations including hotels, cafes, and airports. You have configured Windows Firewall options with exceptions that enable client employees to access product information when in client locations. However, when you are elsewhere, you must block all external computers from accessing your computer regardless of firewall rules that allow connections when you are in client locations. How should you configure Windows Firewall?

a. Select the **Block** option in the Inbound Connections section on the Private Profile tab of the Windows Firewall with Advanced Security on Local Computer Properties dialog box.

Select the **Block all connections** option in the Inbound Connections section on the Public Profile tab of the Windows Firewall with Advanced Security on Local Computer Properties dialog box.

b. Select the **Block** option in the Inbound Connections section on the Public Profile tab of the Windows Firewall with Advanced Security on Local Computer Properties dialog box.

Select the **Block all connections** option in the Inbound Connections section on the Private Profile tab of the Windows Firewall with Advanced Security on Local Computer Properties dialog box.

c. Select the **Block** option in the Outbound Connections section on the Private Profile tab of the Windows Firewall with Advanced Security on Local Computer Properties dialog box.

Select the **Block all connections** option in the Inbound Connections section on the Public Profile tab of the Windows Firewall with Advanced Security on Local Computer Properties dialog box.

d. Select the **Block** option in the Outbound Connections section on the Public Profile tab of the Windows Firewall with Advanced Security on Local Computer Properties dialog box.

Select the **Block all connections** option in the Inbound Connections section on the Private Profile tab of the Windows Firewall with Advanced Security on Local Computer Properties dialog box.

e. Select the **Block** option in the Inbound Connections section on the Private Profile tab of the Windows Firewall with Advanced Security on Local Computer Properties dialog box.

Select the **Block** option in the Outbound Connections section on the Public Profile tab of the Windows Firewall with Advanced Security on Local Computer Properties dialog box.

    f. Select the **Block** option in the Inbound Connections section on the Public Profile tab of the Windows Firewall with Advanced Security on Local Computer Properties dialog box.

        Select the **Block** option in the Outbound Connections section on the Private Profile tab of the Windows Firewall with Advanced Security on Local Computer Properties dialog box.

106. You are a consultant that assists home users in maintaining their computers. A client named Linda has called you for help with her computer, which runs Windows 7 Home Premium. She informs you that her computer does not boot properly after she downloaded and installed a new driver for her network adapter. You start her computer in safe mode. Now you want to configure her computer so that the driver names are displayed as they are loaded during startup. What should you do?

    a. Run `msconfig`, and on the General tab, select **Diagnostic startup**.

    b. Run `msconfig`, and on the Boot tab, select **Boot log**.

    c. Run `msconfig`, and on the Boot tab, select **OS boot information**.

    d. Run `msconfig`, and on the Startup tab, select **Disable all**.

107. Jerri is an application support specialist for a company that runs an Active Directory Domain Services (AD DS) domain. Servers in the domain run Windows Server 2008 or Windows Server 2008 R2. At present, all client computers run Windows XP Professional, but an order is being processed for a shipment of 100 new computers, which will be running Windows 7 Enterprise.

Users of the new computers will need to run several mission-critical applications that were developed five to six years ago. Jerri has encountered compatibility problems on attempting to install these applications on a test computer running Windows 7 Professional. She needs to implement a solution that will enable users of the new computers to run these applications without problems? What should Jerri do?

    a. Install the applications on the new computers, and then configure them to run in compatibility mode for Windows XP SP3.

    b. Install Windows XP Mode on each of the new computers, and then install the applications from within Windows XP Mode.

    c. Install the applications on the new computers, and then specify the **Run this program as an administrator** option.

    d. Apply a shim to the application installation files, and then install the shimmed files on each of the new computers.

108. Scott has been transferred from the accounting department to the engineering department of his company. He takes his computer, which runs Windows 7 Ultimate, from his old office to the new one. The computer has a 600 GB hard disk that is configured as a single volume. He uninstalls several programs and deletes a large folder containing many files used in his previous position. He then installs new applications and data files.

After a few weeks of working in his new position, Scott finds that his computer is not performing as well as it previously did. Operations involving the modification of large data files take an excessive quantity of time. Checking the properties of his hard disk, Scott notes that it still contains over 300 GB of free space. What should Scott do first to improve his computer's performance?

a. Upgrade his RAM.

b. Install a second processor.

c. Install a new hard disk.

d. Defragment his current hard disk.

109. You are the network administrator for Salty Dogs, LLC. The company's Design Director, Elizabeth, uses a portable laptop computer that has been installed with Windows 7 Ultimate. Your company requires that all users use smart cards to access company resources. You have therefore provided Elizabeth with a portable smart card reader. Company policy also requires that all users connect with the highest level of security possible when using an Internet, VPN, or modem link. You are now creating the modem connection for Elizabeth to dial in to the network. Which authentication protocol should you select so that Elizabeth can use her smart card for access to the VPN?

a. Microsoft Challenge Handshake Authentication Protocol (MS-CHAP) version 2

b. Extensible Authentication Protocol (EAP)

c. Challenge Handshake Authentication Protocol (CHAP)

d. Password Authentication Protocol (PAP)

110. You want to create a backup of the Windows settings including the Registry on your computer. You also want to back up your applications and data at the same time, so you access the Backup and Restore Center. Which of the following options should you select?

a. **Create a system repair disc**

b. **Back up system state**

c. **Create a system image**

d. **Create a restore point or change settings**

111. You are installing Windows 7 Home Premium on a computer equipped with a 2.0 GHz processor, 1 GB RAM, a 600 GB hard disk, and a video card with 128 MB video memory. On the final boot the computer hangs, but you are able to

reboot the computer in safe mode. So, you access the log files. Which of the following should you check first when locating the cause of the problem?

a. `Setupact.log`

b. `Setupapi.dev.log`

c. `Setuperr.log`

d. `Netsetup.log`

e. `Scesetup.log`

112. Jennifer is the desktop support specialist and is responsible for updating and maintaining all computers in the company. She is configuring a Windows 7 computer that will be used by a help desk analyst, who has a standard user account on the computer. The help desk analyst will need to run scripts from the command prompt using administrative privileges.

Jennifer must ensure that the help desk analyst receives the User Account Control prompt to elevate his privileges each time without the need to right-click the command prompt option and select **Run as administrator**. Which of the following should she do?

a. From the Shortcut tab of the Command Prompt Properties dialog box, click **Advanced** and then select the **Run as administrator** option.

b. From the Security tab of the Command Prompt Properties dialog box, select the help desk analyst's user account and then select **Full Control** under the Allow column.

c. From the Compatibility tab of the Command Prompt Properties dialog box, select the **Run as administrator** option.

d. Add the help desk analyst's user account to the Administrators group on the Windows 7 computer.

113. You and Catherine are the desktop administrators for your company. You install and share a printer on a Windows 7 Professional computer. You have been instructed to ensure that only members of the Support local group can use this printer, and that only you and Catherine can manage the printer and all print jobs. Members of the Support local group should be able to manage only their own print jobs. In which of the following ways should you configure printer permissions?

a. Grant the Support group the Allow–Print permission. Grant the Allow–Full Control permission to Catherine's user account and your user account.

b. Grant the Support group the Allow–Manage documents permission. Grant the Allow–Manage this printer permission to Catherine's user account and your user account.

c. Grant the Support group the Allow–Print permission. Grant the Allow–Manage this printer permissions to Catherine's user account and your user account.

d. Grant the Support group the Allow–Print permission. Grant the Allow–Manage documents permission to Catherine's user account and your user account.

114. Sandra has completed deploying new Windows 7 Professional computers at her company. The company has 28 computers running Windows XP Professional SP2 that are going to be decommissioned. The president asks whether Sandra can move the information from the old computers to new ones that she has deployed in the organization. Which of the following tools is best used for this project?

a. User State Migration Tool

b. Windows Easy Transfer

c. Sysprep

d. Files and Settings Transfer Wizard

115. Mindy is a consultant in charge of converting a large company's network over to using IPv6 addressing. The company has been using private IPv4 addresses on the private 172.16.0.0/16 network address space. All client computers receive their IP addressing information from DHCP servers, and this must not be changed. Mindy is required to configure the network with the appropriate type of IPv6 addresses. Which address type should she select?

a. Global unicast

b. Link local unicast

c. Site local unicast

d. Multicast

e. Anycast

116. Shelley accesses the Performance Information and Tools applet on her Windows 7 Home Premium computer and notices the following Windows Experience Index scores:

- Processor: 7.1

- Memory (RAM): 7.1

- Graphics: 6.4

- Gaming Graphics: 5.1

- Primary Hard Disk: 5.8

Based on these values, what is her computer's base score?

    a. 5.1

    b. 6.3

    c. 6.4

    d. 7.1

117. Sharon is a network administrator for a company that operates an Active Directory Domain Services (AD DS) network. Two Windows Server 2008 computers are domain controllers and run the DNS service. The network also has three member servers running Windows Server 2003 R2, 80 Windows XP Professional computers, and 35 Windows Vista Business computers.

The company receives a shipment of 45 new computers that are to replace some of the Windows XP computers and provide computers for additional employees expected to be hired in the coming year. Sharon installs Windows Deployment Services (WDS) on a Windows Server 2008 computer to automate the installation of Windows 7 Professional on the new computers. She attempts to install Windows 7 Professional on a new computer but is unable to connect to the WDS server from this computer. She then uses the Windows 7 Professional DVD-ROM to install Windows 7 Professional on another new computer and is successful. The new computers are all located on the same network segment.

What should Sharon do so that the new computers can connect to the WDS server successfully?

    a. Install a DHCP server on the network and authorize it in Active Directory.

    b. Install a WINS server on the network and configure the DNS server to use it for name resolution.

    c. Create an answer file named `Winnt.sif` and copy it into the `RemoteInstall\WDSClientUnattend` folder on the WDS server.

    d. Convert the DNS server zones to Active Directory-integrated zones.

118. Sarah is working on a book project for a major publisher. She receives Internet service by means of a digital subscriber line (DSL) from the phone company. A contractor working on a new building has accidentally severed a trunk line, and Sarah will be without an Internet connection for several days. Because she needs to get a chapter to the publisher immediately, she goes downtown to an Internet cafe and opens Internet Explorer on a Windows 7 computer to access the publisher's website and submit her chapter.

Sarah is concerned that unauthorized individuals might access information she transmits across the Internet. How should she configure Internet Explorer on the Internet cafe machine to reduce the chances of this happening?

a. From the Safety menu in Internet Explorer, she should enable **InPrivate Browsing**.

b. From the Safety menu in Internet Explorer, she should enable **InPrivate Filtering**.

c. From the Security tab of the Internet Options dialog box, she should add the publisher's website to the Restricted Sites security zone.

d. From the Privacy tab of the Internet Options dialog box, she should select **Block All Cookies** for the Internet zone.

119. Ryan is a consultant who frequently visits client sites and requires up-to-date copies of equipment specifications and job progress charts to keep projects running properly. He has configured his notebook computer running Windows 7 Ultimate to synchronize offline files from several different clients by setting up multiple synchronization relationships in the Sync Center.

One of Ryan's clients has made numerous changes to a specification document on her desktop computer, which saves the changes to a shared folder on a Windows Server 2008 computer in her office. Meanwhile, Ryan has made several changes to the same document on his notebook computer. When he arrives at the client's office, he connects his computer to the client network and synchronize files.

What does Ryan need to do to ensure that all changes to the specification document have been incorporated, using the least amount of effort?

a. Download the client's version to his notebook and save it under a new filename. Then edit the document to incorporate his changes into the newly saved version.

b. Download the client's version to his notebook and save it under a new filename. Then manually type his edits into this version.

c. From the Sync Center, perform a manual synchronization. Then manually type his edits into the synchronized document.

d. From the Sync Center, perform a manual synchronization. Choose the option to save both versions of the document, and then edit the newly saved document to incorporate his changes.

e. Rename his version of the document before opening the Sync Center. Then perform a manual synchronization and edit the synchronized document by coping changes from the renamed version.

120. Betsy has installed a copy of Windows 7 Ultimate on a VHD at `d:\w7.vhd` on her Windows Vista Ultimate computer. Now she wants to configure the boot loader so that she can boot her computer to the VHD. She has obtained the globally unique identifier (GUID) of the VHD, which is represented here as *{guid}*. Which commands should she use? To answer, select all the commands she should use and arrange them in the order in which she should issue them.

a. `bcdedit /set {guid} osdevice vhd=d:\w7.vhd`

b. `bcdedit /attach {guid} osdevice vhd=d:\w7.vhd`

c. `bcdedit /set {guid} device vhd=d:\w7.vhd`

d. `bcdedit /copy {guid} osdevice vhd=d:\w7.vhd`

e. `bcdedit /attach {guid} device vhd=d:\w7.vhd`

f. `bcdedit /set {guid} detecthal=on`

g. `bcdedit /copy {current} /d "Boot from VHD"`

Answers to Practice Exam

1. **B, D**. You should attach the card reader first. When you do this, Windows will first display a message that it is installing device driver software. When it is unable to locate the driver software, it will prompt you to insert the CD-ROM. It will then provide instructions to install the drivers and support applications. You should not install the drivers and applications first, so answer A is incorrect. It is not necessary to access Device Manager to install the drivers and applications, so answer C is incorrect. You should attach the card reader before inserting the CD-ROM, so answer E is incorrect. For more information, see the section "Installing Devices and Drivers" in Chapter 7.

2. **B, D**. Joe can configure the computer's power button action to shut the computer down on battery power by selecting **Shut down** from the Power Button Action option in the Power Options dialog box, or by selecting the same option after clicking **Change plan settings** under the current power plan. Either of these actions configures the computer's power button to shut the computer down completely rather than enter sleep mode. The Power Saver power plan by default does not shut the computer down when the power button is pressed, so answers A and F are incorrect. Answer C is incorrect because this action shuts the computer down when Joe clicks the Start Menu power button rather than pressing the computer's power button. Answer E is incorrect because this action prevents the computer from entering sleep mode but does nothing for changing the default action when the computer's power button is pressed. For more information, see the sections "Additional Power Plan Options" and "Advanced Power Settings" in Chapter 13.

3. **D**. You should ensure that Protected mode is enabled for the Internet zone. You can do this by accessing the Security tab of the Internet Options dialog box. Protected mode prevents websites from modifying user or system files and settings unless you provide your consent and is enabled by default on all zones except the Trusted Sites zone. The SmartScreen Filter checks websites against lists of known and suspected phishing sites, but is not relevant to this situation, so answer A is incorrect. The Block All Cookies

option prevents websites from placing cookies on your computer but does not prevent websites from installing software, so answer B is incorrect. The pop-up blocker prevents websites from displaying additional Internet Explorer windows but also does not prevent them from installing software, so answer C is incorrect. For more information, see the section "Configuring Protected Mode in Internet Explorer" in Chapter 8.

4. **B, F**. Shirley should open the Internet Options dialog box and select the Security tab and then select the Trusted sites zone and click the **Sites** command button. From the Trusted sites dialog box, she can add the Cert Guide website to the Trusted sites list. On the same dialog box, she should clear the **Require server verification (https:) for all sites in this zone** check box. The Trusted sites zone is the zone that you should use for sites whose content you trust not to damage a user's computer or data, such as sites of trusted business partners. By default, server verification is required for all sites in the Trusted sites zone, so Shirley should clear this check box to remove this requirement.

The Local Intranet zone is used for websites on your organization's intranet, although you can also add external websites to this zone. By default, this zone does not enable downloading of unsigned ActiveX controls. Consequently, Shirley should not add the Cert Guide site to this zone, so answers A and E are incorrect. Enabling the **Download unsigned ActiveX controls** option would leave your computer open to rogue websites downloading malicious ActiveX controls, so answer C is incorrect. The **Include all sites that bypass the proxy server** option would cause Internet Explorer to interpret local intranet sites as being in the Internet zone rather than the Local Intranet Zone. This setting is not relevant to this situation, so answer D is incorrect. The **Initialize and script ActiveX controls not marked as safe for scripting** option would also leave your computer open to malicious ActiveX controls, so answer G is incorrect. For more information, see the section "Configuring Internet Explorer Security Zones" in Chapter 8.

5. **A, B, D**. Alex can copy the installation files from the Windows 7 DVD-ROM to any of these devices and perform the installation by accessing the BIOS setup screen of the laptop and selecting the appropriate device as the primary boot location. If he is using a network share, he might need to use a Windows PE CD-ROM disc to boot to a command prompt and enter the `net use` command to access the share. Alex cannot use WDS in this situation, so answer C is incorrect. For more information, refer to "Other Windows 7 Installation Methods" in Chapter 2.

6. **B**. The `ipconfig` command revealed that the media was disconnected for the adapter, and because the discussion about Billbored's LLC revealed that computers were often moved around the network, it is likely that the installers

simply didn't plug the network cable into the adapter or wall, or didn't plug it in firmly enough. When the adapter is connected, you can run `ipconfig /release` to remove the existing TCP/IP configuration information and then run `ipconfig /renew` to obtain a new IP address. Answer A is wrong because `netstat -e` will display the Ethernet statistics, but that isn't possible to do without the adapter being connected. Answer C is incorrect because you do not need to reset the connection. Answer D is wrong because there is no need to check the NetBIOS statistics. Answer E is wrong because the DHCP process always uses a broadcast when a DHCP client asks for a lease of an IP address; you never need to know the IP address of the DHCP server until the middle of that process. For more information, refer to "Using TCP/IP Utilities to Troubleshoot TCP/IP" in Chapter 9.

7. **A, E**. Abby needs to convert the two 400 GB disks to dynamic storage and create a striped volume from these disks. A striped volume consists of segments of equal size from 2 to 32 different physical disks combined together as a single entity. Data is written to and read from the striped volume evenly across all hard disks, resulting in improved read/write performance. To create the striped volume, she must first convert the two 400 GB disks to dynamic storage. Abby could convert all three disks to dynamic storage, but this is not necessary, so answer B is incorrect. A spanned volume consists of separate segments of any size on 2 to 32 different physical disks. This configuration does not offer any read/write performance enhancement, so its use is not warranted here; therefore, answers C and D are incorrect. She cannot include the system/boot volume in a striped volume; hence, she cannot create a striped volume from all three disks, so answer F is incorrect. For more information, refer to "Working with Dynamic Disks" in Chapter 15.

8. **C, F**. Sarah should clear the **Block all incoming connections** option on the Customize Settings for Each Type of Network dialog box. She should also open TCP port 80 in Windows Firewall on her computer. In this scenario, it appears that the **Block all incoming connections** option has been enabled on her computer, preventing any type of network communication, including use of the `ping` command. Clearing the **Block all incoming connections** option enables network communication from other computers. To enable port 80 across Windows Firewall in Windows 7, Sarah must access the Windows Firewall with Advanced Security on Local computer dialog box and create a new rule that allows traffic on port 80 across the firewall. The public profile is used for enabling communications in insecure locations such as public Wi-Fi spots. Enabling inbound communications under this profile would not enable communications across port 80 in this scenario, so answer A is incorrect. Turning Windows Firewall off would expose her computer to unauthorized users on the Internet, so answer B is incorrect. Remote Administration enables the management of remote computers

by means of utilities that utilize Remote Procedure Call (RPC), but does not allow other users to access her website, so answer D is incorrect. Unlike the situation in Windows Vista, Windows 7 does not provide the capability of adding ports within the Windows Firewall Control Panel applet, so answer E is incorrect. For more information, see the section "Configuring Security Settings in Windows Firewall" in Chapter 10.

9. **B**. Of the options presented, only MDT 2010 includes the Deployment Workbench, which is the Microsoft solution accelerator for deploying operating systems such as Windows 7 and Windows Server 2008 R2, together with device drivers, applications, and updates. WDS provides many of these functions, but does not include the Deployment Workbench, so answer A is incorrect. DISM is a command-line tool that he can use to service a Windows image or work with a Windows PE image. It also does not include the Deployment Workbench, so answer C is incorrect. RIS was used for deploying Windows XP, Windows Server 2003, and older Windows versions; it is no longer supported in Windows 7, so answer D is incorrect. For more information, refer to "Suggested Deployment Strategies" in Chapter 5.

10. **D**. Brendan needs to reformat the laptop's hard drive and reinstall Windows 7. If the recovery password has been lost, the Windows installation and all data stored on the partition are permanently lost (hopefully a backup is available and Brendan can restore the data from the backup). It is not possible to access the BitLocker applet in Control Panel without first entering the password, so answer A is incorrect. Inserting a USB flash drive also will not work if the user has not selected this option for storing the recovery password, so answer B is incorrect. When the computer starts, it will display the BitLocker Drive Encryption Recovery Console; however, Brendan would need to enter the recovery password to start the computer normally; therefore, answer C is incorrect. If a domain recovery agent had been configured, Brendan could have entered credentials for this recovery agent from the BitLocker Drive Encryption Recovery Console. For more information, see the section "BitLocker Drive Encryption" in Chapter 13.

11. **D**. Ethan should enable the **Password protected sharing** option. This option increases security by limiting access of shared files and printers to only those who have a user account and password on your computer. Windows 7 enables him to specify the usernames of users allowed to access a shared folder. However, this option does not prevent users without passwords from accessing the shared folders or the Public folder, so answer A is incorrect. The **Public folder sharing** option enables others on the network to access files in his computer's Public folder. This option does not prevent users without passwords from accessing the Public folder, so answer B is incorrect. The **Network discovery**

option enables his computer to locate other computers and devices on the network and other computers to locate yours. Disabling this option would prevent users from accessing shares on your computer, so answer C is incorrect. For more information, see the section "Using the Network and Sharing Center to Configure File Sharing" in Chapter 11.

12. **B**. Antivirus (AV) software is known to cause problems during installation or upgrading of Windows operating systems. On the first reboot, these programs might falsely report that the installation files contain a virus and halt the installation. You should uninstall the AV software and disable any AV checking in the computer's BIOS before installing or upgrading to Windows 7. You can always reenable or reinstall antivirus software after you have completed the upgrade. The computer is not actually infected with a virus, so Tom does not need to reboot to Windows Vista or scan for viruses; therefore, answer A is incorrect. The Check Compatibility Online option is used to check a computer for software or hardware incompatibility before upgrading to Windows 7. These problems do not cause the false reporting of a virus, so answer C is incorrect. `Fixmbr.exe` is used to recover corrupted master boot records on existing Windows installations. You cannot use it in this scenario when the Windows installation is incomplete, so answer D is incorrect. Tom does not need to upgrade the RAM to 2 GB, so answer E is incorrect. For more information, see the section "Additional Preparatory Tasks" in Chapter 3.

13. **C, E**. Owen needs to use AppLocker to configure a file hash rule that blocks execution of the specialized applications. He also needs to specify an exception that enables members of the Engineers group to run the applications. He cannot use a path rule or a publisher rule because the applications are not digitally signed, so answers A and B are incorrect. Owen then needs to specify an exception that allows members of the Engineers group to run the application; he can do this from the wizard used for creating the rule. When Owen uses a file hash rule, only programs that correspond to the file hashes he has specified are blocked; therefore, he does not need to specify an exception that allows other programs covered by the rule to execute, so answer D is incorrect. For more information, refer to "Application Control Policies" in Chapter 8.

14. **B**. The Restore Previous Versions option, also known as the volume shadow copy feature, enables Wayne to restore his document to a point in time before corruption occurred. He can access this option by right-clicking the document and choosing **Restore previous versions** and then selecting the most recent time that the document was still good. System Restore does not restore documents to an earlier point in time, so answer A is incorrect. Restoring from the most recent backup would undo all changes made since the previous Sunday at 7 P.M. (the default backup time), so answer C is incorrect. The system repair disc is

used to boot a computer that cannot be started normally, thus causing him to lose all work done on the document since then. Therefore, answer D is incorrect. For more information, refer to "Using Shadow Copies to Restore Damaged or Deleted Files" in Chapter 18.

15. **B**. The `create vdisk` command of `DiskPart` enables Teresa to create a VHD. She must specify the size of the VHD in MB and not GB, so answer A would create a VHD of 40 MB size and is therefore incorrect. Answers C and D are incorrect because these commands would create a primary partition on the VHD; actually, their syntax is incorrect because you would not use `file=` parameter with this command. For more information, refer to "Using DiskPart to Create a VHD" in Chapter 6.

16. **C**. It appears in this scenario that his computer is still configured with the Windows Vista default, which always presented UAC prompts under these circumstances. By selecting the Windows 7 default, he will not receive prompts when he makes changes to Windows settings. Selecting the **Run this program as an administrator** option will result in his always receiving prompts when he runs these programs; therefore, answer A is incorrect. The **Always notify me when** option is most likely the option that is currently enabled on his computer; this option produces behavior similar to that of Vista—consequently, answer B is incorrect. The **Never notify me when** option would disable UAC completely, so Paul would not receive prompts when he attempts to install a program or when websites attempt to make changes to his computer's configuration; consequently, answer D is incorrect. For more information, refer to "Configuring User Account Control" in Chapter 12.

17. **A**. Sheila should instruct the users to run the `ipconfig /flushdns` and `ipconfig /registerdns` commands. The `ipconfig /flushdns` command flushes the contents of the DNS cache, and the `ipconfig /registerdns` command renews all adapters' DHCP leases and refreshes the DNS configuration. It is probable that the users' computers have cached the old IP address of Server1 and are hence unable to locate this computer, so running these commands flushes the cache and loads new DNS information that contains the new IP address of Server1. The `ipconfig /release` and `ipconfig /renew` commands release and renew IP address leases for the client computers. The `ipconfig /displaydns` command displays the contents of the DNS cache. The `nbtstat -R` command displays NetBIOS name resolution statistics. The `nslookup` command accesses the DNS server and displays information records on this server. None of these commands obtain IP address information for Server1, so answers B, C, D, and E are incorrect. For more information, see the section "Using TCP/IP Utilities to Troubleshoot TCP/IP" in Chapter 9.

18. D, E. Nancy should enable the **Require additional authentication at startup policy** and select the **Allow BitLocker without a compatible TPM** option. She should then use a USB flash drive to hold the encryption keys and access password while she enables BitLocker from the BitLocker Drive Encryption applet in Control Panel. If Nancy were to repartition the hard drive by using the command prompt available from the System Recovery Options dialog box, her data would be lost. Therefore, answers A and B are incorrect. Enabling the **Choose how BitLocker-protected operating system drives can be recovered** policy enables a data recovery agent but does not protect her data. Therefore, answer C is incorrect. It is not possible to store the encryption keys and access password on a floppy disk, so answer F is incorrect. For more information, see the section "BitLocker Drive Encryption" in Chapter 13.

19. C. Colby should use Software Restriction Policies to create a policy specifying a path rule that blocks all games. He can apply these policies to any computer running any edition of Windows XP/Vista/7. AppLocker policies can be applied to computers running Windows 7 Enterprise or Ultimate only, so he cannot use AppLocker to create a policy for any of the computers in this scenario. Therefore answers A and B are incorrect. It is not possible to use a Software Installation Policy to uninstall game software installed as part of the Windows installation, so answer D is incorrect. For more information, refer to "Configuring Application Restrictions" in Chapter 8.

20. B. Robert should use a side-by-side migration utilizing a compressed migration store. In a side-by-side migration, data is copied from an old computer to a new one. The Scanstate.exe tool is used to collect information from the old computer, and then the Loadstate.exe tool is used to restore this information at the new computer. USMT supports three types of migration stores: uncompressed, compressed, and hard-link. Of these types, only the compressed type supports encryption and password protection. The wipe-and-load migration is used when you are saving data from a computer and then wiping its hard drive clean and installing a new copy of Windows 7 on the same computer. This is not the proper strategy here, so answers A and C are incorrect. The hard-link migration store does not support encryption and password protection; further, it cannot be used in the side-by-side migration strategy, so answer D is incorrect. For more information, refer to "Side-by-Side Versus Wipe and Load" in Chapter 4.

21. C. Kristin should select the **WPA-Enterprise** security method. This security method uses TKIP as its default encryption type as well as 802.1x authentication. The WPA-Personal and WPA2-Personal security methods both require preshared keys for authentication, so answers A and B are incorrect. The WPA2-Enterprise security method uses AES and not TKIP as its default encryption type, so answer D is incorrect. For more information, see the section "Setting Up a Wireless Connection" in Chapter 10.

22. **A.** Lynn should configure a source-initiated event subscription. This causes each source computer to push the specified events to the collector computer. This type is typically used where there are a large number of source computers configured using Group Policy. A collector-initiated event subscription would typically be used where there are a limited number of easily identified source computers. This is not the case here, so answer B is incorrect. A filter that views logs by event source displays logs according to Windows services, utilities, and components; this is not what is needed here, so answer C is incorrect. You could use a filter that views logs by user and computer, but this would be less convenient than creating an event log subscription, which is new to Windows 7. Therefore, answer D is incorrect. For more information, refer to "Using Event Log Subscriptions" in Chapter 16.

23. **C.** George should boot the computer with the Windows 7 DVD. He should select the option to perform a clean installation, select the third partition, format this partition with the NTFS file system, and install Windows 7 on this partition. This procedure installs Windows 7 while maintaining the XP installation intact. On rebooting, he will receive a boot menu from which he can select either XP or Windows 7. If he were to select the first partition, he would destroy the XP installation, so answer A is incorrect. The upgrade option is not available in this situation because Microsoft does not support a direct upgrade from Windows XP to Windows 7, so answer B is incorrect. If he were to format both partitions and install Windows 7 before reinstalling XP, he would lose all his previously configured settings in XP. Further, he would damage the Windows 7 installation because when you install more than one operating system, you should install the oldest operating system first. Consequently, answer D is incorrect. For more information, see the section "Dual-Booting Windows 7" in Chapter 2.

24. **D.** Mike should uninstall the add-on from the Control Panel Programs applet. While you cannot uninstall add-ons that were preinstalled on your computer, you can uninstall add-ons that you have downloaded. Click **Start** > **Control Panel**, and under Programs, select the **Uninstall a program** option. This starts the Programs and Features applet with a page labeled Uninstall or change a program. Resetting Internet Explorer to the default settings will not undo the effect of the problematic add-on, so answer A is incorrect. Although you could run Internet Explorer with the No Add-ons option by selecting this option from the Start > All Programs > Accessories menu, many websites would be unable to display properly; therefore, answer B is incorrect. It is not possible to uninstall an add-on from the Manage Add-ons dialog box; you can only uninstall ActiveX controls or disable add-ons from this location. Therefore, answer C is incorrect. For more information, see the section "Managing Add-ons" in Chapter 8.

25. **D**. Jill will be granted no access to the FOLDER share. When accessing a shared folder configured with NTFS security permissions, the lowest level of permissions apply. In addition, the explicit denial of permission overrides all other permissions. Therefore, answers A, B, and C are all incorrect. For more information, see "Effective Permissions" in Chapter 11.

26. **A, B**. Ann can remove the Photoshop CS4 installation files from the image by using DISM with the /Remove-Package option. She can then use either DISM with the /Add-Package option or the New Application Wizard in MDT 2010 to add Photoshop CS5 to the image. Note that DISM does not include a /Remove-Apps option, so answer C is incorrect. Note that DISM does not include either an /Add-Apps or a /Remove-Apps option, so answers C and D are incorrect. For more information, refer to "Inserting Applications into System Images" in Chapter 5.

27. **D**. Louise should request that a network administrator open TCP port 3389 on the firewall. Both Remote Desktop and Remote Assistance are based on Terminal Services technology and use this port to establish remote connections. Most firewalls are configured to block incoming connections to this port; therefore, it is necessary to configure the firewall to open this port when using Remote Assistance. These connections usually fail in scenarios where the user requiring assistance is behind a firewall. Remote Assistance enables a user to create a shared connection with a remote expert who can input information to the user's computer and carry on a chat session with the user. Its chief purpose is to enable the expert (Louise in this case) to help a user (Andrew in this case) with a problem that he is having with his computer.

The **Allow connections only from computers running Remote Desktop with Network Level Authentication (more secure)** option is used with Remote Desktop and not with Remote Assistance, so answer A is incorrect. The **Allow this computer to be controlled remotely** option enables Louise to take control of Andrew's desktop session so that she can show him the steps to be followed or actually perform the steps for him. This option should be selected and not cleared, so answer B is incorrect. The Remote Desktop Users local group is used for enabling users to make a Remote Desktop connection, not a Remote Assistance connection, so answer C is incorrect. For more information, see "Remote Desktop" and "Remote Assistance" in Chapter 14.

28. **E**. Maria should select the **Change settings** option. This reopens the wizard that enables Maria to select the items that will be backed up. The **Create a system image** option enables her to back up all items required to restore Windows operation but does not necessarily add the files and folders she wants. Therefore, answer A is incorrect. The **Create a system repair disc** enables her to create a CD or DVD disc that she can use to start her computer if other startup options fail, so answer B is incorrect. The **Back up now** option merely

starts a backup with the current settings, so answer C is incorrect. The **Manage space** option enables her to manage the space used by backups including deletion of older backups, but it does not allow her to change the backup configuration. Therefore, answer D is incorrect. Note that on the exam, a question such as this one might be displayed as a "hot spot" item where you must select the correct answer by clicking on an image of the dialog box as shown in the exhibit here. For more information, refer to "Managing and Troubleshooting Your Backups" in Chapter 17.

29. **D**. Brenda should access the Windows Update applet in Control Panel. She should click **Restore hidden updates**, select the update, and then click **Restore**. Updates might become hidden if she has asked Windows not to notify her or install updates automatically. Selecting the check box labeled **Give me recommended updates the same way I receive important updates** enables her to check for both critical and recommended updates including drivers as well as updated definition files for Windows Defender. This option (which is selected by default) does not enable her to restore a hidden update, so answer A is incorrect. Brenda should not select the **Install updates automatically (recommended)** option because she wants to retain the option to let her choose whether to download and install future updates; therefore, answer B is incorrect. The **View update history** option enables her to view installed updates but not access hidden updates, so answer C is incorrect. For more information, see the section "Configuring Windows Update Settings" in Chapter 7.

30. **B**. Bob can use the most recent system restore point to roll the computer back to the condition that existed before Emily installed the tax calculation application. Using a system repair disc with the most recent system image is a drastic measure that Bob would use only if other restore methods have failed, so answer A is incorrect. It is unadvisable to attempt to edit the Registry in this type of situation; Bob could damage the computer's configuration irreparably by attempting to remove any added settings. Therefore, answer C is incorrect. Using the most recent system image from safe mode is a more drastic move that is not needed in this situation, so answer D is incorrect. The Last Known Good configuration will not work in this scenario because Emily was able to log on before she realized that a problem existed, so answer E is incorrect. For more information, refer to "Running System Restore" and "Safe Mode" in Chapter 18.

31. **E**. Kane should disable the Store passwords using reversible encryption policy. This policy determines the level of encryption used for storing passwords; enabling it reduces security because it stores passwords in a format that is essentially the same as plain text. All other policy settings shown are reasonably set; so answers A, B, C, and D are all incorrect. Note that on the exam, a question similar to this might be presented as a "hot spot" where you must click on the exhibit at the place that you must configure. For more information, refer to "Password Policies" in Chapter 12.

32. C. Erin should install the website certificate to the Trusted Root Certification Authorities certificate store on her computer. She can do this by accessing the Content tab of the Internet Options dialog box and clicking the **Certificates** button. In the Certificates dialog box, she should select the **Trusted Root Certification Authorities** tab, click **Import**, and then follow the instructions provided by the Certificate Import Wizard. None of the other options presented here will install this certificate and permit her to access the secured website, so answers A, B, and D are incorrect. For more information, refer to "Certificates for Secure Websites" in Chapter 8.

33. B. When you create an answer file that will be included on a USB flash drive or floppy disk for users that are installing Windows 7 from a DVD-ROM, you should name the file Unattend.xml. The user should insert this disk after the computer starts to boot from the DVD-ROM. The other files mentioned were used for deploying Windows XP but are no longer used with Windows 7, so answers A, C, and D are incorrect. For more information, see the section "Understanding Answer Files" in Chapter 5.

34. C. Phil should add more RAM. A value of Memory\Pages/sec consistently greater than 20 indicates a shortage of RAM and a potential bottleneck. LogicalDisk\% Disk Time and PhysicalDisk\% Disk Time report the percentage of time that the disk was busy servicing disk requests; in this situation, the high amount of paging results in a busy disk. When PhysicalDisk\% Disk Time is above 50%, it is sometimes necessary to upgrade to a faster hard disk; however, if memory counters are also high, you should add RAM first to improve computer performance. Therefore, answers A and B are incorrect. Paging activity and disk requests might cause an increase in the Processor\% Processor Time; however, the value of 71 for this counter is within acceptable limits. Therefore, answers D and E are incorrect. For more information, see the section "Performance Monitor" in Chapter 16.

35. A. Jason should run the Windows 7 Upgrade Advisor. This tool generates reports describing hardware and software components that might not be compatible with Windows 7, thereby alerting him to problems that might occur when he upgrades his computer. The Windows 7 Program Compatibility Wizard enables Jason to configure older programs to work properly with Windows 7 after he has upgraded, so answer B is incorrect. The Windows Easy Transfer Wizard is used to transfer files and settings from an older computer to a new Windows 7 computer, so answer C is incorrect. Although he can upgrade drivers from Device Manager in Windows XP, he might still have other compatibility issues that would be divulged when running the Upgrade Advisor, so answer D is incorrect. For more information, see the section "Windows 7 Upgrade Advisor" in Chapter 3.

36. **A**. The `dism` command invokes the Deployment Image Servicing and Management utility, which enables Kim to perform offline servicing and updating of a Windows 7 image. The `/Set-Edition:Ultimate` parameter upgrades the Windows edition on this VHD to Windows 7 Ultimate. The `/Get-Edition` parameter is invalid; Kim would use the `/Get-CurrentEdition` parameter to obtain the current edition of the VHD, so answer B is incorrect. The `wdsutil` command is the command-line version of Windows Deployment Services, which Kim can use to deploy new Windows 7 images to VHDs, but not to upgrade existing Windows 7 images. Therefore, answers C and D are incorrect. For more information, refer to "Upgrading a Windows Image to a Higher Edition" in Chapter 6.

37. **C**. You can use Encrypting File System (EFS) to encrypt the contents of the Clients folder by using the `cipher /e` command. To ensure that other tax preparers can use the files, you must add each preparer's file encryption certificate to the Encryption attributes options. Answer A is wrong because that would render users incapable of accessing the resources. Answer B is wrong because it would render the computer fully open to anyone who happened to pass by and log on. Answer D is incorrect because the `/d` switch causes files to be decrypted rather than encrypted. For more information, see the section "Encrypting Files" in Chapter 11.

38. **D**. By configuring the portable computers to enter sleep mode when the lid is closed, Evan can enable the users to rapidly and manually place their computers in a low-power state from which the computers can resume normal operation rapidly. Although the Power saver and Balanced power plans enable sleep mode after a preconfigured time interval, they do not enable the users to manually place their computers into sleep mode, so answers A and B are incorrect. The Critical battery alarm also does not enable the users to manually place their computers in sleep mode, so answer C is incorrect. The computers do not resume normal operating condition as rapidly from hibernation as they do from sleep mode, so answer E is incorrect. For more information, see the section "Power Plans" in Chapter 13.

39. **A**. Donna should select the **Custom (advanced)** installation option to install 7 on the second partition and format this partition with the NTFS file system. The **Upgrade** option is not available because Microsoft does not support a direct upgrade from Windows XP to Windows 7, so answers B and D are incorrect. If she does not format the partition with the NTFS file system, the installation will fail, so answer C is incorrect. For more information, see the sections "File System Considerations" and "Dual-Booting Windows 7" in Chapter 2.

40. C, D. Barbara should select the **High** blocking level in the Pop-Up Blocker Settings dialog box. She can access this dialog box from the Privacy tab of the Internet Options dialog box by clicking **Settings** under Pop-Up Blocker or by selecting **Pop-up Blocker > Pop-up Blocker Settings** from the Tools menu in Internet Explorer 8. The Low blocking level permits pop-ups from secure sites and the Medium level permits many nonautomatic pop-ups; therefore, she would receive pop-ups that she doesn't want. Consequently, answers B and C are incorrect. Adding the website to the Trusted Sites zone does not allow pop-ups to appear when she has specified the High blocking level, so answer E is incorrect. For more information, refer to "Blocking Pop-Ups" in Chapter 8.

41. D. `scanstate.exe` and `Loadstate.exe` are components of the User State Migration Tool (USMT), which can be used for migrating user files and settings from an old computer to a new Windows 7 Professional computer. These utilities can be scripted and provide an automated method of transferring files and settings from one computer to another as required by this scenario. Sysprep is used to create an image of a reference computer for duplicating to a series of new computers, and not for imaging old computers, so answer A is incorrect. You should not copy or import Registry files, so answer B is incorrect. The Recovery console was used with Windows XP computers to repair startup problems. Although you might be able to copy information using this tool, this is not a recommended procedure for transferring data from one computer to another, so answer C is incorrect. For more information, see the section "Migrating Users from Previous Windows Versions" in Chapter 4.

42. B. Leona can view the driver information from Device Manager. Here she can right-click the camera and choose **Properties** to bring up its Properties dialog box. Information on the driver is available on the Drivers tab of this dialog box by clicking the **Driver Details** command button. This includes the driver files and the provider and name of the digital signer. The `sigverif` utility checks a computer for unsigned drivers. It would inform Leona if the camera drivers were unsigned but does not provide information about signed drivers; therefore, answer A is incorrect. Information about signed drivers on the computer is available in the Software Environment (not the Components) node of the System Information tool. This information includes the manufacturer, who is not necessarily the digital signer. Consequently, answer C is incorrect. The Windows 7 Logo Program for Hardware lists all components for which drivers exist that have been certified as Windows 7–compatible, but again does not provide driver signing information, so answer D is incorrect. For more information, refer to "Managing and Troubleshooting Drivers and Driver Signing" in Chapter 7.

43. **A.** John can restart the computer with the Last Known Good Configuration. The Last Known Good Configuration can be used because John didn't log on after the Stop error. Answers B, C, and D are wrong because they all require more time and effort than using the Last Known Good Configuration; John would use one of these only if Last Known Good fails to correct the problem. For more information, see the section "Last Known Good Configuration" in Chapter 18.

44. **A.** You should change the subnet mask on Evelyn's computer to 255.255.240.0. This subnet mask reserves the first four bits of the third octet as part of the network ID and the last four bits of this octet as part of the host ID. The subnet mask of 255.255.0.0 currently on her computer makes the computer think that IP addresses on Subnet 2 are actually on Subnet 1. Consequently, attempts to access Subnet 2 computers do not cross the router and these computers cannot be found. If you were to change the subnet mask to 255.255.255.0, Evelyn's computer would still be unable to access Subnet 2 computers and would also be unable to access some Subnet 1 computers, so answer B is incorrect. The default gateway is correctly specified and changing it would not enable connection, so answer C is incorrect. It does not help to give Evelyn's computer a second IP address on the Subnet 2 network; moreover, this option is not available when IP addresses are statically assigned. Therefore, answer D is incorrect. For more information, see the section "Static IPv4 Addressing" in Chapter 9.

45. **A.** To run a PowerShell cmdlet against a remote computer, Tara must use the `icm` command, specify the computer name, and enclose the PowerShell cmdlet in curly brackets. Answer B is incorrect because the curly brackets are missing. Windows Remote Shell is invoked with the `winrs` command, but Tara cannot use this tool to run a PowerShell cmdlet, so answers C and D are incorrect. The `winrm` command enables her to use a series of command-line tools, but it does not enable the use of PowerShell cmdlets, so answers E and F are incorrect. For more information, refer to "Using Windows Remote Management Service" in Chapter 14.

46. **E, B, F, H.** You can create a script to automate many of the capabilities of the Disk Management snap-in by using subcommands of the diskpart command-line utility. In this situation, Lawrence first needs to select the new disk (disk 1), which shifts the focus to this disk. He then converts the disk to dynamic storage and creates a simple volume on this disk. Finally, he uses the `Mount` command to mount the volume to the `c:\mounted` folder. He should save these commands to a text file, which he can place on a floppy disk or USB thumb drive. At each affected computer, he can execute `DiskPart /s a:scriptname.txt`. Note that on the exam, a question of this type would appear as a drag-and-drop question in which you are required to drag the required actions into a list and ensure that they are arranged in the proper order ("build list and reorder question"). If you have selected the correct items but not placed them in the proper order, the question is still scored as incorrect. For more information, refer to "Using DiskPart to Create Striped, Mirrored, and RAID-5 Volumes" in Chapter 15.

47. **E.** Stephanie should use the `Netsetup.log` error log to see whether a computer was able to join a domain. Answer A is incorrect because `Setupapi.dev.log` records data about Plug and Play devices and drivers. Answer B is incorrect because `Setuperr.log` shows errors related to hardware or driver issues that occur during setup. Answer C is incorrect because `Scesetup.log` shows security-related error information. Answer D is incorrect because `Setupact.log` displays all the actions that Setup performs during installation. For more information, see the section "Troubleshooting Failed Installations" in Chapter 2.

48. **C.** Connie can use any of PPTP, L2TP, SSTP, or IKEv2 to set up a tunneled connection from a remote location across the Internet to servers in the office network and access shared resources as though she were located on the network itself. However, if she is connecting to a server running Windows 2000 Server or Windows Server 2003, these servers use Rivest Cipher 4 (RC4) encryption at a level of either 40 bits or 56 bits. However, her computer uses 128-bit encryption by default; the error observed indicates an encryption mismatch and she must select the **Maximum strength encryption (disconnect if server declines)** option to correct this problem. The other encryption options will not correct the encryption mismatch. Connie will obtain the same error regardless of the type of VPN connection protocol she is using. Therefore, answers A, B, and D are incorrect. For more information, refer to "VPN Connection Security" in Chapter 14.

49. **B.** When you have installed a faulty device driver or application and the computer fails to complete the startup sequence, you can use the Last Known Good Configuration to restart the computer. This restores the computer to its configuration as of the previous successful logon. If this method does not work or if Lisa had been able to log on before receiving the error, she could roll back the driver using safe mode. This is not the first option she should try, so answer A is incorrect. She should use System Restore only if no other recovery methods solve the problem, so answer C is incorrect. The Command Prompt option from the System Recovery Options dialog box can be used to remove or replace faulty or corrupted files if safe mode does not work. It is also not the first method of choice, so answer D is incorrect. For more information, see the section "Last Known Good Configuration" in Chapter 18.

50. **D.** Terri needs to mount (attach) the disk so that she can find it in Disk Management and proceed further with configuring it. She can do this by right-clicking **Disk Management** and choosing **Attach VHD**. She can also do it by

issuing the `Attach` command from within DiskPart. Terri cannot format the disk until she has mounted it and created a partition, so answer A is incorrect. She does not need to convert it to dynamic storage; further, she cannot do this until she has mounted it, so answer B is incorrect. She cannot mark the disk as active until she has mounted it and created a partition. She then needs to format the partition, and only then can she mark the partition (not the disk) as active, so answer C is incorrect. For more information, refer to "Mounting VHDs" in Chapter 6.

51. **A**. The **Use Policy List of Internet Explorer 7 sites** policy enable Harry to add any desired websites to a list of sites that display in Compatibility View. This feature enables websites designed for earlier versions of Internet Explorer to display properly in Internet Explorer 8. Harry can access this policy from the **Administrative Templates\Windows Components\Internet Explorer\ Compatibility View** node under either Computer Configuration or User Configuration. None of the other options provided here will make the websites display in Compatibility View, although users can manually specify that they will display in Compatibility View; consequently, answers B, C, and D are incorrect. For more information, refer to "Configuring Compatibility View" in Chapter 8.

52. **C**. Windows PE is the Preboot Execution environment, used with Windows 7 to boot the computer to a command prompt. You can use Windows PE when capturing an image of a reference computer on which you've installed Windows 7 and used Sysprep to prepare it for imaging, or to start a manual deployment of an image to a new computer. Windows PE boots the computer to a command prompt, which enables you to use the DiskPart tool to create and format a partition suitable for installing Windows 7 from a network share. It is no longer possible to use an MS-DOS floppy disk for this purpose, so answer A is incorrect. You would use a Windows 7 installation DVD-ROM to perform a manual installation but not to start an installation from a deployment share, so answer B is incorrect. A system repair disc is used for accessing repair options for a computer that will not start properly; although you can use it to boot to a command prompt, this is not the standard method for starting an installation, so answer D is incorrect. For more information, refer to "Understanding Windows PE" in Chapter 5.

53. **B**. You should configure the User Account Control: Behavior of the **elevation prompt for standard users policy** to prompt for credentials. The exhibit shows that this policy is set to automatically deny elevation requests, which results in users receiving a denial of access if they attempt to perform an action that displays a UAC prompt. By setting this policy to prompt for credentials, Charles will receive a UAC prompt that asks for an administrator to enter a

password to enable him to perform this action. If you add Charles to the Administrators group, he receives more privileges than required, so answer A is incorrect. If you enable the Only **elevate executables that are signed and validated** policy, this policy would perform public key infrastructure (PKI) signature checks on programs requiring elevated privileges but would still allow programs that pass this check to run. This does not alleviate the problem at hand, so answer C is incorrect. If you enable the **Switch to the secure desktop when prompting for elevation** policy, the secure desktop appears whenever a UAC prompt is displayed. Although you should enable this policy for a secure environment, it does not solve this problem, so answer D is incorrect. If you disable the **Run all administrators in Admin Approval Mode** you turn UAC off. Administrators can run any actions that normally display UAC prompts without receiving a prompt, whereas non-administrators are denied access; therefore, answer E is incorrect. For more information, see the section "User Account Control Policies" in Chapter 12.

54. **A**. When you upgrade to an edition of Windows 7, the Windows.old folder holds subfolders and files from the previous operating system. The Program Files folder holds the current applications only, so answer B is incorrect. The Users folder holds current user-specific documents and settings. It does not hold previous settings, so answer C is incorrect. Software Explorer is a utility that enables you to view and manage programs. It also does not hold previous settings, so answer D is incorrect. For more information, see the sections "Upgrading from One Edition of Windows 7 to Another" and "The Windows.old Folder" in Chapter 3.

55. **B**. Don should select the **Create a system repair disc** option, which enables him to create a CD or DVD disc that he can use to start any Windows 7 computer if other startup options fail (one disc is needed for 32-bit machines and a different one for 64-bit machines). The **Create a system image** option enables him to back up all items required to restore Windows operation but does not create a bootable disc that can be used to start other computers, so answer A is incorrect. The **Back up now** option merely starts a backup with the current settings, so answer C is incorrect. The **Manage space** option enables him to manage the space used by backups including deletion of older backups, but it does not allow him to change the backup configuration, so answer D is incorrect. The **Change settings** option would reopen the Set Up Backup Wizard so that he could change the items that are included in the backup, so answer D is incorrect. Note that on the exam, a question such as this one might be displayed as a "hot spot" item where you must select the correct answer by clicking on an image of the dialog box as shown in the exhibit here. For more information, refer to "Creating a System Recovery Disk" in Chapter 17.

56. A, D, E, H. For DirectAccess connections to work, each client computer must have a computer certificate that enables DirectAccess authentication, and its computer account must be added to the special security group set up on the DirectAccess server—in this case, the DA group. Nolan must also configure a GPO that specifies IPv6 transition technologies as well as DNS security (DNSSEC) and DNS settings for DirectAccess. User certificates are not required, nor should the user accounts be added to the DA group, so answers B and C are incorrect. DirectAccess does not use SSL configuration settings; nor does DirectAccess use WINS name resolution technologies, so answers F and G are incorrect. For more information, refer to "Configuring DirectAccess Clients" in Chapter 13.

57. C. The new Location-Aware Printing feature in Windows 7 enables Helen to specify different default printers according to the network she is attached to. When she moves her computer from one network to another, the default printer automatically changes according to the settings she has specified after selecting **Change my default printer when I change networks**. It is not possible to set more than one printer as default from the Devices and Printers applet, so answer A is incorrect. If she selects **Always use the same printer as my default printer**, this disables location-aware printing, so answer B is incorrect. In previous Windows versions, she would have needed to ensure that the correct printer is selected from the Print menu of the application she is using; however, using location-aware printing removes the need to do this. Therefore answer D is incorrect. For more information, refer to "Location-Aware Printing" in Chapter 10.

58. B. The Change Homegroup Settings dialog box provides the **Choose media streaming options** link that opens the Choose media streaming options for computers and devices dialog box. From this dialog box you can view all accessible devices on your network and select **Allowed** or **Blocked** as required for each device, including the home theater system in this scenario. Simply selecting **Music** and **Videos** in the Share libraries and printers section would share these libraries with the other Windows 7 computers, which is not desired here. Therefore, answer A is incorrect. The **Change advanced sharing settings** option does not provide access to the options for allowing or blocking specific devices or for turning media streaming on or off, so answers C and D are incorrect. For more information, refer to "Modifying HomeGroup Settings" in Chapter 11.

59. A, C, D, E. Reliability Monitor includes categories for Application failures, Windows failures, Miscellaneous failures, Warnings, and Information. Within the Miscellaneous failures category, Sam can obtain information about improper shutdowns and sleep failures, among other problems; however, none of these categories provide information related to logon failures. Therefore, answer B is incorrect. For more information, refer to "Reliability Monitor" in Chapter 16.

60. B. The new Transport Server mode in WDS enables Michelle to install Windows 7 on new computers without the need for an AD DS domain or a DNS server. This mode includes a PXE provider that enables her to perform network booting and multicasting on a network meeting the specifications outlined here. Deployment Server mode requires an AD DS domain, DNS server, and DHCP server. These are not available here, so answer A is incorrect. MDT 2010 uses additional servers and is more complex to set up for an installation of this size, so answer C is incorrect. Use of unattended installation using DVD media would take additional effort including a visit to each of the new computers, so answer D is incorrect. For more information, refer to "Understanding WDS" in Chapter 5.

61. C. Beth should use the volume shadow copy feature to restore the folder in which the file was located. She can right-click the folder and choose **Restore previous versions** and then select the most recent time before she deleted the file. Before she does this, she should copy other files in the folder that have changed since the time of the previous version because they will also be restored back to this time and their changes will be lost. After she restores the folder, she can copy these other files back into the restored folder. Using Windows Backup will recover the file to the time of the most recent backup, losing changes that have occurred since then, so answer A is incorrect. She cannot use volume shadow copy to restore a deleted file, so answer B is incorrect. The System Restore feature restores her computer to an earlier point in time but does not recover document files; therefore, answer D is incorrect. For more information, refer to "Using Shadow Copies to Restore Damaged or Deleted Files" in Chapter 18.

62. E, D, B, G, A. You should perform the installation steps in the following order:

E. Create a network share and copy the Windows 7 Professional Setup files to it.

D. Check the client computer's hardware and BIOS for compatibility.

B. Boot the computer with a network boot disk.

G. Connect to the server's network share containing the Windows 7 Professional Setup files.

A. Run `Setup.exe`.

For the simple action of installing a single new computer before setting up to begin a deployment, you do not need to install WDS or create a VHD, so answers C and F are incorrect. Note that on the exam, a question similar to this might be displayed as a "build list and reorder" question, in which you must drag the required items to a list area and sequence them in the proper order; if they are not in the correct order, the question is scored incorrect. For more information, see the section "Performing an Attended Installation" in Chapter 2.

63. C. Fred should click the down arrow next to the Search area in the Internet Explorer address bar. From the menu displayed, select the desired search provider. This procedure changes the search provider for the duration of the current Internet Explorer session, after which it reverts to the default you have configured. The Settings button on the Privacy tab of the Internet Options dialog box enables him to configure the pop-up blocker and not the search provider, so answer A is incorrect. Selecting a search provider by either clicking **Settings** from the Search section of the General tab or clicking **Manage Search Providers** from the Tools menu changes the search provider permanently, so answers B and D are incorrect. For more information, see the section "Configuring Providers" in Chapter 8.

64. A. Greg should right-click the network adapter and select **Update Driver Software**. The red X indicates that the network adapter does not have drivers installed. Selecting **Update Driver Software** starts the Hardware Update Wizard and initiates a search for the appropriate driver. He might need to reboot to Windows XP to access the network adapter manufacturer's website to download a suitable driver before he runs this wizard. Greg would receive the **Enable** option only if the network adapter were disabled; in this case, it would be displayed with a black downward-pointing arrow icon, so answer B is incorrect. The **Scan for hardware changes** option does not install new drivers, so answer C is incorrect. Windows Update provides updates for Windows 7 and other Microsoft software products. It does not provide Windows 7–compliant drivers, so answer D is incorrect. For more information, see the section "Using Device Manager" in Chapter 7.

65. B, C, E. Keisha should assign Ben's user account the Allow–Full Control permission for the folder, encrypt the folder, and then add Ben's user account to the list of users allowed to open the folder. She should not assign the Users group the Deny–Full Control permission for the folder; doing so would prevent Ben from accessing the folder because all users are automatically members of this group and an explicit denial overrides all allowed permissions. Therefore, answer A is incorrect. If she were to encrypt the files rather than the folder, new files including the temporary files would not be encrypted, so answer D is incorrect. It is not necessary to designate Ben's user account as an EFS recovery agent in this scenario, so answer F is incorrect. For more information, refer to "Configuring Security Permissions" and "Configuring Data Encryption" in Chapter 11.

66. **B**. Windows Easy Transfer facilitates the transfer of a user's documents and settings from an old computer to a new one. This tool enables you to use an Easy Transfer cable, a network share, or an external USB hard disk or flash drive to transfer these items. The user profile would not contain all the required information, so answer A is incorrect. The `Scanstate` and `Loadstate` tools are designed more for transferring data and settings from a series of older computers to new Windows 7 Professional computers. It is easier in this scenario with only one computer involved to use the Windows Easy Transfer; therefore, answer C is incorrect. The Files and Settings Transfer Wizard was used in Windows XP for this purpose. It has been replaced by Windows Easy Transfer, so answer D is incorrect. For more information, see the section "Windows Easy Transfer" in Chapter 4.

67. **A**. Ron needs to type the **`ipconfig /renew`** command at the command prompt. If a computer is configured to obtain an IPv4 address automatically and it is unable to contact a DHCP server, it will use Automatic Private IP Addressing (APIPA) to obtain an IP address. When this happens, a computer will receive an IP address in the range 169.254.*x*.*y*, where *x* can vary from 0 to 255 and *y* can vary from 1 to 254. When configured with APIPA, a computer can communicate with any other APIPA-enabled computers but not with other computers or the Internet.

    The problem is not related to the lack of an IP address for the default gateway or DNS server, so answers B and C are incorrect. If the network administrator has configured these properties for the DHCP scope, Ron's computer will automatically receive these parameters when it successfully contacts the DHCP server. There is no reason to suspect that his computer's network adapter card has become faulty and needs to be replaced, so answer D is incorrect. For more information, refer to "Implementing APIPA" in Chapter 9.

68. **A**. In the Allow programs to communicate through Windows Firewall dialog box, you should enable the Remote Administration option. This option enables the management of remote computers by means of utilities that utilize RPC. Remote Assistance enables a user to seek assistance from an expert on another computer but does not enable RPC-based utilities, so answer B is incorrect. Remote Desktop enables you to connect to your computer from another computer running Windows XP/Vista/7 but does not enable RPC-based utilities, so answer C is incorrect. It is not necessary to enable TCP port 135 because it is simpler to enable Remote Administration, so answer D is incorrect. Remote Procedure Call is not a program that you can add to the Exceptions list using the **Allow another program** button, so answer E is incorrect. For more information, see the section "Basic Windows Firewall Configuration" in Chapter 10.

69. **A, G**. To connect to the executive's computer, you need to enable TCP port 4322 on each router by allowing it for incoming and outgoing traffic. Then, to connect to the computer via the new TCP port, you would use the computer's NetBIOS name of LON182-EX concatenated with a colon (:) and the port number of 4322. Answer B is incorrect because the Registry key is only for listening for incoming connections and you do not need to configure that on the client computer. Answer C and D are incorrect because the **Create invitations that can only be used from computers running Windows Vista or later** check box option is used when configuring Remote Assistance, not Remote Desktop. Answer E is incorrect because the IP address is that of the DNS server. Answer F is incorrect because the IP address is the exec's current IP address; at some point you would not be able to connect via the IP address if the computer leased a different IP address from the DHCP server, so you should use the NetBIOS name. In addition, the port in answer F is incorrectly identified as 4233, not 4322. Answer H is incorrect because the port number is not identified in the Connect text box, so it defaults to TCP port 3389 and the exec's computer is not listening to that port. For more information, see the section "Remote Desktop" in Chapter 14.

70. **A, B**. To service offline Windows images, including updating security fixes, Gerry must mount the images first. He can use either Deployment Image Servicing and Management (DISM) or ImageX for this purpose. Of the commands mentioned, only the `dism /mount-wim /wimfile:x:\image1.wim /index:1 /mountdir:c:\mountedimages` and `imagex /mountrw x:\image1.wim 1 c:\mountedimages` have the correct command syntax. The other commands are invalid, so answers C, D, E, and F are all incorrect. For more information, see the section "Creating an Answer File" in Chapter 5.

71. **D**. By enabling the **Specify intranet Microsoft update service location** policy, Kingsley can specify the name of the WSUS server from which client computers will receive their updates. The **Configure Automatic Updates** policy governs how the computer will receive and install updates. The **Turn on Software Notifications** policy enables him to determine whether users see detailed notification messages that promote the value, installation, and usage of optional software from the Microsoft Update service. Neither of these two policies will prevent clients from accessing the Microsoft Windows Update website across the Internet, so answers A and B are incorrect. The **Enable client-side targeting** policy enables him to specify a target group name to be used for receiving updates from an intranet server such as a WSUS server; however, this policy by itself does not ensure that all computers access the WSUS server to receive their updates, so answer C is incorrect. For more information, refer to "Configuring Windows Update Policies" in Chapter 7.

72. B, C, E, F. This scenario requires that Roberta install BranchCache in Hosted Cache mode, which uses a server running Windows Server 2008 R2 in each branch office that hosts files cached from head office servers. She cannot use Distributed Cache mode because this mode works only with a single subnet with no more than 50 client computers, so answer A is incorrect. She must upgrade the branch office servers because BranchCache does not work on a Windows Server 2003 R2 machine. She must also upgrade branch office (but not head office) client computers to Windows 7 because BranchCache does not work on a Vista machine; therefore, answer D is incorrect. She must also create a GPO including a predefined firewall rule that enables BranchCache messages to pass, and the indicated predefined firewall rule works for this scenario, so she does not need to create any custom firewall rules. Therefore, answer G is incorrect. For more information, refer to "Configuring BranchCache" in Chapter 12.

73. B. You can right-click the program and choose **Properties**. On the dialog box that appears, select the **Compatibility** tab and select the option to run this program in compatibility mode for Windows XP (Service Pack 3). The Previous Versions tab enables her to go back to an older version of a file (which includes the shortcut to the program but not the program itself). It does not enable her to run a program in compatibility mode, so answer A is incorrect. You need to have Windows 7 Professional, Enterprise, or Ultimate to use Windows XP Mode. Because you are using Windows 7 Home Premium, you cannot install Windows XP Mode, so answer C is incorrect. Enabling the Windows Classic theme emulates the desktop appearance of older Windows versions but does not enable a program to run in compatibility mode; therefore, answer D is incorrect. For more information, see the sections "Software Compatibility" in Chapter 2 and "Configuring Application Compatibility Mode" in Chapter 8.

74. C. Laurie should access the Battery section of the Power Options dialog box and increase the **Low battery level** setting. She can reach this dialog box by selecting the **Change plan settings** link for the power plan in use and then selecting **Change advanced power settings**. Increasing this setting enables her to receive a warning sooner and gives her more time to save her work. Setting the **Put the computer to sleep** setting to a higher value would cause the computer to remain active for a longer time, thereby actually increasing the chance of data loss from a sudden shutdown, so answer A is incorrect. Selecting the **Power saver** power plan would allow the computer to run longer on battery power but in itself would not provide more warning of low battery levels, so answer B is incorrect. Increasing the Low battery notification setting is not possible. This is an on/off switch and is normally set to on. Turning it off would result in no warning at all and the computer would shut down without warning; therefore, answer D is incorrect. For more information, see the section "Advanced Power Settings" in Chapter 13.

75. **C**. Lance should access the User Access to Effluents dialog box, click **Add**, and add the other researchers individually to the list of users that can transparently access the file. Windows 7 enables you to enable additional users to access files and folders that are encrypted with EFS. Lance can authorize the users in his group to access the data files in this folder by following the procedure in this option for each of the files in turn. The Encryption Details dialog box does not contain an option for enabling additional users to access the encrypted files, so answers A and B are incorrect. Lance cannot add a group to the list of users who can access the file on the User Access dialog box, so answer D is incorrect. For more information, see the section "Encrypting Files" in Chapter 11.

76. **A, C**. Besides Task Manager, which has been able to do this since the days of Windows NT, Brent can use Resource Monitor to terminate an unresponsive process. The process is displayed in red in the top section of the Overview tab. Right-click the process and choose **End Process** and accept the warning that you will lose unsaved data. The other tools mentioned here do not offer this capability, so answers B, D, and E are all incorrect. For more information, refer to "Task Manager" and "Resource Monitor" in Chapter 16.

77. **C**. Ken should run the Windows 7 Upgrade Advisor. He can download this application by selecting the **Check Compatibility Online** option from the Install Windows screen that appears when he inserts the Windows 7 DVD-ROM. The setup command used for installing Windows 7 does not include the /checkupgradeonly switch, so answer A is incorrect. The winnt32 /checkupgradeonly command was used with Windows XP to produce a compatibility report for upgrading older versions of Windows to this operating system. However, it is not used with Windows Vista or 7, so answer B is incorrect. Because Ken can download and run the Windows 7 Upgrade Advisor to produce a comprehensive report of potential issues, he should not simply install Windows 7 and hope that everything is compatible. Therefore, answer D is incorrect. For more information, see the section "Preparing a Computer to Meet Upgrade Requirements" in Chapter 3.

78. **B**. Amanda should use ZTI. This is a high-volume deployment strategy that is suitable for an AD DS network and enables fully automated installation of client computers without user intervention. All other deployment strategies mentioned here require more amount of user intervention, so answers A, C, and D are all incorrect. For more information, refer to "Zero-Touch, High Volume Deployment" in Chapter 5.

79. **D**. Ellen should use the Wbadmin command. This utility enables her to script the creation and management of backups on Windows 7 and Windows Server 2008 R2 computers. Available subcommands and parameters for this command enable her to perform any action associated with the Backup and Restore Control

Panel applet. The `Ntdsutil` command enables her to perform a large range of computer management actions but not backups, so answer A is incorrect. The `Ntbackup` command was used in older versions of Windows but has been replaced in Windows 7 by the `Wbadmin` command, so answer B is incorrect. The `Wdsutil` command enables her to manage a Windows Deployment Services (WDS) server for deploying multiple Windows 7 images. It is not used with backups, so answer C is incorrect. For more information, refer to "Using the Command Line to Perform a Backup" in Chapter 17.

80. **C, D, E**. The problem exhibited by the one computer suggests a networking problem. Mark should check the physical network adapter and the TCP/IP configuration. He should also check the `netsetup.log` file for networking errors. Answers A and B are incorrect because the device settings are not the problem and the `setupapi.log` file is applicable to device driver installation, not networking. For more information, see the sections "Unavailable Network" and "Troubleshooting Failed Installations" in Chapter 2 and "Using TCP/IP Utilities to Troubleshoot TCP/IP" in Chapter 9.

81. **B, C**. To share the modem, one computer should be connected to both the modem and the network. That computer should be configured with ICS. This automatically begins a simplified DHCP service, with a DNS forwarding service and NAT service, to the rest of the computers. The remaining computers should all be configured as DHCP clients because they receive their IP address information from the sharing computer. Answer A is wrong because there is no need to install a router that uses NAT. You likely do not need to modify the default configuration of Windows Firewall, which means answer D is wrong. Answer F is wrong because the modem either obtains an IP address or is configured with a static IP address—either way, it is still able to be shared. Answer E is wrong because only one computer needs to share the Internet connection. Answer G is wrong because you do not want to create a bridge on any of the computers. For more information, see the section "Using Internet Connection Sharing to Share Your Internet Connection" in Chapter 10.

82. **B**. You should access the Safety menu in Internet Explorer and ensure that the SmartScreen Filter is enabled. This option updates the phishing filter first introduced in Internet Explorer 7 with Windows Vista and checks for malicious websites that attempt to trick you into providing personal data such as credit card or bank account numbers for fraudulent purposes. It sends the addresses of these sites to Microsoft, which maintains an up-to-date list of websites that have been identified as phishing sites. This filter is enabled by default. The pop-up blocker prevents websites from displaying additional Internet Explorer windows but also does not check for phishing sites, so answer A is incorrect. Protected mode prevents websites from modifying user or system files and settings unless

you provide your consent. It also does not check for phishing sites, so answer C is incorrect. Setting the security level for the Internet zone to High disables less secure features of the browser and ensures that the highest security level is maintained; however, it does not check for phishing sites, so answer D is incorrect. For more information, see the section "Configuring the SmartScreen Filter" in Chapter 8.

83. **C**. Credential Manager is a new feature in Windows 7 that enables Pauline to manage credentials for user logon to resources such as websites, terminal servers, and applications. It includes a backup-and-restore feature that simplifies the process of backing up credentials and restoring them to a different computer. Windows Backup and Restore can transfer this data, but it is far more convenient to use Credential Manager for this purpose; therefore, answer A is incorrect. Windows Easy Transfer migrates files and application settings, but not website logon and password information, so answer B is incorrect. The **Import** command on the Privacy tab of the Internet Options dialog box imports cookies and not passwords; therefore, answer C is incorrect. For more information, refer to "Backing Up and Restoring Credentials in Credential Manager" in Chapter 12.

84. **A**. DirectAccess client computers must be running Windows 7 Enterprise or Ultimate; computers running other editions of Windows 7 cannot use DirectAccess. The computer must have a computer certificate that enables client and server authentication; user certificates are not required, so answer B is incorrect. The DirectAccess server, and not the client, must have two consecutive IPv4 addresses, so answer C is incorrect. The computer account of the client computer, and not the user account, must be included in the DA security group, so answer D is incorrect. For more information, refer to "Network Infrastructure Requirements" in Chapter 13.

85. **B, E**. Rupert should ensure that the drivers have been signed by either a Windows publisher or trusted publisher. He should add the publisher's certificate for each driver to the trusted certificates store and place the drivers in the driver store. This process is known as *staging driver packages*, and it is the only way in Windows 7 to enable standard users to install devices without administrator privileges. The publisher's certificate needs to be in the trusted certificates store and not in the driver store, so answer A is incorrect. If you create your own certificates for unsigned drivers, users would still need administrative credentials to install these drivers, so answer C is incorrect. The drivers are placed in the driver store and not the `Windows\System32\Drivers` folder, so answer D is incorrect. For more information, refer to "What's New with Driver Signing in Windows 7" in Chapter 7.

86. **A.** By enabling the **All Removable Storage classes: Deny all access**, Doug denies read and write access to all types of removable storage devices. None of the other policies provide the complete denial required by this scenario, so answers B, C, and D are all incorrect. For more information, refer to "Configuring Removable Drive Policies" in Chapter 15.

87. **B.** An IPv6 address that begins with 2002 is a 6-to-4 address. The address given here maps the IPv4 address 10.254.253.252 to the IPv6 address space. A Teredo address would begin with 2001 and not 2002, so answer A is incorrect. An IPv4-mapped address maps an IPv4-only node and is represented as `::ffff:w.x.y.z` to an IPv6 node, so answer C is incorrect. A link-local unicast address is the IPv6 equivalent of APIPA and does not represent an IPv4 to IPv6 transitional technology, so answer D is incorrect. For more information, refer to "Compatibility Between IPv4 and IPv6 Addresses" in Chapter 9.

88. **B, E.** To delete passwords, cookies, and form data that you have stored on the computer, you should access the Delete Browsing History dialog box, select all the check boxes provided, and then click **Delete**. You can reach this dialog box from the General tab of the Internet Options dialog box. Then, to clear automatically completed names and passwords, you should access the Content tab of the Internet Options dialog box. Click **Settings** in the AutoComplete section, and then clear the check box labeled **User names and passwords on forms**. The Temporary Internet Files and History Settings dialog box does not have an option for deleting browsing history, so answer A is incorrect. Clearing the check box labeled **Turn on feed reading now** stops the downloading of RSS feeds but does not remove stored passwords, so answer C is incorrect. Changing the security level for the Internet zone to High also does not remove stored passwords, so answer D is incorrect. For more information, see the section "Configuring Internet Explorer" in Chapter 8.

89. **B, C.** Wendy should first enable the Windows Remote Management Service, which she can do by typing `winrm quickconfig`. Having done this, she can access Server3 and determine its MAC address by using the command `winrs -r:Server3 ipconfig /all`. The `winrm get server3` command would retrieve management information about Server3 but would not enable remote management, so answer A is incorrect. She must specify the remote computer name using the `-r:` parameter, so answer D is incorrect. The `arp -a` command displays current ARP entries in her local computer's address resolution table but in itself does not provide MAC address information for a remote computer, so answers E and F are incorrect. For more information, refer to "Using TCP/IP Utilities to Troubleshoot TCP/IP" in Chapter 9 and "Using Windows Remote Management Service" in Chapter 14.

90. **C**. The problem is apparently a share permission that is more restrictive than the NTFS permissions because the assistant can log on locally and use the files but cannot make changes to them from across the network. This means that there is no need to make changes to NTFS permissions, so answer A is incorrect. It also means that the share permissions should be increased by allowing Full Control (your only option in this case) rather than denying Read or denying Full Control, which is why answers B and D are incorrect. For more information, see the section "Modifying Shared Folder Properties" in Chapter 11.

91. **A**. The default schedule for Windows Backup to create backups is every Sunday at 7 P.M. If the computer is not running at this time, a backup will not be created; Steve must modify the backup schedule so that the backup takes place on a day and time that the computer is running. It is possible that Steve might not have allocated sufficient space for creation of additional backups, but he would have received an error during the initial backup; consequently answer C is incorrect. Creation of additional backups does not depend on choice of settings such as creation of a system image or use of the **Let Windows choose** default, so answers B and D are incorrect. For more information, refer to "Scheduling Your Backups" in Chapter 17.

92. **A, C, G**. Three things must be in place before Suzanne can connect a Remote Desktop Connection to her home computer: (1) the corporate router and firewall must allow the RDP traffic to be transmitted, (2) Suzanne's home computer's Windows Firewall must be configured to allow an exception for RDP traffic, and (3) Suzanne's home computer must be configured to enable Remote Desktop services with Suzanne's user account granted permission to connect. The standard port is TCP 3389 for RDP. Answers B, D, E, and F are all incorrect because you do not need to configure anything on Suzanne's laptop, nor do you need to enable Internet Connection Sharing. Answer F is also incorrect because the **Create invitations that can only be used from computers running Windows Vista or later** check box is used when configuring Remote Assistance and not Remote Desktop. For more information, refer to "Basic Windows Firewall Configuration" in Chapter 10 and "Remote Desktop" in Chapter 14.

93. **B**. You should choose the option to select another backup to restore files from and then follow the steps presented to restore this backup. The option to save the restored files in a specified location enables you to create a new copy of files or folders backed up on the same computer, so answer A is incorrect. The option to create a restore point or change settings enables you to create a point that can be used for rolling back your computer settings to a previous point in time. It does not restore files from either the same computer or a different one, so answer C is incorrect. The option to recover system settings or your computer is used to restore your entire computer to an earlier point in time. This does not restore files from another computer, so answer D is incorrect. For more information, see the section "Using Windows Backup to Recover Data" in Chapter 18.

94. **C**. Mary should issue the `imagex /apply c:\Windows_Install \install.wim /check 1 p:` command. In this command, the 1 is the image index number of the Windows image being deployed. This number ranges from 1 to the total number of Windows images contained within the `install.wim` file, which is 1 in this scenario. Mary would use the `dism` command for servicing and updating an existing VHD, not for deploying a new copy of Windows 7. Further, the syntax for using this command is incorrect here, and answers A and D are both incorrect. The `wdsutil` command is used to script the rapid deployment of Windows to many computers using Windows Deployment Services (WDS). It is issued from a server and not from a client computer, so answer B is incorrect. The `Image:` and `Set-Edition:` parameters are used with the `dism` command for upgrading an existing Windows image and not for deploying a new one, so answer E is incorrect. For more information, refer to "Deploying VHDs" in Chapter 6.

95. **A, D**. In Internet Explorer 8 on Windows 7, the default setting is to run in Protected mode. So, if you reset Internet Explorer to default settings, it will be running in Protected mode. In addition, it will display the message `Protected Mode: On` in the status bar. If this message is not visible, you should reset the default settings. Protected mode attempts to prevent hackers from hijacking your browser and installing malicious software. Deleting the browser history, disabling add-ons, or disabling RSS feeds will not reset Internet Explorer to Protected mode, so answers B, C, and E are incorrect. For more information, see the section, "Configuring Protected Mode in Windows Internet Explorer" in Chapter 8.

96. **B**. You should upgrade the RAM. All editions of Windows 7 require a minimum of 1 GB RAM. The specifications indicated for all the other hardware components meet the requirements for Windows 7, so answers A, C, D, and E are incorrect. For more information, see the section "Identifying Hardware Requirements" in Chapter 2.

97. **A**. Rachel should select **View update history**. She should then select the **Installed Updates** link and, on the Uninstall an Update page that appears, right-click the problematic update and select **Uninstall**. This action enables her to uninstall the problematic update. Clearing the check box labeled **Allow all users to install updates on this computer prevents** nonadministrative users from installing updates but does not remove problematic updates; therefore, answer B is incorrect. Selecting the **Download updates but let me choose whether to install them** option enables her to choose whether updates are

installed but also does not remove problematic updates; therefore, answer C is incorrect. There is no Uninstall option available on the page that appears after selecting the **Change settings** option, so answer D is incorrect. For more information, refer to "Reviewing Update History and Rolling Back Updates" in Chapter 7.

98. D, F. You can upgrade computers running Windows Vista Home Premium and Windows 7 Home Basic to Windows 7 Home Premium without the need to reinstall all applications and user settings. Answers A, B, C, and E are wrong because all other computers listed in this question require a clean install of Windows 7, which requires that applications and user settings be reinstalled. For more information, see the sections "Upgrading to Windows 7 from a Previous Version of Windows" and "Upgrading from One Edition of Windows 7 to Another" in Chapter 3.

99. B. Bill needs to import a certificate to the certificate store on the BranchCache server. This certificate must be imported under the local computer account so that the client computers in the branch office can trust this server. If it is added under the administrator account, clients will be unable to use this certificate to access the Hosted Cache server, so answer A is incorrect. It is not necessary to import certificates to the certificate store on the client computers, so answers C and D are incorrect. For more information, refer to "Certificate Management with BranchCache" in Chapter 12.

100. D. You should check the network connectivity from her computer to the DHCP server and verify that the DHCP server is operating normally. An IPv6 address in the range fe80::/64 is a link local unicast address, which is the IPv6 equivalent of an APIPA address. The computer configures itself with this address type when it is unable to access a DHCP server to obtain proper TCP/IPv6 information. You should not configure a manual IPv6 address because this might conflict with another address on the network and cause communication problems, so answer A is incorrect. The Alternate Configuration tab is available only for IPv4 and not for IPv6, so answer B is incorrect. You cannot configure an IP address in the Advanced TCP/IP Settings dialog box if the computer is configured to obtain an IP address automatically; this configuration is reserved for computers requiring more than one IP address. Therefore, answer C is incorrect. For more information, see the section "Troubleshooting IPv4 and IPv6 Problems" in Chapter 9.

101. A, B. Kathy must enable the **Provide the unique identifiers for your organization** and **Choose how BitLocker-protected operating system drives can be recovered** policy settings as part of setting up a DRA. She should enable the latter policy in the Fixed Data Drives, Operating System Drives, and/or Removable Data Drives subnodes of the BitLocker Drive Encryption node as required. She might need to enable the other two policies mentioned in this question, but they are not specifically needed for enabling a DRA so answers C and D are incorrect. For more information, refer to "Use of Data Recovery Agents" in Chapter 13.

102.A, D, G. By configuring the Documents library with the Share with Homegroup (Read) option, Edward enables all other family members to view but not modify files and folders in this library. The other options for the Documents library would enable read/write capabilities that are not desired according to this question, so answers B and C are incorrect. To specifically share the Financial folder with Louise while providing her with read/write capability, he needs to place this folder in a new library and provide her with the read/write capability. Configuring this library with either Share with Homegroup option would provide undesired access to the children for this folder, so answers E and F are incorrect. For more information, refer to "Folder Virtualization" and "Modifying HomeGroup Settings" in Chapter 11.

103.A. Windows SIM enables you to create answer files from information included in a Windows image (.wim) file and a catalog (.clg) file. The answer file created by SIM is named Unattend.xml, and you should copy this file to a USB flash drive or floppy disk and insert the disk after the computer to be installed with Windows 7 has booted from the DVD-ROM. Windows XP and older operating systems used the answer file named Unattend.txt. This file is not used with Windows Vista or 7, so answers B and D are incorrect. Sysprep.exe is used to create an image of a Windows 7 installation for deployment to other computers. It is not used to create answer files, so answers C and D are incorrect. For more information, see the section "Understanding Answer Files" in Chapter 5.

104.A. You should use the Startup Repair tool to diagnose and repair the problem. This tool attempts to recover a computer that is unable to start normally. Among the problems this tool can repair is that of missing or corrupted device drivers. You cannot use the Last Known Good Configuration because Kelly logged on successfully after the first reboot, so answer B is incorrect. You cannot access safe mode because Kelly stated the computer would not even boot after it locked up, so answer C is incorrect. The Recovery Console option in Windows 2000 and XP has been replaced by the Startup Repair tool in Windows 7, so answer D is incorrect. You should not reinstall Windows 7 unless you have exhausted all other repair options, so answer E is incorrect. For more information, see the section "Using a System Repair Disk" in Chapter 18.

105.A. You should select the **Block** option in the Inbound Connections section on the Private Profile tab of the Windows Firewall with Advanced Security on Local Computer Properties dialog box. This enables client employees to access shared information on your computer according to the Windows Firewall exceptions you have configured. You should also select the **Block all connections** option in the Inbound Connections section on the Public Profile tab of the Windows Firewall with Advanced Security on Local Computer Properties dialog box. This prevents any unauthorized connections to your computer when you are in an insecure location, while still allowing Internet access. Answer B is incorrect because this option would prevent client employees from accessing required information and would leave your computer open to unauthorized access when in insecure locations. Answers C, D, E, and F are all incorrect because you do not need to configure outbound connections and one of the required inbound configurations is missing. For more information, see the section "Configuring Multiple Firewall Profiles" in Chapter 10.

106.C. You should select the **OS boot information** option from the Boot tab of the System Information utility, which is started by typing `msconfig`. This tool enables you to disable common services and startup programs to selectively troubleshoot which items are preventing a normal startup. By selecting the **OS boot information** option, you can see which drivers are being loaded during startup. This can assist you in determining which driver is causing her computer to not start properly. The **Diagnostic startup** option loads only basic drivers and services but does not display driver names during startup, so answer A is incorrect. The **Boot log** option logs information from the boot procedure to `%systemroot%\Ntbtlog.txt`. It does not display driver names, so answer B is incorrect. The **Disable all** option disables all startup programs but does not display driver names, so answer D is incorrect. For more information, refer to "System Configuration Utility" in Chapter 16.

107.B. Windows XP Mode provides a fully functional virtual computer running Windows XP Professional on top of the Windows 7 desktop, enabling Jerri to install an incompatible application so that users can run it from Windows 7 as though it were running on a Windows XP computer. In this question, Jerri encountered compatibility problems attempting to install the application on the test Windows 7 computer, so any option suggesting that she install them on the new computers and specify compatibility options is incorrect. A shim is a minor compatibility fix, but its use here will not enable installation of the applications on the new computers. For more information, refer to "Windows XP Mode" in Chapter 8.

108.D. Before Scott undertakes hardware upgrades to his computer, he should defragment his current hard disk. After deleting old applications and data files, his disk contains numerous noncontiguous portions of unused space, which are filled in order with the new applications and data. This results in many fragmented files, and the read-write head must search the entire disk for the required fragments during each I/O operation. This degrades performance significantly. If performance is still at subpar levels after defragmentation, Scott should run Performance Monitor to obtain information that can assist him in choosing the best hardware upgrade (although this is most often to upgrade RAM). However, the other choices are not the first actions that Scott should do, so answers A, B, and C are incorrect. For more information, refer to "Disk Defragmenter" in Chapter 15.

109.B. You should use the EAP authentication protocol. This is the only authentication protocol that works with smart cards. None of PAP, CHAP, or MS-CHAPv2 work with smart cards, so answers A, C, and D are incorrect. For more information, see the section "Remote Access Authentication Protocols" in Chapter 14.

110.C. You should select the **Create a system image** option. This option enables you to fully restore your computer in the event of a hardware failure. This image contains your Windows files and Registry, and you can use it to recover from a hardware failure. The **Create a system repair disc** option enables you to create a CD/DVD disc that enables you to boot your computer into the Windows recovery environment but not back up applications or data, so answer A is incorrect. The **Back up system state** option existed in Windows 2000/XP for backing up items such as the Registry, system files, and boot files. It has been replaced by the **Create a system image** option in Windows 7, so answer B is incorrect. The **Create a restore point or change settings** option enables you to create a point that can be used for rolling back your computer settings to a previous point in time. It does not create a backup of any type, so answer D is incorrect. For more information, see the section "Creating a System Image" in Chapter 17.

111.C. You should check the `Setuperr.log` file first. This file records only the errors generated during Setup, including those errors generated by hardware or driver issues. `Setupact.log` records modifications performed on the system during Setup. Although it might display some errors, it is not the best location to look first, so answer A is incorrect. `Setupapi.dev.log` records data about Plug and Play devices and drivers, but not setup errors, so answer B is incorrect. `Netsetup.log` records information about attempts to join a workgroup or domain, so answer D is incorrect. `Scesetup.log` records security settings but not setup errors, so answer E is incorrect. For more information, see the section "Troubleshooting Failed Installations" in Chapter 2.

112.A. Jennifer should select the **Shortcut** tab of the Command Prompt Properties dialog box, click **Advanced** and then select the **Run as administrator** option. This action marks the command prompt to always run with elevated privileges and ensures that the help desk analyst will receive the UAC prompt. She cannot select the **Run as administrator** option from the Compatibility tab of the

Command Prompt Properties dialog box because these options are not available on this tab; therefore, answer B is incorrect. She should not grant the help desk analyst the Full Control permission on the Security tab. This would enable the help desk analyst to modify the properties of the shortcut but would not provide him with the UAC prompt automatically, so answer C is incorrect. Adding the help desk analyst's user account to the Administrators group would provide him with more privileges than required, so answer D is incorrect. For more information, see the section "Running Programs with Elevated Privileges" in Chapter 12.

113. **C.** By default, anyone with the Allow–Print permission can manage their own print jobs. The Manage documents permission enables you to manage other users' print jobs, and the Manage this printer permission enables you to manage all aspects of the printer, so you should grant these permissions to Catherine's user account and your user account. Printers do not have a Full Control permission, so answer A is incorrect. Granting the Support group the Allow–Manage documents permission would enable them to manage other users' jobs, so answer B is incorrect. Granting only the Allow–Manage documents permission to your user account and Catherine's user account would not enable you and Catherine to manage the printer, so answer D is incorrect. For more information, see the section "Sharing Printers" in Chapter 11.

114. **A.** The best tool that Sandra can use for migrating the files and settings from 28 older computers to 28 newly installed Windows 7 computers is the User State Migration Tool (USMT). Answer B is incorrect because Windows Easy Transfer is best used to migrate files and settings of a single older computer to a single new one. Answer C is incorrect because Sysprep does not migrate any settings. Answer D is incorrect because the Files and Settings Transfer Wizard was a Windows XP tool that is no longer used with Windows 7. For more information, see the section "Migrating Users from Previous Windows Versions" in Chapter 2.

115. **C.** Mindy should configure computers on the network with site local unicast IPv6 addresses. These addresses are equivalent to the private IPv4 addresses and are used for communication between nodes located in the same site. This provides addresses that are private to an organization but unique across all the organization's sites. Global unicast addresses are globally routable Internet addresses that are equivalent to the public IPv4 addresses. They are not private, so answer A is incorrect. Link local unicast addresses are equivalent to APIPA-configured IPv4 addresses and are used on networks without a DHCP server, so answer B is incorrect. Multicast addresses provide interfaces to which packets are delivered to all network interfaces identified by the address. This is not appropriate, so answer D is incorrect. Anycast addresses are utilized only as destination addresses assigned to routers, so answer E is incorrect. For more information, see the section "Types of IPv6 Addresses" in Chapter 9.

116.A. The base score is determined by the lowest of the five component-based Windows Experience Index scores. This is because the slowest component exerts a rate-determining effect; in other words, actions performed by the computer are limited by the weakest performing component. The base score is not the mean (6.3), median (6.4), or maximum (7.1) component score, so answers B, C, and D are incorrect. For more information, refer to "Windows System Monitoring Tools" in Chapter 16.

117.A. Sharon should install a DHCP server on the network and authorize it in Active Directory. Besides the WDS server itself, the network requires an AD DS domain controller, a DNS server, and a DHCP server so that she can use WDS to install new computers. Here the DHCP server was not present. The DHCP server configures the new computers with TCP/IP information that enables them to access other computers on the network, including the DNS server, which resolves the name of the WDS server to its IP address. WINS is used to resolve NetBIOS names to IP addresses and is not required on AD DS networks, so answer B is incorrect. Sharon does not need to create an answer file for WDS to work; however, the Winnt.sif file was used with Windows XP and is no longer used with Windows 7. If she wants to use an answer file, she should create an Unattend.xml file and copy it to the RemoteInstall\ WDSClientUnattend folder on the WDS server. Therefore, answer C is incorrect. It is not necessary to create an Active Directory–integrated DNS zone, so answer D is incorrect. For more information, see the section "Automated Deployment of Windows 7 by Using Windows Deployment Services (WDS)" in Chapter 5.

118.A. Sarah should enable InPrivate Browsing. She can do this from the Safety menu in Internet Explorer; once she selects this option, a new Internet Explorer window opens up, from which she can do whatever business she needs to do. When she is finished and closes this window, all personal information such as cookies, temporary Internet files, browsing history, credentials, and so on is discarded. InPrivate Filtering blocks third-party website content from being sent within her browsing session but does not discard personal information when she finishes her browsing session, so answer B is incorrect. Adding the publisher's website to the Restricted Sites zone or selecting **Block All Cookies** for the Internet zone does not offer her the protection she can get from using InPrivate Browsing, so answers C and D are incorrect. For more information, refer to "Using InPrivate Browsing Mode" in Chapter 8.

119.D. Ryan should use the Sync Center to synchronize the document. The Sync Center will report that a conflict exists and offer options to save either or both versions of the document. Choose the option to save both versions, and then edit the newly saved document to incorporate the changes. The Sync Center makes it simple to incorporate edits from different locations by recognizing conflicts and providing this option. Ryan does not need to download the client's version of the document separately and then copy the changes from his version because the Sync Center facilitates the download process, so answer A is incorrect. He does not need to manually type in his corrections because the Sync Center can save both versions, so answers B and C are incorrect. He does not need to rename his version of the document because the Sync Center recognizes the conflicting changes, so answer E is incorrect. For more information, see the section "Use of the Sync Center" in Chapter 13.

120. **G, C, A, F.** Betsy must issue the commands in the following sequence:

```
bcdedit /copy {current} /d "Boot from VHD"
bcdedit /set {guid} device vhd=d:\w7.VHD
bcdedit /set {guid} osdevice vhd=d:\w7.VHD
bcdedit /set {guid} detecthal=on
```

If the first command does not provide Betsy with the GUID of the VHD, she should use the bcdedit command without any parameters before continuing with the next command. The /attach subcommand is used with DiskPart and not with bcdedit, so answers B and E are incorrect. The /copy subcommand is not used with the osdevice parameter, so answer D is incorrect. Note that on the exam, a question similar to this might be displayed as a "build list and re-order" question, in which you must drag the required items to a list area and sequence them in the proper order; if they are not in the correct order, the question is scored incorrect. For more information, refer to "Booting VHDs" in Chapter 6.

Answers to the "Do I Know This Already?" Quizzes

Chapter 2

1. C. A basic Windows 7 installation requires at least 1 GB of RAM. It is desirable to have more RAM for efficient execution of multiple applications at the same time.

2. A. Windows 7 requires a 1 GHz processor. A higher processor speed will increase the speed of application execution but is not required for running Windows 7.

3. C. A 32-bit Windows 7 installation requires at least 16 GB of hard drive space on the system partition. You need additional hard drive space for your applications and data, but not for the Windows installation. Note that a 64-bit Windows 7 installation requires at least 20 GB of hard drive space.

4. D. TCP/IP is the standard networking protocol used by Windows 7 for accessing other computers on the network as well as the Internet. NetBEUI was used by Windows NT as a simplified networking protocol but is no longer supported. NWLink and IPX/SPX are protocols used by Novell NetWare for networking; you would install these only if you need to access a NetWare server.

5. A, B, C, D, F. You should have all of these items on hand before beginning a Windows 7 installation. The Windows 7 installation media is on DVD and not CD, so you do not need a CD-ROM drive.

6. A, C, D. When installing Windows 7 from a DVD-ROM, you can configure the username and password; the date, time, and time zone; and the network settings type during installation. You would configure domain membership and desktop gadgets after installation of Windows 7 is completed.

7. C. Windows 7 uses the bcdedit.exe tool for editing settings for dual-booting Windows 7 with another operating system. The other utilities mentioned were used with older Windows operating systems.

8. B. When setting up a multiple-boot system, you should install the oldest operating system first. In this scenario, you would install Windows 98, and then Windows XP, and finally Windows 7.

9. A. In general, the BIOS is set up to boot from either the hard disk or the floppy drive. If you need to boot from a USB drive, you must specify this option in the BIOS before starting.

10. D. To start installing Windows 7 using WDS, you should press the **F12** key. None of the other keys indicated will start this type of installation.

11. A, B, C, D, E. Any of these problems could cause Windows 7 installation to fail.

12. D. The `netstat` utility is used to display a computer's TCP/IP connections and protocol statistics. The `ipconfig` utility displays the computer's TCP/IP configuration, such as the IP address, subnet mask, and default gateway. The `ping` utility tests connectivity with a remote machine. The `nbtstat` utility displays NetBIOS statistics.

13. C. To access the Advanced Boot Options menu, you should press **F8** before Windows starts loading. The other options do not access this menu; one of them might access the BIOS setup screen according to the manufacturer of the BIOS.

14. D. The `setupact.log` file records modifications performed on the system during Setup. The `netsetup.log` file reports the results of a computer attempting to join a workgroup or domain. The `setuperr.log` file records errors generated by hardware or driver issues during Windows installation. The `setupapi.log` file records data about Plug and Play devices and drivers or about application installation.

Chapter 3

1. A, D. You can upgrade Windows Vista Home Premium directly to Windows 7 Home Premium or Windows 7 Ultimate. To upgrade to Windows 7 Professional, you must upgrade to Windows 7 Home Premium first and then run the Windows Anytime Upgrade. To upgrade to Windows 7 Enterprise, you must perform a clean install.

2. E. You cannot upgrade any edition of Windows XP to Windows 7; you must either upgrade to Windows Vista and then to Windows 7 or perform a clean install of Windows 7.

3. A, C, D, E, F. You should perform all these tasks before beginning an upgrade of Windows Vista to Windows 7. The Windows 7 Anytime Upgrade is used to upgrade one edition of Windows 7 to a higher one, and not for upgrading Vista.

4. B. It is not possible to upgrade a 32-bit edition of Windows Vista to a 64-bit edition of Windows 7, so this would cause the observed result. You must accept

the license agreement before you receive the Which type of installation do you want? page. If you are attempting to upgrade to Windows 7 Professional, you will receive an error message informing you that this upgrade is not accepted. If you are attempting to upgrade to Windows 7 Ultimate, this upgrade is fully supported and the upgrade option will be available.

5. D. The simplest way is to insert the Windows 7 DVD and perform a clean install. It is not possible to upgrade Windows XP directly to any edition of Windows 7. You could upgrade to Windows Vista and then to Windows 7, but this would require additional licensing costs and take much more time.

6. B. When you perform a clean installation of Windows 7 over Windows XP on the same partition, a `Windows.old` folder is created and the Windows XP system files are placed in this folder. You would need to perform the clean installation on a different partition to create a dual-boot system.

7. A. The `Windows.old` folder also stores other Windows XP files, including all subfolders of the `Documents and Settings` folder. Fred can then access his documents and move them to the `Users\Fred\My Documents` folder. It should not be necessary to restore these files from backup; however, it is good practice to back them up before upgrading in case some type of failure occurs during the upgrade process.

8. C. You can use Windows Anytime Upgrade to upgrade Windows 7 Home Premium to Windows 7 Professional. It is not possible to upgrade directly to Windows 7 Enterprise. You cannot downgrade Windows 7 Home Premium to a lower edition, such as Starter or Home Basic.

9. A. Windows Anytime Upgrade enables a rapid upgrade of one edition of Windows 7 to a higher one, in as little as 10–15 minutes in most cases. So, it is not necessary to perform a more complex upgrade.

10. C. The Windows Recovery Environment and the `Windows.old` folder enable you to recover Windows Vista, so it is not necessary to reformat the Windows partition and perform a clean install. No Uninstall option is available in Control Panel, unlike the option that was available a decade ago when you upgraded Windows 98 to Windows 2000.

Chapter 4

1. C. Windows Easy Transfer provides a simple, wizard-based routine that enables a user to migrate documents and settings from an old computer to a new one. It replaces the Files and Settings Transfer Wizard, which was used with Windows XP but is no longer available. USMT would be used for migrating large numbers of users but not a single user (as in this scenario). Windows AIK is used to customize the installation and deployment of Windows 7, including the installation of USMT. It is not used in this situation.

2. B. USMT is suitable for a situation such as this one, where a large number of users are being migrated from old computers to new ones. It would be far more tedious and cumbersome to use Windows Easy Transfer, which would require migrating these users one at a time.

3. A, B, D. USMT 4.0 includes the `ScanState.exe`, `LoadState.exe`, and `MigApp.xml` components. `Migwiz.exe` is part of Windows Easy Transfer and is not included with USMT 4.0. There is no such file as `Migapp.exe`.

4. A. The `ScanState.exe` utility is used to collect user settings and data from old computers when running USMT. `LoadState.exe` is used afterward to place these settings and data on the new Windows 7 computers. `Migwiz.exe` is part of Windows Easy Transfer and is not used in this situation. `Fastwiz.exe` was part of Windows XP's Files and Settings Transfer Wizard and is no longer used with Windows 7.

5. B. You would use `LoadState.exe` to transfer the user settings and data to the new Windows 7 computers. `ScanState.exe` is used to collect the settings and data from old computers and place them on the server. `Migwiz.exe` is part of Windows Easy Transfer and is not used in this situation. `Xcopy.exe` is an old DOS routine and is not used with any of the procedures described in this chapter.

6. D. The Custom (Advanced) option installs a completely new Windows 7 operating system on your computer, rather than upgrading the current installation. Doing so places your documents and application settings in subfolders of the `Windows.old` folder. The simplest way to migrate these items to their proper Windows 7 locations is to use Windows Easy Transfer. It would be possible to copy these items from the backup disk or to copy them from `Windows.old`, but you would need to know exactly where to place them. This procedure requires additional effort. The Files and Settings Transfer Wizard was used with Windows XP but is no longer available.

7. D. When you upgrade your computer directly from Windows Vista to Windows 7 (as described here), the upgrade process leaves the documents and application settings in their expected locations, so you do not need to do anything further with these items.

8. C. Windows AIK includes the files and settings required to run USMT. Unlike Windows Vista, the Windows 7 installation DVD does not contain a `Support\Tools\USMT` folder. Windows PE does not include these tools. Use of `Xcopy.exe` would be far more cumbersome and would probably not work properly.

9. D. In the wipe and load migration procedure, user settings and data from a computer running an older Windows operating system are collected and then the same computer is upgraded to Windows 7 and the user settings and data are restored to this computer. Transfer of these items to a new computer constitutes

the side by side migration procedure. Windows Easy Transfer is not used in either of these procedures.

10. **B.** In the side-by-side migration procedure, user settings and data from an old computer are transferred to a new Windows 7 computer. This procedure transfers data from one computer to another. Installing Windows 7 on the same computers constitutes the wipe and load migration procedure. Windows Easy Transfer is not used in either of these procedures.

Chapter 5

1. **C.** A `.wim` file is a compressed image file used in the deployment of Windows 7 operating systems to multiple computers. Sysprep does not produce any single compressed image file. The file that contains answers to questions asked during Windows 7 setup is called `unattend.xml`. The library of compressed files used with CBS is a `.cab` file.

2. **A.** Windows SIM is used to perform these actions. Windows PE is the Preinstallation Environment, which is a minimal operating system that assists you in preparing a computer for installing and deploying Windows. Windows AIK is the Automated Installation Kit, which is used to customize the installation and deployment of Windows 7. ImageX is a command-line tool that captures, creates, modifies, and applies Windows images. Sysprep is a utility that prepares a computer running Windows 7 with a set of installation applications for imaging and deployment to multiple target computers.

3. **D.** You would use ImageX to capture, modify, and apply file-based disk images during Windows 7 deployment. Windows SIM is used to create or edit answer files. The other options are used as described in the explanation to question 2.

4. **B.** The default answer file used for unattended installation of Windows 7 is called `Unattend.xml`. `Unattend.txt` and `Sysprep.inf` were previously used for automated deployment of Windows XP; these files are no longer used. `Install.wim` is a Windows 7 installation image file available from the Windows 7 DVD.

5. **C.** You would use the `/generalize` parameter of Sysprep to remove system-specific information from a Windows 7 installation. The `/audit` parameter is used when you are adding drivers and applications as required for deployment. The `/oobe` parameter is used so that Windows Welcome and the oobeSystem configuration pass are run at the next reboot. Sysprep does not use an `/unattend` parameter.

6. **A.** You would use the `/audit` parameter to verify hardware and retain the ability to add drivers and applications to your Windows 7 image. The purposes of the other parameters are as given in the explanation to question 5.

7.   D. You would use `ImageX /capture` to capture the contents of a reference computer for deployment to new computers. `Sysprep /generalize` removes system-specific information from a Windows 7 installation. `Sysprep /oobe` causes Windows Welcome and the oobeSystem configuration pass to be run at the next reboot. `ImageX /export` copies Windows system files.

8.   B, D, E. DISM enables you to add, remove, and enumerate packages and drivers; change the language, locale, fonts, and input settings within a Windows 7 image; and upgrade a Windows 7 installation to a higher edition. You would use `ImageX /capture` to capture the contents of a Windows 7 installation for deployment to new computers. You would use the Windows `copy` command to copy Windows 7 images across the network.

9.   C. The `DISM /Add-package` command enables you to add application packages and updates to the mounted Windows image. The `DISM /Get-AppInfo` command displays detailed information about a specific Windows Installer application installed within the image. The `DISM /Get-Apps` command displays basic information about all Windows Installer applications in the offline image. `/Check-apps` is not a valid DISM parameter.

10.   B. You would use `OCSetup` to add system components to a Windows 7 image. `ImageX /config` is used to specify the name and location of the configuration file (`.ini`) when capturing the contents of an image file prepared with Sysprep. The `DISM /Add-package` command enables you to add application packages and updates to the mounted Windows image. The `DISM /Get-AppPatches` command displays basic information about all applied MSP patches installed on the offline image.

11.   A, D. New to WDS in Windows 7 and Windows Server 2008 R2 are the ability to deploy new computers in a workgroup environment and the ability to deploy virtual hard disk images during an unattended installation. Previous versions of WDS allowed the ability to install Windows computers at a remote location across a WAN and the support for Windows PE and the `.wim` format.

12.   C. To deploy new computers to a workgroup, you would use WDS in Transport Server mode. This is a new functionality of WDS in Windows 7 and Windows Server 2008 R2. RIS was previously used in Windows XP and Windows Server 2003 for computer deployment. Deployment Server mode is used for computer deployment in a domain environment only.

13.   A, C. To enable the installation at each target computer to start without the need to press a key or enter data, you would specify the PXE Boot Policy option in the Boot tab of the WDS server's Properties dialog box and a default boot image that will be deployed from the Boot tab of the WDS server's Properties dialog box. The other two options do not enable the required objective.

14. B. If the `Unattend.xml` file contains a syntax error, the computer on which this file is run displays a screen from the Setup Wizard, asking the user to enter the desired option. Default installation options are never used in this scenario, and because this screen is displayed, the computer can continue Windows installation without hanging or rebooting.

15. A. When you use a domain computer to prepare a Windows 7 image using Sysprep, the computer is automatically removed from the domain.

Chapter 6

1. B, C, E. The valid types of VHDs in Windows 7 are fixed, dynamic, and differencing. The other types of VHDs mentioned do not exist.

2. A, E. You can use either DiskPart or Disk Management to create a new VHD. You would use bcdedit to edit the boot loader file. Sysprep and ImageX are used in preparing and imaging Windows installations for deployment. None of these tools is used in creating VHDs.

3. B. Before you can format a new VHD, you must initialize it. This prepares the VHD for partitioning and formatting by writing a master boot record or GUID partition table, as well as a disk signature and end of sector marker. When you initially create the VHD using Disk Management, it is automatically mounted, so you do not need to perform this action. You must initialize the VHD before you can partition it or assign a drive letter.

4. D. The `Attach` command is used in scripts to mount a VHD. The `Create` command is used to create a VHD or a partition on the VHD but not to mount it. The `Active` command marks the selected partition as active. The `Mount` command does not exist.

5. A. The act of mounting a VHD on a computer makes it available for use on this computer. You must perform this task before you can partition or format it or create a path to it.

6. A, B, C, E. To deploy a custom Windows image to multiple VHDs, you must first install Windows and configure applications on a reference machine. You then use Sysprep to generalize the image, ImageX to capture the image to a .wim file, and Bcdedit to configure each computer for booting from the VHD. RIS was used in Windows XP and Windows Server 2003 and is no longer used in image deployment. DISM is used in servicing Windows images, and not in deployment of VHD images.

7. B, C, D. These facts are all true about using a VHD file as if it were a normal hard disk. However, you cannot use a VHD file in this manner to run Windows XP. It is not necessary to have Virtual PC or Virtual Server installed to use a VHD in this manner.

8. C. The `ImageX` `/apply` command deploys (applies) Windows 7 to a previously created VHD. Although DISM supports a large number of options, `/apply` is not one of them. ImageX does not have a `/create` option. `Bcdedit` `/copy` makes copies of entries in the boot configuration store but does not deploy Windows 7 to a VHD.

9. D. The `Bcdboot` command enables you to manage and create new BCD stores and BCD boot entries for booting Windows 7. You can use this tool to create new boot entries when configuring a system to boot from a new VHD. You would then use `Bcdedit` to edit the boot entry and point it to the VHD. You must use `Bcdboot` first before you can use `Bcdedit`. `Ntldr` and `Boot.ini` were used in booting Windows XP and older Windows versions but are not used with Windows 7.

10. D. You would mount the VHD as drive e: on another computer, and then execute the `DISM` `/image:e:\` `/Enable-Feature` `/FeatureName:<name>` command. The `/Get-Feature` parameter displays a list of all available Windows features and whether they are enabled. It does not add features. You must perform this action as an offline servicing action, which refers to updating the image offline without booting it; it is not possible to perform this action in an online manner.

11. A. The `DISM` `/image:<letter>:\` `/Add-Driver:<path_to_driver>` command adds a driver to a previously created VHD. The `/Get-Driver` parameter provides basic information about driver packages in the image but does not add drivers. ImageX is not used for adding drivers to VHDs.

12. B. When a native-boot VHD is running Windows 7 Ultimate, it is not possible to upgrade this edition further; hence, no upgrading options are provided when you run this command. It is not possible to use a native-boot VHD with Windows Vista. The `/Get-Edition` and `/Apply-Edition` commands do not exist.

Chapter 7

1. A, B, C, D. You can install PnP devices from any of these locations.

2. A. A disabled device is indicated in Device Manager by a black downward-pointing arrow. A red "X" indicates that the device is not functioning. A yellow question mark indicates that the device is functioning but experiencing problems. A blue "i" on a white field indicates that the device has forced resource configurations.

3. A, E. You can obtain information about the resources being used by a device by accessing the Resources tab of the device's Properties dialog box or from the Hardware Resources node of the System Information dialog box. The Components node of this dialog box provides information on hardware device properties, including driver information but not resource information. The General

tab of the device's Properties dialog box provides the device's description and status. The Details tab provides a long list of property specifications, but not the resources used by the device.

4. B. By uninstalling a device driver, you remove the driver completely from the computer. You should do this only after you have actually removed the device because Windows will otherwise redetect the device at the next reboot and reinstall the driver. You should also select the **Delete the driver software for this device** check box. None of the other options provided will remove the driver completely.

5. D. The process of staging a driver package involves adding the publisher's certificate to the trusted certificates store, thereby enabling standard users to install the package. Automatic updating is accessible to all users on the computer and is configured by default. The driver manufacturer sends the new driver package to Microsoft, who provides the electronic signature.

6. B. The sigverif.exe utility is used to determine whether any unsigned drivers are present. The sfc.exe utility is the System File Checker, which checks the digital signature of system protected files. Msinfo32.exe is the System Information utility, which provides a large amount of information on hardware and software on the computer but does not provide driver signature information. Gpedit.exe is the Local Group Policy Editor, which is used to apply policies to a computer or a series of computers.

7. B. If the device worked before you updated its driver, you can roll back the driver to restore the previous driver that worked with the device. A further update might solve the problem but would not likely be available because you already updated the driver. Uninstalling or disabling the driver would not work.

8. C. The Resources by type view displays the devices according to the resources used, including IRQ, DMA, and memory addresses. The other views do not provide this information directly, although the Resources by connection view displays which resources are currently available.

9. A. If the installation of a new device on your computer results in another device not working, this indicates that the two devices are attempting to use the same resource (such as an IRQ). Any of the other options provided could result in the new device (the Blu-ray writer) not working, but other devices would still work.

10. D. The Conflicts/Sharing subnode of the Hardware Resources category in System Information provides information on device-related problems but does not provide tools for correcting these problems. Device Manager enables you to correct these problems. Sigverif.exe provides information on unsigned drivers but does not provide information on device-related problems. Action Center provides information on some device problems plus a link for corrective actions.

11. C. An update roll-up is a packaged set of updates that fix problems with specific Windows components or software packages such as Microsoft Office. A critical security update is a single update that Microsoft issues to fix a problem that is critical for a computer's security. An optional update is a potentially useful nonsecurity-related update. A service pack is a comprehensive operating system update that often adds new features or improvements to existing features.

12. A. By default, updates can be installed by all users. To prevent nonadministrative users from installing updates, clear the check box labeled **Allow all users to install updates on this computer.** The check box labeled **Give me updates for Microsoft Products and check for new optional Microsoft software when I update Windows** enables users to receive new optional software or updates for products such as Microsoft Office but does not affect the installation of critical updates. The check box labeled **Show me detailed notifications when new Microsoft software is available** determines whether notifications of new Microsoft software are received.

13. C. The **Specify intranet Microsoft update service location** policy enables you to specify a WSUS server on your network that client computers will access to receive software updates without accessing the Internet. With the other policies mentioned, client computers will still attempt to access the Internet for updates.

14. C. The Windows Update Control Panel applet, found in the Program category, lists all updates the computer has received and installed. These are sorted by Microsoft application, including Microsoft Windows, and can be resorted within each section by attributes such as name and date. The other locations do not provide this type of information.

Chapter 8

1. A. You should select **Run this program in compatibility mode for** and select either Windows XP Service Pack 2 or Windows XP Service Pack 3. Because the application has worked successfully on Windows XP, this is the most likely compatibility mode that would enable it to work with Windows 7.

2. C. Microsoft refers to this type of compatibility fix as a shim. Compatibility mode is a selectable mode that emulates an earlier Windows version or places specified restrictions on desktop properties. A filter is a condition for viewing information on a dialog box or application. A hotfix is a correction for an operating system problem.

3. B. In this case, it is probable that you have not enabled virtualization in your computer's BIOS Setup program. Even if your processor is verified as capable of hardware virtualization, this feature might not be enabled by default in the BIOS. Windows XP Mode requires 2 GB RAM, so you have sufficient RAM. Windows XP Mode does not use Windows Virtual Server. Windows XP Mode

runs on Windows 7 Professional, Enterprise, or Ultimate, so you do not need to upgrade your operating system.

4. **B.** You should use the Internet Explorer Compatibility Test Tool. This tool provides a report on any issues that might exist with your company's websites and web-based applications. Both Windows XP Mode and Application Compatibility Mode can be used to display the website using an older version of Internet Explorer, but they do not provide any compatibility information. The SmartScreen filter detects phishing websites.

5. **A, C, D, E.** You can configure any of these rule types in Software Restriction Policies. There is no such thing as an Operating System Version Rule.

6. **B, D.** AppLocker enables you to gather advanced data on software usage by implementing audit-only mode and to create multiple rules at the same time with the help of a wizard. Disallowed, Basic User, and Unrestricted are the rule settings available with Software Restriction Policies; AppLocker uses Allow and Deny. You can use either Software Restriction Policies or AppLocker with Group Policy.

7. **D, E.** You can use AppLocker with the Enterprise and Ultimate editions of Windows 7 only. AppLocker does not work on any other editions of Windows 7, although you can configure AppLocker policies with Windows 7 Professional.

8. **B, D, E.** Compatibility View, InPrivate Mode, and SmartScreen Filter are new features of Internet Explorer 8, although it should be noted that SmartScreen Filter is an updated version of the Phishing Filter included with Internet Explorer 7. Protected Mode and Pop-Up Blocker were both available in Internet Explorer 7.

9. **B.** By default, all websites are placed in the Internet zone. You must manually configure the sites that will be placed in the other zones.

10. **B.** The Pop-up Blocker Settings Dialog box can be accessed by clicking the Settings button, which is found on the Privacy tab of Internet Options. None of the other tabs contain an access to this dialog box.

11. **A, D.** One of the options available from the Manage Add-ons dialog box is to configure additional search providers. You can access this dialog box directly from the Tools menu in Internet Explorer. From the Internet Options dialog box, you can also select the Programs tab and then click **Manage add-ons** to access this dialog box. The Toolbars option in the Tools menu merely determines which toolbars will be visible. The All Accelerators option determines which accelerators are available for use.

12. **A, B, C.** The Manage Add-ons dialog box lets you configure search providers, accelerators, and InPrivate Filtering. It also lets you configure toolbars and extensions, but you cannot manage the SmartScreen filter from here.

13. D. You should ensure that the SmartScreen Filter is enabled; it is enabled by default. This filter is an upgrade of the Phishing Filter first introduced in Internet Explorer 7, and it detects actions such as that described here. None of the other options perform this action.

14. C. The InPrivate Browsing feature sets up an isolated browser session that discards all personal types of browsing information once you close Internet Explorer, thereby ensuring that all traces of your actions have been removed. None of the other features mentioned enable this.

15. B. The presence of the gold padlock icon indicates that the website is using a secure certificate that has been properly verified. Neither InPrivate Browsing nor Protected mode offers encryption for information sent from your computer; tab color merely indicates the presence of a tab group and says nothing about security.

Chapter 9

1. A, B, D. All these protocols are components of TCP/IP. Although it is used by TCP/IP-enabled computers, DHCP is not considered a component of TCP/IP.

2. C. The default gateway is the IP address of the router that connects your computer's subnet to other subnets on your company's network, as well as the Internet. Although important for your computer's TCP/IP configuration, the other items given here do not address this objective.

3. B. Any IP address in the range 128.0.0.0 to 191.255.255.255 belongs to class B. Class A addresses are in the range 1.0.0.0 to 126.255.255.255; Class C addresses are in the range 192.0.0.0 to 223.255.255.255; Class D addresses are in the range 224.0.0.0 to 239.255.255.255; Class E addresses are in the range 240.0.0.0 to 254.255.255.255.

4. D. CIDR enables you to specify the number of bits used for the subnet mask as part of the network address, in this case 24. WINS is not an address notation, but it is a protocol used for resolving NetBIOS names to IP addresses. Unicast and multicast are types of IPv6 addresses; this scenario deals with IPv4 addressing.

5. A, C. To configure your computer to use DHCP, you should ensure that the **Obtain an IP address automatically** and **Obtain DNS server address automatically** options are selected. You would specify the other two options if you were configuring your computer to use static IP addressing.

6. B. If your computer is using an IPv4 address on the 169.254.0.0/16 network, it is configured to use APIPA. An address on this network is assigned when the computer is configured to receive an IP address automatically but is unable to reach a DHCP server. Private IPv4 addressing is in use if the IP address is on any of the 10.0.0.0/8, 172.16.0.0/16, or 192.168.0.0/24 networks. An alternate

IP configuration is a separate static IP address that you can configure on a computer that is using DHCP; it would not be using this address.

7. A. A global unicast address is a globally routable Internet address that is equivalent to a public IPv4 address. A link-local unicast address is used for communication between neighboring nodes on the same link; a site-local unicast address is used for communication between nodes located in the same site; a multicast address provides multiple interfaces to which packets are delivered; and an anycast address is utilized only as destination addresses assigned to routers. None of these address types are suitable for direct Internet contact.

8. B. A link-local IPv6 address has an address prefix of fe80::/64. This address is equivalent to an APIPA-configured IPv4 address. The other address types have different network prefixes.

9. D. Teredo is a tunneling communication protocol that enables IPv6 connectivity between IPv6/IPv4 nodes across network address translation (NAT) interfaces, thereby improving connectivity for newer IPv6-enabled applications on IPv4 networks. It uses this prefix. The other address types use different prefixes.

10. B. The concept of LLMNR refers to the capability of computers running IPv6 on the local subnet to resolve each other's names without the need for a DNS server. APIPA is used on IPv4 networks and not on IPv6 but is included in Windows 7 for backward compatibility only. WINS is an older name resolution service used by Windows NT and 9x computers. ARP resolves IP addresses to media access control (MAC) addresses and has nothing to do with name resolution.

11. B. You should use the `ipconfig /renew` command. This command forces the computer to try again to connect to the DHCP server and obtain an IP address lease. In this case, the computer was unable to access the DHCP server and configured itself with an APIPA address. The `/release` parameter releases the current IP address configuration but does not contact the DHCP server. The `/flushdns` parameter flushes the contents of the DNS cache. You would use this parameter when the computer has connected to an incorrect network. The `/displaydns` parameter displays the contents of the DNS cache. This is also useful if the computer connects to an incorrect network.

12. D, E. The `tracert` and `pathping` commands both provide routing information. The route command provides routing table information or enables you to configure routers but does not provide the information requested in this scenario. The `netstat` command provides TCP/IP connection statistics. The `ping` command checks connectivity to a remote host but does not provide routing information.

13. D, C, A, E, B. You should perform the indicated actions in the following sequence: Run `ipconfig /all` to validate the IP address, subnet mask, default

gateway, and DNS server, and whether you are receiving a DHCP leased address. Ping 127.0.0.1 or ::1 to validate that TCP/IP is functioning. Ping the computer's own IP address to eliminate a duplicate IP address as the problem. Ping the default gateway, which tells you whether data can travel on the current network segment. Ping a host that is on another subnet, which shows whether the router will be able to route your data. Microsoft exams might ask you to select actions you must perform and place them in the required sequence.

14. C. If two computers on the network are configured with the same IP address, the first one will connect properly, but the second one that attempts to connect will fail to do so and this problem will result. If your computer is configured for static IP addressing, it will never use APIPA. If the subnet mask is incorrect, your computer would not connect to machines on another subnet at any time. If your computer is configured with static IP addressing, the alternate IP address option will be unavailable.

Chapter 10

1. A. B. D. The Set Network Location dialog box enables you to configure your computer for any of the Home, Work, or Public network types. This dialog box does not have options for Private or Domain network types.

2. D. The **Password protected sharing** option requires users attempting to access shared resources on your computer to have a user account with a password. None of the other options enforce this requirement; without selecting the **Password protected sharing** option, others can access your shared resources without a valid username and password.

3. B. ICS is a simple means for enabling computers on a small office or home network to use one computer on the network as the router to the Internet. It is a simplified version of NAT designed for these small networks. The full implementation of NAT would require a server. A simplified version of DHCP is included in ICS; implementing the full version of DHCP requires a server and by itself would not grant shared Internet access. WEP is a security protocol that provides encryption of data sent on a wireless network; it does not enable computers to connect to the Internet.

4. A, B, C, D. You can encrypt data sent on a wireless connection by using TKIP, AES, WEP, WPA, or WPA2. The SSID is a network identifier that is broadcast by many wireless access points (WAPs) to enable you to locate available wireless networks; it does not provide data protection.

5. D. 802.11n is a new wireless networking protocol that is compatible with devices using older protocols but enables a transmission speed of up to 150–600 Mbps. It has the best signal range and is most resistant to interference. No other protocol offers this much transmission speed.

6. B. By default, the WPA2-Personal protocol uses AES encryption and requires a security key or passphrase. WPA-Personal and WPA-Enterprise both use TKIP encryption by default. Both WPA-Enterprise and WPA2-Enterprise do not require the user to type a security key or passphrase.

7. C. You should set up a per-user profile. This profile contains the required settings and is connected when the specified user logs on to the computer. An all-user profile applies to all users of the computer and is connected regardless of which user is logged on to the computer. There are no such profiles as per-computer and all-computer.

8. C. The Public network location locks Windows Firewall down so that others cannot access anything on your computer, although it can also limit your access to external resources. The Work and Home network locations allow others to access any items you have configured for sharing on your computer. The Private location is the same as Work and Home.

9. B, C, E. You can configure Windows Firewall to specify programs that are allowed to communicate, or you can configure Windows Firewall to block all incoming connections, from the Windows Firewall Control Panel applet. You can also specify firewall settings for home, work, and public networks from this location. However, you must use the Windows Firewall with Advanced Security snap-in to configure ports and logging (the Windows Firewall applet in Windows Vista allowed specifying allowed ports, but this function was removed from this location in Windows 7).

10. C. Windows Firewall with Advanced Security does not include any connection security rules by default. You can use the New Rules Wizard to set up connection security rules as well as additional rules for the other rule types.

11. A. You should run the New Inbound Rule Wizard, specify the path to Windows Media Player on the program page, and then specify the **Allow the connection if it is secure** option. The latter option permits only connections that have been authenticated using IPSec. You need an inbound rule, not an outbound rule. Connection security rules do not permit specifying programs that are allowed to connect. The Allowed Programs and Features list does not enable you to restrict connections to only those that have been authenticated using IPSec.

12. D. It is not possible to change a rule from Inbound to Outbound from any setting that is available in the rule's Properties dialog box. It is also not possible to drag a rule from one node to another in Windows Firewall with Advanced Security. You must create a new outbound rule to perform this action.

13. A. The Properties dialog box of Windows Firewall with Advanced Security enables you to perform this action for each of the Domain, Private, and Public profiles. You can access this dialog box by right-clicking **Windows Firewall**

with **Advanced Security** at the top of the console tree and choosing **Properties**. None of the locations mentioned in the other options provides a Properties dialog box.

Chapter 11

1. B. By enabling the **Public folder sharing** option, you enable users at other computers to be able to access folders in your libraries. This is known as the Public folder sharing model. The **File and printer sharing** option enables you to share folders you have specifically configured for sharing, but you must specifically configure the required folders for sharing. Password-protected sharing limits the accessibility of shared folders to users who have a username and password. Media streaming enables sharing of media files with networked devices.

2. B, D, E. Administrative shares are created by default when you first install Windows 7. These shares are suffixed with the $ symbol and are visible from the Shares node of the Computer Management snap-in; they can be accessed by entering the UNC path to the share in the Run command. Because they are hidden, you cannot see them in an Explorer window, nor can you access them from the Network and Sharing Center.

3. A, C, E. You can specify any of Read, Change, or Full Control shared folder permissions. The Modify and Read & Execute permissions are NTFS security permissions; they are not shared folder permissions.

4. A. A library is a set of virtual folders that is shared by default with other users of the same computer. The library also contains folders such as My Documents and My Pictures, which are not shared by default with users of other computers. A library is not a single folder; it is a collection of virtual folders or pointers to the actual folders.

5. B. You should grant Kristin's user account the Manage this printer permission. This permission enables her to do the required tasks. The Print permission grants only the ability to print documents on your printer. The Manage documents permission enables her also to perform tasks such as modifying printer properties or permissions. Full control is not included in the printer permissions; it is only a shared folder or NTFS permission.

6. D. If the network location is set to Work, you cannot join a homegroup. You can join a homegroup even if your computer is joined to an AD DS domain; this facilitates working at home with a laptop that is moved between home and work locations. You can join a homegroup with any edition of Windows 7. A password is automatically created when you create a homegroup; this password is required for another computer to join the homegroup, but you cannot create a homegroup without a password.

7. E. You should assign the Read & Execute permission to enable users to view files and run programs in the folder. The Full Control permission and Modify permission would enable users to edit or delete files in the folder. The Read permission does not enable them to run programs. The Change permission is a shared folder permission only.

8. A. Security (NTFS) permissions are cumulative; in other words, a user receives the least restrictive of the permissions that have been applied, so Bob has Full Control permission to the Documents folder.

9. D. Although NTFS permissions are cumulative such that a user receives the least restrictive permission, an explicit denial of permission overrides all allowed permissions. Therefore, in this scenario, Jim does not have access to the Documents folder.

10. C. If a shared folder has both shared folder and NTFS permissions assigned to it and a user accesses this folder across the network, the most restrictive permission is the effective permission. Therefore, in this scenario, Carol has Read permission on the Documents folder.

11. A. When a user accesses a shared folder on the same computer on which it is located, the shared folder permission does not apply and the user receives only the NTFS permission that has been assigned to the folder. Therefore, in this scenario, Sharon has Full Control permission on the Documents folder.

12. C. When you copy a file or folder from one NTFS volume to another one, the copy inherits the permissions applied to the destination location. Therefore, the Accounts folder receives the Read permission that is applied to the `D:\Confidential` folder.

13. A. When you move a file from one folder to another folder on the same NTFS volume, the file retains its NTFS permissions. Therefore, in this scenario, Jennifer has Full Control permission to the `C:\Confidential\Projects.doc` file.

14. B, C. To encrypt a file or folder, the file or folder must be located on a volume that is formatted with the NTFS file system. So, you need to convert the volume to the NTFS file system or move the folder to another volume formatted with the NTFS file system. If you were to format the `D:\` volume with the NTFS file system, you would destroy the `Confidential` folder. The folder cannot be compressed because this is also a function of the NTFS file system.

15. B. By default, the administrator account created when Windows 7 is first installed is the default recovery agent for files or folders that have been encrypted on this computer, so you can decrypt the file if you log on with this account. Note that this account is disabled by default, so you need to log on with another account and enable the account first. If you recreate Peter's user account, the new account has a different security identifier (SID) so it does not have the capability of decrypting files encrypted with the old account.

Chapter 12

1. D. The dimmed screen and request to confirm your intent is a UAC prompt, which was first introduced in Windows Vista and refined in Windows 7. Nothing is wrong with your Microsoft Office media, and this does not indicate any need for configuring application compatibility options.

2. B. By default in Windows 7, you receive a UAC prompt only if you are using a nonadministrative user account. In Windows Vista, you always received a UAC prompt; in Windows 7, this is true only if you change the UAC settings and select the **Always notify me when** option. You never have to log off from a standard user account and log back on as an administrator; you merely have to supply an administrative password. The latter option occurs only if you've configured the **Never notify me** option in the UAC settings.

3. D. The red title bar and shield indicate that the program is a high-risk program that Windows has blocked completely. You cannot run it in its present form. No command buttons are provided on this message box, so it is impossible to click **Yes** to run the program.

4. C. By enabling the **Admin Approval Mode for the Built-In Administrator account** policy in Group Policy, you configure the built-in Administrator account to display UAC prompts in the manner as governed by the User Account Settings Control Panel applet setting in use. Configuring options in this applet without enabling the **Admin Approval Mode for the Built-In Administrator account** policy does not change the behavior of the built-in Administrator account, which by default does not display any UAC prompts.

5. C. You should enable the **Behavior of the elevation prompt for standard users** policy and then select the **Automatically deny elevation requests** option. This option prevents any applications that require administrative credentials from running. Either of the **Prompt for credentials** options would display a UAC prompt that requests an administrative password, but these would still allow these programs to run. Enabling the **Only Elevate executables that are signed and validated** policy would perform public key infrastructure signature checks on programs requiring elevated privileges but would still allow programs that pass this check to run.

6. A. Credential Manager is a Windows 7 utility that stores logon credentials and makes them available when needed. You can also use this utility to modify or remove existing credentials. Certificate Manager works only with certificates; it does not work with logon names or passwords. The Security tab of the Internet Options dialog box only enables you to configure security zones. The Content tab of the Internet Options dialog box enables you to use certificates for encrypted Internet connections and identification, but not usernames or passwords.

7. B. When you use Credential Manager to back up the credentials from one Windows 7 computer, it is then possible to restore this backup to a different computer so that you can use the credentials for logging on to this computer. You might be able to use Windows Backup, but this backs up far more than what is needed. Because you can use Credential Manager in this manner, it is not necessary to copy the credentials or to reenter them at the websites.

8. A, B, D. E. The Properties dialog box for a certificate enables you to perform all these functions. However, you cannot modify the validity period for the certificate; this action requires that you contact the issuer of your certificate, even if it is a local company certificate server.

9. E. The Store passwords using reversible encryption policy weakens security because it stores passwords in a format that is essentially the same as plain text. You should enable this policy only if needed for clients that cannot use normal encryption.

10. C. By default, the Backup Operators built-in group is granted the user rights for backing up and restoring files and directories, which enables Carolyn to perform these tasks. You could grant her the Back up files and directories user right and the Restore files and directories user right, but it is simpler to make her a member of the Backup Operators group, which is granted these rights by default. The Administrators group would give her more privileges than required. The Power Users group exists only for backward compatibility with Windows XP and older Windows versions; further, it would not give her the required privileges.

11. A. Distributed Cache mode of BranchCache enables users to cache copies of files and folders from the head office server to client computers without the need for a branch office server. Hosted Cache mode would require a Windows Server 2008 R2 server in the branch office. Copying the contents of the head office shared folder to a shared folder would be possible but would not keep this share up-to-date and would not likely minimize bandwidth needs. FRS also would not minimize bandwidth needs.

12. B. Because the branch office has a server available to all users, it is best to use BranchCache in the Hosted Cache mode. It would be possible to use the Distributed Cache mode, but when client computers containing cached content were offline, additional bandwidth would be used to access content on the head office server. Copying the contents of the head office shared folder to a shared folder would be possible but would not keep this share up-to-date and would not likely minimize bandwidth needs. FRS also would not minimize bandwidth needs.

13. B, D. You need to upgrade all client computers to Windows 7 Enterprise and upgrade the server to Windows Server 2008 R2. BranchCache is a new Windows 7 feature that requires client computers to be running Windows 7 Enterprise or

Ultimate and requires servers to be running Windows Server 2008 R2. A lower level of either operating system will not work. It is not necessary to install DNS on the server, nor is it necessary to configure it as a file and print server.

Chapter 13

1. B. In many computers equipped with a TPM, you might first need to enable the TPM in the BIOS before you can set up BitLocker. BitLocker is supported on both Windows 7 Enterprise and Ultimate, so you do not need to upgrade your computer to Ultimate. You need to enable TPM before you can configure a startup key. You do not need to use Group Policy before enabling the TPM.

2. A, B, C, D. All these are possible locations to which a BitLocker recovery key can be saved or backed up.

3. A. If you use BitLocker To Go to encrypt your USB flash drive containing the BitLocker recovery key, the recovery key might become inaccessible if your computer enters recovery mode. On a domain computer, it is good practice to save copies of recovery keys to AD DS. It is possible to use BitLocker without additional keys on a computer that is equipped with a TPM, although this is less secure. If your computer is not equipped with a TPM, you must use Group Policy to enable BitLocker first.

4. A, D. You need to copy the BitLocker To Go reader to the Windows XP computers. You also need to enable the **Allow access to BitLocker-protected fixed data drives from earlier versions of Windows** policy. These actions enable users of older computers to access data on BitLocker To Go-protected portable hard drives. You do not need to enable any of the other options mentioned here.

5. C, E. F. Client computers must be running Windows 7 Enterprise or Ultimate; you cannot use DirectAccess on a Windows 7 Professional computer or any edition of Vista. The DirectAccess server must have two network adapters and be running the Web Server (IIS) server role and the Direct Access Management Console server feature; it does not need to be a domain controller.

6. C. You should try the 6-to-4 technology to connect these computers to the IPv6 network used by DirectAccess. UAG provides enhanced security on the corporate network and enables access to IPv4-only applications on the network but not for IPv4 client computers external to the company. You might need to use Teredo or HTTPS to connect these clients, but Microsoft recommends that you try 6-to-4 first.

7. A, C. Clients must be joined to the domain and belong to the security group configured on the DirectAccess server; they must have a certificate that specifies the Client Authentication and Server Authentication certificate purposes. They do not require a smart card reader. It is preferable to have an IPv6 globally

routable IP address, but clients with IPv4 addresses can use 6-to-4, Teredo, or HTTPS to access the network.

8. D. You should select the **Always available offline** option. The Open Sync Center option enables you to configure certain file synchronization options but in itself does not automatically cache available files. The Disk Usage option merely specifies how much disk space can be used by cached files. The Sync Selected Offline Files option enables you to select which files are available offline.

9. B. You should enable the Enable Transparent Caching policy setting. Transparent file caching enables Windows 7 computers to temporarily cache files obtained across a slow WAN link more aggressively, thereby reducing the number of times the client might have to retrieve the file across the slow link. The Configure Background Sync and Slow link mode settings control synchronization across WAN links but do not enable the transparent caching feature. The Administratively assigned offline files setting specifies network files and folders that are always available offline.

10. C. Sleep mode, first introduced in Windows Vista, ensures that your laptop computer is ready to go within a few seconds and with your previous documents and applications available to you immediately. The Password protection on wakeup setting requires you to enter your password when resuming from sleep mode. Standby was used on Windows XP and older computers only. Hibernation saves the system state to hard disk and shuts down the computer completely; it takes longer to resume from hibernation. BitLocker is not required in this scenario.

11. B, C. Either by choosing the Power Saver power plan or by reducing the maximum power status of the processor from the Processor power management advanced power setting, you can reduce the processor power so that the battery lasts long enough to watch your movie. The Balanced power plan in itself does not accomplish this task. The Sleep setting would make your computer go to sleep during the movie, which is not what you want here. The Multimedia setting controls the sharing of multimedia with others.

12. A, C, E. You can perform any of these tasks by clicking links available from the battery meter. To enable presentation mode, you must access presentation settings from the Windows Mobility Center. To specify hard disk settings, you must configure a Group Policy setting in the Power Management subnode.

Chapter 14

1. C. Remote Desktop enables you to connect easily to a remote computer and display its desktop as though you were working directly on the remote computer. You would use Terminal Services to connect to a remote server and run programs from this server. You would use Remote Assistance to invite an expert

at another computer to assist you in overcoming some problem or learning how to perform a task. You would use VPN to make a connection to a server on a remote network.

2. B. Remote Assistance enables you to invite an expert at another computer to assist you in overcoming a problem that you are having difficulties with. You would use Terminal Services to connect to a remote server and run programs from this server. You would use Remote Desktop to access another computer such as your work computer and work directly on this computer. You would use VPN to make a connection to a server on a remote network.

3. C. The computer to which you want to establish a Remote Desktop connection must run the Professional, Enterprise, or Ultimate edition of Windows 7. The Remote Desktop Connection Software download enables older computers to make a Remote Desktop connection but does not enable a Windows 7 Home Premium computer to receive a Remote Desktop connection from another computer. You can establish a Remote Desktop session with a Vista computer so that you do not need to upgrade your work computer to Windows 7. This scenario uses Remote Desktop, not Remote Assistance.

4. A. Easy Connect requires that both users establishing the Remote Assistance session be using Windows 7 computers. It is possible that the other user is using a nonadministrative user account; however, she might have to provide administrative credentials at a UAC prompt to perform certain actions. If you have not selected the **Allow this computer to be controlled remotely** option, the other user will not be able to perform tasks on your computer, but she will be able to complete a connection and view your desktop. This scenario calls for use of Remote Assistance, not Remote Desktop.

5. A, C, D. PowerShell cmdlets take the form verb-object, so `Get-Process`, `Select-object`, and `Format-data` are valid cmdlets. `Value-output` and `Folder-create` start with nouns and are not valid.

6. D. Internet Key Exchange version 2 (IKEv2) uses IPSec Tunnel Mode over UDP port 500 to create a secure connection. None of the other protocols use this type of connection security methodology.

7. B. All of PPTP, SSTP, and IKEv2 provide data encryption on their own. L2TP does not; you must use IPSec with L2TP to provide encryption of data sent across a remote access connection.

8. A. Password Authentication Protocol (PAP) sends its credentials in clear-text (unencrypted) form, so it is the least secure method of authenticating a remote access connection. All the other protocols mentioned provide some kind of credential security.

9. D. The Networking tab enables you to specify protocols that will be used during your VPN session, including TCP/IPv4, TCP/IPv6, File and Printer

Sharing for Microsoft Networks, and the Client for Microsoft Networks. None of the other tabs enable you to configure these options. Note that the Sharing tab enables you to configure Internet Connection Sharing (ICS).

10. D. IKEv2 is the protocol that is used by VPN Reconnect, which is the new Windows 7 feature that enables you to automatically reestablish a VPN connection if it is temporarily disconnected. None of the other protocols can be used in this situation.

11. B. You should enable NAP Quarantine Remediation. Using this technology, you can test the security of computers requesting incoming connections and ensure that these computers have up-to-date antivirus and antispyware software definitions, Windows Firewall is enabled, automatic updating is enabled, and all available software updates have been downloaded. NAP Quarantine Remediation also can redirect noncompliant computers to servers that update these clients before they are allowed to access other network resources.

12. C. You should enable RemoteApp. Programs enabled using this feature can be accessed remotely through the RD Gateway server. When a user accesses one of these programs, it appears on her desktop as though it were running locally. VPN Reconnect enables a user to reconnect to an interrupted VPN session. NAP Quarantine Remediation enables you to set up a server that checks incoming clients for appropriate security updates and directs them to remediation servers if required. Internet Connection Sharing (ICS) enables you to share an Internet connection among several computers.

Chapter 15

1. B, C, G. You can configure primary and extended partitions on a basic disk and create logical drives within an extended partition. The other volume types mentioned here require that you upgrade your basic disk to dynamic storage.

2. C. You should run the convert gpt command. This command converts the disk's partition style to GPT (GUID partition table), which enables a volume of more than 2 TB. By default, a disk uses the MBR (master boot record) partition table style, which enables volumes of up to 2 TB. It is not necessary to convert the disk to either basic or dynamic storage (it is basic by default) because you can have a 5 TB primary partition on a basic disk.

3. B. This procedure creates a spanned volume, which extends storage on one volume to additional disks without the need for an additional drive letter. A simple volume includes only a single disk. Mirrored and RAID-5 volumes contain two and 3 to 32 disks respectively but are created differently.

4. B. The Tools tab of a volume's Properties dialog box enables you to check the disk for errors, defragment it, or back it up. The General tab provides a pie

chart of the disk's space allocation, specify a volume name, and execute the Disk Cleanup utility. The Hardware tab displays hardware information for the computer's disk drives. The Quota tab enables you to configure disk quotas. The Customize tab enables you to optimize folders for specified purposes. None of these other tabs enable you to check your volume for errors.

5. A. When you move a disk from one computer to another, you need to initialize the disk in Disk Management before it can be accessed in the new operating system. The Resynchronize command resynchronizes members of a RAID-5 volume. It is not necessary to check the disk for errors unless you encounter other problems. It is definitely not necessary to format the disk and restore all the images from backup.

6. D. When you convert your hard disk to dynamic storage, you might not be able to boot any other operating systems on the same disk. So, you must go through all these steps to revert your disk to basic storage and enable both operating systems to be bootable. The moral is this: If you have more than one operating system on the disk, do *not* convert the disk to dynamic storage. You cannot convert a disk that contains any volumes from dynamic to basic. You cannot convert a single volume from dynamic to basic. You also cannot simply repair your Windows XP installation from its Recovery Console.

7. A, B, C. You should have at least 15% of free space on your disk so that the Disk Defragmenter can run in an optimal condition. Any of the first three options will increase the amount of free space.

8. A, C. You can either specify the volumes to be defragmented or use the /E parameter to specify the volumes that will not be defragmented. The defrag /e: command is incorrect syntax and will produce an error. The defrag /E c: d: command will defragment the E: volume but not the C: or D: volumes because it specifies to defragment all volumes except those mentioned.

9. C, D. Mirroring (RAID-1) and striping with parity (RAID-5) are fault tolerant and can withstand failure of a single disk without data loss. Spanning (which is not considered a RAID technology) and striping (RAID-0) are not fault tolerant; loss of a single disk results in loss of the entire volume.

10. A. The maximum space that you can include in a RAID-5 volume is equal to the smallest amount of free space on a single disk multiplied by one less than the total number of disks. Here the smallest amount of free space is 40 GB and the number of disks is 4, so you can have $40 \times 3 = 120$ GB. You require the space equivalent to one disk for parity; without parity you could have $40 \times 4 = 160$ GB, but this is not the desired result. In this scenario you could have created a three-disk striped volume without parity of 180 GB by using disks 0, 1, and 3 only, but this also is not the desired result. You cannot use all the space available when the sizes of the disks are different, so 280 GB is impossible.

11. D. The add disk 1 command in DiskPart creates a mirror on disk 1 of the current volume. This is the only way you can create a fault-tolerant replica of your system and boot volumes. A striped volume is not fault tolerant and cannot be used on the system and boot volumes. A RAID-5 volume is fault tolerant, but you cannot use this technology on the system and boot volumes; further, this technology requires three disks. The create volume mirror command is invalid command syntax.

12. D. You should enable the WPD Devices: Deny write access policy. WPD stands for *Windows Portable Device* and includes all such device types. None of the other policies mentioned would deny this type of access, although you could specify customized classes by GUID that would disable access to specific device types.

Chapter 16

1. A, C, D, E, F. You can access all these tools except for Reliability Monitor from this location, which is a new applet in the Windows 7 Control Panel that represents a comprehensive location for initiating almost all performance monitoring tools available to Windows 7.

2. D. You should look in the Applications and Services logs for this type of information. These logs are located in their own subnode and provide information for single applications, as opposed to the Application log, which logs events related to all applications on the computer. The Security log records information on audited events, and the System log records events related to actions occurring on the computer in general.

3. A. By filtering the log to display only Critical, Warning, and Error events, you can reduce the number of visible events and more easily locate events of interest. Information events make up the vast bulk of events recorded in the System log and do not represent problematic situations. Configuring the log to overwrite events after 48 hours would reduce the number of events appearing in the log but might cause loss of events indicating significant problems unless you always look at the logs more frequently. Event log subscriptions collect data from several computers and are not relevant here.

4. B. You should use a collector-initiated event subscription, which pulls events from the specified computers. A source-initiated event subscription is more appropriate where there are a large number of computers configured with Group Policy. A filter that views logs by event source displays logs according to Windows services, utilities, and components; this is not what is needed here. You could use a filter that views logs by user and computer, but this would be less convenient than creating an event log subscription, which is new to Windows 7.

5. A, C. You need to run the `Winrm` and `Wecutil` commands. The `Winrm` command initiates the Windows Remote Management service that enables a secure communication channel between source and collector computers. The `Wecutil` command enables you to create and manage subscriptions that are forwarded from remote computers. The `Wdsutil` command enables you to manage a Windows Deployment Services (WDS) server. The `Logman` command enables you to manage data collector sets in Performance Monitor. Neither of the latter two commands is associated with event log subscriptions.

6. A. Reliability Monitor provides this type of trend analysis. None of the other tools mentioned here can do this job.

7. B, D. You can use either Resource Monitor or Task Manager to terminate an unresponsive program, although Task Manager is more convenient. To use Resource Monitor, you need to know the process name of the program to be terminated, although this name is often intuitive (for example, `WINWORD.EXE` for Microsoft Word). The other tools mentioned here do not offer this functionality.

8. C. You should configure a Performance Counter Alert Trace Data Collector Set. This feature logs conditions that you specify such as a high processor utilization and alerts you when such conditions occur. An Event Trace Data Collector Set creates trace logs that log data only when a specific activity takes place; however, this type of data collector set does not send messages for specific conditions. An event log is created by Event Viewer and logs a large number of events but not this type of message. A System Diagnostics Data Collector Set creates reports on local hardware resources, system response times, and processes on the computer along with system information and configuration data. It does not provide alerts.

9. C. You should check the Memory\Committed Bytes counter. This counter measures the amount of virtual memory that has been committed to either physical RAM or running processes. Although useful for determining whether additional RAM is needed, the other counters mentioned here do not provide this specific information.

10. D. You should access the Startup tab and clear the check boxes against items you do not want to start when your computer starts. You will likely need to do this repeatedly until you find the item or items causing your slow startup. The **Diagnostic startup** option loads basic devices and services only and does not enable you to check which items are causing slow behavior. Neither the General tab nor the Boot tab provides an option for clearing check boxes against items you do not want to start when your computer starts.

11. D. Computers running a 64-bit version of Windows 7 cannot run 16-bit MS-DOS programs, and you must upgrade the program. None of the other options mentioned here will enable you to run the game.

12. A, B, D. Action Center enables you to check for possible security-related alerts or solutions to possible maintenance problems. Action Center also enables you to configure backup. However, you cannot view alerts generated by data collector sets or close unresponsive applications in Action Center.

13. A. The Dependencies tab of the service's Properties dialog box, accessed from the Services snap-in, provides you with this information. The General tab of this dialog box does not provide this information. The System Configuration tool would let you disable services but would not provide this information. The Services subnode of the Software Environment node in the System Information tool provides information on all services on the computer including those that are running or stopped and their startup type, but this location does not provide the required information.

Chapter 17

1. D. To perform backups to a network location, you must be using a computer that is running the Professional, Enterprise, or Ultimate edition of Windows 7. Windows 7 Home Premium does not include this capability. You do not need to have a homegroup configured to do network backups, and it is possible to use a Windows XP computer as a target provided you have the proper edition of Windows 7. Standard Windows Firewall settings should allow a network backup to take place.

2. A, B, D. The recommended option of letting Windows choose what will be backed up will back up files and folders from all these locations but will not back up data folders on portable hard drives.

3. C. This manually initiated backup procedure creates an incremental backup, which is a backup that includes only the files added or changed since the previous normal or incremental backup. It also marks the files as having been backed up. A normal backup would back up all files specified in the backup set. A differential backup would include all files added or changed since the previous normal backup without marking the files as backed up. A copy backup would create an extra copy of all files specified in the backup set.

4. B. By selecting **Change settings**, you can restart the Set Up Backup Wizard, so that you can modify all settings used by the default backup routine. The **Manage space** option enables you to manage the space used by backups including deletion of older backups, but it does not allow you to change the backup configuration. The **Create a System image** option enables you to back up all items required to restore Windows operation but does not necessarily add the files and folders you want. The **Back up computer** option was one of the options available in the Windows Vista Backup and Restore Center but is no longer present in Windows 7.

5. D. You should select the **Change settings** option. This restarts the wizard so that you can change all settings related to the backup, including the schedule. Selecting **Turn off schedule** prevents scheduled backups from occurring. Selecting **Manage space** enables you to check the space used by backups and to delete old backups. The **Set up backup** option is no longer available after you have run the first backup.

6. C. The `Wbadmin` command-line utility is used in Windows 7 to perform a backup from the command line. You specify the drive to be backed up with the `-include` keyword and the drive on which the backup is to be stored with the `-backuptarget` keyword. The `Ntbackup` utility was used in previous Windows versions to perform backups from the command line, but it is no longer used in Windows 7.

7. C. A system image includes all the Windows files that are necessary to restore Windows from a hardware failure. This is the simplest way to accomplish the task required by this scenario. A system recovery disk enables you to start the Windows Recovery Environment but does not include all the Windows files required to recover your computing environment completely. A system state backup was used in Windows 2000/XP, and a Complete PC Backup was used in Windows Vista for this type of task, but neither is available in Windows 7.

8. A. A system repair disc, also known as a system recovery disc, can be used to boot your computer should you need to recover from a serious error or to restore Windows on your computer. This disc cannot remove updates or restore critical data, nor is it used to fully restore your computer in the event of a hardware failure.

Chapter 18

1. B. The **In the following location** option enables you to specify a different folder in which the restored files are saved. You can then check this folder for the correct files and ensure that they are correctly restored. Watching for messages is cumbersome and time-consuming; in addition, if the backed up files are corrupted, you could lose data. The Search option would also be time-consuming, and browsing the backed up files would not detect corrupted backups.

2. A, B, D, E. Emily's profile does not include applications she has installed; these are found in the Program Files folder. Everything else mentioned here, including her application settings, are included in her profile.

3. A. The Shadow Copy feature retains previous versions of a document and enumerates the available versions in the Previous Versions tab of its Properties dialog box. By selecting the **Copy** option, you can copy an older version of your report to a different location and then merge the missing section with your current document. If you select the **Restore** option, the older version will overwrite your current version, and you will lose your most recent changes.

Restoring from a backup and selecting the options indicated will work but will take more effort.

4.   D. The System Restore feature restores your operating system, applications, and settings to the date and time that you have selected. It removes applications, drivers, and similar settings that have changed more recently. Simply rolling back the affected drivers will not fully complete this task. Restoring your profile does not remove bad drivers or applications. Restoring from a system image backup takes considerably more time and effort than using System Restore.

5.   A. The device driver rollback feature enables you to rapidly restore an older driver to recover device functionality that has been lost. Downloading a new driver or using System Restore would work but would take far more time. Using a system repair disk is more drastic and would likely cause other changes as well.

6.   C. The System Image Backup includes all files necessary to fully restore your computer in the event of a hardware failure or serious corruption such as occurred in this scenario. The Windows Complete PC Backup was a feature of Windows Vista and the System State Backup was a feature of Windows XP; these have been replaced in Windows 7 by the System Image Backup. The System Repair Disk enables you to reboot your computer for recovery from a serious error but would not restore functionality in this situation. The System Restore feature restores your computer to an earlier point in time but is unlikely to remove a virus infestation.

7.   A. The system repair disk provides a simple way to start your computer in this scenario and enables you to access a system image. The system image contains everything needed to replace Windows, your programs, and all your files, thereby restoring your computer to its previous condition. The Reinstall Windows option would reinstall Windows, but you would have to reinstall applications and restore files and settings separately. The System Restore option is not available when starting with a system repair disk. Performing an in-place upgrade would also require that you reinstall applications and restore files and settings separately.

8.   A, B, C. You can select options for startup repair, system restore, or system image recovery from the System Recovery Options dialog box that you receive after selecting the stated option. You can also choose to perform a Windows memory diagnostic or boot to a command prompt. You cannot perform device driver rollback from this option. Recovery Console was used in Windows XP, but its function has been replaced with the Command Prompt option that is included with this tool.

9.   B. When you are unable to log on after performing a change such as this one, you should first try the Last Known Good Configuration option. This option

restores Registry settings to the most recent values that worked. Only if this does not work should you try either Safe Mode or Low-Resolution Video. You do not need to use System Restore to correct this problem.

10. A. It appears as though this driver has modified resources used by your display adapter as well as the network card. Selecting Safe Mode starts your computer with a minimal set of drivers and enables you to roll back the driver. In this scenario, you were able to log on, so you cannot repair the problem using Last Known Good Configuration. System Restore is not an option available when you press F8 at startup; further, this option is not needed to correct the problem you encountered here.

Glossary

access control list (ACL)
The list of permissions granted or denied that is attached to a file or folder.

Action Center
A new Windows 7 tool that replaces the Windows Vista Security Center. Action Center consolidates security, performance, and maintenance issues affecting your computer into a single panel that also includes information on device-related problems. In addition, Action Center provides links to obtain more information and troubleshoot any of these problems.

active partition
A partition or volume on a hard disk that has been identified as the primary partition from which the operating system is booted.

ad hoc network
A peer-to-peer wireless connection between two computers without going through an access point.

Add-on Manager
An Internet Explorer 8 tool that enables you to disable or allow browser add-ons or undesired ActiveX controls.

add-ons
Optional additional features that can be installed in Internet Explorer and provide enhanced functionality. Websites often download and install add-ons to your browser, sometimes without your knowledge and consent.

Address Resolution Protocol (ARP)
A TCP/IP protocol that is used to resolve the IP address of the destination computer to the physical or Media Access Control (MAC) address.

Admin Approval Mode
The default action mode of Windows 7, in which all user accounts—even administrative ones—run without administrative privileges until such privileges are required. When this happens, the user is presented with a UAC prompt.

administrative shares
A series of shares that are automatically created when Windows 7 is first installed. These shares are useful for administrating remote computers on the network.

alert
A notification provided by the Data Collector Sets feature of Performance Monitor that informs you when the value of a counter has exceeded a pre-configured level.

answer file
An ASCII text file that contains answers, in script form, to questions asked by the Windows 7 Setup Wizard during unattended installations. This file, often called `Autounattend.xml`, enables installation of Windows 7 to proceed without requiring users to answer questions during the installation.

anycast IPv6 address
A type of IPv6 address that is utilized only for a destination address assigned to a router.

Application Compatibility Manager
A component of the ACT that enables you to collect and analyze compatibility data so that you can remedy any issues before you deploy a new operating system such as Windows 7.

Application Compatibility Toolkit (ACT)
A Microsoft resource that helps administrators identify the compatibility of their applications with Windows Vista and Windows 7, thereby helping organizations to produce a comprehensive software inventory.

application compatibility
The process of ensuring that a program or application written for a previous Windows operating system will function properly within Windows 7.

AppLocker
An update to the older Software Restriction Policies, providing new enhancements that enable you to specify exactly what users are permitted to run on their desktops according to unique file identities. You can also specify the users or groups permitted to execute these applications.

authentication
A process whereby an individual on a network proves he is who he says he is. The authentication process validates the source and identity of information and includes such tasks as confirming the identity of a user, computer, or digital signature.

authorization
The process by which an authenticated user is granted access to resources she needs to perform her job.

Automatic Private IP Addressing (APIPA)
The dynamic IPv4 addressing system used when DHCP is unavailable.

Backup and Restore applet
A new application in Windows 7 that provides a centralized location and wizards for performing various types of backup and restore procedures.

backup
The creation of a copy of programs or data on the computer as a protection against some type of disaster.

basic disk
A disk partitioning scheme that uses partition tables supported by DOS and many other operating systems, containing primary partitions, extended partitions, and logical drives.

Basic Input/Output System (BIOS)
The firmware application encoded in a computer that initializes the computer before the operating system is loaded. The BIOS manages basic hardware configuration.

battery meter

A small application that runs on mobile computers and displays the percentage of battery power remaining as well as the power plan currently in use.

Bcdboot

A command-line tool that enables you to manage and create new boot configuration data (BCD) stores and BCD boot entries.

Bcdedit

A command-line tool that enables you to manage BCD stores in Windows Vista/7/Server 2008.

BitLocker

A feature of Windows 7 Enterprise and Ultimate that enables you to encrypt the entire contents of your system or data partition. It is useful for protecting data stored on laptops, which are susceptible to theft.

BitLocker To Go

A component of BitLocker that is new to Windows 7 and enables you to encrypt the contents of a USB flash drive or portable hard drive.

BranchCache

A new feature of Windows 7 that enables users to rapidly access data from remotely located file and web servers. BranchCache enables users at a small branch office to cache copies of frequently accessed files from head office servers on a local computer.

built-in group

A predefined local group that is granted specific rights and privileges on the local computer.

cache

A space on the computer's hard disk that is set aside for holding offline copies of shared files and folders from a computer on the network.

certificate

A method of granting access to a user based on unique identification. Certificates represent a distinctive way to establish a user's identity and credentials. They originate from a certification authority (CA). Internet Explorer uses these certificates so that the user can verify that he is accessing the proper website.

Challenge Handshake Authentication Protocol (CHAP)

An authentication protocol that uses a hashed version of a user's password so that the user's credentials are not sent over the wire in clear text.

Classless Inter-Domain Routing (CIDR)

A flexible method of stating IP addresses and masks without needing to classify the addresses. An example of the CIDR format is 192.168.1.0/24.

Compatibility View

A feature of Internet Explorer 8 that enables websites designed for earlier versions of Internet Explorer to display properly in Internet Explorer 8.

Computer Management console

An application that provides access to several of the most commonly used administrative tools such as Task Scheduler, Event Viewer, Local Users and Groups, Performance Monitor, Device Manager, Services, and several others.

Content Advisor
A component of Internet Explorer that enables you to control what Internet content users can view on a Windows 7 computer.

credential
The information provided by a user or computer to gain access to another network resource. Credentials include usernames, passwords, certificates, and other personal identification information.

Credential Manager
A Windows 7 utility that stores credentials for logging on to resources such as websites, terminal servers, and applications. This utility stores credentials in an electronic Windows vault that makes them available for facilitated logon to these types of resources.

Data Collector Sets
A component of Performance Monitor that records computer performance information into log files. This feature was known as Performance Logs and Alerts in Windows 2000/XP/Server 2003.

Data Recovery Agent
A specially configured user account that has the ability to decrypt drives and partitions that have been encrypted using BitLocker.

decryption
Unscrambling the data in an encrypted file through use of an algorithm so that the file can be read.

default gateway
The term applied to the router that leads to other networks.

Deployment Image Servicing and Management (DISM)
A command-line tool that enumerates, installs, uninstalls, configures, and updates system images.

Deployment Server
The default mode of WDS in Windows Server 2008 R2, this mode deploys Windows 7 installations within a domain environment using AD DS, DNS, and DHCP.

destination computer
A computer on which Windows 7 together with applications has been freshly installed and to which user settings and data are to be restored using the USMT.

device driver
The specialized software component of an operating system that interfaces with a particular hardware component.

Device Manager
A tool from which you can manage all the hardware devices on your computer. It enables you to view and change device properties, update or roll back drivers, configure settings, and remove devices.

Differencing VHD
Also known as a child VHD, a VHD that contains only the differences between it and its parent VHD.

Direct Memory Address (DMA)
The process of data bypassing the CPU and accessing RAM directly, designated as channels; for example, a floppy drive uses DMA channel 2.

DirectAccess
A new feature of Windows 7 and Windows Server 2008 R2 that enables users to directly connect to corporate networks from any Internet connection using a seamless, bidirectional, secured tunnel without the need for a virtual private network (VPN) connection.

Disk Cleanup
A program that checks your hard disk for old, temporary, or repetitive folders and files and enables you to remove these items to free up additional disk space. It includes a dialog box that enables you to select which folders should be removed.

Disk Management snap-in
A Microsoft Management Console snap-in that enables you to perform all management activities related to disks, partitions, and volumes.

DiskPart
A command-line tool that enables you to perform all management activities related to disks, partitions, and volumes. You can use this tool to script actions related to disk management.

Distributed Cache
A mode of BranchCache in which each branch office client computer stores its own copy of files cached from the head office server while making them available to other users in the same branch office who request the same file.

Domain Name System (DNS)
A hierarchical naming system that is contained in a distributed database. DNS provides name resolution for IP addresses and DNS names.

driver signing
The digital signature that Microsoft adds to a third-party device driver to validate its usage.

dynamic disk
A disk partitioning scheme supported by Windows 2000/XP/Vista/7 as well as Windows Server 2003/2008 R2 that contains dynamic volumes.

Dynamic Host Configuration Protocol (DHCP)
The protocol in the TCP/IP protocol stack that negotiates the lease of an IP address from a DHCP server.

Dynamic VHD
A VHD that gradually increases in size towards a configured maximum as data is added to it.

Encrypting File System (EFS)
An advanced attribute setting of Windows 2000/XP/Vista/7 and Windows Server 2003/2008 R2 for files and folders on an NTFS-formatted volume that provides certificate-based public key security for those files and folders. EFS encrypts and decrypts files in a manner that is transparent to users.

encryption
Scrambling and rearranging data in a file through use of an algorithm so that the file cannot be read.

event log subscription
An Event Viewer feature that enables you to collect event logs from a number of computers in a single, convenient location that helps you keep track of events that occur on these computers.

Event Viewer
An administrative tool that enables an administrator to view and/or archive event logs such as the operating system, application, setup, and security logs. In Windows 7, this tool also enables you to configure event log subscriptions that collect events from several monitored computers together.

extended partition
One of the primary partitions that can be divided into multiple logical drives.

Extensible Authentication Protocol (EAP)
An extension to PPP that allows arbitrary authentication methods using credential and information exchanges of arbitrary lengths. You can use authentication methods such as smart cards, biometrics, and more.

File Allocation Table (FAT)
The file system that provides a map of the disk clusters within an allocation table. Files written to the disk are not necessarily stored in contiguous clusters, which can vary in size. FAT, the 16-bit version, is the most widely supported file system and the ideal choice for dual-boot machines. The 32-bit version of FAT (FAT32) is available only on Windows 95 OSR2 and later versions.

file systems
The overall structure of an operating system, in which files are named, organized, and stored. FAT and NTFS are types of file systems.

firewall profile
A means of grouping firewall rules so that they apply to the affected computers dependent on where the computer is connected.

firewall rule
A set of conditions used by Windows Firewall to determine whether a particular type of communication is permitted. You can configure inbound rules, outbound rules, and connection security rules from the Windows Firewall with Advanced Security snap-in.

FireWire
Also known as IEEE 1394, FireWire is a fast external bus technology that allows for 800 Mbps data transfer rates and can connect up to 63 devices. FireWire devices, although conforming to standards that Windows uses, usually require software from the manufacturer to utilize the specialized capabilities of the hardware.

Fixed VHD
A VHD that maintains the same size regardless of how much data is contained in it.

global unicast IPv6 address
An IPv6 address that uses a global routing prefix of 45 bits to identify a specific organization's network, a 16-bit subnet ID, and a 64-bit interface ID. These addresses are globally routable on the Internet and are equivalent to public IPv4 addresses.

Group Policy
A feature of Windows 7 and Windows Server 2008 R2 that allows for policy creation, which affects domain users and computers. Policies can be anything from desktop settings to application assignments to security settings and more.

Group Policy object (GPO)
An object that contains settings and con-figuration information that is attached to a container (such as a site, domain, or OU in Active Directory). Settings in the GPO are applied to all the associated container's objects.

hibernation
A condition in which your computer saves everything to the hard disk and then powers down. When you restart your computer from hibernation, all open documents and programs are restored to the desktop.

hidden shares
A shared folder that does not broadcast its presence and is not browsable in the Network folder. A hidden share is indicat-ed by a dollar sign ($) at the end of the folder name.

homegroup
A small group of Windows 7 computers that can exchange shared information easily with each other.

host
A computing device that has been assigned an IP address.

Hosted Cache
A mode of BranchCache in which a server running Windows Server 2008 R2 located in the branch office hosts files cached from the remote server. Users in the branch office retrieve files from the Hosted Cache server rather than from across the WAN.

hypervisor
An additional layer of software below the operating system for running virtual computers.

ImageX
A command-line tool that captures, creates, modifies, and applies Windows images and assists the use of these images in other technologies such as WDS.

incremental backup
A type of Windows backup that backs up all files and folders that have changed since the last normal backup and removes the archive bit, thereby indicating that the files have been backed up. It is used by the Backup and Restore applet for subse-quent backups after you have created the initial normal backup. This backup type is the fastest one to perform but requires that you restore all incremental backups in sequence since the last normal backup.

information bar
A message that Internet Explorer displays at the top of the page under certain cir-cumstances to alert you of possible secu-rity problems. These messages include attempts by a website to install an ActiveX control, open a pop-up window, download a file, or run active content.

InPrivate browsing
A special browsing mode of Internet Explorer 8 that prevents user informa-tion, cookies, and browsing history from being retained on the computer. This is particularly useful for public computers that are accessed by many individuals.

InPrivate filtering
A component of InPrivate browsing that blocks the transmission of third-party content to websites being viewed in Internet Explorer 8. You can customize the types of third-party content that are allowed or blocked by choosing InPrivate Filtering Settings options.

input/output (I/O) port address
Set of wires used to transmit data between a device and the system. As with IRQs, each component will have a unique I/O port assigned. There are 65,535 I/O ports in a computer, and they are referenced by a hexadecimal address in the range of 0000h to FFFFh.

Internet Connection Sharing (ICS)
The simplified system of routing Internet traffic through a Windows 7 computer so that other computers on the network that are not connected to the Internet can access the Internet.

Internet Control Naming Protocol (ICMP)
A TCP/IP protocol that enables hosts on a TCP/IP network to share status and error information. The `ping` command uses ICMP to check connectivity to remote computers.

Internet Explorer Compatibility Test Tool
A component of the ACT that collects issues with your company's websites and web-based applications in Internet Explorer versions 7 and 8.

Internet Key Exchange version 2 (IKEv2)
A tunneling protocol that uses IPSec Tunnel Mode over UDP port 500. This combination of protocols also supports strong authentication and encryption methods.

Internet Protocol Security (IPSec)
An encryption and authentication protocol used to secure data transmitted across a network.

interrupt request (IRQ)
A set of wires that run between the CPU and devices in the computer; they enable devices to "interrupt" the CPU so that they can transmit data.

IP address
A logical address used to identify both a host and a network segment. Each network adapter on an IP network requires a unique IP address.

IP version 4 (IPv4)
The version of the Internet Protocol that has been in use for many years and provides a 32-bit address space formatted as four octets separated by periods.

IP version 6 (IPv6)
A newer version of the Internet Protocol that provides a 128-bit address space formatted as eight 16-bit blocks, each of which is portrayed as a four-digit hexadecimal number and is separated from other blocks by colons.

Ipconfig
The command-line utility that provides detailed information about the IP configuration of a Windows computer's network adapters.

Last Known Good Configuration
A Registry configuration that contains the settings utilized for the last successful logon. If reconfigured settings prevent your computer from proper startup, you can press **F8** during startup and access Last Known Good Configuration to remove the improper settings.

Layer 2 Tunneling Protocol (L2TP)
A protocol used to create VPN tunnels across a public network. This protocol is used in conjunction with IPSec for security purposes.

library
A set of virtual folders shared by default with other users of the computer. It is used to group documents of similar type in an easily accessible place.

link-local IPv6 address
A type of IPv6 address used for communication between neighboring nodes on the same link. Equivalent to IPv4 addresses configured using APIPA.

Link-Local Multicast Name Resolution (LLMNR)
The capability of computers running IPv6 on the local subnet to resolve each other's names without the need for a DNS server. It is enabled by default in Windows 7 IPv6.

LoadState.exe
A utility used by USMT to restore user settings and data to a new computer running Windows 7.

local group
A group that is configured on the local computer only. It can contain user accounts from its own computer as well as user accounts and groups from a domain to which the computer belongs. Local groups are used to define access permissions to resources on the local computer only.

Local Security Policy
The security-based Group Policy settings that apply to a local computer and its local users.

logical drive
A segment of the extended partition that can be assigned a separate drive letter.

Microsoft Challenge Handshake Authentication Protocol version 2 (MS-CHAPv2)
A Microsoft version of CHAP that uses the same type of challenge/response mechanism as CHAP but uses a nonreversible encrypted password. This is done by using MD4 algorithms to encrypt the challenge and the user's password.

Microsoft Deployment Toolkit (MDT)
A Microsoft solution accelerator that assists administrators in the deployment of operating systems and applications to large numbers of computers on a corporate network.

Microsoft Forefront Unified Access Gateway (UAG)
A DirectAccess option that provides enhanced security within and outside the corporate network, enabling DirectAccess for IPv4-only applications and resources on the network.

Microsoft Management Console
An extensible management framework that provides a common look and feel to a large number of management utilities used in Windows 7 and Windows Server 2008 R2.

mirroring
A method of duplicating data between two separate hard disks so that the failure of one disk will not cause the operating system to fail.

msconfig
The command that opens the System Configuration Utility, which you can use to perform actions such as modifying the startup scheme, the default operating system that boots on a dual-boot computer, services that are enabled, and startup programs that run automatically. You can also launch several computer management tools from this utility.

msinfo32
The command that opens the System Information program.

multicast IPv6 address
An IPv6 address that enables the delivery of packets to each of multiple interfaces.

Network Access Protection (NAP)
A feature that protects network resources by requiring that client computers accessing the network from outside provide assurance that they are up-to-date and free of malware. NAP enables you to ensure that client computers do not spread malware to the internal network.

Network Address Translation (NAT)
A specification in TCP/IP that maps the range of private IP addresses (192.168.0.1–192.168.0.254) to the public IP address of an Internet-facing network adapter.

Network and Sharing Center
A feature of Windows 7 that provides a centralized location from which you can manage all networking tasks such as connecting to networks and the Internet and sharing of files and folders with users at other computers.

normal backup
A type of Windows backup that backs up all selected files and removes the archive bit, thereby indicating that the files have been backed up. Such a backup is the most complete backup and provides the fastest means of restoring data. Also called full backup.

NT File System (NTFS)
The file system originally provided with Windows NT that supports volume mounting, compression, encryption, and security.

NTFS permissions
The security feature available in NTFS that allows you to grant or deny local access rights.

offline files
A feature built into Windows 2000/XP/Vista/7 that enables you to cache locally stored copies of shared files and folders so that you can work with them while offline and resynchronize your changes when you go back online.

paging file
Virtual memory stored on disk that enables Windows 7 to run more applications at one time than would be allowed by the computer's physical memory (RAM).

partition
A configured section of a basic disk that is capable of being formatted with a file system and identified with a drive letter.

Password Authentication Protocol (PAP)
The oldest remote access authentication protocol, which sends the user's credentials over the wire in clear text and can easily be sniffed off of the wire by an attacker.

Password policy
A series of Group Policy settings that determine password security requirements, such as length, complexity, and age.

performance counter
A statistical measurement associated with a performance object such as % disk time, queue length, and so on.

Performance Monitor
A Microsoft Management Console (MMC) application that contains several tools for monitoring your computer's performance.

Performance object
Hardware or software components that the Performance Monitor can use for tracking performance data.

Personal Identity Verification (PIV)
A smart card standard devised by the National Institute of Standards and Technology (NIST) that details the specific physical and data requirements of the smart cards, how they are issued, and how long they are valid.

phishing
The use of a fake website that closely mimics a real website and contains a similar-looking URL. This site is intended to scam users into sending confidential personal information (such as credit card or bank account numbers, birthdates, Social Security numbers, and so on).

Plug and Play (PnP)
A standard developed by Microsoft and Intel that allows for automatic hardware installation detection and configuration in most Windows operating systems.

Point-to-Point Protocol (PPP)
A dial-up protocol that supports TCP/IP and IPX/SPX and others with advanced compression and encryption functions.

Point-to-Point Tunneling Protocol (PPTP)
A protocol used to create VPN tunnels across a public network and includes encryption and authentication.

pop-up windows
Additional windows displayed on your browser by some websites that present advertisements or perform other actions, mostly of an undesirable nature. Internet Explorer 8 in Windows 7 includes a pop-up blocker that blocks the appearance of such windows and provides you with an option to display them if you desire.

power plans
A series of preconfigured power management options that control actions such as shutting off the monitor or hard disks or placing the computer in sleep mode or hibernation.

PreBoot eXecution Environment (PXE)
A bootable ROM chip contained on compatible network interface cards (NICs) that enables client computers without an operating system to boot and connect to the network for locating a WDS server.

primary partition

A segment of the hard disk. A maximum of four primary partitions may exist on a single basic disk.

private key

A piece of data generated by an asymmetric algorithm that's used by the host to decrypt data (for example, by using EFS). A matching public key can be used to encrypt data to be decrypted with the private key.

Protected Extensible Authentication Protocol-Transport Layer Security (PEAP-TLS)

A remote access authentication and security protocol that provides an encrypted authentication channel, dynamic keying material from TLS, fast reconnect using cached session keys, and server authentication that protects against the setup of unauthorized access points.

Protected Mode

First introduced with Internet Explorer 7 in Windows Vista, this protects Internet Explorer by providing enhanced levels of security and protection from malware. Microsoft has improved Protected Mode in Windows 7 by restricting its privileges to reduce the capability of an attack that installs malicious code on a user's computer or an attack that modifies or destroys a user's data.

Public folder sharing

A simple Windows 7 folder sharing model that allows others on the network to access files in your Public folders of each Windows library (Documents, Pictures, Videos, and Music).

public key

A piece of data generated by an asymmetric algorithm distributed to the public for general use. Used to encrypt data when using EFS. Such information can be decrypted only by the corresponding private key holder.

RAID-5

A combination of disk striping with parity data interleaved across three or more disks. RAID-5 provides improved disk performance and is fault tolerant.

recovery agent

A user account that has been granted the authority to decrypt encrypted files.

Reliability Monitor

A monitoring tool that provides a trend analysis of your computer's system stability with time. It shows how events such as hardware or application failures, software installations or removals, and so on affect your computer's stability.

Remote Assistance

A service available in Windows 7 that enables a user to share control of her computer with an administrator or other user to resolve a computer problem.

Remote Desktop

A service available in all editions of Windows 7 that allows a single remote control session of a computer running Windows XP Professional, Vista Business, Enterprise or Ultimate, or Windows 7 Professional, Enterprise or Ultimate. Remote Desktop uses the Remote Desktop Protocol (RDP), which is the same protocol used in Terminal Services.

Remote Desktop Gateway (RD Gateway)

A Windows Server 2008 R2 feature that replaces the Terminal Services feature included with older versions of Windows Server. RD Gateway enables you to connect to remote servers on the corporate network from any computer connected to the Internet. You can publish applications to users on RD Gateway by using RemoteApp.

RemoteApp

Applications that users can access remotely through the RD Gateway server. When a user accesses one of these programs, it appears on his desktop as though it were running locally.

Resource Monitor

A monitoring tool that provides a summary of CPU, disk, network, and memory performance statistics including mini graphs of recent performance of these four components as well as tabulated data pertaining to each of these components.

Safe Mode

A method of starting Windows 7 with only the basic drivers enabled so that you can troubleshoot problems that prevent Windows from starting normally.

ScanState.exe

A utility used by USMT to collect user settings and data on an old computer for purposes of migration to a Windows 7 computer.

Secure Socket Tunneling Protocol (SSTP)

A tunneling protocol that uses Secure Hypertext Transfer Protocol (HTTPS) over TCP port 443 to transmit traffic across firewalls and proxy servers that might block PPTP and L2TP traffic.

Secure Sockets Layer (SSL)

A protocol used to secure data transmitted via HTTPS through the use of public key/private key encryption.

service pack (SP)

A collection of updates and fixes to a software package, usually available via download from the Internet. Service packs are available for download from Microsoft and when using the Microsoft automated update service.

Service Set Identifier (SSID)

A network name that identifies a wireless access point.

Setup.exe

The application that installs Windows 7 on a new computer or updates an older Windows computer to Windows 7. Also frequently used as a routine for installing applications.

shadow copies

Backup copies of files and folders automatically created by Windows as you work on them, enabling you to restore them should they become corrupted or deleted.

shared folder permissions

The security feature available when sharing files and folders across a network that allows you to grant or deny access rights to network users.

shared folders

Folders made available for access by users who are working at other computers on the network.

shim

A compatibility fix used to enable an application originally written for an older Windows version to function properly when running in Windows 7.

side by side migration

A type of migration in which user settings and data from an old computer are transferred to a new Windows 7 computer.

sigverif.exe

A utility that checks your computer for unsigned device drivers.

site-local IPv6 address

An IPv6 address that is private to the network on which it is located. This type of address cannot be accessed from locations external to its network, such as the Internet.

sleep mode

A condition in which the computer consumes low power but is available for use. Sleep mode saves configuration information to memory and powers down the monitor, disks, and several other hardware components.

smart card

A credit-card–sized device that stores a user's certificates and PKI keys.

SmartScreen Filter

An enhancement of the antiphishing and antimalware tools first introduced with Internet Explorer 7 that compares website addresses to a database that is continuously updated to protect users from fraudulent websites that attempt to steal identity information or install malicious software.

Software Restriction Policies

A series of settings included in Group Policy and Local Security Policy that can be used to limit the types of software that can run on a Windows XP/Vista/7 computer. You can limit users to running only those applications they need to do their jobs, and you can also prevent malicious applications from installing or running.

source computer

An old computer from which user settings and data are to be collected using the USMT, prior to repurposing or upgrading to Windows 7.

special access permissions

A granular set of NTFS security permissions that enables a single type of access only. Regular NTFS permissions are actually a combination of special access permissions.

Startup Repair

A utility that provides a diagnostics-based, step-by-step troubleshooter that enables end users and tech support personnel to rapidly diagnose and repair problems that are preventing a computer from starting normally.

stop error

An operating system failure that is severe enough to cause the computer to stop functioning. In Windows 7 and previous versions of Windows 2000/XP/Vista/Server 2003 and Windows NT, the Stop error is displayed as white text on a blue screen and is nicknamed the "blue screen of death" (BSOD).

striping

A method of segmenting data and inter-leaving it across multiple disks, which has the effect of improving disk perform-ance but is not fault tolerant.

subnet mask

A set of numbers, 32 bits in length, that begins with 1s and ends with 0s in binary notation. The number of 1s represents the number of bits that are considered the subnet address. The bits that are 0s are the host address. Using a subnet mask, you can create more subnets with a smaller number of computers per sub-net. All computers on a given subnet must have the same subnet mask. Using dotted decimal notation, a subnet mask is written as 255.255.0.0 (which is the default mask for a Class B address).

Sync Center

A program on mobile computers that synchronizes data with other network devices, including servers, desktop com-puters, and other portable computers.

synchronization conflicts

Occur when two users have modified a file that is available offline and Windows detects that conflicting modifications have occurred. Windows 7's Sync Center enables you to save either or both of these versions.

synchronizing files

The act of copying files from a shared folder on the network to an offline files cache on a computer or copying the same files back to the shared folder after a user has modified them.

System Configuration Utility

A tool that enables you to perform actions such as modifying the startup scheme, the default operating system that boots on a dual-boot computer, services that are enabled, and startup programs that run automatically. You can also launch several computer manage-ment tools from this utility. Started with the Msconfig.exe command.

System Image Manager (SIM)

A wizard that helps you create unattend-ed installation files, which minimizes the required amount of user interaction dur-ing an automated installation of Windows 7. Known as Setup Manager in versions of Windows prior to Vista.

System Preparation Tool (Sysprep)

A utility that you can use to remove computer- and user-specific data from a computer's configuration, enabling you to capture an image for deployment of Windows 7 to other computers.

System Protection

A troubleshooting tool that provides sev-eral options for retaining copies of sys-tem files and settings so that you can configure how System Restore works to restore your computer to an earlier point in time.

system repair disc

Also known as a system recovery disc, this is a CD or DVD that you can use to boot your computer into the Windows Recovery Environment after a serious error has occurred that shuts normal Windows operation down.

System Restore
A troubleshooting tool that enables you to restore your computer to an earlier time at which it was operating properly.

Task Manager
A Windows 7 administrative utility that provides data about currently running processes, including their CPU and memory usage, and enables you to modify their priority or shut down misbehaving applications. You can also manage services, including starting, stopping, enabling, and disabling them; obtain information on network utilization; and display users with sessions running on the computer.

Teredo
A tunneling communication protocol that enables IPv6 connectivity between IPv6/IPv4 nodes across network address translation (NAT) interfaces, thereby improving connectivity for newer IPv6-enabled applications on IPv4 networks.

Transmission Control Protocol/Internet Protocol (TCP/IP)
The suite of protocols used on the Internet for communication between computers. TCP/IP is the default networking protocol for Windows 7.

Transport Server
A new mode of WDS in Windows Server 2008 R2 that enables Windows 7 to be deployed in a workgroup environment without the need for AD DS.

update roll-up
A packaged sets of updates that fixes problems with specific Windows components or software packages such as Microsoft Office.

User Account Control (UAC)
A feature in Windows 7 that enables you to work with a nonadministrative user account. UAC displays a prompt that requests approval when you want to perform an administrative task. Should malicious software attempt to install itself or perform undesirable actions, you will receive a prompt that you can use to prevent such actions from occurring. First introduced in Windows Vista, UAC has been updated in Windows 7 to provide new configuration options and reduce the number of prompts.

user profile
A series of desktop settings, configuration data, and user-specific documents automatically created for each user of a Windows 7 computer, stored by default at `C:\Users\%username%`.

user rights
A default set of capabilities assigned to built-in local groups that defines what members of these groups can and cannot do on the network.

User State Migration Tool (USMT)
A program that migrates a large number of users from an old computer to a new Windows 7 computer. This program uses two executables, `ScanState.exe` and `LoadState.exe`, together with a series of `.xml` configuration files, to migrate user files and settings. You can script this program to facilitate large migrations.

virtual folders
Folders that are actually placeholders or pointers to resources located elsewhere on the computer or on shared network folders. Windows 7 uses libraries to contain a series of virtual folders.

virtual hard disk (VHD)
A file that includes all the files and folders that would be found on a hard disk partition

virtual private network (VPN)
A remote access connection technology that uses a protocol such as Point-to-Point Tunneling Protocol or L2TP with IPSec to tunnel through a public network to connect to a private network and maintain a secure connection.

volume
A logical drive that has been formatted for use by a file system. Although often considered synonymous with *partition*, a volume is most specifically a portion of a dynamic disk (or multiple sections of dynamic disks) that is capable of being formatted with a file system and being identified with a drive letter.

Wbadmin
A command-line utility that provides all the functions of the Windows Backup and Restore applet in a scriptable form.

Wi-Fi Protected Access (WPA)
A wireless authentication protocol that uses preshared network key encryption to ensure that only authorized users receive access to the network.

Windows 7 Logo Program
A list compiled by Microsoft that includes all hardware components that are compatible with Windows 7 and Windows Server 2008 R2. It replaces the older Hardware Compatibility List (HCL) and Windows Catalog used with Windows versions prior to Vista.

Windows Anytime Upgrade
A program that facilitates the upgrading of one edition of Windows 7 to a higher one. It enables you to compare features of different Windows 7 editions and purchase the upgrade online.

Windows Automated Installation Kit (AIK)
A series of tools and documentation provided by Microsoft that facilitates the customization and deployment of computers running Windows 7 or Windows Server 2008 R2.

Windows Deployment Services (WDS)
A feature of Windows Server 2003 and 2008 that enables an automated remote installation of the Windows 7 operating system from a specially configured server.

Windows Easy Transfer
A program that facilitates the migration of user files from an old computer to a new Windows 7 computer. Windows Easy Transfer replaces the Files and Settings Transfer Wizard used with Windows XP.

Windows Experience Index
A performance-scoring metric that assesses the capability of several hardware and software components on your computer. It includes such components as the processor, memory, graphics card, and hard disk, and displays a base score that relates to the weakest performing component on your computer.

Windows Firewall

The personal firewall software incorporated in Windows 7 that filters incoming TCP/IP traffic. Windows Firewall was first introduced in Windows XP SP2.

Windows image (`.wim`) file

A compressed file that includes the files and folders required to duplicate a Windows installation on a disk volume. A `.wim` file can include multiple Windows images.

Windows Mobility Center

An application that runs on all Windows 7 mobile computers and that provides a quick view of functions pertinent to mobile computers, such as battery status, wireless network connections, sync partnerships, presentation settings, and so on. You can configure common mobile computer settings, such as display settings, speaker volume, and battery status.

Windows Optional Component Setup tool (`OCSetup.exe`)

A deployment tool that is used to add system components to a Windows image. This tool installs or removes Component-Based Servicing (CBS) packages online by passing them to DISM for installing or removal.

Windows PowerShell

An enhanced task-based command-line scripting interface that enables you to perform a large number of remote management tasks.

Windows Preinstallation Environment (Windows PE)

A minimal 32-bit operating system based on the Windows 7 kernel, used in the preinstallation and deployment of Windows 7.

Windows Recovery Environment (Windows RE)

A diagnostic and recovery tool included with Windows PE. You can also use Windows RE to build a custom system recovery solution.

Windows Remote Management (WinRM) Service

The Microsoft implementation of the WS-Management Protocol, which is a protocol that assists you in managing hardware on a network that includes machines that run a diverse mix of operating systems including remote computers.

Windows Server Update Services (WSUS)

A service that can be configured to run on a server, supplying updates, hotfixes, and other patches automatically to computers on a network. WSUS enables you to deploy and manage updates downloaded from the Microsoft Windows Update website to WSUS servers running on your own network. Client computers simply connect to the local WSUS server to download and install updates.

Windows Update

An application that enables you to maintain your computer in an up-to-date condition by automatically downloading and installing critical updates as Microsoft publishes them. Also enables access to the Microsoft website on which these updates are published.

Windows Upgrade Advisor

A program that you can download from Microsoft that scans your computer and advises you which components and devices you should upgrade or replace before upgrading an older computer to Windows 7. It also alerts you to any programs that might be incompatible with Windows 7.

Windows XP Mode

A virtual copy of Windows XP that runs within the Windows 7 Professional, Enterprise, or Ultimate desktop and enables you to run applications that don't run properly in Windows 7.

Windows.old

A folder created when upgrading an older version of Windows to a newer one. It contains subfolders containing operating system files, user files, and program files, some of which you can migrate to your newer Windows operating system.

wipe and load migration

A type of migration in which user settings and data from a computer running an older Windows operating system are collected, and then the same computer is upgraded to Windows 7 and the user settings and data are restored to this computer.

Wired Equivalent Privacy (WEP)

A protocol used on 802.11-based wireless networks to encrypt data sent between computers on a wireless network or between a computer and its access point.

wireless access point (WAP)

A wireless router or other device that broadcasts signals to computers on a wireless local area network (WLAN). Computers connecting through a WAP are members of an infrastructure (as opposed to ad hoc) wireless network.

wireless network profile

A series of configuration settings that determines the extent of access to external computers according to your computer's location. Windows enables you to create profiles for home, work, and public locations.

Index

R

PEARSON IT Certification

Browse by Exams ▼	Browse by Technology ▼	Browse by Format	Explore ▼	I'm New Here – Help!

Store   Forums   Safari Books Online

Your Publisher for IT Certification

Pearson IT Certification is the leader in technology certification learning and preparation tools.

Visit **pearsonITcertification.com** today to find

- **CERTIFICATION EXAM** information and guidance for IT certifications, including

  CISCO.    CompTIA.    **Microsoft·**

- **EXAM TIPS AND TRICKS** by reading the latest articles and sample chapters by Pearson IT Certification's expert authors and industry experts, such as
  - Mark Edward Soper and David Prowse – CompTIA
  - Wendell Odom – Cisco
  - Shon Harris – Security
  - Thomas Erl – SOACP

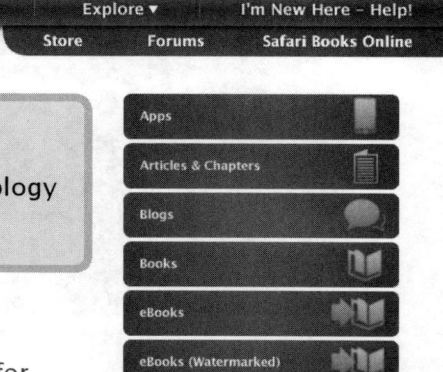

- **SPECIAL OFFERS (pearsonITcertification.com/promotions)**
- **REGISTRATION** for your Pearson IT Certification products to access additional online material and receive a coupon to be used on your next purchase

Be sure to create an account on **pearsonITcertification.com** and receive member's-only offers and benefits.

Pearson IT Certification is a publishing imprint of Pearson

Apps
Articles & Chapters
Blogs
Books
eBooks
eBooks (Watermarked)
Cert Flash Cards Online
Newsletters
Podcasts
Question of the Day
Rough Cuts
Short Cuts
Videos

Connect with Pearson IT Certification

pearsonITcertification.com/ newsletters

 twitter.com/ pearsonITCert

 facebook.com/ pearsonitcertification

 youtube.com/ pearsonITCert

 pearsonitcertification. com/rss/

FREE Online Edition

Cert Guide
Learn, prepare, and practice for exam success

MCTS
70-680
Microsoft Windows 7,
Configuring

Your purchase of **MCTS 70-680 Cert Guide: Microsoft Windows 7, Configuring** includes access to a free online edition for 45 days through the Safari Books Online subscription service. Nearly every Pearson IT Certification book is available online through Safari Books Online, along with more than 5,000 other technical books and videos from publishers such as Addison-Wesley Professional, Cisco Press, Exam Cram, IBM Press, O'Reilly, Prentice Hall, Que, and Sams.

SAFARI BOOKS ONLINE allows you to search for a specific answer, cut and paste code, download chapters, and stay current with emerging technologies.

Activate your FREE Online Edition at
www.informit.com/safarifree

> **STEP 1:** Enter the coupon code: ROHJZAA.

> **STEP 2:** New Safari users, complete the brief registration form.
> Safari subscribers, just log in.

If you have difficulty registering on Safari or accessing the online edition,
please e-mail customer-service@safaribooksonline.com